AF797070

GIAMBATTISTA VICO'S SCIENCE OF HUMANITY

PRINCIPJ
DI
SCIENZA NUOVA
DI
GIAMBATTISTA VICO
D' INTORNO ALLA COMUNE NATURA
DELLE NAZIONI

IN QUESTA TERZA IMPRESSIONE

Dal medesimo Autore in un gran numero di luoghi
Corretta, Schiarita, e notabilmente Accresciuta.

TOMO I.

IN NAPOLI MDCCXLIV.
NELLA STAMPERIA MUZIANA
A spese di Gaetano, e Steffano Elia.
CON LICENZA DE' SUPERIORI.

GIAMBATTISTA VICO'S

SCIENCE OF HUMANITY

Edited by Giorgio Tagliacozzo
and Donald Phillip Verene

Consulting Editors:
Isaiah Berlin, Max H. Fisch,
Elio Gianturco, and Hayden White

Special Advisors:
Ernesto Grassi, Pietro Piovani,
Leon Pompa, and Alain Pons

The Johns Hopkins University Press

Baltimore and London

The preparation of this book and its publication have been assisted through the generosity of the Edgar J. Kaufmann Charitable Foundation, The American Council of Learned Societies, The Johns Hopkins University, and the Andrew W. Mellon Foundation.

The frontispiece is a reproduction of the title page of Giambattista Vico's *Scienza nuova* (Naples, 1744) and was supplied by Giorgio Tagliacozzo.

Copyright © 1976 by The Johns Hopkins University Press
All rights reserved. No part of this book may be reproduced or transmitted in any form or by any means, electronic or mechanical, including photocopying, recording, xerography, or any information storage and retrieval system, without permission in writing from the publisher.

Manufactured in the United States of America

The Johns Hopkins University Press, Baltimore, Maryland 21218
The Johns Hopkins University Press Ltd., London

Library of Congress Catalog Card Number 75–26753
ISBN 0–8018–1720–x

Library of Congress Cataloging in Publication data will be found on the last printed page of this book.

"Joyce and Vico: The Middle Way"
Reprinted with permission from
The New York Review of Books.
Copyright © 1973 Nyrev, Inc.

B
3583
.G48

PREFACE

I

The thought of Giambattista Vico (1668–1744) is both known and unknown to thinkers in the humanities and social sciences today. A growing number of scholars in these fields know Vico's thought directly and involve it in their own thought, but this awareness is small in comparison with the widespread awareness of the thought of other figures in the modern period, such as Descartes, Kant, or Hegel. When regarded in this sense Vico's thought cannot be said to be widely known. It has the appearance of a topic of interest only to specialists in eighteenth-century thought or Italian thought or to those general thinkers whose interests lead them for various reasons to range widely in the history of ideas. There is, however, a second sense in which Vico's thought is known in the present day. This is a sense in which Vico's ideas and the problems to which they were a response are present in the thought and the life of our time. If one reads the works of such figures as Lévi-Strauss, Piaget, Dilthey, Husserl, or Cassirer with Vico in mind, one cannot but be struck by how much ideas forged in response to contemporary problems in various fields have an affinity to those which Vico formulated in the *New Science*. Vico's thought constitutes the center of a wheel out of which many of the themes treated by such contemporary thinkers radiate. In fact, the need generally felt today to recast much of social scientific thinking in humanistic terms and the need in humanistic thought for a comprehensive theory of man are versions of themes present in the *New Science*.

Traditional ways of looking at human knowledge and the mind that have come to us from Descartes, Locke, logical positivism, and much of linguistic analysis, indispensable as they are for the illumination of the logical and cognitive faculties of man, are unable to satisfy the concern of the twentieth century for understanding the noncognitive—the imagination, the will, creativity, feeling, the sensuous, and the aesthetic. There is a need to see these, not simply as support systems for the cognitive activity of the mind or as protoversions of it, but as they fit into man's nature and constitute the bases for significant aspects of his cultural life. Traditional approaches to human knowledge offer little insight into such matters. The French historian Paul Hazard has concisely expressed this as: "If only

76-05189

Italy had lent an ear to Giambattista Vico; if only, as at the time of the Renaissance, she had assumed the leadership of Europe, our intellectual history would have had a very different tale to tell. Our eighteenth-century ancestors would not have believed that everything that was clear was necessarily true. On the contrary they would have looked on clarity as a defect rather than a virtue in the matter of human reason. If an idea is clear, it means that it is finished, rounded off, over and done with. They would have given pride of place in the hierarchy of faculties, not to reason, but to the imagination."[1]

In the face of the identification of human knowledge in modern thought with the cognitive, logical, and commonsensical, Vico asserts the value of the imagination. The activities which the imagination in all of its forms generates are not seen as secondary forms of the rational. The words of the late art and literary critic Sir Herbert Read extend the point made by Paul Hazard. In commenting on Reynolds' view that the painter who aims at the greatest style is one who corrects nature by following a principle of ideal beauty Read wrote: "Here [in Reynolds' view of the grand manner] we have the final formulation of the classical doctrine in art, and this final formulation does not differ essentially from that of Dryden at the end of the seventeenth century, or, for that matter, from that of Alberti in the fifteenth century. Common to them all is the notion that the artist 'makes out an abstract idea'; and that is the feature of the classical ideal to be kept in mind for purposes of contrast with the emergence of a new ideal. Further, the classical ideal is a static ideal, an ideal based on the *status quo* of a particular civilization, that civilization established in Greece and continued in Mediterranean Europe until the present day. If I were to select a single word to characterize the opposing ideal which already in the eighteenth century had made its obscure appearance, that word would be *genetic*. And if I were to select a single name as the originator of this ideal, that name would be *Vico*."[2]

What Vico understood was that the work of the artistic imagination, as well as that of the imagination in general, could be seen, not in terms of its ability to portray an abstract rational ideal, but as an activity capable of producing its own intrinsic structure. Vico's thought offers us the possibility of understanding the imaginative activities of the mind without reducing them to versions of cognitive activity. From Vico's perspective the mind can be understood in other than Cartesian terms; it can be understood in terms which provide for the genetic understanding of the human world. Vico's genetic approach to the human world provides a basis for under-

[1] *European Thought in the Eighteenth Century: From Montesquieu to Lessing*, trans. J. Lewis May (Cleveland and New York: World Pub. Co., Meridian Books, 1963), p. 35.

[2] *Art Now: An Introduction to the Theory of Modern Painting and Sculpture*, rev. ed. (London: Faber and Faber, 1960), p. 24.

standing the unity of knowledge, history, and culture. He puts forth a picture of the human world as a whole by returning to the origins of the human world and seeing in its original state the principles of unity of mind, human life, and reason. Those contemporary thinkers in the humanities and social sciences who are concerned to understand mind, society, and culture in terms of categories of development and wholeness share a common perspective with Vico.

The title of this volume, *Giambattista Vico's Science of Humanity*, arises out of these concerns. It is born out of the editors' deep conviction that Vico's concern to see the human world in its origin and to formulate the principles of its genesis provides a touchstone for recovering the values and internal order of those activities that make up man's humanity. The essays contained herein are intended to further the interpretation of Vico's ideas as they exist in his works and to show some of the systematic connections they have with major viewpoints in the humanities and social sciences. Vico's ideas are an unseen point of origin for many views and perspectives in contemporary thought.

II

This volume is an outgrowth of *Giambattista Vico: An International Symposium*, edited by Giorgio Tagliacozzo and Hayden White, published in 1969 in celebration of the tercentenary year of Vico's birth. It contained essays by forty-one American and European scholars. Shortly after its publication it became apparent that there were many more themes in Vico's thought that have considerable bearing on contemporary problems. Interest in Vico and the approach taken to his thought reached far wider than had been anticipated. The degree of response and the shape it took both in the United States and abroad led to the consideration of a volume of further studies on Vico.

This volume utilizes the same format as the previous volume in that it brings together essays by scholars from various countries, fields, and intellectual traditions; but it differs in its aim. The purpose of *Giambattista Vico: An International Symposium* was in large part exploratory. In it the many facets of Vico's thought were shown; its connections with modern movements of thought were explored; and Vico's influence on many historical traditions and figures were traced. The present volume is less broad in intent. It attempts to go deeper into the structure of Vico's thought and into the viability of his ideas. No attempt has been made, however, to develop within the volume a single interpretation of Vico's thought. Instead, the aim has been to allow whatever differences of viewpoint that exist between authors to indicate genuine divergences of interpretation. Free exchange of perspectives must be the basis for understanding any figure and this is of particular importance in relation to Vico, whose thought has so often in the past served largely as a vehicle for the expression of his supporters' thought.

Although the editors' own interests center on the importance of Vico's thought for questions concerning the unity of knowledge and the philosophy of culture, it has not been our intention to press Vico into the service of yet another position. We have focused the volume around Vico's science of humanity in an attempt to create a perspective broad enough to allow for considerable diversity of thought within a single volume. The editors are acutely aware of their own shortcomings, that there are omissions of topics that might have been covered, and that some topics are not covered as fully as they might have been. It is our conviction, however, that the reader will find here a series of essays that will take him quite far in the analysis of Vico's thought and its bearing on contemporary problems and thinkers.

III

The volume is arranged in five parts. Part I, *Historical and Interpretive Studies*, contains essays focusing primarily on the development of Vico's own thought or on the direct interpretation of some of its most fundamental themes. Part II, *Vico's Conception of History and Historical Knowledge*, is directed specifically to the interpretation of Vico's view of history and its significance for problems in contemporary philosophy of history. Part III, *Vico, Philosophy, and the History of Philosophy*, contains analyses of the relationship of Vico's thought or certain aspects of it to other figures in modern philosophy. No attempt has been made to make this a set of systematic comparisons between Vico's thought and that of all the major figures in modern philosophy. The figures examined are arranged in a broad chronological order. Essays in this section are not primarily comparative studies in the history of philosophy but are generally guided by interest in certain philosophical issues which lie between Vico's thought and that of the other philosophical thinkers involved. Part IV, *Vico and Topics in Humanistic and Social Scientific Thought*, calls attention in various ways to the importance of Vico's thought for views in the social sciences as humanistically conceived and for our understanding of man and society generally. Part V, *Vico and Praxis*, focuses specifically on Vico's views in relation to politics and the role of theoretical thought in the political sphere. The essays of Fisch and Pons are directed specifically to the meaning of Vico's *Pratica*, which is translated into English for the first time in this volume.

The bibliography of Critical Writings on Vico in English, which appears at the end of the volume, presents for the first time a comprehensive list of all work done in English on Vico since the early nineteenth century.

In presenting the twenty-eight essays that comprise the volume in terms of the above scheme of five parts the editors intend little more than that the headings of these parts serve to provide the reader with an overview of the volume. As the reader samples specific essays he will note that many connections are possible between the subjects of essays which tend to cut across and in some cases even to subvert the categories of these headings. It seems in the nature of Vico's thought that in writing about one aspect of it one is almost necessarily led to speak about it as a whole. Thus the purpose of each heading is only to call preliminary attention to the subject matter of any given essay and not to express the final meaning of its content. As Vico's thought itself does not proceed step by step but interconnects topics with each other, so individual essays frequently reflect much of this original interconnection.

Institute for Vico Studies, New York
University Park, Pennsylvania
April 1975

Giorgio Tagliacozzo
Donald Phillip Verene

ACKNOWLEDGMENTS

Work on the present volume has occupied the editors for nearly four years, during which time we have received help and encouragement from many persons in many ways. We would like to thank the consulting editors for the volume, Isaiah Berlin, Max H. Fisch, Elio Gianturco, and Hayden White, and the special advisors, Ernesto Grassi, Pietro Piovani, Leon Pompa, and Alain Pons, who in various ways contributed viewpoints and advice, which are so essential to shaping a project as large and diverse as this.

We would also like to thank the translators of essays, S. J. K. Manco, Azizeh Azodi, and Salvatore Rotella, and to extend special thanks to Margaret Brose, who in collaboration with her husband, Hayden White, translated the balance of the essays. We extend special thanks to Molly Black Verene for compiling the bibliography of critical writings on Vico, for preparing the index, and for the generous donation of her editorial skills to the final shaping of the manuscript. We wish to thank Michael J. Mooney whose assistance in the course of editing the volume led to his writing, for inclusion at the front of the volume, a long-needed note on Vico's writings and their diverse editions. We also wish to acknowledge our considerable debt to Leon Pompa, whose editorial comments and assistance have gone far beyond his duties as a special advisor to the volume.

Financial assistance for expenses involved in the preparation of the manuscript of the volume has been provided most generously by the Edgar J. Kaufmann Charitable Foundation, The American Council of Learned Societies, The Johns Hopkins University, and the Andrew W. Mellon Foundation. Partial funds for European travel connected with preparation of the volume were generously provided for Professor Verene by the Central Fund for Research of the College of Liberal Arts of The Pennsylvania State University. Without support from these sources the volume might never have been completed.

We are also most grateful for the translation of the *Pratica* done especially for this volume by Thomas G. Bergin and Max H. Fisch. All English-speaking scholars of Vico are also forever in their debt for their fine translations of Vico's *New Science* and *Autobiography*.

Giorgio Tagliacozzo and
Donald Phillip Verene

TABLE OF CONTENTS

PART III: VICO, PHILOSOPHY AND THE HISTORY OF PHILOSOPHY

PART IV: VICO AND TOPICS IN HUMANISTIC AND SOCIAL SCIENTIFIC THOUGHT

PART V: VICO AND PRAXIS

CONTRIBUTORS

Gianfranco Cantelli. Professor of Philosophy and History at the Liceo classico "Machiavelli" in Florence and Associate Professor of History of Philosophy at the University of Florence. Author of *Teologia e ateismo, saggio sul pensiero filosofico e religioso di Pierre Bayle* (1969) and *Vico e Bayle: Premesse per un confronto* (1971).

Robert J. Di Pietro. Professor of Linguistics at Georgetown University. Co-author of *The Sounds of English and Italian* (1965) and *The Grammatical Structures of English and Italian* (1965). Author of *Language Structures in Contrast* (1971).

Attila Fáj. Associate Professor of Philosophy at the University of Genoa. Author of numerous publications on topics ranging from Stoic logic to studies in James Joyce and comparative literature.

Guido Fassò. Professor of Philosophy of Law at the University of Bologna. Author of *I "quattro auttori" del Vico* (1949), *La storia come esperienza giuridica* (1953), *Cristianesimo e società* (1956; 2d ed., 1969), *La democrazia in Grecia* (1959; 2d ed., 1967), *La legge della ragione* (1964; 2d ed., 1966), *Il diritto naturale* (1964; 2d ed., 1972), *Storia della filosofia del diritto* (3 vols., 1966–70; 2d ed., 1970–72), *Vico e Grozio* (1971), and *Società, legge e ragione* (1974).

Max H. Fisch. Professor of Philosophy, Indiana University—Purdue University at Indianapolis. His publications have been largely in history of science and history of philosophy. A bibliography of his writings to 1969 appears in *Studies in Philosophy and the History of Science: Essays in Honor of Max Fisch*, edited by Richard Allen Tursman (1970). His Vichian works and translations are listed in the bibliography of the present volume. He is currently engaged in a biography of Charles S. Peirce.

Amos Funkenstein. Professor of History at the University of California, Los Angeles. Author of numerous articles in academic journals and of *Heilsplan und natürliche Entwicklung. Gegenwartsbestimmung im Geschichtsdenken des Mittelalters* (1965).

Howard Gardner. Research Associate at Harvard University and Research Associate at the Aphasia Research Center, Boston Veterans Administration Hospital. Co-editor of *Classics in Psychology* (1973). Author of *The Arts and Human Development: A Psychological Study of the Artistic Process* (1973) and *The Quest for Mind: Piaget, Lévi-Strauss and the Structuralist Movement* (1973).

ALESSANDRO GIULIANI. Professor of Philosophy of Law at the University of Rome. Author of *Il concetto di prova* (1961), *La logica della controversia* (1966), and of numerous articles in academic journals.

MARIA GORETTI. Professor of History and Philosophy at the Liceo classico "M. Minghetti" in Bologna. Author of *Il paradosso Mandeville* (1958), *La scuola e il fanciullo* (1966), and other pedagogical works. Editor of an Italian edition of Vico's *De nostri temporis studiorum ratione* (1958).

ERNESTO GRASSI. Professor of Philosophy at the University of Munich. Editor of *Rowohlts deutsche Enzyklopädie* and *Rowohlts Klassiker*. Author of *Il problema della metafisica platonica* (1933), *Vom Vorrang des Logos* (1946), *Verteidigung des individuellen Lebens* (1947), *Vom Ursprung der Geistes und Naturwissenschaften* (1950), *Kunst und Mythos* (1957), *Die Theorie des Schönen in der Antike* (1962), and *Humanismus und Marxismus. Zur Kritik der Verselbständigung im Wissenschaft* (1973).

STUART HAMPSHIRE. Warden of Wadham College, Oxford University. Author of *Spinoza* (1951), *Thought and Action* (1959), *Freedom of the Individual* (1965), *Philosophy of Mind* (1966), *Modern Writers and Other Essays* (1969), and *Freedom of Mind and Other Essays* (1971).

PETER HUGHES. Associate Professor of English at Victoria College, University of Toronto. Co-editor of *The Varied Pattern* (1971). Author of *Spots of Time* (1969) and *George Woodcock* (1974).

ANGELA MARIA JACOBELLI. Professor of Moral Philosophy in the School of Education, University of Rome. Author of *Tomaso Campanella—La crisi della coscienza di sè* (1953), *G. B. Vico—La vita e le opere* (1960), *Criticità e impegno* (1961), and *Tempo e significato* (1968).

ROBERT WELSH JORDAN. Instructor in the Department of Philosophy, Colorado State University. Author of articles on Husserl and phenomenological topics and the translator of Husserl's inaugural lecture, "Pure Phenomenology, Its Method and Its Field of Investigation" (in *Life-World and Consciousness: Essays for Aron Gurwitsch*, 1972).

DONALD R. KELLEY. Professor of History at the University of Rochester. Author of *Foundations of Modern Historical Scholarship* (1970) and *François Hotman, a Revolutionary Ordeal* (1973).

VITTORIO MATHIEU. Professor of Moral Philosophy at the University of Turin. Author of *Bergson* (1954; 2d ed., 1972), *La filosofia trascendentale e l' "Opus postumum" di Kant* (1958), *Leibniz e Des Bosses* (1960), *Storia della filosofia* (1966), *L'oggettività nella scienza e nella filosofia contemporanea* (1960), *Il problema dell'esperienza* (1963), and *La dialettica della libertà* (1974).

George Mora. Research Associate in the Department of the History of Science and Medicine, Yale University, and Medical Director of the Astor Home and Clinics for Children, Rhinebeck, New York. He is also on the faculty of the medical schools of Columbia University, Union University in Albany, and the New York Medical College and has written extensively on the history of psychiatry and is co-editor of *Psychiatry and Its History* (1970).

John O'Neill. Professor of Sociology at York University, Toronto. Translator of Jean Hyppolite's *Studies on Marx and Hegel* (1969) and Merleau-Ponty's *Humanism and Terror* (1969) and *The Prose of the World* (1973). Author of *Perception, Expression, and History: The Social Phenomenology of Maurice Merleau-Ponty* (1970), *Sociology as a Skin Trade: Essays Towards a Reflexive Sociology* (1972), and *Making Sense Together: An Introduction to Wild Sociology* (1974).

Pietro Piovani. Professor of Moral Philosophy of the Facoltà di Lettere e Filosofia of the University of Naples. Author of *Per un'interpretazione unitaria del Critone* (1947), *Normatività e società* (1949), *La teodicea sociale di Rosmini* (1957), *Giusnaturalismo ed etica moderna* (1961), *Filosofia e storia delle idee* (1965), *Conoscenza storica e conoscenza morale* (1966; 2d ed., 1972), and *Principi di una filosofia della morale* (1972).

Leon Pompa. Lecturer in Philosophy at the University of Edinburgh. Author of numerous articles in academic journals, including "Vico's Science" (*History and Theory*, 1971), and of *Vico: A Study of the 'New Science'* (1975).

Alain Pons. Maître-assistant de Philosophie at the University of Paris-Nanterre. Author of "Nature et histoire chez G. B. Vico" (*Les Etudes Philosophiques*, 1961), a forthcoming French translation of selections from the *New Science*, and a forthcoming French translation of Vico's *Autobiography*.

Emanuele Riverso. Professor of History of Philosophy at the University of Naples and the University of Salerno. Author of *La filosofia analitica in Inghilterra* (1969), *Il pensiero di Ludovico Wittgenstein* (2d ed., 1971) *Dalla magia alla scienza* (1971), *Il pensiero di Bertrand Russell* (3d ed., 1972), *Aspetti della spiritualità europea dal cinquecento al seicento* (1973), and *Il linguaggio nel pensiero filosofico e pedagogico del mondo antico* (1973).

Nathan Rotenstreich. Professor of Philosophy at The Hebrew University of Jerusalem. Author of numerous works, including *Between Past and Present: An Essay on History* (1958), *Spirit and Man: An Essay on Being and Value* (1963), *The Recurring Pattern: Studies in Anti-Judaism in Modern Thought* (1963), *Humanism in the Contempo-*

rary Era (1963), *Experience and Its Systematization: Studies in Kant* (1965; 2d ed., 1972), *Basic Problems of Marx's Philosophy* (1965), *On the Human Subject: Studies in the Phenomenology of Ethics and Politics* (1966), *Jewish Philosophy in Modern Times: From Mendelssohn to Rosenzweig* (1968), *Tradition and Reality* (1972), and *Philosophy: The Concept and Its Manifestations* (1973).

NANCY S. STRUEVER. Associate Professor in the Department of History and Humanities Center at Johns Hopkins University. Author of *The Language of History in the Renaissance* (1970).

GIORGIO TAGLIACOZZO. Former Libero Docente at the University of Rome (1935–38) and Lecturer at the New School for Social Research (1946–61). Editor of the Voice of America-RAI "Università Internazionale Guglielmo Marconi," 1944–1974. Author of *Economia e massimo edonistico collettivo* (1933), *Economisti napoletani dei secoli XVII e XVIII* (1937) and of numerous essays on the history of economics and on the unity of knowledge, including "Une 'unité du savoir' de type vichien" (in *Les Etudes Philosophiques*, 1968), "Vico, oggi" (in *Campanella e Vico*, 1969), and "Unità del sapere e cultura generale—Una tesi moderna, corollario del pensiero vichiano" (in *Vico, Joyce, Lévi-Strauss e Piaget: Saggi di G. Tagliacozzo, I. Berlin, S. Hampshire, N. Rotenstreich and G. Mora*, 1975). Editor of *Giambattista Vico: An International Symposium* (1969).

HOWARD N. TUTTLE. Associate Professor of Philosophy at The University of New Mexico. Author of *Wilhelm Dilthey's Philosophy of Historical Understanding: A Critical Analysis* (1969).

DONALD PHILLIP VERENE. Associate Professor of Philosophy at The Pennsylvania State University. Author of articles on the philosophy of Hegel, Cassirer's philosophy of symbolic forms, and topics in the philosophy of culture. Editor of *Man and Culture* (1970) and *Sexual Love and Western Morality* (1972).

W. H. WALSH. Professor of Logic and Metaphysics at the University of Edinburgh. Author of *Reason and Experience* (1947), *An Introduction to Philosophy of History* (1951), *Metaphysics* (1963), and *Hegelian Ethics* (1969).

HAYDEN WHITE. Professor of Modern European History at the University of California, Los Angeles, currently on leave to serve as Director of the Center for the Humanities, Wesleyan University. Author of *Metahistory: The Historical Imagination in Nineteenth-Century Europe* (1973) and other books and articles on European cultural history. Co-editor of *Giambattista Vico: An International Symposium* (1969).

VICO'S WRITINGS

Obscure writings and a factious history of interpretation—the double legacy of any seminal thinker—are not the only difficulties facing the student of Vico. Due partly to Vico himself, who coined popular titles for several of his published works and cited others in conflicting ways, and partly to Vico's editors, who devised curious abbreviations and acronyms for the works and added new textual divisions to Vico's own, the reader of Vico literature is left often to wonder just what Vico wrote, when he wrote it, and by what title, and to negotiate the diverse styles of citation used by Vichian scholars. To meet this difficulty and to explain the manner of citation used in the essays of this volume the following note on Vico's works is offered.

The Laterza Edition

The standard edition of Vico's writings is the *Opere di G. B. Vico*, 8 vols. in 11 (Bari: Laterza, 1911–41). With the exception of Volume 5, originally prepared by Benedetto Croce, and Volume 1, on which Giovanni Gentile collaborated, the series is entirely the work of Fausto Nicolini. The three parts of Volume 2 are continuously impaginated, and the two parts of Volume 4, though separately impaginated, have continuous paragraph enumeration.

Following are the titles and publication dates of the Laterza edition:

Vol. 1: *Le Orazioni inaugurali, il De Italorum sapientia e le polemiche* (1914)

Vol. 2: *Il Diritto universale* (1936)
  Pt. 1: *"Sinopsi" e "De uno"*
  Pt. 2: *"De constantia jurisprudentis"*
  Pt. 3: *"Notae," "Dissertationes," nota bibliografica e indici*

Vol. 3: *La Scienza nuova prima, con la polemica contro gli "Atti degli eruditi" di Lipsia* (1931)

Vol. 4: *La Scienza nuova seconda giusta l'edizione del 1744, con le varianti dell'edizione del 1730 e di due redazioni intermedie inedite* (4th ed., rev. and enl. with the unpublished notes of a student of Vico, 1953; 1st ed., 1911–16; 2d ed., 1928; 3d ed., 1942)
Pt. 1: *Libri 1–2*
Pt. 2: *Libri 3–5 e appendice*
Vol. 5: *L'Autobiografia, il carteggio e le poesie varie* (2d ed., rev. and enl., 1929; 1st ed., 1911)
Vol. 6: *Scritti storici* (1939)
Vol. 7: *Scritti vari e pagine sparse* (1940)
Vol. 8: *Versi d'occasione e scritti di scuola, con appendice e bibliografia generale delle opere* (1941)

Chronology of Vico's Works

Following is a chronological listing of Vico's writings, with page or paragraph references to the Laterza edition. It has been prepared from the editorial notes in this edition and from the essay, "Gli scritti di Giambattista Vico: storia esterna," which Nicolini inserted as the first section of his revised version of Benedetto Croce's *Bibliografia vichiana*, 2 vols. (Naples: Ricciardi, 1947–48), 1: 7–162.

Omitted from the list are five minor historical sketches, several book dedications, and a number of perfunctory opinions which Vico prepared as a civil censor. Also omitted is a rather large body of commemorations and allocutions, elegies and funeral inscriptions—in short, the commissioned products of Vico's pen deriving from his abilities as a professional rhetorician. Though indicative of Vico's culture and demonstrative of his Humanist heritage, none of the material excluded contributes directly to an understanding of his thought. The interested reader can find it collected in Volume 6 and especially Volume 7 of the Laterza edition.

Included in the list, however, are certain works known to have been written, in whole or in part, but subsequently lost, as well as titles of other works for which Vico prepared sketches or which he indicated an intention to write. They are included in the list because they are referred to regularly by Vico scholars, as indeed by Vico himself, and also because their very mention serves to indicate the development of Vico's thought. The page references for such entries are to Nicolini's comments on the circumstances of these writings and their probable content. Of Vico's verse, three works of special importance are listed by name; the rest are indicated collectively at the end of the list.

All italicized titles in the list derive from Vico: while most are titles of published works, others—as indicated—are later coinages for published writings, or projected titles for works written but never published, or conceived but never written. All non-italicized titles, whether in English or Italian, and whether enclosed in quotation marks or not, were supplied over the years by Vico's several editors, usually to designate untitled works or manuscripts.

Affetti di un disperato (1692) [verse]	5: 313–17
Principum neapolitanorum conjurationis anni MDCCI historia (1703)	6: 301–62
Six University Inaugural Orations (text of 1709) [delivered 1699–1707]	1: 1–67
De nostri temporis studiorum ratione (1709) [Inaugural Oration of 1708]	1: 69–121
De antiquissima Italorum sapientia ex linguae latinae originibus eruenda (1710):	
"*Proemium*" (1710)	1: 123–26
Liber metaphysicus	1: 127–94
Appendix on logic [sketched (1711?); lost]	8: 270–71
Liber physicus [sketched (1709?); lost]	8: 272–75
Appendix: *De aequilibrio corporis animantis* [drafted (1713?); lost]	8: 276–80
Liber moralis [projected only]	
Institutiones oratoriae (edition of 1711)	8: 159–96
Polemic exchanges in the *Giornale de' letterati d'Italia* concerning the *De antiquissima Italorum sapientia* (1711–12)	1: 195–294
Vico's First *Risposta* (1711)	1: 203–21
Vico's Second *Risposta* (1712)	1: 239–76
De rebus gestis Antonii Caraphaei (1716)	6: 3–300
An unfinished commentary on Grotius' *De jure belli ac pacis* (ca. 1716) [lost]	8: 282–83
The University Inaugural Oration of 1719 [lost]	8: 283–84
A first edition of the *Diritto universale* (1719–20) [lost]	8: 284–88
Synopsis of the *Diritto universale* (1720)	2: 1–21
The *Diritto universale* (1720–22), a popular title coined by Vico and retained by scholars to designate collectively:	
De universi juris uno principio et fine uno liber unus, including the "*De opera proloquium*" (1720)	2: 23–263
De constantia jurisprudentis liber alter (1721)	2: 265–589
Notae in duos libros, alterum "De uno universi juris principio et fine uno," alterum, "De constantia jurisprudentis" (1722)	2: 591–760

Giunone in danza (1721) [verse]	5: 318–45
Origine, progresso e caduta della poesia italiana (1723) [verse]	5: 346–51
Solemnis praelectio ad legem primam "Digesti," "De praescriptis verbis": the unpublished trial lecture given in competition for a professorship in Civil Law (1723) [lost; reconstructed by Nicolini]	8: 288–97
Scienza nuova dintorno ai principi dell'umanità (1723–25), the apparent title of an unpublished, and subsequently lost, manuscript, referred to by scholars as "Scienza nuova in forma negativa"	3: 325–29
Scienza nuova prima, Vico's abbreviated title, retained by scholars, for *Principi di una scienza nuova dintorno alla natura delle nazioni, per la quale si ritruovano i principi di altro sistema del diritto naturale delle genti* (1725)	3: §§ 1–529
Vita di Giambattista Vico scritta da se medesimo, referred to by scholars as the "Autobiography" (1725–28; text of 1728)	5: 3–54, 89–91
Vici vindiciae: Notae in "Acta eruditorum" lipsiensia mensis Augusti anni MDCCXXVII, ubi inter "Nova literaria" unum extat de eius libro, cui titulus "Principi di una scienza nuova dintorno alla natura delle nazioni" (1729)	3: §§ 530–84
"Discoverta del vero Dante, ovvero nuovi principi di critica dantesca" (1728 or 1729) [concerning an anonymous commentary on the *Commedia*; Nicolini's title]	7: 79–82
Scienza nuova seconda (1730–44), the title coined by Vico for the edition of 1730, but used by Nicolini and subsequent scholars to designate collectively:	
Principi di Scienza nuova d'intorno alla communi natura delle nazioni (edition of 1744)	4: §§ 1–1112, 1488–92, 1499–1506
Passages from the edition of 1730 and from two unpublished versions (1731 and ca. 1733) omitted or substantially altered in the final edition	4: §§ 1113–1487, 1493–98

Unpublished marginalia made by a student at Vico's direction in a copy of the 1730 edition	4: §§ 1507–67
"Gli *Annali* di Tacito al lume della *Scienza nuova*" (after 1730) [partial sketch of an historical commentary]	6: 401–13
"L'epistola di Orazio ai Pisoni al lume della *Scienza nuova*" (after 1730) [marginal notes; Nicolini's title]	7: 51–77
"Oratiunculae pro adsequenda laurea" (after 1730)	8: 205–7
Supplement to the Autobiography (1731)	5: 55–79
"Poesia e oratoria" (1731) [introduction to the *Rime scelte* of Gherardo degli Angioli; Nicolini's title]	7: 39–41
"Sul diritto natural delle genti" (1731) [written in presenting the *Scienza nuova* of 1730 to Msgr. Ernest von Harrach; Nicolini's title]	7: 25–31
"Le traduzioni poetiche, il *De rerum natura* di Lucrezio e l'antichità e nobilità della medicina" (1731) [preface to the *Sifilide* of Girolamo Fracastoro translated by Pietro Belli; Nicolini's title]	7: 45–49
De mente heroica (1732) [Inaugural Oration]	7: 3–22
"Le accademie e i rapporti tra la filosofia e l'eloquenza" (1737) [speech before the *Accademia degli Oziosi*; Nicolini's title]	7: 33–37
Institutiones oratoriae (edition of 1738)	8: 197–203
"Idea d'una grammatica filosofica" (ca. 1740) [concerning the *Grammatica* of Antonio d'Aronne; Nicolini's title]	7: 43–44
Poetry and Occasional Verse (1693–1743)	8: 1–129 5: 352–66
Correspondence (1693–1743)	5: 137–278 8: 245–53

The Published and Commonly Given Titles of Vico's Works

The three important common titles that Vico coined—*Diritto universale, Scienza nuova prima,* and *Scienza nuova seconda*—appear first in the supplement added to the Autobiography in 1731, that is, in the period just after the publication of the second edition of the *Scienza nuova.* The first of these, *Diritto universale*, was used by Vico to refer to three published Latin works: *De universi juris uno principio et fine uno liber unus*, *De constantia jurisprudentis liber alter*, and *Notae in duos libros*. As the titles make clear, Vico conceived these works as a unity, but unlike the earlier instance of the *De antiquissima Italorum sapientia*, he did not supply them, at publication, with a generic title. One may question whether the omission was totally injudicious, for scholars are rather generally agreed that the three works, notwithstanding Vico's intentions, contain quite different arguments, or at the very least evince a development in perspective that later matured in the *Scienza nuova*.

Following its publication in 1725, the *Scienza nuova* in turn underwent repeated manuscript revisions, leading to new editions in 1730 and 1744. So different were the versions of 1725 and 1730, in fact, that Vico himself chose to refer to them as *Scienza nuova prima* and *Scienza nuova seconda*, and suggested that when the latter was reissued, the former should be printed with it (*Opere* 5: 72). Nicolini, as other editors before him, honored the suggestion, though not without changing the meaning of the title, *Scienza nuova seconda*. Since the final edition of the *Scienza nuova* in 1744 was not as dramatically different from that of 1730 as that of 1730 was from the initial edition in 1725, Nicolini chose to print the edition of 1744 as the *Scienza nuova seconda*, and to include in an appendix the variants in the edition of 1730 and intermediary versions. Subsequent scholars, including those contributing to this volume, have followed him in this usage, but do not as a rule extend the term to include the variants appended to his edition.

Abbreviations of Vico's Titles

However inappropriate or variously applied, Vico's common titles are at least grammatical and clear—qualities wanting in several abbreviated titles currently in use among scholars. From one shortened form—*De ratione*—the reader could conclude that Vico had written a treatise on the rational faculty; only when the further term, *studiorum*, is supplied, does one recognize a work that forms part of a Humanist genre on methods of study. Two other abbreviations suffer an even worse lot: *De antiquissima* and *De uno*, with nouns pared from adjectives, display a violence to grammar that would not be tolerated in the vernacular. The following list of short titles used in the present volume, therefore, includes alternatives to these common, though unfortunate, usages:

Inaugural Orations	Six addresses of various titles delivered in Latin at the University of Naples to initiate the academic year

De studiorum ratione	*De nostri temporis studiorum ratione*
De Italorum sapientia	*De antiquissima Italorum sapientia ex linguae latinae originibus eruenda*
De uno principio	*De universi juris uno principio et fine uno liber unus*
De constantia jurisprudentis	*De constantia jurisprudentis liber alter*
Notae in duos libros	*Notae in duos libros, alterum "De uno universi juris principio et fine uno," alterum "De constantia jurisprudentis"*
The Autobiography	*Vita di Giambattista Vico scritta da se medesimo*
Vindiciae	*Vici vindiciae: Notae in "Acta eruditorum" lipsiensia mensis Augusti anni MDCCXXVII, ubi inter "Nova literaria" unum extat de eius libro, cui titulus "Principi di una scienza nuova dintorno alla natura delle nazioni"*

Other Editions of Vico's Works

Though Vico wished, we are told in the Autobiography (*Opere* 5: 70–71), that the *New Science* alone remain known to history, and thus denied the request of two Neapolitan entrepreneurs for the gift of all his published and unpublished writings, history has succeeded in salvaging the bulk of his works, principally through the efforts of three Italian archivists: Carlantonio de Rosa marchese di Villarosa (1762–1847), Giuseppe Ferrari (1811–76), and Fausto Nicolini (1879–1965). Following years of intense searching in the libraries and private collections in Italy for the lost manuscripts and letters, Villarosa published four volumes of Vico's "minor works," three under the Italian title, *Opusculi di Giambattista Vico* (Naples: Procelli, 1818–19), and the last with a Latin title, *Jo. Baptistae Vici Opuscula* (Naples: Fernandes, 1823). These published volumes, together with the still unedited materials in Villarosa's possession, were incorporated by Giuseppe Ferrari in his edition of the works some ten years later, *Opere di Giambattista Vico, ordinate ed illustrate coll'analisi storica della mente di Vico in relazione alla scienza della civiltà*, 6 vols. (Milan: Società tipografica de' classici italiani, 1835–37; 2d ed., 1852–54). Containing both the major and minor works, and embellished with notes, indices, and a lengthy introduction, this was the first true corpus of Vico's writings.

Shortly thereafter, a lawyer named Francesco Saverio Pomodoro, in association with the publishing firm of Domenico and Antonio Morano, undertook a new edition of the works, with Italian translations of those written in Latin. The first six volumes to appear—between 1858 and 1861—"slavishly imitated" (in Nicolini's words) Ferrari's second edition. But two supplementary volumes, published in 1865 and 1869, included materials not found in Ferrari: that of 1865 reissued, together with Luigi Parchetti's Italian version, Carlo Tipa's 1845 edition of the *Institutiones oratoriae* of 1711, as well as the *Ragionamenti* previously published by Giuseppe Del Giudice; that of 1869 published for the first time, from a manuscript edited by Antonio Galasso, five of the so-called "Inaugural Orations." Together with the six previously published, these volumes formed the Pomodoro, or better, the Morano, edition, *Opere di Giambattista Vico, versione italiana col testo latino a piè di pagina da Francesco Sa. Pomodoro*, 8 vols. (Naples: Morano, 1858–69).

The edition of the works prepared for Laterza by Nicolini not only encompassed the offerings of previous editions, but did so with superior critical and editorial skills. The texts were more accurate and better arranged and the volumes were generously laced with textual and historical notes. The sole exception was Vico's course manual of 1711, *Institutiones oratoriae*, printed in full in the seventh volume of the Morano edition. Citing the high cost of paper and printing at that time (1941), Nicolini chose to omit from the *Institutiones* "the relatively long passages of Cicero, Caesar, Sallust, and other Latin writers adduced as examples, as well as a considerable number of pages devoted to nothing but very familiar definitions and distinctions, endlessly repeated—often in Vico's very words—in innumerable other scholastic manuals, printed or in manuscript, of the seventeenth and eighteenth centuries" (*Opere* 8: 229). It should be noted, however, that these very passages are the ones which at least two contributors to the present volume, Attila Fáj and Alessandro Giuliani, have found useful to recall.

Following the completion of the Laterza edition, a number of Italian presses published partial editions of the works, based generally on the work of Nicolini. Nicola Abbagnano prepared an anthology for the "Classici italiani" series of UTET, Paolo Rossi edited a volume for "I Classici Rizzoli," and Francesco Flora began an edition for "I Classici Mondadori." Nicolini himself prepared an excellent anthology, with Italian translations of the Latin selections, as part of the Ricciardi series, "La letteratura italiana: storia e testi." And most recently, Paolo Cristofolini has edited for Sansoni's "Le Voci del Mondo" two volumes of the works, *Opere filosofiche* and *Opere giuridiche*, with fresh translations of the Latin writings.

Apart from the Laterza edition, then, the editions of Vico's works most frequently cited in contemporary scholarship are these:

Opere (Ferrari)	*Opere di Giambattista Vico.* Arranged and elucidated by Giuseppe Ferrari with an historical analysis of the mind of Vico concerning the science of civilization. 2d ed. 6 vols. Milan: Società tipografica de' classici italiani, 1852–54.
Opere (Morano)	*Opere di Giambattista Vico.* An Italian version prepared by Francesco Sa. Pomodoro, with the Latin text at the bottom of the page. 8 vols. Naples: Morano, 1858–69. Reprint (8 vols. in 4). Leipzig: Zentralantiquariat der Deutschen Demokratischen Republik, 1970.
Opere (UTET)	*La Scienza nuova e opere scelte di G. B. Vico.* Edited, with an introduction, by Nicola Abbagnano. Turin: Unione Tipografico-editrice torinese [UTET], 1952.
Opere (Ricciardi)	*Opere di Giambattista Vico.* Edited, with an introduction and notes, by Fausto Nicolini. Milan and Naples: Ricciardi, 1953.
Opere (Mondadori)	*Tutte le opere di Giambattista Vico.* Edited by Francesco Flora. 1 vol. to date. Milan: Mondadori, 1957–.
Opere (Rizzoli)	*Opere di Giambattista Vico.* Edited, with an introduction, by Paolo Rossi. Milan: Rizzoli, 1959.
Opere filosofiche	Vico, Giambattista. *Opere filosofiche.* Texts, translations, and notes by Paolo Cristofolini, with an introduction by Nicola Badaloni. Florence: Sansoni, 1971.
Opere giuridiche	Vico, Giambattista. *Opere giuridiche.* Edited by Paolo Cristofolini, with an introduction by Nicola Badaloni. Florence: Sansoni, 1974.

English Translations

Three major works of Vico have thus far appeared in their entirety in English: *The Autobiography of Giambattista Vico* (1944; cor. rpt. 1963) and *The New Science of Giambattista Vico* (1948; 2d rev. ed. 1968) were translated by Thomas Goddard Bergin and Max Harold Fisch; and *On the Study Methods of Our Time,* a translation by Elio Gianturco of *De nostri temporis studiorum ratione,* was published in 1965. The Bergin and Fisch translation of the *New Science* is based on the text of the Laterza edition of Nicolini and maintains his paragraph enumerations. Thus the numbered paragraphs of the *New Science* and the *Scienza nuova seconda* are correlative (with the exception of the variants, which appear only in the Laterza edition).

Following is a list of English translations of Vico's writings arranged sequentially by date of original publication:

"Affetti di un disperato." Translated by H. P. Adams. In *The Life and Writings of Giambattista Vico* by H. P. Adams, pp. 223–26. London: Allen and Unwin, 1935.

The Autobiography of Giambattista Vico. Translated with introduction and notes by Max Harold Fisch and Thomas Goddard Bergin. Ithaca: Cornell University Press, 1944. Reprinted with corrections and supplementary notes: Ithaca: Cornell University Press, Great Seal Books, 1963.

The New Science of Giambattista Vico. Translated by Thomas Goddard Bergin and Max Harold Fisch. Ithaca: Cornell University Press, 1948. Second revised edition with an introduction by Max Harold Fisch: Ithaca: Cornell University Press, 1968. Abridged and revised edition with an introduction by Max Harold Fisch: Garden City, N.Y.: Doubleday Anchor Books, 1961. Reissue of the abridged and revised edition: Ithaca: Cornell Paperbacks, 1970.

"Discovery of the True Dante." Translated by Irma Brandeis. In *Discussions of the Divine Comedy,* edited by Irma Brandeis, pp. 11–12. Boston: Heath, 1961.

On the Study Methods of Our Time. Translated with an introduction and notes by Elio Gianturco. Indianapolis, New York, and Kansas City: Bobbs-Merrill Library of Liberal Arts, 1965.

"Gli affetti di un disperato." Translated by Thomas Goddard Bergin. *Forum Italicum,* 2 (1968): 305–9.

"A Factual Digression on Human Genius, Sharp, Witty Remarks, and Laughter" [from the *Vindiciae*]. Translated by A. Illiano, J. D. Tedder, and P. Treves. *Forum Italicum,* 2 (1968): 310–14.

"Practic of the *New Science*" [from the unpublished 1731 version of the conclusion of the *Scienza nuova*]. Translated by Thomas Goddard Bergin and Max Harold Fisch. Published herein.

MICHAEL J. MOONEY

A NOTE TO THE READER

References to the Bergin and Fisch translation of *The New Science of Giambattista Vico* are to the second revised edition of 1968. It is cited throughout as *New Science* followed by the appropriate paragraph number (for example, *New Science*, § 241). References to the Bergin and Fisch translation of *The Autobiography of Giambattista Vico* are to the Great Seal Books reprint with corrections and supplementary notes of 1963. It is cited throughout as *Autobiography* followed by the appropriate page number.

References in most essays to the texts of Vico's works are to the Laterza edition of Nicolini. Citations are given as *Opere* usually preceded by the short title of the work to which reference is made and followed by the volume and page number; exceptions to this are references to the third and fourth volumes which are given by volume and paragraph number rather than page number (for example, The Autobiography, *Opere* 5: 3–10; but *Scienza nuova, Opere* 4: § 1054). When *Scienza nuova* is used without further specification it refers to what in the Laterza edition is called the *Scienza nuova seconda*. "The Autobiography" is used without italics in citing the Italian text, but with italics in citing the English translation. References to editions of Vico's works other than the Laterza edition are given as above, but with the name of the edition in parentheses; for example, *Opere* (Ferrari) or *Opere* (Ricciardi).

Complete bibliographical information on the English translations of Vico's works, the Italian editions of his writings, and the short titles of his particular works employed herein is given in the foregoing note on "Vico's Writings."

References to *Giambattista Vico: An International Symposium*, ed. Giorgio Tagliacozzo and Hayden V. White (Baltimore: The Johns Hopkins Press, 1969) are given herein by title only.

But in the night of thick darkness enveloping the earliest antiquity, so remote from ourselves, there shines the eternal and never failing light of a truth beyond all question: that the world of civil society has certainly been made by men, and that its principles are therefore to be found within the modifications of our own human mind.

New Science, § 331

Guido Fassò

THE PROBLEM OF LAW AND THE HISTORICAL ORIGIN OF THE *NEW SCIENCE*

I

Most students of Vico's philosophy have repeatedly asserted that its basis is the principle of the identification of *verum* and *factum*—the principle that Vico set forth in 1710 at the beginning of the *De antiquissima Italorum sapientia* as an epistemological criterion over against the Cartesian principle of rational evidence. The development of Vico's philosophy on this account must have been the following: in reacting to the dominant philosophy of Descartes, Vico discovered and accepted as a general epistemological principle the notion that only he who has made things can truly know them. Therefore, as he limits himself to asserting in the *De antiquissima Italorum sapientia,* the science of things is possible only for God, the sole maker of them, while the only object of science for man is mathematics, since mathematical concepts alone are human creations. Later, as a result of new developments in his thought which occurred between 1710 and 1719, Vico overcame this original agnosticism, discovering that man is the author, not only of mathematics, but also of history. Thus, history was able to become for him an object of philosophical investigation, and the *New Science* was born, which is precisely a science of the world made by men.

Actually, even those who would not agree with this view of the formative process of Vico's philosophy, which is suggested by both the general conception and many particular aspects of the *New Science,* would have to recognize, by the words of Vico himself, that at its origin stands the principle of *verum ipsum factum.* In fact, immediately after his fundamental affirmation that the civil world had certainly been made by men and that therefore its principles were to be sought in the evolution of the human mind, Vico marvels at the fact that all philosophers had seriously sought to arrive at a science of the world of nature—the science of which only God could know, inasmuch as it was He who had made it—and that they had neglected to meditate on the world of the nations, or the civil world, "which, since men had made it, men could come to know."[1]

Even though they are enunciated only indirectly and incidentally in this

[1] *Scienza nuova, Opere* 4: § 331.

passage from the *New Science* of 1730, the connections to the epistemological thesis of the *De antiquissima Italorum sapientia* and its extension to history are evident. And the same connections appear in a passage a few pages later (this time, however, with an allusion to the theory of the scientific comprehensibility of mathematics originally set forth in 1710). In fact, Vico writes that his new science proceeds like geometry, which creates the world of its concepts in the very act of studying them, but with greater reality because the "deeds of men" have greater reality than geometrical figures. Thus the reader of the *New Science*, in meditating on the "ideal eternal history" of the "world of nations," inasmuch as it has been made by men, knows it as its maker, which ought to provide the reader with a kind of "divine pleasure" since "in God knowledge and creation are one and the same thing."[2]

Vico himself thus reaffirms, almost at the beginning of the *New Science*, the doctrine of the identification of knowing and making and alludes, without actually citing his work of twenty years earlier, to the theories of the *De antiquissima Italorum sapientia* concerning the perfect presence of that identification in God, modifying it only with the assertion that man has a science, not only of mathematics, but also—and better yet—of history. This seems to confirm the historical foundation of the traditional thesis according to which Vico's definitive and finished philosophy was created by his deliberate extension of the principle *verum ipsum factum* from mathematics to history. Difficulties arise here only in establishing the elements and the circumstances that led Vico to recognize the possibility, and thus the necessity, of giving to the principle of *verum ipsum factum* a wider range than he had given it in the *De antiquissima Italorum sapientia*.

Conversely, however, neither in the *Autobiography* (written between 1725 and 1728, that is to say before the *Second New Science* [1730], which contains the development I have just mentioned), nor in the *Diritto universale* (written between 1720 and 1721 and considered to be a preliminary version of the *New Science*), nor even in the *First New Science* (1725) does Vico mention the principle of *verum ipsum factum* and its possible applications. I do not mean to suggest that in the *Diritto universale* or in the *First New Science* Vico did not in effect apply that principle. What I doubt is that before 1730 Vico was aware of the presence in his new work of the principle that he had formulated in the old, that is, in the *De antiquissima Italorum sapientia*; and that, therefore, historically, the *New Science* could be considered the product of Vico's discovery of the possibility of extending the principle of *verum ipsum factum* to history and thus his deliberate extension of this principle to it.

By saying this I do not mean at all to deny the logic of the process of

[2] *Ibid.*, § 349.

Vico's thought; by offering the hypothesis that the principle of *verum ipsum factum* was not the historical cause of the *New Science*, I do not intend to say that it was not its cause in a deep and very real sense. The connection between the *New Science* and the identity of *verum* and *factum*, which we cannot doubt and which, as we have seen, finally was recognized by Vico himself, is already in itself a proof of that. And, I repeat, I wish only to suggest that this doctrine, although conceivably a logical cause of the *New Science*, may not have been its historical cause. Nor do I deny that between that logical cause (which is the principle of *verum ipsum factum*) and the historical cause (which, as we will see, is quite distinct from that) there might be an intimate connection which could indeed be seen as a substantial identity.

It is always necessary to keep in mind that Vico's thought was manifested in works whose unity resembled more a work of art than a true and proper philosophical system; that is to say, it is a spontaneous unity, not willed nor pursued in its determinate form, but actualized in its form by an immanent logic. This logic is certainly truer and deeper, but it is different from that which determined the historical process of the work's formation.

The interpreter capable of grasping Vico's essential thought might be led, therefore, to think that the logical process by which he succeeded in grasping it (and which is, in fact, its deep, true logical process) was also the process historically followed by Vico in his composition of the work. But in fact this was not the case at all. It is not, therefore, a contradiction to suggest that, given the fact that the doctrine of the identity of the *verum* and the *factum* was the real cause of the birth of the *New Science*, historically the latter was constructed by Vico independently of the former and that only much later, once the work was substantially completed, did he become aware of the connection between his final theory and the original one which, twenty years earlier, he had placed at the base of his philosophy.

II

It is really rather strange that, while in the *Second New Science* (1730), Vico asserted so explicitly the relation of his "ideal eternal history" to the doctrine of the identity of making and knowing, in those books which are considered to be earlier versions of that work or in some way expressions of his final philosophical views (the *Diritto universale* and the *First New Science*), he himself never acknowledged such a relationship. Whoever might maintain that the conceptualization of the *New Science* resulted from Vico's deliberate extension of the principle of *verum ipsum factum* to history, would have to find it strange that he does not speak of this at all in the *Autobiography*. It must be assumed that in the *Autobiography* (written between 1725 and 1728 and thus contemporaneous with the *First New Science*) Vico would have recounted everything relevant to the formation of his thought and the birth of his works. Yet in all the *Autobiography* Vico does not suggest any relationship at all between the birth of the *New Science* and the principle of *verum ipsum factum*. Indeed, he does not speak of any relationship between them, not even when he speaks of the *De antiquissima Italorum sapientia*, the book in which he originally set forth this principle. It might even be said that, when he was writing the *Autobiography* (and thus the *First New Science*), he attributed no importance to that principle.

In fact, there are no documents which permit us to assert that when, around 1720, Vico began to elaborate the final version of his philosophy, he was guided by an awareness of the applicability of the principle of *verum ipsum factum* to history. After having formulated this principle in 1710, Vico did not speak of it again even indirectly until 1730; while already in the *Diritto universale* and even more so in the *First New Science*, that is, from 1720 and 1725, he was making history itself the object of his philosophical studies.

It would seem, then, that before becoming aware that man could have a science of history because history is made by man, Vico had to discover that it is precisely man who makes history. First he had to discover that the subject and the creator of history is man and that, thus, to discover the laws of history, it is necessary to investigate the laws of the human spirit; only subsequently could he have stated the connection of this procedure with the doctrine of the identity of knowing and making.

The formative process of Vico's philosophy does not follow a syllogistic pattern: "man can have a science of that which he makes; man makes history; therefore man can have a science of history." The "new science" is not born historically as a science of history, as an investigation of history. Certainly Vico always had a lively historical sense, one that was evident from the days of his anti-Cartesian polemics; but in 1720, when he began the composition of the first part of the *Diritto universale*, the *De uno universi iuris principio et fine uno*, history was not his problem. If one really wants to schematize the formative process of his philosophy, the schema would look something like this: from a certain kind of research (which will soon be specified), Vico was led to try to construct a new science (which also will soon be specified); in constructing it, however, he recognized that it had to be a science of that which was made by man (that is, of history), and that in order to build such a science, it would be necessary—and *a fortiori* possible[3]—to find the principles of the human spirit in it. This, he next recognized, was consonant with his earlier doctrine of *verum ipsum factum*. Finally, the synthesis of the *vero* and the *certo*,

[3] *Ibid.*, § 331.

that is, of the universal and the individual, which was the basis of his new science, was theoretically justified by the identity of the "certain" with the "made," and therefore with the "true." But all that took time; and the synthesis of the true and the certain, which is justified by the identity of the true with the made, inasmuch as the certain is that which is made by man, Vico simply intuited and applied without even suspecting the need for a philosophical justification of it. This justification was worked out by him only after the work had been completed, when the development of the work had carried him very far from the problem with which he had started.

III

As I have said, neither in the *Autobiography* nor in any other of the works written before 1730 did Vico make any mention of the principle of the identity of the *verum* with the *factum*. But in the *First New Science* (1725) he presents his "new science" as one which must contain simultaneously the philosophy and the history of human customs, in such a way that the philosophy would develop a systematic list of "reasons" and the history would give an uninterrupted sequence of "the facts of humanity in conformity with those reasons."[4] The result is that the principles of this "new science" are divided into the two classes, those of ideas and those of languages.[5] That shows (as indeed does the whole structure of the work) that Vico was perfectly aware of the function in his work of the relation between the true and the certain, or between the universal and the individual, or between reason and fact (languages, together with "things," precisely constitute for Vico the certain, the knowledge of which he calls philology). Yet, as I have said, in the *First New Science* he did not in any way acknowledge the principle of the identification of knowing and making.

Even while in the contemporary *Autobiography* he remains silent regarding the principle of *verum ipsum factum*, in his account of the birth of the *New Science* Vico makes his conception of his definitive philosophical position dependent upon his discovery of the correspondence between, indeed the identity of, philosophy, or the science of the true, and philology, or the science of the certain. Vico tells us that he first intuited his new philosophy when, while reading Grotius, he became aware that in the sphere of culture there was still no system by which to relate philosophy to philology with any kind of scientific rigor;[6] and the "ideal eternal history"

[4] *Scienza nuova prima, Opere* 3: § 90.
[5] *Ibid.*, § 44.
[6] The Autobiography, *Opere* 5: 39.

in which he epitomizes his philosophy is founded, he says, on the philosophy and the philology of the human species.[7]

Even in the *Second New Science*, in which indeed one sees a recognition of the value of the principle of *verum ipsum factum*, this principle is hardly stressed at all. Vico does not place it among what he calls his "axioms" (*degnità*), that is, among those principles stipulated as the fundamental presuppositions of the work. And yet, many of these "axioms" refer to the identity of the "certain" and the "true," of "philosophy" and "philology."

If he had been aware that the new science was born from the principle of *verum ipsum factum*, Vico would then certainly have placed among those whom he calls his "authors" the thinker who had suggested it to him.[8] However, he names as his authors (that is, those who had provided the sources of his thought in any way whatsoever) writers who are totally unconnected with such a doctrine—Plato, Tacitus, Bacon, and Grotius. All of these, as I have shown elsewhere,[9] are related by Vico to the problem of the relation between the true and the certain, between the rational universal and the individual historical fact.

It is the principle of the identity of the true and the certain, and not of the true and the made, which, historically, generates the new science. If it is argued that, in their deepest essential meaning, the two principles coincide because both signify the synthesis or the mediation of the universal and the individual, I would agree completely and even grant the *logical* priority enjoyed by the principle of *verum ipsum factum*. But examination of Vico's texts shows that, of the two principles, the one which effectively and concretely operated in the generation of the *New Science* was that of the identity of the true and the certain.

The very expression "new science" appears for the first time in Vico's writings in connection with the assertion of the reducibility of philology to a science of the knowledge of the certain, in a passage of the *De constantia jurisprudentis* (the second part of the *Diritto universale*, which appeared in 1721). Significantly, this passage closes with the assertion that reason is the authority on which the "certain" rests:

Since man consists of intellect and will, everything that man knows is derived from the intellect or the will, and thus everything that is called 'knowledge' is connected either to the absolute necessity of reason or to the will of authority. Philosophy demonstrates the constancy of reason; let us try to demonstrate the

[7] *Ibid.*, p. 51.

[8] On the problem of who this might have been see R. Mondolfo, *Il "verum-factum" prima di Vico* (Naples, 1969).

[9] See my *I "quattro auttori" del Vico* (Milan, 1949) and my *Vico e Grozio* (Naples, 1971).

constancy of authority, to the extent that we have said that authority is a part of reason.[10]

This passage is immediately followed by the chapter entitled "Nova scientia tentatur"; and in fact, what Vico from 1725 on will call *New Science* corresponds to this part of the *De constantia jurisprudentis* in which the "new science is attempted" and which is entitled "De constantia philologiae," or rather, reduction of the knowledge of the certain (which is to say, of history, the knowledge of discrete facts, isolated by human will, by *auctoritas*) to a science or a recognition of the *verum* which is present in the certain.

IV

I stated earlier that the original impulse which led Vico to the conceptualization of his definitive philosophy was not an interest in the problem of history. He came to the problem of history while meditating on another problem, which provided him, thanks to the revelation of the relationship between the true and the certain, with the key with which to then penetrate the larger problem of history; this original problem was that of law. A strong indication of this is the fact that the first manifestation of Vico's mature philosophy is a work which even in its title clearly reveals that the author had proposed for himself and intended to deal with a problem of the philosophy of law—*De universi iuris uno principio et fine uno,* the first part of what Vico himself called, significantly, *Diritto universale,* and which he himself characterized as a "sketch" of the *New Science.*

Now the philosophical problem which law raised for Vico was precisely that of the relationship between the true and the certain—between a natural, or rational, law that was universally valid and positive and historical laws, apparently valid only insofar as they are chosen by human will, by *auctoritas.*

Vico himself comments in his *Autobiography* that when in his youth, following the desire of his father, he turned to legal studies, he found great pleasure in meditating on the general maxims of justice which the ancient interpreters (the glossators) had abstracted from the particular motifs of equity which had inspired the jurisconsults and the emperors; and that this was the aim of the entire study that he subsequently had

10 "Ut autem homo intellectu et voluntate constat, ita quicquid scit homo ab hominis aut intellectu aut voluntate profluxit, ac proinde omne quod discunt "scibile" aut ad rationis necessitatem aut ad auctoritatis arbitrium refertur. Philosophia firmat constantiam rationis: tentemus ut philologia firmet constantiam auctoritatis, qua via diximus auctoritatem partem esse rationis" (*Diritto universale, Opere* 2: 307).

dedicated to the principles of universal law.[11] This can only mean one thing: that, as soon as he had begun legal studies, Vico was led to pose the problem of the relationship between law as a universally and rationally valid idea and law as fact, as a historically determined phenomenon, that is, between the true and the certain in law.

The *Autobiography* offers us another documentation of this. Vico tells us that after having studied the *Ethics* of Aristotle, which deals with the problem of equity or of the relation between justice and positive law, he realized that Roman jurisprudence utilized numerous particular precepts treated by the laws, while by contrast the science of the just taught by the moral philosophers proceeded on the basis of a few eternal truths suggested by a metaphysical ideal of justice.[12] It is a matter of the relation between the certain and the true; but the *Autobiography* speaks of this problem only in the context of Vico's discussion of law.

In the first of Vico's major works, the *De nostri temporis studiorum ratione* (1708), which deals with the study methods of the various disciplines, it is jurisprudence which receives the most attention. Here Vico insists above all on the contrast between the Roman *ius civile*, based on authority alone, and the *ius honorarium*, based on equity or reason: on the contrast, in other words, between the certain and the true in law. This problem was certainly at the center of Vico's interest during those years, and it had been for some time: in fact, in the *Autobiography* he tells us that even before 1695 he had conceived "the idea of considering an ideal eternal law[13] (and, one should note, the "history" with which the *New Science* deals is precisely "ideal" and "eternal"). The idea of an eternal ideal law was obviously juxtaposed to that of a positive, historical or "certain" law. Meditating on the problem of ideal law, Vico was probably led to the idea of the presence of the rational in history, of the absolute in the empirical, of the universal in the individual, and, finally, of the rationality or providentiality of history.

The best proof of all this is the *De universi iuris uno principio et fine uno*, of which not only the title is eloquent. Its *Proloquium* lists, among those things which Vico calls the *scribendi causae*, the foundation of law on both *ratio* and *auctoritas*;[14] and speaking of the relationship between reason and authority in law, Vico criticizes those who are not aware that *auctoritas* is *rationis pars quaedam*. He anticipates Axiom X of the *Second New Science* by deploring that: "A general conflict exists between philosophy and philology, and the philosophers have never inquired into the reasons [that is, the rational and thus absolute necessity] of authorities [that is, the historical facts produced by the will], and the philologists

11 The Autobiography, *Opere* 5: 7.
12 *Ibid.*, p. 11.
13 *Ibid.*, p. 12.
14 *Diritto universale, Opere* 2: 26.

consider the universal theories of the philosophers to be enunciations of historical facts."[15] This is, obviously, the same assertion that Vico will repeat in his definitive work, no longer only in terms of law but also in terms of the whole of history (to which his inquiry will have been expanded): those philosophers who did not render "certain" their "reasons" by the authority of the philologists missed the mark as much as those philologists who did not bother to render "true" their "authorities" with the reason of the philosophers.[16] Vico thus applies to all of history a discovery suggested to him by his meditation on law.

One could cite many passages from the *De uno principio* to confirm the idea that the presence of the true in the certain was suggested to Vico by the history of law, and above all by Roman law. But since that would take up too much space, I refer the reader to my study of Vico cited above,[17] in which I discuss the signs of Vico's earliest interest in law in the *De constantia jurisprudentis* and in the two *New Sciences*.[18] What may be noted here is chapter 82 of the *De uno principio*, in which, with respect to law, and only to law, Vico explicitly indicates for the first time the connection between the certain and the true. The argument of the chapter "Verum legum et certum legum"—the problem of the relationship between the true and the certain in law—leads Vico to the conclusion that *certum est pars veri*.[19]

V

Now, in all of Vico's investigations of the problem of law, from which emerged the essential discovery of that connection between the true and the certain and between philosophy and philology, the principle of *verum ipsum factum* does not play a major role. The fundamental assertion contained in the *De uno principio* that *certum est pars veri* is not at all the result of an extension or of a new application of the principle of *verum ipsum factum*. It emerges instead directly from Vico's investigation of the relation between historical law and ideal law. If the discovery that the certain is part of the true had been suggested to Vico by the application of the principle of the identity of the true and the made, Vico certainly would have said it. Indeed, it would have been an excellent argument for

[15] "Universim philologiae et philosophiae dissidium factum est; neque philosophi auctoritatum rationes unquam investigarunt; et philologi vel ipsa philosophorum dogmata tanquam historias spectant" (*Ibid.*, p. 31).

[16] *Scienza nuova, Opere* 4: § 140.

[17] *I "quattro auttori" del Vico*, pp. 59–63.

[18] *Ibid.*, pp. 71–73; 75–90. Also the presence of Grotius among the "authors" of Vico is to be related to his interest in the problem of the relation between *verum* and *certum* in the field of law. See my *Vico e Grozio*.

[19] *Diritto universale, Opere* 2: 82–83.

the philosophical justification of his daring assertion. The same thing may be said about the place that chapter 82 and those following it occupy in the *De uno principio*. The treatment of this material suggests that this principle originated only from the study of the history of law and from the necessity to explain that history in philosophical terms.

And one should note another fact. In the *Proloquium* to the *De uno principio* Vico says that he had already arrived at the distinction between the true and the certain in the *De antiquissima Italorum sapientia*,[20] that is to say, in the book in which he asserted the principle of *verum ipsum factum*. If Vico had been aware that the relationship in which he had now placed the true and the certain was the same as that between the "true" and the "made," in citing the *De antiquissima Italorum sapientia* he would certainly have referred to this fact which in the other book is stressed greatly; and not referred to the distinction between the true and the certain which in this work is only marginal and not emphasized at all.[21]

The relationship between the true and the certain, between *ratio* and *auctoritas*, which is suggested in the *De uno principio* is not exactly the same as that used by Vico in the *New Science*, because it does not yet signify the synthesis of the universal and the individual, but only the participation of the latter in the former. In the *De uno principio* the doctrine of the synthesis of the universal and the individual remains unclear, as indeed the whole work is unclear, and oscillates between traditional philosophy and historicism. However, the discovery of the simple connection between the true and the certain, whatever this connection might be, is the motive force behind all subsequent developments in Vico's work. As we have already seen, when, in the *De constantia jurisprudentis*, Vico announces the *nova scientia*, that is, the demonstration of the scienticity (*constantia*) of philology, the knowledge of the certain, he justifies this attempt by recalling that *auctoritatem partem esse rationis*.[22] As we have already seen, in Vico's language *auctoritas* is the origin of the *certum*. To say *auctoritatem partem esse rationis* is thus to repeat the assertion of the *De uno principio* that *certum est pars veri*.

Actually, Vico's works from 1720 on are, in a certain sense, all of a piece. His investigation of the relationship between historical and ideal law generated the *De uno principio* and the discovery of the connection between the true and the certain. This discovery, the basis of much of the *De uno principio* itself (though not all of it, which accounts for the want of philosophical coherence between its first and second parts), generated

[20] *Ibid.*, p. 35, n. 1.

[21] *De Italorum sapientia*, *Opere* 1: 147.

[22] *Diritto universale*, *Opere* 2: 307. Vico himself recalls, in a note, chapter 83 of the *De uno principio*, in which, from the affirmation contained in the preceding chapter, that *certum est pars veri*, is deduced, still in reference to law, *auctoritatem cum ratione omnino pugnare non posse*.

the *De constantia jurisprudentis,* which is born of the application of the principle *certum pars veri.* The period between the *De uno principio* and the *De constantia jurisprudentis* was so short (one year only) that Vico himself was not aware of the transition completed in his thought with the extension of the principle *certum pars veri* to all of philology, that is to say, to history. Vico considered the *De constantia jurisprudentis* to be an appendix of the *De uno principio.* He entitled it *jurisprudentis* because he believed it to be merely a continuation of his earlier researches in law. For the same reason, he called the totality of the two works *Diritto universale.*

In turn, *De constantia jurisprudentis* generated, by means of the *Scienza nuova in forma negativa,* the *First New Science.* And in fact, even the *First New Science* is, in part, a "universal law," that is to say a *natural* law possessing absolute validity, but with respect to mankind, which is to say that it is "historical"—a law which is at one and the same time true and certain. This reminds us of the title of the *First New Science*[23] and explains Vico's habit, otherwise inexplicable, of calling history the "natural law of mankind."

VI

At the same time that Vico was extending his research from the philosophical investigation of law to the whole of history, he became increasingly aware that since law as well as history is the work of men, therefore the philosophy of both could be found only in the philosophy of the human spirit. In this way Vico was led to discover the fundamental "single truth" that the world of nations was made by men; this was why its principles had to be sought in the nature of the human mind.[24]

Thus we pass from the *Diritto universale* to the *Scienza nuova prima,* in which the new science is in fact called, with an unconscious reference to its original aspect, a "jurisprudence of the human race," but also, in the same book, an "ideal eternal history."[25] The development of Vico's thought is completed finally in the *New Science* of 1730, in which the "system of the natural law of the gentes" is relegated to only sixth among the seven aspects which, according to the author, the *New Science* is presenting. And only at this point, when the development of his thought has come to the extreme consequences to which the synthesis between philosophy and philology led, is Vico able to acknowledge that his new doctrine, now become "a history of human ideas, on which the meta-

[23] The full title is *Principi di una scienza nuova intorno alla natura delle nazioni, per la quale si ritruovano i principi di altro sistema del diritto naturale delle genti.*

[24] *Scienza nuova prima, Opere* 3: § 40.

[25] *Ibid.,* § 90.

physics of the human mind must proceed,"[26] is perfectly harmonious with the theory of the identity of knowing and making. In fact now, for the first time, after twenty years, Vico explicitly says this. And yet, he cites it not as fundamental, but as a simple confirmation of the truth that "the world of civil society has certainly been made by men and its principles are therefore to be found within the modifications of our own human mind."[27] The principle of *verum ipsum factum* is cited, not as a condition or origin of the new science, but as extra proof of its foundation. Vico evidently knew well that he had come to it by another road, that of the correspondence of the true and the certain that had been suggested to him by his research on the relationship between ideal and historical law.

Translated by Margaret Brose

[26] *Scienza nuova, Opere* 4: §§ 347 and 391.
[27] *Ibid.,* § 331.

Donald R. Kelley

VICO'S ROAD: FROM PHILOLOGY TO JURISPRUDENCE AND BACK

The Vico Road goes round and round
to meet where terms begin.

James Joyce, *Finnegan's Wake*

"History does not yet have its principles."[1] When Giambattista Vico made this observation in 1720, he was already at work on a remedy. It is hardly too much to say that his entire intellectual life was taken up with an unwavering, though not quite single-minded, attempt to do for the human past what Isaac Newton had done for nature, that is, literally to fashion a *Principia* of history. Over two decades before, in his first inaugural lecture at the University of Naples, he had announced the primacy of human culture for the attainment of true wisdom; and in the subsequent quest he became increasingly convinced that, given the weakness of human nature and the corruption of human intelligence, the only route was, not through pure reason, but through the investigation of humanity's past in all of its richness and depravity, in all of its grandeur and absurdity. This lifelong search took Vico along a very circuitous and often unmarked trail. Sometimes he lost his bearings, doubled back, and tried again to find the right path; but never did he give up the journey, which began as early as 1700, when according to Vico's own recollection he "entertained in his mind a new and grand idea of uniting in one principle all of human knowledge."[2] This aim was pursued through an encyclopedic variety of works ending in the successive metamorphoses of the *New Science*.

Vico's lament about the disorder of history applies also to his own career, for his biography likewise lacks its "principles," in his sense of the term, though his *Autobiography* certainly provides materials for such a project. The first and perhaps most significant of Vico's axioms is that one has to begin at the beginnings: "Doctrines must take their beginnings from that of the matters of which they treat."[3] It is the curse of human nature, he assumed, that men cannot apprehend things through pure reason but must proceed gradually, by empirical and historical means, the way children learn. Analogously, on the level of metaphysics, Vico

[1] *Diritto universale*, bk. 1: *De uno principio*, ch. 104, *Opere* 2: 95: "Historia nondum habet sua principia." Cf. *Scienza nuova prima*, bk. 2, ch. 57, *Opere* 3: § 208: "Scoverta de' veri elementi della storia."

[2] The Autobiography, *Opere* 5: 31.

[3] *Scienza nuova, Opere* 4: § 314.

tended to assume that the properties of any changing thing are present in some fashion from its inception, so that in order to understand the character of anything—the *ingenium* of a nation, for example—one had to begin *ab ovo*. As applied to biography this is not quite an invitation to psychoanalysis, but it does imply that a man's ideas and attitudes may be understood most directly in terms of his early studies and enthusiasms, not in terms of his final philosophy. And this assumption is quite in line with certain other features of Vico's thought: that formal philosophy is vastly inferior to the natural workings of the human mind;[4] that the study of language and topics belong to childhood, while philosophy and criticism belong to old age; and that in general mature and reasoned wisdom is actually "derived" from the more creative thought processes of youth—the child is literally father of the man. Moreover, since Vico's "methods" were designed specifically to help historians in the reconstruction of complicated, obscure, and unrecorded processes, it seems most appropriate to apply them to his own mental life.

How does this genetic approach apply to Vico? The pattern seems clear, though the details are few. At the age of seven Vico fell on his head and was unconscious for five hours or so. Now it would be unkind to suggest that this misfortune had a formative impact upon his thinking; yet it was the first event of his life that he thought worth recording, and if nothing else it interrupted his studies and forced him to become his own teacher for some three years. It marked his first departure from conventional education and so the first stage of his growing intellectual independence, and to this extent he never fully recovered from his fall. At the castle of Cilento he continued his solitary habits of study for nine years, continuing to be, in his own word, an "autodidact," and proud of it. Later he "blessed his good fortune in having no teacher whose words he had sworn by. . . ." He was used to being alone in his opinions and out of step with his times—to being, as he put it, "a stranger in his own land." The result was to broaden but hardly to discipline his mind. Despite later vanity about the mathematical design of his work, he had little use and less aptitude for the niceties of geometry, which he thought proper rather to "minute wits" than to "minds already made universal by metaphysics." For logic he had even less patience, and he gave it up altogether. What he wanted was to range over the whole spectrum of human knowledge, especially the preserve of the humanities, in order to find relationships grander than those of Euclid or even of Newton. In Vico's own terms his point of departure, and indeed his final destination, was not philosophy but "philology."[5]

Although we may think of Vico as a philosopher, in fact the subject that he taught for most of his active life, over forty years, was rhetoric; and

[4] First Inaugural Oration, *Opere* 1: 10.
[5] The Autobiography, *Opere* 5: 3, 9–22.

so he was, in the most traditional sense, a professional humanist. He was an accomplished poet, and towards the end of his life he was appointed royal historiographer as well.[6] That he belonged to the grand tradition of Renaissance humanist scholarship is indicated by the substance of his erudition, his ideas about language, his concerns with such problems as world chronology, and even his encyclopedic plan to establish a unified system of knowledge. This allegiance was increasingly obscured by tendencies in his later writing: by the penchant for generalizing and turning every insight into a "principle"; by his fascination with system, geometric design, and circular form; and by the tendency (illustrated in the successive versions of the *New Science*) to suppress citation of "authorities," as if literally to proceed, as he promised in his *Autobiography*, "as if there were no books in the world." Yet beneath the eclectic exterior of this rococo philosophy it seems apparent that Vico's main achievement—his basic inspiration, key concepts, and scholarly instincts—derived from his peregrinations about that humanist circle of learning centering about the *studia humanitatis* and the attitudes associated with these. "How many new arts have been devised!" marveled Vico in a formula that had been part of humanist litany for centuries. "How many new sciences!"[7] He was thinking, too, of course, of the achievements of men like Galileo and Descartes; but it is important to remember that his own great enterprise, his own "new science," was a reconstituted version of that central creation of Renaissance scholarship, *philologia*, which he began by celebrating in the same "encyclopedic" terms as those employed by Lorenzo Valla, Guillaume Budé, and Erasmus. The first phase of Vico's intellectual road, then, coincided with the later stages of Renaissance Humanism.

> A prolonged visit to a house
> of call at Cujas Place.
>
> *Finnegan's Wake*

Yet if Vico was a humanist by calling and by training, he did not want to spend his entire professional career within the confines of the *trivium*, teaching liberal arts to children. His particular goal was not philosophy, however, but jurisprudence, a subject which had been the secondary focus of his studies almost from the beginning and which figured most prominently in his early scheme of learning, as it had in the descriptions of the *studia humanitatis* by many earlier humanists. His approach was through

[6] See the addendum to the Autobiography by the Marchese di Villarosa, *Opere* 5: 84.

[7] *De mente heroica, Opere* 7: 19; cf. *De studiorum ratione, Opere* 1: 78. The orientation of the present discussion, general and specific, arises from my *Foundations of Modern Historical Scholarship: Language, Law, and History in the French Renaissance* (New York, 1970).

the textbooks of Hermann Vulteius and Henricus Canisius and the legal history by Vincenzo Gravina; then he moved on to the sources of civil and canon law and took his degree *utriusque*. He was won over to the tradition of legal humanism associated with the names of Valla, Budé, Andrea Alciato, and especially Jacques Cujas (*interpetri eruditi, Alciatani,* or *Cujaciani*) because of its criticism and critical method, but at the same time he respected the medieval jurists (*giureconsulti medesimi*) because of their philosophical standards.[8] The trouble with modern jurisprudence, he believed, stemmed from the conflict between these two schools. "Why has philology been alienated from philosophical studies?" he asked.[9] The fault lay not only with the traditional hostility of scholasticism and humanism, he suggested, but also with the fashionable naturalistic bias of Descartes and his disciples. The major objective of Vico's legal quest was, by building on the work of a few pioneers like Grotius, to reunite the soul and body of jurisprudence and to restore its essential "constancy."

One of the turning points in Vico's life came in his attempt to achieve professional status by obtaining the chair of law at his University of Naples. His account of the competition is at once comic and pathetic. He described his assigned lecture as a triumph of wit, strategy, and learning. His subject was the *Digest* title "On Prescriptions," and he displayed both his learning and his characteristic eclecticism by defending medieval jurists like Accursius, as well as the humanists Alciato, Cujas, and Hotman.[10] But Vico's curious erudition did not carry the day; and in view of the overreaching and rather bizarre notions expressed in his *Universal Law*, composed with an eye to this chair, the decision of the university authorities may not seem surprising. In any case he spent the rest of his life in his lowly position. Thenceforward Vico was not only isolated, he was without chance of professional advancement. His only hope lay in the future, that is, in literary fame, and the vehicle of this fame would be his *New Science*, already prefigured in his *Universal Law*, in which Vico would create and preside over his own world.

From a genetic and historical—a Viconic—point of view, however, the key work of Vico's career, in Vico's characterization, was the earlier one, the *Universal Law*. Here we can see the first effects of the union between Vico's "new science" of philology and that most perfect form of wisdom, which was jurisprudence. The direction of this, the first major phase of Vico's road, is clear. Vico explained,

[8] The Autobiography, *Opere* 5: 7ff.; cf. *De studiorum ratione, Opere* 1: 100–13; *De Italorum sapientia, Opere* 1: 145–46; *Diritto universale*, "De opera proloquium," §§ 17–18, *Opere* 2: 31–32. In general see Fausto Nicolini, *La giovinezza di Giambattista Vico (1668–1700)* (Bari, 1932), and Benvenuto Donati, *Nuovi studi sulla filosofia civile di G. B. Vico* (Florence, 1936).

[9] *Diritto universale*, bk. 2: *De constantia jurisprudentis*, pt. 2, ch. 1, § 24, *Opere* 2: 318.

[10] The Autobiography, *Opere* 5: 44–47.

Philology is the study of speech and it treats of words and their history, then shows their origin and progress, and so determines the ages of languages, thus revealing their properties, changes, and conventions. But since the ideas of things are represented by words, philology must first treat the history of things. Whence it appears that philologists study human governments, customs, laws, institutions, intellectual disciplines, and the mechanical arts.[11]

If mathematics was the language of the book of nature, as Galileo had taught, philology was indispensable for anyone who hoped to penetrate the book of humanity. As for the target of this philological method, it would be that subject which was at once a cornucopia of learning, the most comprehensive expression of ancient culture, and the most complete reflection of human society and its ideals—namely, jurisprudence, and particularly Roman jurisprudence. Although Vico chose Greek poetry, and specifically Homer, as the vehicle of his masterwork, the *New Science*, it should be understood that most of his insights and ideas and general line of argument were developed first of all in the context of, and with the aid of, the Western legal tradition—the great *respublica jurisconsultorum*, as one of Vico's Neapolitan contemporaries called it, which included all of Europe and almost two millennia within its boundaries.[12]

The debts owed by Vico to jurisprudence are incalculable and in some cases almost indemonstrable, at least in terms of conventional *Quellenforschung*, for they involve matters not only of content but of form and method, not only *exempla* but, much more significantly, also *principia* of human behavior. In many ways Vico may be understood as another in the long line of commentators on the texts of civil law.[13] His discipleship is most clearly apparent in his discussion of such classic rubrics as "On law and justice," "On the origin of law," and "On the meaning of words," as well as in his investigation of such sources as the Law of the Twelve Tables and the post-Roman *Consuetudines Feudorum*. The main difference between Vico and other commenators is that Vico, following the lead of such freewheeling Renaissance jurists as Jean Bodin, departed from convention, not only by changing the order and meaning of topics and, in typically eclectic fashion, by adding extralegal material, but by transmuting

[11] *Diritto universale*, bk. 2: *De constantia jurisprudentis*, pt. 2, ch. 1, § 1, *Opere* 2: 308.

[12] Giuseppe Aurelio di Gennaro, *Respublica jurisconsultorum* (Leipzig, 1733).

[13] A "born glossator" Vico is called by Frank Manuel, *The Eighteenth Century Confronts the Gods* (Cambridge, Mass., 1959), p. 150. Certain aspects of the juridical tradition on which Vico drew I discuss in "The Development and Context of Bodin's Method," in *Jean Bodin: Verhandlungen der internationalen Bodin Tagung in München*, ed. Horst Denzer (Munich, 1973), pp. 123–50; in "Clio and the Lawyers: Forms of Historical Consciousness in Medieval Jurisprudence," *Medievalia et Humanistica*, n.s. 5 (1974); and in "Louis le Caron Philosophe," in *Philosophy and Humanism: Renaissance Essays in Honor of Paul Oskar Kristeller*, ed. Edward Mahoney (Leiden, 1975), pp. 16–35. Unfortunately, there is no useful general treatment of the legal tradition between the late Middle Ages and Vico's time.

them into almost unrecognizable form in order to elaborate his philosophical view of history. Most of his ideas about the origins and processes of historical change, of the structure and values of civilization, and even of the nature of human consciousness can be correlated with, if not derived from, legal formulas. Topics should be studied in youth, when memory is strongest, Vico believed, and philosophy in maturity, when reasoning powers are greatest; and the pattern of his own thought seems to follow this prescription, for it was Roman jurisprudence that provided the topical basis for the first expression of Vico's science of humanity.

No less important, though less obvious, was Vico's reliance upon the hermeneutics developed within the legal tradition; and characteristically his adaptation of the *ars interpretationis* of the jurists was a conflation of humanist and scholastic methods of exegesis—another manifestation of the fusion of philology and philosophy. Like the humanists, he insisted on understanding laws in their specificity and historical context, and in particular he carried on their pursuit of interpolations, that is, of "Tribonianisms," and anachronisms.[14] Yet he transformed these attitudes into a highly theoretical way of "divining" and interpreting antiquity. He was especially fascinated with the possibilities of etymology, though again he refused to be bound by a narrowly literal interpretation. So he rejected Valla's famous criticism of a conventional derivation of "testament" (from a "testifying of the mind") on the grounds that law was not restricted by grammar. His view was not unlike that of another fifteenth-century jurist, namely, that etymology was not merely historical but was designed to get at the "quidditas" of a term (*ex rerum ipsarum vi et potestate*, as Vico put it); and the result was sometimes derivations as outlandish as some of those of Isidore of Seville.[15] But in general Vico preserved the goal of Renaissance jurisprudence: to determine not only the letter but also the spirit (*voluntas, mens, ratio*) of laws, and even to "correct" them according to rational standards. Vico may have gone further than his predecessors, but not necessarily in another direction. In any case the second stage of his road is marked by his adaptation of the forms, methods, and attitudes of Roman legal science.

[14] *Diritto universale*, bk. 1: *De uno principio*, chs. 85 and 211, *Opere* 2: 84–85 and 243–45; and in general, Vincenzo Piano Mortari, *Ricerche sulla teoria dell'interpretazione del diritto nel secolo XVI* (Milan, 1956), and Pietro de Francisci, "L'antitribonianismo di G. B. Vico," *Rivista internazionale di filosofia del diritto* 5 (1925): 428–36. This entire issue of the *Rivista* is devoted to the subject of Vico and law.

[15] *Diritto universale*, bk. 1: *De uno principio*, ch. 170, *Opere* 2: 184–85; *ibid.*, bk. 2: *De constantia jurisprudentis*, pt. 2, ch. 7, *Opere* 2: 342–44; *Scienza nuova prima*, bk. 2, ch. 60; *Opere* 3: §§ 212–18. Cf. Lorenzo Valla, *Elegantiae latinae linguae*, VI, 36, in *Opera omnia*, ed. Eugenio Garin, 2 vols. (Turin, 1962), 1: 217, and Claude de Seyssel, *Speculum feudorum* (Basel, 1566), p. 11.

Long Livius Lane . . .
by New Livius Lane

Finnegan's Wake

"To jurisprudence," Vico declared, "the Romans gave the same definition as the Greeks gave to wisdom, 'the knowledge of things divine and human.' "[16] For Vico this famous formula, derived from the first title of the *Digest*, had a threefold function. First, it provided him with a vehicle for his conception of culture, which was essentially a projection of this traditional idea of *sapientia*. Second, this fundamental distinction, which corresponded to that between philosophy and philology, established, in a temporalized form, the *termini a quo* and *ad quem* of the trajectory of cultural history, which in a sense recapitulated that of individual education. Finally, it offered the Roman experience as the paradigm of historical change.

Remember. O Romans, you keep universal rule over nations
In these ways: by maintaining peace through law,
By doing justice to the lowly, by bringing down the haughty.[17]

These lines of Vergil, which Vico was fond of citing, symbolized also Vico's own adaptation of Roman law, which likewise gave conceptual order to the chaos of human history, gave new significance to primitive creations, and placed the most exalted constructs of civilization in critical perspective. In Vico's vision of history, then, Rome again ruled the world of the *gentes* and established the conditions for *humanitas*, or rather for Vico's science thereof.

The supreme model of *Romanitas* was that great "image of antiquity," as Cicero called it, the Twelve Tables; and in his discussion of this alpha and omega (*finis et fons*) of civil law, Vico once again was carrying on a leading theme of humanist scholarship, which had tried to reconstruct this monument since the sixteenth century.[18] Here was displayed the "heroic

[16] *De studiorum ratione*, *Opere* 1: 101. Cf. also the Sixth Inaugural Oration, *Opere* 1: 66; *Diritto universale*, "De opera proloquium," §§ 2–6, *Opere* 2: 26–28. See also the *Digest*, I, 1, 1, and in general Eugene F. Rice, Jr., *The Renaissance Idea of Wisdom* (Cambridge, Mass., 1958), and Benvenuto Donati, "La definizione di Ulpiano di 'juris prudentia' e l'interpretazione del Vico," *Archivio giuridico "Filippo Serafini"* 98 [4th ser., 14] (1927): 51–74.

[17] *Diritto universale*, bk. 1: *De uno principio*, ch. 186, *Opere* 2: 214, and "Sul diritto natural delle genti," *Opere* 7: 27. See in general Giovanni Baviera, *Giambattista Vico e la storia del diritto romano* (Palermo, 1912); Max H. Fisch, "Vico and Roman Law," in *Essays in Political Theory: Presented to George H. Sabine*, ed. Milton R. Konvitz and Arthur E. Murphy (Ithaca, 1948), pp. 62–88; Elio Gianturco, "Vico's Significance in the History of Legal Thought," in *Giambattista Vico: An International Symposium*, pp. 327–47; and especially Dino Pasini, *Diritto, società e stato in Vico* (Naples, 1970).

[18] *Diritto universale*, bk 1: *De uno principio*, ch. 176, *Opere* 2: 197; *ibid.*, bk. 2: *De constantia jurisprudentis*, pt. 2, ch. 36, *Opere* 2: 564–71; *Scienza nuova*, *Opere* 4: § 154, and the first *ragionamento* appended to the *Scienza nuova*, *Opere* 4: §§ 1412–54.

wisdom" of Rome, of which Vico recognized three elements. The first, as always, was the divine origin and character of primitive law, which caused the founding fathers to enshroud their handiwork in secrecy and led later jurists to style themselves, in Ulpian's phrase, "priests of the law" (*sacerdotes legum*).[19] Second, and correlative to this, was the poetic character of this law, which Vico later referred to as a "serious poem" both because of its mythical overtones and because traditionally it had in fact been chanted. Recalling Justinian's own remark about the "fables of early law," Vico declared that "ancient jurisprudence is poetic throughout."[20] Last, and a function of these, was the extreme formalism of ancient law, which reflected the literalism of a preconceptual period when words had a magic power: "As the tongue has declared so shall it be binding," Vico quoted, and "When the words fail the cause is lost."[21] From these elements came the conservative and almost hermetic nature of Roman law and its intimidating historical force, which, as Vico pointed out, inspired even in the reforming Justinian a great "reverence for antiquity." *Patrios mores servandos* ("the ways of the fathers must be preserved") was the formula Vico cited.[22]

Through the Twelve Tables Vico gained some of his most important insights about the conventional legal *quaestio de origine juris* and so the *principia historiae* which constituted the primary target of his *Universal Law*. Prehistorical times (*tempus obscurum heroicum* or *fabulosum*) were no golden age, no Thomist state of innocence, but rather were filled with crime and acquisitiveness—the brute rule of "mine" and "thine" described by jurists like Lucas de Penna and Bodin.[23] Regulation of this primitive anarchy began with individual action, which is to say, in terms of private law. *Lex ex facto oritur* ("law originates in fact") was the old formula. Vico illustrated this process through the etymologies of terms designating early means of acquiring possessions, such as *mancipatio* (*res manu captae*, "by hand"), *usucaptio* ("by use"), and *heredity* (related to *hero*), and also through discussion of paterfamilial practices and the notorious *patria potestas*. Testamentary succession itself was a legal act based on individual will and thus, according to Vico, an antecedent of the famous political principle that the prince's will was law (*quod principi placuit legis habet vigorem*). In general, he assumed, "familial or domestic authority" (*aucto-*

19 *Diritto universale*, bk. 1: *De uno principio*, ch. 168, *Opere* 2: 180; cf. *Digest*, I, 1, 1, 1.

20 *Diritto universale*, bk. 1: *De uno principio*, ch. 182, *Opere* 2: 200–201; cf. Justinian's prefatory edict to the *Digest*, "Tanta." See also *De uno principio*, ch. 124, *Opere* 2: 114; *Scienza nuova*, *Opere* 4: §§ 469 and 1027.

21 *Diritto universale*, bk. 1: *De uno principio*, ch. 180, *Opere* 2: 198.

22 *Ibid.*, chs. 141 and 215, *Opere* 2: 132–34 and 250.

23 *Ibid.*, ch. 104, *Opere* 2: 95–101. Cf. Jean Bodin, *Method for the Easy Comprehension of History*, trans. Beatrice Reynolds (New York, 1945), p. 297, and Lucas de Penna, cited by Walter Ullmann, *The Medieval Idea of Law as Presented by Lucas de Penna* (London, 1946), p. 47.

ritas oeconomica seu familiaris) constituted the "first foundation of government" (*rerum publicarum rudimentum*).[24] At one point Vico departed from the common view of Bodin and others, and that was in his belief that aristocracy, not monarchy, was the first type of government. According to the formula of Pomponius cited by Vico, "When the institutions themselves dictated it, kingdoms were founded."[25]

For Vico, then, might made right, or rather right originated in might: at first, as he put it, *bonus* meant simply *fortis*. This heroic form of justice he called the "law of private violence" (*jus privatae violentiae*), and within this he recognized three protolegal categories. These were lordship, liberty, and self-defense (*dominium, libertas, tutela*), of which the last two comprised what the jurists had called "prior natural law," and the first, "posterior natural law." To these correspond also, it is important to note, a series of other basic and completely homologous triads which expressed, in Vico's characteristically systematizing way, various aspects of *humanitas*. These included the three parts of human nature, which are knowledge, will, and strength (*nosse, velle, posse*); the three heroic moral qualities, virtue, temperance, and fortitude; the three parts of jurisprudence, philosophy, history, and judgment; and even the three species of government, monarchy, aristocracy, and democracy.[26] It was in terms of these categories that the historical process itself unfolded, and here again the pattern was juridical in nature. The movement was from a private to a public sphere, specifically to the political categories of eminent domain, civil liberty, and sovereignty (*summum imperium*). "Out of lordship, liberty, and self-defense," as Vico summed it up, "all republics are born." So in that "adolescence of the human race" men passed from a fabulous and heroic age into historical time (*tempus historicum*), and so Vico laid the foundation for another of his theories of humanity, that "the order of ideas proceeds according to the order of things."[27]

The remaining question was the cause of this social transformation, and again Vico had recourse to a legal convention. What impelled men to move from a state of nature to a state of society was not mere natural utility, as such infidels as Machiavelli and Grotius had argued. Rather it was that fundamental concept of civil law, equity—*aequum bonum* was the term Vico adapted from Ulpian's famous definition of law as *ars boni et aequi*—which was the "source of all natural law" (*fons omnium naturalis juris*); and this in turn was inseparably bound up with that motive

[24] *Diritto universale*, bk. 1: *De uno principio*, chs. 100ff., *Opere* 2: 90ff.

[25] *Scienza nuova, Opere* 4: § 584.

[26] The heroic moral qualities and protolegal categories are discussed in *Diritto universale*, bk. 1: *De uno principio*, chs. 71ff., *Opere* 2: 75ff.; corresponding triads appear in the "De opera proloquium," esp. §§ 2, 25, and 28, and in chs. 10 and 138ff., *Opere* 2: 26, 34f., 44, and 128ff.

[27] *Diritto universale*, bk. 1: *De uno principio*, chs. 87, 108, and 124, *Opere* 2, 86, 104, and 114; *Scienza nuova, Opere* 4: § 238.

force of civilization, the drive toward truth (*vis veri*).[28] Here is another conspicuous illustration of Vico's aversion to naturalistic explanations. Utility was merely the occasion for social organization; the cause was a kind of moral instinct (*honestas*). "The true reason of state" (*giusta ragione di stato*) was not animal self-interest but human equity (*aequitas civilis*). So the "principles of history" were linked directly with the "principles of jurisprudence" (*legitimae scientiae principia*).[29] This transmuted and temporalized form of jurisprudence, Romanoid if not Roman, constitutes the third stage of Vico's road.

> Panoptical purview of political progress and the future Presentation of the Past.
>
> *Finnegan's Wake*

In his own eccentric and eclectic fashion Vico fulfilled another part of the enterprise of late medieval and early modern jurisprudence, which was to rationalize and to systematize law and especially to raise it above its Romanist context. Yet even this work was carried out in terms provided by the civilian tradition; namely, the field defined by ancient jurists as "the law of nations" (*jus gentium*), though as usual Vico transformed this concept. In the first place Vico, again like Bodin two centuries before, in effect equated this field with that of universal history, which represented the combined life stories of all the *gentes* and their customs and institutions. Secondly, he altered the *jus gentium* in historical terms by distinguishing between the law of the greater nations (*jus majorum gentium*) and that of the lesser (*jus minorum gentium*)—that is, between the "heroic" jurisprudence and wisdom of the fathers and the civil institutions of the first governments. Vico summed it up in this way: "From the principle of self-defense [*tutela*] comes the *jus gentium*, which can be defined as the law of violence, and as self-protection is the first law of human life, so it holds first place in history, which is the life of the human race."[30]

[28] *Diritto universale*, bk. 1: *De uno principio*, chs. 34ff. and 55, *Opere* 2: 49ff. and 61–62; cf. *Digest*, I, 1, 1. In general see Nicola Petruzzellis, "*Vis Veri e Societas Veri* nel pensiero di G. B. Vico," in *Giambattista Vico nel terzo centenario della nascita* (Naples, 1971), pp. 37–51, and for the Renaissance background, Guido Kisch, *Erasmus und die Jurisprudenz seiner Zeit* (Basel, 1960).

[29] *Diritto universale*, bk. 1: *De uno principio*, chs. 46, 53, 179, and 185, *Opere* 2: 54–56, 60–61, 198, and 209–13; cf. *Scienza nuova*, *Opere* 4: §§ 320 and 948.

[30] *Diritto universale*, bk. 1: *De uno principio*, ch. 100, *Opere* 2: 90. Among many studies, see Guido Fassò, *Vico e Grozio* (Naples, 1971), Girolamo Cotroneo, "A Renaissance Source of the *Scienza nuova*: Jean Bodin's *Methodus*," in *Giambattista Vico: An International Symposium*, pp. 51–59, and Elio Gianturco, "Character, Essence, Origin and Content of the *Jus Gentium* according to Vico and Suarez," *Revue de littérature comparée* 10 (1936): 167–72, and "Bodin and Vico," *ibid.* 22 (1948): 272–90.

One of the consequences of this principle was that, on a priori grounds, Vico could not accept the idea of appreciable cultural "influence" in the early stages of a national history. Although every nation experienced the same general process, each had its own *ingenium* (*genius* was the humanist term) and cultural style. In general terms Vico accepted the humanist commonplace about the antihistorical character of Greek thought and the nonphilosophical character of Roman thought, and so he rejected as a fable the account, given by Pomponius and accepted by all previous commentators, about the trip made by the *decemviri* to consult with the wise men of Athens before drawing up the Law of the Twelve Tables.[31] This view was reinforced by Vico's study of feudal law, that is, of the *Consuetudines Feudorum*, which jurists had persisted in regarding as an authentic part of Roman law. According to the *communis opinio*, the institution of fiefs was Roman in origin, and the usual source, suggested by humanist and scholastic jurists alike, was the ancient *clientela*. Only a minority argued, largely on terminological grounds, that feudalism had to be acknowledged as modern, and specifically Germanic, in origin. Here again Vico constructed a kind of metahistorical synthesis out of these two interpretations. While agreeing that fiefdom and vassalage were Germanic in character and in no way an imitation of Roman practices, he nonetheless insisted upon the analogy with the ancient *clientela*. But he reversed the practice of the jurists by applying "barbaric" terminology to early Roman society instead of applying classical terminology to feudal institutions. "Roman law emerged from feudal law," as he expressed it, "not feudal from Roman," by which he meant that "feudalism" represented an early stage of every society.[32] So the old rubric *de origine feudorum* became the starting point for another of Vico's principles of history.

For Vico the period of barbaric culture, or "heroic wisdom" (*heroica sapientia*), was crucial in the establishment of these principles; thereafter it was simply a question of the way in which they were worked out. In general the pattern of civilization was remarkably similar to the evolution of jurisprudence—as well as to the education of a legal-minded scholar like Vico. The movement of history was from particularity to uniformity, from the private sphere to the public, from anarchy to order, and from philology to philosophy. The signs of this transformation in the period of "human jurisprudence" included the appearance of standards of comfort instead of

[31] *Diritto universale*, bk. 1: *De uno principio*, ch. 176, *Opere* 2: 197; *Scienza nuova*, *Opere* 4: § 1031, and the first *ragionamento* appended to the *Scienza nuova*, *Opere* 4: §§ 1412–54; cf. *Digest*, I, 2, 2: "De origine juris."

[32] *Diritto universale*, bk. 1: *De uno principio*, chs. 129 and 192, *Opere* 2: 119–20 and 222–23; *ibid.*, bk. 2: *De constantia jurisprudentis*, pt. 2, ch. 21, esp. § 41ff., *Opere* 2: 450–78, esp. 467ff.; *Scienza nuova prima*, bk. 2, ch. 31, *Opere* 3: § 149; *Scienza nuova*, *Opere* 4: § 599. See also Fausto Nicolini, *Commento storico alla seconda Scienza nuova*, 2 vols. (Rome, 1949–50), 2: § 1057, and more generally my "De Origine Feudorum," *Speculum* 39 (1964): 207–28.

utility, natural equity instead of special interests, and popular government rather than oligarchy. Similarly Roman jurisprudence had been organized in rational terms, and jurisconsults had become philosophers of the law (*philosophi legum*) instead of mere practitioners (*pragmatici*, the traditionally derogatory term of humanists).[33] Law became at once more equitable and more general: cases became members of instead of substitutes for general categories, and the primitive *ingenium* of Rome was transformed into true wisdom. In this final period of enlightenment there also emerged what Vico called the "constancy" of jurisprudence, philosophy, and philology, and consequently the means for acquiring a true understanding of humanity. It is precisely at this point, indeed, that for the first time Vico proclaims: "a new science is attempted."[34]

On the most general level of all, Vico saw the process of history as operating between another set of terminals corresponding to what was perhaps the most fundamental of all of Vico's concepts, distinguishing between the certain (*certum*), which belonged to human consciousness, and the true (*verum*), which was the province of nature and of God.[35] In law the distinction was between the standards of authority, which extended from human will, and reason, which applied to "the necessity of nature"; and human experience, historical as well as individual, naturally proceeded from the first to the second—from standards that were *de facto*, arbitrary, and perhaps irrational to those that were *de jure*, equitable, and perhaps philosophical. Before being amenable to reason, Vico said, men had first to become accustomed to authority; and so it was not always possible (according to an admission which Vico adapted from Justinian) to understand the rationale of some early laws. In general, Vico thought, "ancient jurisprudence neglected the true for the certain," that is, equity for the "propriety and origin of words." On the other hand the medieval "interpreters" tended to dogmatize unhistorically without a proper understanding of philological "authority." These were the conditions of that discord of philology and philosophy which Grotius, that philologist of universal understanding—"jurisconsult of mankind" Vico called him—began to repair, and which spurred Vico to his effort to reconstruct the essential "constancy of jurisprudence" and to establish the "natural law of nations" (*jus naturale gentium*).[36] This system of universal law constitutes one facet of the *New Science* (where it is termed *diritto naturale delle genti*) and one of the last stretches of Vico's road.

[33] *Diritto universale*, bk. 1: *De uno principio*, chs. 19 and 84, *Opere* 2: 46 and 84.

[34] *Ibid.*, bk. 2: *De constantia jurisprudentis*, pt. 1, ch. 1, and pt. 2, ch. 1, *Opere* 2: 272 and 308ff.

[35] *Diritto universale*, "De opera proloquium," § 30, *Opere* 2: 35; *ibid.*, bk 1: *De uno principio*, chs. 83 and 180, *Opere* 2: 83–84 and 198.

[36] *Diritto universale*, bk. 1: *De uno principio*, chs. 136 and 218, *Opere* 2: 126–27 and 254–55; cf. *Scienza nuova*, *Opere* 4: §§ 31, 154, and 394, and "Sul diritto natural delle genti," in *Opere* 7: 25–31.

By a commodius vicus
of recirculation. . . .

Finnegan's Wake

"The true principles of history," Vico announced in the first version of his *New Science*, "are those rules of morality, politics, law, and jurisprudence of the human race, discovered by this new science of humanity, by which the universal history of nations is governed, and which determine their rise, progress, maturity, decline, and fall."[37] So at last we reach the final and most traveled portion of Vico's road, the part where it begins to circle around and join with its beginnings by considering the nature of poetry, myth, religion, and other aspects of "poetic wisdom" in terms of a number of hybrid pseudosciences, including a "philosophy of authority," a "civil theology," and a "rational chronology," as well as a "philosophical grammar," a "system of universal law," and a myriad-formed "philosophy of history."[38] As Galileo had begun to decipher the great book of nature through mathematics, so Vico began to decipher, likewise in a "new science," the book of humanity through language; and what finally emerged was not so much a *philosophia perennis* as a *philologia perennis*.

Despite "geometrical affectations," the orientation of Vico's thought was always historical and indeed (one need not be a Crocean to say) historicist; and his principal sources of inspiration were the *studia humanitatis* and the human "science" of law (*legitima scientia*, it is called in the *Digest*). Jurisprudence was scientific, as jurists had argued for centuries, both because it dealt with things in terms of cause and effect and because it was universal, though, unlike natural philosophy, it had as its goal human welfare; and such were precisely the claims that Vico made for his "new science."[39] Jurisprudence differed from natural philosophy, moreover, in that its arrangement was topical (in a rhetorical sense) rather than logical, and its categories—persons, actions, things, relations—were those of society rather than metaphysics. It was this human system of moral, social, and political thought, it may be suggested, rather than the tradition of Greek, scholastic, or Cartesian metaphysics that provided Vico with his principal model and central ideas. Indeed, in laying the foundations for his new science of humanity, Vico was quite directly fulfilling the old Roman ideal set down in the very first sentence of the *Digest* (and quoted approvingly by him), that "jurisprudence is the true philosophy."[40]

Even while transcending the European legal tradition, however, Vico

[37] *Scienza nuova prima*, bk. 2, ch. 57, *Opere* 3: § 208.

[38] *Scienza nuova, Opere* 4: §§ 385–99; *Diritto universale*, bk. 2: *De constantia jurisprudentis*, pt. 2, ch. 1, *Opere* 2: 308–19.

[39] A characteristic discussion is Barthélemy de Chasseneuz, *Catalogus gloriae mundi* (Paris, 1529), X, 9.

[40] *De studiorum ratione, Opere* 1: 101; cf. *Digest*, I, 1, 1, 1.

continued to be affected by its habits and techniques; for the older jurists, too, had transcendental pretensions—hoping, in Vico's terms, to understand not only the certain, from authority, but also the true, through reason. "To understand laws," according to the formula of Celsus cited by Vico, "is not only to know their letter but also their spirit and intention."[41] In legal terminology the "spirit of law" (*mens* or *ratio legis*) referred basically to the intention of the lawmaker as contrasted to the *verba* of the law itself, but it connoted also the rational justification of the text. Vico was quite in agreement with the standard sixteenth-century view that "the *mens* represents the soul of the law, the *verbum* its body," though as usual he fitted this idea into his own dialectical scheme. Specifically, his point was that the *mens legis* had to do with the authority of the law (and so belonged to the realm of the *certum* and to the standard of utility), while the *ratio legis* had to do with its rationality (and so involved the *verum* and equity). The consequence for Vico, as for Montesquieu, was that comprehension of "the spirit of laws" required both historical and legal—both philological and philosophical—analysis.[42] Indeed these two processes, together with their practical application to society, constituted the essence of jurisprudence, whose purpose was thus one of restoration of natural and divine law. What was true of jurisprudence held for wisdom in general: "The first principles of all sciences are from God," Vico declared at the outset of his *Universal Law*,[43] and yet the "true principles" of Vico's science lay only at the very end of his road.

Old Vico roundpoint.

Finnegan's Wake

"So turns the circle of divine law," Vico wrote.

As all human law begins with divine law, so by the succession of things which we have followed, it returns to divine law. And as society was begun among men by God through that succession of the law of the major nations, common civil law, and the law of the minor nations through war, so it endures in God Himself.[44]

The parallel with the pilgrimage of Dante, noted over a century ago by Michelet and by many others since, is striking. Like Dante, Vico regarded language as the gateway to the truth and "poetic wisdom" as the most

[41] *Diritto universale*, bk. 1: *De uno principio*, ch. 84, *Opere* 2: 84; cf. *Digest*, I, 3, 17.

[42] *Diritto universale*, bk. 1: *De uno principio*, ch. 81, *Opere* 2: 82. Cf. Stefano Federici, "De interpretatione legum," in *Tractatus universi juris* (Venice, 1584), I, 210, and in general Piano Mortari, *Richerche sulla teoria dell'interpretazione del diritto nel secolo XVI*.

[43] *Diritto universale*, bk. 1: *De uno principio*, ch. 1, *Opere* 2: 43.

[44] *Ibid.*, ch. 156, *Opere* 2: 162.

essential starting point, yet a transcendental vision as the final destination. Like Dante, he took the experience and values of the Roman tradition as his guide. Like Dante, too, he traversed a number of circles, rising from the elementary learning of the liberal arts to the exalted certainty of philosophy and theology, of divine wisdom, before reaching his final vision. The difference is that Vico's path did indeed circle back upon itself, ending up with a system of human science, a theory of history, language, and culture, and with a revelation not about the destination of humanity but rather about its origins—about the *principia* of history and the roots of language, the baby-talk of the human race.

Vico's own intellectual *corso* exhibits a similar circular pattern, especially in the convoluted, multilayered, multiversioned *New Science*; for to arrive at his destination he had indeed to become as a child. He returned not only to the elements of grammar and primitive speech of childhood, to the credulity and creativity of that stage of life, but also—the main aspect of his new science—to his catechism. But in another sense, of course, he was not really back at his starting point at all: the element of self-consciousness was added; he was at the beginning of a *ricorso*, so to speak. Emulating the divinity, he had transcended humanity by—in intellectual terms—recreating it, and so finding his end in humanity's beginning. Having begun with a state of natural law as a divine given, Vico offered his own system of natural law as a rational construct, thus indeed, in his role of philosophical demiurge, transforming the *factum* into the *verum*, the realm of *coscienza* into that of *scienza*. There are countless ways of looking at Vico's grand construct—as an encyclopedic summary of centuries of Western scholarship, as a cornucopia of new and previously undefined disciplines, or perhaps merely as a giant cryptogram of curious learning—a "vicous circle," in one of Joyce's apter coinages. But as for comprehending the past of humanity, it must be said that Vico transcended rather than resolved the problem, offering instead a sort of codification of his own reading of the humanistic and especially the legal traditions and one of the largest *petitiones principii* on record. The original dilemma remains: "History does not yet have its principles."

Alessandro Giuliani

VICO'S RHETORICAL PHILOSOPHY AND THE NEW RHETORIC

. . . verum . . . est intellectus humani ingenitus appetitus . . . homines sicut delectantur veris, ita indolent falsis.

Vico, *Institutiones Oratoriae, Opere* (Morano) 7:98

Introduction: The *Institutiones oratoriae*

The return to Vico of contemporary humanism coincides, not casually, on the one hand with a widespread dissatisfaction with Cartesianism considered as philosophy of the social sciences and on the other with the reappraisal of the topical method, submitted for reconsideration by the school of the "new rhetoric." This essay, inspired by a prevailing theoretical interest, intends to be a first attempt to identify the relationship between Vico and the contemporary revival of rhetoric. Only in recent times have we rediscovered the logical and philosophical dimension of rhetoric, for long relegated to the role of theory of the ornate form. This revival encourages us to inquire into the work of Vico as professor of rhetoric, as evidenced by the much neglected *Institutiones oratoriae*.[1] Over these, in truth, there still weighs the heavy judgment of idealistic historiography, according to which "in vain one would look [into that work] for a shadow of his true thought."[2] Even those who have not neglected his rhetoric lectures have concluded them to be a "manual of style," belonging to the first "literary" phase of the Vichian speculation.[3]

The contribution of his rhetoric teaching, which began in 1699, seemed in truth to be inconsequential, but from the beginning his speculation seems to have a juridical as well as a rhetorical orientation. Research on the didactic activity of Vico can throw light on the form of his dialectical

[1] On the various manuscripts and the various editions, prepared by students of the University of Naples, of Vico's rhetoric lectures see B. Donati, *Nuovi studi sulla filosofia civile di G. B. Vico* (Florence, 1936), p. 134. Citations to the *Institutiones oratoriae* in this essay are to the 1711 text as published in the Morano edition of Vico's works. In the more recent Laterza edition of Vico's works the manual of 1711 was not considered worthy of complete publication, although some precious citations from its 1738 edition are included (see the Laterza edition, *Opere* 8: 197–203).

[2] Benedetto Croce, *Estetica come scienza dell'espressione e linguistica generale*, 9th ed. rev. (Bari, 1950), p. 253.

[3] Donati, p. 148.

thinking, to which Pietro Piovani has called attention.[4] The influence of the *Institutiones* can be found in his entire vast production, and even in the *Scienza nuova*; special attention from this point of view is due to the *Inaugural Orations* from 1699 to 1708, which we here consider in close relationship to the *Institutiones*. Vico himself calls for a unitary interpretation; his lectures do not lack some explicit *Selbstzitat*. Such a point of view is confirmed by his Autobiography: "What later on unfolded in my mind, I had been searching for since the early inaugural orations."[5]

In this essay we hope to show that Vico cared neither for the theory of the ornate form nor for the emotive rhetoric. Logic and philosophy were always his primary concern: that is, the relationships "rhetoric-logic" and "philosophy-rhetoric." Thus he stands out in contrast with an epoch that had failed to question the legacy of the previous centuries; rhetoric had emerged from the Renaissance impoverished, once its divorce from logic had been decreed. A theory of ornamentation had resulted which progressively came close to poetry; the most apparent result is found in the baroque era. By establishing once again the ties of rhetoric with philosophy and law, Vico returned to the classical tradition; this appears to us as one of the most significant aspects of Vico's debt not only to Roman thought (especially Cicero's)[6] but also to Greek thought. From that tradition Vico derived some principles that could be thus summarized:

(a) the aim of rhetoric is the search for truth, and diverting from this end represents an abuse;

(b) rhetoric is a methodology for the exact application of words to things, to facts; but it is a matter of things and facts that can be changed through human choice; and

(c) the relationship between rhetoric and truth is the reflection of an aspiration of human reasoning, of a natural disposition towards truth which Aristotle called νοῦς and the Romans *intellectus*.[7]

We would like to call attention to the last point, which represents a constant reference to his first philosophical reflection. It is said in the *Institutiones* that truth is *intellectus humani ingenitus appetitus* (p. 98); but Vico's intellect is not—as the modern concept of intellect—an instrumental reason, that is a means towards the search for truth, but a source of truth. He is aware that modern rationalism has been at the heart of the corruption of the classical meaning of intellect and that philosophical reason has been transformed into scientific reason. In the whole development of

4 Pietro Piovani, "Vico without Hegel," in *Giambattista Vico: An International Symposium*, p. 103.

5 *Opere* (Ricciardi), p. 50.

6 Pietro Piovani, "Il debito di Vico verso Roma," *Studi Romani* 17 (1969): 15, asserts that: "Vico's philosophy from many points of view could be called Ciceronian."

7 On the historical and methodological aspects of the rhetoric (and of the dialectic) as theory of the argumentation see A. Giuliani, "Logica giuridica (teoria dell'argomentazione)," *Enciclopedia del diritto*, vol. 25 (Milan, 1974).

his thought there is a constant reference to a reason that does not deal with means but with ends (from those suitable to human nature to political ones); but the terminology varies. In the first oration of 1699 the reference to the tendency of human nature for truth is central (*natura enim nos ad veritatem fecit . . . ita errare, nescire, decipi humanae menti inimicum*). The tendency towards acquiring knowledge is a divine gift; the fool who renounces knowledge is his own worst enemy.[8] In the *De uno principio* Vico insists that the intellect is a faculty; the *vis veri*, like the Aristotelian intellect, is an intellectual virtue (*vis veri quae errorem vincit est virtus dianoethica*).[9] For Vico, therefore, men are created first of all to know truth, even before utility. A fundamental problem, then, is the equitable exchange in truth; the society of truth (*societas veri*) seems to be inherent in the society of the useful (*societas aequi boni*).

The principle of veracity implies the social use of reason and the exchange of truth. From this point of view, science itself is not different from common knowledge. This is why Vico seems to have been fascinated by the processes through which the human mind learns. His faithfulness to the classical concept of the intellect must be gleaned from a varying terminology: common sense, intelligence, *ingenium*, etc. Fantasy is the eye of the intellect. If, however, nature *nos ad veritatem fecit*, the conquest of truth is difficult, because it can be achieved only in a situation of controversy. Vico was quite conscious, to quote freely from Price, that "clarity is not enough."[10] The methods are determined by the object of the inquiry; the domain of human truth requires a method which analyzes the points of view, the opinions according to a juridical model of reasoning.

It is up to that "art of learning the truth,"[11] which is dialectics, to regulate communication and information; in fact, as there exists the abuse in exchange relative to utility, there exists also the abuse in the exchange relative to that good which is truth. Dialectics—like rhetoric—inasmuch as it aims at establishing a situation of reciprocity in the search for truth, is juridically oriented. In this emerges that connection between truth and

[8] Inaugural Orations, *Opere* 1: 13. See also Donati, p. 165 and M. Candela, *Diritto e umanità in G. B. Vico* (Empoli, 1968), p. 125.

[9] *Opere* 2: 50. See N. Petruzzellis, "*Vis Veri e Societas Veri* nel pensiero di G. B. Vico" in *Giambattista Vico nel terzo centenario della nascita* (Naples, 1971), p. 37.

[10] H. H. Price, "Clarity is not Enough" in *Clarity is Not Enough*, ed. H. D. Lewis (London: Allen and Unwin, 1963, p. 15. Note what Vico said in the famous *Risposta* of 1711: ". . . clear and distinct knowledge is a vice and not a virtue of human understanding. . . ." (*Opere* [Ricciardi], p. 324).

[11] ". . . questa [la topica] è l'arte di apprender vero, perchè è l'arte di vedere per tutti i luoghi topici nella cosa proposta quanto mai ci è per farlaci distinguer bene ed averne adeguato concetto; perchè la falsità dei giudizi non altronde proviene che perchè l'idee ci rappresentano più o meno di quello che sono le cose: del che non possiamo star certi, se non avremo raggirata la cosa per tutte le questioni proprie che se ne possano giammai proporre" (*Risposta all'articolo X del tomo VIII del "Giornale dei letterati d'Italia"* [1712], *Opere* [Ricciardi], p. 356).

justice which will remain a central aspect of Vichian speculation; truth has not only a logical value but also an axiological value.

What is the relationship between dialectics and rhetoric in Vico? It seems to be a relationship of "connection-distinction": they are neither wholly divided nor wholly identified. Useful elements can be found in the paragraph of the *Institutiones* devoted to the topical art (p. 10), dealing with rhetorical and dialectical proofs. The logical means of the dialectician are the same as those of the orator (and of the jurist); the latter in fact cannot do without the *argumenta docentia*, which Perelman would classify among the quasi-logical arguments.[12] But Vico does not rely on these arguments, limiting himself to examples, since it is not the function of a rhetoric treatise to give rules: *tradere praecepta nostrae provinciae non est* (p. 11). How can such indifference be explained? We shall attempt to show that rhetoric must concern itself, according to Vico, with the application of logical evidence to argumentative situations. The knowledge of logical proofs is a prerequisite of their application; but to discuss them is not the function of a rhetoric manual. For Vico, rhetoric is essentially logic of argumentation, technique for the presentation of argumentative data; but rhetoric—and this must be emphasized—is not divorced from truth because the orator holds his audience by truth (*veritate tenet*): only the learned (*qui vera sequuntur quia vera sunt*) are content with the truth; to the masses the truth is disagreeable if it is not rendered attractive (*illecebris iucundum*) (p. 2).

One could suspect that Vico sought in the *ratio artificialis* of rhetoric the new sense of producing and acting which was unknown to the techniques of modern reason. He seems to find here the premises for the study of the social functions of reason, for the sketching out of a psychology of the associated minds. It is true that, after the first oration, the problem of knowledge is posited in the field of what ought to be done, which is fundamental for rhetoric. But such study is not possible independently of the analysis of those moral and natural dispositions of man, which are the virtues. The phenomenology of exchange is analyzed not only from the point of view of the utility (*societas aequi boni*), but also from that of human communication (*societas veri*). The problem of good faith and *veriloquium* emerges from the society of truth. From the same emerges ultimately the interest in error, that is, in fallacy, which had been neglected, at least in appearance, in the *Institutiones*.

The rhetoric is divided under five heads—invention, disposition, elocution, pronunciation, and memory—but most of the emphasis is on those heads more intimately tied to a theory of argumentation, to invention, and above all to elocution. Profoundly innovative, Vico treats elocution, not

[12] Ch. Perelman and Lucie Olbrechts-Tyteca, *Traité de l'argumentation* (Paris, 1958), p. 259. English trans.: *The New Rhetoric*, trans. J. Wilkinson and P. Weaver (Notre Dame, 1969).

from the stylistic point of view, but from the logical point of view of argumentation. The distinction between invention and elocution seems relative; invention is subordinated to elocution, which is a methodology for the presentation of argumentative data. While by the previous tradition elocution had been considered merely as an accessory, on the contrary Vico accorded it a primary situation and seems to have identified it with rhetoric itself: *huius artis pars potissima est* (p. 72). He bases this on the fundamental idea that the study of expressive means cannot be disassociated from that of the mental procedures. Linguistic communication is also mental communication. For this reason—getting away from the order of the *Institutiones*—we start by dealing with elocution; here one can see the pattern of Vico's rhetorical philosophy, of the subordination of philology to philosophy. Later we shall take up the theory of controversy which is discussed—in the chapter on invention—apropos of the *genus judiciale.*

The main head of rhetoric: elocution. The tripartition of elocution: elegance, dignity, and composition

Attention should be called to the fact that more than half of the *Institutiones* is dedicated to the chapter on elocution, with which rhetoric itself seems to be identified. Elocution is a methodology for the application of words to things: *est autem elocutio idoneorum verborum, et sententiarum ad res inventas, et dispositas, accomodata expositio* (p. 74). It is therefore a technique for the presentation of argumentative data—a technique of presence. Language is intimately tied to thought; the study of expressive means makes possible an analysis of the internal constitution of the human mind and its social operations. Even if Vico accepts the classical tripartition of elocution—into elegance, dignity, and composition—the heading of composition is of little importance: composition, really, is the more stylistic part, and he spends little time on it.

In relation to elocution, let us examine the various points considered by Vico:

a. Elegance. Elegance is a virtue of oration which serves to select the appropriate expression; but the expressive phenomenon is not separated from the mental one: *ad explicanda quaeque mentis sensa deligimus verba, quae ad ea ipsa significanda . . . nata sunt* (p. 81). The choice of words must be related to common language, which is the most important manifestation of a mental communion, the vehicle of a collective experience, including not only the *vocabula propria* but also the metaphor (*translata ex causa necessitatis*). Metaphoric language—and this topic will be taken up more extensively in the section on *dignitas*—is ordinary language inasmuch as it is born from the poverty of speech. Closely connected with a theory of argumentation is the thesis that synonyms do not exist: *in nulla lingua reperiri ista quae synonima appellantur* (p. 82). No word means exactly the same as another. Vico's work, when it deals with the distinction between meanings and with etymologies, seems closely connected to such a thesis.

Vico gives extensive treatment to metaphoric language represented by conceits, maxims, and aphorisms; the problems found in this discussion are reconnected to the sixteenth-century polemics concerning *dicta acuta.* His "author" here seems to be Aristotle, who saw in the gnomic knowledge one of the most important manifestations of collective knowledge; it seems that Vico learned from Aristotle that the philosophers' task is the analysis of common wisdom. Getting away from some authors of treatises of the seventeenth century, he distinguishes between *dicta acuta* and *arguta;* only the former are connected with the truth, inasmuch as they facilitate the process of learning and therefore are related to intellect.

From a general point of view, elegance appears to be subordinated to *dignitas.* The latter teaches us the appropriate expression (*ut dicamus apta, et quae deceant* [p. 101] and therefore constitutes the central head of elocution.

b. Dignitas. While the previous tradition had fallen into heavy and scholastic casuistry, Vico treats tropes and figures in a logical perspective. Metaphorical character is not independent from cognitive value; it derives from the insufficiency of the linguistic patrimony, which is rooted in the nature of things. Metaphor, metonymy, synecdoche, and irony are mentioned among the tropes, but the metaphor enjoys an absolute pre-eminence: *ex omnibus . . . facile princeps metaphora* (p. 102). Once the metaphors "for ornament" are distinguished from the "necessary" metaphors,[13] attention is focused on the latter. Metaphors based on necessity presuppose (*a*) the poverty of the language (*verborum inopia*) and (*b*) an analogical reasoning (*ratio similitudinis*).

The point of departure of the reflection on the metaphoric and analogic character of the language is found in rhetoric itself; since the metaphor is reasoning based on similitude (*contracta in unam vocem similitudo*), it must correspond to things; and the treatment of the cases of *viciosa metaphora* assumes a profound familiarity with the pathology of argumentation, and especially with the theory of fallacies. Vico will remain faithful to the superiority of the metaphor—in the *Scienza nuova prima,* the three evolutive phases of language are related to the three tropes: metonymy, synecdoche, and metaphor—he will realize that irony and lie are born from reflection.

[13] *Institutiones oratoriae, Opere* (Morano), p. 101. Of the change in meaning: "duae videntur causae: necessitas et ornatus. Necessitas ea fuit, quod cum verba, ut inquit iurisconsultus, sint rerum notae, et multo plures sint in natura res verbis. . . ." The distinction between the metaphors by "necessity" and those by "ornamentation" has its roots in the classical topical tradition. See Aristotle, *Soph. El.,* 165ª II; Cicero, *De orat.,* 3, 153.

From the point of view of a theory of argumentation the scholastic classifications of the figures have no value, especially the distinction between the figures of speech and the figures of thought, which concerns only stylistics. Vico's criticism aims at devaluating the figures of speech:

> their nature is such that their artifice has nothing of value, and they aim more at appearance than at substance. They please indeed, but are of no use to things. In as much as they are sudden and manifest, they distract the audience from things, instead of calling attention to them. And since they are obvious, they manifest the artifice, they annul any credibility. (p. 115)

The distinction between figures of speech and figures of thought therefore has no logical value; only the latter *non aures, sed mentem occupant.*

Vico accepts traditional examples and terminology but attempts to single out logical classifications from the *figurae sententiarum*—for instance, *ad probationem, ad explicationem, ad exprimendos mores, ad affectus.* The reference to a juridical model of reasoning, to the scheme accusation-defense, is always assumed. The figures, in short, are means of evidence, of confutation, of justification; and among them should be included exclamations, interrogations, and imperatives. Every classification is to be understood in a relative sense; only the interest for the argumentative utilization of figures is relevant. Here we will limit ourselves to mentioning some of the figures *ad probationem*: "prolepsis," through which we confute in advance a possible accusation; "communication" (or anocenosis), which, involving the appeal to the impartial judgment of the judge, assumes a sympathetic attitude.

The figures, in short, like the metaphors, are not ornaments of speech, but mental procedures. The tension between letter and spirit, which is tied to every figurative utterance, is a constant which cannot be eliminated; departure from normal use must be justified by the argumentative situation, and with respect to this it appears appropriate. Vico, unlike the moderns,[14] is no victim of the so-called descriptivistic fallacy, inasmuch as he is aware that the descriptive use of language does not exhaust the area of its functions. Figurative language has a prescriptive, normative function; the human world and its institutions are dependent on it. Speaking of Terence, Vico says that from the many examples of civil customs, "one could assume a definite criterion about the duties of men."[15]

The theory of figures, especially, reveals that rhetoric is a technique of presentation, since the choice by the orator must take into account the argumentative situation: *pro rerum de quibus agit diversitate* (p. 110). The discourse on the metaphors and figures goes back to philosophy, inasmuch as the notion of presence is tied to a metaphysic of the human mind. There is an implied reference to true and real intellect,[16] that is, to

[14] M. J. Charlesworth, *Philosophy and Linguistic Analysis* (Louvain, 1961), p. 178.
[15] *Opere* (Ricciardi), p. 960.
[16] *De Italorum sapientia, Opere* (Ricciardi), p. 293.

a reason not instrumental, which permits us to analyze procedures of evaluation and of justification, to sympathize, to look at the rules from an inside point of view.

The theory of controversy

The interest in the logical aspect of Vico's rhetoric is confirmed by the incisive and, in some respects, original treatment of the theory of judicial controversy (*status*). Through his lecture on this topic, Vico obtained the chair of rhetoric, as he tells us in his Autobiography: "So Vico competed with an hour's lecture on the opening lines of Fabius Quintilian's very long chapter *De Statibus Caussarum*, limiting himself to the etymology of the term *status* and the distinction of its meaning, full of Greek and Latin erudition and criticism. . . .[17] Vico was quite aware that the theory of controversy,[18] closely tied to a juridical model of reasoning, represented the most logical chapter of rhetoric: *ista de statibus caussarum inveniendis praecepta sunt vere logica.*[19] It should not be forgotten that the classical theory of *status* had made it possible to go beyond an emotive and irrational rhetoric. The distinction among the various types of conflict has an objective, impartial, and neutral value; from this perspective rhetoric appears structurally as the art of distinguishing (*ars distinguendi*). The díalectician does not simplify; he distinguishes. He is aware that the clarity which takes no consideration of the nature of the problems is wrong because it ends up by ignoring the question. The controversy, understood as a center of argumentation, is complex, and the rhetorician must distinguish within it a plurality of questions (principal, subordinate, preliminary, etc.)

The breaking down of the questions makes us aware of the entire gamut of the conflicts; to understand their nature represents a first step in getting out of a controversial situation. Hence, the importance for the orator to identify the preliminary question (*questio princeps*): *est autem iudicatio questio princeps, de qua iudices iudicare, et quam orator confirmare debet* (p. 30). Even if there is no specific treatment of the theory of the relevance of the questions, Vico—under the heading of confutation—points to the importance of the preliminary questions, which logically prevent the treatment of the main issue: *Caput aggredimur si inde caetera tamquam annulis catenata dependant* (p 69).

Truly, the theory of controversy has philosophical implications which must be sought from the changes in the scholastic classifications; hence the

[17] *Opere* (Ricciardi), p. 30.

[18] On the theory of rhetorical controversy (*status*) see A. Giuliani, *Il concetto di prova: contributo alla logica giuridica* (Milan, 1961), p. 55.

[19] *Institutiones oratoriae* (1738 edition), *Opere* 8: 201.

importance of identifying the theory proposed by Vico. In general he seems to depart from the prevailing Roman tradition which distinguished between logical questions (*status rationales: coniectura, definitio, qualitas*) and legal questions (*status legales*), that is, controversies concerning the interpretation of the law—*antinomia, ambiguitas, ratiocinatio, translatio*. Vico is a profound innovator. He accepts the tripartition: controversy on the fact (*coniectura*), on the name (*definitio*), and on the quality (*qualitas*).[20] He places the *status legales* in the realm of the *qualitas*. We would like to call attention to this latter aspect, inasmuch as it assumes the primacy of the controversy concerning quality; and this is the reflection of a concept of rhetoric, axiologically and philosophically oriented, to which Vico will always remain faithful. For this reason—getting away from the order of Vico's treatise—we shall deal first with "quality," and later with "definition;" the controversy on the fact (*coniectura*) is of minor relevance to the scope of this essay.

Let us consider the main controversial issues:

a. "Quality" (normative issue) and the theory of confutation. The controversy on quality is the model of the practical problems and has strong judicial basis. The philosophical question itself, like the juridical controversy, belongs to quality; we could say that it involves the domain of values. In short, there is no structural difference between thesis and hypothesis; we read in the Autobiography that Vico "resorted always to the practice of advancing universal arguments."[21] If one recognizes the juridical nature of the qualitative area, as Vico does, its confutatory character emerges.[22] Confutation is in this case the normal procedure of justification, of proof, the analysis of the rules, of the proposed models, cannot be independent from the judgment of the parts. The practical problem appears to us from this perspective as an argumentative situation. Every participant, arguing from relevant circumstances, indicates the limits of the applicability of the rules. Even if only in his own interest, he enlarges the field of information and, though it is not his intention, serves the cause of truth. We have reason to assume that the realization of this might have suggested to Vico the famous principle that *homo non intelligendo fit omnia*.

The normative issue is divided into dialectical question (*status quali-*

[20] The distinction between *coniectura, definitio,* and *qualitas* becomes more intelligible if one accepts the terms "existential issue," "conceptual issue," and "normative issue" which are recommended by Mortimer J. Adler, "Philosophical Discussion and Controversy," in *Idea of Freedom* (New York, 1957), p. 16.

[21] *Opere* (Ricciardi), p. 33.

[22] The "confutatory" character of the research is constituted by the problems of quality. On the distinction between "absolute" and "relative" confutation in the topical tradition see A. Giuliani, "La logique juridique comme théorie de la controverse (a propos du *περί τῶν στάσεων* d'Hermogène de Tarse)," *Archives de philosophie du droit* 15 (1966): 87.

tatis rationalis) and legal question (*status qualitatis legalis*). (1) *Qualitas rationalis* is a controversy related to values and choices the techniques of which have a confuting and justifying character. The confutation can be absolute (*absolute*), or relative (*assumptive*). The absolute refutation is like an aggression whose aim is to paralyze the accusation, by questioning the premises, the preliminary questions. One does not deny the existence of a fact and of its definition, but its quality (*recte factum esse defendimus*), moving from causes of extralegal justification (*naturae instinctu, nationum consensu, sapientum virorum iudicio*, etc.). The relative confutation does not deny the quality of the fact; it actually puts it in a certain time dimension concerning exceptional circumstances. For example, in the case of the *concessio*, we recognize the unlawfulness of the fact, but we find a justifying cause in *imprudentia*, in *necessitas*, in *fortuna*.

(2) *Qualitas legalis*. The attraction of the controversies related to the legal interpretation in the area of "quality," implies transferring the mechanism of information peculiar to the latter one. This assumes the rejection of a conception of interpretation as interpretation of a legal text, of a written document; the text is but an element in the interpretative process: the primacy of the case, as well as that of the "nature of things," on the abstract norm is assumed. Using the dialectical method in the domain of interpretation makes it possible to give information about the relevant circumstances. The ambiguity of the normative language appears, then, not only inevitable but even beneficial, inasmuch as it makes its adaptability possible. The conflict between the letter and the spirit of the law, to which Vico devotes much space, seems to be implicit in the figurative character of the normative statements. However, the most important of all *status legales* is the form of analogical reasoning based on the similitude, that is, the *ratiocinatio* (*in quo statu stant omnes fere de iure disceptationes*). The *a simili* reasoning in fact remains outside any systematic claim, inasmuch as it is tied to the opinion and therefore to a dialectical procedure of research.

b. "*Definition*" (*conceptual issue*). We would like to call attention to the *status definitionis* because it seems possible to find here the first intuition concerning the relationship between "truth" and "fact". A juridical element is present, since the logical activity of *defining* constitutes the most significant manifestation of the *doing* of the jurists. It seems clear to Vico that the problems of definition in argumentation are tied to those of the social operations of the human mind:[23] (1) The definition assumes the existence of topical agreements, of *loci communes*; (2) it aims at establishing a relationship with common sense; and (3) it is the result of justificative procedures of research.

[23] "In statu finitivo loci utrique parti communi sunt: ut definiat uterque quam maxime potest ad communem sensum, et vim verbi accomodata" (*Institutiones oratoriae, Opere* [Morano], p. 31).

The definitions, because of their appeal to common sense, are outside the "real" as well as the "nominal" definition; the rhetorical definition, like the dialectical one,[24] is tied to opinion and concerns the domain of law, ethics, and politics. In the dialectical tradition—which Vico knew well—the definition, conceived as a center of argumentation, was the most important part of dialectics; and it was intimately connected both to the theory of fallacies in argumentation and to the theory of controversy. The definition had the purpose of determining, not the essence, but the limits of the proposed definitions; the philosopher qua dialectician inquired into the definitions advanced by common knowledge through slogans, aphorisms, and etymologies. The theory of definition resulted in an analysis of ordinary language, in a methodology for the exact application of words to things. The agreement on the definition appears from this perspective to be the result of a dialectical inquiry and the substitute for an ontological order; the dialectical definition is not a definition of essences, but one of things that might be changed as a result of human choice.

Vico seems to grasp from the very early stages of his philosophical speculation (which in our opinion is closely connected to rhetoric) that man, to use freely one of Austin's expressions,[25] has the possibility of doing things with words, first of all through "giving names." And it is there that the fact becomes one with the truth, and Vico himself has the pleasure of attesting to it. In the *De antiquissima*,[26] after reminding us that for Roman authors the expressions *quaestio nominis* and *quaestio definitionis* had the same meaning, he asserts: *et tunc quaerere definitionem putarent eum quaerebant quid, verbo prolato, in communi hominum mente excitaretur.*

The definition, then, is an act of human creation, inasmuch as it implies assigning a value to a situation, to a fact. The dialectical method, and not the scientific demonstration, affords us the definition in the domain of the opinion. This is why Vico's reflection on the definition appears to be the point of departure of his principle that the human mind participates in a creative manner in the real. The definition, like the *modus operandi* of the jurist, is in relation to an order which is not preconstituted but is in a continuous state of self-renewal.

Vico and the topical tradition

References to the theory of rhetoric occur frequently in all of Vico's works. Particularly important is the connection between Grotius' theory of legal interpretation and the rhetoric theory of legal controversies: *Hugo*

[24] See A. Giuliani, "The Aristotelian Theory of Dialectic Definition," *Philosophy and Rhetoric* 6 (1972): 129.
[25] J. L. Austin, *How to Do Things with Words* (London, 1962).
[26] *Opere* 1: 136.

Grotius doctrinam de interpretatione magna ex parte rhetorum praeceptis, quae de statibus caussarum tradunt, illustrat (*De uno principio*, Proloquium, § 5). Grotius appeared initially to be a dialectician, bound by the techniques of the *ratio artificialis*: "*si eius principia ad exactae criticae trutinam expendantur, magis probabiles verisimilesque quam necessariae sunt et invictae rationes.*" (*De uno principio*, Proloquium, § 20). It is not by chance that such an assertion is found in the context of a comparison between Grotius and the jurist and dialectician Goveanus, who had been Ramus' adversary and had restored the true meaning of the Aristotelian dialectics as logic of the opinion and of the probable. If, as we believe, Vico interprets Grotius dialectically, further arguments could be added to Guido Fassò's thesis that Grotian philosophy, as we know it from his commentators, was unknown to Vico and also to the Neapolitan culture of his time.[27] In Vico's doctrine of common sense there is the echo, as Fassò indicates, of Grotian thought, according to which the reason different peoples have the same concept of natural law "can hardly be anything else than the feeling which is called the common sense of mankind."[28] Perhaps in reading the *De iure* which emphasizes the axiological function of that activity, *humano intellectui conveniens*, aimed at preserving society (Prolegomena, § 8), Vico sensed in it the classical concept of the intellect as immediate intuition, common sense, and awareness of right and wrong. This is not the place for inquiring into the relationships between intellect, prudence, and topics in Aristotelian thought, well known to Vico; it is certain, though, that in his *Institutiones* (p. 6) he asserts that common sense is *omnis prudentiae, eloquentiae norma*.

From whom could Vico have derived the inspiration for such a conception of rhetoric, which, in a certain sense, was original? Who then were his "authors"? He himself has given some indications in his Autobiography about his lecture in competition for the chair; namely, "that it was replete with Greek and Latin erudition and criticism." It is not difficult to identify the Latin sources, especially Cicero and Quintilian.[29]

We would like to advance here some hypotheses concerning the Greek sources. The first seems to be Aristotle the dialectician, the author of the *Topics*, the *De Sophisticis Elenchis*, the *Rhetoric*, and the *Ethics*. Vico was well aware that modern rationalism had contributed to the corruption of the authentic Aristotelian thought: *hodie nec Carthesiana nec nostri temporis Aristotelea* (*doctrina*) *rebus oratoriis plurimum confert* (p. 7). When he contrasted the method of the orator to that of the scientist (p. 75) and warned against the use of mathematics in the domain of the

[27] *Vico e Grozio* (Naples, 1971).

[28] "Alis autem existimationis causa vix ulla videtur posse praeter sensum ipsum, communis qui dicitur" (Grotius, *De jure belli ac pacis*, bk 1, ch. 1, § 12). Cf. Fassò, *Vico e Grozio*, pp. 91f.

[29] A. Sorrentino, *La poetica e la retorica di G. B. Vico* (Turin, 1927).

probable truth, Vico borrowed the famous arguments of the *Nichomachean Ethics*. Apropos of the study of mental faculties, of the learning processes, we would like to recall the invitation that he extended to his students in the 1701 oration:[30]

Pay attention to how perceptively Aristotle embraced all the faculties of reasoning. Other philosophers have added nothing to his Treatise but some explanations, some arguments and some examples . . . examine his complete system of moral philosophy and you will discover spontaneously the miraculous character of this 'work.'

For Vico as for Aristotle, the relationship between rhetoric and truth is a constant theme of concern,[31] and therefore Vico's discussion of rhetoric makes reference to philosophy, law, and ethics. It is not possible to prescind from those moral and natural dispositions of men which are the virtues; among them should be counted intellect, or the *vis veri*, to use Vico's language. The speculation on rhetoric is therefore intimately connected to ethics, understood as philosophy of human conduct: Vico's morality is not that of obligation but of virtue.[32] The rejection of the morals of Stoics and of Epicureans as morals of solitary minds is based on a rhetorical philosophy which originates from the social function of reason: *nec Epicureorum, nec Stoicorum doctrina eloquentiae utilis erat* (p. 7). Passions are not blind with regard to values and are considered in a dialectical perspective in contrast to the scientific one. The Cartesian treatise on the passions can be more useful to medicine than to morality.[33] We could consider Vico as philosopher of the praxis, if praxis is considered in the classical, Aristotelian sense; doing (πράττειν) in fact is considered with regard to the use of freedom, and in contrast to making (ποιεῖν), where, regardless of the intention, one looks only at the results. Among the assertions that support this interpretation must be remembered Vico's contrast between *homo prudens* and *homo faber*.

With regard to the logic of controversy, Vico's rhetoric seems to have been influenced by the Byzantine tradition, which evolved in a series of commentaries on the rhetoric of Hermogenes from Tarsus, a dialectician of the second century A.D. In the text of the *Institutiones* of 1738, there is a significant assertion: "*de statibus caussarum spinosissimam tractationem Quintilianus . . . et Hermogenes integro libro exequuntur.*"[34] In Hermo-

[30] Inaugural Orations, *Opere* 1: 31.

[31] The relationship between rhetoric and truth remains a constant motive of Vico's speculation. Among many assertions on this recall the speech delivered at the inauguration of the Accademia degli Oziosi in 1737: "There is no eloquence without truth and dignity; and wisdom is composed of these same two parts" (*Filosofia ed eloquenza, Opere* [Ricciardi], p. 940).

[32] Pietro Piovani, "Pensiero e società in Vico" in *Giambattista Vico nel terzo centenario della nascita* (Naples, 1971), p. 131.

[33] The Autobiography, *Opere* (Ricciardi), p. 23.

[34] *Opere* 8: 201.

genes' tradition we find some of Vico's views: the primacy of "quality," which implies an axiological orientation of rhetoric; the reference to extralegislative sources (*μόρια δικαίου*) as causes of justification; the interest in the figures of speech. Hermogenes' work could also have influenced Vico through the medium of the numerous authors of treatises on rhetoric and poetry who, from the time of the Renaissance, reverted to Hermogenes. Among them one should not ignore Bacon,[35] from whom Vico might have found encouragement to elevate elocution to an important head of rhetoric. In the *De Augmentis,* in fact, rhetoric is considered to be the art of transmission and elocution. And one should not forget—as Perelman has shown —the importance of the presence in the argumentation for Bacon.

Vico and the "new rhetoric"

Our reference to Perelman is not accidental, since in Vico's rhetoric it seems possible to single out the more vivid instances of the movement that is at the head of the "new rhetoric." Perelman is one of the few contemporary scholars who shows awareness of Vico's *Institutiones,* which he used extensively in his *Traité de l'argumentation* (1958).[36] In Vico and in Perelman's works it is possible to find, even if by opposite ways, an ideal point of encounter. The young Neapolitan professor of rhetoric discovered in Bacon one of his "four authors." In more recent times a young Belgian logician dissatisfied with the conclusions, in the domain of action, of the logic of the rational, has rediscovered the rhetoric that for centuries had been relegated to the modest role of theory of the ornate form. By reverting to such tradition it was possible for him to defend the claims of an historical reason in contrast to a *raison éternelle.* Here, too, the point of departure has been the struggle against the Cartesian idea of reason and of evidence:

> Les luttes incessantes qui, depuis Descartes ont, opposé les rationalistes à leur adversaires dans la tradition philosophique occidentale, ont contribué a renforcer une thèse commune aux deux camps, celle de la liaison de la raison aux raisonnements nécessaires. Le rationnel s'étend aux domaines que l'ont soumis aux preuves apodictiques, et tout ce qui n'est pas susceptible de preuve nécessaire relève de l'irrationnel.[37]

Such limitation of the concept of reason and of its techniques in the domain of the necessary is responsible for the lack of a philosophical

[35] Hermogenes represents one of the sources of Bacon's rhetoric. See K. R. Wallace, "Bacon's Conception of Rhetoric," in *Historical Studies of Rhetoric and Rhetoricians,* ed. R. F. Howes (Ithaca, 1961), p. 114. For Hermogenes' influence on the Renaissance see A. M. Patterson, *Hermogenes and the Renaissance* (Princeton, 1970).

[36] See above, n. 12.

[37] Ch. Perelman, "Raison eternelle, raison historique" in *Justice et Raison* (Brussels, 1963), p. 95.

methodology of the human sciences. Perelman therefore proposes another concept of reason, *qui découle d'une théorie moin limitée de la preuve*, by reevaluating the rationality of the procedures of argumentation and of justification, analyzed by the classical tradition of rhetoric. The purpose of argumentation is to bring the audience to the conclusion of the orator; it is here impossible to resort to demonstration and to verification. A large part of the *Traité* is therefore devoted to the classification of argumentative techniques: quasi-logical arguments similar to the formal structure of logical and mathematical reasoning (for example, contradiction and incompatibility, identity and definition, etc.); arguments based on the structure of reality (causality, pragmatic argument, etc.); arguments attempting to establish the structure of reality (example, model, analogy, etc.). The initial interest of Perelman was perhaps that of the logician interested in the study of the mechanics of thought in the argumentative use of reason. Students of formal logic were quick to show that the theory of argumentation is not incompatible with logic and that it is *empreinté de positivité*; formal premises have been sought in Perelman's inductive method, from which the schema of argumentation have been singled out.[38]

Perelman, however, has clarified the foundations of his rhetorical philosophy in connection with more profound investigation of the problems of law and language.[39] Because of the insufficiency of theoretical reasoning in the domain of choice and of action, law becomes a "model of reasoning worthy of the logician's interest." The philosophical question is not structurally different from a judicial controversy, and the philosophical enterprise as a whole is "justificative." The philosopher, like the jurist, cannot hope for absolute clarity. The area of leeways has a function, which is to permit a division of knowledge implying a practical, social use of reason.

We would like to call attention to the problem of language, inasmuch as Perelman rejects the rationalistic theses—(realism and nominalism have ended up by agreeing on them)—that the language is a disturbing element of knowledge. On one hand, the realists, in order to render inoffensive the intervention of language, imagine a perfect language the terms of which coincide with objective essences; on the other hand, the nominalists consider it a mere conventional instrument, since the different languages can be perfectly translated, transmitting the same language without ambiguity.[40] The recognition of a cognitive value of ordinary language (proverbs, maxims, slogans) links Perelman to the best dialectic tradition, from Aristotle to Vico. In Perelman, too, the reevaluation of the cognitive value

[38] For a critique of the formalistic interpretation of the theory of argumentation, in which the philosophical presuppositions are however ignored, see my review: "Il campo dell'argomentazione. Su di un recente volume di Ch. Perelman," *Rivista internazionale di filosofia du diritto*, 49 (1972): 100.

[39] From this perspective, especially significant is the collection of more recent essays of Ch. Perelman, *Le Champ de l'argumentation* (Brussels, 1970).

[40] De l'évidence en métaphysique," *ibid.*, p. 236.

of the metaphor occurs through a distinction between "explicative" and "expressive" metaphors.[41] The philosophical use of metaphors is different from the poetic as well as the scientific, it is, in fact, limited to those metaphors based on analogy, and thus assumes an axiology or even an ontology. The philosophical work is in a certain sense a correction of the analogical material, which is peculiar to a particular culture.

The reevaluation of a practical use of reason is closely tied to the secular ideal of philosophy as love of wisdom and as rational knowledge that leads to happiness and to virtue. Such an idea is in irreducible antithesis with that of a calculating reason; only a practical reason can offer us criteria of valuation of the actions "independent from the ends, at times unreasonable and often opposed." The need to establish a contact between the new rhetoric and other currents of contemporary thought is quite pressing; even if originally Perelman demonstrated some sympathy for the irrationalistic currents such as existentialism, today—aware of the achievements of a new rationality—he seems inclined to reinterpret the Hegelian dialectic or Peirce's logic.[42] We hope that we are not being too nationalistic if we express the wish that—next to the names of Hegel and Peirce—the new rhetoric will attempt to establish a rapport with the rhetorical philosophy of Giambattista Vico.

Translated by Salvatore Rotella

[41] "Analogie et métaphore en science, poésie, et philosophie," *ibid.*, p. 271. For the philosophy of language of the new rhetoric see A. Giuliani, "Nouvelle rhétorique et logique du langage normatif," *Logique et Analyse* 49–50 (1970): 65.

[42] Ch. Perelman, "The New Rhetoric: A Theory of Practical Reason" in *The Great Ideas Today* (pub. by *Encyclopedia Britannica*, 1970), p. 306. See also Max H. Fisch, "Vico and Pragmatism" in *Giambattista Vico: An International Symposium*, p. 401, which calls attention to the similarity between Vico and Peirce.

Gianfranco Cantelli

MYTH AND LANGUAGE IN VICO

The *New Science* could be considered as a detailed and systematic interpretation of the myths left to us by pagan peoples. Vico accepts the historical significance of the ancient fables, yet at the same time he interprets the myths as a language, in fact as the natural language of the primitive ages of mankind. The identification of language and myth forms the basis of his historical reconstruction of the origins of civilization. This study proposes (1) to clarify the Vichian identification of myth and language, (2) to establish the problems which led Vico to propose this identification, and (3) to indicate what might have been the linguistic theories and the mythological systems which suggested to him both his interpretation of myths and his interpretation of language.[1]

According to Vico, the fables of ancient peoples were "true and severe histories of the customs of the most ancient peoples of Greece." This interpretation of the fables thus signifies for Vico the opening of a path to the understanding of the very origins of civilization and to the knowledge of the general lines of the history of primitive peoples, since all the histories of barbaric races "have fabulous beginnings." This conception of the myths as true and severe histories, which recurs constantly in Vico's works, is cited by Vico as the "master key to this science," which discovery, he insists, "has cost us the persistent research of our entire literary life." What Vico proposes is, therefore, a historical interpretation of myths, and in this sense his work is closely allied to the new directions proposed for historiography in his own time and which found in Jean Leclerc their major exponent.[2]

We should not undervalue the influence which Leclerc's mythographic studies might have had on Vico. Many of the fundamental principles implicit in the historical interpretations of fables proposed by Vico in the *New Science* have their immediate antecedents in the canons established

[1] Here it would be well to note the limits of this essay. It is meant simply to indicate some possible arguments and it serves as a kind of *pro-memoria* to a series of analyses and investigations which are being undertaken to reconstruct in their historical presuppositions, not only the linguistic doctrines of Vico, but also those of Warburton and Condillac.

[2] On the relations between Vico and Leclerc see G. Cantelli, *Vico e Bayle, premesse per un confronto* (Naples, 1971), pp. 57ff.

by Leclerc, by which the mythic accounts of pagan antiquity could be related to profane history. Among these canons are: the principle of a primitive, crude, and barbaric humanity whose concepts of virtue and truth were incommensurable with those of more civilized peoples; the notion that myths are not born from a corruption of Biblical tales and that their genesis should be traced back to the internal history of the gentile peoples; the recognition of the isolation of the Hebrew people and of the separation of their history from that of other peoples; the refusal to see the myths as evidence of the cleverness of legislators and priests, used for the maintenance of political power and the imposition of a civil order on the mass of crude and uncivilized mankind; and, finally, the rigorous critical-historical attitude of rejecting every interpretation which might seek to view ancient fables as allegories of sublime philosophical truths.

Whatever we might finally conclude regarding Vico's originality, it is impossible to deny a decisive influence of Leclerc on Vico's interpretation of myths. However, it is especially on the matter of the evaluation of myth as a historical document that Vico is to be rigorously distinguished from Leclerc. For Leclerc, myth is a true and proper historical account, to be understood exactly like a modern historical narrative, once its original nucleus is disengaged from the fabulous shell in which the crude and uncivilized men of those times had encased it, and once the linguistic obscurities which, in the course of its transmission, had distorted its sense are clarified by philological analysis. For Vico, myth constituted instead a primitive expression of fantasy, in a language so fitting that it would not be possible to distinguish a nucleus of truth from the fantastic form in which it was expressed. This differentiation leads us to Vico's definition of myths as "poetic characters."

These "poetic characters" have been much studied by Vico's interpreters, and their nature as a mute primitive language has been fully recognized. However, the common tendency of the majority of Vico's interpreters has been to approach the problem from a point of view too exclusively aesthetic and linguistic,[3] which has left obscured the perhaps decisive fact that, for Vico, the investigation of the origins of poetry grew out of a predominantly historical inquiry and that his true intention was less to establish the manner in which poetic language was born than to examine the formation of myths, to clarify the origins of religion, and to determine its role in the civil development of mankind. Therefore, it seems worthwhile to raise once more the question of myth in Vico, considering it from this historical perspective.

[3] See esp. Santino Caramella, "L'estetica di G. B. Vico" in *Momenti e problemi di storia dell'estetica* (Milano, 1959), pt. 2, pp. 840–64; for an analysis of the linguistic theories of Vico see the penetrating article of A. Pagliaro, "La dottrina linguistica di Vico," *Atti dell'Accademia nazionale dei Lincei, Classe di Scienze morali, Storiche, e Filologiche* (Rome, 1959), ser. 8, vol. 8, fasc. 6.

Myth comes to be interpreted by Vico as *parola*, a true and proper linguistic character, a signifying character capable of expressing a certain reality, or at least a certain interpretation of reality. Perhaps the clearest expression which Vico gives of his theory of myths as poetic characters is to be found in "The Idea of the Work" set forth in the *New Science*:

We find that the principle of these origins both of languages and of letters lies in the fact that the first Gentile peoples, by a demonstrated necessity of nature, were poets who spoke in poetic characters. . . . The [poetic] characters of which we speak were certain imaginative genera (images for the most part of animate substances, of gods or heroes, formed by their imagination) to which they reduced all the species or all the particulars appertaining to each genus. . . . These divine or heroic characters were true fables or myths, and their allegories are found to contain meanings not analogical but univocal, not philosophical but historical, of the peoples of Greece of those times (§ 34).

Among these many, perhaps too many, things which Vico seeks to tell us in this passage, we might distinguish those most useful for clarifying what he meant by poetic characters, namely: (1) that primitive peoples were poets and spoke in poetic characters; (2) that such poetic characters were images, for the most part endowed with animated essences; (3) that the fables were actually these poetic characters, whether divine or heroic; (4) that such fables were (according to the etymology which Vico gave to the term *favola*) true fables, that is to say, true and proper language; and (5) that allegory was a similar language, according to a meaning of the term *allegoria* that we shall try to establish later.

Myth, therefore, is a character which becomes defined as an image of animated substances, which are in their turn identified as gods and heroes. The language of myths is thus revealed, not as an articulate language, but as an essentially mute figurative language. This is the discovery that Vico presents as "the master key" of the *New Science*, the discovery which had required the "persistent research of almost all [his] literary life." In chapter 4 of the *New Science*, entitled "Origins of Languages and Letters" and conceived as a corollary of theology, metaphysics, and poetic logic, Vico makes clear the terms of his discovery, the fundamental principle of which is that we cannot separate the origins of letters from the origins of languages, which "were by nature conjoined" (§ 429). According to Vico, it was precisely because they had ignored this natural conjunction and had separated the origin of language from the origin of writing that scholars of times past had failed to discern the true nature of poetic characters, fables, and hieroglyphs.[4] Thus we see how, according to Vico, one ought to

[4] "Thus, in their hopeless ignorance of the way in which languages and letters began, scholars have failed to understand how the first nations thought in poetic characters, spoke in fables, and wrote in hieroglyphs. Yet these should have been the principles, which must by their nature be most certain, of philosophy in its study of human ideas and of philology in its study of human words" (*New Science*, § 429).

understand poetic characters, that is, the fables, or indeed the images of those animated substances which are gods and heroes: one is dealing with hieroglyphics; in short, the fables and myths of Greece are the analogue of what appear in Egypt as hieroglyphics.[5]

Now, if we seek to specify what inspired Vico to join together the origins of language with those of writing and to make of hieroglyphs, not the first form of writing, but the first language of a childlike humanity, we discover his conviction that the first "gentile men" used a "mute language of signs and physical objects having natural relations to the ideas they wished to express" (§ 32). All the first peoples expressed themselves by means of gestures, real characters, images, and hieroglyphics, which are thus all poetic or fabulous characters. Their mode of expression accorded perfectly with the necessity of their nature, which was that of men "wanting in speech" but yet needful, in society's earliest times, of explaining themselves and of making themselves understood. The entrance to the earliest epochs of mankind does not, then, remain closed to the historian. In fact, myths constitute the most authentic evidence of a possible entrance. They are not, however, like a simple historical document; they are the very language in which primitive peoples expressed their ideas, conceived and delineated their social relationships, their work, and the rise of their customs and arts, and established, finally, their conception of nature. It is Vico's contention that he has found the key to this language, reconstructed its vocabulary, discovered its syntax, and finally, armed with these discoveries, penetrated the human, civil, and physical world that was the object of that language. It might be argued, indeed, that all of Vico's works, from the *Diritto universale* on, are nothing but an audacious and systematic attempt to decipher hieroglyphics, or better, that analogue of Egyptian hieroglyphics which, according to Vico, were the Greek fables.

But mythic language, one could argue, is a language which is today forgotten, and it was Vico himself who stressed that philological criticism could never alone reconstruct its meaning. Mythic language takes us back to the dawn of humanity, into a context of experiences radically different from those of civilized men. The interpretation of the language of that time is, then, before being a philological problem, first of all a philosophical problem. In order to understand such a language, in fact, it is necessary to perceive the transition of men from their original ferine state to their human state. One must try to imagine and to understand what would have been their first thoughts, their responses to the physical world that surrounded them and to the civil world which they were so arduously con-

5 "Thus the divine fables of the Greeks and Latins must have been the true first hieroglyphs, or sacred or divine characters, corresponding to those of the Egyptians" (*ibid.*, § 437).

structing. This is a great and most complex task, the difficulty of which Vico stressed constantly in his works.[6]

A correct interpretation of mythic language, which is at once a critical, philosophical, and metaphysical endeavor, must be preceded by a philological-critical analysis. In order to understand "poetic characters," one must go through the reverse of the process necessary for deciphering articulated languages. In the latter case, one moves from words to thoughts; in the former, however, in order to decipher the original language of humanity, one must first penetrate the thoughts (or better yet, the signs in which the thoughts of the first men were expressed) so as to reconstruct the words. The metaphysics of the human mind which Vico sets forth in the *New Science* is, therefore, the fundamental presupposition which permits a successful understanding of mythic language.[7]

If the philosopher and the historian are to succeed in reconstructing the world of primitive men, in understanding, on the one side, the universal necessities of human nature and, on the other side, the ideas, also universal, which arose and were defined in the strictest relation to those necessities, then they cannot ignore the mode in which these ideas were expressed. Language in fact—and this is another hinge of Vico's philosophy—is not an arbitrary instrument born of convention; all human languages, and in particular that of primitive times, are natural and correspond perfectly to the needs, ideas, and passions of a people in a given stage of its history. Human nature and language are intimately interconnected with one another. They are, in fact, two corresponding aspects of a single reality: to enter into the interior structure of the one is to discover the key which permits us to penetrate the meaning of the other. But a discussion of the merits of this metaphysics of the human mind and of the critical method, also metaphysical, which is derived from it, would require, in fact, a discussion of the whole philosophy implied by the *New Science*. Let us examine instead how Vico allows us to witness the birth of the first thought within the human mind and with it the concomitant birth of the first poetic character (fable, divine image, hieroglyphic, or perhaps gesture), which was the expressive sign of that first thought.

6 "Our treatment . . . must take its start from the time these creatures began to think humanly. In their monstrous savagery and unbridled bestial freedom there was no means to tame the former or to bridle the latter but the frightful thought of some divinity, the fear of whom is the only powerful means of reducing to duty a liberty gone wild. To discover the way in which this first human thinking arose in the gentile world, we encountered exasperating difficulties which have cost us the research of a good twenty years. [We had] to descend from these human and refined natures of ours to those quite wild and savage natures, which we cannot at all imagine and can comprehend only with great effort" (*ibid.*, § 338).

7 "In search of these natures of human institutions our Science proceeds by a severe analysis of human thoughts about the human necessities or utilities of social life, which are the two perennial springs of the natural law of the gentes. In its second principal aspect, our Science is therefore a history of human ideas, on which it seems the metaphysics of the human mind must proceed" (*ibid.*, § 347).

Vico tells us that two hundred years after the Flood, this being the time necessary for the land to dry out, it became possible for the earth "to send up dry exhalations or matter igniting in the air" to produce lightning: "the sky fearfully rolled with thunder and flashed with lightning" (§ 377). The few giants who in that moment were dispersed throughout the forests on the mountain heights, terrified by the noise and sight of the spectacle and ignorant of its causes, raised their eyes and for the first time "became aware of the sky" (*ibid*). Vico's whole effort is concentrated on the penetration of the minds of these giants, not yet men but on the point of becoming such, so as to grasp what meaning that "awareness of the sky" could have had in their crude and ignorant minds. This first experience of a natural phenomenon was violent and terrifying and dominated them by its extraordinary power.

When men are ignorant of the natural causes producing things, and cannot even explain them by analogy with similar things, they attribute their own nature to them. [So that:] the human mind, because of its indefinite nature, wherever it is lost in ignorance makes itself the rule of the universe in respect of everything it does not know (§§ 180–81).

All knowledge is an interpretation of that which is unknown on the basis of that which is known; it is a referring of that which is far to that which is near and daily in our view. The giants wandering through the great woods of the earth two hundred years after the Flood became aware of the sky but could not attribute to it anything other than their own nature:

and because in that state their nature was that of men all robust bodily strength, who expressed their very violent passions by shouting and grumbling, they pictured the sky to themselves as a great animated body, which in that aspect they called Jove, the first god of the so-called greater gentes, who meant to tell them something by the hiss of his bolts and the clap of his thunder (§ 377).

In this way was born the first thought in the human mind, and with it, the first poetic character, "the first divine fable, the greatest they ever created: that of Jove, king and father of men and gods, in the act of hurling the lightning bolt" (§ 379). The first "word" is thus intimately connected to the first experience and the first thought of man.

The above passage states that Jove, the sky, pictured as a great animate body, was understood by the giants to be speaking to them through "the hiss of his bolts and the clap of his thunder." Here also one must immerse oneself in the mind and in the passions of those first founders of nations, the giants inhabiting the woods on the highest mountains. Terrorized by the strange phenomena of the lightning and thunder, they became aware of the immeasurable power of a reality which, although able to annihilate them, had however spared them, limiting itself simply to a manifestation of its will. "From the first great benefit he conferred on mankind by not destroying it with his bolts, he received the title *Soter*, or savior" (§ 379).

Jove is, therefore, terrifying because of his unlimited power but also beneficent because he spared men and placed them under his authority. Hence the necessity of submitting oneself to his power and interpreting his manifestations (the lightning and the thunder above all) as his signifying and revelatory signs.[8]

We can recognize in all this a fundamental aspect of Vico's linguistic theory. The sky, interpreted as a living being, has for the first men a significance intrinsic to its nature and which reveals itself explicitly as a language: nature itself and its manifestations—first those most apparent (thunder and lightning), then with time those less evident (eagles, movements of the intestines of animals, etc.)—are all aspects of the language of Jove. This interpretation is in full harmony with what we can imagine to have been the nature of the human mind in the dawn of civilization; the mind of primitive men was all sensation and passion, and in their total ignorance the first men made of themselves the measure of the universe.

The first language is thus born divine; it is the language of the sky, of Jove, who by means of the things of nature (real characters) manifests his will and imposes his rule on men. The language of men can only be a copy, an imitation (a picture) of this divine language; human language derives from the discovery that natural things have a meaning and that it only remains to men to grasp the revelation contained in them by replicating their structures exactly.[9] Fantasy and imitation are not then, for Vico, two opposed concepts, the one excluding the other, but are rather complementary of one another. Original language is an imitation of nature, but this nature was of a sort which primitive men were able to imagine and to fantasize: an animate being whose members were enlived by that very force which they felt to be flowing in and animating their own bodies.

Myth and language, which is to say, religion and language, are thus born together. Vico's thesis, set forth in total opposition to that sustained by Bayle, is that it is impossible to speak of men and of civil society apart from some kind of religion. A people without some form of religion is as

[8] "The first men, who spoke by signs, naturally believed that lightning bolts and thunderclaps were signs made to them by Jove; whence from *nuo*, to make a sign, came *numen*, the divine will, by an idea more than sublime and worthy to express the divine majesty. They believed that Jove commanded by signs, that such signs were real words, and that nature was the language of Jove. The science of this language the gentiles universally believed to be divination, which by the Greeks was called theology, meaning the science of the language of the gods" (*ibid.*, § 379).

[9] "Thus . . . Jove was born naturally in poetry as a divine character or imaginative universal, to which everything having to do with the auspices was referred by all the ancient gentile nations, which must therefore have been poetic by nature. Their poetic wisdom began with this poetic metaphysics, which contemplated God by the attribute of his providence; and they were called theological poets, or sages who understood the languages of the gods expressed in the auspices of Jove; and were properly called divine in the sense of diviners, from *divinari*, to divine or predict" (*ibid.*, § 381).

impossible to conceive as a human society without some form of language. Atheism presupposes a stage of humanity without any kind of language and therefore without any kind of social bond. It would be improper to call such a stage human; in fact, we should have to call it ferine. Another extremely important consequence of the identification of myth with a particular form of language is the solution which Vico succeeds in giving to a problem which for centuries had bothered scholars and theologians, the problem of pagan polytheism, considered as a monstrosity when contrasted with the principles of reason.[10]

We need not examine here the development which, according to Vico, the myths underwent in the interior of a language that was progressively enlarging its vocabularly in relation to the enrichment of the political and social experiences of primitive peoples. However, from what has been said above, we could easily discern the line that Vico followed, both in the reading and interpretation of the individual myths and in the reconstruction of the whole system of pagan mythology. All myths, understood as poetic characters and divine images, express, in their very multiplication, complication, and enrichment of civil society, the new deeds and the new experiences of men; they portray the rise of new arts and the discovery of new instruments of war and work. The transition from this fleeting monotheism proper to the very first times, expressed in the fable of Jove, to polytheism signals, not a regression—a forgetting of a higher and purer conception of divinity, but rather the natural enrichment of a language which multiplies its own linguistic signs in perfect correspondence with the complication of social life and human experiences, whether in relation to the community of which it is a part or to the nature which surrounds it. If, therefore, as the Jesuit fathers report to us after their missions to the Far East, the Chinese utilize some 120,000 hieroglyphic characters, we should be no more surprised than if, as Varro reports, the Latins appear to have numbered in their Pantheon some 30,000 deities. Thus, Vico says:

> There can be no doubt that among the Latins Varro occupied himself with the language of the gods, for he had the diligence to collect thirty thousand of their names, which would have sufficed for a copious divine vocabulary, with which the peoples of Latium might express all their human needs, which in those simple and frugal times must have been few indeed, being only the things that were necessary to life. The Greeks too had gods to the number of thirty thousand, for they made a deity of every stone, spring, brook, plant, and offshore rock. Such deities included the dryads, hamadryads, oreads, and napeads. Just so the American Indians make a god of everything that exceeds their limited understanding. Thus the divine fables of the Greeks and Latins must have been the first true hieroglyphs, or sacred or divine characters, corresponding to those of the Egyptians (§ 437).

[10] See David Bidney, "Vico's New Science of Myth" in *Giambattista Vico: An International Symposium*, p. 273.

The identification of myth and language also permitted Vico to resolve, in a rather elegant way, full of decisive consequences, a difficulty which had threatened to compromise the new historical interpretation of ancient fables promoted by Leclerc and becoming predominant in the years in which Vico was formulating the *New Science*. In the first decades of the eighteenth century, the thesis that myths might have an allegorical meaning was still indissolubly linked to the tradition of mystical interpretation of pagan religion promoted by Neo-Pythagoreanism and Neo-Platonism since the first centuries of the vulgate era. The quest for the allegory in myth was always identified with the discovery of an arcane wisdom, fraught with the highest philosophical concepts, in the letter of the fable. From the beginning the historical interpretations of fables proposed by Leclerc had been reduced to a narrowly euhemeristic horizon. It had not seemed possible to conceive an allegorical meaning for the fables different from that consecrated by tradition: to discover the allegory in the primitive and the symbolic in the naive and rude imagination of a savage mind was a prospect utterly foreign to the majority of the mythographers, who, on the model of Leclerc, wished to resolve mythology into profane history without any residue.

How was it possible to imagine that the most ancient populations of Egypt, Mesopotamia, Phoenicia, Greece, and Latium had been capable of rising to the heights of philosophical conceptualization found in Pythagoreanism, Platonism, and Stoicism? The idea of an ancient wisdom of the human race—heritage of exiguous priestly castes and restricted philosophical sects, depositories also of political power—was an antihistorical thesis which ignored the true condition of primitive peoples, immersed, as the savage populations of America and Africa showed, in a condition of rudeness, barbarism, and ignorance more like that of animals than that of men. The sovereign founder of a state, the ancient legislator of a people, was not a sage or philosopher but a violent man, full of unchecked passions, who, by force, cruelty, and an animal cunning, united the populations ruled by him—populations which, struck by his *virtù*, subsequently would have divinized him. Only euhemerism seemed reconcilable with the single historically plausible idea of a barbarous and uncivilized humanity, once the interpretation of the myths as a misunderstanding of sacred history had been rejected.

But while euhemerism seemed to be the only solution, it also impeded any historical interpretation from realizing all the possibilities of research inherent in its method. In Vico, by contrast (and of this discovery he was fully conscious), the notion that symbolism was precisely characteristic of a primitive mentality was recognized and asserted with extraordinary evocative power. Myth is a symbol in the same way that spoken or written language is a symbol. In his view, men began to write and to speak, not in order to express profound philosophical conceptions, but in order to resolve their practical problems, to found the first families, to organize their work, and to satisfy the stringent necessities of survival. Vico accepts without reservation the principles underlying the historical interpretation of ancient fables: the rudeness of primitive men, the distinction between sacred and profane history, the denial of an ancient hidden wisdom, and so on. But at the same time, with his theory of poetic characters, which linked together language and myth as a unique product of the symbolizing activity inherent in primitive mentality, Vico surmounted traditional euhemerism and furnished the historian with an instrument much better suited to penetrate into the origins of human civilization and to reconstruct those primordial facts which had conditioned its future development. Allegory once more becomes the characteristic trait of myths, but Vico's concept of allegory has nothing in common with the traditional concept of allegory.

These divine or heroic characters were true fables or myths, and their allegories are found to contain meanings not analogical but univocal, not philosophical but historical, of the peoples of Greece of those times.

Since these genera (for that is what the fables in essence are) were formed by most vigorous imaginations, as in men of the feeblest reasoning powers, we discover in them true poetic sentences, which must be sentences clothed in the greatest passions and therefore full of sublimity and arousing wonder. Now the sources of all poetic locution are two: poverty of language and need to explain and be understood. Heroic speech followed immediately on the mute language of acts and objects that had natural relations to the ideas they were meant to signify, which was used in the divine times (§ 34).

In his "Poetic Logic" Vico sets forth the rules which inform the language of myths; these rules almost comprise a treatise on rhetoric, in which all of the laws of traditional rhetoric are utilized to illustrate his new conception of language in general and of primitive language in particular. Metaphor, synecdoche, metonymy, hypotyposis, episodes, and turns—all the classical figures which in traditional rhetoric are attributed to the acuteness of the mind and are identified as the highest, most sublime product of the intellect—are now explained as the natural and unconscious operation of a fantasy bound to the sensible and to the particular expression of immanent and unreflective passions.

Myth is born, Vico asserts, in the act of attributing life and senses, under the press of terror, hope, admiration, and curiosity, to that which in itself lacks both sense and life. The sky is interpreted by the first authors of the nations as an immense animated body which expresses itself and speaks, thereby revealing its immeasurable power with terrifying thunder and lightning. And metaphor itself is, therefore, simply the attribution of senses and passions to that which in itself is insensate and lacking in passion.

All the first tropes are corollaries of this poetic logic. The most luminous and therefore the most necessary and frequent is metaphor. It is most praised when it gives sense and passion to insensate things, in accordance with the metaphysics above discussed, by which the first poets attributed to bodies the being of animate substances, with capacities measured by their own, namely sense and passion, and in this way made fables of them. Thus every metaphor so formed is a fable in brief (§ 404).

And it is not by chance, Vico observes immediately afterward, that in all languages the expressions which indicate inanimate things were coined on the basis of a metaphor of the human body and its parts, or rather with a metaphor of its passions, sentiments, and desires; and that: "in every language the terms needed for the refined arts and recondite sciences are of rustic origin" (*ibid.*).

It constantly recurs in the history of Western philosophy that the greatest decisive revolutions in thought are achieved by a radical reversal of preceding modes of thought. If this may be taken as a correct criterion for judging the novelty and originality of a theory, few philosophies would have a greater claim to innovation and originality than that constructed by Vico in the *New Science*. And yet, without meaning to detract at all from his stature as an original and innovative philosopher—his is a gaze that penetrates far, envisioning aims which perhaps even today are not fully realized—it must be asked whether Vico, however radical and systematic his revolution, might not have conserved unwittingly the most beautiful and suggestive aspects of the very thought which he was attempting to overturn. This too is a common recurrence in the history of philosophy: the most profound and radical, the most beautiful and humanly universal revolutions have often conserved and carried to full maturation the fruits that were germinated in the light and warmth of that very past which these revolutions intended to overcome. Hoping that such an auspicious event might occur yet in our own epoch, we can certainly assert that this was precisely what happened with Vico and with his philosophy of history, myth, and language.

The thesis that myth might be a language had in fact been suggested, more or less clearly, by those theories which sustained the allegorical significance, rich in a profound wisdom, of the ancient fables—the theories, that is, which constituted the principal objects of Vico's criticism. Such a thesis became directly explicit and defined in all of its particulars when myth, the narrative of the actions of a god, came to be considered, not merely as the story of the actions of a god, but as an *image* of the divinity and its actions. That literature which, from the Italian Renaissance down through the whole of the seventeenth century, saw in the images of the gods a figurative language, analogous or almost completely similar to Egyptian hieroglyphics, is practically unlimited. That is a thesis, for example, which one finds formulated both in the *Hieroglyphica* of Pierio

Valeriano[11] and in the book of Celio Augusto Curione,[12] which, after its early editions, was added as an appendix to the work of Valeriano. In this work, as the title of the first book indicates, are contained accounts of "those things that are signified by the various statues and images of the gods." Here Egyptian hieroglyphics and pagan fables (images and statues of the gods) are considered as parts of a single symbolic mode of expression, parts that oftentimes are not even distinct, since myths, even the Greek myths, are treated as direct derivations from Egyptian hieroglyphics, the allegorical significance of which they conserve even if in a corrupted form.

We have mentioned the sixteenth-century texts of Valeriano and Curione, but there are innumerable works which propose a similar thesis; indeed, the principle of the essential identity of hieroglyphics and myths is central to the whole of that copious literature concerned with emblems, arms, devices, standards, and so on. Neo-Platonism and Hermetism, by now common opinions and vulgar conceptions of the world, are the philosophies which sustain this interpretation of symbolic language. The strict dependence of Greek fables on Egyptian hieroglyphics was thus asserted, to take another example, by Abbé Alessandro Farra in his *Settenario:*

> That the poets sing divinely has been demonstrated at length elsewhere, and thus fables used by these poets will be filled with high mystery . . . and the most ancient wise men of Greece, who were in Egypt to learn the foundations of the noblest sciences, began to use them in place of hieroglyphics, so as to conceal by these means from the common knowledge the venerable secrets of divine wisdom.[13]

One need only open any of the many works of the late sixteenth and seventeenth centuries to find these same ideas repeated, with infinite variations and diverse classifications. The only difference is that, in these later texts, the confines of figurative language are progressively extended to include a greater number of species punctiliously and pedantically differentiated and classified: parables, aphorisms, enigmas, moral tales, and Aesopian fables, as well as emblems, devices, shields, liveries, standards, medallions, coins, and so on. It is hieroglyphics, however, which continue to serve as the original matrix of these various symbolic languages; and it is always from hieroglyphics, as we can see in the works of Ruscelli, Taegio, and Palazzi,[14] that heraldic devices are derived, directly or indirectly. All

[11] Pierius Valerianus (Gian Pietro delle Fosse), *Hieroglyphica, sive de sacris Aegyptiorum aliarumque gentium literis* (Basel, 1556).

[12] *Hieroglyphica . . . I. P. Valeriani . . . a Caelio Curione duobus libris aucti et multis imaginibus illustrati* (Basel, 1556).

[13] A. Farra, *Del Settenario* (Venice, 1594), p. 320.

[14] G. Ruscelli, *Discorso di Girolamo Ruscelli intorno all'inventione dell'Imprese, dell'Insegne, de'Motti e delle Livree* (Venice, 1556), pp. 123ff.; Taegio, *Il Liceo* (Milan, 1572); and Giovanni Andrea Palazzi, *I discorsi sopra le Imprese* (Bologna, 1575), pp. 6ff.; see also Giovanni Ferro, *Teatro delle Imprese* (Venice, 1623), p. 34.

of this constitutes a veritable *topics* of symbolic expression. "Symbol," maintains Ercole Tasso in his *Trattato della realtà e perfettione delle imprese,*

is understood sometimes as genus and sometimes as species. Taken as genus, it includes the following: words without figures; characters without figures; colors with letters, with or without words, in clothing or standards; colors on shields, with characters, words and figures together, and with only a few of them, and even without any; figures completely without words or letters, but with or without gestures; figures without the need of words or colors, but sometimes with both the former and the latter; figures with words and without the combination of which the figures would neither signify nor the words have sense.[15]

Giulio Cesare Capaccio dedicates a chapter of his *Trattato delle imprese* to hieroglyphics and "how they might conform to devices," and under the same symbolic genus he places also enigmas, fables, parables, insignias, the reverses of medals, and so on.[16] Francis Bacon also insists on this familiar connection between fables, enigmas, emblems, gestures, and hieroglyphics,[17] even though his own philosophical reflection was, at the same time, moving within a completely original domain of problems. The Jesuit Silvestro da Pietrasanta, in turning his attention to the various symbolic modes of expression, observes in his treatise *De symbolis hieroicis* (book 4, chapter 1) that the ancients above all and even some moderns practiced a language that was neither written nor spoken but meaningful nonetheless: "Sometimes the ancients, even without uttering or writing a word, succeeded nonetheless in clearly expressing what they thought."[18] And in this regard he cites two famous anecdotes: one concerning Tarquinius the Proud, who in order to express his thought on the fate of the city of Gabi, beseiged by his son, cut off with his rod the crown of some poppies growing in his garden; the other concerning Idanthyrsus, king of the Scythians, who sent to Darius the Elder the famous message written in real characters, which included a mouse, a frog, a bird, a bow, and a plough. Silvestro da Pietrasanta's interpretation simply refers this observation to a similar symbolic mode of expression, which includes hieroglyphics, devices, medals, and so on, to that art of signs and silent speech which Giovanni Bonifacio had discussed in his huge and interesting vol-

[15] Ercole Tasso, *Della realtà e perfettione delle Imprese* (Bergamo, 1612), pp. 6ff.

[16] Giulio Cesare Capaccio, *Delle Imprese* (Naples, 1592), pp. 5ff.

[17] See esp. *De sapientia veterum*. Consult esp. the penetrating analysis of Paolo Rossi "Le favole antiche" in *Francesco Bacone, dalla magia alla scienza* (Bari, 1957), chap. 3. See also Rossi's *Le sterminate antichità* (Pisa, 1969). The latter work is important for its linkage of Vico's linguistic theories with those of the Hermetic tradition of the Renaissance, providing a perspective which this essay seeks to recapture and to develop.

[18] *De symbolis heroicis libri IX, auctore Silvestro Pietrasancta romano, e Soc. Jesu* (Antwerp, 1634), p. 123.

ume.[19] The Jesuit father Athanasius Kircher opens the second volume of his *Oedipus Aegyptiacus* with a book devoted to symbols in general, codifying in a systematic manner what by then had become a traditional doctrine. Included as species under the genus *symbol* are: emblems and devices, grifs and logogrifs, parables, proverbs, moral tales, and, once again, the fables of the poets, the origins of which are naturally traced back to Egyptian hieroglyphs.

> The Egyptians in fact were the first peoples to celebrate the deeds of gods under the veils of fables, for which reason I dare to assert that the hieroglyphic wisdom of the Egyptians was nothing but the science of divinity and of nature, presented under various fables and allegorical fictions of animals and of other natural things, so that one can say that nothing comes closer to hieroglyphics than the creation of fables and moral tales.[20]

John Marsham, also, in taking up the problem of hieroglyphic characters, continues this tradition, by linking together the symbolic script of the ancient Egyptians and the images of the gods;[21] and similarly, Johannes Spencer appeals to fables and hieroglyphics as a proof of the tendency, common to the ancients, to hide science under the veil of a symbolic mode of expression: "No one with any literary sophistication could fail to recognize that science in its earliest periods was wrapped in the veils of symbols, types, hieroglyphs, emblems, fables, enigmas, or parables."[22]

Of all the treatises on rhetoric of the seventeenth century, the *Cannocchiale aristotelico* of Emmanuele Tesauro is the most suggestive and the best known. One must not forget, however, that the work, in the original project of the author, was born as a treatise on heraldry, and that precisely these symbolic heraldic figures, drawn rather than written, were taken as the poetic language *par excellence* and as the exemplary model of metaphor.[23] It is, in fact, with the heraldic device ("the noblest, most heroic, and most ingenious and acute of all symbols") that allegory reaches its highest expressive culmination, so that "whoever knows how to compose heraldic devices will also necessarily know how to compose emblems, hieroglyphics, masks, trophies, and all other symbolic products of the intellect."[24] Metaphor finds its most perfect realization in a symbolic transposition of images; and according to Tesauro, heraldic devices, emblems, hieroglyphics, masks, and trophies are nothing but metaphors. In this, his doctrine of metaphor, Tesauro was simply making himself the

[19] Giovanni Bonifacio, *Dell'arte de' cenni, con la quale formandosi favella visible si tratta della muta eloquenza che non è altro che un facondo silenzio* (Vicenza, 1616).

[20] Atanasio Kircher, *Oedipus Aegyptiacus* (Rome, 1653), vol. 1, pt. 1, p. 40.

[21] J. Marsham, *Canon chronicus aegyptiacus, hebraicus, graecus, et disquisitiones*, 2d ed (Frankfort, 1696), pp. 37ff.

[22] J. Spencer, *De legibus Hebraeorum ritualibus earumque rationibus libri* IV, 2d ed. (Tübingen, 1733), p. 211.

[23] E. Tesauro, *Il cannocchiale aristotelico* (Venice, 1663), p. 2.

[24] *Ibid.*, p. 575.

interpreter and exemplary expositor of a thesis that had already been widely upheld in earlier literature on heraldic devices.[25]

We should recall here Vico's harsh words against Father Kircher, his criticisms of Marsham and of Spencer, and his constant polemics against that type of literature which from the Renaissance on, following the false path of Neo-Platonic philosophy and hermeticism, interpreted myths and hieroglyphics as mysterious symbols, depositories of a sublime and archaic wisdom. The novelty of Vico's thought in this polemic has been noted often and with justification. The point of view from which Vico considers all of this material is not only different, it is diametrically opposed to the traditional view, so that it would be difficult to imagine a more radical innovation. And yet, despite this absolute revolution, the structural elements of this new edifice remained the same. The foundations were changed, but the relations between the various parts of the system of symbolic language were not altered. For example, Vico retains the thesis that myth is a language and that this language is identical with that of hieroglyphics; what is more, he maintains that images and figures, even before the characteristic words and letters of articulated speech, are the very characters of that language. Gestures and, along with gestures, regal figures are the original signs of that mute speech which was characteristic, according to him, of the first ages of mankind. Vico also cites the famous anecdotes of Tarquinius the Proud and Idanthyrsus. It is highly probable that the idea that the origin of languages must be linked to the origin of letters, which Vico numbers among his principal "discoveries," had been suggested to him by the traditional identification of fables and hieroglyphics, once he realized that myths and hieroglyphics had been the first language of the nations. The thesis that myth might be a metaphor and that every metaphor might be in embryo a small fable finds its antecedent in the *Cannocchiale aristotelico* of Tesauro, who in much the same way had seen metaphors in heraldic devices, emblems, and hieroglyphs. And the *Cannocchiale aristotelico* is a work that could not have been unknown to Vico.[26]

[25] See for example Ercole Tasso, who writes: "A device is a symbol consisting necessarily of a natural figure . . . or even an artificial figure naturally understood, and of words belonging to it or simply borrowed; separated, figures and words signify nothing, but combined they express, not a property belonging to this figure, but rather some immediate feeling, action, or resolution" (*Delle Imprese*, p. 24.); and Cesare Ripa: "Leaving aside that image which is used by the Orator and with which Aristotle deals in the third book of the *Rhetoric*, I will speak only of that which pertains to painters or to those who by means of colors or any other visible things are able to represent things different from them and conforming to the thing represented; this is why the painter persuades by means of the eye just as the Orator by means of words moves the will, and thus even he looks to metaphors of things which are extrinsic to man and to metaphors which, because they are joined to man, are called essential" (Della *Novissima Iconografia del cavaliere Cesare Ripa Perugino* [Padua, 1625], Proemio, p. 1.).

[26] Fausto Nicolini, *Commento storico alla seconda Scienza nuova* (Rome, 1949), vol. 1, p. 197. Nicolini observes that in Tesauro Vico found the principle that "the

In this analysis of Vico's text I have limited myself to "divine" language; for reasons of space I did not deal with "heroic" language. But we should not forget the great attention, in the various editions of the *New Science*, and especially the first, that Vico pays to the origins of heraldic devices, medals, coins, standards, and so on, and his observations on Aesop's fables, parables, moral tales, and proverbs. The traditional thesis regarding the affinity between these symbolic forms and hieroglyphics is here rigorously observed. Although Vico gives us very few citations in this respect, it can be suggested that he had in mind heraldic devices, medals, and hieroglyphics. Every language is representative of a world which constitutes its corresponding and appropriate object; and the world which underlies the erudite language of heraldic devices, hieroglyphics, fables, enigmas, gestures, and regal characters is an enchanted world, impelled by an internal vital force which pervades all its parts, a world rich with infinite significations, itself a symbol of God's continual creativity. It is a world which articulated language is incapable of representing in all of its fecundity and complexity. Only images, gestures, hieroglyphics, fables, and the most daring products of fantasy are adequate to its expression. Allegory and metaphor are not bold ends in themselves; they are, rather, the means which, through continual transposition of images, permit man's mind to adjust to the infinite multiplicity of meanings of a living universe. And it should be observed that Vico, too, saw the language of fables, hieroglyphics, and heraldic devices—proper to a youthful humanity—as corresponding to an animated world and its multiplication of gestures, images, sounds, and colors. In allowing us to witness the birth of the sensual and passionate soul of primitive men, Vico presents us with the same symbolic world which had delighted all those who praised the acuteness of the human mind.

The proof of this is the engraving designed under Vico's direction by Domenico Antonio Vaccaro for the frontispiece of the 1730 edition of the *New Science* and reproduced in subsequent editions. It was meant, according to Vico, "to give the reader some conception of this work before he reads it, and, with such aid as imagination may afford, to call it back to mind after he has read it" (§ 1).

It was thus an image tied to the most traditional rules of the art of memory but also a heraldic device, a hieroglyphic or almost, one might say, the tutelary spirit of the *New Science*. It was certainly not by chance that Vico, a professor of rhetoric, after having drawn out an entire uni-

perfect device is a metaphor" and also the "association (*raccostamento*) of devices with hieroglyphs." It should be noted, however, that the "principle" just as much as the "association" had been used, the first operating implicitly, the second explicitly formulated, in numerous treatises on devices which preceded that of Tesauro. Here Nicolini is inclined, as he always is, to defend the absolute originality of Vico's speculations and draws no consequences from his observations.

verse of symbols from the fantasy of the first men, came to condense his own doctrine in an erudite heraldic device and thus to retrace the path traversed by his own thought. It was probably a *lapsus*, but it was all the more significant therefore. The current relevance of Vico's linguistic theories cannot be challenged. And his identification of myth and language is still fascinating today, especially in the light of the most recent linguistic and mythographic studies. That Vico's theories remain ripe for investigation and development teaches us once again how much that is modern comes to us from the past.

Translated by Margaret Brose

Hayden White

THE TROPICS OF HISTORY: THE DEEP STRUCTURE OF THE *NEW SCIENCE*

The first edition of the *New Science* of Giambattista Vico was published in 1725; the second and third editions of the work, published in 1730 and 1744, respectively, were so different from the first that they virtually constituted a new work, which has come to be known as the *Second New Science*. It is to this work that scholars normally refer when they speak of Vico's achievement and the ways in which he anticipated the social theories of thinkers as diverse as Hegel, Marx, Nietzsche, Dilthey, Freud, and Lévi-Strauss. Vico's claim to originality cannot be seriously doubted, though the extent to which he anticipated and influenced later thinkers will probably remain a subject of debate for some time to come. In his own time, his originality consisted primarily in his insistence, against both the Cartesians and some of the jus naturalists, on the necessity of a different conceptual apparatus for the analysis of social and cultural phenomena from that which might legitimately be used to analyze the processes and structures of physical nature. The formula in which this insight was expressed asserted the "convertibility" of the "true" and the "fabricated," or the principle of *verum ipsum factum*.

This principle asserts that men can know only that which they themselves have made or are in principle capable of making. As an enabling postulate, it provides the means, for Vico, of distinguishing between the heuristic potentiality of the sciences of physical nature on the one side and the projected sciences of human nature, of culture, and of society on the other. It suggests that, whereas physical scientists may aspire to a kind of knowledge about the physical cosmos, they can never legitimately aspire to complete knowledge of it; for, since they are unable to make the physical world, as God did, they have no way of definitively confirming their claims to knowledge of its most fundamental structures and processes. Only God, who made the cosmos, can have perfect knowledge of its operations. Therefore, the knowledge produced by the physical sciences will always be more or less probable and always incomplete as the truth about the cosmos.

Knowledge produced by students of social and cultural phenomena is, however, a different matter, for, unlike the physical cosmos, the world of social and cultural artifacts is a creation of men themselves and therefore is in principle completely knowable by men. The criterion of knowledge is the capacity of the knower to *produce* that of which he has knowledge. Whereas our knowledge of the physical world does not permit us to reproduce that world, our knowledge of social and cultural artifacts does permit us to reproduce those artifacts, as when we demonstrate our ability to speak the languages of the ancient Greeks or Romans, to write poetry or dramas in the way they did, to borrow our laws from them and apply them to the regulation of our own societies, or to take up their ethical beliefs and use them for regulating our own lives. This line of thought appears to make of Vico a precursor of the Hegelian and late-nineteenth-century efforts by thinkers such as Durkheim and Weber to create sciences of society and culture, efforts finally consummated in the foundation of anthropology, sociology, psychology, and political economy as autonomous disciplines with their own unique objects of study, methods of analysis, and aims. Thus, Vico appears to merit attention as a theoretician of the social sciences and as a defender of their claims to autonomy vis-à-vis the physical sciences and their right to seek their own relational and predictive laws in their own conceptualizations.

A second achievement for which Vico is alternatively praised and damned is that which is expressed in his aphorism (Axiom LXIV in his list of principles): "The order of ideas must follow the order of institutions" (*New Science* § 238). This aphorism and Vico's application of it to his theory of cultural evolution appears to anticipate the Marxist conception of the relation between the superstructure of a culture (the publicly sanctioned forms of consciousness incarnated in the art, religion, jurisprudence, philosophy, and literature of an age) and the social praxis of that culture (which, in Marx's view, is in turn determined by the modes of production and the interests of the group controlling them).

There is more than a little justification for this conception of Vico's anticipation of Marx's theories, for unlike many of his contemporaries, Vico did not believe that culture was primarily a function of environmental, and more specifically of climatic, conditions. He viewed culture rather as a product of the interaction of consciousness with its milieu, both social and natural, and in such a way as to make of the main forms of art, religion, philosophy, and even science little more than retrospective rationalizations of the forms of mediation of men with their milieu in the specific situations in which they found themselves.

But the differences between Vico and Marx are as significant for a proper understanding of Vico's thought as the similarities between them. Most importantly, Vico did not believe that the mental climate of an age (or, to put it in Marxist terms, the "ideology") was merely a reflection of the modes of production and the relations with them sustained by the different classes in the society in question. Men's relationship with their worlds, social and natural, was mediated by consciousness in a crucial way, and especially by speech, which was not, for Vico, merely a verbal representation of the world of *praxis*, a reproduction in consciousness of the world of things and the actual relations between them, but a productive and creative, active and inventive power. Vico in fact anticipated the notion, later identified by Georg Lukács as the Achilles heel of Marxist theory, of *false consciousness*, the capacity of the mind to misconstrue the actual relationships between man and his world and to make of this error the basis of a project to change, revise, and reform the actual world.

Vico defines human nature as composed of body, mind, and speech (§ 1045) with speech serving as the makeweight of the impulse to transform or sustain the modes of relationship actually achieved in any given society or culture against the natural impulse of the human organism to remain content with whatever modicum of security and well-being it enjoys as a result of those achieved modes of relationship. In this respect, Vico appears to resemble Hegel more than Marx, Bergson more than Comte, Croce more than Taine, in short, the idealist strain of nineteenth-century European thought rather than the materialistic one, the vitalist tradition more than the mechanistic.

This apparent proto-idealism is seemingly confirmed by the "philosophy of history" which Vico articulates in books 4 and 5 of the *New Science*. In book 4, entitled "The Course [or Cycle] the Nations Run," Vico lays out what he calls the "ideal eternal history" that all nations (or cultures) not informed by the redeeming truths of Christian revelation must reproduce, as they pass from their birth and adolescence through their period of maturity to their old age and dissolution. In Book 5, entitled "The Recourse [or Recycle] of Human Institutions which the Nations Take When They Rise Again," he deals with the problems of progress through recapitulation of the original cycle. Here he appears to anticipate the concept of transcendence by sublation which Hegel used to account for the fact that, although individual societies may be governed by a law of rise and fall similar to that which governs any organism, culture in general is incrementally progressive and developmental over the course of many such cyclical recurrences. For Vico, as for Hegel, human culture, like human consciousness, continues to develop in spite of the cyclical nature of the lives of the individuals who possess it.

The stages through which all cultures must pass (save the Hebrew and Christian, which enjoy the benefits of divine enlightenment in the principles governing them [§ 948]) Vico characterizes as the ages of gods, of heroes, and of men (§ 173). In each of these ages, men sustain a specific relationship with nature, based on their conceptions of the natural and social world in each age and reflected in the kinds of institutions they construct for satisfying their needs, as they conceive them, in each time.

The first age of a culture is characterized by the kinds of relationships children have with their worlds, and the modes of organization devised in such ages are always derived from the essentially religious consciousness of such ages of naive faith in immediate experience. Hence the first age of a culture he calls the age of the gods, for in it men are presumed to have projected onto the natural world their conceptions of their own passional and sensate natures, to have endowed all aspects of nature with an animus, or spirit, and to have conceived themselves to be governed by and to have worshiped these products of their own febrile imaginations.

The second age of a culture Vico calls the age of heroes, inasmuch as in it men have begun to identify themselves with the spiritual forces with which they have endowed nature, and in such a way as to justify the privileged position that certain men or a certain class of men—usually the most powerful, who are therefore regarded as the most wise, or at least as the custodians of the wisdom of the race—enjoy at the expense of the weaker members of their communities, namely, children, women, and aliens. The institutions of this age reflect the fractured nature of the society they sustain: class division, disparity of privileges and responsibilities between strong and weak, and an ideology which ascribes to the upper classes the attributes of the gods (from which the heroes are supposed to descend) and to the lower classes the attributes of beasts (from which they are supposed to have arisen).

In the third age, the age of men, however, the humanity actually shared by upper and lower classes is asserted as a right by the lower classes and is made the basis of a new kind of polity, governed by written laws. Conflicts between the classes on the one side and between the private individual and the public weal on the other are subjected to the mediation of judges in the name of the abstract concept of justice. This is the age of reason in the history of a culture or society, an age of reflection and of meditation rather than of power and struggle, and it is an age which, by the very fact of its rational nature, contains within it the seeds of its own destruction; for ages of reflection and meditation, Vico argues, inherently tend toward relativism in morality and scepticism in belief. Piety, the basis of any sound commonwealth, is undermined; each citizen becomes increasingly aware of the purely human origins of the institutions, laws, and customs he is supposed to honor as governors of his conscience; and all are driven to pursue private pleasures at the expense of the public good. Therewith, the society or culture passes into its phase of decline and dissolution, which brings on a "second barbarism," more barbarous than primitive savagery, inasmuch as it is unrestricted by the fear and ignorance which drove men to impose restrictions upon their desires in primitive times. And the culture sinks into decadence on its own accord, in the one instance, or falls prey to external enemies in the other, thereby providing the conditions for the beginning of a new cycle and a new recycle, world without end. . . .

Throughout all his works, Vico exempts Christian civilization from the law of *corso* and *ricorso*, which he insists is the ineluctable fate of every culture (save the Hebrew) not succored by the true faith, the Christian religion. This exemption is made on the basis of a distinction between the direct revelation of man's proper relationships to god, nature, and man (vouchsafed to the Hebrews through Abraham, Moses, and the Prophets and to the Christians through Jesus, the Apostles, and the Church) and the indirect revelation of the Creation itself, on which gentile wisdom is founded. Since the ancient Hebrews and the Christians had the benefit of direct knowledge of what God prohibited to men, they possessed rules by which to guide themselves in the construction of communities that might escape the gentiles' fate and progressively realize the ideal *communitas* that would prefigure, even if it did not perfectly represent, the City of God promised for the elect in Heaven (§ 948).

Vico is both quite explicit and quite consistent in his defense of this conception of the history of the chosen peoples of the world. Their histories do not present the problems of interpretation that the histories of the gentile (or pagan) peoples do; for the principles for interpreting the histories of Hebrew and Christian societies are contained in the same Holy Writ which provides the bases and informing principles of their governance. His problems as a philosopher of history are two: (1) to account for the level of civilization attained by pagan peoples, which in its highest examples (the Greek and Roman) very closely approximated that to which the Christian peoples attained, but which was attained *without* the benefit of direct revelation of the sort the Hebrews and the Christians enjoyed; and (2) to determine the relationship between the cycles of growth and decay manifested in the histories of the pagan peoples (and especially of the Greeks and Romans) and the progressive histories of the Hebrews and Christians. These two problems involve him in investigations on two levels of historical existence: that of the specific pagan societies and that of the whole genus of societies, pagan, Hebrew, and Christian. Thus, in order to solve the two problems differentiated above, Vico was compelled to generate two kinds of historical laws: intrasocial (governing the dynamics of different kinds of society) and intersocial (governing the structural relations between different kinds of societies).

Vico solved these two problems in a manner similar to that of Hegel, which is to say that he made a qualitative distinction between different kinds of social orders (pagan and Christian) and then translated this distinction into spatial and temporal terms, making that which was contiguous in space (Greek, Roman, Hebrew, Christian) convergent in time, so that the first three could be treated as components of the synthesis achieved in the fourth. Greek culture is characterized as exceptional by virtue of the brillance of its cultural achievement, and Roman culture is viewed as exceptional by virtue of its long duration and achievement in the spheres of politics and law. As in Hegel, Greece is the "poetry," and Rome the "prose" of the world of pagan peoples.

Hebrew culture, by contrast, is presented as a consequence of the rule of divine law partially known, that is, as a set of prohibitions (specifically against uncleanliness and divination), which made it righteous in a way superior to anything attained by the pagan peoples. And Christian culture is regarded as a consequence of a definitive revelation of God to man, which not only kept it on the path of righteousness but permitted it to expand and flourish, to the point where in Vico's own time (by his lights) it gives promise of encompassing the globe.

These four cultural streams—Greek, Roman, Hebrew, and Christian—come together and are fused into a new and definitively progressive social order in Western Europe after the fall of the Roman Empire, between the fifth and twelfth centuries, after which time the whole of human history is placed on a new basis, permitting the anticipation of a time when the whole world will be ruled by Christian principles of governance, in which the true and correct relationship between power and justice will not only be known but also will be applied to create a virtual Heaven on earth, a semblance of the New Jerusalem promised in Scripture.

Now, all of this is reminiscent of Hegel and, as Karl Löwith has noted in *Meaning in History*, points to a possible affiliation of Vico's thought with the Joachite, or millenarian, tradition of the late Middle Ages, from which Hegel himself is sometimes presumed to derive. But while the similarity to both Hegel and to millenarian conceptions of the meaning of human history may be admitted, the significance of this similarity is unclear. Moreover, its utility as a heuristic device is very questionable. By concentrating on the superficial similarities between Vichian (and Hegelian) and Joachite (or millenarian) traditions of metahistorical speculation, the true originality of Vico's historical reflections is obscured altogether or at least reduced to a position in which they must receive less credit than they deserve. For at the interior of Vico's thought there resides a principle of interpretation, or to use a recently revived term, "hermeneutical principle," of which no other thinker in Europe prior to Hegel even glimpsed the possibility. This principle derives from the perception, original with Vico in the form that he gave to it, that speech itself provides the key for interpreting cultural phenomena and the categories by which the evolutionary stages of a given culture can be characterized. Here the basic distinction is between poetic expression on the one side and discursive prose representation on the other. The former is conceived to be a creative and active force by which consciousness confiscates its world; the latter a receptive and passive operation in which "things as they are" are mirrored. The effect of these two aspects of speech on consciousness sets up a tension, within consciousness itself, that generates a tendency of thought to transcend itself and to create out of the sensed inadequacy of language to its object the conditions for the exercise of its essential freedom.

What is the nature of the creative power of language? The answer to that question is not to be found in Vico's general remarks on the functions of poetic imagination (as when he says that the function of great poetry is to invent fables suitable to the popular understanding, to excite, and to sanctify belief [§ 376]); it is rather to be found in his discussion of the nature of metaphor, at the beginning of book 2 of the *New Science*.

Vico's theory of metaphor is developed within the context of and as the key to his discussion of "poetic logic." In Vico's usage, poetic logic designates the forms by which things, as apprehended by primitive man, are signified (§ 400). Since the first men were "stupid, insensate, and horrible beasts," their knowledge of things was not "rational and abstract," only "felt and imagined" (§ 375). Their "metaphysics," Vico says, was "their poetry," or, to put it another way, out of their poetic capability they created, or intuited, a metaphysics—a sense of the nature of things (*ibid.*). Projecting images of their own sensed natures upon the larger inanimate world—the earth, the sky, and the sea—they made "of all nature a vast animate body which feels passions and effects" (§ 377).

Now, "poetic logic" is Vico's term for the modes of operation of this primitive consciousness, the ways in which it works; and knowledge of these modes of operation provides the principles by which the creations of that primitive consciousness are to be interpreted. Thus, Vico begins the discussion of poetic logic with a distinction:

> That which is metaphysics insofar as it contemplates things in all the forms of their being, is logic insofar as it considers things in all the forms by which they may be signified. Accordingly, as poetry has been considered by us above as a poetic metaphysics in which the theological poets imagined bodies to be for the most part divine substances, so now that same poetry is considered as poetic logic, by which it signifies them (§ 400).

The connection between metaphysics, the science of things in all the forms of their being, and logic, the science of the forms by which they may be signified, is explicated in the philosophy of language which Vico develops in this section of his book. Poetic logic, the logic of primitive man, Vico maintains, differs from the logic of modern men (or, as he calls them, reflective men) by the direction which thought takes in its attribution of characteristics to things. In primitive times, the direction taken by thought is from the familiar to the unfamiliar and from the concrete to what we would call the abstract, so that the "forms by which things are signified" in primitive times must always be interpreted as a projection onto the unfamiliar of attributes felt to characterize the familiar. The origins of human knowledge, and *a fortiori* of human society and culture, are to be found in the onomathetic powers of primitive men, the power of "naming" objects, of distinguishing them from other objects, and, in the process, endowing them with specific attributes. Hence Vico's identification of the meaning of Greek *logos* with both *word* and *logic,* since the logic of primitive men was nothing but the operations by which they "named" and thereby "comprehended" the objects and processes of the world around and within themselves. The first language, he says, "was not a language in accord with the nature of the things it dealt with . . . but was a fantastic [in the sense of imaginative] speech making use of physical substances endowed with life and most of them imagined to be divine" (§ 401). It is these primitive identifications of the unfamiliar and threatening world of natural things with the familiar attributes of human nature, and especially of the senses and passions, which are, Vico surmises, the true contents and meanings of the myths and fables handed down by primitive peoples to our own times.

But it is not enough to read these myths and fables as if they were simple allegories, for poetic logic has, by virtue of the original metaphorical nature of its contents, its own inner dynamic or, as we might say, dialectic, so that the relationship between language and the world of things is not simply reflexive. Primitive linguistic representations of the world of things are not simply reversed images of the world given in sense perception, as they would be if they were only a product of thought reflecting on the world of things in a language restricted to metaphors based on the identification of the external world with internal emotional states. For metaphorical identifications have their own logic, which is not that of the syllogism *or* the sorites (§ 499), the two conceptions of the chain of reasoning known to Vico from classical sources, but rather the logic of the figures of speech or tropes, the "sensory topics" of primitive man (§§ 495–98).

Vico argues that all figures of speech may be reduced to four modes or tropes: metaphor, synecdoche, metonymy, and irony (§§ 404–09). This contention follows Aristotle but with this difference: Vico restricts the meaning of the mental operation indicated by each trope. Moreover, he makes of metaphor a kind of primal (generic) trope, so that synecdoche and metonymy are viewed as specific refinements of it, and irony is seen as its opposite. Thus, whereas metaphor constitutes the basis of every fable (or myth), the escape from metaphorical language and the transition into the use of a consciously figurative language (and thus into literal and denotative, or prose, discourse) are made possible by the emergence of an ironic sensibility. It is thus that the dialectic of figurative (tropological) speech itself becomes conceivable as the model by which the evolution of man from bestiality to humanity can be explained. Or to put it another way, the theory of metaphorical transformation serves as the model for a theory of the autotransformation of human consciousness in history. How Vico developed such a view can be shown only after we have considered his theory of the tropes.

According to Vico, "the most luminous and therefore the most necessary and frequent" of the tropes is metaphor, but metaphor of a specific kind, that is to say, that in which "sense and passion" are ascribed to "insensate things." It was by this kind of metaphorical projection that "the first poets attributed to bodies the being of animate substances, with capacities measured by their own, namely sense and passion, and in this way made fables of them" (§ 404).

It must be recalled that the term "fable" here refers, not to a story, but to a kind of naming operation in which the unfamiliar is identified with the familiar, so as to constitute a field of perception populated with (fantastic) particulars, each of which is related to some aspect of an apprehended self by both resemblance and difference. Thus, for example, the primitive's identification of thunder with anger, caused by savage man's fear of the sound, and his recognition of it as the emotional state that he naturally associated with that sound presuppose a similarity between kinds of noises (that made by an angry man and that heard in the thunder) and a difference between them (based on the fact that their volumes are unequal). The difference in volume is as crucial as the similarity in tone, for the difference is what makes it necessary for primitive man to identify the sound. The identification of the sound as anger at once familiarizes and defamiliarizes it; that is, it makes the sound recognizable as a specific kind of sound and makes of it a manifestation of a special kind of sound-making agency, in this case providing the basis for the presumption that it is made by, or is a manifestation of, a superhuman agency. Thus, the naming of the thunder creates implicitly what Vico calls an imaginative class concept (*genere fantastico*), which can in turn serve as the subject of other attributes of the natural world similarly awesome in aspect. This is the meaning of Vico's assertions that "every metaphor . . . is a fable in brief" (§ 404) and that the "mythologies are the proper languages of the fables" (§ 403), that is to say, allegorical extensions of the characteristics of the class concepts (constructed by fabulation) to "the diverse species or the diverse individuals comprised under [the] genera" (*ibid.*).

Vico's most important contention is that this primitive classification of phenomena by simple metaphorical identification of the unfamiliar sets up the tension between things and the words used to characterize them which makes further specification of the nature of things necessary and the further refinement of language possible by tropological variation. Once the thunder is identified as anger, then the notion of anger itself in the exceptional form in which it is apprehended becomes an object to which other attributes can be ascribed. The thunder's anger becomes particularized by virtue both of its identification as an emotional state and recognition in it of an exceptional degree of power. It becomes both known and unknown, known inasmuch as it has a name, unknown inasmuch as the name given it does not account for certain of its aspects, specifically the power or volume of the sound. The unknown aspect of the particular thing thus provisionally classified as an emotional state invites further attempts at classification, the modes of which Vico himself classifies in terms of the tropes of metonymy and synecdoche.

The fund of names which primitive man had available to him for characterization of unknown things or those aspects of known things which required further characterization Vico presumes to have been fashioned from "the most particular" and "the most sensible" ideas. That which is most prominent in the perceptual field, that which is experienced most vividly, that which is noticed most immediately *has* particularity. That which is experienced most vividly is the body and its various parts on the one hand and the emotions and their various states on the other. These provide the references for the most primitive kind of metaphorical identification and the bases for the ascription to a natural process, such as thunder, of the attributes of the emotional state resembling it in human experience. Once thunder is particularized as anger, it becomes the subject of further specification by two kinds of tropological reduction: metonymy and synecdoche.

By metonymy of cause for effect, the most sensible aspects of the thunder's anger become endowed with the attributes of agency. What we would call the effect of thunder is apprehended by primitive man as being itself a causal agency. By metonymy of agent for act, the act being itself the most sensible aspect of this putative causal agency, it is further endowed with the attributes of purposive activity. And by metonymy of subject for form and accident (or of primary for secondary characteristics), this agency is personalized, thereby creating the conditions for the foundation of the institutions of primitive religion: divination (the effort to determine the will of the gods) and worship (the effort to placate them). By metonymic reductions, the thunder is endowed with all the characteristics necessary to permit the conceptualization of it as a powerful, willful, and purposeful being, a great spirit which, because it is similar to man in some of its attributes, can be treated with, served, and placated.

Once such a being has been constituted, that is to say, made into a particularity with specific attributes, it becomes further characterizable by synecdoche as a conceptual unity. Just as metonymy represents a movement of thought from the most sensible idea to the less sensible, so that the abstract is experienced as a tangible or concrete reality, so Vico conceives synecdoche to move from the most particular idea to the most general, which results in the "elevation" of particulars into universals and of parts into wholes. Vico gives a number of examples:

Thus [he says] the term "mortals" was originally and properly applied only to men, as the only beings whose mortality there was any occasion to notice. The use of "head" for man or person, so frequent in vulgar Latin, was due to the fact that in the forests only the head of a man could be seen from a distance.

The word "man" itself is abstract, comprehending as in a philosophic genus the body and all its parts, the mind and all its faculties, the spirit and all its dispositions (§ 407).

The three tropes thus far distinguished by Vico—metaphor, metonymy, and synecdoche—provide him with the bases of a theory of linguistic dynamics. The three tropes and the structural relations between them outlined above serve Vico as the categories of what he calls poetic logic. Primitive thought operates, in his view, on precisely the same principles as figurative (or poetic) language but with the difference that, whereas the modern poet is capable of distinguishing between figurative and literal language and of using the former self-consciously to gain specific kinds of poetic effects, primitive man is presumed to have been able at first to speak only figuratively and to think in allegories and to have taken these figures and allegories as literal truths, or denotative representations, of the world external to himself. And, Vico says, it was only after the recognition of disparities between these figurative representations of reality and the objects they were meant literally to characterize that the fourth major trope, irony, became possible.

Irony, Vico says, "is fashioned of falsehood by dint of a reflection which wears the mask of truth." Irony represents a stage in the evolution of consciousness in which language itself has become an object of reflection, and the sensed inadequacy of language to the full representation of its object has become perceived as a problem. Ironic speech presupposes an awareness of the possibility of feigning or of lying or dissimulating. Thus, Vico says: "Irony certainly could not have begun until the period of reflection," for "since the first men of the gentile world had the simplicity of children, who are truthful by nature, the first fables could not feign anything false. . ." (§ 408). That is to say, the fables of primitive man were taken to represent a true report of reality.

Irony presupposes awareness of the distinction between truth and falsehood, of the possibility of misrepresenting reality in language, and of the difference between a literal and a figurative representation. Therefore, Vico maintains, the tropes ought not to be considered as the "ingenious inventions" of sophisticated ages of high civilization, but rather as "the necessary modes of expression" of primitive men (§ 409). They become the *bases* of figurative language only when, "with the further development of the human mind, words were invented which signified abstract forms or genera comprising their species or relating parts with their wholes" (*ibid.*). Thus the trope of irony, in which falsehood is presented as the truth, constitutes the limit of figurative characterizations of reality; for an ironic utterance is not merely a statement about reality, as metaphor, metonymy, and synecdoche are, but presupposes at least a tacit awareness of the disparity between a statement and the reality it is supposed to represent. Ironic speech implicitly invokes the distinction between truthful and false speaking and thus points to the distinction between literal and figurative representation, thereby constituting the basis of all those sciences which, through use of stipulated meanings, consciously seek not only to make true statements about the world but also to expose the error or inadequacy of any given figurative characterization of it.

Now, the important point is not whether Vico's theory of inventive language is correct or even whether his characterization of the major tropes and the relation between them is valid, but the role the tropes play in his theory of primitive consciousness. For in fact his tropological conception of what he calls poetic logic serves him not merely as the basis of a method for interpreting the myths, fables, and legends of ancient Greek and Roman times and of relating them to the social institutions of which they are conceived to be reflections or rationalizations, but also as a model by which to describe the structural characteristics of ancient societies and as a schema for relating the phases through which they pass in their evolutions.

It will be recalled that Vico postulates three stages through which all cultures pass in their cycles from primitivism to high civilization—religious, poetic, and prosaic—each with its own distinctive form of human nature (religious, heroic, and human) and a reprise of the cycle with the return of barbarism when these cultures have reached their terms. Actually, in his discussion of the *corsi*, these three stages are further refined into subphases: birth, growth, maturity, decadence, and dissolution. But the subphases are related to the stages by the conceptual equivalents of the relationships between man and his world analyzed in the discussion of the master tropes. The table on the facing page will illustrate the point:

As a system of classification of cultures or societies, Vico's schema is neither more nor less original than those of Aristotle and St. Thomas Aquinas or, to take modern examples, those of Machiavelli, Montesquieu, Hegel, Marx, Spengler, or Toynbee. Nor is his conception of human nature as mind and body mediated by speech particularly novel; nor his conception of the relationship between consciousness on the one side and its different social milieux on the other. Even the kind of distinction he draws between poetic and prosaic language is anticipated by Aristotle, as is that drawn between the two kinds of "logic" required for the assessments of scientific statements on the one side and poetic statements on the other. What *is* original is his use of the tropological analysis of figurative language for the construction of a model by which both the stages in the evolution of consciousness can be defined and the transitions from one to another of them can be accounted for in terms of "the modifications of the human mind." As a theory of the historical development of human nature from bestiality to civilization, the *New Science* asserts a strict analogy between the dynamics of metaphorical transformations in language and the transformations of both consciousness and society. This is Vico's dialectic,

STAGE:	RELIGIOUS	HEROIC	HUMAN ⟶ REPRISE	
Transition:	metaphor to metonymy	metonymy to synecdoche	synecdoche to irony	
Subphase:	birth and growth	maturity	decadence and dissolution	
Type of human nature:	poetic	heroic	human	(§§916–18)
Type of society:	theocratic	aristocratic	democratic	(§§925–27)
Type of language:	mute	heraldic	articulate	(§§928–31)
Type of law:	divine	contractual	forensic	(§§937–40)
Type of reason:	divine	natural	civil	(§§947–51)
Type of writing:	hieroglyphic	imaginative	vulgar	(§§932–35)

which is not a dialectic of the syllogism (thesis, antithesis, synthesis) but rather the dialectic of the exchange between language on the one side and the reality it seeks to contain on the other. Put most simply, the analogy states the following generic similarities between transitions in societies and the tropological transformations of speech:

1. The transition from primal metaphorical identifications by naming external reality in terms taken from the most particular and most sensible ideas of the parts of the body and the emotional states to metonymic reductions is analogous to the transition in society from the rule of the gods to the rule of aristocracies;

2. The transition from metonymic reductions to synecdochic constructions of wholes from parts, genera from species, and so on is analogous to the transition from aristocratic rule to democratic rule; and

3. The transition from synecdochic constructions to ironic statement is analogous to the transition from democracies ruled by law to the decadent societies whose members have no respect for the law.

This idea is sustained by Vico's belief that the mode of social organization of a given stage of cultural development is analogous to the modes of relating the unknown or problematical aspects of human experience to the known or cognitively secured aspects of it characteristic of the four master tropes. In the first stage, men project upon the gods their own sensed human attributes, imputing to them the power they see manifested in cataclysmic natural events, such as thunder, lightning, volcanic eruptions, floods, and so on. They effectively conceive themselves to be lesser creatures, servants, or slaves of these higher powers and order their lives in terms of these functions. Fear drives men into caves, floods drive them into caves high on the sides of mountains; lust drives them to take women with them and to cohabit with them in the caves; and necessity, the threat of physical destruction, keeps them in the caves, thereby forcing the formation of the first families. Within the families, relations are governed by the rule of the strongest; just as between the families and the gods from whose wrath they are fleeing, fear of powers stronger than the strongest man lays the foundation of the first religious practices: worship and divination. So too, in the first men's conceptions of the relations between the generations, fear and strength are the governing principles (the children's fear of the fathers and the fathers' fear of the dead). The men of these first times are totally alienated from themselves by virtue of their (purely human) capacities for metaphorical projection of their own natures upon the circumambient nature. As Vico says, they lived in fear of themselves, that is, of those aspects of their own natures which they had projected onto the physical world and imagined as gods. In their consciousnesses, men were nothing, and the gods were all, even though the gods were products only of their own imaginations and nothing but projections of their own animal and human capacities.

This relationship of total alienation is mediated by changes in consciousness analogous to those reflected in the presumed differences between simple metaphor on the one side and metonymy on the other. Within the primal family, relationships are in fact determined by the rule of the strongest, the father who both exploits his own family and protects it from other predators—from animal and human predators by his physical strength and from divine and spiritual predators by his religious wisdom and his command of magic and ritual. This mode of social praxis characteristic of the family becomes in turn the basis for attribution of specific characteristics to the gods; they are identified as exercising the same kind of powers over men that the fathers do over the families, so that by analogy, the radical differences felt to exist between gods and men are mediated, at least partially and selectively, by the progressive humanization of the gods and the progressive divinization of the fathers.

The internal differentiation of status, functions, privileges, and responsibilities within the family on the basis of strength is attended by the extension of power of the patriarchs to include aliens driven from the forests and plains below, where the primal struggle of all against all continues to consume the weakest or forces them to seek protection by the established families in the caves above. These refugees form the basis of the *socii*, who in return for protection by the patriarchs perform the services of slaves to them, in the same way that the first men performed their services as slaves to the gods. This creates a division within socialized humanity both in practice and in consciousness, in that members of the servile class are denied the status of men, are defined as beasts, and are treated as such. Thus, the patriarchs are given an occasion for the further definition of their own humanity by negative example, not as contrasted to the gods but as contrasted to the animal men on whose labor they come increasingly to depend. Thus, the heroic societies are formed out of the divine societies, and the age of gods gives place to the age of heroes (aristocracies).

The consciousness of these heroic societies is expressed in the mode of metonymic identification. It is essentially reductive, not in the mode of metaphor, but primarily in that of metonymy. For among the strongest and most powerful and among the weakest and most servile, the social order is sustained by acceptance of the divided social order as being in the nature of things. That is to say, among both rulers and ruled, the act of ruling is taken for the agency of rule; the form and accident of rulership are taken for the essence or subject of it; and the effect of rulership is taken for the cause of its being what it is. And all this in accordance with the principle that the most vivid objects of experience, in this case the strongest and most terrifying men in the group, are treated as the primitive data of consciousness to which all extrinsic apprehensions of human existence must be referred for determination of their significance. The cultural products of this kind of society are similarly metonymic, in that the elevated style of the epics, which have as their subject matter the acts of the "heroes" or most noble of men, presupposes the nobility, the divine descent, of their protagonists and stresses the essential differences between the heroes and ordinary men. And so too for the laws of this period. They have to do primarily with the privileges enjoyed by the nobility and are guarded by it lest the plebeians, by simple knowledge that a law exists, be driven to demand a law for regulating relations between themselves and the nobility.

The transition from the age of heroes to the age of men, from rule by the aristocracy to the rule of law conceived as a mediator between the classes, is effected, Vico states, by a change in consciousness among the lower orders, which change is analogous to the progression from a metonymic mode of perception to a synecdochic mode. For the rebellion of the servile class has as its presupposition the perception of the unity of the individual with the species and of the species with the genus. Therefore, in accordance with the principle that, in primitive synecdoche, the identification is always made in reference to the attributes which are most sensibly apprehended, this perception invests the servile class with the humanity which the nobility had originally claimed for itself alone.

Primitive synecdoche takes the part for the whole or the species for the genus. It thereby provides the explanation of the plebeians' ascription to themselves of the attributes originally ascribed to the gods and later claimed by the nobility. Vico describes the transition from the heroic age to the human age in the following way:

the family fathers, having become great by the religion and virtue of their ancestors and through the labors of their clients, began to abuse the laws of protection and to govern the clients harshly. When they thus departed from the natural order, which is that of justice, their clients rose in mutiny against them. But since without order (which is to say without God) human society cannot stand for a moment, providence led the family fathers naturally to unite themselves with their kindred in orders against their clients. To pacify the latter, they conceded to them, in the world's first agrarian law, the bonitary ownership of the fields, retaining for themselves the optimal or sovereign family ownership. Thus the first cities arose upon reigning orders of nobles. And as the natural order declined which had been based, in accordance with the then state of nature, on [superiority of] kind, sex, age, and virtue, providence called the civil order into being along with the cities. And first of all [civil orders], that which approximated most closely to nature: that in virtue of nobility of humankind (for in that state of affairs nobility could be based only on generating in human fashion with wives taken under divine auspices) and thus in virtue of a heroism, the nobles should rule over the plebeians (who did not contract marriages with such solemnities), and now that divine rules had ceased (under which the families had been governed by divine auspices) and the heroes had to rule in virtue of the form of the heroic governments themselves, that the basic institution of these commonwealths should be religion safeguarded within the heroic orders, and that through this religion all civil laws and institutions should belong to the heroes alone. But since nobility had now become a gift of fortune, providence caused to arise among the nobles the order of the family fathers themselves, as being naturally more worthy because of age. And among the fathers it caused the most spirited and the most robust to arise as kings whose duty it should be to lead the others and gird them in orders to resist and overawe the clients who rebelled against them (§ 1100).

This long passage contains the principles of Vico's philosophy of history *in nuce*, presenting images of both the structural relationships obtaining between consciousness and social practices and a schema explaining the transition from one stage to another. It is followed by another passage, equally representative, in which the emergence of synecdochic consciousness is explicitly invoked as the cause of class conflict and as the basis of the popular government arising from it.

But *with the passage of the years* and the *far greater development of human minds*, the plebs of the peoples *finally became suspicious* of the pretensions of such heroism and *understood themselves* to be *of equal human nature with the nobles*, and *therefore* insisted that they too should enter into the civil institutions of the cities. . . . In this way . . . the popular commonwealths were born. . . . In such commonwealths the entire peoples, who have in common the desire for justice, command laws that are just because they are good for all (§ 1101) (italics mine).

It is only in such "human" communities, Vico surmises, that there arises that philosophical consciousness which seeks to mediate between truth and falsehood, and in the same way that the law explicitly mediates between justice and injustice. "All this was ordained by providence," Vico remarks, "to the end that, since virtuous actions were no longer prompted by religious sentiments as formerly, philosophy should make the virtues understood in their idea, and by dint of reflection thereon, if men were without virtue they should at least be ashamed of their vices" (*ibid.*).

But this kind of consciousness contains within it the seeds of its own dissolution. Just as irony presupposes consciousness of the distinction between truth and falsehood, so too the vision of an internally differentiated though legally unified human community is inherently fated to promote a decline from the condition of virtue to that of vice. The sign of corruption is given in the "descent" of philosophy to scepticism and of oratory from eloquence to eristic. Thus Vico says:

But as the popular states became corrupt, so also did the philosophies. They descended to skepticism. Learned fools fell to calumniating the truth. Thence arose a false eloquence, ready to uphold either of the opposed sides of a case indifferently. Thus it came about that, by abuse of eloquence like that of the tribunes of the plebs at Rome, when the citizens were no longer content with making wealth the basis of rank, they strove to make of it an instrument of power. And as furious south winds whip up the sea, so these citizens provoked civil wars in their commonwealths and drove them to total disorder. Thus they caused the commonwealths to fall from a perfect liberty into the perfect tyranny of anarchy of the unchecked liberty of the free peoples, which is the worst of all tyrannies (§ 1102).

When this condition arises, Vico says, providence provides a remedy of one or another of three kinds: calling forth a strong man (such as Augustus), unleashing upon the decadent society a conquering barbarian horde, or permitting the internal logic of the relation between virtue and vice to work itself out in self-destruction. The last "remedy" represents the effect of ironic consciousness serving as the rule governing social relationships. Thus, Vico writes:

But if the peoples are rotting in that ultimate civil disease and cannot agree on a monarch from within, and are not conquered and preserved by better nations from without, then providence for their extreme ill has its extreme remedy at hand. For such peoples, like so many beasts, have fallen into the custom of each man thinking only of his own private interests and have reached the extreme of delicacy, or better of pride, in which like wild animals they bristle and lash out at the slightest displeasure. Thus no matter how great the throng and press of their bodies, they live like wild beasts in a deep solitude of spirit and will, scarcely any two being able to agree since each follows his own pleasure or caprice (§ 1106).

Through "obstinate factions" and "desperate civil wars," the cities are turned into "forests and the forests into dens and lairs of men." "*In this way,*" Vico concludes, "through long centuries of barbarism, rust will consume the misbegotten subtleties of malicious wits that have turned them into beasts made more inhuman by the *barbarism of reflection* than the first men had been made by the *barbarism of sense*" (§ 1106) (italics mine). This creates the conditions for the return to "piety, faith, and truth" by the same kind of transformations of consciousness described in the analysis of the tropes and in the same order of transformation, so that the *corso* of the original transition from barbarism to civilization is lived through again, as a *ricorso,* with new contents but ruled by the same laws of structure and process.

Vico's conception of "The Recourse of Human Institutions Which The Nations Take When They Rise Again," set forth in book 5 of the *New Science,* is less clearly formulated than his conception of their original course. And this for the reason that whereas he deals with two principal examples of the courses, Greece and Rome, he deals with only one example of the recourse, early medieval Europe. The import of this example is rendered ambiguous by the fact that, in the medieval European case, the contents of consciousness are of two orders, Christian *and* pagan, rather than of the single order that Vico conceives them to be in the original barbaric age. Still, the structural relationships between consciousness and its objects are presumed to be the same as in the original primitive times, and the transitions from one stage to another are analyzed on the same analogy with linguistic transformation.

The exceptional nature of this single example of *ricorso* is signaled in Vico's remark, at the beginning of book 5, to the effect that in the early Middle Ages, God "permitted *a new order of humanity* to be born among the nations" so that the true religion "might be firmly established according to the natural course of human things (*cose*) themselves" (§ 1047). But the mode of relationship of the Christian religion to the pagan peoples, Vico maintains, was the same as that which primitive man sustained with nature; and its truth for pagan humanity was established by the same means, on the basis of its appeal to the most particular and the most sensible ideas of things in the childlike consciousness. "Working in superhuman ways," Vico says, "God . . . revealed and confirmed the truth of the Christian religion by opposing the *virtue* of the martyrs to the power of Rome, and the teaching of the Fathers, *together with the miracles*, to the vain wisdom of Greece . . ." (§ 1047) (italics mine). In short, the truth of the Christian religion was first established by the *acts* of the martyrs, the *teachings* of the fathers, and the *miracles* wrought by God, which is to say by a kind of divine *poesis* appropriate to the understanding of childlike natures reduced to fear and anxiety by the anarchy of their condition. Thus, from the "caves" of the ruined cities men fled for protection to "asylums" in the countryside, provided by "bishops and abbots" who were "comparatively humane in the midst of such barbarism," thereby forming the Christian counterpart of the first families of the patriarchs in the original divine ages (§ 1056).

These "divine times" were followed, Vico then says, "by certain heroic times, in consequence of the return of a certain distinction between almost opposite natures, the heroic [that is, aristocratic] and human" (§ 1057). This mode of social relationship corresponds to the metonymic consciousness which flourished during the original heroic times. And it is transcended, not by a change in the social relationships themselves, but rather by a change of consciousness corresponding to the synecdochic identification of the general with the specific, or the specific with the individual instance of humanity. Thus Vico argues:

> But finally, with the opening of schools in the universities of Italy and the teaching of the Roman laws contained in the books of Justinian, laws therein based on the natural law of the human gentes, *minds now more developed and grown more intelligent* were dedicated to the cultivation of the jurisprudence of natural equity, which makes the common people and their nobles equal in civil rights, just as they are equal in human nature. . . . The plebeians, *once they know themselves to be* of equal nature with the nobles, naturally will not submit to remaining their inferiors in civil rights; and they achieve equality either in free commonwealths or under monarchies (§§ 1086 and 1087) (italics mine).

But because the religion of the Europeans is the *true* religion (§ 1094), the new society which took shape in Western Europe in the early Middle Ages is, in Vico's view, guarded in a special way against the fall into ironic consciousness which beset its pagan counterparts. For the truth which opposes falsehood in Christian societies, Vico asserts, is superior to the natural truths arrived at by natural means in minds not informed by Christian faith. Thus Christianity stands as the divinely provided solvent of ironic consciousness, as the measure of all truth, and as the criterion by which every merely human belief and all human knowledge are to be judged. It is from the standpoint of Christian truth that Vico is permitted, in his own mind, to view, with self-conscious irony, the courses which the gentile nations run in their passage from birth and growth through maturity to decline and dissolution. It is this irony which gives to him the detachment necessary for the construction of the laws governing the gentile nations' developments. This detachment, in turn, permitted him to conceive their histories as purely autonomous processes of development, governed by providence only insofar as it provided, in the constitution of human nature itself as body, mind, and speech, the three variables whose interactions the pagan histories represent. And by assigning primacy as mediative force to speech rather than to either mind or body, he was permitted to claim that he had accounted for the evolution of reason out of emotion, of humanity out of bestiality, and of civilization out of savagery in a way that no one before him had ever been able to do.

The root metaphor of Vico's conception of history, then, is to be found in the theory of linguistic transformation that he used as a model of both consciousness's relation to its objects and the dynamics of consciousness's transformations in time. The internal dynamics of the system represents a projection of the theory of the tropes and of the relationships between them that he took over entire from classical poetics. His emplotment of human history is elaborated on two levels: the Hebrew-Christian, which describes a progressive evolution of consciousness in the light of revealed truth; and the pagan, which describes a pattern of cyclical recurrence, the phases of which are described in tropological terms, on the analogy of the linguistic evolution from simple metaphor, through metonymy and synecdoche, to irony.

The attitudes which Vico assumes before his data are twofold in kind: with respect to the data of Hebrew-Christian history, it is pious and utterly uncritical; with respect to all pagan histories, it is ironic, inasmuch as what all pagan thinkers take for *the* truth, Vico himself takes for a mixture of truth and error. The voice with which Vico speaks of historical events is that of one privy to *the* truth reflecting on the mixtures of truth and error which the pagan thinkers produced, but with sympathy for their attempts to discover truth and praise for their attainment to the distinction between truth and error. This sympathy is generated by his conviction, product of his Christian faith, that they were congenitally incapable of rising to the higher truth which he, along with all other Christians, possessed. Therefore, the voices in which he addresses his contemporaries are of two kinds: one produced by the assumption of a shared religious belief, the other used to address those beyond the pale of correct belief. His pride arises from his conviction that he has met the enemies of Christian faith on their own grounds and that he has derived from the consideration of the evidence alone a justification for belief in the operations of providence even among these peoples not privy to Christian truth. And his contention is that his new science provides a way of dissolving the ironic consciousness of which modern philosophers of chance on the one side and of strict determinism on the other are representatives. It achieves this effect, in Vico's view, by reversing the relationship between the components of ironic consciousness so that the false is seen, not to oppose the true, but to be contained within it as a necessary stage in the attainment of the whole truth. This is the higher irony, praised and practiced by Erasmus, who perceived that folly is not the opposite of reason or sanity, but dialectically related to it, the basis and presupposition of the attainment of rationality and health. Thus, to the dualisms and monisms of his age, Vico opposed a third alternative, based on the recognition that just as death is contained in life and life in death, so too savagery is contained in civilization and civilization in savagery and, perhaps more importantly, based on the recognition that the bestial exists in the human in the same way that the human exists in the bestial.

Attila Fáj

VICO AS PHILOSOPHER OF *METABASIS*

Metabasis as a constructive fallacy

Metabasis reveals itself, from the perspective of philosophy of science, as the main characteristic feature of the scientific method followed by Giambattista Vico. What is *metabasis* in Aristotelian-scholastic logic? *Metabasis* (μετάβασις εἰς ἄλλο γένος) means, first and foremost, an illicit transition from one genus (or species) to another, based mostly on ambiguity. In order to avoid fallacies caused by ambiguity, both the exact definition of terms and their consistent use are required.[1] One cannot, for example, discuss reasonably the virtue of high-mindedness (μεγαλοψυχία) without defining the concept precisely and always giving it the same meaning. We soon realize, Aristotle notes,[2] that, when it is used to characterize the high-mindedness of Alcibiades or Homer's Achilles and Ajax, the concept has a meaning completely different from when it is used to characterize the virtue of Lysander or Socrates. The former are called high-minded because of their intolerance of dishonor, the latter because of their indifference to bad or good fortune. There seems to be no transition from one species of this virtue to the other, since the kind of high-mindedness that shows itself in war (Alcibiades), by flying into rage (Achilles), or by committing suicide (Ajax) is by no means identical with the high-mindedness that manifests itself in indifference to the vicissitudes of fortune (Lysander and Socrates). From the perspective of Achilles, Socrates is not high-minded, and vice versa. Only by passing from one species of this virtue to the other can we infer that both are intolerant of dishonor, as well as indifferent to fortune.

The transition from the nature of "civilized men" to that of "men without moral restraint" is considered illicit for the same reason. The two senses of *nature* are each caught by the following statements: "Natural law agrees with nature" (in the first sense); "Nature" (in the second sense) "contests every kind of law." The conclusion (transition) drawn from these statements, if they serve as premises, would lead to the paradox "Natural law agrees with nature in contesting every kind of law," that is,

[1] For the main passages on *metabasis* in Aristotle's logic see *An. Pr.* I. 27; *An. Post.* I. 7, 9; II. 13.
[2] *An. Post.* 97b. 15–25.

including natural law. This is an example of the fallacy of four terms (*quaternio terminorum*), one of the most frequent occurrences of *metabasis* in syllogism. In this fallacy the middle term is taken in the first premise in a sense different from that in which it is taken in the second premise. By using four terms rather than three, the syllogism yields a false conclusion.[3]

Most instances of sliding from one field of science to another in the course of a proof or a demonstration are considered by Aristotle to be an illicit *metabasis*. The arithmetical proof of a geometrical proposition,[4] or any other "jump" into an alien field by apparently far-fetched inferences, is an unjustified logical transgression. Such a transgression is, for example, the deduction of a change of color from a change of figure,[5] or an eccentric inference ("stating the middle term in too remote a form"), such as accounting for the absence of female flute-players among the Scythians by the circumstance that in Scythia there are no vines.[6] Sometimes Aristotle allows for a *metabasis* from one science to another when one discipline is concerned with the collection of empirical facts while the other is concerned with discovering the reasons for the facts. This is the situation, occasionally, he admits, not only between "lower" and "higher" sciences (physics affords the facts, and mathematics discovers the reason for them) but also between sciences equal in rank. A geometrical proposition, for example, can be used to give us the reason for the physiological fact that circular wounds heal more slowly than regular ones.[7] But Aristotle never examined the conditions under which a logical *metabasis* was permitted.

The linguist who reads the *New Science* for the first time remains perplexed about the huge number of false etymologies and arbitrary interpretations the author puts forward to support his philosophy of history. The critical editions of the work are full of footnote rectifications of illicit etymologies and illations. In the great mass of these only "here and there sparkle some real pearls."[8] The reason for these errors is not that philology and historical sciences were not evolved enough at that time to provide critical methods. These errors are not merely such traditional errors as the repetition of mistaken etymologies already existing and interpretations of myths, literary texts, and so on. In many cases the author of the false illations is Vico himself, and where he is not, he cannot evade the responsibility for his bad choice from the body of inherited etymologies. According to Croce, Vico's faults are more deeply rooted. They rise from the

[3] Cf. C. L. Hamblin, *Fallacies* (London, 1970), pp. 196ff.
[4] *An. Post.* 75a. 38ff.
[5] *Metaph.* 1057a. 26ff.
[6] *An. Post.* 78b. 29–32.
[7] *An. Post.* 78b. 33–79a. 17.
[8] Antonino Pagliaro, "La dottrina linguistica di G. B. Vico," in *Atti della Accademia Nazionale dei Lincei, Classe di Scienze morali, Storiche, e Filologiche* (Rome, 1959), ser. 8, vol. 8, fasc. 6, p. 467.

confusion of three fields—philosophy, history, and empirical sciences—a confusion that leads to free and easy passages from one field to another. Thus, empirical (linguistic and historical) data are used to prove the philosophically determined stages of the regular succession of civilizations, states, languages, styles, and moral systems. Moreover, in Croce's opinion, Vico commits also the illicit generalization from a kind of manifestation of the mind to the spirit of a historical age. He passes, for example, from poetry to the barbaric epoch of humanity as such and certifies the latter as the ideal age of poetry.[9] Undoubtedly Vico was aware of the mistakes committed by the learned who gave philosophical explanations to linguistical and mythological data. He deemed misleading Plato's word analyses in *Cratylus*, as well as Bacon's erudite interpretations of ancient myths and poetical fictions in *De sapientia veterum*.[10] Nevertheless, he continues to make similar transitions, giving priority, however, to the socializing and historizing analysis of words and decipherings of myths and other poetical creations of the human mind.[11]

[9] B. Croce, *The Philosophy of Giambattista Vico*, trans. R. G. Collingwood (London, 1913), chap. 3 et passim.

[10] Is, for example, the Baconian interpretation of the figure of Pan, regarded by the English philosopher as the universal framework of nature, a forced interpretation (see *De sapientia* in *The Works of Francis Bacon*, ed. Spedding, Ellis, and Heath, 14 vols. [London, 1858–74], vol. 6, pp. 635–41) in comparison with the view held by Vico, who considers this half-man and half-beast the symbol of the social situation born from the union of the ancient nobility with the plebeians (see *New Science*, § 654)?

[11] The failure to distinguish between poetry and social philosophy leads Vico to consider even the Homeric poems as emblematical representations of historical forces and social movements. The Homeric heroes become symbols of abstract political processes, "puppets in a mechanistic theory of civilization," says W. B. Stanford, because Vico "fails to see that the primary function of the Homeric poems is to tell a story about human beings and to rise (especially in the *Odyssey*) above class distinctions and social conventions." Consequently, he continues, his attitude is anti-Homeric, nay, "more radically destructive: it is antihumanistic." Vico is "a prophet of Marxism" who outrages the facts and paves the way for pseudo-sciences. (See W. B. Stanford, *The Ulysses-Theme* [Oxford, 1954], pp. 185f.)

Stanford's caricature is not entirely without foundation and relevance. In the history of pseudo-sciences, a particular place is reserved for the vulgar Vichianism. The linguistic theory of Nikolay Ya. Marr (1864–1934), whose "new doctrine" was the ruling glottogonical theory in the thirties and forties in the Soviet Union, seems in many respects an adoption of Vico's erroneous transitions. (On Marr, see *Bolshaya Sovyetskaya Entsiklopediya*, 2d ed. [1954], vol. 26, s.v. "Marr, Nikolay Yakovlevich." Marr's *Izbrannye sochineniya* [*Selected Works*] have been published in five volumes, Leningrad, 1933–37.

The most obvious affinities are revealed by Marr's hypothesis of a prehistorical silent, or hand language and by that of four elements supposed to constitute the basis of every language (for analogies, see the *New Science*, § 452); further by his theory of a primordial prelogical thinking or speaking, absolutely different from the logical way of thinking and speaking (see analogies in the *New Science*, §§ 378f., 391, 400), which did not exist in prehistory; and, last, by his predilection for considering the language of a nation as superstructure or class language closely depending on the revolutionary social-economic changes. These parallel features of the two conceptions did not escape the attention of the Soviet Vico popularizers (for example, V. N. Maksimovsky, "Esteticheskye vzglyady Dzh. Vika" [The Aesthetic Views of Giambattista Vico], in

Although in the history of logic *metabasis* has long been known as a paradigm of erroneous reasoning, we must not overlook its constructive aspect when handled correctly; at least it seems at times to be a *felix culpa*. The positive *metabasis* often appears in Vichian philosophy; moreover, it may be said without exaggeration that every impressive result of the *New Science* originates in a train of thought with one or more illicit logical transitions. Sometimes even the choice of examples makes one feel that Vico wants to challenge Aristotle by proving the validity of some transitions which Aristotle branded as errors. Vico, like Aristotle, clearly sees the incompatibility of Socrates' high-mindedness with that of the Homeric Achilles. He notes that the two kinds of this virtue are incompatible only when they are considered from the same point of view and from the same point of time but that they become compatible when the points of view and the times are changed.[12] The transition from one kind of high-mindedness (the heroic) to the other (the human) is quite natural even from the logical point of view. The Socratic indifference to fortune conceived as a heroic will free from passions is, as a matter of fact, also a kind of intolerance of dishonor, since it is a reaction by a dispassionate reasoning about common utility and rightness for everybody and by a behavior consistent with the results of such reasoning. Thus indifference to fortune and intolerance of dishonor constitute two opposite aspects of the same idea of high-mindedness, which is divided in two only by the human mind, that is, by the operation of the definitory dissection (διαίρεσις).[13] The idea of high-mindedness, like any idea, is not independent from time, circum-

---

Literaturnyi kritik, 11 (1935): 10–27), who intended to do Vico's philosophy a service by presenting him as a forerunner of Marr. The publication of the first Soviet translation of the *New Science* in 1940 is partly due to these presentations.

It is a curious episode of Vico's fortune in the Soviet Union that, when Stalin decided to attack Marr's "new doctrine" in a series of articles, "Concerning Marxism in Linguistics" (Moscow, 1950), and to give free play to the criticism of Marrism, he created the preconditions for a rediscovery of valid Vichian thoughts. (See B. I. Sharevskaya, "Protiv antimarksistskikh izvrashcheniy v osveshchenii voprosov pervobytnogo myshleniya i pervobytnoy religii" [Against anti-Marxist distortions in the interpretations of the primordial thinking and religion], in *Sovyetskaya Etnografiya*, 1953, no. 3, pp. 9–26.) For example, Sharevskaya's insistence on stressing that in prehistory the prelogical mood of thinking and speaking exists parallel to a fully logical one agrees with the Vichian thesis of a kind of synchronical coexistence of the divine and the human languages and of the primitive poetical and the scientific languages (see *New Science*, §§ 412, 446, 629).

[12] Cf. *New Science*, §§ 666f., 708, and 879.

[13] *Ibid.*, §§ 1041f. It should be noted that here Vico's statement is more general. He asserts the compatibility of the idea of the dispassionate research after common utility and rightness with a passionate striving after private utility and interests. The Vichian passage is an obvious reference to Plato's *Parmenides* 129b–e, a passage where Socrates says how marvelous it would be if someone succeeded in demonstrating that the kinds and ideas in and by themselves possess opposite qualities. The rest of this dialogue is a series of such demonstrations.

stances, and individuals; in different times and under changed conditions it unfolds with a wide range of regular modifications.[14]

Using a similar train of thought, Vico demonstrates that the *quaternio terminorum* is not a logical fallacy, if we keep in mind the manifold points of view, times, and circumstances:

> Natural law agrees with human nature.
> Human nature contests every kind of law.
>
> ---
>
> Natural law agrees with human nature contesting every kind of law.

Natural law, in the *New Science,* has several meanings,[15] in accordance with the several meanings of human nature in the different historical ages. Therefore, the *metabasis* from one meaning of the middle term, "human nature," to another is in order. Let us accept as a basic hypothesis that in every epoch natural law agrees with human nature. Now, if it is true that in the epoch of men (democracy) natural law agrees with the nature of civilized men (major premise), but human nature in the epochs of gods (theocracy) and heroes (aristocracy) contests every kind of a highly civilized conception of law (minor premise), then, consequently, it is true that natural law in the epochs of gods and heroes agrees with human nature contesting such a developed conception of law.

Vico states definitely that human nature varies in conformity with the age of the individual.[16] From the fact that children like playing (*lusus*) and lasciviousness (*lascivias*), young people like parties (*convivia*) and physical rivalry (*campum*), adults like honor (*honores*) and power (*potentiam*), and old people like wealth (*divitias*) and comfort (*opes*), Vico concluded by a metabasical induction that it is an inherent property of man in every age to be fond of certain things according to his age.[17] By analogy, he inferred also that mankind is already fond of something according to the different epochs; for example, in the human epoch, that of democracy, men enjoy honor, power, wealth, and comfort, whereas in the heroic epoch, that of aristocracy, they are generally fond of amusements

[14] *New Science,* § 1039. Cf. Plato's analysis in *Parmenides* 153c–e, according to which the idea as *genus* ("one") is younger than the species and the individuals ("others"), as it will exist completely only when all possibilities have already developed from it; but the same idea is also contemporary with the species and individuals come out of it, because the idea itself is living and developing together with them.

[15] See *New Science,* § 9. Cf. Opere (Ricciardi), p. 373, n. l.

[16] *Institutiones oratoriae, Opere* (Morano) 7: 61.

[17] It is Vico who calls this method induction. For Aristotle such a passing from the species to the genus is only a transition by which we get a definition (*An. Post.* 97b. 26ff.).

and physical rivalry. Consequently, in the heroic epoch, natural law agrees with the joy to display antagonistic forces.[18]

In summary, human nature is universal, not because it manifests itself from the philosophical viewpoint in an absolutely determined way (the sort of *metabasis* deprecated by Croce), but because it is identical in *hypothetically* equal times and circumstances and different in *actually* different times and circumstances.[19] The *metabasis* from one meaning of human nature to the other is indispensable for the comprehension of mankind and natural law in progress.

Forms and uses of the metabasis: *Vico's theory of science*

In Vico's philosophy there is a particular "art" which makes allowance for personal, temporal, local, and other circumstantial factors and brings to light the necessary changes of meaning in reasonings and thereby assists every scientific progress. On the authority of Aristotle, Cicero, Boethius, and Bacon, Vico calls this part of logic *topics* and considers it as an art of invention. By the aid of the *topoi* (that is, "commonplaces," "points of view," "schemes")[20] the terms and arguments unfold their complex and contradictory meaning, and we get a deeper and more exhaustive knowledge of the subject at issue. The wide range of *topoi* varies in conformity with the questions to be dealt with. Cicero and Boethius sharply distinguished two kinds of *topoi*, or *loci*: the *loci dialectici* and the *loci rhetorici.* The former concern theses, or categorical propositions, which deal with a subject in itself, that is, independently of circumstances, and rest, ultimately, on self-evident, basic truths. The latter concern hypotheses, namely, questions about persons, places, times, actions, facts, and other circumstances, and furnish only probable truths.[21]

The greatest difference between the traditional and the Vichian interpretation of *topoi* undoubtedly lies in the fact that the Italian philosopher

[18] Vico's analogy between individual nature and the nature of humanity is not invariable in his works. In the *Institutiones,* for example, he states that man likes lasciviousness in his childhood, while in the *New Science* (§ 879) we read about a humanity particularly keen on it at the end of the heroic epoch (the age of *Odyssey*). Besides, the main human strivings after pleasure, victory, honor, and so on, being in Vico the manifestations of one and the same metaphysical principle (conation), are distinguished only relatively, and each of them is only the relatively prevailing feature in an epoch.

[19] *New Science,* § 147. Cf. Thomas Aquinas, *Summa theologica* II, II, 9, 57, *articuluma* 2.: "Natura autem hominis est mutabilis. Et ideo quod naturale est homini potest aliquando deficere."

[20] This last translation corresponds more closely to Aristotle's *Rh.* 1403a. 18f.: "elements (or topic) is a head under which several enthymemes are included." Cf. also *Rh.* 1358a. 12ff.

[21] Cf. Cicero, *Top.* II. 73f.; Boethius, "De differentiis topicis," in *Opera* (Basel, 1570), p. 859.

removes the contrast between the *loci dialectici* and the *loci rhetorici*. In his opinion the former have as their concern, besides fundamental and self-evident *theses*, common beliefs or preconceptions (*notiones communes*) characteristic to the human mentality at specific times, surroundings, and stages of social evolution. Bacon would have regarded such *loci* as prejudices of the human mind (*idola*) which deform true knowledge, but in Vico the same *loci* are essential to the discovery of the stages of the historical and social processes and of the rules inherent in them.[22] Moreover, when we want to make a true reconstruction of the history of the sciences, it is not sufficient to enumerate revolutionary discoveries; it is also necessary to reconstruct the commonplaces. Indeed, the radically new very often appears embedded in accepted commonplaces, even in preconceptions and prejudices. Besides, the scientific preconceptions and ideas developed in an earlier stage of cognition are not corpses interred once for all; the cognitive process often revivifies old preconceptions and ideas by viewing them from new perspectives. Therefore, in order to gain a possible total picture of the history of scientific development, the historian must make use of the commonplaces and paradigms domesticated in the "normal sciences," that is, in the common scientific conception and practice of an epoch.[23]

One general question remains, however: Are the *loci*, considered as preconceptions, useful for discoveries in mathematics and in the natural sciences, or do they impede directly every revealing operation? I believe that Vico had a notion of the fertility of *topoi* as preconceptions even in fields outside the historical sciences; in fact, in these fields he could operate with several cognate theories in ancient philosophy and rhetoric. In the Stoic—Neo-Platonic sciences *prolēpsis* (πρόληψις), besides meaning "unclear, primitive preconception," also means "untaught pre-notion" developed in a natural way. Such a pre-notion is, for example, that of straight

[22] For example, *idola tribus*, the prejudices caused by the *actively* deforming human nature, "rise either from the homogeneity of the substance of the human spirit, or from its preoccupation, or from its narrowness, or from an infusion of the affection," etc. (Bacon, *Novum Organum*, bk. 1, sec. 52. The translation is taken from John M. Robertson, ed., *Philosophical Works of Francis Bacon* [London 1905], p. 267). Hence such prejudices, on the one hand, presuppose the Vichian axioms (*New Science*, XIII, §§ 144–46; XIV, § 147) about the relative equality of human nature; on the other, they are indispensable to the ascertainment of the characteristic mentality, way of life, and so on, in determined times. The *idola fori* are prejudices caused by the *passively* deforming human nature, inclined to accept false commonplaces, conventional meanings, and faulty and unskillful abstractions (Bacon, *Novum Organum*, bk. 1, secs. 59f.). The laws of the spiritual inertia and the respective prejudices are implied in many Vichian axioms (II, § 122; IX, § 137; XI, § 141; XVI, §§ 149f.) and reasonings. *Idola fori* are equally indispensable to the identification of an epoch.

[23] For the importance of the "normal science" in the history of sciences, see Thomas S. Kuhn, *The Structure of Scientific Revolutions*, 2d ed. (Chicago, 1970); and idem, "Reflection on my Critics," in *Criticism and the Growth of Knowledge*, ed. I. Lakatos and A. Musgrave (Cambridge, 1970).

and circular lines.[24] In the Stoic rhetoric *prolēpsis* is the anticipation of the opponent's objection by means of questions raised and replied to by the rhetorician himself, even if those questions and their answers or solutions lead to another field, such as politics.[25] A rhetorical question, by anticipating objections, according to the rhetorician Hermogenes, implies what emerges spontaneously in every hearer.[26] The transition from the *prolēpsis* as *locus* and preconception to the *prolēpsis* as anticipation of the opponent's objections by rhetorical questions is by no means forced or artificial, since, for Hermogenes and for Vico, the latter *prolēpsis* is spontaneous though not unconsidered, groundless, or immature. The rhetorical question concerns always either something formerly demonstrated (περὶ τῶν τῷ λόγῳ προαποδεδειγμένων) and accepted tacitly by the audience or something on which everybody agrees by nature (περὶ τῶν φύσει ὁμολογουμένων). In both cases these questions emerge spontaneously and contain preconceptions developed in everybody in a natural way. For this reason they cannot be contradicted (ἀναντίρρητόν ἐστι),[27] and they become generally accepted. How could one ever contradict the questions "In a house with a wall made a breach in, you were found taking away a suit, and you are not a thief?" and "Is there any useful thing that takes place and is not a transformation?"[28] Even the most general rhetorical questions, such as "Does this thing really exist?" "What is this thing from the quantitative and qualitative point of view?" "How did it come into existence?" and "How does it function in relation to other things?" cannot do without containing preconceptions rooted in human nature, that is, without categories and *loci*.[29]

Vico uses *prolēpsis* in all the above meanings and stresses that the questioning by means of categories and *loci*, like every pertinent question that

[24] Proclus Diadochus, *In primum Euclidis Elementorum librum Commentarii*, ed. G. Friedlein (Lipsiae, 1873), pp. 118. 21–119. 1. Cf. Max Pohlenz, *Die Stoa* (Göttingen, 1948–49), vol. 1, p. 231; vol. 2, p. 117.

[25] In other terms for the Stoics rhetoric includes politics by preconception because "it is ridiculous to separate the political faculty from perfect rhetoric, for it is included in the concept of rhetoric, just as those skilled in the art of medicine possess a knowledge of what is healthful and harmful." See Philodemus, *Volumina rhetorica*, ed. S. Sudhaus (Lipsiae, 1896), vol. 2, p. 266. The translation is taken from Harry M. Hubbell, "The Rhetorica of Philodemus," in *Transactions of the Connecticut Academy of Arts and Sciences*, vol. 23 (1920): 357f.

[26] Hermogenes, *Opera*, ed. H. Rabe, in *Rhetores Graeci* (Lipsiae, 1913), vol. 6, pp. 425f.

[27] *Ibid.*, p. 425.

[28] The first quotation is from Hermogenes, *ibid.*; the second from Marcus Aurelius Antoninus, *Meditationes* VII, 18.

[29] For the four categories used by the Stoics as basic questions or methodological principles in any philosophical investigation—*substance, quality, disposition,* and *relative disposition*—see Phillip de Lacy, "The Stoic Categories as Methodological Principles," in *Transactions and Proceedings of the American Philosophical Association* 76 (1945): 246–63.

anticipates the opponent's objections, entails preconceptions.[30] "The modern physicists," he writes,[31] "in the application of their method, proceed by placing primary axioms first.[32] The skillful orator, instead, omits things that are well known, and while impressing on his hearers secondary truth,[33] he *tacitly reminds them of the primary points* he has left out, and while he carries through his argument his listeners are made to *feel that they have formulated it by themselves*."[34] For Vico, the physicists who "proceed by placing primary axioms first" are the Cartesians, whereas the physicists who follow Galileo, the careful researchers and followers of the experimental method,[35] like the orators, impress on their auditors secondary truth, while tacitly reminding them of primary points and making them feel that they themselves have formulated the arguments. The formulation of such arguments, as in Galileo's *Dialogues*, proceeds by the anticipation of an imaginary opponent's questions and objections, introduced by phrases such as: "Now someone will object to me," "Perhaps somebody will wonder," "Lest it seems strange," "Perchance someone will object to me," "If someone asks me," and so on.[36] In fact, Vico insists, "eloquent rhetors as well as extremely careful scientific researchers will spring from the same sources,"[37] as both raise pertinent questions supplied by topics, and examine the problems critically in every respect.[38]

Before illustrating the threefold function of preconception or anticipation in inferences of the Vichian type, let us reconstruct the main features of Vico's logic of scientific discovery.

1. For Vico the procedure of invention has to be inductive. It furnishes only the probable truth, compensating us, however, with richness, fertility, and efficacy.[39]

2. The scheme of the inventive induction, roughly speaking, looks like a syllogism combined with topics.[40]

[30] *De Italorum Sapientia, Opere* (Ricciardi), p. 299.

[31] Giambattista Vico, *On the Study Methods of Our Time*, trans. and introduction by Elio Gianturco (Indianapolis, New York, Kansas City: Bobbs-Merrill, 1965), p. 25, hereinafter cited as *On Study Methods.*

[32] Cf. what has been said above on *theses* in Cicero and Boethius.

[33] Cf. what has been said above on *hypotheses* in Cicero and Boethius.

[34] Italics and the slight modification of the translation are mine.

[35] For experimental method in physics see *De Italorum sapientia* and *Seconda risposta, Opere* (Ricciardi), pp. 303 and 356.

[36] Vico defines *prolēpsis*, or *occupatio*, as "a figure by which we foresee, prevent and confute what our opponent may object" ("*. . . prolēpsis sive occupatio, qua quod ab adversario obiici posse coniicimus, praevertimus, ac diluimus.*") This definition is followed by a series of stereotypic phrases introducing *prolepses.*

[37] *De Italorum sapientia, Opere* (Ricciardi), p. 299.

[38] *Ibid.*, p. 300. We note that already in the *Institutiones Oratoriae,* of twenty-six examples of *loci* thirteen are in the interrogative form! See *Opere* (Morano), pp. 11–16.

[39] *Institutiones oratoriae, Opere* (Morano), pp. 14f.; *De Italorum sapientia, Opere* (Ricciardi), pp. 301f.

[40] *De antiquissima,* in *Opere*, pp. 298ff.: "neither invention can be sure without judgment, nor judgment without invention"; "topics will be changed into criticism."

3. The syllogistic form combined with topics is similar to the mode *Darapti* of the third traditional figure,[41] but with the important difference that now the premises, instead of being universal affirmative, are particular affirmative, and the conclusion, instead of being particular affirmative, is universal affirmative with a purport of certainty or high probability.[42]

4. The *metabasis* from particular premises to a probable universal conclusion results from the transition from one meaning of the middle term to the other, in strict relation with a closer approach to the proper nature of what is symbolized by the middle term.[43]

5. The penetration into the deeper meaning of the middle term is realized by the topics.[44] *Topoi* (*loci*) are neither fixed nor invariable, like a complete list of stereotyped viewpoints, indifferent to the content and to the kind of scientific statement to which they are applied, nor are they completely attached to them.[45] The choice of *topoi* is not chained to one field of science.[46] Even the anticipations of the opponents' questions and the respective answers are *topoi*.[47]

6. *Topics* discovers and accumulates; criticism divides and removes from what is accumulated. Topical *minds* are more copious and less true,[48] but

[41] In one of the traditional ways of symbolizing, it is: where *S* and *P* are used respectively for the subject and predicate terms of the conclusion wherever they appear, and *M* stands for the term which appears in both premises but not in the conclusion and which is called the middle term.

For example:

All *M*'s are *P*.	Every diamond is combustible.
All *M*'s are *S*.	Every diamond is stone.
Hence, Some *S*'s are *P*.	Hence, Some stones are combustible.

[42] Symbolically:

Some *M*'s are *P*.	In this form consider the Vichian example: These living beings (children, young people, etc.) are always fond of something in every age.
Some *M*'s are *S*.	The same living beings are men.
Hence, certainly every *S* is *P*.	Hence, certainly every man is always fond of something in every age.

[43] *On Study Methods*, pp. 14f. and 32f.; *Seconda risposta*, *Opere* (Ricciardi), pp. 356f.

[44] *On Study Methods*, pp. 14–19; *De Italorum sapientia* and *Seconda risposta*, *Opere* (Ricciardi), pp. 299 and 356.

[45] *Seconda risposta*, *Opere* (Ricciardi), p. 299. Cf. Aristotle, *Rh.* 1358a 10–31. In the presented Vichian induction (see above notes 16, 17, 36) the *topoi* are the various characteristic objects (play, parties, honor, etc.) of human affection, in conformity with the human ages.

[46] *On Study Methods*, pp. 23f.; *De Italorum sapientia*, *Opere* (Ricciardi), 295f.

[47] *On Study Methods*, pp. 24f. In his *De dignitate* Bacon mentions anticipation in this sense. For him, too, *topoi* are mixtures of logical arguments (questions included) and elements drawn from the subject at issue. See *The Works of Francis Bacon*, vol. 1, bk. 5, ch. 3, pp. 633–39.

[48] *Seconda risposta*, *Opere* (Ricciardi), p. 358.

topical *reasoning* is an art by which we obtain truth and the clearly distinguished, proper meaning for which we are searching.[49]

7. The inventive induction, unlike the syllogism, is not linear, unidirectional, but ramifying and eccentric.[50]

Let us illustrate the Vichian induction by two examples. Aristotle allows (without motivation) the *metabasis* from medicine to geometry in the same way as Vico does when he counsels, on the one hand, to use induction in medicine and not to stick to one genus during a diagnosis[51] and, on the other, to apply geometry to disciplines apparently very distant from that science.[52]

M	P
These wounds	heal slowly when compared to the wounds of the same type and of the same perimeter.
M	S
The same wounds	are circular.
	TOPICAL REASONING
	But what does the circular form of a wound mean from a geometrical point of view? It means that these wounds have the greatest area relative to their perimeter; therefore, from a medical-geometrical respect, their healing parts are further separated than in non-circular wounds of the same kind and perimeter; consequently, nature has more difficulty joining them up.
S	P
Probably all circular wounds	heal slowly when compared to the wounds of the same type and of the same perimeter.

In the topical reasoning of this induction[53] we can observe all three kinds of anticipation: as rhetorical question, as untaught geometrical notion of the circular line, and as a quite primitive, anthropomorphic notion about the behavior of the almost personified nature. To complete this scheme we must add that before the introduction of topical reasoning that gives certainty to the conclusion, and before a circumstantial analysis made by the researcher, the following presyllogism may flash across his mind:

Do these wounds heal relatively slowly?
Yet the same wounds are circular!

Therefore, do circular wounds heal relatively slowly?

[49] *Ibid.*, p. 356.
[50] *De Italorum sapientia, Opere* (Ricciardi), pp. 295 and 301.
[51] *On Study Methods*, pp. 32f.
[52] *De Italorum sapientia, Opere* (Ricciardi), p. 303.
[53] For the topical reasoning see Philoponus, *Commentarii in An. Post.* (Berlin, 1909), p. 182. 10–27.

A similar problem-raising (rhetorical-questioning) presyllogism may be formulated if the Vichian inductive reasoning is applied to a case which stands nearer to the modern sciences and concerns, for example, the discovery of radioactivity:

Do these things photograph themselves in the dark?
But the same things are only pitchblende, polonium, etc.!

Therefore, do pitchblende, polonium, etc. photograph themselves in the dark?

The Vichian induction would look like this:[54]

Experience	*Syllogistic Scheme*	*Topical Reasoning*
1st observation	M — P These things—leave traces on the photographic plate.	But P means, per definitionem, to provoke characteristic chemical alteration by rays. ———————— Therefore, these things, per definitionem, must be thought as things provoking alteration by rays (D). But in that case, whatever be "these things," if they cause this chemical alteration, they must necessarily and always be thought as provoking alteration by rays (D) But according to the minor premise of the presyllogism the same things are pitchblende, polonium, etc. (S) ———————— Therefore, S must be thought as matters acting by a special kind of ray (SDn).
2nd observation	M — SDn The same things	

[54] For schemata of such inductive reasoning in modern science see J. Szamek, "The Theory of Induction" (in Hungarian) in *Bölcseleti Közlemények* (Budapest, 1943), pp. 28–48.

are really matters acting by a special kind of ray, i.e., they are radioactive matters.

SDn P
Therefore, all radioactive matters—leave traces on the photographic plate.

We must note that in this example the conclusion is clearly universal, since here the topical reasoning, unlike in the former example, does not contain any primitive notion. On the basis of the empirical premises in themselves, we are permitted to register exclusively a casual coexistence between the physical matters at issue and radiation; by topical reasoning we obtain, however, a new, speculative coexistence, according to which the radiation must necessarily coexist with the examined substances, because we must think "these things" necessarily and always together with radiation. The empirically controlled minor premise is formulated, and the universal conclusion is drawn on the strength of the topical reasoning. We called the middle term "these things" in order to express that we are searching for the unknown aspect of apparently well-known things.

As we have already seen in the two inductions of a Vichian type just presented, the *metabasis* from the two particular affirmative premises to a universal affirmative conclusion originates in a *metabasis* from one sense of the middle term to another and involves a *metabasis* from one branch of science to another. Thus new intermediate sciences rise from the Vichian inductive method. Indeed, the motivated conclusion in the first induction presented ("Probably all circular wounds heal slowly, since they have the greatest area relative to their perimeter") belongs to a discipline which may be called geometrical medicine. In *On the Study Methods of Our Time* and in *De antiquissima Italorum sapientia,* much before the *New Science,* Vico partly records, partly anticipates a number of new intermediate sciences, among others chemical medicine (pharmacology),[55] mechanical medicine, chemical physics, geometrical physics, and so on.[56] In our age, when new intermediate disciplines, such as biochemistry, biophysics, cybernetics, chemogenetics, nuclear physics, earth science, and others spring up almost daily, it hardly needs to be pointed out that the traditional division of disciplines arose merely out of convenience and that the denial of transitions between the branches might easily prove incon-

[55] He gives this meaning (pharmacology) to *spargirica,* which was disdained by Bacon as a pseudo-science or a kind of alchemy.

[56] *On Study Methods,* chaps. 1 and 2; *De Italorum sapientia, Opere* (Ricciardi), p. 303.

venient and a hindrance to both knowledge and scientific progress in general. Therefore it is quite natural, or obligatory, to pass from one science to another when the object is to slip through the traditional limit of a discipline and enter into another.[57]

The origin and order of sciences

Whatever the immediate concern of the *New Science*, it is undeniably metabasical in many respects. First of all the work anticipates a large group of "intermediate" disciplines, such as comparative history, comparative linguistics, sociology, cultural anthropology, depth psychology, and so on. Moreover, by means of these sciences and the metabasical method peculiar to them, Vico discovered the intermediate character of many ancient "sciences," such as, in heroic times, poetic geography, poetic chronology, poetic physics, poetic cosmography, poetic astronomy, and so on. They are not intermediate between two sciences but rather between science and poetry. Thus, for example, poetic geography and chronology appear to be poetic inventions when compared with the authentic, though primitive geography and chronology of the heroic times. On the other hand, they have an informative, or scientific character in comparison with a free and unbound, or truly poetical character. Here we must pay attention to the exact meaning of these discoveries. Vico does not claim that the sciences of divine and heroic times are exclusively poetic. In contrast to vulgar Vichianism (see above, Marr's "new doctrine," n. 11), he does not always assert that in the prehistoric and heroic epochs there was no scientific knowledge and that merely a poetic knowledge existed. On the contrary, he admitted the parallel existence of a poetic and a nonpoetic knowledge, or science, in ancient times.[58] It was only that he was much more interested in examining the poetic science than the nonpoetic.

One might be inclined to think that the axioms of the *New Science* laid the foundation of those intermediate sciences which have nothing to do with any real geographical region or particular ethnic group and inform us, at best, about some collective social phenomena or about the mental regions and patterns of the collective subconscious.[59] Vico's discovery,

[57] The Aristotelian refusal of the transition from color to scheme (see *Metaph.* 1057ᵃ. 26ff.) proved to be indefensible. It is a textbook commonplace by now that colors, in substance, are reducible to special wave schemes. The necessity of this transition (in polemic with Aristotle) was stated for the first time by the Stoic Zeno. See I. ab Arnim, *Stoicorum Veterum Fragmenta* (Lipsiae, 1905), vol. 1, p. 26. 1f.

[58] For the passages and their analysis see G. Tagliacozzo, "Epilogue" in *Giambattista Vico: An International Symposium*, p. 601.

[59] Vico himself says that the new science uses a metaphysical geography and chronology based on the common sense of "an entire class, an entire people, an entire nation, or the entire human race," on a common sense determined by the necessary convenience of identical human things (*New Science*, Axiom XII, § 142; § 348).

however, had no such limited metabasical character. Indeed, by the aid of a number of his axioms and of concrete phylogeographical data,[60] we are able to explain also particular usages and customs of a country and also particular linguistic facts. Unlike Aristotle, Vico would have explained the absence of the female flute-players among the Scythians by the fact that in Scythia there were no vines; that is, he would have applied his axiom that any nature—human nature included—is a modification of time and environmental factors (Axioms XIV, XV; §§ 147, 148), as well as the axioms that names, ideas, and customs take their beginning from the matters they denote or reflect (Axiom LXIII, §§ 236, 237; Axiom CVI, § 314) and that the order of human things (names, ideas, and so on) must follow the order of those matters existing in reality (Axioms LXIV, LXV; §§ 238, 239f.). The same axioms allow for many important inferences from concrete linguistic facts to biogeographical facts,[61] and through these to the original dwelling places, life, and culture of concrete ethnic groups. Such a valid *metabasis* is contained, for example, in the following reasoning of linguistic paleontology: If in a single family of languages the same plants and animals have the same names, we must presume that these common names come from the common original language, that is, from the stock of words of the respective proto-ethnic group which must have known these plants and animals and, consequently, lived in a land where all these plants and animals were to be found together.[62]

In *De antiquissima Italorum sapientia*, as well as in the answers to the objections provoked by this work, Vico returns to the question, What are the characteristic features of a science that joins metaphysics, the trunk of all human knowledge, with physics? According to him, Aristotle and Descartes avoided this important question when they denied the intermediary function of geometry. Aristotle treats physics metaphysically and absorbs it completely into his metaphysics. Descartes, instead, submerges metaphysics in physics, the latter in geometry, and geometry in mathematics. Therefore, he first quashes the intermediary function of geometry by considering *physics* as an intermediary between metaphysics and geometry and then deprives geometry of its relative independence by merging it, together with physics and metaphysics, with mathematics. At the time of *De antiquissima Italorum sapientia* Vico still believed that the Car-

60 Phylogeography is a science that deals with the distribution of the plants on earth.

61 Biogeography deals with the distribution of the living organisms on earth.

62 This kind of inference has led, for example, to the discovery of the Finno-Ugrians' original country in northeastern Europe, more precisely in the woodland between the Volga bend and the Ural mountains in the Kama-Belaya region. See F. P. Keppen (Köppen), *Materialy k voprosu o pervonachal'noy rodine i pervobytnom rodstve indo-evropeyskogo i finno-ugroskogo plemeni* [Contributions to the question about the earliest fatherland and the original relationship of the Indo-European and Finno-Ugrian tribes], offprint from *Zhurnal Ministerstva Narodnogo Prosveshcheniya* (St. Petersburg, 1886); Miklós Zsirai, *Finnugor rokonságunk* [Our Finno-Ugrian relationship] (Budapest, 1937), pp. 112f.

tesian analytical geometry was only the result of such an attempt at merger and that analytical geometry, far from being a link between geometry and mathematics, constituted a kind of mathematics subserving the unfounded liquidation of geometry.[63]

Against Aristotle and Descartes Vico maintains that physics cannot be merged with metaphysics, nor metaphysics with physics, since the objects of physics are extended and moving, and the objects of metaphysics—God, the "metaphysical points"—are unmoving and unextended. If there is no science whose object is halfway between extended and unextended, moving and unmoving things, then there is no relation between metaphysics and physics. Geometry is the intermediate science that deals with objects patterned after metaphysical objects, first of all after the metaphysical points. A geometrical point is what the human mind can conceive about a particular property of the metaphysical point, that is, about the "indivisible power (*virtus*) of extension and motion."[64] Every geometrical invention is achieved by starting from the concept of this power called conation (*conatus*). The objects of geometry are not obtained from the empirical world by means of abstraction,[65] but by the human inventive force availing itself of the conation of the mentally reproduced metaphysical points. Vico is firmly convinced that it was Zeno and the other Stoics who laid the foundation of geometry by means of the concept of metaphysical points and conation.

The Stoic origin of the Vichian conception of geometry is usually denied on the authority of Croce and Nicolini. When Vico ascribes this conception to Zeno and the Stoics, he is thought to disguise his (or Leibniz') concept in classical garb; or even to confess doing so, as when he says: "That if, finally, you do not want to accept this sentence as Zeno's, I shall—although reluctantly—give it to you as mine; still I shall give it to you, even though alone and unsupported by big names."[66] But this passage means, in my opinion, only that Vico acknowledges the Stoic priority of the foundation of geometry on the concepts of metaphysical points and on the principle of conation but also that, independently of the Stoic authority, he deems valid such a foundation. Only thus can we understand why he continues to call Zeno and the Stoics the discoverers of the new foundation of geometry.

I think Vico was right in doing so. In fact, conation, the metaphysical principle, defined by him as "the tension (*sforzo*) of the whole by which the whole emits and sustains every particular thing, even the smallest

[63] *De Italorum sapientia* and *Risposta a tre opposizioni, Opere* (Ricciardi), pp. 276 and 322.

[64] *De Italorum sapientia, Opere* (Ricciardi), p. 271.

[65] *Ibid.*

[66] *Seconda risposta, Opere* (Ricciardi), p. 348.

one,"[67] is related to the Stoic principle of tension (τόνος).[68] Zeno's followers applied this principle thoroughly to geometry, down to the smallest geometrical object, the point which, according to them, posseses an unlimited hidden cohesive and creative force.[69] For the Stoics the concept of geometrical points, modeled after the metaphysical points, the so-called seminal reasons (λόγοι σπερματικοί),[70] is created "merely by human inventive force"[71] like every other geometrical concept. Simplicius stresses that this tensional geometry is absolutely incompatible with the Aristotelian conception of geometry; what is more, by introducing tension, the Stoics "destroy the essence of mathematics [geometry and arithmetic] which is static and free from every change and therefore also from tension."[72] Obviously the Stoics were convinced of the contrary and thought that geometry and arithmetic would be destroyed if their objects were conceived and handled in the Aristotelian way, viz., as unmoving, absolutely static entities.

But how does the unlimited, static, cohesive and creative power show itself in the single limited geometrical objects? How does the tension manifest itself, for example, in the geometrical point or in the straight line? Is there no contradiction between movement and rest, boundlessness

[67] *Risposta a tre opposizioni* and *Seconda risposta, Opere* (Ricciardi), pp. 324, 327, and 350.

[68] See Arnim, *Stoicorum Veterum Fragmenta*, vol. 4. The Stoic physics, based on tension, re-emerges in the garb of a physics based on the *conatus* (that is, the elastic force of the ether which "intus omnia pervadet") in the early work of Leibniz, *Hypothesis physica nova* (1671). (See G. W. Leibniz, *Die philosophischen Schriften*, ed. Gerhart, Berlin, 1880, vol. 4, pp. 177–219.) In a letter to Honoré Fabri (quoted on p. 11 of *Die philosophischen Schriften*) Leibniz says that he has discovered this thought by a happy coincidence while reading some ancient texts. He does not specify the authors; however, in explaining his physical hypothesis he allows the understanding that these must have been authors who reported some Stoic thoughts. Thus, for instance, Cicero, who, when he speaks of the metaphysical conception of Zeno of Citium (*De natura deorum*, II. 58; see also *Stoicorum Veterum Fragmenta*), adds on this conception that: as individual natures contain in their seeds what is born and grows, so in the same way does the nature of the world ("omnis motus habet voluntarios conatusque et adpetitiones, quas ὁρμάς Graeci vocant"). Those movements, *conatus*, aspirations, he continues, manifest themselves in reasonable acts which are similar to the acts of men who use the intellect and the senses. Philo of Alexandria identifies the ὁρμή (*Leg. Alleg.* I and 30; see *Stoicorum Veterum Fragmenta*, vol. 2, p. 229, fragment 844) with the tensional force (τονική δύναμις). Lucretius says, after the manner of the Stoic cosmology, that as a universal force it drags the cosmos toward the general conflagration (ἐκμύρωσις μάντων) even if the efforts (*conatus*) of the sun and of every fire do not yet achieve this effect (*De rerum natura*, bk. 5, lines 383–85). The Stoic physics, based on the *tonos-conatus*, seems to have inspired Vico both through the reading of these and other classical passages and through the reading of Leibniz' *Hypothesis physica nova*.

[69] Diadochus, *In primum Euclidis Elementorum librum Commentarii*, pp. 88.4f; 90.3ff.

[70] See Arnim, *Stoicorum Veterum Fragmenta*, vol. 4, (σπεερατικὸς λόγος).

[71] Diadochus, *In primum Euclidis Elementorum librum Commentarii*, p. 89.16f.

[72] Simplicius, *Commentarium in Aristotelis Categorias*, ed. Kalbfleisch (Berlin, 1907), p. 264.34ff.

and limit? The Stoics avoided these and similar questions by shaping new and more refined geometrical preconceptions than the primitive untaught Euclidean preconceptions (that is, definitions). In their new premises the point is both limited and unlimited: it is the limit of a line obtained through countless and imperceptible steps.[73] According to the tensional meaning, the straight line is a line stretched to the utmost among an infinite number of lines connecting two points.[74] It was the tensional conception of geometry that suggested to Chrysippus the inkling of the process of convergence towards a limit and thereby the anticipation of the method of fluxions.[75] At the same time the tensional geometry was more compatible with physics than was Euclidean geometry and constituted, therefore, a convenient mediation between metaphysics and physics. Indeed, the dynamic element introduced by the Stoics, writes Sambursky, "consists essentially of a physicalization of geometry by endowing geometrical figures with the elastic properties of material bodies."[76] Moreover, the Stoic tensional motion (τονικὴ κίνησις) also explained the physical phenomena between rest and movement satisfactorily. Galen illustrates this state of a body with the example of the swimmer against the current in a river, who will remain in the same place "not because he does not move at all, but because he is carried forward by his own movement by the same amount that he is carried back by the external movement."[77]

The question of how the boundless binding power of the cosmos, that is, the tension of the pneuma or "the aether which penetrates and fills everything"[78] manifests itself in individual geometrical objects is also for Vico a fundamental problem. It is not easy to deduce the singular definite powers of extension and motion from the "indefinite power of extension and motion."[79] Deductive processes like this are used in analytical geometry, although they seem thoroughly uncertain.[80] On the other hand, the theory of abstraction remains likewise unacceptable[81] because the human mind, while disregarding empirical properties, cannot dispense with em-

[73] Diadochus, *In primum Euclidis Elementorum librum Commentarii*, p. 101.20–25. This conception of the point is obviously suggested by the third Euclidean axiom ("the limits of a line are points"), which can be considered as a positive definition of the geometrical point. In methodological respect this definition is better than the negative definitions like "what has no parts" (Euclid) or "what has no extension" (Heron, Psellus), and so on. Cf. D. D. Mordukhay-Boltovsky, trans. and comm., *Nachala Evklida* [Euclid's Elements] (Moscow and Leningrad, 1950), vol. 1, pp. 224f.

[74] Simplicius, *Commentarium in Aristotelis Categorias*, p. 264.34ff; Diadochus, *In primum Euclidis Elementorum librum Commentarii*, p. 110.18.

[75] S. Sambursky, *Physics of the Stoics* (London, 1959), pp. 93–96.

[76] *Ibid.*, pp. 85f.

[77] Arnim, *Stoicorum Veterum Fragmenta*, vol. 2, fr. 450. Cf. also Sambursky, *Physics of the Stoics*, pp. 32f. My quotation is from Sambursky's translation.

[78] *New Science*, § 379.

[79] *De Italorum sapientia, Opere* (Ricciardi), pp. 274f.

[80] *Ibid.*, p. 262.

[81] *Ibid.*, p. 271.

pirical objects. Abstraction is a loss of the human inventive strength, which is the underlying principle of geometry and itself part of the universal tension.[82] Vico opts for the Stoic way to resolve his dilemma. He cautiously extends the metaphysical conception of conation by stating that it is the "hindered power of motion from which the extended things draw strength";[83] then he passes over it and accepts the new meaning, that of conation as a restraining, arresting power.[84] He reshapes the notion of conation in geometry after the model of this refined metaphysical conception to form a new notion, according to which conation is the striving towards a limit in numberless imperceptible steps.[85] Applying the notion to geometry, he can easily get new preconceptions, like the definition of the straight line: the line toward which numberless defective lines linking two points strain. In short, the straight line is the norm of the distorted lines (*pravorum regula*).[86] The Stoic origin of this tensional definition is manifest. Probably, the new concept of conation made Vico understand later the main point of the Cartesian analytical geometry, where "magnitudes are devoid of forms,"[87] and the essence of the infinitesimal calculus. On the other hand, his tensional geometry, similar to that of the Stoics, is also applicable to physics. Vico adopts Galen's example of the swimmer against the current to illustrate the Stoic tensional motion, which is neither rest nor movement.[88]

Besides geometry, Vico sought to establish the exact places of other intermediate disciplines in the classification of sciences. Although he did

[82] *Ibid.*, p. 278.

[83] *Ibid.*

[84] *New Science*, §§ 340 and 504. Vico surely had no doubt about the double meaning of *conation* (inciting power and arresting power), and he knew that for the classical authors the word means above all "effort," "endeavor," "inciting, instinctive power." His favorite author, Cicero, used the word in this sense, and interestingly, in a passage of the famous *Oratio in Catilinam* (I, 5. 11) he places *conatus* in contrast with the arresting power: Cicero thanks *Jupiter Stator* for having stopped Catilina's infamous *conatus*. In his *New Science* Vico regards the arresting power of *Jupiter Stator* (and *fermator*) as the only authentic *conatus*. Cf. *New Science*, § 504.

[85] *New Science*, §§ 340 and 689.

[86] *De Italorum sapientia, Opere* 1: 281. In my opinion Vico borrowed the Stoic idea of tensional geometry from two main sources: the reading of the classics (Proclus, Simplicius, in a Latin translation) and from Leibniz' *Theoria motus abstracti* (see *Die philosophischen Schriften*, pp. 221–240). This Stoic-inspired work of Leibniz, which was written after his *Hypothesis physica nova* (1671) lays the foundations of a geometry of the *conatus*, in which, for instance, the elementary *conatus* or geometric point is "initius finisque motus" (*Die philosophischen Schriften*, p. 229). The elementary *conatus* which Leibniz elsewhere calls "conatus embryonati" (see *Opuscules et fragments inédits*, ed. L. Couturat, Paris, 1903, pp. 525ff:) correspond to the "metaphysical points" of the *Monadology* and to the σπερματικοὶ λόγοι of the Stoics. Concerning the straight line in the geometry of the *conatus* Leibniz affirms that if this line coincided with the curved line, then, in a absurd way, the *conatus* of the straight line and the *conatus* of the curve and the respective movements would be identical (see *Die philosophischen Schriften*, pp. 231f.).

[87] *Della mente eroica, Opere* (Ricciardi), p. 924.

[88] *De Italorum sapientia, Opere* (Ricciardi), p. 278.

not make a detailed exposition of the classification of sciences, we may nevertheless elicit some information concerning the hierarchy of the principal sciences, about the places of the interconnected sciences on that scale, and about the relations between the main and the interconnected sciences. In *On the Study Methods of Our Time* and in *De antiquissima Italorum sapientia*,[89] Vico establishes the following hierarchy:

mathematics (geometry, arithmetic)
mechanics
physics
chemistry
biology (medicine)
moral sciences

Advancing in the direction of the arrow, sciences, he says, get more and more uncertain, due to their "sinking more and more into the corporeal matter" (*magis in materia corpulenta immerguntur*).[90] Although the justification of this statement is erroneous because the uncertainty may rather derive from the sinking into the sphere of the spirit, where the laws of mechanical causality have no absolute validity, the statement in itself is worthy of consideration. We can interpret it as follows: advancing in the direction of the arrow, the sciences get more and more uncertain because they get more and more complicated. On the principle that the less complex the science, the more certain, the followers of a genetical epistemology would set up a nearly Vichian scale of the following sciences:[91]

1. mathematics
2. mechanics
3. physicochemistry
4. biology
5. psychosociology
   etc.

The complexity consists in the fact that the object of a science marked with a lower number is always added to that of the sciences marked with a higher number.

1. mathematical thing = the most simple thing (quantity)
2. mechanical thing = mathematical thing + concept of force
3. physicochemical thing = mechanical thing + changeable substance
4. biological thing = physicochemical thing +developing organism
   etc.

[89] *Il metodo degli studi del tempo nostro, Opere* (Ricciardi), pp. 174f. and *De Italorum sapientia, Opere* (Ricciardi), pp. 254f.
[90] *De Italorum sapientia, Opere* (Ricciardi), p. 254.
[91] J. Mouhasseb, *Essai sur la classification des sciences* (Damascus, 1953), pp. 166–83.

The order remains the same, if we consider movement as the object of the sciences; in this case too the movement of the "lower" sciences is added to that of the "higher" sciences. By means of the classificatory scale it is easy to establish the subdivisions of a science. Let S be the symbol of the sum of the subdivisions of a science, n the number indicating the degree of a science on the scale, and s the number of the intrinsic subdivisions, then:

$$S = (n - 1) + s.$$

For example, in the case of biology: $n = 4$, $s = 2$ (anatomical and physiological biology). Thus:

$$S = (4 - 1) + 2 = 5.$$

The five subdivisions are:

$$\left.\begin{array}{l}\text{1. mathematical biology}\\ \text{2. mechanical biology}\\ \text{3. physicochemical biology}\end{array}\right\} (n - 1) = 3$$

$$\left.\begin{array}{l}\text{4. anatomical biology}\\ \text{5. physiological biology}\end{array}\right\} s = 2$$

The main interconnected sciences are indicated by $(n - 1)$. Obviously, the number of the interconnected sciences is always larger than $(n - 1)$ because, according to the formula, the crossed main sciences bring along their own intrinsic subdivisions. Consequently, mathematical biology, in conformity with the subdivisions of mathematics, will be divided into algebraic, geometrical, topological, and other biology. It is the same with the other interconnected science, the physicochemical biology. Since acoustics and electronics are intrinsic parts of physics, physicochemical biology must have among its subclasses both acoustical and electronic biology.[92]

In *On the Study Methods of Our Time*, Vico states similarly that when a science is "carried in" another, the transported science conveys its own subdisciplines in the other. With chemistry its "daughter," pharmacology, also enters into biology (medicine).[93] This kind of transition of a subdiscipline takes place not only in the advanced human wisdom but also in the "poetic wisdom" of the heroic epoch. Naturally, in the second case it is a poetic subdiscipline that is transferred with a poetic science to another field. Consequently, we have to look for the exposition of this

[92] These subdisciplines actually exist. For example, biotopology establishes that abstract topological spaces correspond to every living organism and that these spaces can be obtained one from another by the same transformation formula. Electronic biology (bionics) is the application of the knowledge about living organisms to the planning of electromechanic driver and communication systems.

[93] *Il metodo deli studi del tempo nostro, Opere* (Ricciardi), p. 175.

kind of transition in the *New Science*, the most brilliant parts of which are devoted to the analysis of "poetical wisdom." Let us take an example.

We saw before that according to the formula establishing the subdivisions of a science, an interconnected science called acoustical biology must *a priori* exist. Undoubtedly, we can *a posteriori* ascertain this mixed science in the human wisdom of today. Indeed, bioacoustics exists and deals with the structure and physical characteristics of the acoustical phenomena of living beings. Moreover, this science establishes how the mentioned phenomena, produced either by a sound-forming organ or in a mechanical way, fulfill the function of communication in the life of living beings and examines the prerequisites, conditions, and contents of such communications.

How does Vico deduce the existence of a "poetic bioacoustics" in ancient times? Poetic biology, he states, is born from poetic physics by the transference of a fictitious, poetic physics onto biological phenomena.[94] Poetic acoustics is a part of poetic physics. This poetic subdiscipline takes the acoustic phenomena (a thunderclap, blowing of the wind, roaring of the sea) in a metaphorical and metonymical sense, that is, as the communications of Nature's personified figures (as Jove's threat, the wind's whistle, the waves' murmur).[95] The use of metaphors and metonymies rises originally, not from the search for a "poetic" effect (in speaking of ancient times we should continually put the word "*poetic*" in quotation marks), but from a hard necessity. Metaphors and metonymies are necessary means for men in the heroic ages, because their stock of words is very poor. They have not a proper word for each thing, each natural phenomenon, like the blowing of the wind, the roaring of the sea, and so on, and thus they are compelled to use improper words.[96] In Vico's opinion, also the transference of poetic acoustics to biological phenomena is a kind of metaphor or metonymy, as it arises from the same necessity. In heroic periods, men need to adopt such a *poetic metabasis* because of lack of appropriate explanations and terms for bioacoustic phenomena. Therefore, when living things communicated their passions, warnings, and so on, not through words, but in the most primitive speechless language of the "mutes," that is, by shapeless, inarticulate sounds,[97] unavoidably men of the heroic times described and explained these phenomena by some kind of poetic bioacoustics. The history of languages and the etymologies corroborate *a posteriori* that this deductively inferred poetic bioacoustics actually existed.

94 *New Science*, §§ 367 and 692–702.

95 *Ibid.*, §§ 404–7.

96 *Ibid.*, §§ 402–11. See also *De tropis* in *Institutiones oratoriae*, *Opere* (Morano) 7: 101.

97 *New Science*, §§ 228–31, 694, and 701f. This kind of speechless language of the "mutes" is more primitive than the gesture and picture-writing language and is used by every living being, even by the "mute" animals like fish.

In conclusion we can state that in Vico uses of *metabasis* are often to be found both as erroneous and as correct logical transitions. Correct *metabases* have a particular function in the Vichian induction, that is, in Vico's logic of scientific discovery, which I have tried to reconstruct. Vico's merit is not confined to the foundation of a single new science, since he discovered and anticipated, by using *metabasis*, a great number of new interconnected sciences, inconceivable in both Aristotelian logic and philosophy of science.

Part II VICO'S CONCEPTION OF HISTORY AND HISTORICAL KNOWLEDGE

Vittorio Mathieu

TRUTH AS THE MOTHER OF HISTORY

The Platonic Content of History

Only an extraordinary concurrence of circumstances could have given birth to the paradox that forms the nucleus of Vico's philosophy—history as the priviledged seat for Platonic ideas. Traditionally historical evolution would seem to be least suitable to such a role: indeed, far less suitable than nature, which, though variable and varied, is at least subject to immutable laws. History is the realm of the accidental, whereas Platonic ideas are eternal laws for that which never changes. Theology has trained Christians to view history as the enactment of a providential pattern, with its roots sunk in eternity; but this pattern is a *unicum*, derived from God's will to lend unified significance to the historical sequence of events. It is not a universal law valid both for real events and for possible ones and constituting an "ideal eternal history." Several conditions were necessary before this paradoxical idea of an ideal eternal history could be conceived.[1] First the Plotinian concept (which Vico, in the wake of tradition, calls "Platonic") of the individual universal, as opposed to the Aristotelian concept of a generic universal, is required. Indeed, according to Plotinus, each universal is the entire hypostasis of the intellect in a particular projection; thus it is individual, indivisible, and subsistent. For this reason Plotinus accepted ideas of individuals as well, much to the surprise of his disciple Porphyry; and in so doing he paved the way for Vico's theory because only as an individual can the universal be introduced into history.

One has only to think of Vico's "imaginative universal" to realize the importance of the Plotinian precedent, even though Vico's knowledge of this can only have been indirect. The imaginative universal is a personage, like Jupiter or Hercules, an idea in personified form, or, in Vico's own words, *un carattere*, an individual type very close in meaning to the English *character*.[2] Since not generic universals, but only such typified universals, appear in history, had Vico not understood the Platonic idea in this light,

[1] "The fifth aspect [of the *New Science*] is an ideal eternal history traversed in time by the histories of all nations" (*New Science*, § 393).

[2] "Thus, in accordance with what has been said about the principles of the poetic characters, Jove was born naturally in poetry as a divine character or imaginative universal . . ." (*ibid.*, § 381).

he could never have made history the scene for the revelation of Platonic truth.

The kind of Neo-Platonism that filtered through to Vico via Italian Renaissance sources or by even more indirect routes, such as Malebranche or Leibniz, would not have been enough on its own to direct his attention to history; an essentially Baroque conception of Humanism was necessary. In fact the pre-Romantic elements in Vico which so impressed his Victorian readers were nothing more than a residue of Baroque ideas still present in Neapolitan culture at the beginning of the Enlightenment. The Baroque period had developed a new sense of the historical that was at once tragic and metaphysical. Instead of the idea of eternal recurrence of identical cycles, derived from Pythagoras, the idea of the possible recurrence of constants was formulated, coupled, however, with a sense of the irrepeatable. In the Baroque conception of history successive periods began to separate and at the same time to be interconnected. Baroque painting was the first to clothe characters from distant epochs in a manner different from their contemporaries; nevertheless, recondite affinities between events of the distant past and contemporary aspirations were ferreted out. Underlying this attitude was an idea of recurrence, no longer as the indefinite repetition of the identical, but rather as a continual referring back to a constant and mysterious law by means of variable signs that made up its cipher.

Historical reality, in the Baroque age, was the cipher to something that was metahistory. However this concept, usually implicit, was never formulated clearly before Vico. The process is refined and decanted in Vico: on the one hand, what was a cipher in the Baroque conception becomes a *myth*, that is, a fable; on the other hand, the myth itself implies and requires a rational justification. No doubt Vico "mythifies" the whole of history, but not merely from his own natural inclination: he justifies this procedure in terms of his theory.[3] According to him there is only one historical sphere, which includes the gods, the heroes, the ancients, and the new barbarians up to and including modern man and his contemporaries, the scientists. However, this unique and continuous sphere is differentiated internally by an essential law that separates the various periods qualitatively, even when they are repetitive. In each an identical truth is revealed, but the *way* in which it is revealed changes.

The myth, the "true narration,"[4] then becomes a common denominator that makes the connection and continuity of periods possible, not only by reason of their very existence, but also in essence, even when they are quite different qualitatively. Only when mythified can history reflect, in its

[3] "The seventh and last of the principal aspects of this Science is that of the principles of universal history" (*ibid.*, § 399).

[4] ". . . since the first men of the gentile world had the simplicity of children, who are truthful by nature, the first fables could not feign anything false; they must therefore have been, as they have been defined above, true narrations" (*ibid.*, § 408).

infinite variety, an unchanging truth; conversely, an unchanging truth cannot become history unless it is expressed in mythical form.

This, then, is the relationship that links ideal eternal history to myth, by virtue of the imaginative universal. Bacon's interpretation of ancient fables was undoubtedly a decisive precedent. Bacon, however, simply compared the ancient to the modern by means of a parable; in Vico there is no break between the mythical and the contemporary, because of a complex yet exquisitely clear, speculative structure linking our age to the age of heroes and of gods. Only mythology could trace the connection between exploits so far removed in quality as those of Hercules and Torricelli. More amazing still, Vico is able to explain *why* and *how* mythology can do so. It is worth examining his explanation because it allows us to understand how history becomes the sphere in which truth is revealed.

God's Purpose in Creation

To understand how truth unfolds itself in history, one should remember that Vico, as a Christian, believes that truth is first and foremost God Himself. God is subsistent truth, according to the words of John: "I only am the way, the truth, the life."[5] Therefore, as early as *De Antiquissima Italorum sapientia*, Vico points out that in essence truth escapes us, since we are unable to comprehend the manner in which "the word of the mind is properly generated in God." This process may only be apprehended by analogy with the way in which the word of the mind is generated "improperly [imperfectly] in man."[6] Original truth is not, in fact, *God's* creature but is *generated* by Him, coeternal with the Father and identical to Him; we call it the Word. Tradition and theology had always distinguished between *genitum* and *factum*, and so does Vico.

Despite the gulf that divides us from the way in which truth endures as God, it is here that we look for the origin of those truths, both multiple and particular, that are the component parts of truth as we know it: "Since truth exists only in the divine intelligence, we must accept as indubitably true all that has been revealed by God, without allowing ourselves to question the form or the reason why it is true, since it is totally beyond our comprehension. From this point we are able to rediscover the human sciences, and finally to find a criterion which will enable us to recognize which of them are true."[7]

[5] John, 14, 6.

[6] "Et verbum mentis proprium in Deo, improprium in homine fiat" (*De Italorum sapientia*, *Opere*, 1:187). Also see below, n. 8.

[7] "Ex quibus antiquorum Italiae sapientum de vero placitis, et hac, quae in nostra religione adhibetur, *geniti* et *facti* distinctione, principio habemus, quod cum in uno Deo exacte verum sit, omnino verum profiteri debemus, quod nobis est a Deo revelatum; nec quaerere genus, quo modo verum sit, quod id omnino comprehendere nequeamus. Indidem originem scientiarum humanarum repetere, ac denique normam ad dignoscendum quae verae sint, habere possimus" (*ibid.*, p. 133).

The truth immanent in the creation is therefore contained in the divine purpose, in His design for doing what He does. Truth has become the *ratio* of things, the criterion for God's operation; and the human *verum-factum* is achieved inasmuch as we are able to perceive this criterion and make it our own: "And since with regard to God the criterion of truth is indeed contained in the communication of His goodness and His thoughts to creation—*vidit Deus, quod essent bona*—in man this criterion is to be found likewise in that he does what he understands."[8]

To advance from this *analogy* between human truth and divine truth, described in *De Antiquissima Italorum sapientia*, to the far more typical *participation* of the human mind in the divine truth, explained in the *Scienza nuova*, one should replace an epistemological viewpoint with a historical viewpoint, not because man shapes history on his own, but because history exemplifies the collaboration of God and man. If God on the one hand should engender truth in His own mind, and man on the other should engender truth all on his own, in the sphere of historical events, one cannot see how the former could express the latter. In reality history is not made in this manner. Because of the mysterious ways of Providence, man takes an active part in God's operation; thus his knowledge, as well as his actions, participates in the original truth. It is important that man impart shape to history precisely because it is God who shapes history.[9] History is the privileged seat of truth because here what man does is brought into contact with what God does. For this reason the *Scienza nuova* may be thought of as a "rational theology of divine providence."[10]

Man's Share In God's Operation

Once this point is clear, we can examine the extraordinary and concrete manner in which the operations of God and man are brought together in history. There can be no greater gulf than that which divides these two, since God's operation, being perfectly conscious, is performed instantly and intuitively,[11] whereas man's actions are merely imperfectly conscious and

[8] "Et veri criterium, quemadmodum apud Deum inter creandum est suis cogitatis bonitatem communicasse: 'vidit Deus, quod essent bona'; ita apud homines sit comparatum, vera quae cognoscimus, effecisse" (*ibid.*, p. 137).

[9] See for example *New Science*, § 1088: ". . . But the Romans . . . proceeded with even steps, being ruled by providence through the medium of vulgar wisdom."

[10] "So that this Science becomes in this principal aspect a rational civil theology of divine providence, which began in the vulgar wisdom of the lawgivers, who founded the nations by contemplating God under the attribute of providence . . . (*ibid.*, § 385).

[11] "Deorum voluntatem dixere 'numen', quasi Deus . . . suam voluntatem facto ipso significet, et tanta celeritate et facilitate significet, quam celer et facilis nutus est oculorum" (*De Italorum sapientia, Opere* 1:188).

their performance discursive and progressive, extending over a period of time. In order for the former to participate in the latter, this gulf must be bridged, and providence is the cipher that signifies how God's operation bridges the gulf. To comprehend truth is to comprehend how providence is able to reconcile the difference in quality between the two moments of history—the eternal moment, whose roots are in God, and the temporal moment, with man as its instrument. And although from one point of view the action of providence transcends our ability to comprehend it, from another it can and should be explained and interpreted by man, who is a participant in it, for the very reason that his participation is not merely that of a purely passive instrument. The *Scienza nuova* may be read, therefore, as an hermeneutics of Providence.

An essentially new element, characteristic of all forms of Neo-Platonic philosophy, is thus introduced into the circle connecting the intelligible world to the world of events. The classical Alexandrine cycle did indeed follow the metaphysical transition from the absolute supra essential unity through the noetic unity of the intellect that generates truth within itself, to the psychic unity that has given way to dispersion, and finally to the *punctum flexus contrarii* (or *epistrophé*) towards the consciously rediscovered unity that is to be found in man. However, this "phenomenology of essential transcendence," if it may be so termed, did not lead, in the Neo-Platonic cycle, to a corresponding "phenomenology of existential transcendence," as it does in Vico; ancient philosophers were, in fact, interested in essence and the differences between essences. They were therefore interested in studying the ideal mutations through which the essence contained within the intelligible world passed in order to become the essence displayed in the sensible world, and vice versa. Modern philosophers are interested in existence. They wish to examine in what manner the "history that runs through time," that is, the history of that which exists, shows the progressive unfolding of the contents of the idea; and the whole of this unfolding takes place entirely on a lower, temporal and sensible level that a degraded metaphysics defined after the soul was incarnated in the world. As a result, whereas the Alexandrine cycle unfolded in what we might call a vertical dimension, in relation to our terrestrial horizon, the Vichian cycle unfolds in a horizontal dimension and is, in accordance with the Platonic definition of time handed down to us by Timaeus, in a species of "moving image of eternity".[12] The *Scienza nuova* is therefore a science that answers the question, What does the "moving image of eternity," or the image of eternity imprinted on time, look like?

Hence the apparently contradictory concept of an "ideal eternal history." The *mobility* of this imprint is inevitable for the very reason that we are on the sensible level of dispersion in multiplicity, in which immobility

[12] Tim. 37 d.

would be the immobility of death, and not of life, as in the sphere of the eternal. But this mobility, which is the very stuff of historical development, is not abstract formal movement, subject to rigid laws of conservation, as in the case of a change of place or even of physical evolution in general. In this case it could not bear the imprint, albeit dispersed, of God's most concrete and instantaneous autogeneration, but its refutation. This imprint must therefore reflect a self-made concrete becoming, a unified development, a history, as a set of events pregnant with meaning. From this point of view history acquires, or at least develops as never before, an organic unity that transforms it into an organic whole. The unity that Augustinian theology had began to impart to history reappears, thanks to a wholly human philosophy of history, as a process that develops *iuxta propria principia.*

Furthermore, in Saint Augustine, the providence—which imparts a unified meaning to history—was a Biblical providence, the expression of God's *deliberate* will accomplishing a predesigned pattern. Whereas Vico's providence, though never explicitly opposed to the Biblical conception, is much closer to the Plotinian *prónoia,* that is, to an *automatic* manifestation of divine unity which endows the sensible world with its admirable order but which also, in a manner likewise automatic, leaves behind it *hiati,* imperfections, contrasts, for the very reason that this unity takes place on a level which is not its own: the level of sensible dispersion. On the whole, Biblical providence, the Mohammedan concept of fate being its extreme form, excludes the accidental, and therefore the more obscure aspects of history should be justified as negative moments in the function of the positive whole, as the mysterious instruments of the accomplishment of the divine pattern. The Vichian providence does more than offer a justification for the obscurity of these aspects; it requires their presence because the progressively unfolding pattern of history reflects God's will in the temporal sphere, but it transposes it into a dispersive medium, in which God's purpose seems to have been turned upside down, because this dispersive medium is the exact opposite of divine unity: it is an inert and opaque multiplicity.

If providence is so conceived, history becomes a *sequence of inadequacies* through which providence shines (like Luther's God) *abscondita sub contrario:*[13] right is born of violence, profit is the result of avidity, and technical progress of avarice, while truth is born of illusion.[14] Vico's cycle,

[13] ". . . divine providence, apprehended by such human sense as could have been possessed by rough, wild, and savage men . . ." (*New Science,* § 385).

[14] "Men mean to gratify their bestial lust and abandon their offspring, and they inaugurate the chastity of marriage from which the families arise. . . . The reigning orders of nobles mean to abuse their lordly freedom over the plebeians, and they are obliged to submit to the laws which establish popular liberty. The free peoples mean to shake off the yoke of their laws, and they become subject to monarchs" (*ibid.,* § 1108).

which takes us from the age of early brutish man to the age of the Academies via the ages of the gods and the heroes, poetic wisdom, and inventive genius, is therefore a process by which man's ability to manifest truth is gradually transformed in qualitatively different ways but never ceases to be intrinsically inadequate. The courses and recourses are the periodic succession of inadequate forms of participation in truth, passing continuously from one phase to the next because in none of these does truth find a completely satisfactory ground.

The Sequence of Inadequate Forms of Truth

Vico's truth is therefore possessed of a history, not because its very roots are changeable (these are always identical because they are in God's image), but because it is revealed, on the human level, in an upside-down form. Up to this point Vico is in agreement with the ancients; history begins with the Fall of Man, which the story of original sin explains in a historico-mythical form but which, rather than an event, is a Neo-Platonic degradation of essence. A modern historicism wishing to preserve the historical value of truth while leaving aside the mythico-metaphysical concept of the Fall, could not, therefore, claim to have descended from Vico. Rather, since Providence is revealed in history *abscondita sub contrario*, one might say that for Vico the history of truth is error—an "error" which, originally, has an etymological meaning, coming as it does from the wandering (Latin *errare*) of early brutish men (*bestioni*) about the *ingens silva* of the earth, and which later acquires the meaning of a wandering that is no longer physical but intellectual, itself a myth. However, when the thought of truth should wish to settle, to cease its wandering, this illusory disappearance of error, and of the relevant myth, would in fact be the most radical obnubilation of truth.

This is exactly what happens, in tendency at least, during the last period of the age of the Academies, when truth is "frozen",[15] or rather is transfixed in a conceptual immobility which, though it hopes to free truth from the mists of its myths, never achieves more than the fixity of death. Man is under the illusion that, in setting myth aside, he has reached truth, that he has finally found its "proper" form by eliminating the fanciful superstructures that hid it; and he is encouraged to pursue this illusion when he notices how truth, according to this conception, becomes ever more functional and pragmatically easier to apply. Truth, while it is always a *factum*, has now become a fact appertaining to man, something that man can do by following a technique now under his control; it is a scientific

[15] See Vico's letter to Gherardo degli Angioli (26 December 1725) on "Dante and the nature of true poetry," *Opere* (Ricciardi), p. 121, ". . . a wisdom that freezes all that is most generous in the best poetry."

truth and can indeed be termed "human," since it belongs to a sphere in which man operates under his own initiative and is no longer guided by a mysterious "inspiration." And yet, at the very moment when truth is humanized it is flattened out and becomes abstract, losing an essential dimension: the dimension of that contact with divine truth thanks to which *fact*, and therefore *truth*, were concrete realities. Science is the only serious attempt to relieve human truth of its inadequacy; but from this point of view it cannot be said to have succeeded. Quite the opposite. Paradoxically scientific truth reveals the greatest inadequacy of all—a radical evaporation of truth. If man were indeed able to fabricate this truth on his own and to cease to be a participant in God's work, truth would be cut off at the root, providence would remain suspended in the void, and history would come to a halt.

The Moving Principle Underlying History

Therefore, if it were possible for Vico to imagine the death of history and of truth, it would be the result of death from freezing. But the cyclical movement of history saves us from such a tragic destiny. During the cyclical recurrences providence is able to take history in hand once again, which had been wasting away and flattening out and generally tending to escape from its control. And in so doing providence inevitably appears to us in a somewhat catastrophic guise. The self-assurance which appeared to have been achieved becomes questionable, and history resumes its motion under the negative sign of a renewed "barbarism".[16]

These catastrophies, however, far from being surprising, are no more than the usual method by which providence appears to us in an upside-down form. Even during the period when truth was becoming more human and civilization more refined, providence was standing on its head; but man took no notice and could hardly foresee providence as an impending catastrophe, since the cycle, in that particular phase, was going in his own direction, the direction of a truth placed at the disposal of mankind. Only when this phase is reversed and truth is once again dehumanized does man perceive how providence acts upon history in an upside-down form. Although he may see this as a catastrophe, it is also the salvation of history, in that man is again brought into contact with God. The irremediable end of history would be, then, the permanent stagnation of civilization in the "barbarism of refinement" phase, which would leave man totally barren.

That this had never come about, up to his own time, is one of the

[16] "The nations mean to dissolve themselves, and their remnants flee for safety to the wilderness, whence, like the phoenix, they rise again" (*New Science*, § 1108).

reasons for Vico's optimism. This is what we might term a "transcendent," (and not simply a "transcendental") optimism, in that it is dependent on the divine root of historical development and may therefore coexist quite happily with an empirical pessimism, which sees providence as permanently upside-down. Despite every confidence in the transcendent, it is conceivable that the history that runs through time is destined—one might even say certain—to come to an end. Although as a Christian Vico rather conceives as inevitable an apocalyptic ending of history, as a philosopher he could easily imagine this end in a different light: as a tranquil death, a repetition devoid of direction in which all movement is dispersed without recurring cyclically in its own tracks, which therefore empties itself without renewing its contact with the divine meaning of history. Whereas this end would preserve its lifelike appearance, it would furnish the final proof that history had been abandoned by providence. The apocalyptic ending, on the other hand, gives us further evidence of the workings of providence; or rather, it would be its supreme manifestation, since "apocalypse" means "revelation." How is it then that Vico is such an optimist as to believe in this apocalyptic ending to history, rather than fearing its definitive descent into insignificance?

Apart from his generic confidence in providence, there is a special form of truth which fills him with hope. Truth, for Vico, possesses a privileged form, the form of "poetic knowledge," and this is the cause of Vico's optimism. It is true that within the providential development of history no form and no phase should be more privileged than another, since each is necessary to the economy of the whole. But Vico is not exempt from showing a preference which, despite attempts to tie Vico to the Enlightenment, is not related to the latter. The Enlightenment showed a preference for truth in form and in science, Vico preferred truth under the guise of poetic wisdom—which possessed, in his view, excellent reasons for being preferred. On the one hand truth, in form and in poetic wisdom, has not yet lost touch with its divine origins, so much so that the inspiration for poetic wisdom is always explicitly indicated as coming from a god. On the other hand, thanks to poetic wisdom, man slowly became aware of this inspiration as he emerged from the mists of sensibility that shrouded him in primitive times. It hardly matters if the forms in which the imagination clothes divine truth are, even in this instance, turned upside-down and the divine content presented as a series of myths, which our conceptual consciousness rejects as irremediably false, as in the case of the Homeric myths. What matters is that truth is already felt to be present as truth, and not as a bestial impulse, as it had been in the age of early brutish man. However, it has not yet become an abstract operative schema: this only comes about in civilizations that have grown old.

No doubt the workings of poetic wisdom (one should not forget that wisdom, according to its biblical meaning, as well as its archaic Greek meaning of $\sigma o \phi \acute{\iota} \alpha$, is an operative faculty, not one of pure contemplation)[17] are subject to risk and uncertainty. Its technique is not entirely in our hands, since it is still a providential technique, exercised in fact by God Himself. But it is precisely this quality that makes it so elating. Thanks to poetic wisdom, we participate consciously in God's operation. Thus the function of the human *poietés*, which in Vico's view embraces all forms of creation, from the fine arts to law, politics, and even craftsmanship, is "truth".[18]

Between the early brutish man, who exists as a blind instrument of Providence, and the perfectly intelligent man, who knows what he is doing but can only operate on a human plane (and for this very reason is involved in a species of *Seinsvergessenheit*, as Heidegger would put it, that is far more radical than such a plane), is the middle phase, which is the happiest. Here consciousness is already ours and yet is still the vehicle for divine action, the extension of a transcendent *numen*. Indeed, it is precisely in the guise of poetic wisdom that truth achieves its maximum propulsive effectiveness for history. It is poetic wisdom which returns history to its cyclical course and prevents its coming to an end.

The Spread of Poetic Wisdom

At this point we should note that Vico tends to extend the realm of poetic wisdom as far as he can in time and space. In space it includes all forms of human activity, including human crafts, which, according to Vico, are "poems, and to a certain extent, real" in their inventive phase.[19] In time poetic wisdom persists far beyond the chronological phase to which it ought to belong and reappears persistently, though sporadically, in the exercise of a wisdom that has been conceptualized, reviving it with brilliant intuitive perceptions that prevent its final congealment. If it was enough for his friend Gherardo degli Angioli to spend a short time in the woods to give new life to his poetic vein,[20] then poetic wisdom continues to slumber within us, even when circumstances seem to have suffocated it.

[17] ". . . wisdom in its broad sense is nothing but the science of making such use of things as their nature dictates" (*ibid.*, § 326).

[18] "And since naturally the discovery or invention of things comes before criticism of them, it was fitting that the infancy of the world should concern itself with the first operation of the human mind, for the world then had need of all inventions for the necessities and utilities of life, all of which had been provided before the philosophers appeared . . ." (*ibid.*, § 699).

[19] ". . . all the arts of the necessary, the useful, the convenient, and even in large part those of human pleasure, were invented in the poetic centuries before the philosophers came; for the arts are nothing but imitation of nature, and in a certain way 'real' poems [made not of words but of things]" (*ibid.*, § 217).

[20] See Vico's letter to Gherardo degli Angioli, *Opere* (Ricciardi), p. 121.

True, real poetic wisdom can only belong to the heroic age, with which only the barbarians are in spiritual contact, but this direct contact, soon to be obscured by the progress of thought, is not altogether severed and can, at times, reemerge. Vico's method of dividing history into periods is equally characteristic. In the letter to Gherardo degli Angioli, just cited, and also in a passage from the 1730 edition of the *Scienza nuova* which was not included in the 1744 edition, Vico goes so far as to place "the close of the barbarian age" in the age of Galileo, that is, towards the end of the Renaissance.[21] This has a fairly obvious purpose: to show how all inventions, from spectacles to the compass, from sailing ships to the discovery of the new physics, all come from the matrix of the "barbarian age," or in other words, are due to the use of poetic wisdom.

This division of history into periods is in itself a myth, a form of expression very dear to Vico. Nevertheless *genius*, which Vico considers to be the highest expression of the barbarian age, extends the age of poetic wisdom into the age of the Academies (and sometimes into the Academies themselves). The genius (and Vico, in *De Antiquissima Italorum sapientia*, is one of the first eighteenth-century philosophers to expound a theory of genius)[22] is, as it were, a latter-day primitive who, in an age in which truth tends towards abstraction, preserves his ability to become aware of the profound effects of providential action. His mind is an "heroic mind," according to the title of Vico's inaugural oration of 1732,[23] because it has not lost touch with divine inspiration. This does not mean, of course, that the genius conceives Providence or God thematically; rather it means that in his actions he shows a capacity for invention that had seemed to have become extinct, in an age when ideas were gradually congealed.

Among all the possible forms in which human truth can be inadequate, the "poetic" form (in the broad sense I have mentioned above) is therefore the most effective. It is that in which truth is brought closest to man, without losing its divine dimension. For this reason we may call it the propulsive principle of history, that peculiar form of truth that gives life and movement to history. Thanks to this principle, Vico's historicism reverses the Renaissance conception of *veritas filia temporis*, which now becomes *veritas mater temporis*. Whereas poetic wisdom persists, at least potentially, far beyond the historical phase to which it belongs, even into the age of frigid abstraction, it enables historical motion to continue and avoids its dispersion in indefinite vibrations without unified direction; in fact it saves history from the *Seinsvergessenheit* with which it is threatened.

[21] *Scienza nuova, Opere,* §§ 1246, 1247. See also the letter to Gherardo degli Angioli in which, after referring to Brunelleschi's "cupola resting on four points," Vico mentions, ". . . towards the end of the age of barbarism, the telescope, that has produced new methods of research in astronomy" (*Opere* [Ricciardi], p. 122).

[22] *De Italorum sapientia, Opere* 1: 178.

[23] *De mente heroica,* Vico, *Opere* 7: 3–22.

The Myth as an Historically Operative Truth

If poetry (in a broad sense) is the vehicle for truths which makes history, then it is unavoidable that an immanentist historicism (as, for instance, that of Italian historicism) fails to understand Vico adequately. This type of historicism will tend inevitably to view the participation of man in God's providential operation as the immediate expression, in man, of the self-determination of the All in One. But where the transcendental dimension is absent one fails to understand why the most effective human expression of truth should be an extrinsically mythical, and hence metaphorical, form "translated," that is, transferred, into a sphere different from its original one. Nor, inversely, can one see how myths could be "true fables" even when, taken literally, they contain falsehoods. Once deprived of its transcendent dimension, myth should be considered at most a superstructure that must be removed if one wishes to discover authentic truth. Vico, on the contrary, is so deeply convinced of the opposite that he has presented his own thought in a form we might often term mythical. It would be foolhardy to assert that he did so deliberately so that his philosophy would belong to the sphere of poetic wisdom rather than to the sphere of abstract speculation. He would have had difficulty in admitting to such an artificial purpose even to himself, let alone to others. Instead it was probably Vico's attraction for poetic wisdom to exercise a spontaneous influence over his writing as an almost instinctive form of expression. After all, despite the relation Vico establishes between philosophy and philology, more than one of the examples he gives us of the results of his philological reflections are far closer in form to his own definition of myth as a true fable. However, if, quite apart from his natural inclinations, one considers his theory on its own, it is easy to justify his preference for poetic wisdom. The truth it contains, which is not an entirely human form of truth but is ours only by participation, is the form of truth which moves history.

Translated by S. J. K. Manco

Leon Pompa

VICO AND THE PRESUPPOSITIONS OF HISTORICAL KNOWLEDGE

I

One of the most impressive features of the *Scienza nuova* is its attempt to make intelligible modes of thought and kinds of attitude proper to societies which were in many ways very different from that in which Vico himself lived. It is strange therefore that although the present revival of interest in Vico coincides with a lively debate on the nature and possibility of cross-cultural understanding, little attempt has been made to show the relevance of Vico's theories to this problem.[1] This is partly because Vico approached the problem in its connection with history, concerning himself with the nature of the difficulties raised for historians by the fact that the societies of the past which they want to understand are often very different from their own,[2] whereas the contemporary debate has been

[1] A notable exception here is provided by P. Winch in his article "Understanding a Primitive Society," *The American Philosophical Quarterly*, 1 (1964). Although he is concerned with the problem as it arises for anthropology, Winch notes the resemblance between certain "limiting notions" within which cross-cultural understanding can take place and Vico's "three first principles." See below, n. 5.

[2] Awareness of the possibility of conceptual and linguistic anachronism was one of the prime motives for the critical reexamination of historical documents by a whole tradition of scholars from Renaissance humanists such as Petrarch and Lorenzo Valla up to Spinoza, Casaubon, and Selden. (See Peter Burke, *The Renaissance Sense of the Past* [London, 1969], pp. 50–69.) The critical writings of these scholars were known to Vico, who, while rejecting many of their specific reinterpretations, never disputed the epistemological difficulties raised by acceptance of the notion of cultural difference in history. The same difficulties, however, were also raised in the sixteenth and seventeenth centuries by the wealth of information regarding the practices and institutions of primitive peoples brought back by explorers in America and the Far East and, especially, by Catholic missionaries in their attempts to extend the frontiers of Christianity. A third area of research which directly connected the problem of cross-cultural understanding with that of historical understanding concerned the interpretation of myths, including both those of contemporary primitive societies and those of past societies. Vico's own cultural upbringing and personal interests directed his attention to the state of debate with regard to the first and third of these areas of controversy, but by his day the issues involved in all so impinged on one another that it was impossible to have knowledge of one without knowledge of the others. For a particularly illuminating account of the historical background to this see: Gianfranco Cantelli, *Vico e Bayle: Premesse per un confronto* (Naples, 1971).

I would like to express my gratitude to Professor W. H. Walsh of the University of Edinburgh for reading a draft of this paper and for suggesting a number of changes which have made it clearer than it would otherwise be.

pursued largely by cultural and social anthropologists and philosophers of the social sciences. It is also in part due to the failure of the traditional interpretations of Vico to clarify certain problematic aspects of his thought, involving in particular the exact nature of his distinction between what is necessary and what is contingent in history and the epistemological status of this distinction. In the nineteenth century the Italian positivists ascribed to him the view that the content of history was wholly contingent and our knowledge of it wholly empirical. Their neo-Hegelian successors, among whom Croce was preeminent, went to the other extreme, attributing to him the view that the content of history was wholly necessary, our knowledge of it wholly a priori. Current research has shown that neither of these interpretations can be sustained but has produced no systematic alternative by which to replace them. In what follows I hope to outline such an alternative and to indicate its relevance for the problem of cross-cultural understanding.

II

The connection between historical knowledge and cross-cultural understanding may be seen in the following way. The historian's aim, we are often told, is to establish the truth about man's past. This could mean that he aims to establish truths about the past in the same terms as those in which the agents and societies of the past themselves thought about them.[3] His task would thus involve elucidating and making intelligible conceptual schemes in many ways very different from his own. Alternatively it could mean that he is to establish such truths from a wholly different point of view, utilizing concepts and theories, often causal, which presuppose his own conceptual scheme but not that of the societies and historical agents about whom he writes.[4] An historian who recreated the events of, say, the Black Death as contemporary observers felt about them, describing them in terms of an obsolete medical terminology and explaining them as divine punishment for worldly sin, would be engaged in the first task. An historian who described them in terms of current medical theory and explained their occurrence by reference to climatic and economic theory would be engaged in the second.

It might be tempting to think of these as alternative ways of doing history between which one could choose according to one's interests. But this becomes impossible as soon as it is accepted that there may be large

[3] This was the view, for example, of R. G. Collingwood, in *The Idea of History* (Oxford, 1961), and, more recently, of P. Winch in *The Idea of a Social Science* (London, 1970), pp. 131–33, and in "Understanding a Primitive Society."

[4] Such a view is advocated by A. C. Danto, in *Analytical Philosophy of History* (London, 1965), chap. 7.

differences between the ways in which different societies look at and explain their experience; for it then seems that neither can be pursued on its own without dispensing with certain crucial features of historical knowledge. If we try to take historical events solely in terms proper to the historical culture in which they occurred, we shall have to dispense with all facts which cannot be stated in those terms. That people die from cancer or have neurotic tendencies might be facts about our own society, but they could not be considered to describe many past societies. Historical thinking would thus involve considerable conceptual reorientation and would provide understanding of a sort very different from, and sometimes much poorer than, that which we ordinarily enjoy. If, on the other hand, we were to look at past events solely in our own conceptual terms, we should lose sight of what is distinctive and different about the thought of past societies. We would, for example, be unable to appreciate the differences between the thought of classical Greece, medieval France, and our own modern society. Thus, on the first view history would cease to be a species of contemporary knowledge, and on the second it would cease to be historical.

This point may be reinforced by the following consideration. The historian cannot confine himself to taking a past culture entirely in its own terms for it is part of his job to establish that his interpretation of these terms is correct. And this requires the establishment of facts in conformity with the criteria appropriate to the concept of a fact as it exists in his own conceptual scheme.[5] Yet, despite this, he cannot afford entirely to dispense with understanding the past culture in its own terms. For, whatever factual account he gives requires support, which will involve him in construing certain historical remains (pieces of stone, parchment, wool, and so on)

[5] This has been denied by Winch in "Understanding a Primitive Society." Addressing himself to the same problem as it arises in anthropology, Winch claims that the aim is not to understand concepts which are integrally embedded in one conceptual scheme while presupposing a standard of rationality proper to a different scheme, for such a task is theoretically impossible. Instead, he suggests that the aim is to achieve an extension of wisdom by taking the beliefs of other cultures in their own terms and learning what are the standards of rationality they presuppose. Nevertheless, Winch makes some concessions to the necessity for finding some ground common to the two schemes in his admission that we could not find out what are the terms in which to understand another culture if there were not some "limiting notions" (i.e., the ideas of birth, death, and sexual relationships) which "are inescapably involved in the life of all known human societies in a way which gives us a clue where to look if we are puzzled about the point of an alien system of institutions." ("Understanding a Primitive Society," p. 322). Winch goes on to note the similarity between these limiting notions and Vico's "three first principles," upon which "he [Vico] thought the possibility of understanding human history rested." It will become apparent below that I accept this claim if it means that Vico's three principles are necessary for such understanding but think that it must be considerably augmented and modified before we reach an acceptable account of what Vico thought sufficient for such understanding.

as *human* phenomena (parts of buildings, documents, clothes, etc.)[6] and thus in ascribing certain beliefs, practices, and institutions to past historical agents. He thus requires some grasp of the conceptual content of the system of practices and institutions of which any historical evidence was once a part and in which it acquired its original human significance and intelligibility before he can go on to explain it in terms of theories to which he himself subscribes.

These considerations point to the need for a set of conditions which will provide an intelligible connection between some aspects of the historian's conceptual scheme and those of the different historical societies about which he writes. Somehow the historian must be able to relate concepts proper to his own scheme to events, actions, and processes structured by concepts proper to a different conceptual scheme. Yet these conditions must not provide grounds for a complete assimilation of the two schemes, for in trying to make the past intelligible from a viewpoint which reflected the intellectual interests of his own society, the historian would deprive himself of the possibility of recognizing what is different and distinctive about the past. What is required here is a set of conditions which can provide the grounds for an understanding of both the similarities and differences between the thought of the historian's own society and that of the societies of the past he wishes to study.

A further difficulty concerns our knowledge of such a set of conditions. Most historians, and some philosophers of history, have thought that it was empirically based.[7] However, this cannot be correct, for the question could then be decided only by a comparative inquiry into the similarities and differences between present and past conceptual schemes. But if knowledge of past conceptual schemes presupposes knowledge of these conditions, the former cannot be used to establish the latter. On the other hand, to treat it as a wholly a priori matter involves the risk, of which historians are rightly conscious, of pressing the thought and activities of the past into a mould of our own devising, lacking any claim whatsoever to historical accuracy.[8]

[6] It is helpful to remember Collingwood's instructive account of the difference between the archaeologist's evidence and the palaeontologist's: "The archaeologist's use of his stratified relics depends upon his conceiving them as artifacts serving human purposes and thus expressing a particular way in which men have thought about their own life, and from this point of view the palaeontologist, arranging his fossils in a time-series, is not working as an historian, but only as a scientist thinking in a way that can at most be described as quasi-historical" (*The Idea of History*, pp. 212).

[7] For example, Hume, who wanted to base historical knowledge upon an *empirical* science of human nature.

[8] It is worth noting that Croce, who ascribed to Vico the view that our knowledge of history was wholly a priori, accused him of precisely this fault. See *La Filosofia di G. B. Vico* (Bari, 1965), p. 45. From what follows it will be seen that Croce only arrived at these results through his failure to distinguish on the one hand between what is empirical and what is contingent and on the other between what is a priori in the sense of being an unchallengeable assumption and what is a priori in the sense of being conceptually true.

These two unacceptable approaches to the question approximate fairly closely the positivist and idealist interpretations of Vico, mentioned earlier. In ascribing to Vico a different view I shall therefore be presenting a third possibility with regard to the solution of these difficulties.

III

It will be useful to begin by recalling certain facts about the development of Vico's theory of knowledge. In *De antiquissima Italorum sapientia* Vico laid great stress upon the causal nature of knowledge. He accordingly claimed that it was accessible to man only in those sciences, among which mathematics was preeminent, in which men themselves created everything (that is, the rules, definitions, axioms, and methods) upon which correct demonstrations of the truths of the science depended. Knowledge thus included not merely an account of what it is that is true but an understanding of that by virtue of which it is true, that is, of the causes of its truth. At this stage Vico believed that history could not be a proper branch of knowledge: if men do not create their own natures, in which are to be found the causes of their deeds, practices, and beliefs, they cannot know them. Human history was not therefore a species of *scienza* but of *coscienza*, that is, of unilluminated, brute fact.

The extension of this early theory of knowledge to accommodate historical knowledge was made possible by Vico's realization that the men who are the agents in history are *in some sense* identical with the men who later write that history: "the world of civil society has certainly been made by men . . . its principles are therefore to be rediscovered within the modifications of our own human mind."[9] In modifying his theory of knowledge to meet this claim it became necessary for Vico to modify the relationship between understanding and knowledge. In the theory of *De antiquissima Italorum sapientia,* knowledge of mathematical propositions involved understanding the conventional nature of the system in which they inhere: a mathematical proposition is "known" when we understand that it is (essentially) nothing but what it is proved to be. In the theory of the *Scienza nuova,* however, the identity between historian and historical agent does not imply that the deeds of the historical agent are nothing but the consequences of applying the methods and rules proper to historiographical construction. Vico does not claim that by virtue of the identity between the historical agent and historian the latter *knows* the historical world, but that by virtue of it he *can come to know it.*[10] The suggestion is that the identity in question makes the historical world *intelligible* and therefore a possible object of knowledge. That it should obtain is thus a

[9] *New Science,* § 331.
[10] *Ibid.*

necessary but not sufficient condition of historical knowledge. It is this prizing apart of the concepts of intelligibility and knowledge which distinguishes the theory of knowledge in *De antiquissima Italorum sapientia* from that in the *Scienza nuova* and which allowed Vico to ascribe to historical evidence its proper confirmatory role in the latter work.[11]

The intelligibility of the historical world depends therefore upon certain causal features which are identical with those of "our own human mind" and which can be rediscovered from the latter. The crucial questions here are, of course: What are these features? How can we rediscover them? and, How do they suffice to establish the intelligibility of history?

IV

In seeking to answer these questions it is convenient to begin by drawing attention to certain features of Vico's reconstruction of the structure, content, and development of historical conceptual schemes, beginning with some which he mentions explicitly. These are contained in the concept of a common sense. Common sense is a basic capacity human beings have for formulating those beliefs about what is necessary or useful to themselves, upon which their subsequent activities depend.[12] According to Vico the largest part of human beliefs, including the most abstruse and intellectual as well as the most immediate and practical, arise, directly or indirectly, from the operation of this faculty.[13] Two points of importance are to be noted about it.

1. It is a social faculty. The capacity to reach such beliefs is "shared by an entire class, an entire people, an entire nation or the entire human race."[14] This claim is an application of the principle that man is essentially social.[15] It is thus a basic assumption in Vico's conception of history that man responds to, recognizes, chooses, and acts in pursuit of ends which presuppose his place in a social context.[16] Man's nature is such that he

[11] I have discussed the role of empirical evidence in Vico's later theory of knowledge in my article "Vico's Science," *History and Theory* 10 (1971): 49–83.

[12] I omit here consideration of complications raised by the extension of the list of objects of common sense to include comforts, pleasures and luxuries (*New Science*, § 241), since this extension raises no difficulties of principle.

[13] The best-known example of this thesis is Vico's claim that the sources of the content of Socratic philosophy are to be found in the social, economic, and legal life of classical Athens. See *New Science*, §§ 1040–43. The importance of the primacy of social and economic beliefs in the culture of a given society is well brought out by Werner Stark, "Giambattista Vico's Sociology of Knowledge," in *Giambattista Vico: An International Symposium*.

[14] *New Science*, § 142.

[15] *New Science*, §§ 134–36; 308–9.

[16] It is not, however, Vico's claim that man pursues these ends because he recognizes that they are social. Rather, man pursues social ends unknowingly because they are identical with the personal ends which he does knowingly pursue. He thus produces something of social value while seeking something for himself. Cf. *New Science*, § 341.

cannot avoid living in and being conditioned by a network of social relationships, and his beliefs, choices, actions, and institutions are affected by this.

2. The character of this capacity changes in accordance with a sequence of different kinds of mental activity, which is natural to man in his various necessarily social contexts: "men first feel without perceiving, then they perceive with a troubled and agitated spirit, finally they reflect with a clear mind."[17] This principle is elsewhere described as the sequence of three phases—poetic, heroic, and human—through which human nature naturally develops.[18]

It is necessary to note that these conditions are causal in character, insofar as they are conditions which affect the structure of human conceptual schemes, and that knowledge of them is indispensable to historical knowledge. Both claims come out via the use Vico makes of the concept of "modifications of the human mind" in his reconstruction of the beliefs of poetic man. The latter, he writes:

> [should begin] with metaphysics which seeks its proofs not in the external world but within the modifications of the mind of him who meditates it. For since this world has certainly been made by men it is within these modifications that its principles should have been sought. And human nature, so far as it is like that of animals, carries with it this property, that the senses are its sole way of knowing things. Hence poetic wisdom . . . must have begun with a metaphysic not rational and abstract like that of learned men now, but felt and imagined as that of these first men must have been who, without power of ratiocination, were all robust sense and vigorous imagination.[19]

Vico subsequently goes on to show how such a being, by use of his "robust sense and vigorous imagination," which work in accordance with purely natural principles, would invest his world with certain conceptual properties. He would come to see the world as a vast living being and certain parts of it (such as thunder and lightning) as this being's way of communicating with men.

It is not possible here to follow the rest of Vico's account. It is necessary to stress, however, that in producing it Vico uses knowledge of certain natural psychological principles in accordance with which, he claims, the various imaginative and associative connections in it are made.[20] The claim is thus that the conceptual scheme of primitive man is structured by the operation of a number of natural principles of the imagination which the historian can rediscover by appeal to the modifications of his

[17] *Ibid.*, §§ 218–19.
[18] *Ibid.*, §§ 916–18.
[19] *Ibid.*, §§ 374–75.
[20] For a most interesting account in which it is maintained that the fundamental natural principles here are the linguistic connections involved in the various *tropes*, see the essay in this volume by Hayden V. White.

own mind, that is, to some knowledge he can have of the principles upon which his own imagination works.

This is not an isolated example of Vico's appeal to natural properties of the human mind to support his reconstruction of historical conceptual schemes. All his reconstructions involve such an appeal. Axioms XXXI through XXXIX, for example, consist almost entirely of statements of such properties: "wonder is the daughter of ignorance," "once men are seized by a frightful superstition they refer to it all they imagine, see or even do or make," "when men are ignorant of the natural causes producing things . . . they attribute their own nature to them," and so on. In stating this series of properties Vico is giving a specific account of the principles upon which common sense works and therefore of certain natural conditions by which human conceptual schemes are structured and upon knowledge of which historical knowledge itself depends.

V

Vico's account of the *content* of historical conceptual schemes involves further features to which he does not explicitly draw attention. They make it clear, however, that on his account only the historian can have *scienza* because only he is in a position to utilize the distinction between the causes and the content of a conceptual scheme upon which *scienza* depends. This becomes obvious if we attend to Vico's explanations of the beliefs of poetic man. The latter, we are told, lives in a world of violent natural phenomena, involving the frequent occurrence of floods, thunder, and lightning. For these events themselves Vico offers purely physical explanations, to which nothing corresponds in the conceptual scheme of poetic man.[21] For poetic man the things he sees and hears *are* the commands and orders of Jove. They thus constitute part of the content of his belief. But in claiming that poetic man sees thunder and lightning as the commands and orders of Jove Vico is giving an account which poetic man could neither give nor understand. For such a claim can only be made within a conceptual scheme which contains a distinction between thunder and lightning, or natural events, on the one hand and the commands and orders of Jove, or supernatural events, on the other hand. And this distinction does not obtain in the conceptual scheme of poetic man. The latter would accordingly be unable to comprehend the suggestion that what he saw as a series of divine commands was really a series of natural phenomena. For the historian, however, who does have such a distinction in his conceptual scheme, it is perfectly proper to refer to these natural phenomena when giving his account of the causes of the content of the conceptual scheme of poetic man.

[21] *New Science*, § 377.

It follows that the kind of account Vico is offering does not consist in taking the beliefs of an historical culture entirely in its own terms. It involves, rather, showing how reality as it is conceived in the historian's own culture was conceived in former historical cultures. It thus presupposes the historian's right to introduce certain truths, the statement of which can be made only within his own conceptual scheme. The legitimacy of this procedure is obviously crucial for only by virtue of it can Vico give an account in which he tells us not only how poetic man conceived his world and what he thought of himself as trying to do in it but also what his world really was and what he was really doing in it.

It is important to note that some appeal to an independent knowledge of reality, such as this account involves, is necessary if the historian is to allow for the relativity of historical conceptual schemes and yet to substantiate his claims about their content. For he cannot do the latter by showing that his account is consistent with the evidence, since it is logically possible for an infinite number of accounts to be consistent with any given evidence. Nor, again, can he establish it by showing how the beliefs it contains were conditioned by prior beliefs, since this would only put in question the establishment of these prior beliefs ad infinitum. It is true that the beliefs of an historical society are conditioned by prior historical beliefs, but this process of conditioning does not wholly determine their content, and were it to do so, historians would never be able to substantiate their accounts of that content. They must, in addition, appeal to knowledge of the causal context in which historical men really lived. They must, therefore, assume their own conception of reality in order to reconstruct the ways in which historically men have conceived it.

VI

Sections IV and V have been concerned largely with the beliefs of what Vico calls common sense, but what might better be called *relative* common sense, since the beliefs it contains change in accordance with a sequence of modes of mental functioning natural to human beings. Its content for an historical society may therefore be in many ways different from that in the historian's own society. The suggestion is that the knowledge of it is accessible to the historian only because he has some prior knowledge both of this natural sequence of modes of mental functioning or thought and of the causal context in which it operates.

It is necessary now to note certain other features of this causal context. What has come to light so far is Vico's reliance upon a number of physical and geographical facts in his reconstruction of the thought of poetic man. His right to assume these can hardly be questioned. Obvious though it may seem, it is nevertheless an important truth that historians could make little of a nation's history if they could not assume that the latter took place in, and was causally affected by, a physical context much of the sort as that in which the historian finds himself. It is thus necessary that at all points in history there be some beliefs which the historian can explain in such a way that he can see how they can be beliefs about what *he*, the historian, calls the physical world. But this assumption, though necessary, is not sufficient, for not all historical beliefs are of this sort. Were it the only assumption to which historians were entitled, they would not advance very far in their reconstruction of historical conceptual schemes.

Vico's further account of this causal context is given in what he calls the "three principles of this science,"[22] that is, the institutions of religion, marriage, and burial of the dead, which he claims to be necessary conditions of any form of civilized life. Their necessity, however, is a consequence of certain vices, ferocity, ambition, and avarice, to which man is naturally prone and which, were he able to live nonsocially, would lead quickly to his total destruction.[23] The claim that the institutions are necessary arises directly from this fact: religion is necessary because it is the only institution which can force men to accept the concept of law,[24] which is itself an essential aspect of social life;[25] marriage is necessary because it alone can provide the causal context in which parents will look after and educate their children and thus ensure the preservation and transmission of the products of civilization as they exist at any one time;[26] and burial of the dead is necessary because it is intimately bound up with hope of an afterlife and thus with an element of prudential idealism in human conduct which, again, is necessary but not to be found in man's basic capacities.[27]

The claim is that individual man is a self-centered and vicious creature who, were he able to live out of society, would quickly bring about his own destruction. This is averted, however, by the civilizing or humanizing influence of three basic institutions which condition these vices in socially constructive ways. These institutions are not, of course, created by men with foresight: such an explanation would be incompatible with the vicious nature Vico attributes to man. They are, rather, the unforeseen but necessary consequences of certain ways of experiencing and existing in the world which are natural to man. They thus arise from men's exercise of their basic natural propensities in a given causal context.

[22] *Ibid.*, § 130.. Cf. § 332 where they are described as the "universal and eternal principles . . . on which all nations were founded and still preserve themselves."

[23] *Ibid.*, §§ 132–33.

[24] *Ibid.*, §§ 177–79.

[25] *Ibid.*, § 309.

[26] *Ibid.*, § 336. Cf. also § 629 where marriage is described as the "recognised source of all authority" and §§ 504–13 where it is a necessary condition of morality, itself a social bond.

[27] *Ibid.*, §§ 12–13; 337; 537.

It must be emphasized that these three principles are not in any sense conceptually necessary. They are causally necessary, man's nature being what it as a matter of fact is. This is made very clear by the arguments Vico presents to support two of them. Marriage, he claims, is necessary because children born out of the context of such an institution either would be abandoned to die by their parents or would fail to receive the teaching upon which many of their human characteristics depend. In the absence of such an institution, any given society would simply revert to barbarism.[28] Similarly, burial of the dead is necessary, for if it were not practised, disease would become rife and would prevent civil development.[29] Neither of these arguments implies that the institutions in question, or the human characteristics upon which they depend, are conceptually necessary. In the case of the second, which rests upon a claim about the physical corruptibility of the human body, this is very evident. In the case of the first, the assumption is that unmarried parents would not provide the education that social development requires. This assumption itself presupposes Vico's account of man as a vicious creature but does not presuppose that this is some sort of conceptual truth. The claim is simply that since men are what they are, spiritually degenerate and physically corruptible, no society could endure and develop which did not contain certain institutions which counterbalanced these factors.

The principles are therefore causally but not conceptually necessary. They are also, however, epistemologically necessary, in that knowledge of them is a necessary condition of any acceptable historical knowledge. The historian can reconstruct the changing ways in which men have seen their world in the past only if he can know what they were *really* thinking about, and he can know this only if he can assume that in some cases, at least, they were doing their thinking in the context of an objective reality identical with his own. One aspect of this reality, as we have seen, is a common physical world which they inhabit. The other is a common social world in which they live, that is, a social world in which the three basic institutions are causally operative. And this implies, of course, that they share those features of human nature upon which this operation itself depends. Thus, as we have seen, there must at all points in human history be some beliefs which the historian can explain in such a way that we can see how they can be beliefs about what he, the historian, calls the physical world. In a precisely analogous way, however, there must also be others about the institutions the historian calls "religion," "marriage," and "burial of the dead," the necessity for which, again, arises from what he recognises as "ferocity," "avarice," and "ambition."

[28] *Ibid.*, § 336.
[29] *Ibid.*, § 337.

VII

From the foregoing account it would seem that Vico is resting our capacity to reconstruct and render intelligible past conceptual schemes upon some knowledge of the causal conditions upon which such schemes depend. This claim gives rise to two further problems upon which I shall briefly comment: How do we come by such knowledge? And in what way does it contribute to the intelligibility of past conceptual schemes? The answers to both these questions lie in the important but strangely neglected concept of self-reflection.[30] It is to be noted that when Vico explains why the real knowledge of the *Scienza nuova* has been overlooked in favor of the pseudo-knowledge of the natural sciences, it is to the difficulty of self-reflection that he refers:

> this aberration was a consequence of that infirmity of the human mind by which, immersed and buried in the human body, it naturally inclines to take notice of bodily things and finds the effort to attend to itself too laborious, just as the bodily eye sees all things outside itself but needs a mirror to see itself.[31]

It is possible to overlook the importance of this passage by taking it as nothing more than a general complaint against past scholars for attending to the natural sciences rather than to the human sciences. But this can hardly be all that Vico means, for on his view the natural sciences are a legitimate species of human construction even though, since they are created without regard to the genesis of their basic conceptual presuppositions, they cannot rise above the level of *coscienza*, or unenlightened belief. The complaint is not against man for having beliefs about the natural world but for having failed to reflect upon how he has come to have those beliefs and, hence, for attributing to them an unjustifiable epistemological status, that is, taking them for *scienza* rather than *coscienza*. In terms of Vico's own analogy with the eye and the things seen by the eye, the natural scientist is concerned solely with the things seen and ignores the nature of the eye which conditions what is seen. The historian, on the other hand, understands the things seen as a species of conditioned belief because, by self-reflection, he can understand how his own beliefs were conditioned and what particular human characteristics conditioned them.

[30] Croce and the Hegelian school in general did not disregard this concept. But they mistook Vico's references to it as a recommendation to some sort of a priori and conceptual reflection upon the principles which condition history. If, as I have suggested, these principles are almost all natural and causal, this cannot be what Vico intended in his references to the concept.

[31] *New Science*, § 331. Cf. also § 263: "the human mind is naturally inclined by the senses to see itself externally in the body and only with great difficulty does it come to understand itself by means of reflection."

To see what Vico has in mind here it is useful to recall his frequent attempts to use our understanding of children to illuminate the beliefs of poetic man.[32] If this is connected with the claim that we can have knowledge of the requisite modifications by self-reflection, it would seem that Vico is suggesting that our capacity to reflect upon ourselves as children teaches us not only what it is like to see or to think of the world in a certain way but also how our doing so results from the operation of certain natural propensities. Children, and poetic man, of course, lack this kind of understanding. They see the world in a certain way but have no capacity to reflect upon, and hence to understand, why they see it in this way: their mode of consciousness being unreflective,[33] they are confined to *coscienza* of their world. But a rational adult, that is, an adult born in the age of fully developed human reason,[34] can reflect upon the beliefs of his childhood and see how their main characteristics were a consequence of natural associative principles of thought, memory, and imagination. Precisely because it is his own experience he is recalling and reflecting upon, that is, because it is self-reflection in which he is at once the subject and the object of his reflection, he can see how the main features of his beliefs were conditioned by his natural propensity to connect things in certain ways and by the context in which he lived. Similarly, the capacity for self-reflection, when exercised upon his beliefs in social situations, can teach him how his specific social contexts condition him to think and believe in one way rather than another. If these are the modifications to which self-reflection gives us access and upon which historical knowledge itself depends, the special characteristic which Vico ascribes to the latter is its capacity to enable us to understand both how and why an historical society thought about things in the way it did.

It is important to stress that the claim is not that because the things we learn by self-reflection are true of ourselves they must be true of other societies. It is that only insofar as they are true of ourselves and of other societies can we understand the latter. It remains, on this view, a logical possibility that there be societies of which none of the things we learn of ourselves by self-reflection were true. But we could not have historical knowledge of such societies because in a very fundamental sense, a sense which distinguishes the human sciences from the natural sciences, we would not be able to understand what caused them to think about things in the ways they did.

[32] Vico often refers to the age of poetic man as the "childhood of the human race" and his accounts of the natural propensities of poetic man are constantly supported by references to similar propensities in children. Cf. e.g. *New Science*, §§ 211–13 where a claim about the nature of memory in children is presented as "the principle of the expressiveness of the poetic images that the world formed in its first childhood."

[33] This gives added significance to Vico's claim that the beliefs of common sense are "without reflection" (*New Science*, § 142).

[34] *Ibid.*, § 350.

VIII

If this is correct, one of the most crucial features of Vico's account of the nature of historical knowledge is that it presupposes a certain kind of understanding which itself involves beliefs about certain fundamental but contingent conditions under which human conceptual schemes are shaped. Some of these conditions pertain to the natural principles which structure the development of human consciousness, others pertain to the physical and social contexts in which human beings must live and by which, accordingly, the content of their thought is affected. The requirements of historical understanding thus are not satisfied by the purely formal adequacy of the concepts we use but must be supplemented by certain facts about the natural conditions which affect the growth of human cultures.

It is not possible, within the scope of this essay, to undertake a lengthy inquiry into the acceptability of these general claims, even less into that of the particular set of contingent propositions upon which Vico's own account of history rests. In conclusion I shall confine myself to some remarks concerning the most crucial general point: whether *any* contingent truths are among the presuppositions of historical understanding.

One way of evaluating Vico's claim is to consider what would be the position were we to deny it, as we would were we to maintain, for example, that the only presuppositions of historical understanding were of a purely formal nature. The peculiar weakness in such a position is that it cannot rule out historical accounts which, though formally correct, are too bizarre to be understood. To appreciate this we might consider the position of an historian who was prepared to accept Vico's own account of the formal categories involved in historical understanding but denied the necessity for any contingent truths. He might, for example, be prepared to accept the claim that modes of consciousness develop causally in history and that these condition human conceptual schemes but not to accept that we had any prior knowledge of the specific principles upon which the development of modes of consciousness depended. The latter, he might claim, was a purely empirical matter, to be discovered from history and not, therefore, a presupposition of history.

It would be compatible with this view for a history to be written in such a way as to present imaginative and anthropomorphic modes of thought and belief as a development of more rational and materialistic modes of thought, for there need be nothing formally incorrect about such an account. It could, for example, satisfy Vico's formal requirement that people's actions be described in terms which connected them internally with their aims and intentions and that the latter be explained by reference to social roles and institutions. But as long as we confined ourselves to demanding that historical accounts be formally correct there would be no way of rejecting accounts in which superstitious and pre-scientific modes of thought arose from highly sophisticated modes of thought or in which the whole of what happened was explained as the outcome of men's desire to initiate and complete actions directed towards a common good.

It might be thought that such accounts could be falsified empirically, but this cannot be so. Empirical falsification in history depends upon knowledge of historical fact. The latter in turn depends upon the interpretation of evidence and thus involves some hypotheses about the structure and content of human nature and its relationship to the evidence. Given, however, the theoretical possibility of an infinite number of such hypotheses, it would always be possible, with enough ingenuity, to find some hypothesis to support any given account, no matter how improbable the latter might seem.

It follows therefore that if formal correctness were the only condition historical accounts had to satisfy, there would be a large number of conflicting accounts between which we could not justify a choice, even though many of them struck us as frankly incredible. Indeed, the notion of historical credibility would itself have no meaning in such circumstances, since we could not cash it by any appeal to a prior knowledge of human nature or of any principles of the development of human consciousness. The point is not merely that we would not be able to falsify such accounts (and we certainly would not be able to do so) but that we could not decide whether they were intelligible in the sense of resting upon a recognizable view of human nature.

It might be objected to this that we ought not to reject accounts merely on the grounds of their nonformal unintelligibility, for people of the past may have been very different from us, and such accounts may indeed be true. This objection would rest upon the point that it is logically possible that there be societies of the sort mentioned (though how far the concept of a society can be stretched to allow for this possibility is itself debatable) and would conclude from it that there are no limitations upon the kinds of historical accounts possible. But while it may be true that we cannot antecedently reject the possibility of such societies, we can and do antecedently reject the possibility of our understanding them historically. For in understanding something historically we presuppose a partial identity of contingent truths about that society and our own. And without this it is difficult to see how history could have the human significance it has for us.

Historical understanding therefore presupposes a number of basic contingent truths common to the historian's own society and that in which he is interested. This presupposition cannot determine a priori what happened in the past, but it can, and does, determine a priori the limits of our understanding of what happened in the past. It is conceivable that there were peoples in the past whom we just cannot understand historically, but it is inconceivable that we should understand any people or society whatsoever without falling back upon our own convictions concerning certain contingent truths about human nature. To this extent Vico is committed to some sort of insight into the relationship between the natural properties of human nature and systems of human belief.

W. H. Walsh

THE LOGICAL STATUS OF VICO'S IDEAL ETERNAL HISTORY

Anyone who reads Vico's *New Science* with a little attention must be struck by the extraordinary confidence Vico shows in the correctness of his general view. He comes on the scene as a man with a theory to offer and applies the theory wherever opportunity allows. If facts or apparent facts conflict with the theory's requirements, they are discounted as illusions or explained away as not what they seem to be. Thus the theory requires monarchy to arise only "as a result of the unchecked liberty of the peoples" (*New Science*, § 737); Assyria constitutes an apparent exception to this rule. Vico assures us that Assyria "must have passed through the successive stages of divine and heroic regimes and then of popular liberty in order to reach that of monarchy" (*ibid.*); he even takes credit for thus filling in "purely by understanding, without benefit of memory . . . the beginnings of universal history" (§ 738). There is in fact no evidence for these pre-monarchical stages of Assyrian history, but to suppose that it might have begun with a monarchy is to suppose an impossibility, like thinking that a frog is born from a summer shower (*ibid.*). Reason requires us to say that the truth must be otherwise. Vico is in general free in his use of "must" and similar words. The gentile nations, he tells us, *could not* have been founded without religion and *could not* grow without valor (§ 198). The first fables *must* have contained civil truths (*ibid.*). Solon *must* have been "a sage of vulgar wisdom, party leader of the plebs in the first times of the aristocratic commonwealth at Athens" (§ 414). Theseus *must* have been a poetic character typifying "the Athenian youths who, under the law of force practised on them by Minos, are devoured by his bull or pirate ship" (§ 635). Vulcan's being thrown out of heaven *must* "refer to a struggle of the plebeians to secure from the heroes a share in the auspices of Jove" (§ 650). That there had stood on the shores of Latium a Greek city which had taught the Latins their letters is "a *necessary* conjecture" (§ 763). Homer *must* belong to the end of the heroic age, since the sentiments, actions, and attitudes depicted in his poems were real only at that time (§ 808). There is no record of dueling in the period of the first barbarism, but "*it passes our understanding*" how the Cyclopes could have endured wrongs without any means of retaliating, and so we are justified in postulating Cyclopean duels (§§ 962–63). And there are of course countless other instances of the same sort of thing.

I have brought together this evidence, not because I want to suggest that Vico was wrong to rely on theory in this way, but to call attention to a feature of his thinking which is not often emphasized by commentators, namely its strongly rationalist character. To describe Vico as a rationalist sounds paradoxical for a number of reasons. One is Vico's own protest against a priori speculation in the sphere of human affairs, expressed in the famous declaration that "the philosophers failed by half in not giving certainty to their reasonings by appeal to the authority of the philologians" (§ 140). It is clear from this that there is a kind of rationalism which Vico deplores and repudiates, the kind which relies on reason unaided by any reference to fact. A second ground for finding it odd to pin the tag of "rationalist" on Vico is the very concrete nature of much of his own thought. His interest in empirical questions is intense, so intense indeed that it often impedes effective discussion of general issues. For one who ranks as a philosopher, Vico is both shy of explicit abstractions and unusually bad at handling them, thanks to the fact that his mind moves all too readily from universal principles to their concrete application. If we asked where his greater interest lay, in elaborating the general shape of an ideal eternal history or in considering how such a history was embodied or reflected in individual cases, we might well find ourselves answering that it was in fact in the second.

Nevertheless, as Leon Pompa has demonstrated at length,[1] Vico was a student of human affairs whose approach to his subject was, in one sense of the term, decidedly theoretical. He was certainly far from being a simple empiricist. It is not, for example, true that he sought to deduce the stages of his ideal eternal history from reflection on particular histories; indeed, he could not have done so, since it was his thesis that the particular histories available in his own time were full of mistakes and mythology. An ideal eternal history was needed to supply a corrective to mistakes of this kind; without it, reliable particular histories could not exist. Nor could it have been Vico's intention, as it is sometimes said to have been,[2] to arrive at a theory of how historical development must proceed by generalizing from a single case, that of Rome. The simple fact is that the history of Rome, as presented by Livy, for instance, was in Vico's view not a genuine history at all. As it stood it contained no properly authenticated facts and so could not supply a basis for any sort of dependable induction. The 'facts' of Roman history needed to be scrutinized critically and got into

[1] "Vico's Science," *History and Theory* 10 (1971): 49–83. I owe many points to this impressive article. I am also grateful to Dr. Pompa for helpful comments on the present paper.

[2] "The 'new science' was Rome idealised and generalised" (Robert Flint, *Vico* [Edinburgh: Blackwood and Sons, 1884], p. 166).

perspective; one of Vico's most impressive achievements was his success in meeting this need. But he reached this result by *using* the ideal eternal history, which was thus *presupposed* in his work on Roman history rather than derived from Roman history itself.

But if the ideal eternal history was not arrived at by induction, how was it come by? A possibility which can be set aside at once is that it was the product of straight conceptual reflection. Whatever else they are, the propositions of which it consists (that there are three kinds of natures, three kinds of customs, etc. [§ 916 ff.]) are not analytic propositions; they would not be of much interest if they were. Vico's aim in the *New Science* can scarcely have been to *legislate* about what institutions and forms of life are to be taken as distinctively human. It might be argued that he comes near to legislation of this sort when he specifies religion, marriage, and burial of the dead as his three fundamental institutions. The point is by no means certain, for we find in fact that Vico argues his case here by talking about the causal effects of these institutions, or of what would result if they were removed. But even if it were granted, it would not follow that the main body of Vico's conclusions was to be seen as simple deduction from these premises. Even if Vico was dogmatic in holding that human society must display certain forms, we need not see his account of social behavior as shaped exclusively by that fact. Men act in situations, certainly, and what they do is determined in important respects by how they see their situation. But you cannot, just by thinking about the nature of a situation, deduce how men will act in it. To arrive at knowledge here you require additional premises of another kind altogether.

The point I have been arguing could be put more shortly by saying that the idea that Vico in the *New Science* is engaged in an enquiry which is basically conceptual is quite inconsistent with his remarks about the need to marry philosophy with philology in this area. Vico says in effect that the project he is pursuing can be neither an affair of pure reason nor one of the pure recording of fact. Philosophy has to be given certainty "by appeal to the authority of the philologians," whilst the "authority" of philology has to be given the sanction of truth "by appeal to the reasoning of the philosophers" (§ 140). What these cryptic words mean will need further discussion, but at least it is clear that they rule out any suggestion that *mere* thought could arrive at reliable results in the social sphere. If mere thought could do the trick, there would be no need for the new scientist to appeal to the authority of the philologians. Indeed, the latter would simply have no standing in the matter, any more than they have in what would be the parallel case of mathematics.

If Vico in the *New Science* is neither a simple empiricist nor a simple rationalist, what is he? The obvious answer is a modified or moderate rationalist of the type admired by Professor Karl Popper; such a person does not approach his task with a blank mind but thinks up hypotheses which, however, he is prepared to accept only so far as they stand up to empirical testing. I think myself that this answer is correct: in a broad sense Vico does use something like the hypothetico-deductive method. But it is not very enlightening to say so. It is not enlightening in the first place because the hypotheses here in question are themselves far from logically simple: they are not so much suggestions or conjectures as conclusions from a complex argument, an argument whose nature needs careful scrutiny (it is not a matter of purely *logical* deduction) and whose premises require to be made explicit. From one point of view the whole ideal eternal history must be seen as an hypothesis; from another it is a result asserted to be true. How it can be both, if indeed it can, is a question which needs to be pursued further. So too is the question of how on Vico's own assumptions the ideal eternal history can be tested. The problem here is that of finding a suitable body of independent data with which to confront it; the arguments about empiricism above suggest that Vico might be embarrassed if asked to specify such data. The difficulty turns on what he means by "philology" and whether philologians can produce any truths which are not colored by "philosophical" theory. Unless this difficulty can be solved, the easy formula about Vico being a moderate rationalist is not going to be of much help.

I shall be devoting the rest of this paper to an attempt to elucidate and, if possible, meet these difficulties. I begin rather obliquely by asking to what extent Vico relies on empathetic understanding in arriving at his conclusions about the ideal eternal history. Idealist commentators such as Croce have explained the peculiar confidence Vico felt in these by referring to the celebrated passage (331) in which Vico said it was "a truth beyond all question that the world of civil society has certainly been made by men, and that its principles are therefore to be found within the modifications of our own human mind." They interpret these words as implying that the truth about civil society can be recovered if only we can contrive to rethink the ideas which those who made that society had in mind; Vico, the implication is, was convinced that he had done just that. But even if he had it does not follow that the problem would be solved, as reference to another famous passage should make clear. At the very end of his book Vico, while reiterating that 'men have themselves made this world of nations', goes on to claim that "this world without doubt has issued from a mind often diverse, at times quite contrary, and always superior to the particular ends that men had proposed to themselves; which narrow ends, made means to serve wider ends, it has always employed to preserve the human race upon this earth" (§ 1108). What this says, in effect, is that the social world is made by God rather than by man, a point which Vico proceeds to illustrate by a series of examples. Thus men "mean to gratify their bestial lust and abandon their offspring" (*ibid.*): what they want and hope to get is simply sensual satisfaction. In fact circumstances are such that, in trying to carry out this aim, they "inaugurate the chastity of marriage from which the families arise" (*ibid.*). Marriage and the families are here unintended consequences of men's actions and as such cannot be understood exclusively in terms of men's thoughts. To make empathetic understanding a sufficient condition of social comprehension is accordingly a mistake.

But though it is not sufficient for such comprehension, it may all the same be necessary, and I think Vico's thesis is that it is. His position, as I see it, is roughly as follows. First of all, he bids us to do our best to enter into the minds of the persons, whether past or present, whose activities we propose to investigate. In many, indeed in most, cases this will not be a simple matter of putting ourselves in their shoes, since, in order to fulfill the injunction properly, we need to divest ourselves of many assumptions which are entirely natural to us but which would not be seen in that way by those with whom we are concerned. We may have to undertake complicated enquiries in order to establish how our subjects see or saw the world, what they take words or other symbols to mean, what they think the proper way of responding to this or that situation should be. Vico says several times that we can scarcely understand, still less imagine, the thoughts of those who "founded gentile humanity" (§ 378; cf. §§ 34, 338, 700). He is certainly not complacent about the difficulty of the task. But equally he believes that the task can be accomplished succesfully, given sufficient patience and skill. What happens if it is? Not, as the idealists and even Sir Isaiah Berlin seem to suggest,[3] that we shall find ourselves possessed of a special kind of knowledge of human nature, as a result of which we shall see at once why things went as they did. Certainly we shall be in a position to say how the people in question saw their situation and what they thought it proper to do when so circumstanced. But though this might, for example, make it intelligible that primitive men alarmed by thunder when engaged in promiscuous fornication should each flee to caves accompanied, by a single shy, indocile woman, it will not explain the subsequent consequences of their act. That in these conditions radically new social arrangements would arise is something which the men in question were hardly in a position even to *forsee*; that they *intended* them to arise is excluded by Vico's own description of the situation (it was Providence which did the intending.) Knowledge of their minds, however complete and reliable, will thus not be enough to account for what came about; knowledge of the causal connections between one type of situation and another will be needed as well.

Writers on the problem of historical explanation have long disputed about whether it depends on a special sort of insight into men's minds or requires a knowledge of causal connections broadly similar to that found

[3] "A Note on Vico's Concept of Knowledge" in *Giambattista Vico: An International Symposium*, esp. pp. 375–76.

in the natural sciences. As Vico saw the matter, it requires both. But to put the point in that way is perhaps misleading, since it fails to bring out the intimate way in which the two sorts of knowledge are used together. As already explained, an historical or social investigator begins by trying to get inside the minds of the persons with whom he is concerned; if successful he will see the world as they saw it and understand, as it were from within, why they reacted as they did. Having got that far, he can turn his attention from the agents to the objective situation and explain, on the basis of causal knowledge, why it should have developed as it did quite apart from any particular intentions. But he will not stop at this point. In this kind of context a situation is of interest primarily because of its effects on what men think and do; when situations change, men's minds tend to change as well. Hence the social investigator's next step will be to turn back to the agents and discover their reactions to the changed situation, to find out how they responded to the altered state of affairs as they saw it. What they did will in turn produce effects in the objective world, some of them intended but others unintended; and the investigator will again need to bring causal knowledge to bear to explain what came about. But he will do this only to put himself in a position to look at things once more from the agents' point of view, a process which in due course will take him back to the objective situation. This dialectic can clearly be carried on indefinitely.

I suggest that in working out his ideal eternal history Vico thought along the lines just sketched. He began by supposing that the first men had certain very clear characteristics: they were violent, sensual, incapable of abstract thought, compact of imagination, and exclusively concerned with short-term selfish ends. He then asked what would ensue if men with such natures were to be confronted with a certain unexpected contingency when in a certain situation—the situation and contingency mentioned above. We are supposed to see directly, thanks to our knowledge of "the modifications of our own human mind," that they would have taken thunder to be the expression of anger on the part of beings whose nature was like their own but whose power was much greater; we are further supposed to appreciate that their reactions to the situation would be as Vico says they were. Given that they did react in this way, Vico next asks us to allow that certain very important changes would come about in the objective state of affairs. In place of a condition in which men wandered about the face of the earth leading a purely animal existence, some men would form lasting unions with particular women, and this would lead eventually to the founding of families. More immediately, the changed situation would involve the practice of religion in a rudimentary form, thus introducing into men's minds an all-important factor of which they had previously been quite innocent—fear of the gods. Subsequent developments, explicable by alternate reference to what men thought and did on the one hand, and to the effects of their thoughts and deeds on the other, follow on naturally from these simple beginnings. Hence Vico's entire story about the age of the gods, the age of heroes and the age of men.

One way of putting what has just been described is to say that Vico here works out a priori a model of general social development. I think this is substantially correct, but certain caveats need to be entered. Vico's procedure may be said to be a priori inasmuch as he deals with an abstract case rather than a series of concrete cases (he considers what *would* happen rather than what *did* happen) and insofar as he arrives at his results by thinking instead of consulting fact. But this is not to say that he uses premises which are a priori in the sense of necessarily true. The premise about the nature of primitive men—that they are selfish, violent, imaginative, and so on—is clearly put forward as being a simple truth of fact. Propositions to the effect that one kind of objective situation gives rise to another, which are, as I have claimed, necessary for his argument, cannot be established by attention to the meaning of words and the laws of logic but must to be significant be synthetic. Nor is it true that we know a priori what men whose minds answer a certain description will think or do when placed in an envisaged situation, though we may be able to find the answer by thinking ourselves into the position once we discover what that position is. There can be no question here of adducing a few simple definitions and then discovering what follows from them, despite the curious array of axioms with which Vico begins the *New Science*. What he says about the ideal eternal history may be fanciful, even absurd, but it is certainly intended to have empirical content. And the deduction involved in arriving at it is more like the deduction of the detective, who relies on insight into his subject matter to make connections between facts, than that of the mathematician, who confines himself to what strictly follows according to logical rules.

When Vico is said to be concerned here with a model of general social development, it must not be thought that he supposes that the model will be followed in every conceivable concrete instance. He need not have supposed it would be followed in any, because a model is of its nature abstract, even unreal. To construct a model is to discover what happens when everything works as it should, without regard to extraneous circumstances. The model shows that in ideal conditions—when we have what might be called a pure case of the development in question—things will work out in this or that particular way. But when we turn from the sphere of theory to that of fact, all sorts of factors may be present for which the model makes no allowance but which nevertheless distort or prevent the result which ought to follow if it is accepted. It is important to realize that a model is not necessarily discredited if it fails of empirical application in a particular case. An empirical generalization can be refuted by producing a counter-instance. But a theory like that of the ideal eternal history is not invalidated by the existence of a recalcitrant case, provided that it can be shown that there were special circumstances which prevented things happening as they should.

Vico's own grasp of points like these was naturally imperfect, but in general it seems reasonable to suppose that he took the ideal eternal history to be what its name implies: an account of what happens in ideal conditions. He certainly recognised that not all "nations" have managed in his own words "to accomplish this course of human civil institutions" (§ 1088). Carthage, Capua, and Numantia in the ancient world are given as examples, and in each case Vico adduces special reasons for their failure to conform, though not perhaps very convincing ones (the Carthaginians "were prevented by their native African shrewdness, which was further sharpened by their maritime trade" [*ibid.*]; the Capuans avoided the cycle thanks to their mild climate and the fertility of their country). Similarly, "in the new world the American Indians would now be following this course of human institutions if they had not been discovered by the Europeans" (§ 1095). Vico is quite right in believing that, in principle at least, he can acknowledge such exceptions without destroying his theory. He is perhaps less satisfactory in holding that the ideal eternal history has a perfect instance, that of Rome, which "having none of these obstacles, proceeded with even steps, being ruled by providence through the medium of vulgar wisdom" (§ 1088). Strictly, a social theory of the kind Vico sets out to elaborate cannot have a perfect instance, just because it is and must be *schematic*. But his failure to appreciate this was not in practice of major importance.

It should now be possible to see how the ideal eternal history can have the ambiguous character mentioned above, being from one point of view an hypothesis of a complicated kind, whilst appearing from another as a result asserted to be true. It can be said to be an hypothesis insofar as it proffers a principle, or rather a set of connected principles, for interpreting social data; the final test of its acceptability lies not in itself, but in the light it throws on the data. To say this is to say no more than that the ideal eternal history is a theory which needs to be brought to bear on facts before we can pronounce on its value. But it is not an arbitrary or idle theory, but one which is carefully worked out on the basis of premises which struck its author as being true and by a series of steps which he took to be entirely justified. Because the conclusions of which it consists are the natural if not exactly the logical consequences of premises taken to be true,[4] it is not extravagant to claim truth for them as well. But at best the truth concerned can only be provisional, since the propositions in question have still to be brought to the test of experience. Or to put the point in another way, they take the form of a series of hypothetical statements, to

[4] I am thinking here of what was said above about the kind of deduction involved in social investigation.

the effect that *if* or *where* conditions are so and so, then such and such consequences will ensue. Hypothetical statements can be said to be true, but they are not true in the same way as are categorical statements of fact. As logicians say, they perform a different function in enquiry. They need to be correct, but their correctness is not shown by pointing out some feature of reality to which they correspond precisely. Much of the confusion surrounding Vico's ideal eternal history springs from failure to take account of these elementary points.

Was Vico justified in displaying such confidence in the ideal eternal history? As was pointed out at the beginning, his approach to the explanation of social phenomena is a highly theoretical one. Throughout his work he takes his stand on his theory and asserts boldly that what it says ought to have happened must have happened. Much of the history he puts forward is what is called in one place (heading to § 905) "rational history"; history, that is to say, which rests not so much on evidence as on "philosophical" principles (cf. § 464) or is arrived at by exercising a "metaphysical art of criticism" (§ 348). If challenged on his justifications for following this procedure he would almost certainly have replied by pointing to the successes he had achieved in dealing with particular problems on the basis of the theory, above all in the sphere of Roman history. But he might have argued that, quite apart from its applications, the theory carried conviction when considered in itself and therefore ought to be followed by a rational inquirer. Unlike the speculations of the natural-law theorists, it began with premises about the nature of primitive man which were critically thought out and had every appearance of being reasonable. It recreated the situation and outlook of these men, made their supposed reactions intelligible and made apparent how what it said had to happen might well come about. It then went on to work out details of a progression which was not merely linear but had ramifications in many fields, as book 4 of the *New Science* makes clear. It was a theory which was not just closely argued, but had an admirable internal spread; a theory with wide consequences, offering many opportunities for empirical testing. That Vico should have reposed confidence in a theory of this sort is not at all to his discredit.

This is not, of course, to suggest that the theory is quite free of difficulties. There are obvious problems over its beginning for anyone who cannot accept the Biblical story of the Flood and Vico's postulation of the feral wanderings which followed it. That these are not of significance is suggested by Vico's acceptance of the doctrine of "recourses." According to this a second barbarism ensued after the first cycle was run through, but there was no second Flood or second age of giants. More important is the question of how Vico is supposed to come by the causal propositions which, according to the account given above, are needed to work out the ideal eternal history. Vico argues that, in the ideal circumstances he is examining, social development proceeds through a series of distinct stages, none of which was deliberately planned by the agents concerned; what he has to do is make clear that each stage led on necessarily, or at least naturally, to its successor. His way of doing this is to concentrate on the minds of the agents and show that, given certain pressures of a mainly institutional kind, men will modify their behavior in a definite manner, with the result that new institutions develop. If this is correct, the causal propositions involved will be arrived at not by noting regularities, but through the medium of a special sort of thought-experiment which, it is argued, each of us is in principle able to perform. That this is possible, if indeed it is, would depend on the items here connected being of a particular kind: they could not be Humean events but must have to do with human behavior and human responses.[5] That Vico himself had any clear perception of this seems unlikely, but it is at least possible that he was thinking of something like it when he spoke of the importance for the new science of knowledge of "the modifications of our own human mind."

I end this section of my paper with two parenthetical remarks. The first concerns Vico's originality in regard to the new science. Vico writes as if he had found nothing in the works of his predecessors which anticipated what he was after, though he sometimes adds generously that if only philosophers and philologians had joined forces they might have done so (§ 140). The philosophers he considers in this connection are Grotius, Selden, and Pufendorf, the three natural-law theorists, together with Thomas Hobbes; the philologians presumably include Polybius and Tacitus. It is curious that Vico did not think in this connection of another author he greatly admired, namely Plato. In books 8 and 9 of the *Republic* Plato produced an account of the decline of the soul and the state through a series of distinct stages; some have taken him to be attempting a form of history here, others to be engaged in constructing a philosophy of history. I argued in a paper published some years ago,[6] that what he says here should be taken neither as straight history nor as philosophy of history but as sociological or political theory written up in narrative form. Plato is concerned to investigate what happens in conditions which may, in fact, never be actual; the stages he traces are stages in an ideal progression, which would develop and continue along the lines sketched if everything went as it should. Plato begins as Vico does with certain assumptions about the springs of human action, and though he has little sense of historical development, he shows himself very much alive to the way in which men's minds and behavior can change in response to changed

[5] Our earlier assertion that Vico appealed both to empathetic understanding and to knowledge of causal connections of a broadly scientific type needs amendment if this point is accepted. The causal propositions necessary for constructing the ideal eternal history do not link events which are totally loose and separate. But equally they do not link situations whose connections with one another are purely conceptual. See below on von Wright.

[6] "Plato and the Philosophy of History," *History and Theory* 2 (1962): 3–16.

environmental conditions. It would not be entirely extravagant to credit him with the same insight as Vico into the joint importance of personal and institutional factors in accounting for historical change. His work in this area is less significant than Vico's, not only because it is on a much smaller scale but also because it takes its start not from primitive men but from philosopher kings; there is, further, no attempt in Plato's case to show that the theory has concrete application. But despite these differences Plato and Vico are engaged in the same kind of inquiry, and the only reason I can suggest for Vico's failure to see this is that Plato's intentions in this part of his work were persistently misunderstood by critics from Aristotle onwards.[7]

My second remark concerns the logical structure of the explanations of social change which Vico puts forward. In chapter 4 of his *Explanation and Understanding*,[8] G. H. von Wright discusses what he calls "quasi-causal explanations in history" and analyzes their logic. He argues that when historians claim that, for example, the murder of the Austrian archduke at Sarajevo caused the outbreak of the first world war they first of all think of certain agents with particular aims and ambitions in certain situations and then consider what happens when a change is introduced into such a situation. A changed situation calls for a fresh response, which will in turn change the situation of the parties involved and probably evoke a fresh response from them. Von Wright wants to say that the connection of cause and effect in a case like this is made through a series of practical inferences. Situations give rise to one another by figuring in the "motivation background" for the actions of particular agents, and because this is so, knowledge of causal *laws* connecting this type of situation with that is not required. Individual connections are made intelligible without being purely conceptual. It seems to me that this corresponds pretty closely to Vico's actual practice in the *New Science*. It has the great merit of showing how men's thoughts on the one hand and situations as reflected in men's thoughts on the other combine to determine what happens in history.

I turn now to a different subject, that of how the ideal eternal history is to be tested. Vico, as we have seen, says that the new science demands collaboration between philosophy and philology. Philosophy needs to be given "certainty," which it can do by appealing to the philologians; philology needs to be given the "sanction of truth," which it can get from the reasoning of philosophers. The obvious interpretation of this is that philosophy provides theories, and philology facts. Theories need to be tested by being brought to bear on facts; facts need to be made intelligible

[7] Aristotle (*Politics*, V, 12) took Plato to be putting forward a series of empirical generalizations and then advanced counter-examples to refute him. See my article, "Plato and the Philosophy of History," pp. 7f.

[8] London: Routledge and Kegan Paul, 1971, pp. 139–43.

in the light of appropriate theories. Broadly, this must be what Vico means to say. But there are difficulties about his saying it.

First, the setting up of the ideal eternal history, that is, the elaboration of the theory to be tested, requires the acceptance as true of a number of factual propositions. That there was a universal flood, that after it men wandered over the earth behaving like beasts, that some of them were frightened by thunder when engaged in fornication are among these. If Vico's theory is to be defensible as it stands, it must be possible for propositions of this kind to be known to be true. But it is not clear how Vico provides for this, in view of his association of truth with reasoned knowledge, that is, with fact backed up by philosophy.

Second, the ideal eternal history cannot be tested except against facts which are independent. But where is Vico to find such facts? The answer we should expect him to give is in philology, among the exponents of which he includes "all the grammarians, historians, critics, who have occupied themselves with the study of the languages and deeds of peoples: both at home, as in customs and laws, and abroad, as in their wars, peaces, alliances, travels and commerce" (§ 139). The facts of philology are the facts of history, the facts of language, and the facts of law, among other things. But Vico himself has emphasized from the first the lack of solidity in such supposed facts. There *are* facts in these areas, but in order to discover them we must sort out appearances according to principles, principles which are provided by the ideal eternal history itself. It would be begging the question to test the ideal eternal history only against such facts, since they are clearly not independent of it.

Can we get over the problem by contrasting facts with evidence and making the latter the independent something to which successful theory must conform? We might try to develop an argument to this effect on the following lines. People alive today tell certain stories of the past, make certain memory claims about it, engage in certain ceremonies, follow certain procedures in their dealings one with another, use certain formulas on particular occasions, and use words with certain meanings. These may be described as *phenomena*, or *appearances*. Historians claim to make sense of such phenomena by revealing what lies behind them, that is, by producing true statements about the past. The test of the truth of an historical statement is in its ability to do justice, not just to selected phenomena, but to each and every phenomenon relevant to it. And the truth of a high-level historical or social theory such as Vico's would also be shown in whether or not it covered the appearances. To test it properly we should have to look for recalcitrant data in a wide variety of spheres and satisfy ourselves that the theory could deal with them adequately. The existence of an unexplained phenomenon here and there would not in itself refute the theory, though it might weaken confidence in it. The existence of many such phenomena in many different areas would make it necessary to abandon the theory altogether.

In general, Vico proceeds in the *New Science* as if he thought on these lines, with one significant difference. He starts out by assuming the existence of a body of phenomena in the sense described, insofar as he acknowledges historical traditions, popular mythologies, legal procedures, linguistic practices, and other similar things. And he certainly claims it as a major merit of his theory that it can do justice to such phenomena: it can explain why they are what they are and in so doing can transform itself from abstract speculation into concrete truth. Vico is tireless in his search for evidence on which to bring his theory to bear; his ingenuity in finding such evidence in hitherto unexplored quarters is quite remarkable. But it has to be admitted that he looks all the time for material which will *confirm* his theory or show that it *has application*. He shows little or no sense of the need to seek out evidence which apparently conflicts with what the theory requires, in order to test its ability to handle unfavorable material. For all his admiration for Bacon, he does not really know about the force of the negative instance.[9]

To claim genuine intellectual respectability for the ideal eternal history a modern defender of Vico would have to show that it could meet this further requirement. But to put the theory on a fully sound basis it might be necessary to introduce more fundamental alterations in Vico's theory of knowledge. His distinction between philosophy and philology runs parallel to the traditional philosophical antithesis of knowledge and belief. Philosophy purveys rational but abstract knowledge; philology "observes that of which human choice is author, whence comes consciousness of the certain" (§ 138). For concrete knowledge the two need to be combined, the unargued beliefs of the philologians getting grounds in the reasonings of the philosophers. The trouble about this, as we have already seen, is that it leaves no room for what might be called free facts, items of *knowledge* which are independent of theory and can hence be used to test theory. In practice Vico behaves as if he knew that many perceptual and even some memory statements are true (think, for example, of what he says about the behavior of children and deaf mutes), and yet does not explain how they can be. If he replied that he only took them to be certain, in effect as matters of belief, that would not do, since a proposition taken to be certain may very well be false. Vico at least needs to provide for the possibility of perceptual and memory knowledge. He may even have to allow that historical knowledge is possible apart from theory, since he appeals to some seemingly historical propositions in setting up his theory ("that there was a Flood") and to others in applying it ("that there was a second barbarism"). How far such concessions would damage his overall position is a question which cannot be raised now.

[9] *Novum Organum*, I, 46.

Peter Hughes

CREATIVITY AND HISTORY IN VICO AND HIS CONTEMPORARIES

In offering his tragedy *Bajazet* to a civilized audience of *honnêtes gens*, Racine excused the nearness of its events in time by pointing out their exotic distance in place, in the seraglio of the Turkish sultan at Constantinople. The outlandish and the antique are convertible: "Distance of country compensates in some sort for nearness of time; for people do not distinguish between that which is, if I may venture to say so, a thousand years, and that which is a thousand miles away from them."[1] This theatrical discovery that distant places and the distant past merge in our imagination was to become, in the generations that followed Racine, above all in the generation of Vico, Swift, and Montesquieu, the basis of a much greater discovery. As Vico discovered in his *Scienza nuova*, reality is historical, concrete, and aesthetic; and to explore that reality we must embark on an imaginary voyage whose limits and subject are the varieties of human experience.

These new human studies, or *sciences humaines*, which originate in Vico and his contemporaries, are the most complete rejection of the angelic and geometric sciences of Leibniz and Descartes.[2] They turn instead toward what Vico called the "world of nations" to create rivals for the sciences that Leibniz and Newton, whom Vico called "the two foremost minds of our age" (§ 347),[3] had derived from the world of matter. And in so doing they led a new movement; for the Enlightenment is above all the quest for sciences of human society analogous to those attained in the cosmos of mathematics and physics. In arguing here that Vico, Swift, and Montesquieu all took part in this quest, I am not reviving false (and in the end pointless) hopes of direct or biographical connections between Vico and his

[1] "L'éloignement des pays répare en quelque sorte la trope grande proximité des temps. Car le peuple ne met guere de différence entre ce qui est, si j'ose ainsi parler, à mille ans de lui, et de ce qui est à mille lieues" [Seconde] Préface, in *Oeuvres complètes*, ed. Raymond Picard, Bibliothèque de la Pleiade, vol. 2, pp. 530–31.

[2] H. P. Rickman, "Vico and Dilthey's Methodology of the Human Studies," *Giambattista Vico: An International Symposium*, pp. 447–56. Rickman's *Understanding and the Human Studies* (London, 1967) is both a valuable critique of modern failures to find a better model for human studies (both the arts and social sciences) than that provided by the physical sciences and a bold proposal of such a model.

[3] All citations in the text preceded by a paragraph sign (§) are to the *New Science*. Vico's phrase in the paragraph cited here is "questo mondo di nazioni."

contemporaries. I intend to show instead how and why the works of these three writers, of similar educations and of the same generation, present so many affinities in method, scope, and style. And in its longer aim this essay is another short step toward the liberation of literary studies from Aristotelian mimesis and Kantian aesthetics, a step toward their renewal through cultural and linguistic history. By considering Swift's *Gulliver's Travels* together with Vico's *Scienza nuova* and Montesquieu's *De l'Esprit des lois*, I wish to suggest that what makes them all literature is the synoptic irony they have in common, and not any trivial distinction between fiction and nonfiction. Literature, perceived for the first time not as fiction but rather as figurative history, is at once the map and compass of their search.

Every step of this quest was difficult; at every uphill step into the past and the far-off world of nations Vico and his contemporaries had to breath the thin air of Cartesian abstraction. Leibniz had tried to disprove the independent reality of space and time.[4] Hobbes, who disparaged space as *phantasma existentis*, attacked the shadows of the imagination. In Buckingham's verses:

While in dark ignorance we lay, afraid
Of fancies, ghosts, and every empty shade;
Great Hobbes appear'd, and by plain Reason's light
Put such fantastick forms to shameful flight.[5]

Descartes, as Collingwood has pointed out, "did not believe history to be, strictly speaking, a branch of knowledge at all,"[6] and he denounced as two faces of the same idol the literature and history that formed the basis of his Jesuit schooling. Descartes admits the charms of his human studies, but like many other thinkers of his age, he puts them behind him as childish things.

I was brought up from childhood on letters, and, because I had been led to believe that by this means one could acquire clear and positive knowledge of everything useful in life, I was extremely anxious to learn them. But, as soon as I had completed this whole course of study, at the end of which it is usual to be received into the ranks of the learned, I completely changed my opinion.[7]

Even more significantly, he anticipates Racine's connection between space and time only to condemn it:

. . . I thought I had already given enough time to languages, and even also to the reading of the Ancients, to their histories and fables. For to converse with

[4] *The Monadology and other Philosophical Writings*, trans. Robert Latta (London, 1898), esp. pp. 101–3.

[5] John Sheffield, Duke of Buckinghamshire, "On Mr. Hobbes and his Writings," in *The Works of the English Poets*, ed. Alexander Chalmers, 21 vols. (London, 1810), vol. 10, p. 97.

[6] *The Idea of History*, Oxford Galaxy edition (New York, 1956), p. 59.

[7] *Discourse on Method and other Writings*, trans. F. E. Sutcliffe, Penguin edition (Harmondsworth, 1968), pp. 29–30.

those of other centuries is almost the same as to travel. . . . But when one spends too much time travelling, one becomes eventually a stranger in one's own country; and when one is too interested in what went on in past centuries, one usually remains extremely ignorant of what is happening in this century.[8]

Against all of these Cartesian views, Vico asserts the value of histories of our humanity and joins Montesquieu in attempting through them the "conquest of Cartesianism."[9] He finds in them the revolutionary principle that we can know only what we have made. And this principle, which defends the claims of consciousness (*coscienza*) against those of knowledge (*scienza*),[10] is a principle discovered in antiquity itself:

. . . in the night of thick darkness enveloping the earliest antiquity, so remote from ourselves, there shines the eternal and never failing light of a truth beyond all question: that the world of civil society has certainly been made by men, and that its principles are therefore to be found within the modifications of our own human mind. Whoever reflects on this cannot but marvel that the philosophers should have bent all their energies to the study of the world of nature, which, since God made it, He alone knows; and that they should have neglected the study of the world of nations, or civil world, which, since men have made it, men could come to know.[11]

Swift's hostility to Descartes is obvious in the *Battle of the Books* and elsewhere; with Hobbes and Gassendi he leads the modern bowmen in that battle, in which he is slain by Aristotle and swept away "into his own Vortex."[12] And Montesquieu's entire approach opposes Cartesian method: his account of the three forms of government in *De l'Esprit des lois*—republic, monarchy, and despotism—depends on such historical realities as Venice, France, and Turkey, not on Cartesian deductions from prior definitions. When he speaks of republics he observes, "I have said that the nature of a republican government consists in this, that the people in a body, *or certain families*, have the sovereign power. . . ."[13] That phrase

[8] *Ibid.*

[9] See Yvon Belaval, "Anti-Cartesianism," in *Giambattista Vico: An International Symposium*, pp. 77–91, and Werner Stark, *Montesquieu: Pioneer in the Sociology of Knowledge* (Toronto, 1961), pp. 1–24.

[10] *New Science*, § 137: "Men who do not know what is true of things take care to hold fast to what is certain, so that, if they cannot satisfy their intellects by knowledge (*scienza*), their wills at least may rest on consciousness (*coscienza*)."

[11] *Ibid.*, § 331. This passage also implies the necessity for an historical approach, for Vico is here arguing that our knowledge must begin where its subject begins: in remote antiquity.

[12] *The Prose Writings of Jonathan Swift*, ed. Herbert Davis and Irvin Ehrenpreis, 14 vols. (Oxford, 1939–68), vol. 1, pp. 152, 156. All subsequent volume and page references to Swift's prose works are keyed to this edition.

[13] "J'ai dit que la nature du gouvernement républicain est que le peuple en corps, ou de certaines familles, y aient la souveraine puissance," *Oeuvres complètes*, ed. Roger Caillois, Bibliothèque de la Pléiade, 2 vols. (Paris, 1949–51), vol. 2, pp. 251. References throughout are to this edition.

"or certain families" reflects the realities of power in Genoa, or Venice, or Holland, not the abstract notion of a republic in Cartesian theory. And while Swift mocks the geometric contortions of natural shapes in Laputa—"In the first Course, there was a shoulder of Mutton, cut into an Aequilateral Triangle. . . . The second Course was two Ducks, trussed up in the Form of Fiddles. . ." (XI, 145)—Montesquieu attacks such Cartesian aesthetics both in principle—"The principles of geometry are very true; but if one were to apply them to matters of taste, one would rob reason itself of its reasonableness" (II, 1165)—and in practice—"Excessive regularity is sometimes, and indeed often, disagreeable. There is nothing so beautiful as the sky; yet it is covered with stars without order. The houses and gardens around Paris have . . . the fault of being too much alike: they are perpetual copies of Le Nôtre. . ." (I, 1265).

Against this chaos of forms, this discord of the spheres in which words and natural shapes are regimented and distorted by geometry and music, Vico and his contemporaries advance the languages of the world of nations, the languages of literature and history. Vico perceived that these languages, through which the antique and exotic were to be expressed, were at once a means of expression and an object of knowledge. Swift, as we learn in his *Proposal for Correcting, Improving and Ascertaining the English Tongue,* wanted to pacify the warring dialects within English culture, what he called the "Enthusiastick Jargon" of "Fanatick Times," and having done that, to stabilize "the perpetual Variations of our Speech" (IV, 3-21). Montesquieu, even though he gloried in the bizarre variety of customs and laws revealed by his travels, reading, and observation, remained convinced that his aim was "to describe the world in a unique language, but a language neither technical, quantitative, nor mathematical: in the reasonable language of *honnêtes gens.*"[14] Swift's satirical treatment of proposals for the abolition of words in Gulliver's "Third Voyage"; and Montesquieu's trust that writing was the most trustworthy witness to the world of nations[15] are both signs of confidence in a world of words. But just as Newton showed that apparently white light can be analyzed into colors that are not "Qualifications of Light" but rather "original and connate properties,"[16] Vico discovered that even the most neutral and abstract language can be analyzed into metaphorical and concrete dialects.

Vico's "eternal and never failing light," which shines out of "the night of thick darkness enveloping the earliest antiquity," can be analyzed into the prismic flames of bacchanalia, funeral pyres, and holocausts. And those who voyage outward rather than backward may find themselves, like Vico among the Olympian gods, Montesquieu among the despotic Japanese, or

[14] Jean Starobinski, *Montesquieu par lui-même* (Paris, n.d.), p. 22.

[15] "L'écriture est un témoin qui est difficilement corrompu" (II, 862).

[16] In his letter communicated to the Royal Society, 6 February 1672, printed in *Philosophical Transactions of the Royal Society,* vol. 80.

Swift among the Yahoos, suddenly cast into the heart of darkness. In turning back to the age of the pagan gods, Vico is appalled and yet fascinated by their promiscuity, in much the same way as Montesquieu is by the sexual displays of the distant Chinese and Swift by that of his Yahoos:

> . . . Orpheus then founds the humanity of Greece on the examples of an adulterous Jove, a Juno who is the mortal enemy of the virtues of the Herculeses, a chaste Diana who solicits the sleeping Endymion at night, an Apollo who gives oracular responses and pursues to the point of death modest maiden Daphnes, a Mars who, as if it were not enough for the gods to commit adultery on earth, carries it even into the sea with Venus. Nor is this unrestrained licentiousness of the gods satisfied by forbidden intercourse with women: Jove burns with wicked love for Ganymede; indeed this lust reaches the point of bestiality and Jove, transformed into a swan, lies with Leda (§ 80).

The subjects raised by these explorations of the world of nations, the words that must be used, violate the purity of any well-bred style. And the horror of the past cannot be concealed by exalting it to tragic or sublime heights. The rhetorics through which that might have been done had been utterly discredited. The concision of Swift, the *style coupé* of Montesquieu, and the sardonic idiom of Vico are negations of tragic grandeur and fanatical belief.[17] They are anti-heroic and sceptical dialects, devised to cope with the infamy that lay so close to the surface of ancient grandeur and to question the lies of travelers back from distant parts. Whether its subject is long-past or far-off, the style of the new rhetoric always opposes what we see in the frontispiece to Faulkner's 1735 edition of *Gulliver's Travels*: the insolent pride, the projector's complacent gaze and smile, and below it all, the mocking Horatian caption: *splendide mendax*. And the more closely this style grapples with its dangerous subjects, the more it risks being subverted by what it opposes, corrupted by grandeur, taken in by lies, turned itself into a fable or fiction. Irony and truth are the only means by which such a style can save itself from fabulous credulity.

There were others in the eighteenth century who perceived what Vico seized upon. As Geoffrey Hartman has pointed out, many felt poignantly a gap between what Collins described as their false themes and their gentle minds, between themes of ancient and modern romance and their own civilized awareness, between the language of the tribe and the language of *la cour et la ville*.[18] The lyric poets, except those content to apply to themselves Voltaire's defense of what La Chaussée called the language of the

[17] For valuable discussions of the rhetorical aspects of Swift, Montesquieu, and Vico, see Martin Price, *Swift's Rhetorical Art* (New Haven, 1953), pp. 1–35; Peter France, *Rhetoric and Truth in France* (Oxford, 1972), pp. 3–33, 69–111; Antonino Pagliaro, "Lingua e poesia secondo Vico," *Altri saggi di critica semantica* (Messina and Florence, 1961), pp. 299–444.

[18] "False Themes and Gentle Minds," in *Beyond Formalism* (New Haven, 1970), pp. 283–97.

gods,[19] swung toward the internalizing of romance that triumphed in later romantic poetry.

But doubts about fiction and romance had sunk in too deeply. Vico and Montesquieu abandoned lyric poetry and fiction, with which their writing careers had begun, and Swift purged his prose and verse of both fiction and romance. They had come to suspect that fiction could only survive by consuming the truth of experience and that romance could only flourish in an oppressively feudal culture. Montesquieu saw quite clearly that even the greatest theme of romance, the Genesis myth of *Paradise Lost* (a theme Milton chose after long considering an Arthurian subject), required the subversion of religion by the *splendide mendax* of fiction: "Fictions are so much of the essence of the epic poem that Milton's, based on the Christian religion, only began to be admired in England after Religion there passed for a fiction" (I, 1224). Vico and his contemporaries were independently engaged in an attempt to turn religion and literature, laws and customs, into objects of knowledge. They grasped the need to study objectively and to transform into new sciences the privileged moral fictions of pagan, Christian, and feudal myth.

The one privileged fiction Vico rightly felt it would be impious and dangerous to examine objectively was that of sacred or providential history, which is why the *Scienza nuova* explicitly limits its scope to the world and history of the Gentile nations, from whom he excludes the covenanted nations of Israel and the people of God who form the Christian Church. Vico's prudence is understandable. Galileo had paid for the intrusion of his discoveries into Biblical cosmology; the Inquisition, which was active in Naples, had earlier condemned many of Vico's friends. But Montesquieu, who had seen something of this Neapolitan culture during his visit there in 1729, had less to fear. He once noted as a book he wanted to write "a civil history of the kingdom of France, as Giannone has written the civil history of the kingdom of Naples" (I, 1256). In that civil history, which like so much of the historical writing of the Enlightenment in Italy, France, and England was aimed at reform,[20] Giannone separated the two cities of God and man and then ironically showed how collusively they were interwoven. Another of its readers was Gibbon, who found in it "the use of irony and criticism on subjects of Ecclesiastical gravity."[21]

In order to free history from credulity and superstition, Vico freed literature from fiction. Paul Ricoeur has pointed out that Cartesian doubts about material reality lead directly to the even more radical doubts of

[19] See David Williams, "Voltaire and the Language of the Gods," *Studies on Voltaire and the Eighteenth Century* 62 (1968): 57–81.

[20] See the valuable essay by Franco Venturi, "History and Reform in the Middle of the Eighteenth Century," in *The Diversity of History: Essays in Honour of Sir Herbert Butterfield*, ed. J. H. Elliott and J. G. Koenigsberger (London, 1970), pp. 223–44.

[21] *Autobiographies*, ed. John Murray (London, 1896), p. 235.

Marx and Freud: "After doubt about things, we have entered into doubt about consciousness itself."[22] In renouncing Descartes and all his doubts, Vico insisted upon the bedrock validity of consciousness throughout the world of nations, even among the most unlearned or uncertain: the will stood firmly founded on *coscienza* even when *scienza* was utterly lacking (§ 137 and n. 9 above). Vico held with Goethe that man is the first speech that Nature holds with God; a dialogue in which consciousness is expressed through language, and language through poetry. What Vico calls the poetical characters of primitive thought are in fact metaphors that consciousness offers as objective correlatives for its perception of reality.

As our powers of abstraction and transference increase through historical experience, the linguistic bond between name and nature changes into an historical bond between event and structure. The understanding of history therefore depends upon an understanding of language, since there is in fact no theoretical distinction between these two ways of knowing. Myths are revealed to be historical metaphors, and fictions give way to irony and allusion as the means by which the human imagination recreates and knows its history. As Stuart Hampshire has put it, "Philology is the supreme historical science."[23] It also implies that both historical and literary studies begin and end in hermeneutics. As Dilthey perceived, all of these studies interpret reality through written memorials. Paul de Man has gone further, arguing that "what we call literary interpretation—provided only that it is good interpretation—is in fact literary history . . . the bases of historical knowledge are not empirical facts but written texts, even if these texts masquerade in the guise of wars or revolutions."[24]

The converse of this suggestion becomes clearer if we recall that until the end of the eighteenth century the boundaries of literature extended far beyond mimetic fiction to include many more kinds of written texts than we would include today. In the age of Vico literature was thought to consist of all written texts with a claim to permanence arising from their expressive quality. In that age and in ours, fiction may be no more than what Earl Miner has called a symptom of literature;[25] fictive structures may be nothing more than historical events in need of interpretation. Vico's prolonged study of Homer in the *New Science*, for example, is an attempt to fill that need. But if the fictional symptom turns epidemic, it may become necessary to quarantine fiction, to cast out those modes of expres-

[22] "Après le doute sur la chose, nous sommes entrés dans le doute sur la conscience," *De l'Interprétation: essai sur Freud* (Paris, 1965), p. 41. See also his essay "Le Conscient et l'inconscient," in *Le Conflit des interprétations: essais d'herméneutique* (Paris, 1969), pp. 101–21.

[23] "Vico and the Contemporary Philosophy of Language," in *Giambattista Vico: An International Symposium*, p. 478.

[24] "Literary History and Literary Modernity," *Daedalus* (May 1970), p. 403.

[25] "Literary Diaries and the Boundaries of Literature," *Yearbook of Comparative and General Literature* 21 (1972): 46–51.

sion characterized by vision or fictional mimesis. In one of the most gnomic of his *Pensées* Montesquieu seems to be doing just that: "In this century of ours," he mutters, "no more Greek, no more verse, no more sermons"—("*Dans ce siècle-ci, plus de grec, plus de vers, plus de sermons*") (I, 1232).

From the standpoint of these new sciences of enlightenment, a literary work is a figurative history. On one obvious level this description suggests a work that *continues*, that has a noticeable extension in time. And that may explain why brief, lyric, and iconic literary modes fell out of favor (some of them into oblivion) during the first half of the eighteenth century. It also implies a mode of writing whose aim is discovery rather than invention. The distinction between finding or unearthing and making up or creating out of nothing is a major difference between these new human sciences of the Ancients and the old mathematical sciences of the Moderns. Chosen models for narrative, furthermore, show how widespread the aesthetic reciprocity between time and space had become in the half-century since Racine proposed it, how various and remote the figurative meaning of discovery could be. Choosing at random from English literature alone, we might mention some titles that name some of these models: Defoe's *Journal of the Plague Year*, Smollet's *Expedition of Humphrey Clinker*, Fielding's *History of Tom Jones*, Goldsmith's *Chinese Letters*; and we might recall Swift's full title: *Travels into Several Remote Nations of the World*.

We shall return to the larger implications of these "models," but let us note for now that on the smallest and most exact scale of narrative structures, the new sciences of man had to destroy the balanced equations between words and things demanded by Descartes, Locke, and the Royal Society. The demand that there be a thing for every word and a word for every thing could only be satisfied in a world without remote time or space, a world of discourse that, as we know from Swift's satires, speaks only in the present tense, falls silent about the past, and raves about the future. Vico's discovery that the process of linguistic change is from the concrete to the abstract implies on the contrary that all discourse in civil societies will be characterized by an excess of words over things.[26] This excess, which it is the task of linguistic history to consider, is increased by learning, by which we can recover past *metaphorical* links between words and things through genetic studies of metaphor and etymology. It follows, moreover, that if philology is the "supreme historical science," the first science is mythology: ". . . the first science to be learned should be mythology or the interpretation of fables; for, as we shall see, all the histories of the gentiles have their beginnings in fables, which were the first histories of the gentile nations" (§ 51). Myths themselves are therefore historical

[26] A discovery attributed to him by even the most limiting appraisals of his achievement: See Robert A. Hall, Jr., "G. B. Vico and Linguistic Theory," *Italica* 18 (1941): 145–54.

metaphors, and the displacement of myths into literary fictions—a problematic process in Northrop Frye's latter-day new science of literary criticism[27]—is in Vichian terms the growth of figurative histories through changing contexts for metaphor. The increasingly civil and vicarious nature of these contexts, as each culture in turn says with Prufrock "I am not Prince Hamlet, nor was meant to be," alters metaphor into simile, simile into allusion, allusion into perspective, and perspective into delusion, so that in any literate and enlightened society metaphor is likely to be a mistake.[28] Once such histories are perceived as poetic wisdom, all of the expressive texts and memorials of past and distant societies aspire toward the status of literature: laws, constitutions, meditations, libels, prayers, voyages, and above all histories themselves; for history increasingly becomes both the dancer and the dance, the way of knowing and the object of knowledge.

The convergence of language, literature, and history becomes clearest in the approach of the new scientists to classical antiquity. Vico, Swift, and Montesquieu all follow Bacon in recognizing the historical completeness of Greek and Roman culture: ". . . antiquity is like fame, *caput inter nubila condit*, her head is muffled from our sight. For the History of the Exemplar States [of Greece and Rome], it is extant in good perfection" (*Advancement of Learning*, II, ii, 7). The exemplary character of that history for Bacon and his eighteenth-century followers (and he was one of Vico's four great authors) was however radically different from its status during the Renaissance. On both sides of the Alps, Renaissance humanists sought in classical culture exact rules, standards, and icons; their ideal was to write exactly like Cicero or Virgil. To differ from the ideal was to fail; to surpass it was inconceivable. But for Vico and his contemporaries the "exemplar" offered by antiquity was not a rule or standard to be mimicked. It was rather a model to be employed in the projection of realities or the solution of problems. On a stylistic level, we need only think of what Erasmus did for Cicero, as opposed to what Pope did to Horace, to grasp the difference: it is the difference between copying and re-imagining.

In his remarkable book *The Structure of Scientific Revolutions*, Thomas Kuhn uses these very terms—"exemplars" and "models"—in ways that suggest a deep affinity between the new sciences of the eighteenth century and scientific revolutions in other ages. After mentioning Michael Polanyi's concept of "tacit knowledge" (a highly Vichian notion in its merging of knowing and making), Kuhn clarifies his general theory that scientific

[27] "Myth, Fiction, and Displacement," in *Fables of Identity* (New York, 1963), pp. 21–38.

[28] The stages of this history of metaphor can be traced, in order if not in perfect agreement, through the opening chapter of Bruno Snell's *The Discovery of the Mind* (Cambridge, Mass., 1953); Claudio Guillén's *Literature as System* (Princeton, 1970), pp. 365–71; and Walker Percy's remarkable essay "Metaphor as Mistake," *Sewanee Review* 66 (1958): 79–99.

change is discontinuous, socially influenced, and unaffected by laws and rules by making the following distinction:

When I speak of knowledge embedded in shared exemplars, I am not referring to a mode of knowing that is less systematic or less analyzable than knowledge embedded in rules, laws, or criteria of identification. Instead I have in mind a manner of knowing which is misconstrued if reconstructed in terms of rules that are first abstracted from exemplars and thereafter function in their stead.[29]

This is an excellent analogy to Vico's methodology and to his radically historical use of models rather than rules. The new sciences tend in fact to collapse rules into models. In Montesquieu, laws and governments are continually criticized, revalued, and denounced through the concrete realities they entail; Vico is continually tracing back to human activities and conflicts the apparently stable and serene maxims and customs of Roman law and religion; and Swift satirically demolishes the proud certainties of European man by confronting them with the pigmy, gigantic, futuristic, and reductive models from which those certainties were derived.

Kuhn's emphasis on shared exemplars or paradigms (or "concrete achievements") most closely resembles the sense shared by Vico and his contemporaries that the exemplary history of classical antiquity is a record of social struggle manifested in language, art, and myth.[30] It is I think revealing that Swift, in *A Discourse of the Contests and Dissentions between the Nobles and the Commons in Athens and Rome, with the Consequences they had upon both those States*, and Montesquieu, in his *Considérations sur les causes de la grandeur des Romains et de leur décadence*, provide what their titles promise: unillusioned recreations, satirical on the one hand, reflective on the other, of the class struggles that Vico analyzed so boldly in his genetic study of Roman history (esp. §§ 599–665). Their Rome was in no sense the *Roma aeterna* of the humanists. It was instead a disturbing and revolutionary paradigm for their own societies, a cyclic irony rather than a focus for nostalgia. Vico interprets the written texts of this Roman history through a series of comparative readings in other distant societies, both ancient and primitive. As he does so, he demolishes the dream of a golden age, replacing it instead with a painful struggle toward civility (§§ 517–19), a continuing clash of social groups that manifests itself in the styles and metaphors of their languages and literatures.

It is in this clash of linguistic levels that literature and history become one. Through the linguistic theories of Benjamin Lee Whorf we have become accustomed to the thesis that the structure of language decides the

[29] 2d ed. (Chicago, 1970), esp. "Postscript," pp. 174–210. The quotation is from p. 192.

[30] These three activities, as Cassirer has pointed out, are a "triad" that constitute according to Vico "the true unity of human culture." *The Philosophy of Symbolic Forms*, trans. Ralph Mannheim, 3 vols. (New Haven, 1953–57), vol. 2, p. 3.

structure of reality. This is a thesis that Vico consciously accepts in the *Scienza nuova,* that Swift presents ironically in the crazed jargons of *A Tale of a Tub,* that Montesquieu implies both in his view of literary language and in his own *style coupé.* But we need to consider a more complex thesis if we are to interpret their major works *as they are experienced by the reader.* In reading each of these works, the rhetoric of enlightenment[31] increasingly clashes with the enormities, absurdities, and extremes they relate. The author's irony becomes increasingly necessary. We need to hear Vico's summing-up of an age of cannibalism: "Such a mild, benign, sober, decent, and well-behaved time it was!" (§ 517); and yet our involvement in the horror outweighs our detachment through irony. We join in the Brobdingnagian king's crushing dismissal of Gulliver's countrymen as "the most pernicious Race of little odious Vermin that Nature ever suffered to crawl upon the Surface of the Earth" (XI, 116), and yet we are closely related to those vermin and to their exploits. We note the ironic request made by Montesquieu, "I beg that no one take offense at what I have said; I follow all the histories" (II, 255), and yet we notice that "all the histories" justify in the passage that follows a scorching attack on courtiers. That attack, like similar ones in Vico and Swift, is written in the form of a catalog or avalanche of accusations: candor assaults irony at every turn in the literature of the new sciences. The history is at war with the historian, and the reader is caught between them.

This conflict may be the source of both the thesis and the explanation we seek. We have already seen that the exemplary history of each of these three works develops through clashes between opposed social groups: nobles against populace, Japanese against Europeans, Romans against barbarians, Yahoos against Houyhnhnms, heroes against the gods. I suggest that if we examine their figurative and rhetorical aspects we will discover that these conflicts are reflected in continually shifting and opposed stylistic levels. What Whorf describes as a structure may be more accurately described in Benveniste's terms as a series of events, of changes in levels of expression and usage.[32]

All of these works are characterized by the author's intrusion into the work, by his mutiny against his narrative or self-liberation from barbarism. An excellent example occurs in the *Scienza nuova*'s account of the origins of satire. This starts off on the well-trodden etymological ground that the satyr play was a satire and a primitive form of tragedy. But it shifts suddenly, first into the present, into the Italian countryside, then just as suddenly back into the pagan past:

And satire kept this eternal property with which it was born: that of expressing invective and insult; for the peasants, thus roughly masked and riding in the

[31] I am indebted for this phrase and for an excellent discussion of the rhetorical aspects of my subject to Peter France, *Rhetoric and Truth in France,* pp. 68–96.

[32] Émile Benveniste, *Problèmes de linguistique générale* (Paris, 1966), pp. 119–31.

carts in which they carried the grapes, had the license—as the grape-pickers still have in our happy Campania (once called the dwelling of Bacchus)—of hurling abuse at their betters (§ 910).

In a note on this passage, Fausto Nicolini suggests that this account is a probable allusion to the false Neapolitan legend devised to explain the mask of Pulcinella. The legend may have been false, but Vico's impulsive linking of masks, satire, and social upheaval is an interpretive truth. Masquerades and charivaris have historically been tinged with rebellion; for they often symbolize both the desire to turn the world upside down and the attempt to make it happen.[33] Satire itself has from its origins had overtones of malediction and revolt.[34] Montesquieu and Swift join Vico in associating satires and rebellion with the anarchic world of forests and Yahoos that lies beyond the city limits of the civil world.

Swift extends this analogy between remote histories and conflicting dialects throughout *Gulliver's Travels*. Each of the voyages offers a parodied edition of an exemplary history, and in each of these histories the satire arises out of an utter disjunction of languages. And what Yeats noted of Swift's *Discourse* is equally true of *Gulliver's Travels*: they are both Vichian works, figurative histories that project past and remote conflicts into the present.[35]

It should be clear by now that irony is central to all these histories and voyages. That irony, which takes the place of discarded fiction, is the language of historical perspective. After the three languages posited by Vico (of gods, heroes, and men), we encounter this fourth language of modernity, the language he and his contemporaries actually wrote in. Vico recognizes that irony is appropriate to his own age: "Irony certainly could not have begun until the period of reflection, because it is fashioned of falsehood by dint of a reflection which wears the mask of truth" (§ 408). That language translates, compiles, edits, and criticizes foreign and dead languages but it is always distanced from them by the irony of retrospect and historical narrative. It is moreover precisely *because* the literature of the new sciences is concerned with truth that it is so steeped in historical irony: Without truth, irony has no significance.[36] Unlike Rousseau and Diderot, who internalize the ancient and remote, thereby making it paradisal and exotic, Vico, Swift, and Montesquieu gain creative strength from this dual principle only by keeping it external, at the arm's length of irony. Only through irony could they achieve what they all sought: the alignment

[33] Natalie Zemon Davis, "The Reasons of Misrule: Youth Groups and Charivaris in Sixteenth-Century France," *Past and Present* 50 (1971): 41–75.

[34] Robert C. Elliott, *The Power of Satire* (Princeton, 1960), esp. pp. 1–99.

[35] Introduction to "The Words upon the Window-Pane," in *Explorations* (London, 1962), pp. 343–69.

[36] This is the theme of Antonino Pagliaro's recent and suggestive book, *Ironia e verità* (Milan, 1970), which treats a series of ancient and modern myths as Vichian historical metaphors.

through narrative of the order of events and the nature of things. "What I say," claims Montesquieu, "is confirmed by the whole of history and fully conforms to the nature of things" (*"Ce que je dis est confirmé par le corps entier de l'histoire, il est très conforme à la nature des choses"*) (II, 251). The reader is led toward a sharing of that alignment through a narrative which plays on his yearning for distant wonders and yet recurrently subdues his aroused credulity through irony, drawing him out of his solipsist dream.

In reading such a narrative the ironic author persuades us at each stage to put behind us the horror of the past, to return finally like Rasselas and Candide from distant parts. As a consequence, these narratives are what Plato offers in the *Phaedrus*, what Stanley Fish has called self-consuming artifacts. The purpose of such a dialogue with the reader—and the works we are concerned with share that purpose—"is, paradoxically, to bring the reader to the point where he is no longer interested in the issues it treats; no longer interested because he has come to see that the real issues exist at a higher level of generality."[37] That movement toward a higher level of generality, which is the state of enlightenment, is in fact curiously similar to a Platonic ascent. But in aspiring to the wisdom of Socrates, the reader is at the mercy of his editor, Plato.

And this is perhaps the most remarkable aspect of these figurative histories: in each of them the author plays the role of the godlike editor. The editorial panoply of eighteenth-century works is immense. Among the major satires we find mock books and travesties of learned editions. *The Dunciad* for one, *A Tale of a Tub* for another. Richard Sympson edits *Gulliver's Travels* on one level, Gulliver re-edits them on another. Montesquieu devotes twenty years to the compilation and ordering of his synoptic research on the laws; Vico battles throughout the *Scienza nuova* against the errors and corruptions of other editors and jurisconsults. Voltaire's absorption in the sources for his histories is if anything exceeded by Gibbon's for his *Decline and Fall*. Johnson's heroic *Dictionary*, Diderot's *Encyclopédie*, Muratori's *Rerum Italicarum Scriptores*—in all of these the editor towers over the mere author and reader, and he claims this stature by right of his ability to write a more perfect history.

This curious phenomenon makes sense if we reflect on the consequences for literature of its new historical model. If all historical interpretation is of written texts rather than of events, it follows that the world we inhabit is a world of words, a world in which a pandemonium of conflicting or corrupted texts demands an editorial hero, demon, or god to put matters right. This has been a badly neglected development (and one with nineteenth- and twentieth-century parallels), but in some spirited remarks Christopher Ricks has pointed out its most important consequence. The editor, as he has observed, can become a blasphemous godsmith, the Maker

[37] Stanley Fish, "Literature in the Reader: Affective Stylistics," *New Literary History* 2 (Autumn 1970): 123–62. The quotation is from p. 136.

of makers: "God may indeed be our Author, but there is one person who can (with guilty pride) trump even authors: an editor. In the beginning was the Word, and the Word was with God, and the Word was God—and I edited it, cackles the lunatic editor."[38] There can be little doubt that this is the voice we hear in the unmaking of the world that is at the center of *The Dunciad* and *A Tale of a Tub*. Its echoes can be heard in Montesquieu scorching some wretched legal drudge ("*Ce malheureux compilateur des capitulaires*") (II, 802) for a blunder concerning Roman law, in Vico's repeated contempt for the conceits and obtusities of scholarly false prophets, and in Gulliver's indignant or complacent defenses of his various discovered societies. And the editor's godlike power in all of these works is increased by the fact that he is translating and interpreting sacred texts and languages—Latin, Greek, hieroglyphs, Gothic laws, Gulliver's unknown tongues—into the vernaculars of modern Europe.

The new scientist's final and proudest claim, however, is that he is a hero of the human mind. Montesquieu compares his work of twenty years to Theseus's victory over the labyrinth. Gulliver vindicates himself and his works and proudly denounces human pride. Vico closes by praising providence for ordering the world of nations in such a way that man—and the scholar above all—might be filled with wonder and veneration at "the matchless wisdom of the ancients" and by "the ardent desire" to attain that wisdom (§ 1111), thereby enabling him to recreate his history. And even though these feelings can be corrupted by what he calls in this same passage "the conceit of scholars and the conceit of nations," Vico clearly did not think they had corrupted him. On the contrary, as he told a friend in a letter written a year after completing the first version of his *Scienza nuova*:

> I no longer lament my hard lot and . . . denounce the corruption of letters that has imposed that lot; for this corruption and this lot have strengthened me and enabled me to perfect this work. Moreover (if it not be true, I like to think it is) this work has filled me with a certain heroic spirit, so that I am no longer troubled by any fear of death, nor have I any mind to speak of rivals.[39]

From the writer's perspective, this heroic role is the creative analogue of Vico's theory of *ricorso*, which "as the principle of universal history is the act by which the human spirit renders present and contemporaneous to itself the life of all the individual nations in their eternal and ideal principles."[40] We might understand the significance of this heroic act for literature and history if we recall Vico's theory of cultural sequence. "This

[38] In a review of two books on Carlyle: "Pale Fire," *New York Review of Books* 11, 7 (24 October 1968): 31–34.

[39] Letter to Father Bernardo Maria Giacco, 25 October 1725 in *Opere* (Ricciardi), p. 118.

[40] Robert Caponigri, *Time and Idea: The Theory of History in Giambattista Vico* (London, 1953), p. 141.

was the order of human institutions," he declares, "first the forests, after that the huts, then the villages, next the cities, and finally the academies" (§ 239). The act of *ricorso* is the imaginative telescoping of this order into a single aesthetic perception. This is the meaning and value of Vico's *Scienza nuova,* of Pope's symbolic life at Twickenham;[41] its utter reversal is a key to the satirical meaning of *Gulliver's Travels.*

Its chief aim and consequence is the unifying of human experience through language and written texts, which can most perfectly unite our divided awareness of events and structures. At the very end of his great work, Montesquieu suddenly interjects into his conclusion the quotation "Italiam, Italiam. . . ." This was the shout of Aeneas' companions on seeing for the first time the land where they were to renew Troy and its history. And that perhaps is the final significance of the creative discoveries considered in this paper: they bring about an imaginative discovery of the new Troy, a restored city of man.

[41] See Maynard Mack, *The Garden and the City: Retirement and Politics in the Later Poetry of Pope,* 1731–1743 (Toronto, 1969), esp. pp. 3–76.

Part III

VICO, PHILOSOPHY AND THE HISTORY OF PHILOSOPHY

Nancy S. Struever

VICO, VALLA, AND THE LOGIC OF HUMANIST INQUIRY

There are two major historical interpretations of Vico in Karl Apel's *Die Idee der Sprache in der Tradition des Humanismus*.[1] First, he claims that Vico points to the German theorists of language, that the full implications of his thought appear only with Herder, Hamann, and their followers. The difficulty with this interpretation is that it reads Vico through the eyes of the idealists. Recently, two powerful articles, P. Piovani's "Vico without Hegel," and H. V. White's "What Is Living and What Is Dead in Croce's Criticism of Vico,"[2] have explicitly warned us against idealist, and particularly Hegelian, distortions of Vico: they see Hegel and Croce in their role of intellectual historian as "boa constructors," to use the phrase of Panofsky,[3] developers of concepts which can swallow scores of thinkers whole.

However, Apel puts forward a second interpretation as well. Using one of Hegel's boa constructions, he claims that Vico functions as the "owl of Minerva" in relation to Italian Humanism; that is, coming at the end of a long and brilliant development, he both summarizes and illuminates its major tendencies.[4] To use the less mythical terms of Leonard Meyer, Apel seems to claim that "it is through the realisation of implications, through the completion of process, that patterns have become closed and events are thought to be defined."[5] Thus to choose Apel's second perspective is, in the first place, to assume that it is more rewarding to study an historical achievement as the end rather than the beginning of an intellectual development: it is richer, more revealing, illuminated as the cadence rather than the opening chords of a movement. But further, to emphasize the connection between Renaissance Humanism and Vico is to focus on their most idiosyncratic preoccupation. Vico, after all, was a professor of rhetoric, and the study of language provided the master key to his new science.[6] For

[1] Bonn, 1963.

[2] In *Giambattista Vico: An International Symposium*.

[3] In E. H. Gombrich, "The Evidence of Images," in *Interpretation: Theory and Practice*, ed. C. S. Singleton (Baltimore, 1969), p. 71.

[4] Apel, *Die Idee der Sprache*, p. 321.

[5] Leonard Meyer, *Music, the Arts, and Ideas* (Chicago, 1967), p. 91.

[6] *New Science*, §§ 34, 35, 145, and 161. All citations in the text preceded by a paragraph sign (§) are to the *New Science*.

the Renaissance Humanists rhetorical discipline was primary: it was a protoscience, a general propaedeutic to all others.[7] Perhaps it is possible to hypothesize that, after the break in continuity, what Mazzacurati calls the crisis of humanist rhetoric of the late sixteenth and early seventeenth centuries, where rhetoric loses its programmatic seriousness and becomes merely the technique of ornament,[8] Vico once again employs and transforms rhetorical structures in a general program of reform of humanist studies. What Vico shares with the earlier Humanists, then, is a mode of investigation. The logic of Humanist inquiry would be a rhetorized logic; in order to make specific and concrete the connections of Vico with Renaissance Humanism, I would like to suggest some parallels in the relation of rhetorical and epistemological strategies between the fifteenth-century Humanist Lorenzo Valla and Vico.

Interestingly enough, at least three of the leaders in the lively and reforming intellectual milieu of Naples in the late seventeenth century specifically named Valla as a precursor, an early philosophical reformer. Leonardo di Capoa, author of the fascinating intellectual history the *Parere*, speaks of Valla as the first to liberate philosophy from its blind and miserable servitude to Aristotle.[9] These words are echoed somewhat later in Giuseppe Valletta's brief history of modern philosophy,[10] and the passage is quoted by Francesco d'Andrea in his defense of the *Parere*, which had been attacked by the Inquisition.[11] D'Andrea notes that Valla, the renovator of the Latin language, the first to write against the logic of Aristotle, had been a fellow Neapolitan for a period and had also been hated and persecuted for his bravery against the superstitious Aristotelians.

In short, the Neapolitans see Valla as engaged in their own intellectual battle, whose slogan was *libertà di filosofare*, "liberty to philosophize."[12] More specifically, it is the linguistic mode of liberation which Valla and Vico share.[13] In another treatise inspired by the Di Capoa controversy, Costantino Grimaldi laments that it is exactly the domination of Aristotelian logic which ruined theological and philosophical studies for so many centuries.[14] I would suggest that Valla and Vico mount two separate but related attacks on Aristotelian linguistics: Valla criticizes the logic of Aristotle and his followers as presenting a barrier to the disciplined research

[7] R. Barilli, *Poetica e retorica* (Milan, 1969), p. 181.
[8] G. Mazzacurati, *La crisi della retorica umanistica nel '500* (Naples, 1961).
[9] *Parere* (Naples, 1681), p. 633.
[10] *Lettera di Signor G. V. in difesa della moderna filosofia* (Rovereto, 1732).
[11] *Difesa di Di Capoa*, MS Biblioteca Nazionale di Napoli, quoted in N. Badaloni, *Introduzione a G. B. Vico* (Milan, 1961).
[12] M. Donzelli, *Natura e humanitas nel giovane Vico* (Naples, 1970); see also Valla, "Praefatio," *Dialecticae disputationes, Opera Omnia* (Basileae, 1540; photoreproduced, Turin, 1962), I, p. 644.
[13] Tullio de Mauro, *Introduzione alla semantica* (Bari, 1965); see also P. Rossi, "Linguisti d'oggi e filosofi del Seicento," *Lingua e stile* 3 (1968): 1–20.
[14] *Discussioni Istoriche, Teologiche, e Filosofiche* (Lucca, 1735), p. 36.

of the real; Vico attacks Aristotelian theory as making absurd and ahistorical statements about the origins of language "as if the peoples that invented the languages must first have gone to school to [Aristotle]!" (§ 455) Further, for both Valla and Vico rhetoric is the first of the *artes sermocinales*; both start from classical rhetorical structures of explanation and description and transform them for their own purposes: Valla to correct logic, enrich expression, and sharpen a historical awareness of language, Vico to develop a new theory of the origins and progress of language and thus of the origins and progress of man.[15]

In order to attempt to understand the Vichian transformations of rhetorical structures, let us refer to one of Vico's typical, and therefore exasperating, condensations of his language theory. In the chapter entitled "Poetic Logic" he first establishes that *logos* ("language") is *favella* ("speech" and "fable"). Then, in paragraph 403 he equates fables with imaginative class concepts and defines mythologies as the allegories corresponding to them. The allegories signify the diverse species or diverse individuals under these genera (fables)

> so that they must have a univocal signification connoting a quality common to all their species and individuals (as Achilles connotes an idea of valor common to all strong men, or Ulysses an idea of prudence common to all wise men); such that these allegories must be the etymologies of the poetic languages, which would make their origins all univocal, whereas those of the vulgar languages are more often analogical.

The juxtaposition of etymology and analogy recalls the passage in Quintilian (*Institutio Oratoria* I. 6. 1) which describes the four foundations of correct *Latinitas*: "Language is based on reason, antiquity, authority, and usage. Reason finds its chief support in analogy and sometimes in etymology."[16] But where etymology contributes to the rhetorical aim of correct usage in Quintilian, etymology relates to the rhetorical, that is, holistic description of specific languages in Vico. We can note here two things:

[15] Tullio de Mauro, "From Rhetoric to Linguistic Historicism," in *Giambattista Vico: An International Symposium*, pp. 279–96; on the transition from rhetoric to metaphysics, see A. Pagliaro, "G.V. tra linguistica e retorica," in G.V. *nel terzo centenario della nascita* (Naples, 1971), pp. 133–62.

[16] "Sermo constat ratione vel vetustate, auctoritate, consuetudine. Rationem praestat praecipue analogia, nonnumquam et etymologia." Cf. Cicero, *Topica*, X, 35–37. See Kurt von Fritz, "Ancient Instruction in 'Grammar' according to Quintilian," *American Journal of Philology* 70 (1949): 345–56, on the concept of *ratio* in this passage. On etymology see J. Cousin, *Études sur Quintilien*, 2 vols. (Paris, 1935–36), vol. 1, p. 54; I. Opelt, "Etymologie," in *Reallexicon für Antike und Christentum* (Stuttgart, 1964), vol. 6, cols. 797–844; P. Zumthor, "Fr. Etymologie," in *Etymologica: Walther von Wartburg zum siebsigsten Geburtstag* (Tübingen, 1958), pp. 873–93; Guy de Poerck, "Etymologia et origo à travers la traditione latine," in *ANAMNHCIC: Gedankboek Pr. Dr. E. A. Leemans* (Brugge, 1970), pp. 191–228; and P. Guiraud, *L'étymologie* (Paris, 1964).

1. The poverty of the language available to Vico to describe language (Pagliaro claims that he lacks a metalanguage).[17] Thus where analogy, which refers to similarities of grammatical structure, and etymology are two parallel sources of rational system for Quintilian, Vico must use analogy on another, substantive level of meaning as well; thus the etymologies of poetic language (referring to a pre-logical plane) are univocal; those of vulgar language (referring to "ordinary" language) are analogous.

2. That Vico has his own priorities: He views languages as systematic in the sense that there is some methodical process at work in the formation of words. Vico's etymologies must be the most difficult aspect of his work for modern readers. Certainly they are harassing: De Mauro has said that when Vico and Leibniz "engaged in etymological research the results were absurd; thus, in that respect, they deserve a negative verdict or a compassionate silence."[18] But it seems ahistorical, to say the least, to pick and choose which methodological elements to study; they make up a unified approach, after all. And indeed, Vico's mistakes are often as significant as his successes.

Thus, for example, by referring to Quintilian, we see that Vico is using the classical rhetorical system to define his purpose; etymology and analogy are the two supporting frameworks of a rational semantics, a science of meanings.[19] Like Quintilian, he presumes a deep, perhaps hidden structure of genuine insight and efficacy; unlike Quintilian, who is interested primarily in style, he does not have in mind an appeal to antiquity (*vetustas*), authority (*auctoritas*), or custom (*consuetudo*). What he is about in his etymologies is a reconstruction from the evidence of language of historical layers of pre-logical encounters with reality, the definition of hidden process, the linguistic system of processing experience which existed, and still exists, outside rational or logical processing which is marked primarily by the use of analogy.

Guiraud has published an article, "Étymologie et Ethymologia," which casts some light, I think, on Vico's notion of etymology.[20] Guiraud distinguishes between the scientific etymology of modern historical linguistics and etymology as rhetorical figure, a mode of literary invention which characterized much of medieval literature and popular usage in all periods. In this second sense etymology invents connections between words in such a way that they do not simply represent reality but control our apprehension of it—he calls this an example of retro-motivation—things do not call

[17] Pagliaro, "G. V. tra linguistica e retorica," p. 151.

[18] De Mauro, "From Rhetoric to Linguistic Historicism," p. 284; but see Edward Said, "Vico: Autodidact and Humanist," *Centennial Review* 11 (1967): 336–52. Said characterizes Vico's etymologies as "brilliant, courageous, if frequently inaccurate" (p. 336).

[19] K. von Fritz, "Ancient Instruction," p. 349.

[20] *Poétique* 3 (1972): 405–13.

up words, but words create the basis, the name creates the character, the word engenders the thing. Thus one sees a relation between phonemes (units of sound), one desires one between sememes (units of meaning), and one simply creates a historical occasion to justify it; or, one wishes a relation between sememes and simply fudges one between phonemes. In both cases the etymological resemblances become stronger than any connection with reality. One can also see the operation of folk etymologies as an "abusive" investing of the signifier with the traits of the signified. In any case, the system of relations of reality is only the reflection of a system of relations between signs; in a truly Whorfian sense, the sphere of language is the operative one, structuring and controlling the world of mere "facts."

Now to recognize this linguistic operation is to recognize one aspect of the dynamics of language. "In fact," Guiraud says, "all pre-scientific knowledge—and this continues to include almost the totality of our immediate and daily experience—reposes on a priori codages, in which a system of signs already constituted imposes its form on reality."[21]

Now it is precisely this linguistic dynamism which Vico attempts to explore in his etymologies; Vico uses etymology as a logical (systematic) study of etymology as rhetorical (creative) process. To take an isolated and controversial example, Vico in his *Autobiography* begins with the word *coelum* and shows how it generates a whole cosmology.[22] The rules of poetic logic demonstrated here involve the priority of the concrete over the abstract—*coelum* can mean both *wedge* and *heavens*, but wedge becomes the operative meaning—and domination of the simple by the complex, that is, the necessary conflation of aspects of words—gender, voice, phonetics, lexicon, syntax. Thus, for example, that we speak of *anima* and *animus* is deeply significant; gender distinctions have the resonance of generative distinctions. Further, the relations between separate etymologies are vital; in Guiraud's terms, they can be described as relations between signifieds, which lead to relations between signifiers; in the case of *coelum* and *ingenium* there is no phonological relation, but there is a shared concept of "wedginess," of instrumental shaping, which recalls the mythopoetic function.

In all, there are three characteristics of pre-logical mental processing disclosed by etymologies:

[21] "Étymologie et Ethymologia," p. 408; cf. p. 409: "En fait, la science moderne est le premier effort de l'homme pour immuniser sa pensée contre ce mirage lexical en créant des codes artificiels qui protègent la structure signifiée contre les déformations du système signifiant. Mais la 'pensée scientifique' est récente et n'intéresse qu'une faible partie de notre activité mentale. Pour l'essentiel de nos pensées, de nos jugements, de nos décisions, de nos comportements, nous continuons à nous en remettre, plus ou moins aveuglément, au pouvoir des mots. On peut donc être assuré que les phénomènes décrits ici loins d'être de simple curiosités constituent les fondements même de notre activité verbale."

[22] *Autobiography*, (Ithaca, 1963), pp. 148–49; see Said, "Vico: Autodidact," pp. 343–45, on the *coelum* etymology.

1. It is natural and necessary. Although Vico's starting point is undoubtedly Plato's etymologies in the *Cratylus,* he criticizes Plato as attributing too rational procedure to the primitives; his etymologies are based on analogies, similarities, proportions determined in a logical fashion. On the contrary, words are born out of a poverty of language; they are necessitous as historical events (§§494, 401, 336, 456).

2. It is, to borrow a famous pair of adjectives, "clear and distinct" (§ 444); like the logical universals the poetic universals expressed in the roots of words represent a single intuition predicated of many individuals; univocity emphasizes the legal nature of its mental processing; all verbal connectedness, all ambiguity stems from a "delight in the uniform" which characterizes the mind (§§ 403, 933).

3. It is a self-contained system. Vico's focus is not on symbolism but on the use of symbolism. The etymological language systems are closed, circular, precisely manifesting that autonomy of man-made culture noted in Vico's *verum-factum* equation. In his dictum *Homo non intelligendo fit omnia,"* he is delineating the utter self-sufficiency of this sphere of attributed meanings (§ 405), a self-sufficiency, we must observe, Vico himself forgets when he tries to reconnect sign with referent, with external reality in the etymology from the *Autobiography* quoted above.

In one sense, then, Vico's etymologies are a simple acknowledgment of the force of words, a special case of linguistic relativism. What Vico is aware of, and what modern linguistics is aware of, is exactly the dynamic complexity of language behavior. But Vico not only describes, he employs the figure *ethymologia* in the sense Guiraud explains. He does not use the scientific techniques of historical phonetic linguistics to verify his assumptions about connections; he does not know and probably would not be impressed by the importance of these phonetic legalisms. Rather, his process of description mirrors the process of retro-motivation he describes. We are shocked by Vico's retro-motivation, but we are probably surrounded by it, not only in popular usage, as Guiraud describes, but in inquiry itself: Freud, Lacan, and N. O. Brown share Vico's enjoyment of word play, puns, the raw generative power of words. And it is precisely this autonomy, this separation from "objective" reality of this linguistic world, which holds a charm.

If we look at Valla's etymologies we see a very different and possibly much more sympathetic technique. Valla also is searching for system, for mechanism of linguistic processing, but in his inquiry Quintilian's notion of *analogia* dominates. And, as in Quintilian, grammatical and logical techniques are embedded in a rhetorical strategy; in his *Elegantiae* and in the *Dialecticae Disputationes* Valla intends to cure usage, to resemanticize discourse. The truly revolutionary implications of his method are obvious in his treatment of key words in philosophy and theology—*substantia, essentia, persona.*[23] What the etymologies disclose is grammatical possibility; the grammatical functions should engender one, and only one, proper sense. Vico is interested in basic phonetic and semantic units, roots, Valla in structural relations; or, in Valesio's terms, Vico is interested in *icon*, Valla in *schema*.[24] In a sense, Vico and Valla recreate the *physis-thesis* dispute over language. Vico focuses on motivated words, while Valla underlines the precise expressivity of the unmotivated forms, of the arbitrary aspects of language. Where Vico delights in the richness of poetic ambiguity revealed in his etymologies, Valla wishes to correct ambiguity: his etymologies are speech therapy. Like Vico, Valla understands the self-sufficiency, the dynamism of language, and like Vico, Valla turns to common usage, to popular processing as significant. But for Vico the etymologies disclose the people as poet; Valla looks to common usage as canonical in its common sense, in its straightforward approach to grammar. For Valla, the philosophical language he confronted was simply a series of grammatical mistakes. Aristotle was an anarchist who treated his units of grammatical form with semantic irresponsibility.

Vico goes on to use rhetorical codes to define the modes and the successive stages of the linguistic behavior revealed by etymology. He employs the rhetorical doctrine of the tropes, quite clearly set out in Quintilian, whom Vico studied assiduously,[25] but available in many rhetorical texts. To be sure, Vico's interest in etymology and his use of alliteration and of the trope or figure *paronomasia* are intimately connected in a virtuoso playfulness, a "verbal alchemy."[26] But most importantly, he regards the tropes primarily, not as inventions for ornament, but as providing a taxonomy, as defining stages of information retrieval, of giving names that take cognizance of other names. In the *Scienza nuova prima* (pp. 303f.) metonymy, connection by contiguity, describes the divine-mute phase of language formation; synecdoche, connection of part to whole, the heroic phase; metaphor, connection by similarity or analogy, the articulate or vulgar phase. In the *Scienza nuova seconda* he adds irony as also describing the vulgar phase; irony as profoundly reflective and self-conscious demonstrates by its absence the unself-conscious, the "truthful" nature of earlier linguistic

[23] See Valla's strictures on the word *persona*, in *Elegantiae*, VI, c. 34, O.O., I, pp. 215–16; on the words *substantia* and *essentia* in *Dialecticae disputationes*, I, in O.O., I, pp. 635f. On Valla's use of Quintilian see Salvatore Camporeale, *Lorenzo Valla: Umanesimo e teologia* (Florence, 1972), pp. 149f.; see also Valla's panegyric of Quintilian at the end of book 2 of the *Dialecticae disputationes*. Also important is Cesare Vasoli, "Filologia, critica, e logica in Lorenzo Valla," *La dialettica e retorica dell'Umanesimo* (Milan, 1968), pp. 50f.

[24] P. Valesio, "Icone e schemi nella struttura della lingua," *Lingua e stile* 2 (1967): 349–55.

[25] F. Nicolini, *Commento storico alla seconda Scienza nuova*, 2 vols. (Rome, 149–50), vol. 1, p. 151.

[26] On alliteration and the figure of *paronomasia* see P. Valesio, *Strutture dell'allitterazione* (Bologna, 1967); Andrea Battistini, "Semantica fonica nella prosa della *Scienza nuova*," *Lingua e stile* 6 (1971): 15–49.

processing.[27] Thus in the *coelum* etymology of the *Autobiography*, metonymy, synecdoche, and metaphor successively delineate language as plurisystematic and historical. Vico emphasizes the temporal nature of the process: a primitive concept struggles to reach the next level of elaboration or sophistication. Language relates to a limited repertoire of modifications of the mind, a repertoire which has one privileged direction of usage.

Vico's use of the rhetorical tropes celebrates, then, on the one hand, the progressive nature of our distinction and connection-making capacity, and, on the other, the ambiguity and oblique richness of language (§ 445). Vico presumes that language is by nature ambiguous; that is to say, we tend to name one thing by reference to another. Just as, for example, our biological competence engenders basic patterns or syndromes, such as repression, so, Vico seems to be telling us, our linguistic competence engenders basic patterns of obliqueness. Man is the oblique animal. Thus when he asserts that metaphor makes up the most of language, he is by no means insulting language (§ 444). On the contrary, his idiosyncratic definition of autonomy —*homo non intelligendo fit omnia*—isolates our relation-making competence. All tropes express relationships; the etymologies of the pre-logical phases, the analogies of the logical phases anatomize the possibilities of connectedness.

There is no exact equivalent to Vico's use of tropes in Valla, but his *Elegantiae*, a grammar for rhetoricians, illustrates his assumption of the importance of connectedness, of interrelatedness, in the study of language. Valla, like Vico, prefers not to discuss words as isolated lexical entries; he engages in the description of large semantic structures, fields we might call them.[28] The organization of books 4 and 5 of the *Elegantiae* is particularly striking: only rarely does a word appear alone in a chapter; most usually formal (etymological and analogical) similarities and differences are the instruments of classification, or a group of words are shown to constitute a substantive, a notional field—they divide and share a spectrum of meaning. Where Vico exploits the tropes as a repertoire of figurative strategies, Valla exploits the repertoire of grammatical morphemes as an index to the combinative powers of language. And in the *Dialecticae Disputationes* he demonstrates how the suppression of connection, as in the insensitivity to participial form, can lead to false reification. For Valla, each word casts a semantic and stylistic shadow larger than itself, impinging on neighboring words. Further, like Vico, Valla insists on the legal and temporal nature of the relationships: analysis discloses the lawful connections possible, the

[27] I have followed Pagliaro, "G.V. tra linguistica e retorica," p. 154f; on the other hand, H. V. White, *Metahistory* (Baltimore, 1973), chap. 1, has a different notion of succession: he emphasizes Vico's discussion of concrete metaphor as one of the first tropes (*New Science*, § 404) of the poetic phases, rather than abstract metaphor as pertaining to the vulgar, or reflective, phase.

[28] See Vasoli, "Filologia," p. 52.

successions of meaning, and enables the reader to use the word in the most powerful way.

Vico's references to a third instrument of classical rhetoric, the topics, are most important for his epistemology; they are evidence of predilections for the anti-reductionist, anti-solipsist moments of rhetoric. Here, perhaps, the similarities of his approach to that of Valla are most obvious. For example, Vico states that "the first founders of humanity applied themselves to a sensory topics, by which they brought together those properties or qualities or relations of individuals and species which were, so to speak, concrete, and from these created their poetic genera" (§ 495). This notion of a sensory topics enhances the role played by experience, rather than reason alone, in creating expression; it underlines his presupposition that logic and reason cannot exhaust experience (§ 405).[29] Similarly, Valla's program of reducing the number of logical categories has as its purpose, not simply greater economy and elegance, but greater contact with the innumerable things of reality we experience.[30] For example, the abstractions of the philosophers generate religious error, since they move away from the shared perceptions of divine things; Valla's emphasis on a religious vocabulary of affect is a moral imperative: for "nothing is useful which is not felt."[31] Valla carries further Quintilian's rhetorical imperialism, his rearrangement of dialectical instruments within a framework of topoi as concretely apprehended lines of argument. For Valla, dialectic is simply invention, one of the five parts of rhetoric.[32]

Their rhetorical attitudes bespeak a quantifying urge. Vico defines a topic as "an art of regulating well the primary operations of our mind by noting the commonplaces that must all be run over in order to know all there is in a thing that one desires to know well; that is, completely" (§ 497). True knowledge is seriatum, not syllogistic.[33] An excellent metaphor for this humanist assumption is Nicholas of Cusa's notion of the human mind as an infinite-sided polygon gradually approaching, although never coinciding with, the infinite circle of God's creation.[34] Or, to put it another way: recall that Vico claimed that linguistic ambiguity was a reflex of clarity, of a delight in the uniform. For both Vico and Valla the research of mental linguistic processes is not to rest in the apprehension of simple structures, but to lead to the appreciation of the infinite riches of

[29] On the priority of invention see *New Science*, §§ 495f., and E. Gianturco, trans., *On the Study Methods of Our Time* (Indianapolis, 1965).

[30] See Vasoli, "Filologia," pp. 61, 72.

[31] "Nihil est utile quod non sentiatur"; *MS Otto. lat.* 2075, f. 154r, quoted in Charles Trinkaus, *In Our Image and Likeness*, 2 vols.. (London, 1970), vol. 1, p. 113.

[32] "Proemium," bk. 2, *Dialecticae Disputationes*, O.O., I, p. 693; first redaction quoted in Camporeale, *Lorenzo Valla*, p. 83.

[33] On the topics see *On the Study Methods of Our Time*, chap. 3; *Autobiography*, p. 124.

[34] *De docta ignorantia*, I, chap. 3, in Nicolai de Cusa, *Opera Omnia* (Leipzig, 1932), vol. 1, p. 9.

linguistic expression which the simple structures generate. Neither Vico nor Valla could be content with a knowledege of generative structures; they wish to move beyond the explanatory mechanism of systems to a description of the cultures, to an exceedingly complex map of achievement; their aim is a holograph, not a system. Vico's goal is not the universal grammar of Port-Royal, but a universal mental dictionary; Valla attempted in his *Elegantiae* a dictionary of *Latinitas*, a list, open-ended in form, of enabling conventions which give access to a universal culture.

In sum, the logic of Humanist inquiry in Vico and Valla is rhetorical, since only rhetorical structures are generous enough to encompass the cultural wholes they wish to study. But if one were to choose the most central and characteristic insight of their Humanist mode of inquiry, it would have to be, I think, their predication of the *social* nature of innovation, that *society* invents. Note that a topics consists of commonplaces, a shared inventory of a shared consciousness. Vico and Valla's rhetorical taxonomies describe a linguistic relativism which does not underwrite subjectivity; socially determined words mold our consciousness. Our mental constructs are not, cannot be, solipsistic: they assume the priority of social discovery. For Vico the locus of meaningful change is on the collective level; innovation is circumscribed but also mandated by a publicly shared vocabulary—language is hero. Notice the lack of personal names in Vico: important historical moments are moments of shared activity. And recall Valla's encomia on *Romanitas*, on the molding, enriching force of the Latin language, and his subordination of political to linguistic hegemony.[35] To be sure, Vico's axiom "human nature is social" (§ 309) is a classical and Renaissance commonplace. But it is a bold step then to refine one's notion of linguistic innovation to the point of referring to Homer as "lost in the crowd of the Greek people" (§ 882). The major thrust of Vico's rethinking of the processes of language is to emphasize both the universality and historicity of process. Thus, speaking of the tropes of metonymy in *Scienza nuova prima,* he points out that "they revealed themselves to be born from the nature of the first nations, not from the caprice of particular men, able in poetry" (§ 305).[36] Nor is the social nature of innovation limited to the poetic phase; in the third edition Vico claims that, by a feat of consummate genius, the people went on to form the vulgar genera, by means of which "the minds of the peoples grew quicker and developed powers of abstraction, and the way was thus prepared for the coming of the philosophers, who formed intelligible genera" (§ 460).

Social invention is not social uniformity, however. Just as Vico celebrates the ambiguity and richness of poetic expression, so he becomes a celebrator of Babel—of the range and variety of points of view of the vari-

[35] "Praefatio," *Elegantiae*, I, O.O., I, pp. 3–5; *De reciprocatione*, O.O., I, p. 249.

[36] F. Nicolini, ed. *Scienza nuova prima* (Bari, 1968) 305; quoted in Pagliaro, "G.V. tra linguistica e retorica," pp. 157–58.

ous nations so brilliantly displayed in the variety of their languages (§445). George Steiner has pointed out that both Vico and Leibniz developed a remarkable combination of universalist and relativist theories.[37] Vico can most winningly discuss the genius of the national languages and then postulate the universality of Latin. And his project, after all, is a civil history of providence, a universal dispensation constituted by historical speech acts.

This construct of the social nature of innovation bears upon two major issues in the history of humanist ideas: the relation of humanism to classicism and the centrality of "civic" humanism. This is not to consider humanist classicism in the sense of a naive classical style, but in the difficult sense of the perverse, to us, classical relationship between tradition and innovation summarized long ago by T. S. Eliot in his "Tradition and the Individual Talent." But this connection, in Vico's epistemology, must subsist in relation to what we now call the *langue-parole* distinction. Saussure has taught us that *langue*, as social convention, is restrictive; and *parole*, individual speech, is the source of innovation. In Vico our normal equation of the social or traditional with necessity and the individual with innovation is reversed: language, a social invention, is liberating in that it offers infinite riches of expression. Tradition and the individual talent are not locked in some agon, as in the Romantic model; tradition nourishes the individual.

There is a kind of classical clarity, modesty, and economy to Vico's notion of individual creativity. He does not predicate more than possible inventive powers of the author: the individual's potential is necessarily circumscribed by the community's language. This anti-heroic moment in rhetorical humanism is implicit in Valla as well; his point is that Aristotle can't make language say more than it can say, and he holds up the simplicity of common usage as a model. For both Valla and Vico the problem of the mind is not the problem of subjectivity, and a cult of Romantic originality cannot subsist on a theory of language whose lexicon lacks the word *subjective*. Vico's notion of his own intellectual role seems to be the discovery of relationships which are preexistent, the private discovery of social discovery.[38] The historian is a species of the genus poet; he remakes connections between insights and activities hitherto seen as disparate. It is a limited but positive evaluation of historical discovery: the evidence, language, is related to the limited repertoire of modifications of the mind—all insights are available.

This classicism, and this notion of creativity, I believe, is germane to our difficulty in reading the Humanists. In Romantic and post-Romantic criticism there is not the classical sense of the reinforcing and liberating

[37] "Whorf, Chomsky, and the Student of Literature," *New Literary History* 4 (1972): 15–34.
[38] *On the Study Methods of Our Time*, pp. 9, 38; *Autobiography*, p. 123.

influence of linguistic wholes; on the contrary, Riffaterre's analysis of stylistic power depends on the isolation of deviations from the norm as the source of literary merit.[39] The difference between "modern" and classical notions of style seems to present the old half-empty, half-full dilemma in terminology. For the moderns, deviation, *écart*, brings out latent insights we share; for the classicist resonance makes viable, powerful, originality, and, as in the doctrine of imitation, helps locate artistic identity. The Humanist historian, then, believes in resonance, is engaged in imitation, and is fascinated by survival, where survival is related to a command of the past, of the full temporal range of language. There is a striking reciprocity between humanist history and classicism: the search for classical artifacts is in the first place a process of self-confirmation, a verification of community identity. Vico's *New Science*, for all its implications for the future, has obvious affinities with humanist historiography as a genre which subverts solipsism and validates a common conscience.

Just as certainly, Vichian ideas of language relate to the issue of the political nature of Humanist thought, of civic humanism as a dominant or recessive aspect of the Renaissance. Surely the civic Humanists regarded the *polis*, or *civitas*, as the organizing focus of the classical thinkers who were of such authority for them. And surely both Vico and Valla emphasize the social goal as well as the social character of knowledge. For Vico, science is the explanation of human structure and process; wisdom, which he equates with "metaphysics" (§ 365), is the complete knowledge of human generative activity which has pragmatic value in the "great city of the human race" (§ 342). Similarly, in the preface to book 1 of the *Elegantiae*, Valla celebrates the "transcendent," nonegoist nature of the civilizing force of language—learning Latin is a process with a social aim, truly Christian in its charity. Paul is hero as the channel of Christian eloquence, and sacred eloquence, in Valla's humanism, provides the solutions to problems of conscience.[40]

It is not at all new to suggest that Burckhardt's thesis of Renaissance individualism is a misleading characterization of the Italian Humanists. What is most striking to me, however, is that both Valla and Vico hypothesize politicality on the deep level of epistemology as well as on the surface level of cultural program. Both move from a scientific establishment of linguistic wholes to holistic theories of history: Valla uses the concept of stylistic resonance to construct historical periods; Vico uses the concepts of the etymon and trope to develop a thesis of continuity and change in collective consciousness.

I would maintain that Vico attempts nothing less than an epistemological basis for a theory of community. His achievement, I think, illumines

[39] "Criteria for Style Analysis," *Word* 15 (1959): 154–74.

[40] On Valla's notion of Christian eloquence see Mario Fois, *Il pensiero cristiano di Lorenzo Valla* (Rome, 1969), esp. pp. 251–60.

both his isolation in early modern European intellectual history and the basic contrast between the declining Italian Humanism and the French rationalism dominant in the seventeenth and eighteenth centuries. Recall Lucien Goldmann's delineation of the destructive (bourgeois) individualism of French rationalism, which, by its epistemological solipsism, undermines the foundation of any social theory and leads to social nihilism.[41] Nor is the Humanist identity simply archaic, continuous with medieval Christian elites; the group identity of the Humanist intellectual is not the same as that of the medieval Scholastic intellectual. It represents a very different notion of social development and destiny. But society dominates. Man is the language-using animal, and the social, intersubjective nature of his language provides both condition and vehicle for his politicality. The moral connectedness of language and politics finds expression in Vico's phrase *Humanitas potissimum linguis conciliata* or in Valla's great metaphor of the word as sacrament. Where Scholastic discourse, even in dialogue form, provokes the reader to a private discourse on verity, the Humanist continuously exalts the truth, the subtlety, and the necessity of civil conversation—a celebration of community which we approach today with wistful iconoclasm.

[41] L. Goldmann, "La pensée des 'Lumières,'" *Annales: ESC* 22 (2) (1967): 752–79.

Amos Funkenstein

NATURAL SCIENCE AND SOCIAL THEORY: HOBBES, SPINOZA, AND VICO

The Problem

With his "system of the natural law of the gentes" Vico attempted to mediate between contradicting political theories. On the one hand he sympathized with the intentions underlying the long tradition of natural law and even the search for ideal states, but on the other hand he recognized that purely teleological justifications of social orders rest altogether on wishful thinking. "Philosophy considers man as he should be and so can be of service to but very few, those who wish to live in the Republic of Plato. . . ."[1] Far from ignoring the persuasive strength of mechanistic-egotistic accounts of the origin and growth of social orders, Vico maintained as much as Hobbes, Mandeville, or Spinoza that neither social instinct nor indeed the urge for a perfect society are immediate facts of man's original nature. Public benefits arise at best out of private vices: "Legislation considers man as he is in order to turn him to good uses in human society. Out of ferocity, avarice, and ambition. . . . it makes civil happiness."[2] Society, in other words, is not a natural product, but an artifact; Vico shared with Hobbes the fundamental principle that "we make the commonwealth ourselves."[3] But if it is not a product of human nature, must the social orders and institutions be seen as mere conventions or impositions? Vico denied this Hobbesian consequence and developed instead his doctrine of man's collective, acquired, or "historical nature" as mediating between nature and society. The continuous dialogue with Hobbes is a distinguishing mark of modern political theories. Vico belongs to the small but important list of those who were irritated by Hobbes but

[1] *New Science,* § 131.

[2] *Ibid.,* § 132; cf. also *Autobiography,* p. 138: "Up to this time Vico had admired two only above all other learned men: Plato and Tacitus; for with an incomparable metaphysical mind Tacitus contemplates man as he is, Plato as he should be."

[3] Thomas Hobbes, *Six Lessons,* in *The English Works of Thomas Hobbes,* ed. W. Molesworth (London, 1844), p. 184. Cf. J. W. N. Watkins, *Hobbes' System of Ideas* (London, 1965), chap. 4, esp. p. 69. On the principle *verum et factum convertuntur,* see below.

This work was aided by a grant from the American Association of Learned Societies.

did not seek to reject him outright on the grounds of opposite premises.[4] Instead, they absorbed the whole force of Hobbes's argument before transforming it into a different, possibly even a contrary, theory. In the first parts of this essay we will try to reconstruct the elements of Hobbes and the Hobbesian tradition to which Vico reacted.

And yet while Hobbes based his claim to have founded "civil philosophy" on the use he made of Galileo's *metodo risolutivo e compositivo* for the analysis and reconstruction of the body politic, Vico challenged the paradigmatic role of either mathematics or the "new science" of mechanics. His mediation between nature and society is founded on the tradition of philological—or, as we shall call it later, contextual—reasoning. The last part of our essay must deal with this conscious methodical distance which separated Vico from the Hobbesian tradition.

Gassendi and Hobbes

Hobbes's insistence on the thoroughly positive, thetic character of laws was not an altogether new position. Vico, among others, recognized that the modern brand of political realism stood within a long tradition.[5] The contraposition of φύσις and νόμος was introduced by the sophists[6] and adopted by the atomists. Strangely enough, few of Hobbes's modern interpreters have commented on the obvious link between the revival of the

[4] Some of the immediate opposition to his metaphysical positions is described by S. I. Minz, *The Hunting of Leviathan* (Cambridge, 1962). If, with F. Meinecke, *Die Idee der Staatsraison, Werke I*, 2d ed. (Munich, 1960), pp. 249–55, we want to see Hobbes as a defender of an "inner" *raison d'état*, then much of the opposition to the separation between morality and the state hits Hobbes too, although he is then taken to be but an annex to the Machiavellian leitmotif. The dialogue with Hobbes is, however, much more fundamental (and more theoretical) than the question of the *raison d'état*.

[5] *De uno principio, Opere*, p. 32: "Quare adhuc Carneadem de iustitia an sit in rebus humanis, aequis momentis in utramque partem dissertare, adhuc Epicurum, Nicolaum Macchiavellum *De principe*, Thomam Obbesium *De cive*, Benedictum Spinosam in *Theologo politico* et nuper Petrum Baylaeum in magno *Dictionario* gallice conscripto, illa obstrudere vulgo audias: ius utilitate aestimari, temporique locoque servire; imbecillos postulare ius aequum; at 'in summa fortuna,' ut Tacituc ait, 'id aequius quod validius.' Ex quibus colligunt et concludunt metu contineri societatem humanam, et leges esse potentiae consilium, quo imperitae multitudini dominetur." Cf. also *New Science*, § 1109 where Vico sees the belief in Providence guiding the course of human institutions vindicated and both Epicurus, Hobbes, and Machiavelli, who believed in "chance," and Zeno and Spinoza, who believed in "fate," refuted. The distinction is important: Hobbes, determinist as he might have been, appeared to Vico as a philosopher of "chance" because of his insistence on the arbitrary character of human institutions. Cf. Grotius, *De iure belli ac pacis* (Lausanne, 1751), I, prolegomena 2, p. 2; 16, p. 10.

[6] W. K. C. Guthrie, A *History of Greek Philosophy* (Cambridge, 1969), vol. 3, pp. 55–147.

classical corpuscular-mechanistic cosmology in the seventeenth century and the revival of the radically thetic interpretation of social institutions likewise characteristic of the atomists.[7] A superficial comparison between Epicurus and Hobbes cannot fail to reveal the congruence between some of their main positions. These similarities should be stated before they are discarded (and justly so) as peripheral. Epicurus's ἀνάγκη and Hobbes's determinism have the same positional value in their respective systems: the elimination of teleological considerations. Hobbes, however, could do without the complementary assumption of the slight original declination (παρέγκλισις) of the atoms to account for chance or free will,[8] much as he could abandon the strictly corpuscular theory itself. Both ascribe an actual and denumerable material substrate for every discrete entity, including the soul (Epicurus) or even God (Hobbes). The epistemology of both consists in the sensualistic interpretation of impressions, "images" (*simulacra*), and their mechanical association. A similar account of man's emotional economy leads both systems to an abrogation of man's social nature.[9] To their grim description of the natural state corresponds the rejection of idealizations of primitivity as an *aurea aetas* and the famous, detailed description found in Lucretius of the bestial, anarchic state of primordial man[10] and of the rise of religion out of somnial images and frights.[11] The strictly contractual origin of laws is likewise a part of Epicurus's doctrine, the stress on the function of political order as a crime-preventing agency only (τό τῆς φύσεως δίκαιόν ἐστι σύμβολον τοῦ συμφέροντες εἰς τὸ μὴ βλάπ τειν

[7] Cf., however, L. Strauss, *Natural Right and History* (Chicago, 1953), pp. 188ff, who sees the main differences as (1) that between merely ethical and mainly political interests, and (2) Hobbes's adherence to a new concept of natural right. The first difference is merely of intention; the second is not convincing.

[8] C. Bailey, *The Greek Atomists and Epicurus* (Oxford, 1928); S. Sambursky, *Das physikalische Weltbild der Antike* (Zurich and Stuttgart, 1965), pp. 328–35, esp. p. 334; the systematic exposition of E. Zeller, *Die Philosophie der Griechen in ihrer geschichtlichen Entwicklung, Teil III*, Abt. 1, 5th ed. (Leipzig, 1923; reprint ed., Darmstadt, 1965), pp. 390–429, is still indispensable (see esp., pp. 408, 421 and n. 5).

[9] Zeller, pp. 455, 471 n. 1; cf. Gassendi, infra. On the theory of motivation cf. also E. Schwarz, in *Charakterköpfe aus der Antike*, ed. J. Stroux, 2d ed. (Leipzig, 1943), pp. 149ff. (Ethics); and G. Kafka and H. Eibl, *Der Ausklang der antiken Philosophie und das Erwachen einer neuen Zeit, Gesch. d. Phil. in Einzeldarstellungen*, hg. G. Kafka 9 (Munich, 1928), pp. 58–67 (the assumptions common to Epicurus and the Stoics; these are the reasons that it was easy to mistake Hobbes's doctrine of affections to be of Stoic origin).

[10] On the atomistic demythologization of the *aurea aetas* see G. Vlastos, "On the Pre-history in Diodorus," *American Journal of Philosophy* 67 (1946); and A. O. Lovejoy and G. Boas, *Primitivism and Related Ideas of Antiquity* (Baltimore, 1935), esp. pp. 222ff. (Lucretius).

[11] W. Jaeger, *Die Theologie der frühen griechischen Denker* (Stuttgart, 1964), has demonstrated the sophistic origins of many latter genetic-culture speculations on religion. See also W. F. Otto, "Epikur," in *Die Wirklichkeit der Götter* (1963), pp. 10–43. On the later transformations of the Epicurean demythologization see Leo Strauss, *Spinoza's Critique of Religion* (New York, 1965), pp. 37–52.

ἀλλήλους μηδὲ βλάπτεσθαι) and even the demand for an unconditional submission to authority.[12]

Hobbes had direct access to both Diogenes Laertius and Lucretius, and we can only speculate as to the depth of his doxographic knowledge (which he must have possessed even if we see a grain of truth in Clarendon's remark that he was a "man of . . . some reading, and somewhat more thinking"[13]) and as to the part, if any, this knowledge had in the formation of his thought. Nevertheless it is important to note that a revival of Epicurus's doctrines, even in *politicis*, was conceived by Gassendi and was well underway when Hobbes elaborated his political ideas.[14] Hobbes knew of Gassendi after his third visit to France; we may at least assume some mutual stimulation. Again, a superficial examination will reveal a number of common features to Hobbes's and Gassendi's systems even apart from the atomistic substratum of both. Both share interest and conviction in the new mechanics. Gassendi's formulation of the inertial principle is earlier (at least in publication) than Descartes' and closer to the formulation adopted by Hobbes.[15] Two points in Gassendi's ethics and political theory merit particular stress in respect to Hobbes. Defending Epicurus's alleged abrogation of all natural human ties, Gassendi stressed the advantage of seeing man's inclination towards his fellow-men, or even towards his family, as an outcome not of blind instinct (*caeco quodam impulsu naturae*) but of education and self-elevation.[16] Social attitudes, Gassendi seems to indicate, are not innate, but a product of man's labor on himself. This is the essence of Hobbes's (and Vico's) opinion later. Indeed, a long section in Gassendi's *De justitia, iure et legibus* may already

[12] Diogenes Laertius X, 150 (H. Usener, Epicurea, Leipzig 1887) 78, 8; on the history of "conventionalism" in antiquity see Leo Strauss, *Natural Right and History* (Chicago, 1965), pp. 81–119.

[13] Edward Earl of Clarendon, *A Brief Survey of the Dangerous and Pernicious Errors to Church and State in Mr. Hobbes' book entitled Leviathan* (Oxford, 1676), p. 2.

[14] Gassendi's literary plans to make Epicurus acceptable date back to 1631: see B. Rochot, *Les Travaux de Gassendi sur Epicure et sur l'Atomisme* (Paris, 1944), pp. 31ff. In 1647 his *De vita et moribus Epicuri* appeared, and in 1649 the commentary on the tenth book of Diogenes Laertius. His main positions and plans were well known during this time. Hobbes's first encounter with Gassendi (through Mersenne) occurred during his stay in 1634–37. The "first tract" may have been written before; but the interest in problems of sensation, his first reading of Galileo's *Dialoghi*, occurred during this crucial time. Some share might be attributed to the encounter with modern Epicureanism. For the date of the composition of the "tract," see Watkins, *Hobbes' System of Ideas*, pp. 40–46. On Gassendi's (and Epicurus's) influence in France, see J. S. Spink, *French Free-Thought from Gassendi to Voltaire* (1960; reprint ed., New York, 1969), pp. 85–168. Cf. also above n. 13.

[15] Cf. F. Brandt, *Thomas Hobbes' Mechanical Conception of Nature* (Copenhagen and London, 1928), pp. 282–85, 327; H. Dijksterhuis, *The Mechanization of the World Picture* (Oxford, 1961), pp. 429–30; and K. Lasswitz, *Geschichte der Atomistik vom Mittelalter bis Newton* (Hamburg and Leipzig, 1890), pp. 150–54, 172–73.

[16] Petri Gassendi, *Syntagmatis philosophia*, tomus II, par. 3 (Lyons 1685), p. 754. Gassendi's social philosophy is thus much clearer than as interpreted by F. Borkenau, *Der Übergang vom feudalen zum bürgerlichen Weltbild* (Paris, 1934), pp. 430–34.

show the influence of the confrontation with Hobbes. A review of the tradition of pessimistic descriptions of man's natural state concludes with the remark that the brutal *status naturalis* is not necessarily a historical reality, but a necessary fiction.[17] Its purpose is to understand society as it would be now without legal agreements, rather than to describe society as it once was;[18] in other words, it is a limiting case, much as the (mechanical) principle of inertia is not a description of any existing motion, but an imaginary limiting case of motions considered under ever diminishing impact of outer forces.[19]

Unlike Gassendi, Hobbes did much more than justify or revive a broken (if not forgotten) tradition. The many affinities to Epicurus's ethics do not bear on the determining concepts and concerns of Hobbes's political thought. Hobbes is first and foremost interested in political power and collective security, that is, in the state rather than in the happiness or autarky of the individual. But beyond the difference in interest, (1) Hobbes's contraposition of "nature" and "convention" is far more radical and far more methodical than in any of the doctrines of his forerunners. And yet (2) precisely this elaborated contraposition enabled Hobbes to anticipate a mediating formula. Finally, (3) Hobbes's methodical and conceptual borrowings from the new science of mechanics were sufficient to lend his concepts of both "nature" and "society" a new appeal and greater precision.

No classical or medieval author ever drew the line between the realm of nature and the realm of convention (or artificial constructs) as sharply as Hobbes and nevertheless tried, as he did, to mediate between both. With his characteristic vigor, Hobbes set out to prove that even though all human institutions—language, culture, religion, law—might have had their formative challenge *in* nature, they should be understood as essentially artificial constructs. They belong to nature only by virtue of the mediation of *foresight* (and Hobbes will go a long way towards a plausible,

[17] Gassendi, p. 795: "Itaque quicquid sit de illa seu suppositione, seu fictione status, in quo seu Epicurus, seu alii vixisse aliquando discunt primos hominos, tam esse protecto vidatur ipsa societas hominum, quam illorum est origo, antiqua; ac non eo quidem solum et modo, quo bruta generis eiusdem sociabilia inter se sunt; verum illo etiam, quo quatenus sunt et intelligentes, et ratione praediti, agnoscunt non posse ullam inter se societatem esse securam, nisi ea conventionibus, pactique mutuis constabitur." Gassendi maintained, even after his turn from scepticism to Epicureanism, the insistence on the *hypothetical* structure of science, as did Hobbes, albeit not an atomist. Cf. T. Gregori, *Scetticismo e Empirismo. Studio su Gassendi* (Bari, 1961), esp. pp. 179ff.; and R. H. Popkin. *The History of Scepticism. From Erasmus to Descartes* (New York, 1964), pp. 100–112, 145–54. The most serious shortcoming of this book, especially vis-à-vis Descartes, is the utter neglect of later scholastic scepticism or relativization of the *communis cursus naturae* when confronted with God's omnipotence.

[18] Among modern interpreters of Hobbes, C. B. MacPherson, *The Political Theory of Possessive Individualism. Hobbes to Locke* (Oxford, 1962), pp. 17–29, stresses this aspect of the natural state most.

[19] See below.

naturalistic aetiology); they derive their validity, not directly from nature, but from human imposition. Only a deliberate act, and not any etiological insight, will lend to human institutions—beginning with language itself—what they need in order to become valid or to *endure*: absolute univocation.

On the one hand, language has its origin in "natural signs"; on the other, the natural connections between regular sequences of events are always ambiguous, and no "sign" is actually natural.[20] Inasmuch as they are part of our language, they are always arbitrary, disregarding their origin.

Whatever is, is by "nature" ("nature," however, is again a mental construct); but the definite meaning of human institutions cannot be derived by appeal to the laws of nature, nor do these suffice as a condition of their validity. Natural necessities (the weakness and equal vulnerability of all men in the state of nature, and hence the fear not to survive) may have generated our submission to contractual obligations, conferring our "rights" to the sovereign; but necessities of nature do not and cannot explain why such obligations must be severed altogether from considerations of expediency, in other words: why they must be *absolutely* binding.[21] The

[20] "Natural signs," we learn in *De corpore* I. 2. 2, in *Opera Philosophica quae latine scripsit omnia*, ed. W. Molesworth (London, 1839), vol. I, are such things which can be used to signify other things which follow them regularly. But Hobbes warns against any inference from signs as to such regularities (*ibid.*, I. 5. 1): clouds may be a sign for rain, but they do not predict it. Only an arbitrary act makes such (ambiguous) signs into univocal "names" (*ibid.*, I. 2. 4), and yet the objective causal nexus guarantees a rough approximation of our system of names to the order of things. The very same structure permeates Hobbes's epistemology and theory of science. We do not perceive things in themselves, only their phantasms; yet Hobbes's belief in the strict chain of material causes guarantees our knowledge of the outer world. Truth is sometimes seen as a property of sentences only in virtue of the consistent usage of names; at other times, it rests on basic intuition. His theory of science emphasized at times the thetic-arbitrary beginnings of science (from definitions), at times the hypothetical-experimental beginnings. Cf. A. Pacchi, *Convenzione e ipotesi nella formazione della filosofia naturale di Thomas Hobbes* (Firenze, 1965), esp. pp. 194–215. Rather than seeing such assertions as expressions of very distinct phases of development, we can regard them, without denying changes of emphasis, as aspects of the following state of things: although there is a general congruence between phantasms and things, it is not a one-to-one relation; the congruence is guaranteed by the strict material causation in the universe; the task of systematic knowledge is at times to remove mistaken or abundant "names" and connections between names, at times to anticipate (infer) new connections. Language and science have their origin *in* nature, although they are arbitrary throughout. Only when made arbitrarily univocal can language help to "understand" nature.

[21] Hobbes's pronouncements to that effect induced much discussed revisions in the interpretation of his ethical and political doctrines. A. E. Taylor, "The Ethical Doctrine of Hobbes," *Philosophy* 13 (1938): 406–24, interpreted Hobbes's theory of obligations, and, correspondingly, his insistence on *mala per se*, as almost foreshadowing Kant's categorical imperative, while H. Warrender, *The Political Philosophy of Hobbes: His Theory of Obligation* (London, 1957), chose to see in Hobbes's natural laws divine precepts. For a discussion, cf. S. M. Brown, "The Taylor Thesis," in *Hobbes Studies*, ed. K. C. Brown (Oxford, 1965), pp. 31–34, 57–71; and Watkins, *Hobbes' System of Ideas*, pp. 85–99. Our suggestion is, again, that both the absolute and the relative

absolute allegiance to the sovereign knows no exception, allows no rebellion. And yet, should a rebellion succeed, and Hobbes sees most states as a dominion by acquisition, the very same allegiance is due to the new, illegitimate sovereign.

This peculiar, almost dialectical relationship between nature and convention, as a clue to the understanding of the structure of all human artifacts, is at the core of Hobbes's argument. The argument draws its strength precisely from the fact that it is not utilized in the analysis of the state only but to explain all manifestations of sociality, actual and potential. The most obvious instance in which Hobbes can be shown to seek for a mediation between "nature" (necessity) and "imposition" (volition) is his theory of conatus (endeavor).[22] Only a few among Hobbes's contemporaries, and fewer still among his later interpreters, have grasped this consistent dualism and its mediation; most of them tend to stress either the materialistic-egotistic or the "nominalistic"-voluntaristic aspect of his thought. Hobbes's concept of nature, natural laws, and language allowed him to deny a one-to-one correspondence of words and things, of imposed constructs and the fully determined chain of physical motions, and yet to insist on an overall congruence between both. So also the state. It is, we believe, neither a simple mechanical compound nor an organism: it has no discrete body. Its "matter" and "artificer" are the diverse human beings who constitute it.[23] Bodies, simple or complex, are distinguished by their force, or "natural resistance," which allows them to endure and maintain their integrity. The state has no such natural durability: its endurance cannot be calculated with the help of any physical laws. The contract on which it is founded is an *ens rationis*. The state is a *creatio continua* and always in danger of dissolution. It is a condition of man fighting *against* nature (including his own) with the aid of devices and designs taken *from* nature and driven by natural necessities.

It might be objected that the classical question whether social entities exist φύσει or θέσει was in antiquity raised not only *in politicis* but also in all spheres of human activity, including language. Yet never before was the

character of obligations are but *aspects* of the notion—the natural genesis of obligations both demands their imposition as absolutely binding and relationizes their validity *in praxi*. Our view of Hobbes's mediation between teleological and mechanistic models is close to that of R. Polin, *Politique et philosophie chez Thomas Hobbes* (Paris, 1953), pp. 7ff., 12–23, 51ff., 176ff.

[22] The best recent discussion is Watkins, *Hobbes' System of Ideas*, pp. 120–37. Cf. R. Hönigsward, *Hobbes und die Staatsphilosophie* (Munich, 1924) pp. 81–83, also with reference to Leibniz. On the basis of his theory of *conatus* Hobbes can hold that an action may be both causally determined throughout *and* voluntary.

[23] Thomas Hobbes, *Leviathan*, ed. M. Oakeshott (Oxford, 1955), p. 5. The analogy of the human body, with which Hobbes commences, is not to indicate that the state is a natural body, but that it is an imitation thereof, much as its constitutive act, the covenant, "resembles that *fiat*, or the *let us make man*, pronounced by God in the creation" (*ibid.*).

disjunction elaborated or its dialectical structure stressed so consistently as in Hobbes. One important difference between the cultural philosophy of Epicurus and that of Hobbes is that the former was interested in the natural substrate of language;[24] Hobbes, while not denying a natural origin, is rather interested in the *validity* of language. In the concept of "natural signs," as a product of both a natural sequence of images and an artificial function, even though this function is itself a product of causal necessity, Hobbes finds a model for analyzing other human constructs, including "natural laws" and obligations. Hobbes's state is likewise both: a product of natural (determined) causality *and* an arbitrary construct.

As against the traditional way of posing the question, Hobbes is interested both in the physical mechanism by which the social order is constructed and in the unique laws that govern these constructs *qua* constructs. In the main tradition of political thought, those who did not derive social order exclusively from necessity or nature or natural law did not investigate much further; once having postulated the thetic character of legal institutions, they went no further. They knew that human laws were not merely a reflection of nature, but they did not inquire into the question of what devices could be applied for their validation. Hobbes's inquiry begins where the classical positivistic tradition ended.

This contraposition, albeit for the sake of an ultimate mediation, of nature and society could not have been defended without the new laws of motion and the new method of eliciting them represented by (if not originating in) Galileo's mechanics. The new laws of motion had, since the seventeenth century, two separate paradigmatic functions. Inasmuch as they relied on *imaginary experiments*, they taught the heuristic value of counterfactual hypothetical reasoning of a specific kind: the "preservation of a body in its state of either rest or movement," for example, is not the absurd consequence of an absurd assumption of the void, as it was for Aristotle;[25] nor is it a critical admonition to reflect on the possibility, *de potestate dei absoluta*, of natural orders other than ours, as it was in the middle ages. The principle of inertia is rather conceived as the limiting case of all actual movements. The use of counterfactual conditionals as *limiting cases* since the seventeenth century made the medieval separation

[24] Whereby "nature" differed from society according to its different impressions. H. Steinthal, *Geschichte der Sprachwissenschaft bei den Griechen und Romern*, 2d ed. (1891; reprint ed., Hildesheim, 1961), pp. 325–29; for a detailed description of the genesis and background of the controversy the book is still most useful, in spite of its strongly Hegelian vocabulary. Cf. also E. Cassirer, *The Philosophy of Symbolic Forms*, trans. R. Mannheim (New Haven and London, 1955), vol. 1, p. 148.

[25] For the following see A. Funkenstein, "Aristotle, Imaginary Experiments and the Laws of Motion," *Festschrift for Lynn White* (in press); and idem, "The Dialectical Preparation of Scientific Revolutions," *The Copernican Achievement*, ed. R. Westman (Berkeley and Los Angeles, 1975).

between logical and physical necessity methodologically fruitful. Counterfactual conditionals became a constructive rather than critical principle; the *methodus interpretandi naturae* thus was founded on operations with purely mental constructs rather than on immediate generalizations from sense perception. The "mathematization" of physics was also a corroboration of the insight that a true understanding is spontaneous rather than receptive, that *verum et factum convertuntur*. Hobbes's theory of science as a systematization of mental constructs thus corresponds immediately to his theory of society as an autonomous (though necessitated) human construct, and his concept of state of nature is nothing but a limiting case analogous to the inertial principle. Both are derived by severing a phenomenon (body, society) from its actual contexts and seeing it "in itself."[26] It is the very same principle of idealization which Vico uses when he equates "nature" with an ideal process, that is, a process of the enfolding of the spontaneous contexts of the "common sense" of a social group if imagined as isolated from the influence of other groups;[27] and like

[26] This, at any rate, was the way in which Cartesians defined the difference between their method and the Aristotelian—Johann Clauberg, *Differentia inter Cartesianam et in scholis vulgo usitatam philosophiam*, *Opera omnia philosophica* (Amsterdam, 1691), 1217–35: ". . . natura est, set potius prout se habet in respectu aliorum, quo ipso tamen interna ejus natura plerumque occulta manet." The "inner nature" of things regarded "in themselves" are the Cartesian "simple natures": Descartes, *Regulae ad directionem ingenii*, Rule VI, *Oeuvres*, ed. Adam-Tannery, 13 vols. (Paris, 1897–1913), Vol. 10. Indeed, to sever a body from its context—to put it under counterfactual conditions, for example, to ask how it would move without being in a medium, how it would move in the void—was, for Aristotle, only a means of *reductio ad absurdum*, (whereby he already anticipated the inertial principle as the absurd consequence of an absurd assumption, the assumption of movement in the void. The Middle Ages regarded the same circumstance as a possibility to God but as a physical impossibility or improbability. Only with Galileo were such counterfactual conditions construed as the limiting case of all actual conditions of a body. The extrapolation of a body (or a relation between bodies) from its contexts was foreshadowed by the terministic technique of "annihilation": only such things which can be imagined as existing *alia re absolute destructa* (Ockham, *Quodlibeta*, Vi, p. y, in *Ockham: Philosophical Writings*, ed. Ph. Boehner [Edinburgh, 1957], p. 26; and E. Hockstetter, *Studien fur Metaphysik und Erkenntnislehre Wilhelms von Ockham* [Berlin and Leipzig, 1927], pp. 56–57). Both Descartes and Hobbes make extensive use of this method of annihilation, not, as in the Middle Ages, with a critical intent only, but with a constructive use of the method. Hobbes commenced his analysis of phenomena by imagining the whole outside world destroyed; left are then, he argues against Descartes, not only the self, but likewise its memories, from which the concept of space as a phantasma of things outside us may be reconstructed: *verum est factum*. Hobbes's analysis of the *status naturalis* of society without a sovereign is likewise a repetition of the method of annihilation. Thomas Hobbes, *De corpore*, II, 7. 1–2. *Opera*, ed. W. Molesworth (London, 1839–45). The importance of Hobbes' method of annihilation for both his methodology of science and his political theory was recognized by Hönigswald, *Hobbes und die Staatsphilosophie*, p. 123, and M. Goldsmith, *Hobbes's Science of Politics* (New York, 1966).

[27] See below.

Hobbes he also legitimatized his application of the *metodo risolutivo* on the epistemological principle of convertibility of *verum* and *factum*.[28]

At the same time, the laws of motion could be taken as the ultimate laws to which social phenomena could be reduced if indeed there is nothing but matter in motion; or at least they could be taken as a material metaphor or paradigm of the laws governing society. The conception of the relationship between political and physical bodies will, throughout the seventeenth century, oscillate between the merely *methodical* and the *material* analogy. Hobbes, in our interpretation, tended towards the former, which does not exclude the *metaphorical* use of mechanical terms. Whether we read him correctly or not, Hobbes himself based his claim to have founded "civil philosophy" on his methodical ingenuity, not on the novelty of his opinions.

Spinoza

Hobbes's argument for the provisional separation between natural and social phenomena could be reversed on his own premises. Spinoza agreed with Hobbes on most physical and anthropological principles. He reversed the emphasis, however. A more subtle account of man's emotional balance (enabling him to dethrone *fear* from the almost absolute monopoly it held in Hobbes's system) and a more realistic outlook of the state (as only one of the many possible social formations) enabled him to place society once more within nature, to deal with the state as a complex physical body (or balance of power), and to ascribe also to the state the *conatus suum conservandi motum* which Hobbes seems to have denied it possesses.

Although, properly speaking, extension (or substance as extended) is but one in number, Spinoza insists on the existence of definite physical bodies—on the right to see not only in simple but also in compound or compound of compounds discrete physical entities.[29] Physical bodies are defined by the *conatus suum conservandi motum*, which depends in part on their individual *quantitas motus*, that is, balance of motions. Descartes' general formula of conservation of momentum in the universe (m.v) is

[28] On the history of this *topos* of the seventeenth century from Hobbes to Vico and on its origin, see B. Croce, *Die Philosophie Giambattista Vico's*, trans. E. Auerbach and Th. Lucke (Tübingen, 1927), pp. 3–17; and K. Löwith, "Vico's Grundsatz: verum et factum convertuntur," *Aufsätze und Vorträge 1930–1970* (Stuttgart, 1971), pp. 157–88. [See also R. Mondolfo, "Il Verum-Factum Prima di Vico" (Naples, 1969) —*ed. note*.]

[29] Spinoza's theory of bodies is contained in some of his letters, and as a separate series of axioms and lemmata in *Ethica*, in *Opera*, ed. J. van Vloten and J. P. N. Land (The Hague, 1913), I, 85–88. The section is clearly an insertion, perhaps out of an intended composition on physics. Cf. A. Rivaud, "La Physique de Spinoza," *Chronicon Spinozanum* 4 (1924–26): 24–57.

used as a definition of *single* bodies,[30] as a physical *principium individuationis.* As long as the body retains its basic "proportion," its specific balance of motions, it remains *one* body (an individuum), even if parts of it are replaced by others.[31] Organic bodies are mechanical complexes capable of assimilating other bodies or of regenerating substitutes (not necessarily copies) of a lost element. Spinoza did not abandon altogether the Cartesian relativization of single bodies or movements; he gave it a positive meaning, much as he did in the case of the corresponding ideas.[32] Every piece of extension in motion may be seen as one, or many, bodies, depending on our point of view. A worm in our blood will recognize the blood, not as one body, but as a universe full of many (microscopic) entities; neither do *we* recognize the *facies totius universi* as what it is—one huge organism.[33] The *unity* of an individuum is its form of organization and consciousness thereof.

These reflections have grave implications—psychological, anthropological, political, and ethical. Some of these Spinoza shared with Hobbes; in many cases, he is more consistent. Against Hobbes, he can view society literally as an organism of sorts, as a body.[34]

1. He agrees with Hobbes that man's emotions and actions are a function of his *conatus esse conservandi* only, but he draws a different picture of the emotional economy and its political relevance. Spinoza emphasizes the conflict of affections due to their origin in inadequate self-consciousness. Hobbes regarded man as one soul, one person, one body; Spinoza's definition of a body and its image allows him to see in man many bodies, many

[30] For Descartes, only the whole, universal continuum of the extended substance really deserves the name of a body and has a constant momentum, that is, an absolute and unchangeable proportion of motion and rest (*quantitas motus*). The single body can be said to have neither any distinct boundaries nor a distinct absolute motion: its inclination to retain its uniform movement in a straight line is never actualized. Cf. A. Kenny, *Descartes: A Study of His Philosophy* (New York, 1968), pp. 200–215. Descartes, then, lacks a physical *principium individuationis*; and Spinoza (much as Hobbes before him) construes his theory of bodies so as to remedy these difficulties. Cf. M. Guerolt, "Spinoza: Dieu," *Ethique* 1 (1968), 529–56. Except for Guerolt and A. Rivaud, "La Physique de Spinoza," little attention has been paid to Spinoza's physics.

[31] *Ethics*, pt. II, p. 13, lemma 4; post. 4. Cf. also *Epistulae, Opera*, ed. J. van Vloten and J. P. N. Land (The Hague, 1913), III, 120: "Per partium igitur cohaerentiam nihil aliud intelligo, quam quod leges sive natura unius partis ita sese accommodant legibus sive naturae alterius, ut quam minime sibi contrarientur. . . ."

[32] Spinoza, contrary again to Descartes, seems to describe a positive function to "confused and indistinct," that is, "inadequate" ideas. They correspond to indistinct entities (or *individua*) and thus have a legitimate ontic status.

[33] *Epistula* XXXII, *Opera*, III, 120.

[34] Spinoza, however, does not explicitly declare societies to be physical bodies; the nearest expression to this effect is in the *Tractatus Theologico-Politicus*, III, in *Opera*, ed. J. Van Vloten and J. P. N. Land (The Hague, 1913), II, 124: "Ad quod nullum certium medium ratio et experientia docuit, quam societatem certis legibus formare, certamque mundi plagam occupare, et omnium vires ad unum quasi corpus, nempe societatis, redigere." Yet our analysis has shown that every single corpus short of the whole universe is only a body in a relative sense.

sometimes conflicting ideas, and souls.[35] For Hobbes, fear of death was the only emotion powerful enough to force man into the social contract and keep him in the state; Spinoza allows for a whole gamut of sometimes contradicting manifestations of self-interest—ambition, gain, fear, care of others—to participate in the creation and maintenance of the *respublica*.[36] Society cannot be maintained by fear only, especially abstract fear as the realization of what would happen without laws. Society is a balance of more or less enlightened self-interests, and only if they converge is the body politics durable. The prudent sovereign is he who does not attempt to eliminate such private interest and opinions (which cannot be achieved even through terror) but utilizes these private interests, without the subjects' awareness, to his own purpose. In this part of his doctrine, Spinoza perhaps found use for Maimonides' "cunning of God," in a manner reminiscent of Mandeville's "private vices, public virtues," or Vico's "providence."[37] This is true for monarchies, aristocracies, and republics alike: the quality (or power) of a constitution depends not on the form of government so much as on the coordination of private interest it achieves, its delegation of power and systems of mutual control of instances.

2. Society, both Hobbes and Spinoza assume, is antagonistic. Yet Hobbes's sovereign is exempt from this antagonism: either the state has the power by delegation of natural rights or it is no state at all. Such delegation by social contract, Spinoza seems to maintain, has no absolute meaning. The state has, identically with its subjects, as many rights as it has the power to enforce them. The sovereign merely participates in the antagonistic, permanent *libido dominandi*.[38] Of course, he can enforce his will by sheer terror; such permanent slavery Spinoza sees as the basis of

[35] *Epistula* XXIV, *Opera*, III, 107: "Unde sequi videtur, sicut corpus humanum ex millenis compositum est corporibus, ita etiam humanam mentem ex millenis constare cogitationibus; et, quemadmodum humanum corpus in millena resolvitur, unde componebatur, corpora, sic etiam mentem nostram, ubi corpus deserit, in tam multiplices, ex quibus constabat, cogitationes resolvi. . . ."

[36] On Spinoza's theory of passions and its consequences on his political theory, see A. G. Wernham, *Spinoza: The Political Works* (Oxford, 1958), pp. 6–11. Lack of any reference to Spinoza's theory of bodies is the only omission in this excellent analysis. Cf. also M. Wartofsky, "Action and Passion: Spinoza's Construction of a Scientific Psychology," in *Spinoza: A Collection of Critical Essays*, ed. M. Grene (Garden City, N.Y., 1973), pp. 329–53.

[37] See below.

[38] Wernham, *Spinoza*, pp. 28–35. In his *Political Theory of Possessive Individualism*, C. B. MacPherson presents Hobbes's analysis of the state as close to the Marxistic analysis of the antagonistic structure of the bourgeois society. Certainly, Spinoza offers even a better analogy. The Marxistic analysis of the modern state insists on the inclusion of the state within the antagonistic members of society. The bourgeois state only *appears* as an embodiment of collective aspirations and as being above the antagonism of society. In fact, it is the guardian of the right to antagonize, that is, exploit, radically as never before. The separation betwen state and society is a bourgeois myth.

the endurance of the Turkish Empire.[39] Yet when such a state collapses, it collapses totally: no change of design, no accommodation is possible. If not a reign of terror, a constitution has to be, in order to endure, in permanent reconciliation of all self-interests of individuals, groups, and the sovereign himself. At any rate, Spinoza's state has no surplus dignity over its constituents; nor is its unity of a higher ontological level than that of individuals, groups, or estates. A complex physical body in general may be stronger or weaker than each of its parts, more primitive or better developed.

3. The more enlightened a society is, the clearer its self-image and the consciousness of its deficiencies will be.[40] An enlightened society will always seek to achieve greater consistency by complying with its basic "pattern" or change its pattern if necessary. Spinoza's *Tractatus Politicus* is a reflection on how to define these patterns for existing constitutions. Aristocracies, for example, consist of a given proportion between patricians and subjects, which must be not smaller than one to fifty;[41] Spinoza implies that De Witt's administration failed because of the lack of this proportion. In order to achieve a maximization of consent, an aristocracy must keep the patriciate mobile—a mercantilistic oligarchy suits this idea best—and a high degree of decentralization. Spinoza's ideal constitutions were, in Vico's language, polities of merchants and shopkeepers.[42]

4. Rigid, throughout unified political organisms are not necessarily more durable. The simpler a body, the more dependent on outer circumstances; a balanced, closed system becomes all the more durable, the richer its inner movements, since its power of regeneration, or "replacement," is increased.[43] Tyrannies, or rigid constitutions, could last longer than complicated systems of balanced particular interests, but for outer pressures and circumstances: in the face of those, a rich flexible system has the better chance. A rigid "unification" is as useless as total anarchy. A stone might last longer than an organism, yet if it does collide and break, it will have lost its identity totally. If a human organism suffers the loss of a hand, it can replace its function through other organs. A tyranny that loses its tyrant is gone; a republic, a monarchy, or a polity with enough organized delegation of powers and active groups has a better capacity to withstand outer crisis. This is, in the long run, why the Israelite theocracy failed: it was too rigid; it collapsed when external pressures loosened. In

[39] Spinoza, *Tractatus Theologico-Politicus*, preface and chap. 7.

[40] This is one inference. Spinoza, however, assumes (*Ethics*, pt. III, prop. 58; pt. IV, prop. 35–37) that the wiser a man is, the more he recognizes the similarities and similarities of interest between himself and his fellowmen.

[41] *Tractatus Politicus*, chap. 8, ed. Wernham, *Spinoza*, p. 379.

[42] *New Science*, § 335, quoted in Wernham, *Spinoza*, p. 343.

[43] That is, its *elasticity*. One can view Spinoza's account of physical bodies as a theory of degrees of elasticity. F. Brandt, *Thomas Hobbes's Mechanical Conception of Nature*, has shown that this conception already underlies Hobbes's critique of Descartes.

short, Spinoza's political theory is a commentary on his fundamental axiom that *ordo et connexio rerum idem est ordo et connexio idearum.*[44]

The history of social theories since antiquity is not devoid of fresh starts and novel approaches. Nor were the best of them short of systematic arguments. The constant search for a new and specific method to ground every new interpretative effort is nevertheless a peculiar feature of modern times. The methodical consciousness of political theories in the seventeenth century and long after took natural sciences as a model. Not only were the *metodo risolutivo e compositivo* or its equivalents copied; the vocabulary of post-Galilean mechanics was applied to "political bodies." Instead of the organological metaphors describing society and its institutions in the tradition of political thought, mechanical metaphors start their eminent career. In the seventeenth century, Hobbes and Spinoza stand for the most consistent attempts to integrate natural sciences and social theory. Their argument is interesting in itself. It also teaches something about the possibilities and limitations of scientific analogies. For historians of the age, they are instructive in yet another way. They reflect a persistent and influential mood of the times.

The mechanical analysis (methodical or material) of "social bodies" assumed more than it could prove. Mechanical terms were, in their use for political theory, in no way better grounded than the organological-biological terms they replaced. But they served as a most adequate expression for a new conviction. Society and its institutions ceased to be an *immediate* product or reflection of nature. They became artificial bodies, a product of man's deliberation and labor, not of his alleged social "instincts." As such, they were believed to be capable of a thoroughly rational design.

In a certain way, the motif was inherited from the political thought of previous centuries. *Der Staat als Kunstwerk* may or may not have been, as Burckhardt believed, the reality of Renaissance Italy; it certainly was a typical Renaissance dream. The last in a certain kind of utopias, and the most interesting, was Campanella's *civitas solis*, a design for the perfect *polis*. The utopian city is artificial in all respects. It represents the perfect environment, capable of transforming man's nature by transforming his circumstances. The reformation or transformation of man is its goal. In summing up this tradition, Campanella's utopianism has become at the same time a prototype of future utopian ideologies. Ideologies can often be defined, not merely by their positive contents, but also by a systematization and forced unification of the adversary's points of view: "dialectical materialism" in the vulgar version of Lenin most clearly reveals its logic through the alleged unity and continuity of "idealism" which it postulates. Campanella found a continuity of diabolic logic in the "Aristotelian"

[44] *Ethics*, pt. II, prop. 7.

point of view: *exiit Machiavellismus ex Peripatetismo*.[45] Aristotle, believing in the eternity of the world and hence in the periodical repetition of all its constellations, could not but assume the unchangeable nature of man also. To accept mankind "as it is" means to confine political philosophy to a "realistic" and deplorable logic of *raison d'état*.[46] Yet since science can prove that the world progresses to its goal, so mankind must be conceived as capable of perfection.[47] The polity which can and will breed a new type of man, not least by planned eugenics, is a true outcome of *poiesis*, an act of designed creation after the pattern of eternal ideas. Whether Campanella drew these last conclusions or not, his *civitas solis* is a true picture of the cosmos, shaping matter by imitating the ideas.

Hobbes and Spinoza, to name only them, when negating utopian thinking, did not simply return to the Aristotelian and medieval tradition of political realism. True, they insisted again on the assessment of "man as he is" as the only basis of any possible political theory; nor did they believe in a possible transformation of human nature or of the anthropological conditions of society. But they retained, against the Aristotelian or medieval transition, the belief in the power of man to affirm the state or to negate it, to design all its institutions or to change them deliberately. Society is an artifice, and only inasmuch as man's mind is a part of nature and obeys natural laws can society be called natural. Some implications of this new sense are obvious; some were actually drawn, some were not. If the state originates in a necessary fiction and thus has neither a body nor an inborn *conatus suum esse conservandi*, then it takes more than a virtuous monarch nourished by a wise instruction (*speculum regale*) to sustain it. Maintaining society must be, for Hobbes, a continuous effort of all society; the making of the state is a *creatio continua*. Or, if we regard a polity, with Spinoza, as a complex body or a self-correcting balance of adverse forces, then the sovereign is hardly a demiurge, but he should certainly be a decent mechanic. The determining force of society is not nature (as instinct or climate) but a man-made constitution. Certainly constitutions, since only of functional value, might be changed when appropriate. A possible implication of the mechanization of politics was the preparation of the rational idiom of revolutions. Political theory

45 Th. Campanella, *Atheismus Triumphatus* (Paris, 1636), p. 20; cf. the introd. to *Metaphysica*, ed. G. di Napoli (Bologna, 1967), I, 22, and also III, 114: "Qui vero negant religionem, sunt indocti, sophistae, ac scelesti, exitium mundi, ut Aristotelici, Sadducei, Averroistae, Epicurus et Machiavellus." Cf. Vico's list of the adherents of *raison d'état* (above, n. 5). It should be added that Campanella's *Metaphysica* had some influence on Vico, cf. K. Werner, *Giambattista Vico als Philosoph und gelehrter Forscher* (Vienna, 1879), p. 145 (the doctrine of *primalitates: posse, nosse, velle*).

46 Meinecke, *Die Idee der Staatsraison* (above, n. 4), pp. 115–29.

47 On Campanella's "scientific" eschatology see also A. Doren, "Campanella als Chiliast und Utopist," *Kultur und Universalgeschichte* (Festschrift to W. Goetz) (Leipzig and Berlin, 1927), pp. 242–59.

began to conceive revolutions as neither illnesses of the organism nor as quasi-natural catastrophies (*revolutiones*),[48] but as deliberate changes of design.

Vico

Vico's links to Hobbes and the Hobbesian tradition are manifold. He, too, stresses the epistemological primacy of matters political over the physical sciences: *verum et factum convertuntur,* and civil society is for him as it was for Hobbes a human artifact. Social structures are neither a product of innate social inclinations nor part of the state of nature. In a way, Vico even radicalizes Hobbes's initial polarization of the natural and civil state. Hobbes could not endow all men, even in *status naturalis,* with a modicum of reason. Indeed, only the faculty of "foresight" accounts for the boundless antagonism within the stateless society. Animals, far from a *bellum omnium contra omnes,* may form natural societies.[49] Antagonism springs from man's knowledge of his vulnerability and of the finitude of natural resources. Foresight breeds acquisitiveness and the urge for protection. But foresight also enables, for the very same reasons, the total transition from the natural to the civil state. Man's fear in the state of nature is rational. Against Hobbes, Vico returns to the conceptions of primitive man as a sheer brute: "From these first men, stupid, insensate, and horrible beasts [*stupidi, insensati ed orribili bestioni*] all the philosophers and philologians should have begun their investigations of the wisdom of the ancient gentiles; that is, from the giants in the proper sense. . . ."[50] The very humanity of man is an artifact.

Is this to say that being within civil society means *contra naturam vivere* and that natural law, even in the minimal sense of "dictates of reason" which Hobbes preserved, is a vacuous phrase? Hobbes, we remember, mediated between nature and society by reference to the natural etiology of the state. Its origin is dictated by the sense of self-preservation. Spinoza, on the other hand, relativized altogether the distinction between bodies natural and artificial; the state and its institution, much as any

[48] The history of the term and the concept from a passive concept of radical changes occurring to the active concept of changes aspired has been sketched by R. Griewank in *Der neuzeitliche Revolutionsbegriff, Entstehung und Entwicklung,* 2d ed. (Frankfurt, 1969).

[49] Thomas Hobbes, *Leviathan,* bk. I, par. 17. Some of the phraseology in this passage was taken over by Mandeville.

[50] *New Science,* § 374. Vico also characterizes the dominant passion of his primordial man as fear—but fear of gods rather than of his fellow-men. Others emphasized timidity: so Montesquieu, *De l'Esprit des Lois,* I, 2, in *Oeuvres,* ed. R. Caillois (Paris, 1951), p. 235—again, arguing against Hobbes's view of the brutality of man in his natural state. Cf. also E. Leach, "Vico and Lévi-Strauss on the Origins of Humanity," in *Giambattista Vico: An International Symposium,* pp. 309–12.

physical compound, are nothing but a balance of forces. Vico sought the mediation between nature and society along an altogether different path. He reinterpreted nature to stand for the very *process* through which man acquires a *second*, social nature. Consequently, he claimed that topical, or historical reasoning is the only instrument with which one can grasp the phases of this process and its driving moments.

"This New Science or metaphysic," Vico announced his program, "studying the common nature of nations [*la comune natura delle nazioni*] in the light of divine providence, discovers the origins of divine and human institutions, [*divine ed umane cose*] among the gentile nations, and thereby establishes a system of the natural law of the gentes, which proceeds with the greatest equality and constancy [*che procede con somma egualità e constanza*] through the three ages. . . . The age of the gods . . . The age of the heroes . . . The age of men, in which all men recognized themselves as equal in human nature. . . ."[51] The term "common nature" is ambiguous. It stands both for a homogeneous process of development *and* for any one of its states, the last of which being the age, if a Marxist term may be used, of "social emancipation" or "true equality." "Natural law" is thus founded neither on social instincts nor on a computation of enlightened interests. It is rather the very immanent, regular, "ideal" process through which civilization emerges time and again as man's acquired collective "second nature." "The nature of peoples is first crude, then severe, then benign, then delicate, finally dissolute."[52]

Vico names this process of transformation an "ideal eternal history [*storia ideal eterna*] traversed in time by every nation in its rise, development, maturity, decline and fall."[53] The ambiguous use of the term "ideal" corresponds to the ambiguous use of the term "natural." The latter had a formal and a material connotation: it stood for a process as well as for the distinctive features of each of the phases of the process, predominantly the original phase. The former stands, again, both for the process and for its goal. More precisely, the "ideal history" does not describe the actual historical course of a definite social entity; rather it measures the actual history against the (methodical) norm of the regular sequence of periods of social creativity. These periods and their immanent sequence are truly *ideal types*. They stand for the course of a "nation" if imagined in and by itself, bare of outer influences.[54] The "ideal history" is a limiting case or

[51] *New Science*, § 31. On the history of the *topos* of the three ages of mankind, cf. A. Funkenstein, *Heilsplan und Natürliche Entwicklung* (Munich, 1965).

[52] *New Science*, § 242.

[53] *Ibid.*, § 245.

[54] The appearance of theologians precipitated, in twelfth-century France, the "premature passage from barbarism to the subtlest sciences," just as the appearance of the philosophers in ancient Greece (*ibid.*, §§ 158–59); the course of Roman history was partly determined through the circumstance that it was founded in the proximity of well-developed cities (*ibid.*, § 160).

a necessary fiction, much like Hobbes's state of nature. Such is Vico's use of the Galilean *metodo risolutivo,* though we look in vain for an awareness of his debt.

"Nature" is not only a given state but also a "process," and what is more, it is not a process reducible to external "necessities." The sequence of human social institutions, though initiated by man's physical environment, is not governed by them throughout. Of itself, albeit "occasioned" by outer necessities,[55] the human spirit, which is one in all its manifestation, emanates all human institutions in regular phases. The order of man's collective institutions determines the order of his ideas. Here, as so often, Vico extrapolates key concepts of heterogeneous philosophical systems from their ontological context to use them in the realm of history only. His theory of occasioned spontaneity bears reminiscences of the occasionalists; the principle *l'ordine dell' idee dee procedere secondo l'ordine delle cose* is a polemical limitation of Spinoza's axiom.[56] The emphasis on human history as a history of man's spontaneous creativity allows Vico to challenge the mechanistic-deterministic interpretation of the foundation (and progress) of civil society. In direct polemics against Hobbes, he intends to show how "divine providence initiated the process by which the fierce and violent were brought from their outlaw state to humanity. . . . It did so by awakening in them [*con risvegliar in essi*; my italics] a confused idea of divinity, which they in their ignorance attributed to that to which it did not belong. Thus through the terror of this imagined divinity, they began to put themselves in some order. . . . This principle of institutions Thomas Hobbes failed to see among his own 'fierce and violent men' . . . and fell into error with the 'chance' of his Epicurus."[57] Between the challenge and the human response Vico inserts the mediation of imagination.

The mediatory function of imagination, immanently developing into "reason," prohibits a purely mechanistic reconstruction of the origins and advancement of "nations." *Verum et factum convertuntur* means, therefore, not only (as it did to Hobbes) that the inquiry into the nature of society is "nearer to us" than the inquiry into the nature of the physical world. Vico set out to prove that the method of historical inquiry is throughout different from the method of reconstruction of physical laws. Assuming the intellect to be uniform in all its "guises," introspection,

55 *De uno principio, Opere* 2:55. "Non igitur utilitas fuit mater iuris et *societatis,* sive metus, sive indigentia, ut Epicuro, Machiavellio, Hobbesio, Spinosae, Baylaeo adlubet: sed occasio fuit, per quam homines, natura sociales et originis vitio divisi, infirmi et indigi ad colendam societatem, sive adeo ad celebrandam suam socialem naturam raperentur."

56 *New Science,* § 238; Spinoza, pt. II, prop. 7; Vico limits the validity of the assertion to the *cose umane*. Cf. F. Nicolini, *Commento storico alla seconda Scienza nuova* (Rome, 1949), I, 94.

57 *New Science,* §§ 178–79; cf. n. 55 above.

that is, the imagination turned inwards, became for Vico the main instrument of historical understanding. Vico seems to see in the Protagorean *homo mensura omnium* principle a natural mode of cognition, serving the construction of society (imagination) as well as its reconstruction (the understanding of its origin). The principle in this, its second, reflective sense, is misleading if used statically. "It is another property of the human mind that whenever men can form no idea of distant and unknown things, they judge them by what is familiar and at hand."[58] The uncritical, or static, projection of one's own image on alien societies or remote phases in *their* own society engenders the "conceit of nations" as well as the "conceit of scholars." But the same principle turns into a constructive tool of understanding if used as a dynamic principle, as a method to reconstruct the phases of society out of the analogy to our own development. Vico thus gave new foundation to the traditional speculative *topos* that the *aetates hominis* are a recapitulation of the *aetates mundi*.[59]

Employed with discipline, the imagination (or introspection) of the historian is not to be understood as the rational isolation of causes or narrative revivification of the past. It rather means the capacity to reconstruct the network of images and corresponding institutions constituting each phase within the "ideal" process of socialization. Imagination was the driving force of cultural transformation, and it is the driving force of the interpretative endeavor to reconstruct them. This interpretative reconstruction, aided with a knowledge of the universal structures of imagination acquired through introspection, has three distinct scopes. (a) Vico's "poetic logic" is, much as primitive thought for Lévi-Strauss, a "logic of the contingent" or of the *a posteriori*.[60] Imagination responds spontaneously to similar circumstances with the same structuring categories (tropes). Their knowledge enables the reconstruction of the original circumstances—the "occasions"—of images (*topoi*) and their corresponding social institutions; the fear of the gods, induced by natural phenomena, acts as the "occasion" for the emergence of the family. Such original images are constructive errors, permitted or even evoked by the cunning of providence.[61] (b) The interpreter will not succeed in rendering meaning

[58] *Ibid.*, § 122.

[59] A. Funkenstein, *Heilsplan*, esp. pp. 36–50, 55, 171 n. 21.

[60] C. Lévi-Strauss, *La pensée sauvage* (Paris, 1962), chap. 2; cf. also E. Leach, "Vico and Lévi-Strauss."

[61] Cf. A. Fáj, "Vico as Philosopher of Metabasis" in this volume. A most striking analogy can be drawn between Vico's theory of "constructive errors" as a manifestation of the "cunning of providence" and the attempt of Maimonides to show how a good portion of the ceremonial law of the Old Testament, notably the sacrifices, was nothing but the attempt of God to detract the nascent Israel from the universal polytheistic cult of the Sabeans. Rather than changing their mentality "from one extreme to the other all of a sudden" (*min ha'hefech el ha'hefech pite'om*), in contradiction to the laws of nature, God allowed for some anthropomorphic institutions to remain but changed their meaning and direction. Maimonides speaks of God's "cunning" (*talattuf*

to discrete, disparate images, institutions, or cultural instances unless he uncovers the patterns of cross-references underlying them, that is, their *context*. Imagination enables the interpreter to find, for example, in Zeus the symbol of class structures. Vico assumes that all spheres of human activity in one age express the same mental configuration. (c) This done, the interpreter will be able to uncover the immanent logic in the transformation of one set of images into another, of one cultural matrix to the next in the line of growth.

The second aspect of Vico's method is of particular interest to the historian of modern historical reasoning. The novel, revolutionary methodical concept which underlies Vico's historical as well as political reasoning is the concept of historical-social *contexts*: each society in each of its successive (ideal) "times" can be determined through some internal, integrating principle rather than, as hitherto, in contraposition to other segments of the historical time. Helped by his imagination, the historian uncovers the "harmony" of an age, the "correspondence" of "accommodation" to each other of all of its manifestations.[62] All human affairs and institutions (*cose umane*) of a society in a given period correspond to and reflect each other. Each of the ideal successive ages of every "nation"—the divine, the heroic, and the human times—brings forth its own significations and achievements, its own language, its own jurisprudence, its own religious imagery. Historical interpretation is an exercise in contextual reasoning.

The awareness that no fact and no piece of historical evidence is self-explicatory outside its context broke with a long methodological tradition. Since antiquity and through the Middle Ages historical facts were considered to need no further interpretation than the verification of their sources and the identification of motives of their agents. History was the

---

fi 'alla, ormat, hashem utebunato). Cf. A. Funkenstein, "Gesetz und Geschichte: zur historisierenden Hermeneutik bei Moses Maimonides und Thomas von Aquin," *Viator* 1 (1970). Maimonides did more than to indicate that parts of the law were a measure against heathenism and "accommodated" to the mentality of nascent Israel. Had this been his only scope, then he could hardly be said to have surpassed the previous exegetical hints or the Christian doctrine of accommodation; and we could see in his detailed account of the Sabean society, as did already H. Graetz, *Die Konstruktion der judischen Geschichte* (1846; reprint ed., Berlin, 1936), p. 86 (note), an example of ahistorical thinking. But he did more inasmuch as he recognized the necessity to alienate Biblical legal institutions from their present meaning and to reconstruct in detail their original context. Maimonides was widely read by Christian scholars in the seventeenth century, and particularly this part of his guide was discussed time and again. Vico may well have been influenced either directly or indirectly (through Spencer, Selden, or Grotius).

[62] *New Science*, § 32 ("Convenevolmente a tali tre sorte di natura e governi, si parlarono tre spezie de lingue . . ."); § 311 ("tra loro conformi"); § 348; § 979 ("mode of the time"). In the following pages I rely on my article "Periodization and Self-Understanding in the Middle Ages and Early Modern Times," forthcoming in *Medievalia et Humanistica*.

simple narrative (*simplex narratio*) of events whose importance was self-evident to their times, wherefore the eyewitness, if only truthful, was regarded as the ideal historian.[63] But Vico was not the first to comprehend that no historical fact is in itself meaningful. Ever since the sixteenth century, philologists, legal historians, and Biblical critics have developed a method of *understanding through alienation and reconstruction*: past monuments and institutions can be understood only if severed from actual connotations and associations and seen in their remote original setting. History became *eo ipso* interpretation.

The *mos gallicus* in the interpretation of the *Corpus Iuris Civilis* was a reaction against the elevation of the Roman law to the status of a universal, inexhaustible paradigm, an ideal law valid for all times. Several humanistic-historical interpretations stressed the irrelevance of Roman law for recent political circumstance. Hotman, the contemporary of Jean Bodin, denied the validity of the *Corpus Iuris Civilis*, not only because the historical conditions underlying it were unique, but also on the strength of the argument that even in its own time, the Justinian code was but an ideal-abstract, never actualized constitution. In the tedious discussion between the adherents of the *Loi écrite* and the adherents of the *coutumes* ("customs"), some of these humanists ended with the realization that there could never be an ideal-rational constitution, valid for every society at all times.[64] Vico accepted these positions and systematized them; in particular, he shared the conviction that custom is the origin of all legal institutions.

Vico must likewise have been aware of the beginnings made in the late seventeenth century of a systematical Biblical criticism. An "understanding through alienation" was also Spinoza's reconstruction of the image of God in the Pentateuch. The interpreter of the Scriptures should not import into them his own dogmatic or philosophical positions but should elicit from the Scriptures themselves the criterion of permissible allegorizations. He will then discover that while the corporeal attributes of God are meant to be a reference to divine passions and affections, the references to God's soul are understood literally. The original *mens auctorum* is thus reconstructed as the philosophically absurd image of a God having

[63] "Dicta autem Graece historia ἀπό τοῦ ἱστορεῖν id est videre vel cognoscere. Apud veteres enim nemo conscribebat historiam, nisi is qui interfuisset, et ea quae conscribenda essent vidisset." Isidor of Sevilla, *Etymologiorum sive originum libri* XX, I, 41, 1 (ed. Lindsay). On the medieval concept of historical facts, see Funkenstein, *Heilsplan*, pp. 70–77.

[64] On the origins of the new hermeneutics in legal theories, cf. J. G. A. Pocock, *The Ancient Constitution and Feudal Law* (Cambridge, 1957), esp. chap. 1; D. R. Kelley, *Foundations of Modern Historical Scholarship; Language, Law and History in the French Renaissance* (New York, 1970). Both lack reference to the important insights of W. Dilthey, *Weltanschauung und Analyse des Menschen seit Renaissance und Reformation*, *Werke* II (Leipzig and Berlin, 1927), pp. 11ff., 113.

a soul but not a body.[65] And it is this image of God which underlies the Israelite theocracy. A reconstruction of the original context of the latter serves as an admonition that it is by no means as ideal a constitution as the Calvinists depicted it, but rather obsolete and unimitable. Vico could refrain from a historical analysis of the Scriptures, for he narrowed his scope. The history of the nations, not of the *populus Dei*—that is, the acts of general rather than particular "providence"—was his declared concern. But the very circumstance that he artificially preserves Augustinian categories shows his awareness of the areas into which contextual reasoning already had penetrated. In short, by the time Vico conceived his "new science," it already had become a truism to warn against those who "mold their notion of past affairs after their resemblance to the present" (*de rebus antiquissimis secundum sui temporis conditionem notionem forment*).[66]

Yet Vico's idea of socio-historical contexts expresses, beyond the insight in the necessity of immanent contextual interpretation, an almost aesthetical category; they constitute an *Einheit in der Manningfaltigkeit*. All manifestations of an age are facets of one and the same collective mental configuration. Vico uses, in a sense peculiar to him, the term "common sense" to name this definite mental configuration of each age,[67] the harmonic principle of each period. This, in essence, is what K. Mannheim was later to call *der totale Ideologiebegriff*, based on the "collective experience" of groups.[68]

In the emphasis on the spontaneous and immanent harmony as the frame of intelligibility we detect Vico's affinity to Leibniz, even if we discard Vico's adherence to the doctrine of "metaphysical points" as insignificant. Indeed, with his distinction between possibility and compossibility,[69]

[65] Spinoza, *Tractatus Theologico-Politicus*, chap. 7. In this theory of an immanent criterion of permissible allegorizations Spinoza relies, beyond particular references, on the hermeneutical theory of Ibn-Erza.

[66] Franz Budde, *Historia Ecclesiastica*, 3d ed. (Jena, 1726), Praef.; quoted by L. Diestel, *Geschichte des Alten Testament in der Christlichen Kirche* (Jena, 1869), p. 463.

[67] *New Science*, § 142: "Common sense is judgment without reflection shared by an entire class, an entire people, an entire nation, or the entire human race."

[68] K. Mannheim, *Ideologie und Utopie*, 4th ed. (Frankfurt, 1965), pp. 60–64, 154–55. The difference between Vico's *sensus communis* and Bacon's *idola fori* lies, to speak Mannheim's language, exactly in that Bacon's idols have the function of uncovering (collective) errors, that they are not universal or *wertfrei*, that they belong to the *partikularer Ideologiebegriff* (p. 58). He does not mention Vico in his historical survey (Vico, however, mentions the idols theory of Bacon as a forerunner of his own inquiries). Cf. also Werner Stark, "Giambattista Vico's Sociology of Knowledge" in *Giambattista Vico: An International Symposium*, pp. 297–307 (without discussion of the "common sense"). It is also interesting to note the similarities and differences between Vico's "common sense" and Ibn Khaldun's *Asabiyah* (*The Mukaddimah*, ed. F. Rosenthal, 3 vols. [Princeton, 1958], vol. I, p. lxxvii; 261–65, and *passim*). Both concepts occupy approximately the same positional value in their systems, but the latter indicates rather an emotional configuration, the former an intellectual.

[69] The best recent discussions are those of Jakko K. Hintikka, "Leibniz on Plenitude, Relations, and the Reign of Law," *Leibniz: A Collection of Critical Essays*, ed. H. G.

Leibniz had already developed the logical foundation of the concept of contextual harmony and made it a cornerstone of his metaphysics. If the predicate-in-notion principle (*predicatum inest subjecto*) is to be taken literally, the monads are contexts of attributes. And monads cluster into "possible worlds," inasmuch as they are, beyond their logical possibility, compossible on the grounds of the principle of sufficient reason.[70] They are a logical, epistemological, but also an aesthetical category of contextual unity.[71]

Vico's "collective mentality of an age" thus has two complementary aspects. On the one hand it secures the anonymity of historical processes: from now onwards, heroes, cultural or political, become ever more dethroned from the outstanding place they had occupied in genetic accounts. *Zeitgeister* of all kinds are imagined as force fields mightier than the mightiest individual. On the other hand, we remember that Vico stressed time and again the spontaneity of this collective mentality of an age. By itself, though indeed "occasioned" by outer necessities, the human spirit emanates all human ideas and institutions in regular phases. Because of this universal though ideal regularity,[72] introspection, that is, imagination, became for Vico the main instrument of historical understanding. Again

---

Frankfurt (New York, 1927), pp. 155–90; and N. Rescher, "Logical Difficulties in Leibniz Metaphysics," *Essays in Philosophical Analysis* (Pittsburgh, 1969), pp. 159–70. It is interesting to note that a modern interpretation suggests reading Leibniz's "Laws of Nature" as having the status of "analogies" or symbols: G. Buchdahl, *Metaphysics and the Philosophy of Science* (Cambridge, Mass., 1969), pp. 394–405; as already L. Couturat, "Sur la Métaphysique de Leibniz," *Revue de Métaphysique et de Morale*, 10 (1902).

[70] What we call context, Leibniz called actual (existing) world, with the greatest degree of "compatible" singulars obeying the least number of principles; this "harmony" or *nécessité physique* (*architectonique*), as differing from mere *nécessité logique*, is grounded on the law of sufficient reason. Each possible "world" and each monad expresses the (undefinable) context of singulars respectively, "states" of singulars. *Die philosophischen Schriften*, ed. C. I. Gerhardt, 7 vols. (Berlin, 1875–90), vol. 6, 50, 321, 612.

[71] On the various aesthetic presumptions and influences of Leibniz cf. for example, A. Bäumler, *Das Irrationalitätsproblem in der Ästhetik und Logik des 18. Jahrhunderts bis zur Kritik der Urteilskraft* (Halle, 1923), pp. 38–60 and *passim*.

[72] The lack of a sense for "individuality" in Vico was argued by F. Meinecke, *Die Entstehung des Historismus*, *Werke* II, ed. E. Hofer (Munich, 1955), pp. 63–69. Meinecke's sense of individuality consists not merely in insistence on singularity, but involved at least in the view of those who tried to find a systematic formula for "historicism" an *epistemic resignation*. The concept demands historical constructs to contain "einen starken unvertilgten Rest von Anschauung" which makes them "individuelle Totalitätsbegriffe" (E. Troeltch, *Der Historismus und seine Probleme* [Tübingen, 1922], p. 36). Meinecke recognizes a few "forerunners"; cf. also his "Klassizismus, Romantizismus und historisches Denken im 18. Jh.," *Werke*, ed. E. Kessel (Munich, 1959), vol. 4, p. 264. Vico, although he recognized the different "guises" of social expression and the singularity of each historical phase (for example, *New Science*, § 148), could not argue their total individuality precisely because he insisted on the basic similarity of the human collective imagination and the phases of its productivity in every society.

we detect the affinity with Leibniz, whose monads represent, as do Vico's societies, a genuine unity only because they produce their perceptions and apperceptions of themselves: they "have no windows"; they are spontaneous. As in his ontology, Leibniz gave also the most radical epistemological meaning to the logical postulate *praedicatum inest subjecto*.

With his own conception of spontaneity of the collective imagination (or *sensus communis*), or rather in his theory of occasioned spontaneity, Vico believes to have mediated between the reality of man's original brutal nature and the ideal of eternal law, between Hobbes and Grotius. Society emerged neither by nature nor by convention but by both, since man could and did transform his brutal nature by himself; he acquired a "historical nature." Leibniz, we remember, attempted a similar mediation between mechanical and teleological models of causation in the field of physics.[73] Vico insisted that "natural law" was based neither on social instincts nor on deliberate reasoning or of necessities (or norms) but on the very immanent, regular, "ideal" *process* through which civilization emerges time and again as man's acquired nature. This is Vico's version of a *List der Vernunft*, of how private vices transform into public benefits.[74] He calls it "providence," a term standing also for immanent dynamics accounting for the regular transformation of one phase into another. The final phase of human egalization, while envisaged as necessarily monarchial, bears nonetheless all the marks of a successful state in Spinoza's terms. It is a balance of conscious, enlightened self-interest.

Thus, in a paradoxical turn of expressions, "providence" came to signify man's emancipation from nature or even from God, the autonomy and spontaneity of his social endeavors. Here Vico expresses, beyond any particular correspondence we might find between his thinking and this or that contemporary theory, the sense and self-understanding of modern thought which stressed, in endless variation, the thesis of man's or nature's autonomy. Vico's aim is to demonstrate the gradual growth of human independence, that is, the rational determination of man's collective fate.

In this sense Vico introduced both historical philology, or contextual reasoning—and the Galilean *metodo risolutivo*—as a means by which to

[73] This interpretative possibility has been pointed out by Y. Belaval, "Vico and Anti-Cartesianism" in *Giambattista Vico: An International Symposium*, pp. 90–91. On Leibniz' *conatus* as mediating between "freedom" and "necessity," see Watkins, *Hobbes's System of Ideas*.

[74] On the origin and development of Mandeville's *topos*, see W. Euchner, *Egoismus und Gemeinwohl: Studien zur Geschichte der bürgerlichen Philosophie* (Frankfurt, 1973), pp. 82–125 and *passim*. The cunning of providence has, for Vico, two distinct functions: the permission of constructive errors of the imagination (above, n. 61) and the sense captured in Mandeville's phrase, or in similar later conceptions (Smith's "invisible hand," Kant's "Verborgener Plan der Natur," Hegel's "List der Vernunft"). On Mandeville and Vico see M. Goretti, "Vico et l'hétérogenèse de fins," *Les Etudes Philosophique*, 3,4 (1968): 351–59 and "The Heterogenesis of Ends in Vico's Thought: Premises for a Comparison of Ideas," in this volume.

mediate between the mechanical and teleological interpretations, between nature and reason through the concept of history. With the help of this version of a *List der Vernunft*, Vico can reintroduce providence into history and thus resume, on a richer base, a tradition of Christian philosophy of history going back to Irenaeus of Lyon, seeking to establish the correspondence between the divine plan of salvation and the immanent nature of man.[75]

Vico's impact was negligible. But his main themes—the contextual harmony within each period, the necessary regularity in the succession of periods (nature), and the growing spontaneity of the social endeavor (freedom)—whether accepted or challenged, maintained a regulative role in the formation of modern historical reasoning.

A Final Comparison

This almost logical sequence, in which Hobbes, Spinoza, and Vico tried to define society in terms of nature, and with procedures taken from natural science, should not be mistaken as a purely dialectical scheme. Dialectical positions, antithetical or mediating, may often characterize the conscious attitude of one system of thought against another; in our case we find also a gradual accumulation and differentiation of similar points of view and methods and, above all, a similarity of scopes. Hobbes, Spinoza, and Vico strive to defend and to define existing political institutions on the basis of a realistic assessment of "man as he is, not as he should be." They represent basic prototypes of anti-utopian thinking grown out of the experience of the modern state. Their defense of political realism is based on a radical interpretation of society or the state as a product of human efforts, that is, of labor.

Yet, an ultimate difference separates Vico from both Hobbes and Spinoza. Hobbes and Spinoza believed society to be an outcome of rational design, though Hobbes believed only one design to ensure the durability of the state. Vico, on the other hand, believed it to be a product of a long evolution in which the individual or a group could not, and should not, interfere. The "mechanization" of political theory or its rejection thus helped to formulate two basic patterns in the varieties of conservative ideologies to come. We can call them, in anticipation, the positivistic and the evolutionary defense of existing orders. Hobbes and Spinoza believed that the state needs the mature participation of each of

[75] With the links between the tradition of the principle of accommodation in Christian philosophy of history I have dealt elsewhere (above, nn. 51, 62). The difference between the medieval principle of accommodation and such modern counterparts as Vico's "providence" is precisely that the latter assume the mediation of human autonomy between the transcendent plan and its adaptation to different human capacities in different ages.

its members; every order, inasmuch as it is genuine order, is worth conservation, yet conserving it is an incessant and conscious task for all. This type of conservatism shares its premises with the utopian or revolutionary ideologies it detests, namely, the recognition of the state as a product of design; it merely negates the wisdom of radical changes. Unwillingly, one could say, Hobbes and Spinoza even prepared the rational idiom of revolutions, while Vico, well aware of the dangers implied in regarding the state as a design always in need of deliberate accommodations to new realities, insisted on the anonymous, almost instinctive amelioration of the human condition.

Maria Goretti

THE HETEROGENESIS OF ENDS IN VICO'S THOUGHT: PREMISES FOR A COMPARISON OF IDEAS

The aim of this essay is to offer a comparison of ideas for the purpose of assessing the importance of what is usually called today the Wundtian law of the heterogenesis of ends for Vico's thought and its significance for our era. It is recognized that the Wundtian law seems to be foreshadowed in numerous passages in Vico's works, all essentially similar to the famous *Axiom* VII,[1] and that it is easy to find some more or less obvious analogies between the Vichian position and that of other thinkers, as different as Mandeville and Smith, Hegel, Marx, and Weber.[2] The comparison has more than a scholarly or historiographical interest; it helps to clarify important aspects of Vico's thought, above all those which concern both the role of egoism in the evolution of customs and the interpretation of providence as Vico conceived it.

Whether or not one considers Mandeville to be an apologist of vice, as his contemporaries generally considered him, or a moralist or sociologist, as the more recent assessments have it,[3] Mandeville considered humanity to be dominated by the mechanism of the passions, gathered under the concept of vice-egoism, which results finally in the creation of power, wealth, and happiness. Obviously Mandeville resolves the heterogenesis of ends into a chemical mechanism, in which, from the mixture of certain elements (in themselves negative) emerge others which are completely heterogeneous with the first and therefore positive. For Vico, the hetero-

[1] *New Science,* §§ 132–33; cf. §§ 341, 344, and 1108.

[2] The connection between the thought of Vico and the authors cited regarding the heterogenesis of ends was also pointed out by Bergin and Fisch in the *New Science.* See Introduction, § F. 6. Cf. also in this regard Duncan Forbes, who writes: "The *locus classicus* of the law of the heterogeneity of ends is the conclusion of the *Scienza nuova*" ("Scientific Whiggism: Adam Smith and John Millar," *The Cambridge Journal* 8, 11 [1954]: 643–70); see also Maria Goretti, "Vico et l'hétérogenèse des fins (Vico et Mandeville)," *Les Études philosophiques* 3–4 (1968): 351–59. For the specific relations between Vico and Mandeville, see Eugenio Garin, "Bernardo de Mandeville," *Civiltà moderna,* 1934, pp. 70–91, and *Per una storia dei rapporti tra Bayle e l'Italia* (Florence: Accademia Colombaria, 1959), p. 212.

[3] Cf. Eugenio Garin, "A proposito di Bernardo de Mandeville," *Giornale critico della filosofia italiana* 37 (1958): 506, 508; and Maria Goretti, *Il paradosso Mandeville* (Florence: Le Monnier, 1958).

genesis of ends operates, not by chemical means so as to yield a "product" —in which case "human" history would become "natural" history[4]—but as a process of self-constitution determined by general principles having neither the a priori character of theological presuppositions nor the necessitarian character of physical laws.[5] This is why Mandeville sees law, justice, and virtue as "social lies," while for Vico they are acquisitions of civilization.[6] In fact, in the transformation from the bellicose to the civilized state, Vico sees the hand of providence; that is, providence determines the heterogenesis of ends. In the light of this proposition one might ask the following questions: (a) Is the auto-transformation of amoral and asocial forces into a social form (civil institutions) and a moral form (justice, the basis of human law and life) a result of a "design" constituted *ab aeterno*, in which case history becomes the theater of a supernatural Mind which operates on two levels, natural and supernatural? (b) Or is such an auto-transformation caused by energies inherent in man, so that the term "providential" assumes the meaning of a natural force, as when we assert that pain is providential because it warns us of danger?

We have already mentioned that, for Vico, history is determined by general principles that do not have the a priori character of theological presuppositions. It would seem obvious, then, that the first question requires no answer. And yet, it has recently been suggested that from certain medieval perspectives, as, for example, the "political theology" of Eusebius or the thought of Anselm of Havelberg, "society emerges out of (enlightened) self-interest" and that this view is connected with the modern, secularized principle of the heterogenesis of ends.[7] One would be tempted, as Amos Funkenstein observes, to connect "the cunning of God" and the Hegelian "cunning of Reason." However, "Medieval evolutionary models defied the apocalyptical insistence on the utter passivity of man in history . . . they did not, as the modern successors of the principle of accom-

[4] A connection between Vico and Dilthey was noted precisely in relationship to the well-known distinction, popularized by Dilthey, between the human and the natural sciences. See H. A. Hodges, "Vico and Dilthey," and H. P. Rickman, "Vico and Dilthey's Methodology of the Human Studies" in *Giambattista Vico: An International Symposium*, pp. 439–45 and 447–56, respectively.

[5] See Leon Pompa, "Vico's Science," *History and Theory* 10 (1971): 49–83, where one reads: "The theory is thus deductive and rests upon necessary ('eternal') or unchallengeable propositions." Pompa deals with the problem of the relation between the "true" and the "certain" in order to determine the scientific validity of Vico's thought.

[6] See Sław Krzemień, "La vision de la science chez G. B. Vico," *Organon* 3 (1966): 185–200. Krzemień shows the secondary aspect of egoism in Vico's thought and writes: "Egoism, as depicted by Hobbes, is not a primary but a secondary quality of human nature." In fact, it is one thing to say that human behavior is motivated by savage and voluptuous instincts (as Vico does) and another to assert that man is defined by such instincts (as do Hobbes and Mandeville). In the first case we have a statement of fact, in the second an a priori and therefore gratuitous value judgment.

[7] Amos Funkenstein, "Periodization and Self-Understanding in the Middle Ages," forthcoming in *Medievalia et Humanistica*. See also the same author's *Heilsplan und natürliche Entwicklung* (Munich, 1965), pp. 34–35.

modation, use the term of providence as a cover for the absolute autonomy of the process in which 'man maketh himself'. . . ."[8] Thus, it is suggested, among the moderns the concept of "providence"—variously translated as "invisible hand" (Smith) or as "cunning of Reason" (Hegel)—would be a kind of metaphor for or actually a masking of the principle of the autonomy of human action. With respect to Vico, one would have to ask if the hypothesis of masking could be accepted. It would be necessary, then, to consider the importance of religion in Vico's thought.

In the concept of religion, one can distinguish two well-known meanings, one referring to an objective datum as revealed truth and the other to a subjective datum as an awareness of the divine, which ends by being assimilated to moral consciousness. The disjunction or juxtaposition of these two meanings was present in the religious drama manifested both in the bloody battles of the Wars of Religion and in the great metaphysical thoughts of the seventeenth century. Such a juxtaposition is, however, totally alien to Vico's thought. Vico, concentrating on the concrete problem of the formation of civil society, assumes that religiosity is the first and most powerful motive force of human action (from which it follows that egoistic motives must be secondary) and that, therefore, internal and subjective motives are externalized in the reality of the objective datum in its meaning as a revelation of truth. Thus, Vico asserts, "fear made the gods."[9]

Putting aside the traditionalist question, however, there could still remain the question regarding the "divine plan," which would place Vico in the deistic atmosphere of his age, in the providentialist mode of Adam Smith. It has already been noted that the principle of the heterogenesis of ends characterizes the philosophy of history of Smith.[10] However, in Smith, as in the other deists, the providential order is a kind of "confirmation" of a rational order; thus the moral imperative does not derive its authority and validity from the notion of God, but the notion of God, rather, derives from the moral imperative. Thus, if Smith's image of the "invisible hand" tends to dissociate human history from theological pre-

[8] Funkenstein, "Periodization and Self-Understanding," pp. 22–23.

[9] Vico does not raise the problem, metaphysical and theological in nature, of the "essence" of God, having already stipulated that it was impossible to know how God acted. See R. Flint, *Vico* (Edinburgh and London, 1884), pp. 194–95, where he writes: "Vico does not try to explain the facts by the doctrine of Providence, but to evolve a doctrine of Providence from the facts." Cf. also F. Vaughan, "*La Scienza nuova*: Orthodoxy and the Art of Writing," *Forum Italicum* 2, 4 (1968): 348, where it is observed: "I suggest that Vico had no interest in vindicating Christianity's place in history. His was a merely philosophical concern . . . the obscurity of the *Scienza nuova* was a device deliberately chosen . . . in order to conceal an unpopular teaching." We are not convinced, however, because, as we have said, we think that the absence of religious drama in Vico's thought is manifest. See, however, G. F. Cantelli, *Vico e Bayle: premesse per un confronto* (Naples, 1971), p. 82.

[10] See L. Limentani, *Le morale della simpatia* (Genoa, 1914), p. 240.

suppositions (and in this way recalls the Vichian position) on the one side it presents the transcendental God as the revelation of human *ratio*, and, on the other side, it constitutes God as surety of the moral truth of utilitarian principles.[11] In other words, Smith, not unlike the traditionalists, claims to know how God operates.[12] Vico rejected this claim as unscientific. Man, in fact, "knows" his own history, of which he is the "cause"; and this "science" reveals the providentiality of history in that very possibility of knowledge. This explains, therefore, how Vico, in opposing the rationalistic abstraction of deism, opposes also the hypothesis of fate, chance, and fortune, inasmuch as, as Croce noted, these are all concepts which tend to separate man from his own acts. The concept of providence as the hidden plan of history fits well with the Cartesian cosmology but not with that of Vico, in which the notion of *conatus* permits one to substitute the concept of dynamism for that of mechanism.[13]

Let us turn now to the second question, which has to do with the identification of God's plan with the "cunning of Reason." Let us remember that since for Hegel history was a theogony, that is to say, a progressive incarnation of the Logos, individuals are only "means and instruments of something higher." Moreover, he adds, "The particular is too unimportant to be compared to the universal: individuals must be sacrificed and abandoned to their fate."[14]

This conception is tied, in part at least, to a well-known tradition of Neo-Platonic mysticism in which individuals lose their personal characteristics. Thus Hegelian thought could easily be used to justify totalitarian regimes. For Vico, however, *determinatio* is not *negatio*, but rather enrichment, as it is for Dilthey. Thus individuals, whether as single persons or as peoples, are neither means nor instruments, even though individuals may use well or badly the means given to them by nature. This "nature" is provident, not so much because it operates as necessity or according to a preestablished plan (as both the "invisible hand" and the "cunning of reason" presuppose), but in the degree to which men can make use of it. In other words, the "divine providence" of which Vico speaks is the very nature of men, who know how to transform themselves from animals into civil beings and who also know how to lose themselves once more in the shadows of a ferine existence. Thus, it is logical that Hegel should speak of a "Providential plan, in which the world spirit realizes its freedom

[11] *Ibid.*, p. 157.

[12] Werner Stark, "Max Weber and the Heterogeny of Purposes," *Social Research* 34, 2 (1967): 264, in which the theological substructure of Smith's thought is pointed out.

[13] Y. Belaval, "Vico and Anti-Cartesianism" in *Giambattista Vico: An International Symposium*, pp. 77–91; Robert Nisbet, "Vico: The Anti-Descartes," *The American Scholar* 39, 4 (1970): 714–18.

[14] G. W. F. Hegel, *Sämtliche Werke, Vorlesung über die Philosophie der Geschichte*, (Stuttgart: Fr. Fromanns Verlag, 1928), vol. 9, p. 63.

in its successive incarnations and peregrinations,"[15] and that his history should take on an optimistic and eschatological meaning.

This same eschatological and optimistic meaning is also found in Marxist doctrine. "The twilight of the bourgeois class and the victory of the proletariat are both inevitable," we read in the *Manifesto*; the social struggle will lead to the paradise of the socialist state, which will be the concrete realization of liberty. Viewing the heterogenesis of ends from such a perspective, it is obvious that the development of social structures presupposes a mechanistic play of forces and that man is identified with economic activity, even if Marx proclaimed that "history only uses man as a means" and that "[history itself] is nothing but the activity of men in pursuit of their own ends."[16] Thus the Marxist heterogenesis of ends could be assimilated both to the mechanistic principle of Mandeville and to the Hegelian cunning of reason from which it derives. As a result, thanks to its eschatological and optimistic basis, the Marxist doctrine takes on a logico-emotive value similar to that which the mortification of the senses assumes in positive religions as a means of extra-mundane salvation and thus assumes the significance of a social-prophetic message.[17] Vico, however, works in a completely different mode, not a metaphysical or utopian one, but an empirical-deductive one, which permits us to consider it in comparison with the positions of Wundt and Weber.

According to Wundt's psychological theory, myth, language, and custom are considered as products of a social spirit by which the end of beings is being modified at the same time that the beings are undergoing transformation: from which one can derive the idea of the heterogenesis of ends.[18] If one took this in a purely literal way, one could see obvious analogies with Vico's thought. And yet, it would be well to recall Weber's objection to Wundt, which was that Wundt had essentially elevated a purely psychological consideration into a world view. It is this very psychologism, it would seem, which differentiates the Vichian from the Wundtian positions. For Vico, the heterogenesis of ends is not to be explained simply in terms of psychological causality, but by the principle of historical causality, which in Vichian thought provides the only means of empirical certainty and thus of verification.[19] The comparison with Weber seems

[15] See Pietro Piovani, "Vico without Hegel" in *Giambattista Vico: An International Symposium*, which brilliantly demonstrates the divergence between the thought of Vico and Hegel, by sustaining the thesis of a persistent Cartesianism in Hegelian thought.

[16] Marx and Engels, *Gesamtausgabe*, I, 3, *Die Heilige Familie*, p. 286.

[17] Stark writes: "Pain as historically experienced is therefore to Marx merely a part of the price which mankind must pay for its salvation, for the coming of the kingdom" ("Max Weber and the Heterogeny of Purposes," p. 259).

[18] See Wilhelm Wundt, *Grundriss der Psychologie* (Leipzig, 1896), and *System der Philosophie*, 4th ed. (Leipzig, 1919), pp. 339ff.

[19] See G. Vadalà-Papale, *Dati psicologici nella dottrina giuridica e sociale di G. B. Vico* (Rome, 1889), p. 151, n. 175, in which it is maintained that the ontological nature of Vichian providence must be denied.

more appropriate. For both Vico and Weber, historical causality is characterized by the motive; hence Weber's "understanding" of the historical fact seems to resemble the "science" of the historical fact posited by Vico; furthermore, the Weberian concept of "ideal types," considered not as historical forces but as heuristic devices serving the historian in his interpretation, presents many points of contact with Vico's ideal eternal history, considered not as a "parameter" but as an heuristic instrument of interpretation. And when Vico writes that "our science is therefore a history of human ideas,"[20] his thought corresponds to that of Weber, who regarded his studies of capitalism as a contribution to the understanding of the ways in which ideas function in history. Affinities between Weber and Vico could be found also in the fact that Weber, in his work on the sociology of religion, opposed the Marxist theses concerning the exclusive dependence of historical processes on economic development. Vico, too, in his examination of the formation of civic institutions, stressed that if economic phenomena affect customs, juridical rules, and civil structures, these economic phenomena are conditioned in turn by the form and nature of such structures.[21]

It is true that Weber, not unlike Smith, Hegel, and Marx, believed it possible to give a metaphysical meaning to the interpretation of history; but while Smith, Hegel, and Marx gave a positive sense to the idea of the heterogenesis of ends, Weber gave it a negative one. This is the point emphasized by Stark.[22] For Smith, Hegel, and Marx, that is, the heterogenesis of ends presupposes a providential force which creates good out of evil; for Weber, the best ideals (the puritan virtue of Calvinism) are condemned to produce bitter fruits (the rise of capitalism and thus the sacrifice of virtue to the golden calf). Stark has stressed the anti-scientific nature of such notions, in which one has recourse to a *deus ex machina*, whether it be God or the Devil, which have virtually no logical content.

In Vico, neither God nor the Devil functions as a *deus ex machina* in history; we find instead the traditional Renaissance notion of man as an "immortal god"—man in his fallible yet perfectionable nature, who by means of errors, illusions, and imaginings succeeds in becoming aware of himself as creator of both reason and justice, driven not by a preordained "plan" or by a "cunning reason" but guided by his own humanity, which is both flesh and spirit, bestiality and divinity, who dies and is reborn like the

[20] *New Science*, § 347.

[21] See Pompa, "Vico's Science," p. 82, which stresses the sociological implications of Vico's work; also, R. Rontchevsky, "G. B. Vico, philosophe de l'histoire et du droit," *Études politiques* (Strasbourg, 1960), pp. 35–49.

[22] See once more the work of Stark in which, precisely because of this recourse to the *deus ex machina*, he denounces the anti-scientific nature of the heterogenesis of ends, as expressed by Wundt and Weber, and *ante litteram* by Mandeville, Hegel, and Marx. Our discourse has been meant to show how the heterogenesis of ends as conceived by Vico avoids the "impasse" denounced by Stark.

Phoenix. Vico does not view history as portending the triumph of either good or evil, but as the justification of man himself.

We hold, therefore, that one of Vico's outstanding contributions was to have suggested precise orientations for a methodology of the human sciences, free from eschatological principles and from optimistic or pessimistic qualifications, so that history does not turn out to be a "comedy of errors," as we find in Croce, or a "divine comedy of truth," as with Löwith, but appears as the revelation of the humanity of man even in spite of the animality of the passions. Vico teaches us that history is not to be read in the light of ideologies, but he also warns us that ideologies have their own historical reality and thus their own way of operating in history, so that it is necessary that both the historian and the sociologist exercise toward them their critical function of understanding.

Translated by Margaret Brose

Nathan Rotenstreich

VICO AND KANT

The exploration of the relationship between Vico and Kant is a clear case of an investigation into a possible affinity of ideas, which is not grounded in a biographical or factual dependence of Kant upon Vico. Our procedure will thus be to interpret Vico in the light of Kant and to interpret Kant in the light of Vico.

We may start the present exposition by outlining the broad sphere of the proximity between the two systems insofar as their respective thrusts are concerned. The two systems have in common the notion of human creativity. Human creativity is not a copy of the course of events of the extra-human world; nor is it fully determined within the human scope itself. Vico clearly belongs to the Renaissance tradition of interpretations of human creativity insofar as the various expressions or modifications of the human mind are concerned—language, poetry, myth, and history. Kant, within his own system, gives the notion of creativity its own particular seal insofar as knowledge and morality are concerned. There are differences between the two thinkers in their elaborations of the theme of creativity, but, just the same, that very theme sets the common ground of the two philosophers.

The heritage the two share can be formulated more poignantly by referring to what could be called the spontaneity of the finite being. Let us take spontaneity in this context as connoting the capacity of bringing about certain products initiated by the mind. We do not at the outset confine the notion of spontaneity to the production of representations as Kant had it, since, as we shall see, Kant himself takes a broader concept of spontaneity than that. We take spontaneity as being concomitant with creativity. Hence the main emphasis has to be laid on the aspect of finiteness in its combination with spontaneity. The human being is a finite being, and both Vico and Kant share the view as to the finiteness of man. In spite of his finiteness, man is endowed with spontaneity and thus creates his own world within the confinement of his finiteness. It is in this sense that Vico and Kant perpetuate the same tradition and formulate variations on the same guiding ideas, though in their respective formulations there are significant divergences of opinion between them on several issues. We shall attempt now to present and to analyze some specific points within the boundaries of the two systems.

The Cogito

Vico's position on Descartes' *Cogito ergo sum* is well-known. It attracted rightly a great deal of attention among the interpreters of his system. Let us sum up briefly Vico's position and then move to Kant. Vico does not take the view that the *cogito* constitutes a basis of what he calls *scientia*. It cannot be the basis of *scientia* because *scientia* is by definition *scientia* of causes. To know truly is to know *via* causes, while in knowing one's own consciousness or thought one does not know the causes; one does not know how and why he thinks. Not knowing the causes of his consciousness, one does not know his existence. The thought as such is not a cause or an explanation of an existence; it is a sign of my being a mind, but the position of a sign is by no means the position of a cause. Hence we have to observe the distinction between knowledge and awareness, or between *scientia* and *conscientia*.[1]

It has to be made clear from the beginning that Vico uses, in his context and generally in his criticism of the Cartesian position, the notion of the cause in a rather definite sense. A cause is, for him, a cause of existence (*causa essendi*). In the Aristotelian sense a cause denotes, at least partially, that out of which something comes about. A cause has for Vico, in a way, an emanating position—that out of which an existent fact emerges. Vico's criticism of Descartes, centering around the distinction between *cogito* and *sum*, is grounded in the view that the *cogito* is not the *causa essendi* for the *sum*. The distinction Vico himself suggests, that between a sign and a cause, is a very adequate way of summing up the main point of his criticism: real knowledge would amount to the knowledge of the emanating process from thinking to existence, and that knowledge is out of reach for the finite mind.

Kant expresses his criticism of the Cartesian view in a way which is similar to that of Vico. Since for Kant, too, "I cannot determine my existence as that of a self-active being; all that I can do is to represent to myself the spontaneity of my thought, that is, of the determination; and my existence is still only determinable sensibly, that is, as the existence of an appearance. But it is owing to this spontaneity that I entitle myself an intelligence."[2] A closer reading of Kant's text will bring into prominence the difference between Kant and Vico. The first item pertaining to that

[1] The main reference in the subsequent analysis is to *De Italorum sapientia, Opere* (Ricciardi), pp. 248ff.

[2] *Kritik der reinen Vernunft*, *B*, p. 158n. (p. 169). Page numbers in parentheses refer to the Norman Kemp Smith translation (New York: St. Martins Press; Toronto: Macmillan, 1965). References to the first edition will be cited as A and to the second edition as *B*.

difference is related to the different understanding of the notion of cause, or of being a cause. While Vico, as we have seen, takes cause to be a cause of existence, Kant understands the relationship described by a cause as one of dependence, or more closely, of a dependence within a context of a sequence of events, *a* and *b*, against the background of time. Kant does not stress the aspect of emergence, characteristic of the position of the cause: causality is related to the succession of the manifold insofar as that succession is subject to a rule.[3] It is clear from this preliminary exposition that while Vico speaks about a cause and its emanating capacity of positing existence, Kant starts his exploration of the principle of causality or the notion of the cause from the given manifold; causality is the principle, not of the emergence of the manifold, but of the regularity of succession and relation within the manifold.

For that reason Kant could not argue against the notion of the *cogito ergo sum* that the *cogito* is not the emanating power of the *sum*, though he shares the preamble of Vico's criticism that *cogito* indicates self-awareness only and thus cannot imply existence. Kant shares Vico's view that *cogito* is a reflective activity, related to the ego itself, and not an existential proposition. But he differs from Vico in his understanding of existence. Kant says that the proposition "I think" is taken only problematically, which means it is taken insofar as it may contain perception of an existent;[4] or put differently, the "I" as such does not contain in itself the least manifoldness because it is merely a logical unity, and as a logical unity it is an absolute unity.[5] We cannot make the transition from the expression "I" to the soul since to know about the soul calls for experience, and that which depends upon experience cannot be inferred from the concept "I."[6] Hence we face a dilemma: either the "I think" is merely a logical proposition and does not entail any statement about existence or the "I think" is an empirical proposition and as such contains within itself the proposition "I exist." "For it must be observed, that when I have called the proposition 'I think,' an empirical proposition, I do not mean to say thereby, that the 'I' in this proposition is an empirical representation. On the contrary, it is purely intellectual, because belonging to thought in general. Without some empirical representation to supply the material for thought, the *actus* 'I think,' would not, indeed, take place; but the empirical is only the condition of the application, or of the employment, of the pure intellectual faculty."[7] On the negative aspect, Kant takes the view Vico takes, namely: the self-reflective or intellectual character of the "I think" does not imply an existential position. But they differ as to the

[3] *B*, p. 183 (185).
[4] *B*, p. 405 (332).
[5] A, p. 354 (337).
[6] *B*, p. 423, note (378, note).
[7] *B*, p. 423, note (378, note).

reason for this want of application: for Vico existence has to emerge from its cause, but as things stand it does not emerge out of the *cogito*. For Kant existence cannot emerge out of the *cogito*, and thus, in order to introduce in the context the concept of existence, we are bound to rely on a manifoldness which lies beyond the boundaries of the *cogito*. For Vico, existence does not emanate from the *cogito*; therefore the *cogito* cannot be the cause of existence. But ideally there has to be a relationship of emanation between a cause and an existence. For Kant the *cogito* in its logical unity is not a cause at all; the emergence of existence is excluded as a matter of principle, because existence is related to what Kant calls "positing."[8]

A parallel structure of reasoning appears in the context of the ontological argument for the existence of God. Vico's argument against the ontological proof can be summed up briefly by saying that according to him an attempt to prove a priori the existence of God exhibits an impious curiosity. This proof is a kind of arrogance on the part of the finite human beings to set themselves up to the position of God. The fundamental mistake of the ontological proof lies, therefore, in the attempted transgression performed by the finite mind pretending to reach the level of infinity and to argue and reason on that level. We may add here, following the previously explored aspect of Vico's doctrine, that to know a priori God is to know the cause of his existence; this is prohibited by the very status of the finite man.

Kant's argument criticizing the ontological proof runs differently and is grounded in Kant's conception of existence. Before moving to that point, let us examine a random observation by Kant on the concept of substance. Kant says that the concepts of necessity and accidentality seem not to be applicable to substance. In addition, we do not ask the question about the cause of the existence of a substance. This is so, since substance is by definition that which is, what always was, and is bound to remain. In terms of the concept of substance, there is no room for the concept of cause. Substance is itself a cause but not a result.[9] Kant seems to suggest in that statement that if we apply at all the concept of cause to the concept of substance, that concept is bound to carry the connotation of being a cause in itself (*causa sui*). Thus via the concept of cause, substance is not lodged in a context, while as a rule the concept of substance refers to a contextual view in terms of the time sequence, or in terms of the relationship between cause and its effect. Speaking about God as a substance connotes the self-contained character of God. Thus the concept of cause can have a meaning only in terms of the *set-up* network of relations in which God is posited.

[8] *B*, p. 626 (504).

[9] *Kants Gesammelte Schriften*, ed. Preussischen Akademie der Wissenschaften, 22 vols. (Berlin: Walter de Gruyter, 1942), pp. 329–30.

Hence, Kant's criticism of the ontological argument does not center around the alleged transgression of the boundaries of finitude. On the contrary, since the ontological argument relates to the attempted demonstration of the existence of God, the question raised is that of the meaning of existence. The meaning of existence as applied to data, that is, the contextual meaning of existence, is the guiding notion even in Kant's criticism of the ontological argument. Hence Kant says that *being* is not a real predicate and cannot be related intrinsically or immanently to God, or else as immanent there would be no distinction between the real and the possible. This is so, since the object as it actually exists is not analytically contained in my concept. It is added synthetically to that concept, or, to put it differently, existence is a position outside my concept. The ontological argument of Descartes is in Kant's eyes, not a transgression, but a way of waste labor and effort: "We can no more extend our stock of (theoretical) insight by mere ideas, than a merchant can better his position by adding a few noughts to his cash account."[10]

The difference between Vico and Kant is visible in their respective criticism of both the Cartesian notion of the *cogito ergo sum* and the ontological proof in its Cartesian variation. For Vico existence is an outcome of the process of emanation, while for Kant existence is an involvement in a network of relations. The existence of the *sum* for Vico cannot be traced to its source in the *cogito*, and thus "the ontological proof" of the existence of the ego is precluded. For Kant the existence of the ego is his involvement in a network of relations and as such cannot emanate from the ego as a logical unity. For Vico the existence of God cannot be demonstrated a priori, since the existence of an infinite entity cannot emanate from a finite mind. For Kant the existence of God cannot be demonstrated a priori because the concept of existence which pertains to the finite ego pertains to the infinite God as well, since existence is the conceptual rendering of a position and not a result of an emanation. Both Vico and Kant put their anchor of criticism of the Cartesian ideas in the self-awareness of the ego or in its reflexivity; but this phenomenological character of the ego does not contain the existential locus of the ego.

It is at this point that we find Vico and Kant's teachings respectively as seminal notions of the subsequent development of the philosophical thought. For Vico, as we have seen vis-à-vis the ontological argument, the discrepancy between the finite mind and the infinite entity of God is the ultimate word of the system. Hegel's attempt to redeem and save the ontological proof of the existence of God can be located here. Hegel does not accept Kant's view that the concept of existence or reality applicable to sensuous data is applicable to God. On the contrary, the truth of the finite is the absolute spirit, and the character of the absolute is the

[10] *B*, p. 630 (507).

identification of being with itself.[11] Once the barrier between the finite and infinite is removed, and the infinite reveals itself through the finite and the finite finds its consummation in the infinite, the validity of the ontological argument is warranted. Hegel accepts here Vico's view as to the chasm between the finite and the infinite only as a point of departure. In addition, he accepts Vico's view that existence or reality can be of an immanent character, once immanence is understood as a self-activity and self-positing, or once there is no distinction between reflection and the position in terms of reality or actuality, that is, when actuality is an outcome of self-activity. Hegel does not accept Kant's view—indeed he criticizes it explicitly—that a category of thinking applicable to encountered data is by the same token applicable to an absolute entity in whose orbit there are not-to-be-encountered data, only self-activity and its outcome.

On the other hand, in some of the existentialist descriptions and analyses we find an echo of Kant's view according to which the ego is involved in a network of relations of which it is not the originator. Thus characteristic of the ego is its existential involvement in situations whose determination lies beyond its boundaries. The ego is primordially involved in a non- or anti-rational situation.

Having explored the first aspect of the systematic confrontation between Vico and Kant against their common meeting ground, we may now move to the second aspect of that confrontation.[12]

Creation and Transubstantiation

Vico's theory of the identity of *verum-factum*, or of the certainty of a truth as being grounded in the fact that one has made that truth himself, is the most renowned aspect of his system and, as such, does not call for any further elaboration in this context. What is needed here is an exploration of Kant's view, keeping in mind the question of whether Kant follows here Vico's line at all and, if so, to what extent he follows it.

The interpretation of the *verum-factum* principle which guides the present interpretation is implied in our previous analysis. Let us state the following: underlying the *verum-factum* principle is the notion that an object can be known only when it is ontologically of the character of the

[11] Georg Wilhelm Friedrich Hegel, "Religion philosophie," *Sämtliche Werke*, ed. H. Glockner, 26 vols. (Stuttgart: Fr. Fromanns Verlag, 1927), vol. 16, pp. 539, 551.

[12] Vico's relation to Descartes has been frequently explored. Consult Robert Flint, *Vico* (Edinburgh and London: Blackwood and Sons, 1884) pp. 50ff.; Benedetto Croce, *The Philosophy of Giambattista Vico*, trans. R. G. Collingwood (New York: Russell and Russell, 1964), chap. 1, pp. 1ff.; Isaiah Berlin, "The Philosophical Ideas of Giambattista Vico," in *Art and Ideas in Eighteenth Century Italy* (Rome: Edizioni di Storia e Letteratura, 1960), pp. 156ff.; Yvon Belaval, "Vico and Anti-Cartesianism" in *Giambattista Vico: An International Symposium*, pp. 77ff.; and Giorgio de Santillana "Vico and Descartes," in his *Reflections on Men and Ideas* (Cambridge, Mass., and London: M.I.T. Press, 1968), pp. 206ff.

knowing subject; in other words, true knowledge is a knowledge based on adequacy. Adequacy in the strict sense amounts to homogeneity between the knower and the known object. That homogeneity is warranted by the emanation of the object from the knower. This is so on the divine level in the total sense: God can know the world because he created it. Man can know history because he created it.

Let us start with Kant's own famous metaphor, or comparison of his own theory with Copernicus' primary notion. Kant says that if intuition must conform to the constitution of the objects, there can be no ground for the assumption that we could know anything of those objects a priori. On the contrary, if the objects must conform to the constitution of our faculty of intuition, there is no difficulty in conceiving such a possibility of knowing of the objects a priori.[13] Kant amplifies his supposed affinity with Copernicus in his emphasis of the distinction between placing the observed movements in the heavenly bodies as against placing them in the spectator; he says that Copernicus could discover the invisible force which holds the universe together only by shifting that force from the observed movements to the spectator.[14] In both statements it is clear that Kant presents an analogy between his position and that of Copernicus as related to the dichotomy between the objects and the subject, and he seems to follow Copernicus in placing the center in the subject. This is summed up in Kant's description of the true method, which cannot be found by way of inspecting that which is discerned in the figure. The true method lies in bringing out that which was necessarily implied in the concepts; and they are formed a priori. These concepts are necessarily put into the figure in the construction by which he presented that construction to himself. "If he is to know anything with *a-priori* certainty, he must not ascribe to the figure anything save what necessarily follows from what he has himself set into it in accordance with his concept."[15]

There can be no question that this very presentation of the Copernican hypothesis as applied to the sphere of knowledge, or the emphasis laid by Kant on the proportional relationship pertaining between knowing anything with a priori certainty and imposing the a priori concepts on the objects, is a variation on Vico's theorem of *verum-factum*. But already at this point we cannot be oblivious of the significant systematic change which occurred in the transition from Vico to Kant: Kant applied the formula of the relationship between a priori concepts and a priori certainties to physics, while Vico tried to show precisely that that applicability is precluded, and the formula can hold good for history and not for physics.

The affinity between Vico and Kant has been pointed out in the fre-

[13] *B*, p. xvi (22).
[14] *B*, p. xvi (25).
[15] *B*, p. xii (19).

quently quoted statement by Jacobi. Jacobi sums up Kant's philosophical position by saying that we comprehend an object only insofar as we let the object emerge in thought before us, insofar as we are able to create it in understanding. Jacobi refers subsequently to Vico, who at the beginning of the eighteenth century wrote that we demonstrate in geometry because we create; before we demonstrate in physics we must be able to create there.[16] The question which we are about to ask at this point is, Since Jacobi has seen correctly the affinity between Vico and Kant, is his interpretation of that affinity adequate or exhaustive? Or, to put it differently, has he not over-interpreted Kant in order to make him more Viconian than Kant really was? Our task will not be to present a whole view of Kant's philosophy, but only to concentrate again on those topics capable of shedding light on Vico's view on the one hand and on Kant's view on the other.

Having said this, and reiterating the kinship between Vico and Kant, we have to qualify Jacobi's statement in some rather significant aspects. Let us start with an additional reference to Jacobi, since he prefaces his own description of the affinity between Vico and Kant by his particular interpretation of Kant, which we can now follow. Jacobi says that the objects of different kinds of knowledge lend themselves through a sort of transubstantiation to transformation into mathematical and logical entities. This transformation and transubstantiation cannot be performed vis-à-vis the proper objects of metaphysics—God, freedom, and immortality—and therefore these objects are out of the reach of knowledge.[17] It goes without saying that Jacobi rejects the implied pretense of knowledge and the quasi-transubstantiation performed by it. Reason or understanding are capable, according to him, of achieving only a dismembering of the objects, but the primary articulate structure of members (*ursprüngliche Gliederung*) is a secret of the creation.[18] It is not by accident that Jacobi employs in his description that Christological concept of transubstantiation, since he seeks eventually to reject the notion that knowledge can introduce changes in reality, while, according to his own systematic conception, knowledge has to take—and can take—reality as it is.

But precisely at this point Jacobi fails to do justice to Kant, and hence

[16] Friedrich Heinrich Jacobi, Von den *göttlichen Dingen und ihrer Offenbarung*, zweyte wohlfeilere Ausgabe (Leipzig: Gerhard Fleischer, 1822), pp. 121–23. The relevant passage is quoted in English in the Introduction to the Fisch and Bergin translation of Vico's *Autobiography*, pp. 68–69.

[17] Jacobi, *ibid.*, pp. 121–22.

[18] *Ibid.*, p. 29, note. Jacobi's interpretation of Kant in the light of Vico might suit Schelling's *Naturphilosophie*. "We *know* only the self-created, knowledge in the *strongest* sense of the word is therefore pure knowledge a-priori." This is so since nature is but the visible organism of our understanding. See "Einleitung zu dem Entwurf eines Systems der Philosophie oder über den Begriff der spekulativen Physik und die innere Organisation eines Systems dieser Wissenschaft 1799" in *Schellings Werke*, vol. 1 (Leipzig: Fritz Eckhardt Verlag, 1907), pp. 684, 688.

he exaggerates the supposed affinity between Vico and Kant. In the preface to the second edition of the *Critique* Kant refers to knowledge and its relation to its object, exhibited in one of two ways, either as merely determining it and its concept or as also making it actual. The former mode of knowledge is theoretical, while the latter is practical.[19] This is indeed a programmatic statement, and we may render Kant's position while being aware of its proximity to Vico's position as follows: The investment into knowledge of a priori principles does not amount to the creation of the objects of knowledge. The creative character of knowledge does not lead to the assumption of the created character of objects, or else that the creative cognitive agent is not by the same token the creative ontological agent. One may even go a step further. In Vico there is a kind of a realistic innuendo—knowledge has to follow the objects, and it can follow them only when there is an identity of the process bringing about the objects and the process, or procedure, formulated in the knowledge of the object. This indeed is the other side of the emanative trend characteristic of Vico, the trend we discussed in the analysis of his confrontation with Descartes. Kant's position, precisely at this point, is of a different character; the presence of the data has to be acknowledged, and the mind can only express or formulate that presence by applying to it the category of existence. The question is, How can knowledge be possible when the object is present, at least in terms of the data supporting the object? It is at this point that Kant's view emerges, that is to say, that the spontaneity of knowledge cannot be a total spontaneity, since it does not create both knowledge and its objects. Being confined to knowledge only, it still can know the objects, though they refer to data which do not stem from the "tree" of knowledge. Vico's limited spontaneity refers to the distinction between the knowable, which is created by man, and the unknowable, which is not created by man, while Kant's limited spontaneity amounts to the contraction of spontaneity to knowledge only, excluding the extension of spontaneity vis-à-vis the objects. Thus for Vico, the horizon of knowledge is the horizon of created objects, the orbit of history as against the orbit of nature, while for Kant there is no fundamental distinction between the orbit of nature and the orbit of history, since both are penetrable for knowledge and its apparatus. It is in this sense that Kant refers to the a priori achievement of the understanding only as to the achievement of anticipating the form of a possible experience in general.[20] The very distinction between the determinable material and the determining form is grounded in the distinction between the status of the objects and the status of the apparatus of cognition. The well-known characteristic features of a priori knowledge listed by Kant, that is, necessity and strict universality, can be meaningful only when they are confined to the realm of statements of knowledge and

[19] *B*, p. x (18).
[20] *B*, p. 303 (269).

do not embrace the realm of objects. The two features are characteristic of propositions and are by no means characteristic of objects. Hence there is no transubstantiation in Kant, and insofar as that notion is presented by Jacobi as the common ground for Vico and Kant, we cannot accept that presentation.

This comment leads us to a further one which is necessary in its own right and relevant also for the subsequenet exploration of the position of mathematics in Vico and in Kant. We do refer to Kant by using the terms of creativity and spontaneity, and to some extent these terms are rightly introduced into our discourse; moreover, the term spontaneity is used by Kant himself. But let us not forget the particular character of the a priori forms in Kant. Insofar as intuitions go, what we find in Kant is the notion of an *a priori manifold.* This notion is significant in Kant's analysis of the space—There is space in both the manifold and the unity. Hence space is both a pure intuition and a form of empirical intuition.[21] What is important for our analysis is that the a priori or formal position of space does not connote that space is created by the form. The form presupposes the to-be-united, or unified, manifold. *Mutatis mutandis,* the same applies to the concepts and propositions of understanding: understanding is basically an activity of unification. The concepts and categories are explications of that activity, or they are different modes in which the activity of unification takes shape. For instance, the mode of assuming the permanent substance is a unification between the permanent and the changeable element, while the mode of assuming causality is the unification of a cause and its effect. Spontaneity is to be taken as a legitimate description of Kant's view in two senses: (1) neither intuition nor understanding derive their manifold (space) or the trend toward unification (understanding) from a source outside their own respective realms; and (2) the application of the structures of both intuition and understanding to externally given data is a product of the forms as such and does not depend upon the data subsumed under these forms. But what we do find in Kant vis-à-vis both intuition and understanding is the structure inherent in them. The activity does not create the structure but is in a sense the other side of the coin of the structure. The activity is exhibited in the application of the structures to the data.

At this point we may refer to Vico's and Kant's respective views of mathematics.[22] Indeed here again there is an affinity between the two systems, a negative affinity at that: both take the position that mathematics is of a nominalistic character, that mathematical concepts are not

[21] *B,* pp. 160–61, note (170–71, note). See my "The Forms of Sensibility and Transcendental Phenomenology," in *Life-World and Consciousness, Essays for Aron Gurwitsch,* ed. Lester E. Embree, (Evanston: Northwestern University Press, 1972), pp. 397ff.

[22] Consult Antonio Corsano, "Vico and Mathematics," in *Giambattista Vico: An International Symposium,* pp. 425ff.

derived from objects. But Vico draws the conclusion from the nominalistic character of mathematics in the direction that mathematics is not applicable to nature by way of creating a mathematical science of nature in the sense envisaged by Descartes, Newton, and Kant. Kant has drawn the conclusion that since mathematics is of a synthetic character, and as such presupposes intuitions, formal intuitions or forms of intuition and concepts (space and time and the concept of magnitude), data of nature are subsumable under mathematical concepts and theorems. Since data of nature are placed within space and time, they are subsumable under mathematical concepts. On this issue Kant follows his general trend indicated before, that of the applicability of forms of knowledge to data, though Kant, because of the gulf between forms and data, returns every once in a while to a mediator, or to a *tertium quid* between form and data.[23] But the mediator, again, is of a cognitive character, and not of a creatively ontological nature.

We can therefore reiterate at this point the first issue presented between Vico and Kant—the different renderings of the anti-Cartesian trend. That rendering, which took shape in the first place vis-à-vis the transition from the *cogito* to the *sum*, takes now an additional shape vis-à-vis the spontaneity on the level of the a priori and the spontaneity in terms of objects.

Nature and History

The theme of the distinction between knowledge and existence reoccurs in the sphere of history. It is because of this recurrent theme that we cannot see Kant as following Vico precisely in the sphere of history. Given the importance of the sphere of history in Vico's system, the dividing line between the two is even more striking.

Let us start with a statement by Kant which seems to sound like an echo of Vico. In "The Contest of Faculties," Kant asks: "How is it possible to have history a priori?" The answer is that it is possible if the prophet himself occasions and *produces* the events he predicts. It was all very well for the Jewish prophets to foretell that a state to which they belonged would sooner or later suffer not only decline but also complete dissolution, for the prophets themselves were the architects of their fate; these same priests stubbornly stuck to their belief in the untenable constitution they had themselves created, so that they were themselves able to foresee the consequences with infallible certainty.[24] This statement sounds like a rehearsal of Vico's formula of *ipsum factum*, but it is not. In the first

[23] Consult my *Experience and Its Systematization, Studies in Kant*, 2d enlarged ed. (The Hague: Martinus Nijhoff, 1972), pp. 26ff.

[24] Consult the English translation of the *Contest of Faculties*, included in Kant's *Political Writings*, ed. with intro. and notes by Hans Reiss, trans. H. B. Nisbet (Cambridge: At the University Press, 1970), p. 177.

place, Kant speaks here about the a priori knowledge of the future; he does not speak about the knowledge of history in general and does not relate that knowledge to the overriding creativity of man. The second point is that the whole statement has rather a polemical character. The prophets who know the doom of the future know it because they are the architects of that doom. This is not knowledge of the future in general, but a kind of self-fulfilling or self-fulfilled prophecy, not in the direction of seeing the future as the locus of progress, but as the locus of decline and disintegration. Kant is rather inclined to take exception to this dubious success of knowing the future. He takes exception to what is called the prophetic tradition (and not only from the statutory laws of Judaism), and he is not impressed, to say the least, with either the prophecy as the knowledge of the future or with the material message, the apocalyptic message at that, characteristic of prophecy.

The basic reason that Kant could not follow Vico vis-à-vis history is the reason presented in our preceding exploration. There is, even in terms of history, a substrate which is not created by man but is presupposed by him and taken advantage of by him in his strifes and aspirations: the substrate of nature. We shall briefly list some of Kant's expressions related to the support given by nature to the historical progress. The first reference is of a broad character, expressed in the *Third Thesis* of Kant's *Idea for a Universal History*: "Nature has willed that man should, by himself, produce everything that goes beyond the mechanical ordering of his animal existence, and that he should partake of no other happiness or perfection than that which he himself, independently of instinct, has created by his own reason." If we take reason as the faculty or agent of human creativity or the sum total of the spontaneous interventions of man, we find in Kant's view of history a sort of harmony between nature and reason. It is the design of nature to have human creativity while, generally speaking, nature has to be taken in cognizance insofar as knowledge goes. From the point of view of history, nature is incorporated into the total orbit of history. The historical development takes advantage of the opportunities provided by the design of nature, or by what Kant calls in the *Eighth Thesis* the secret plan of nature. Hence the conclusion in the *Ninth Thesis* refers specifically to the natural plan leading to the civic union of the human race, and that union contributes to the end of nature.

An empirical expression of the support extended by nature to the development of human capacities lies in the fact that the natural status of men is their involvement in antagonism.[25] Antagonism, or even war, is taken in Kant's treatise "On Perpetual Peace" as leading eventually, by a kind of "cunning of morality," to bringing about a cooperation between individ-

[25] *Idea for a Universal History from a Cosmopolitan Point of View*, trans. Louis White Beck, in Immanuel Kant, *On History*, ed. with intro. by Louis White Beck (Indianapolis: Bobbs-Merrill, 1963), pp. 13, 21, 23, 15.

uals and nations. Natural factors are not only not separated from the historical development, but they serve historical objectives. Though as natural factors they cannot be motivated but caused, or cannot be guided by moral aspirations, they lend themselves to the utilization for the sake of moral achievements, mainly by way of the establishing of the civic society. In any case, we cannot find in Kant a clear-cut separation between the rhythm of nature and the rhythm of history. Eventually this leads Kant to the predominance of the concept of progress in his view of history, and on this too, Kant is, to say the least, more outspoken than Vico.

In terms of the idea of progress, we find again in Kant a conjunction of the impact of nature with the moral principle guiding the development of humanity. Nature, in its own structure, contributes to the progress of humanity, not only in the sense of realization of the secret plan, but also in the sense that the natural capacities which are directed to the use of man's reason are to be fully developed only in the race, and not in any single human individual.[26] To be sure, one could suggest that in the emphasis laid on the race as opposed to the individual, Kant is close to Vico's conception of history as history of peoples. But precisely at this point we have to be aware of the difference between the two philosophers: a people is for Vico a historical entity, and thus there is a variety of peoples; while for Kant race, which amounts to mankind or the human species, is a natural entity supporting the historical process, and thus the historical process is a process of the all-embracing mankind and not of individual peoples, at least insofar as the overriding progress is concerned.

Speaking about progress, we have to point again to a kind of linearity of progress present in Kant. In a way, the linearity is due to the fact, analyzed before, that even forces of nature join historical processes for the objective of the attainment of the historical progress, which for Kant is civil society. But, in spite of the detours present in the historical process, Kant points to the importance of accumulation of historical experience. In one of his analyses of the impact of the phenomenon of revolution on history, he says: "I can predict from the aspects and signs of our times that the human race will achieve this end, and that it will henceforth progressively improve without any more total reversals. For a phenomenon of this kind which has taken place in human history *can never be forgotten*, since it has revealed in human nature an aptitude and power for improvement of a kind which no politician could have thought up by examining the course of events in the past."[27] There seems to be a difference between the gloomy future of the prophets and the prediction of the future based on new data in Kant's own historical presence, once those data reveal the human aptitude for improvement. The prophets are rejected because they themselves create the atmosphere of dissolution and fail, while the predic-

[26] Kant, *On History*, p. 13.
[27] *Political Writings*, p. 184.

tion based on the projection of the new historical experience on the future is based on fundamental human capacities and thus runs counter to the situation artificially created by the gloomy prophets. There are new vistas in human history, and thus Kant rejects implicitly the notion of *ricorsi* when he refers to the fact that total reversals are improbable since the newly accumulated human experience and the forward movement can never be forgotten. In a sense we can say that Kant rejects the identification of *ipsum* and *factum* once the apocalyptic future is involved; but he relies on the combination of nature and freedom once an optimistic outlook is at stake which as such can be forecasted, though the precise time at which this will occur must remain indefinite and even dependent upon chance.[28] In any case the Platonic idea is not an empty figment of the imagination, but the eternal for all civil constitutions.[29]

This leads us to a further point in the conception of history. Kant differs from Vico because of what might be called the moralistic aspect of history; Vico is in a sense more factual-minded. Vico tends to present the plurality of historical factors and does not focus historical process on an issue, including the issue of progress. When Kant asks himself about the sequence the notion of progress can be expected to follow, his answer is that the sequence is not the usual one from the bottom upwards, but, on the contrary, from the top downwards.[30] This would mean that the historical objective has a moral character, or at least a legal character—civic society and the constitution—and that character prescribes the course of events. The dependence of the historical process on the moral objective is stressed very clearly by Kant himself in one of his *Reflections*, where he says that no theory leads us to a justified assumption that the world in its broad contours progresses constantly towards the better. It is only practical reason which makes it mandatory to act according to such a hypothesis in a dogmatic way. In accordance with such a principle, practical reason creates for itself a theory which, in turn, satisfies fully reason in its moral-practical concern but is outside the theoretical interest.[31] Interestingly enough, in this comment Kant applies to his own exposition the term "dogmatic," which can mean only that the expectation of the historical progress grounded in practical reason or in the ethical interests cannot be expected to be warranted by historical events as such. The expectation is a historical projection determined by moral considerations leading from the top downwards. In a sense the expectation of historical progress or objective does not need to stand the test of historical events; and even when Kant speaks about certain events whose impact can never be for-

[28] *Ibid.*, pp. 184–85.
[29] *Ibid.*, p. 187.
[30] *Ibid.*, p. 188.
[31] *Kant's Gesammelte Schriften*, vol. 20, p. 307. See my "The Idea of Historical Progress and its Assumptions," *History and Theory* 10 (1971): 197ff.

gotten, he expresses an expectation and does not express a conclusion factually supported.

It is obvious that Kant takes the historical process as expressing an idea or an ideal of convergence between the ethical imperative and the factual process as it is. Vico is more empirical: he does not deal with history from the bird's-eye view of the moral principle but explores events and facts, though he structures them in cycles. Kant had to struggle a great deal with the discrepancy between the moral postulates and the reading of the historical events; perhaps the most telling example of this struggle are Kant's diverse interpretations of the war and the strifes present in the human condition. Kant is exposed to the criticism centering around the questionable aspects of the whole idea of progress, insofar as progress is meant to be of a total historical character. Vico, by the very fact that he is more empirical, is more immune to criticism.

This leads us to our final conclusion with regard to the difference between Kant and Vico in terms of their respective historical conceptions: Vico is more concerned with historical knowledge, while Kant is more concerned with the character of the historical process or with the historical objective. This is determined by the establishment of the clear relationship between history and morality. Therefore, the last point of our analysis will be the Viconian theme in Kant's theory of morality. Anticipating our subsequent analysis, we may say that in the sphere of morality Kant is more Viconian than Vico was.

Bonum-Ipsum Factum

Let us start this part of our investigation by returning to Kant's distinction between two ways of knowledge: the knowledge whose characteristic feature is the determining of the concept and the spontaneous application of the concept to data supplied from elsewhere, and the knowledge whereby the objects are made actual by knowledge itself. The former is in Kant's view theoretical knowledge, while the latter is practical knowledge and as such is the full expression of the spontaneity of reason. While in the area of theoretical knowledge the maximum to be achieved by reason is the creation of concepts to be applied to data, in the sphere of morality reason creates the full orbit, or to put it negatively, the distinction between form and matter is removed. Form is matter, and matter is form, since the matter is the outcome of the creation of the form. To come back at this point to our previous reference to the differences in the understanding of the notion of cause, we may say that cause and causality in the sphere of knowledge connote the rule of the interrelationship between events against the background of time, while cause in the sphere of ethics connotes the aptitude to create, to produce. It is in this sense that Kant speaks about the causality of reason,[32] and that causality connotes here *causa essendi*, and not the principle of relation between facts or events.

In the area of ethics or morality, Kant is not confined to the distinction, with its anti-Cartesian innuendo, between the sum total of predicates and the position of existence. Hence a kind of ontological argument is possible in his eyes in the sphere of ethics, while it is not possible in the sphere of knowledge or in the sphere of existence cognitively conceived. An interesting example appears in one of the notes in the *Critique of Practical Reason*, in which Kant takes exception to a criticism of his contemporary, Thomas Wizenmann, who argued against his theory as to the right to conclude from a need to the objective reality of the object of the need. Kant quotes Wizenmann, who illustrates his point by an example of a man in love who fools himself with an idea of beauty; yet that idea is merely a chimera of his own brain, and he tries now to argue that the object he entertains in his own mind really exists somewhere. At this point Kant suggests the distinction to be made between a need based on inclination and a need based on reason. A need based on inclination cannot be a sufficient ground to postulate the existence of its objects, let alone the existence of an object which will be valid for everyone. An object, conceived from the position of inclination, has to have its existence independent of the inclination. But whatever holds good vis-à-vis the transition from an inclination to an object does not hold good vis-à-vis the transition from reason to its object. Here the object does not exist independently, since it is related to a duty to realize the highest good, and the duty to do that leads to the assumption that it must be possible to do that.[33] We move here from the duty to existence or from the imperatives of reason to existence. Therefore reason does not have to acknowledge existence conceptually or to render conceptually data via the category of existence. Reason creates its own objects, which is why previously we used the metaphor of ontological proof in terms of Kant's notion of morality, though that proof is lacking ground in terms of Kant's theory of knowledge. The shift from reason to object is, to be sure, of a particular character. The object is not one to be known, but one to be obeyed; that is, the content is not one to be subsumed under consciousness, but one which emanates from the very structure of consciousness. Hence the Viconian notion of the identity between self-creativity and knowledge, or the notion as to the condition for knowledge which lies in the fact to be emanated by the human mind, is transplanted by Kant to the moral field. In that field the concern ceases to be with objects to be known and becomes the concern with laws to be

[32] *Kritik der praktischen Vernunft*, ed. K. Vorländer (Leipzig: Felix Meiner, 1929), p. 94 (*Critique of Practical Reason*, trans. L. W. Beck [New York: Library of Liberal Arts, 1956], p. 83.

[33] *Ibid.*, p. 169n. (English trans., p. 149n.).

obeyed. Kant's theory of autonomy becomes the moral transubstantiation or transformation of Vico's notion of *verum* and *factum*.

A comment on the notion of autonomy will be apposite at this point in the context of the moral interpretation of the Viconian theme.

Kant's ethics is the ethics of autonomy precisely because it is an ethics of reason: "For just as appearances do not exist in themselves, but only relatively to the subject in which, so far as it has senses, they inhere, so the laws do not exist in the appearances, but only relatively to this same being, so far as it has understanding."[34] Laws, therefore, are related to understanding, or to reason in general, the latter being the underlying capacity of understanding. The manifestation of reason is the sum total of laws. Laws of knowledge apply to data but do not create data. In this sense a distinction has to be made between laws and facts, or between determinations and the to-be-determinable data. The structure changes when we move from the philosophy of nature, which deals with all that is, that is to say with facts, to the philosophy of morals, which deals with that which ought to be and thus prescribes the course of action and does not apply to a state of affairs.[35] It is in this sense that reason provides laws; since these are not applicable to data, they are imperatives, or objective laws of freedom.[36] Freedom is introduced in this context, because freedom connotes the capacity to create a course of action; freedom is but the active aspect of reason. Reason expresses itself in laws of freedom, or freedom is manifest in laws. In this context we find the basis for the concept of autonomy. Autonomy in its positive sense connotes the intrinsic legislation of pure, and thus practical, reason.[37] The subjective aspect or resonant of this legislation is the obedience to the law. Since the law is the active formulation of the lawfulness of reason, the ethical law is universal in the first place; universality, and not applicability, becomes the very characteristic feature of the moral law.

Autonomy is thus interrelated with Kant's notion of the primacy of practical reason; indeed we have to understand the notion of primacy in a sense even broader than that suggested by Kant.[38] Primacy amounts to the creation of a universe or a kingdom, or a realm, out of the sources of reason. Such a creation cannot address itself to given data, since the very encountering of data runs counter to the concept of creation. Creation can be a concept or a principle only in a sphere where there are and can be no data, where both the form of universality and the matter are funda-

[34] *B*, p. 164 (172).
[35] *B*, pp. 868–69 (658–59).
[36] *B*, p. 830 (634).
[37] *Kritik der praktischen vernunft*, p. 39 (33).
[38] On Kant's *Concept of the Primacy of Practical Reason*, compare my two analyses: *Experience And Its Systematization, Studies in Kant*, pp. 111ff; and *On the Human Subject, Studies in the Phenomenology of Ethics and Politics* (Springfield, Ill.: Charles C Thomas, 1966), pp. 134ff.

mentally united. Such a sphere is the sphere of morality, and more specifically here, the universality of reason is the very content of reason. This is the meaning of the suggestion in the heading of this section, that Kant identifies *bonum* with *ipsum factum*, and reversely only *ipsum factum* can be *bonum*.

From the negative point of view, the thrust of Kant's system is expressed in the rejection of the notion of the dependence of freedom on any given objects. What follows from that is the rejection of the notion of pleasure as an intrinsic notion of morality. Pleasure presupposes the existence or reality of the object addressed by the subject and thus cannot coincide with freedom as creation of a course of action. Pleasure is the response of the subject to a given state of affairs. The introduction of the principle of pleasure to the sphere of morality would therefore amount to carrying over the aspect of factuality, intrinsic for knowledge, to the sphere of morality, which, being the full expression of reason proper, cannot presuppose any factuality.

This is not to say that Kant follows Vico insofar as Vico's random observations on morality are concerned. These observations are rather scarce, but to the extent Vico comments on morality, he follows the traditional line, referring to ethics in the context of human character, its dispositions, and its passions. Moreover, he rejects the assessment of human affairs by the inflexible standard of abstract right. He rather prefers what he calls Lesbic rule, which does not conform bodies to itself but adjusts itself to their contours.[39] This comment would certainly preclude the direction of Kant's ethics, which is obviously opposed to the Lesbic rule. The argument presented here is that Kant's ethical system is the ethical transplantation of Vico's maxim, precisely because according to Kant Vico's maxim is not applicable in the context of its original formulation, that is, in the context of knowledge. Kant identifies practice with creativity and thus goes beyond the traditional understanding of practice as the activity of shaping the character of man. Kant is led to the new meaning of practice as the activity of creating rules formulated by man and accepted by him because of the self-legislation implied in those rules.

On the level of practical reason Kant eventually comes back to the question of consciousness and existence, the question which we explored before in the context of knowledge; there as we have seen existence cannot be integrated in consciousness. But the structure is different in the realm of moral legislation:

> in certain laws of the pure employment of reason—laws which are not merely logical rules, but which while holding *a-priori* also concern our existence

[39] *On the Study Methods of Our Time*, trans. Elio Gianturco (Indianapolis, New York, Kansas City: Bobbs-Merrill, 1965), pp. 33–34. The evaluation of morality and its cognitive status brings back the notion of *conscientia* versus *scientia*. Eventually this leads Vico to point to the relation between human behavior and common sense. Consult *New Science*, §§ 131–45.

—ground for regarding ourselves as *legislating* completely *a-priori* in regard to our own *existence*, and as determining this existence, there would thereby be revealed as spontaneity through which our reality would be determinable, independently of the conditions of empirical intuition. And we should also become aware that in the consciousness of our existence there is contained a something *a-priori*, which can serve to determine our existence—the complete determination of which is possible only in sensible terms—as being related, in respect of a certain inner faculty, to a non-sensible intelligible world.[40]

To use Vico's terminology, we may say that on the level of practical legislation the difference between *conscientia* and *scientia* disappears, and *conscientia* is inherently *scientia*. This, again, is a manifestation of the primacy of practical reason, and again a manifestation not specifically underlined by Kant himself, but only read indirectly from his text.

We may sum up our analysis of the affinity between Vico and Kant as follows: Kant shares Vico's view of human finite spontaneity, but Kant differs from Vico as to the sphere of application of that underlying notion. Vico suggested that there are facts created by human spontaneity or modification of mind, and they can be known as such by the selfsame mind. Vico argues that only facts created by the mind can be known by the mind. Kant maintains that no facts can be created and thus no facts can be known according to the maxim of the identity between the subject and the object. The very position of the object removes the possibility that facts could be known fully or exhaustively. Spontaneity is warranted only in the sphere where there are no objects, only contents. These contents have to be known, but their status transcends knowledge and becomes an imperative. Vis-à-vis the imperatives there is precisely the identity of subject and object, that identity which cannot be maintained in the sphere of knowledge.

Hegel's system has to be viewed as a sort of synthesis of Vico and Kant. This amounts to an attempt to accept the identity between subject and object limited by Kant to the sphere of ethics and to transplant it to the sphere of knowledge as envisaged by Vico. But that synthesis eventually leads to the notion of an infinite spontaneity as against the notion of a finite spontaneity. It is obvious that because of the notion of infinite spontaneity known by the finite mind Hegel goes in his synthesis beyond both Vico and Kant.

Hegel assumes the convertibility of reason (*Vernunft*) and actuality (*Wirklichkeit*), which can be seen as a variation of the *verum-factum* theme. How could Hegel argue such a position, having in mind Kant's notion of the finitude of human understanding, as well as, whether he knew it or not, Vico's criticism of the possibility of applying the principle to nature? Two points seem to be essential in this context. The first relates to one aspect of Hegel's dialectic: the very fact that we know the finitude

[40] *B*, pp. 430–31 (382–83).

of our understanding places us already beyond or above that finitude. After all, the *Critique of Pure Reason* is written as a critique of *pure reason,* which amounts to the fact that understanding is analyzed from the perspective of reason. The question is only to find bridges of a dialectical character between the assessed finitude and the perspective of infinity which is the perspective of reason. But the first step toward establishing the continuum from understanding to reason lies in the awareness of finitude, which as such transcends finitude.

The second dialectical point is related to nature. Looked at on the surface, nature is alien to reason or to spirit, and thus the *verum-factum* principle could not be applied to it. At this point Hegel takes refuge in the notion of estrangement (*Entfremdung*), which allows him to look at nature as an antithetical expression of the manifestation of spirit—though antithetical, still a manifestation. These are the two devices employed by Hegel in order to overcome the problematic situation as delineated by Vico and Kant on Hegel's way toward his attempt at a synthesis.

At this point we can reemphasize the affinity between Vico and Kant, because both analyze the final understanding and are aware of the difference between finitude and infinity. The difference between them relates to the fact that Kant shifted the Aristotelian notion of form from its position as the end of motion or of an entity to its position as a condition, or functional-relational structure. Because of that new meaning assigned to the term "form," Kant presented the view, which Vico could not present, that knowledge of amorphous data is possible. Data are not known as such, but only insofar as they are integrated in *formal* frameworks of relations.

Howard N. Tuttle

THE EPISTEMOLOGICAL STATUS OF THE CULTURAL WORLD IN VICO AND DILTHEY

In his essay "Wilhelm Dilthey and the Idea of Life," Ortega y Gasset remarked that by 1900 Dilthey had discovered a new intellectual continent which he called "the idea of life." Ortega also claimed that this idea elaborated not only a new historical method but the primacy of the "lived" actuality of human experience.[1] Without denigrating the originality and import of Dilthey's work I would like to suggest that this "new continent" was actually sighted about one hundred and fifty years earlier by a then obscure Italian scholar named Giambattista Vico. One of the quiet revolutions that Vico wrought was his establishment of the integrity and primordiality of the ordinary world in which man exists and creates his culture. Also Vico's work anticipated some of what would later be elaborated into a major tenet of nineteenth-century historicism, namely, that there is a fundamental distinction between the subject matters of the natural sciences (*Naturwissenschaften*) and the human sciences (*Geisteswissenschaften*).

I will clarify these ideas by suggesting that both Vico and Dilthey presupposed a fundamental intuition or metaphor in their theory of knowledge. This metaphor suggests that there is a "within," or internal pole, and a "without," or external pole to all experience. Further, they claimed that the actions and creations of men are experienced as certain because they have a self-evident aspect given in this "inner" dimension of human existence. I will try to show that both thinkers considered this internal pole as the true subject matter for the human studies. I will also show that Vico and Dilthey developed their epistemology in reaction to the then current attempts to subsume the human studies under the methodological aegis of rationalism and the natural sciences.

It is necessary to begin our inquiry by a general description of the genesis of the philosophic milieu against which Vico would react in the eighteenth century. The previous scientific *Weltanschauung* of Galileo, Descartes, and Newton held that any generally valid scientific knowledge would seek to disjoin itself from the ambiguities of human subjectivity.

[1] Ortega y Gasset, "A Chapter from the History of Ideas—Wilhelm Dilthey and the Idea of Life" in *Concord and Liberty* (New York: Norton, 1963), p. 132.

The Copernican revolution declared that our ordinary, subjective mental habits and life experiences would not provide the originating concepts required for the rise of natural science. From Descartes to Comte it was widely assumed that both the natural and human worlds could only be comprehended by the methods of mathematical science. Both Vico and Dilthey believed that this assumption could have a detrimental effect upon the human studies generally. Vico held that a novel approach, a "new science," must be created to penetrate the "thick darkness" which obscures human life in its individual and social dimensions.[2]

With the possible exception of the Baconian tradition, seventeenth-century science can be characterized generally as follows. The world is composed of physical elements whose motion can be mathematically expressed as "the laws of nature." Given any physical cause, such as the gravitational influence of one celestial body on another, there was supposed a mathematically determined effect, such as the predictable orbit of a planet around the sun. Provided with this clocklike regularity, explanations of physical phenomena were believed to exhibit the same necessity that theorems bear to axioms. In Galileo's *Discourses* and Descartes' scientific writings, for example, science was conceived as the discovery of relations between physical phenomena. These relations were expressed in the measurement of the quantifiable, or "primary" properties of matter, namely, weight, velocity, figure, position, magnitude, and number. These so-called primary qualities were the universal, quantifiable properties of nature. The same properties were also thought to be the essence of matter, in that they revealed the external world as it is in itself apart from its individuating, perceptual appearance to man. Conversely, the world of ordinary sense experience, that is, the perceptible qualities of physical things, such as colors, smells, and human emotive states, etc. were termed "secondary qualities." These qualities were the mediated and illusory images of nature as it is in its primary states. For example, Galileo believed that our perception of heat is a subjective illusion. The primary, or real status of heat was nothing but the friction of elementary physical bodies.

But it is in Descartes that we first feel the impact of these premises for the humanistic and social studies. In his *Discourse on Method* and *Meditations on First Philosophy*, Descartes claimed that the classics, history, and scholastic philosophy revolted him because of their subjective nature, their lack of certainty and universally valid method. They are subrational by nature. Descartes sought instead a *mathesis universalis*, a method to provide a system of self-evident and deductively ordered truths. Descartes was here advocating what I will call a monomethodological approach to knowledge. In his epistemology of science we have the assertion that there is but *one* universal method of reasoned inquiry, and this is the mathe-

[2] *New Science*, § 331.

matical comprehension of the quantifiable world of primary qualities—the *res extensa*. All the secondary or qualitative characteristics of experience were equated with the illusions of subjective states, which are neither real nor subsumable under the *mathesis universalis*.

As both Vico and Dilthey realized, the implications of such a monomethodology for the human studies are fatal. The very material of the human studies is in fact a subjective world of ordinary qualitative experience. The human studies are not elaborated in deductive, quantitative conceptions, nor can they be reduced to the primary status of the *res extensa* without eliminating everything that the human studies are about—actions, emotions, intentions, the data of the five senses, first-person states of awareness, cultural material, and the significance of ordinary language. In short, I would maintain that because Descartes' monomethodological conception of reality is incompatible with these states—because they cannot be accounted for by his method—he was forced to confine the human studies to a subjective or subrational status.

In response to the Cartesian challenge Vico proposed a defense of the *litterae humaniores* in his *De nostri temporis studiorum ratione*. Among other things he objected here to Descartes' rejection of what Vico would call the *verisimilar* notion of truth, by which term Vico indicated those secondary or probable truths about those particulars that compose the subject matter of ordinary life. Vico was aware that in the humanistic tradition of philosophy there had been provision for such a concept since Aristotle. Aristotle's φρόνησις, or practical wisdom, was a logic of rhetoric and of the practical, probable demands of human experience. Descartes and his monomethodological tradition had actually subverted this epistemological category. Along with the *verisimilar*, the philological studies, that is, the humanities and social studies, were also relegated to the limbo of the uncertain and subrational. Cartesianism would give epistemic priority to what Plato and Aristotle reserved for θεωρία, that is, the purely intellective faculty which cognizes the transmundane subjects of metaphysics, mathematics, and physics. Here spirit is equal only to theoretical intellect, and the objects of this intellect are excluded to the certain and unchanging world of pure θεωρία. As a logical or epistemic organon Vico saw then that the new rationalistic method seemed to leave no provision for the practical and probable world of the *verisimilar*, nor for human studies per se. All of this had been ignored by exclusive devotion to the *ratio geometrica*.[3]

In summary so far, then, Vico believed the truths of human prudence, or the *verisimilar*, to be founded in the commonsense world of human activity and habitual response. The truth that originates in the *verisimilar* is not adequately accounted for in the *ésprit géometrique*. Nor will the

[3] *On the Study Methods of Our Time*, trans. Elio Gianturco (Indianapolis, Kansas City, New York: Bobbs-Merrill, 1965), p. 39.

Cartesian method account for the reality which the human studies express. Thus, Cartesianism and the thought milieu which accompanied it never achieved a true unity of method, but only one species of it, namely, the mathematical deductive method, which is only applicable to a rationalistic conception of nature.[4]

I must now turn to what I believe is the central aspect in Vico's and Dilthey's search for adequacy in humanistic method: the "internality" of knowledge. Vico had a formula for truth which he called *verum et factum convertuntur*: the idea that the concept of truth converts into the created or actually performed effect of some human action. In this notion Vico developed the thesis that man, unlike God, is a finite creature whose being is not immanent in all things. Because God created the world, He has a perfect knowledge of all His works. God created both the *logos*, or knowable aspect of nature, and its material aspect. He knows nature because its *logos* is a creation of His own Being. Man, on the other hand, grasps nature only externally through sense appearance. He does not know nature from the inside, as it is in itself. Only God's knowledge is implicit within His creation. In other words, man can never know the innermost element of nature because he did not make it. Any mathematical-scientific conception of the world will not reveal nature's innermost parts because these methodological tools are human creations. While man may create the points, lines, axioms, and theorems of science and apply these to nature in its primary state, he will at best understand nature only as a hypothetical and probable entity.[5]

However, in the civil or cultural world, Vico tells us, certainty is attainable. Here man understands the world he makes because he is the cause of the cultural effects which are the products of his own making. Our knowledge of the civil world is not mediated or uncertain because, Vico claims, its principles are "to be found in the modifications of our own human mind."[6] But how can we clarify and exemplify this crucial and seemingly obscure notion in Vico? I am proposing that for both Vico and Dilthey the created cultural world has two aspects: a physical, or "external" side and an "inner" side. By this "inner" side they indicated the significance which a given cultural expression is meant to have.

Let us note examples from the conceptions of Vico himself: the institution of burial, human speech, and the science of philology. The overt physical motions that attend a burial service, the physical sound waves of a speech act, or the ink and paper of a classical document are the sensate, physical, or "outer" side of these cultural creations. But these "outer" physical features are not sufficient conditions for a complete understanding of the artifacts and actions. It is true, of course, that man's creations must

[4] *Ibid.*, pp. 34–35.
[5] *Ibid.*, p. 23.
[6] *New Science*, § 311.

take some material embodiment. But the further implication here is that the concept of culture has what we would today call a self-conscious, or intentional aspect: it is constituted as meaning- and value-laden, as expressing human ends, and as the inner coherence of our experience. Culture, then, is always significant beyond its outer physical dimensions. For example, Vico tells us that the act of the burial of the dead has a universal significance that transcends its overt physical aspects. Here all humanity recognizes the various symbolisms of human finitude, grief of the family, the acts of prayer, the meaning of the death for religious beliefs, and so on. Vico goes on to say that the establishment of the fundamental and universal principles of culture must be derived from the particular symbolic or inner meanings of such human institutions. This is the purpose of his *New Science*.[7]

Vico further developed the notion of the inner-outer metaphor by claiming that the "infirmity of the human mind" originates in its being "buried" in the body. The mind has always tried to understand itself by sensory observation of external bodies, but the mind can only grasp its own true nature by self-reflection.[8] In the case of language Vico argued that the human mind first sees itself in terms of outer physical bodies, but then it comes to attend to itself by reflection on these objects through words which express the significance that man assigns to objects and creations. In fact, there is a common mental structure in all peoples which is able to grasp the same meaning through the diverse sounds and symbols of natural languages.[9] In other words, Vico is telling us that different men, cultures, and eras understand each other because common meanings correspond to overt cultural creations such as speech. The *verum-factum* formula is true because knowing and being in the civil world—epistemology and ontology—are unified. The truth signifies the conversion of intelligible structures into human creations.

It is my contention then that knowing, making, and doing are interrelated, because in human action the agent deliberately performs the subjective symbolic operations that constitute the meaning or truth of his doing and making. The many forms of the civil world, then, are meaningfully constituted by the internal operations of our own and others' self-conscious reflections on our doing. We can be said to understand our creations in the civil world when we can self-consciously refer to the states of awareness that constituted the meaning of our creations. The innermost being of the cultural creation is understandable, because the very consciousness which recognizes itself in the object is the cause of the intelligibility of the object made.

At this point we must note Vico's concept of philology as the means for

[7] *Ibid.*, §§ 333, 347.
[8] *Ibid.*, § 236.
[9] *Ibid.*, §§ 161–62, 198, 355.

grasping the meaning of the cultural world. Man's knowledge of his creations has certainty because he "owns" the epistemic and emotive elements that constitute his creations. Vico has supposed here that human creations and actions can be universal in their significance because they are the expressions of a common human nature.[10] Hermeneutics, or what Vico would have called philology, is the meaningful interpretation of human artifacts, and this process is fundamental to the *New Science*. This method allows us to conform ourselves to the various conscious states of others, that is, to reexperience the meanings that were generated for an actor while creating a cultural object. For Vico all cultural creations are apprehended first as particular and immediate sense residues, which he called the *certum*. But for Vico the new science must be able to interpret from this initial sensory state the symbolic significance of the object. Now we are at the stage of the *factum*. Here the attempt is to determine the species or type of spiritual product implied in the initial sense object. The Rosetta stone, for example, first contained graphic material that was merely marks upon a surface—a sensory *certum*. Then these undecipherable symbols were correlated with other symbols whose meaning was understood. The *factum* of the stone was attained when Champollion penetrated the inner significance of hieroglyphics by his philological methods. Here in philology the spirit of the creator became present to the spirit of the interpreter. Knower and object became one.

In sum, I have argued that the thrust of Vico's thought on the epistemic nature of the culture world refers to an "inner" status which can be reexperienced and known as it actually is or was. We understand the culture world because it is an expression of the common humanity in which we all share. We have certainty with respect to the culture world because to understand it is to refer necessarily to the self-conscious subject, which is assumed to be of the same nature as ourselves. Knowing and being are in principle united. The reader must note here that I use the phrase "in principle" to mean that the unity of thought and being, of knower and known, is only epistemologically possible. This does not imply that we in fact have empirical, discursive knowledge of any or all cultural objects. Our discussion so far only implies that in principle it is possible to know human creations with certainty. The concrete hermeneutical and philological processes by which Vico and Dilthey would come to make empirical-truth claims about any actual state of cultural affairs are an extensive and complicated topic, which cannot be developed here because of lack of space.[11]

Vico's methodology of the human sciences, which implied a self-referential or "internal" knowing-making mechanism, was rediscovered by

[10] *Ibid.*, §§ 6–15.

[11] For a more systematic development of this problem see Howard Tuttle, *Wilhelm Dilthey's Philosophy of Historical Understanding: A Critical Analysis* (Leiden: E. J. Brill, 1969), chaps. 2, 3, and 5.

the German philosopher Wilhelm Dilthey (1833–1911). The concerns which stimulated Dilthey's search were largely duplicative of Vico's. However, the enemy now was not Cartesianism per se but the positivistic attempt to model all explanation after the natural sciences of that day. We may note that Dilthey was not self-consciously a follower of Vico. In the twelve or thirteen published volumes of Dilthey's work there are only a few passing references to Vico by a philosopher who was always scrupulous in citing sources and intellectual debts. But like Vico, Dilthey rejected the positivism of Comte, who believed that he had completed Descartes's program by the extension of his method into the social sciences.[12]

For Dilthey as for Vico, history and culture are the products of man and as such bear a unique meaning for him as the objects of the human studies.[13] The meaningfulness of the socio-historical world derives from our subjective interpretation of a symbol, action, or cultural object. In this same vein all human actions and creations have a significance for the agent performing or making them. Understanding in the human studies is a re-living or re-creating in ourselves the meaning-emotive-volitional complex that an analogous experience has created in another. Also for Dilthey the sole method of understanding in the human sciences is called *Verstehen*, or the systematic interpretation of the self-conscious actions and creations of another. Dilthey called these actions and creations "life assertions" (*Lebensäusserungen*). In connection with the general theme of this essay we must note that these "life assertions" of others have an "outer" or physical side manifest as records, artifacts, symbols, actions, and creations. The complicated process of interpreting these outward "life expressions" back to their "inner" significance Dilthey called hermeneutics.[14]

Like Vico, Dilthey maintained that the scientific understanding of the outer, material nature of an object will not allow us to penetrate to the "inner" meaning of a life assertion. For example, the analysis of the specific gravity of a crucifix will not reveal to us the lived significance of this object for a Christian martyr. Also Dilthey maintained that in the natural sciences the senses mediate our understanding of the material object. The senses must be translated into the formal quantitative properties of experience in order to be subsumed under hypothesis formation and the objective laws of nature. Vico made a like point in his early work on the study methods of his time: neither hypothesis formation nor the objective laws of nature give us a certain or self-evident conception of the natural object as it is "in itself."

In the *Geisteswissenschaften*, or human studies, however, explanation

[12] Auguste Comte, *The Positive Philosophy*, trans. and condensed by Harriet Martineau, 3 vols. (London: George Bell and Sons, 1896), vol. 3, p. 385.

[13] Wilhelm Dilthey, *Gesammelte Schriften*, 12 vols. (Leipzig and Berlin: Teubner, 1921–65), vol. 1, p. 116.

[14] *Ibid.*, vol. 7, pp. 205, 318.

refers, not to the physical laws and dimensions of matter, but to the significant structure implied in our acting and creating. Alexander's cutting of the Gordian knot was a significant action not because of its outer physical aspects, but because it signified that Alexander desired the mastery of Asia with all the meaningful, emotive, and volitional content implied in such an idea. This inner significance cannot be sensed externally, for its content has a self-presentational character. We can know immediately by reference to our own existence what *desire, mastery*, and so on, really present themselves as being. There is no other source from which they can gain meaning. They are the creations and properties of subjective experience, not the material properties of external objects.[15]

In sum, in both Vico and Dilthey man acts upon the outer world, and in so doing creates culture as an effect of his "doing." Vico called this "effect" the civil world. Dilthey called it the world of life. But I believe that both thinkers intended the same thing, namely, that man in his acting and creating endows culture objects with his own subjectivity. For both thinkers these objects possess an "outer" material dimension which is the world of nature. But they also possess an "inner" dimension. This realm is entirely knowable by man because in his creative action he has "externalized" the significance that he intends for any act or creation. This "inner-outer" distinction in epistemology, then, allowed Dilthey to reserve the inner domain for the human studies and to provide them an authentic subject matter. These were among the ends of Vico's labors one hundred and fifty years previously.

We can now examine a few important differences between Vico and Dilthey. The first difference to which I will refer briefly is in the area of the philosophy of history. For Vico human society was conceived as a kind of potency that fulfills itself in ideal forms of growth. Indeed, one of the ends of philological study is to construct the typical stages of a society's evolutionary growth in time. In Vico, too, there was an attempt to delineate the patterns of generation and decay. At the height of its historical development a given culture falls back into a *ricorso* or a reversion to a primitive stage. But the *ricorsi* formula does not imply that historical development is arbitrary. For Vico each stage of growth reflects a principle or law of historical development. Dilthey, however, made no provision for any such discernible pattern of historical development. His emphasis was always methodological, and he rejected any speculative or nomothetic interpretation of the historical process. Dilthey admitted of historical generalization only to the level of ideal types. These typical constructions are always unique in historical time, and they do not repeat any cyclic process. For him all history is idiographic, that is, it is not involved with eternal

[15] *Ibid.*, p. 191.

principles of development, but only with the individual and unique configurations of historical eras, such as the Protestant Reformation.[16]

But for Vico historical truth had an absolute status. There is a universal meaning in history. This truth is revealed through God's providence. Part of the task of the *New Science* was to reveal this providence, by the light of which the relative phases of historical time take their meaning. Mere human actions promote the ends of God for the race. For Vico the end of historical inquiry is man's self-knowledge and knowledge of the eternal providence of God.[17] These notions are impossible in the historicism of Dilthey. For him truth is relative to different historical ages, and any notion of final truth is dissolved into mutually exclusive "world views." Dilthey even went so far as to suggest that historical knowledge is relative to the normative and methodological developments operative in the present.[18] Dilthey tried all his life to overcome his historical relativism, but he never succeeded.

What, in conclusion, is the general import of Vico's and Dilthey's thought today? Perhaps we can approach this question by noting that the fundamental issue in the philosophy of the social sciences now divides into two alternatives: (1) Shall these sciences be premised on the methods and subject matter of the natural sciences, or (2) have they an autonomous basis of their own? I do not know if Vico and Dilthey can provide a definitive answer to this problem. But this much can be said: Vico and Dilthey can supply a powerful and corrective method if we accept the first alternative to mean the following. (1) Causal explanation of human action and creation can be reduced *in toto* to nonmental physiological responses to the physical environment; (2) all human action is only an expression of physical and somatic conditioning, which if understood, can prescribe the laws of all human behavior; (3) a neutral, external observer can in fact explain human action without reference to the subjectively constituted meanings and valuations that the action has for the agent and other men.

I believe that Vico and Dilthey have shown that these supposed criteria do not and cannot provide an adequate social science. Our thinkers would contend that there can be no understanding of man, "laws" of human behavior, or an adequate empirical method without the participation of the researcher in what I have called the "internal" dimension of human existence. Without a participation in the interiority of man there can be no presentation of the significance that actions and objects have for him. In the absence of hermeneutic or philological method, then, significant behavior is invariably reduced to overt bodily behavior, which is purportedly described by external sense experience alone. The interiority of

[16] *Ibid.*, pp. 133, 173.
[17] *New Science*, §§ 1107–08.
[18] Dilthey, *Gesammelte Schriften*, vol. 7, p. 161.

existence is lost in a new *mathesis universalis,* which explains man nomothetically as a body which behaves in space. But as Vico, Dilthey, and thinkers in their tradition from Marx to Weber to Heidegger have pointed out, the predicates which describe external bodies in space simply do not apply to human life as it is actually lived. Man reveals himself in his work and in the subjective meaning with which he interprets his own behavior and creations. Man lives and works in a world of objects which he has created and endowed with expressions of his own being, objects which can only be understood with reference to the interior modifications of the mind that constituted them as human creations. The "within" side of human existence necessarily entails interpretation in terms of motivation, value, and meaning. These cannot be merely observed as objects but must be lived and interpreted as conscious intentions. We are citizens not only of nature but of a life world, a world to which the genius of Vico first drew formal philosophic attention.

Finally, the work of Vico and Dilthey is relevant today because their insights present an alternative to any static determinism that often results from the behavioralistic imitation of what is taken to be natural science. Both thinkers point to the autonomy and responsibility with which man must make his historical world. For them there can be present in human history ideal and novel conditions which man alone can envision, construct, and achieve. If the ideal possibilities of life are ignored, if responsible reconstruction of our world can gain no footing amid the trials and demands of the twentieth century, then modern man will passively and surely suffer the most violent commotions.

Robert Welsh Jordan

VICO AND HUSSERL: HISTORY AND HISTORICAL SCIENCE

The doctrine of Vico that to be true is the same as to be made leads him to the idea of a new science of man, or perhaps more accurately, a new science of things historical. It was to be a science of the man-made world and would enjoy among the sciences a strange preeminence.[1] Unlike pure mathematics, its subject matter would be factual. And, unlike the sciences of objective nature, the new science has access from within to its subject matter; the new science has at hand the power to comprehend the man-made world as it is in itself. In projecting his new science, Vico uncovers as its subject matter a region of subjectively relative being, one which coincides almost exactly with the one that will need to be uncovered anew two hundred years later by Edmund Husserl. Husserl called it by the now familiar name "the life-world." Like Vico he will be astonished that this, the only sphere of facts accessible in all its concreteness, had seemingly been so long ignored. And he, too, will conceive it as a field of research for a universal historical science and for his own phenomenological philosophy, thought of as absolute and ultimate historical science.[2]

Vico's principle that the true is identical with the created leads to a distinction within the real (the true) between those things created by God alone and those made by man.[3] To the former belongs the sphere of nature as it is in itself and for God alone. This can be an object for human thought and is the object of natural science. But the natural sciences, when taken straightforwardly as assertions about nature, do not and cannot produce an account of nature known to be true. To know nature man would have to create her. Yet the same sciences are things of the second sort; they are entities created by men. He who constructs the science knows

[1] The importance for Vico's new science of his conception that a mind can know genuine only what it creates has been stressed in Benedetto Croce, *The Philosophy of Giambattista Vico*, trans. R. G. Collingwood (New York: Russell & Russell, 1964), pp. 19–35, and in Richard Manson, *The Theory of Knowledge of Giambattista Vico* (Hamden, Conn.: Archon Books, 1969), pp. 11–32.

[2] Edmund Husserl, *Phänomenologische Psychologie*, ed. Walter Biemel, vol. 11 of *Husserliana* (The Hague: Martinus Nijhoff, 1962), appendix 5, pp. 376–79, hereinafter cited as *Phänomenologische Psychologie*.

[3] Croce, *The Philosophy of Giambattista Vico*, p. 24.

the science and knows his construct as it is in itself, for it *is* his creation. This yields the ideal of truth in historiographical science. The historian who reconstructs the science—or any artifact or, to use Vico's word, any institution[4]—would know it in the same way as its creator. As creations of man, the products or institutions have once been perfectly known by someone. To reconstruct them is to know them as they are in themselves.

The analogy between divine creation and knowledge on the one hand and human creation and knowledge on the other yields, when carried a step farther, further suggestions concerning the way Vico conceived the subject matter for his new science. It is by no means to be occupied merely with what is observably certain in the human world, that is, with the products that express or indicate the activity, the praxis of men in history. For Vico, the "certain" always appears as the revelation of the creative activity by which the world of nations is generated. The "data" are the traces left by the creators of historical reality. And the "certain" is far from being what is true, the reality itself:

> "Men who do not know what is true of things take care to hold fast to what is certain, so that, if they cannot satisfy their intellects with knowledge (*scienza*), their wills at least may rest on consciousness (*coscienza*). . . . philology observes that of which human choice is the author, whence comes consciousness of the certain."[5]

The traces left by the creators of the human world require interpretation just as much as would revelations by the divine creator. In this Vico appears to anticipate Dilthey's conception of a hermeneutical psychology to serve as foundation for the moral sciences. But Vico's new science, whose task is to be the comprehending or understanding of the decisions by which human praxis generates its products, remains preeminently a theology rather than a psychology. Vico's moral science is intended to be a "rational civil theology of divine providence in human affairs." The notion of divine providence remains central to the new science, even though Vico excludes from its subject matter the history of the chosen people who were aided by supernatural means (grace), choosing to limit its theme to gentile nations whom providence aids by natural means alone.[6]

Disregarding for the time being the role of providence in the world of nations, it remains true that the theme of Vico's science and the manner in which he arrived at it agree almost exactly with Husserl's conception of his phenomenology as absolute historical science (*absolute Geisteswissenschaft*). On this conception, the (psychological) phenomenological reduction has as one of its principal effects the restriction of the scientist's theoretical interest exclusively to subjective phenomena as such, to con-

[4] M. H. Fisch presents a detailed discussion of the manner in which *institute* and *institution* are used in the English translation of the *New Science*, §§ M1-M10.
[5] *New Science*, §§ 137–38.
[6] *New Science*, § 136.

sciousness and to its objects as these appear to consciousness. Phenomenology is seen as a thoroughgoing science of the life-world. The world and all of its constituents are conceived as products (*Leistungen*) which arise by virtue of synthetically combinative consciousness. All products of art or praxis emerge within this life-world. These include whatever has resulted from man's attempts to determine what things are in themselves, apart from their subjectively relative "appearances." The efforts and their results, whether these be myths, religions, poems, or objective sciences, belong alike to the theme of a universal, historical science.

In a manuscript written in 1926,[7] Husserl notes that each particular positive science isolates a field of investigation and that every excision of a special field involves a hypostatization (*Verabsolutierung*) when it is done without being aware of the delimitation as a limitation. What happens in such a case is that a non-self-sufficient part of an all-inclusive concretum is taken to be something which exists absolutely. Each particular natural science has always understood itself to be adapted to a particular and only relatively self-sufficient field within a more inclusive whole, universal nature. In contrast, particular historical sciences, or at least those which have actually been developed as sciences, have never understood their fields of research to be parts of a universal concretum. They have never inquired into the possible scope of a universal historical science, a universal "moral science." Instead they have accepted the hypostatization of nature by natural science; they have taken *its* field of investigation to be the truly concrete. They do not see through this hypostatization and so in turn hypostatize their subject matter, mundane minds existing within the world, as a sort of psychophysical appendage dependent somehow or other on nature which has first been taken as absolute. These hypostatizations result from a characteristic "one-sidedness" in the attitude with which the "naive," positive sciences confront their subject, from the way in which they preconceive it. The subject matter first gets thematized, and only then can a *reflective* attitude apprehend the thematizing as one which *limits* the field, the interest as a *limited* one.

Such one-sidedness can be overcome only by adopting a radically historical (*geistige*) attitude, an attitude which, instead of accepting the hypos-

[7] Published as appendix 5 in *Phänomenologische Psychologie*. The view expressed in this manuscript concerns issues to which he returned again and again. They formed in fact a central theme of his phenomenology at latest from about 1913, when he worked on the manuscripts published in *Ideen zu einer reinen Phänomenologie und phänomenologischen Philosophie*, ed. Marly Biemel, vol. 2, *Husserliana* IV (The Hague: Martinus Nijhoff, 1952), esp. §§ 1–11, 49–53 and appendices 9–12. In *Phänomenologische Psychologie* the theme of appendix 5 is also discussed in §§ 1, 5–7, 11, 16–18, 26–27, 43–45. The same topics are treated again intensively throughout *The Crisis of European Sciences and Transcendental Phenomenology*, trans. with intro. by David Carr (Evanston: Northwestern University Press, 1970), esp. §§ 1–24, 28, 33–39, 53, 54, 71–72, hereinafter to be cited as *Crisis*; accurate summaries of some of these passages may be found in Joseph J. Kockelmans, *Edmund Husserl's Phenomenological Psychology* (Pittsburgh: Duquesne University Press, 1967), esp. pp. 77–86.

tatization of nature, regards historical things purely as mental. From this attitude, nature can enter into the theme of one's radically historical science only insofar as she is made thematic by the mind and only *as* she is mentally included (intended to) in the mind's experience and in its cognition: ". . . only then does one discover that the very nature posited as absolute by the natural scientific and naturalistic orientation toward the world is something "formed" by the mind and that the very same nature which one has consequentially been excluding from consideration is something brought about within the sphere of the mind itself and brought about there as substrate for natural science, something constructed by the mind."[8] It should be emphasized that a science, when viewed from the standpoint of Husserl's universal historical science does not by any means appear to be merely tautological; it would not then be considered an arbitrarily chosen system of analytically related propositions, a system of statements concerning merely relations between ideas, to use Hume's phrase. Considered as an historic construct of the mind, the science is inseparable from the relevant evidence on which it is based; its essence can be understood only by reference to the confirming empirical intuitions and the manner in which experimental situations have been structured so as to bring these intuitions about. The science, its practitioners, their activities, and so on, all are parts of the essentially historic world as it is given us concretely, the world as it is experienced. And, considered historically, the science is unthinkable apart from experienced realities which it has idealized and transformed.

As a world whose experienced realities are conceived and transformed by the sciences, the "life-world" is the foundation on which such formations arise; it is, as has often been emphasized, a pre-scientific world. What has not been adequately emphasized is that what Husserl calls the "original life-world" is *not* the world as we find it, that is, it is not a world of everyday life, within which the sciences occupy a limited place. It is a world through which we all have surely passed. In this sense, it is a "place" with which each *may* once have been familiar; if so, then it is long since forgotten. The very notion of it is now most strange. The notion of an "original life-world" will seem alien perhaps most of all to historians and social scientists. For, like the natural scientists, they too, as positive and objectivistically oriented scientists, have delimited their subject matter; and the original life-world is not merely pre-scientific, but pre-predicative and pre-cultural as well.[9] The life-world is the foundation for *all* praxis, for all creative activity. Idealization of what is given in pre-predicative experience does not originate by any means with the European sciences. There is an idealization involved even in the communicative function of

[8] *Phänomenologische Psychologie*, p. 377.

[9] A point brought out by Kockelmans in *Edmund Husserl's Phenomenological Psychology*, p. 285.

language—in taking for granted that an object is valid for the members of a linguistic community.[10] A consciousness of such an original life-world, a purely natural, pre-cultural world, can be uncovered as a stratum in any consciousness of a concrete world of artifacts. Husserl thinks of this pure nature as being the world the way it appears in sense perception only. Consciousness of the purely natural would thus exclude any reference at all to other subjects; what is perceived would, as purely natural, never appear to be *expressive* of another mental life. Moreover, all consciousness of value determinations would be excluded, whether these stem from the subject's own valuings or from those of others.[11]

Now Husserl is entirely right in the fundamental points he is making:

1. There is no nature in itself apart from the world as given in perception.

2. The artifacts composing the historio-cultural world can be understood only by reference to the formative activities in which they were made, an understanding which must extend to the materials that got transformed in the process.

3. The historical sciences can avoid hypostatizing society, history, culture, tradition, language, and so on, only if it is shown how the consciousness of a socio-cultural tradition can arise psychogenetically for individuals through the individual history (tradition) of each.

4. The historical sciences have a built-in one-sidedness or naïveté by virtue of which they exclude from consideration the necessary preservation of the natural—as what pertains to the original life-world rather than as a natural scientific construct—within the historical.

5. His phenomenology is capable of providing the critique of historical reason required to overcome this sort of naïveté, as well as the hypostatization of objective history.

6. The formative activities peculiar to human praxis and to culturally determined praxis generally are possible only on the basis of a consciousness of "natural" entities belonging to the original life-world, entities of a sort that can be given only in sensuous experience.

As Vico would have been quick to point out, consciousness of such a purely natural world, a consciousness having no reference to other minds or to affective-valuational consciousness, does not occur concretely and, historically speaking, never has. But there is nothing to indicate that Husserl thinks of the consciousness of his "original life-world" as anything but a level of consciousness which can be made thematic through an abstractive process. He makes no claim either that such a world or the consciousness of such a world can exist separately and on its own.[12]

[10] E. Husserl, *Erfahrung und Urteil Untersuchungen zur Genealogie der Logik*, ed. Ludwig Landgrebe, rev. ed. (Hamburg: Claassen Verlag, 1954), §§ 11, 12.

[11] *Ibid.*, pp. 56f., 68f.

[12] *Ibid.*

In contrast to the region of "pure nature" as Husserl conceives it, that is, as an aspect involved in all experience of any concrete world, the identification of what is with what is made seems, as Vico understands it, to require a quite different conception of nature. Vico's sense of "making" seems to require a basic opaqueness of the (natural) things worked on in fashioning institutions. Natural things, being God's product rather than man's, are opaque from any human point of view. The *facts* with which he deals are facts of objective praxis. The human facts with which his new science is concerned are the things men, including "primal" men, have established through actions in response to their passions and needs. When considered as what is true, they are also things providence has established by means of savage and human passions and needs.[13] Historical institutions are indeed modifications of these same passions and needs. History, so far as it can be understood at least, is the story of the modifications by which members, or at least some members, of a species of brute have become and are becoming human. The historian can understand history only because and only to the extent that his own nature is susceptible of these modifications and of savagery as well.[14]

The view that human institutions originate from purposeful activity is one that Husserl shares with Vico. Thus, for both the sciences are to be understood as institutions—subjective formations, to use Husserl's term. They are, to be sure, a very particular sort of institution but nevertheless a sort that belongs as much as any other to the totality of such institutions which make up human history. *As products of practical activity*, the sciences belong to the proper subject matter of the science of history.

The Vichian and the Husserlian views, however, seem to diverge when it comes to Vico's important doctrine of the convertibility of truths and facts. Vico's doctrine is defensible because of his qualification to the effect that the true is created either by man or by God. That productive human actions should generate all truths, thereby making man the measure of all things, is excluded by the first axiom of the new science.[15] The existence of God guarantees the existence of a sphere of nature in itself. The sphere of nature in itself serves in part as the matter upon which productive activity works. The matter in itself par excellence for this activity is the nature of the beast which, as providence purposes, is to become human. Apparently we can have no notion of what that bestial mind might be like or might have been like prior to all humanization. What it is most primitively we cannot know. That is a creation of God alone. Here we reach one of the "first beginnings beyond which it is vain curiosity to demand others earlier."[16] The mind can be known, can be a subject for

[13] *New Science*, §§ 141–45, 341.
[14] *Ibid.*, §§ 331, 339, 341.
[15] *Ibid.*, § 120.
[16] *Ibid.*, § 346.

the new science, only to the extent that it is a human product, the result of education.[17] What is true of nature or creation in general is true of minds as well; so far as they are created by God alone they are known and knowable only by God. The new science can reconstruct mental life only on the basis of historic data, its products; mental life can be part of the theme only to the extent that its own transformations or modifications are products or by-products of its own creative activity. Here, Vico anticipates both the Kantian separation of mind, into empirical mind and mind in itself, and the essentially Kantian separation of psychology from other sciences of the mind, including the historical sciences, as well as transcendental philosophy. Husserl emphatically rejects both separations.[18] His rejection, however, is based in part on grounds that, superficially at least, are curiously Vichian. From the standpoint of Husserl's transcendental phenomenology, anything which might conceivably enter as intended material into any practical activity—whether human or not and no matter how primordial or "savage"—could exist for consciousness only as something "made," that is, as a synthetic product of *the conscious life in which the activity occurs.*

Husserl appears to regard parts of a mind that are in principle not accessible to observation and description in his absolute historical science, not just as things about which it is vain curiosity to inquire, but as essential impossibilities. But he does acknowledge that nonhuman mental lives —including "subhuman"—*are* essentially possible and that there occur in human mental lives conscious processes more primordial than any specifically human praxis. The type of "observation" involved in explicating such phenomena is radically different from any empirical intuition. Indeed, Husserl's absolute historical science is not primarily a science of empirical fact. It is fundamentally *eidetic* transcendental phenomenology, a science concerned not with actualities as such but with essential possibilities, impossibilities, and necessities. More than anything else, Husserl's very explicit separation of sciences of the essential from sciences of the factual sets his historical science apart from other theories of history. Like any other eidetic science, Husserl's absolute historical science would be based on intuition, not of facts, but of essential relations, and its method would be that of "free phantasy variation." Starting from a mental process actually observed reflectively, the investigator takes it as a pure possibility rather than an actuality and varies it in some respect in order to ascertain the range of variability for conscious processes of the kind in question. What such a science claims to establish is the kinds of mental lives that can occur, the kinds of mental processes that can occur in them, and the kinds of statements which may be, must be, and cannot be true of mental processes of a particular kind or of mental lives of a particular

[17] *Ibid.*, § 520.
[18] *Crisis*, §§ 27–32.

kind.[19] As Vico might say, Husserl's historical science aims to establish which properties may, must, or cannot belong to mental life or to mental processes and what sort of "modifications" mental life is capable of. But this also indicates an enormous difference between a phenomenology and any "necessitarian" theory—whether it be Vichian, Kantian, Hegelian, Marxist, or any other—of the historical. In contrast to empirical intuition, eidetic or essential intuition may provide evidence of essential necessity but *never* of factual necessity. It can provide evidence that *if* an event of type *x* occurs, then it must have properties *a, b, c,* etc. It can, however, provide no evidence *that* an *x* actually has occurred, is occurring, or will occur. The discovery and evaluation of evidence for actuality would fall entirely within the province of empirical disciplines within the science of the historical.

Vico and Husserl are both convinced of the need to investigate the "origins" of human history and its institutions. The two also agree that the subjectiveness of the subject matter of their several sciences does not require that the judgments made within the sciences be arbitrary in any way. And there seems even to be partial agreement on what makes such a science possible: that the formative activity being investigated is among the "modifications" of which the investigator's mind is susceptible. Moreover, Vico, like Husserl, seems to regard his new science as one whose judgments are apodictic. However, Husserl's "absolute" historical science is conceived as an eidetic science rather than as a science of fact. In such a science, investigating historical origins would mean showing the *type* of foundation on which an institution of a given *type* can arise, showing the *kinds* of conditions which must be realized *if* a given sort of artifact is to be formed.

Thus, there is a considerable divergence between Husserl and Vico on the issue of what their historical sciences can achieve. Eidetic sciences, as Husserl understands them, are based on intuitive evidence and yield apodictic propositions concerning what is possible, impossible, and necessary. Empirical sciences are sciences of what is actual, and intuitive evidence of actuality is limited to a comparatively narrow range of mental phenomena—the ones called "my own"—beyond which historiography, if it is interested in them at all, soon passes. As a science of the actual course of history, historiography is an empirical rather than an eidetic science. The concepts, theories, and results of historiography and those of an eidetic science of things historical would have to be mutually consistent. A synthesis of the two disciplines which would yield an apodictic historiography is, however, an essential impossibility so far as Husserlian phenomenology—in contrast to Hegel's—is concerned.

[19] E. Husserl, *Ideas: General Introduction to Pure Phenomenology*, trans. W. R. Boyce Gibson (London: George Allen and Unwin, 1931), §§ 1–17, hereinafter to be cited as *Ideas*.

Vico, on the other hand, often seems to regard his new science as just such a synthesis.[20] He clearly seems to believe that the new science, in spite of its being a science of fact, is derived from evidence comparable to that which founds judgments in pure mathematics. The same factor which makes for certainty in geometry is present in the new science.[21] Indeed, a claim of this sort can scarcely be absent when the new science claims to be a rational civil theology of divine providence in human affairs. Vico provides intriguing interpretations of the human sense of the divine, of the role it plays in human history, and of the ways it is expressed in human institutions. But it is also clear throughout that he considers God and providence, not just as senses expressed in specific works, but as actual forces influencing and in fact guiding the courses of nations. Moreover, providence is the ultimate guarantor for the truth of the new science.[22] Its three first principles are human institutions taken by Vico to be the primal origin of humanity in all societies. Since these three customs are common to all, they are construed to be eternal and universal. They are customs taught to man by common sense; they have, therefore, a common ground of truth, since common sense is of divine origin. Divine origin is employed by Vico to establish the universal applicability in fact of his first principles, excluding a priori contradictory claims.[23] He converts in this way what would otherwise be very rough empirical generalizations to essential necessities.[24]

The actuality of providence in history also assures that human actions will always achieve something more and something better than human agents intend: "Since [divine providence] has for its end its own immeasurable goodness, whatever it institutes must be directed to a good always superior to that which men have proposed to themselves."[25] Human actions are regarded as having in themselves definite properties unknown, and apparently unknowable, to the agents. Human history, and not just the sphere of the purely natural, has a determinate being in itself. How this is to be reconciled with the doctrine that history, being a human product, is thoroughly knowable, is far from clear. *The truth* about human actions as about the stages of human development will emerge later, and

[20] *New Science*, §§ 138–41.

[21] *Ibid.*, § 349. For a contrary opinion see Manson, *The Theory of Knowledge of Giambattista Vico*, pp. 14, 19.

[22] *New Science*, § 348. For a contrary opinion concerning the importance of providence in Vico's science see Manson, *The Theory of Knowledge of Giambattista Vico*, pp. xii–xiii.

[23] *New Science*, §§ 334, 336.

[24] In rejecting procedures of this sort, it is virtually certain that Husserl would have agreed with Franz Brentano and incidentally with legal positivists. See Brentano's *The Origin of Our Knowledge of Right and Wrong*, ed. O. Karus, trans. R. M. Chisholm and E. H. Schneewind (London: Routledge & Kegan Paul, 1969), § 4, p. 5.

[25] *New Science*, § 343; see also § 1107.

providence guarantees that what later emerges has been the truth about the earlier all along.

Thus, the real, consensual nature of customs and of positive law emerges, for Vico, with the coming of the "human" era, when laws come to be *understood as* institutions, and universal legal concepts are formulated. Rights emerge as universal, spiritual, and eternal and hence are God-given. Legal obligation turns out to have its grounds in an understanding of rights which shows their divine origin, so that legal obligation carries moral obligation as well.[26] Vico's theory of natural law and legal obligation rests upon supposed facts about the nature and origins of positive law. To that extent, it appears to be a "naturalistic" theory of obligation, in the pejorative sense of the word established by G. E. Moore; it attempts to derive a notion of how things ought to be from the way they have actually occurred.

The role of providence and "natural" purpose in Vico's theory of history serves to foreshadow much of the subsequent philosophy of history from Lessing, Kant, and absolute idealism down even to so recent a Kantian as Cassirer. It also serves to indicate the scope of tasks facing phenomenology as an historical science. Since Husserl's transcendental phenomenological *epochē* is to reduce the field of theoretical interest to pure consciousness, it excludes any statements concerning a god, along with all statements about transcendent beings, except as object or sense for consciousness, that is, as a phenomenon. Any historical science that is to be phenomenological can make no utterances and no suppositions concerning either a transcendent God or providence as an actual force operating in human history and exerted by such a god.[27] The sense of things as "divine" or as "providential" would still be proper subjects for inquiry, but the inquiry could derive no guarantees for its own truth from the "divinity" or "providentiality" of its theme.

A phenomenological science of the subjectively relative will also have to provide its own account of how there originates *for the human agent* a sense which his life and his acts have of occurring in a much wider historical context. It is certainly true that we are almost invariably aware of our actions as bringing about much more than we foresee. But the awareness of a *definite* "something more to it" can emerge only after the fact. Before that it belongs to a more or less indefinite horizon of things yet to come, a horizon in virtue of which his action can and does have for the agent the sense of a venture. However, a definite "more to it" will be given in the future, as it has been in the past. In the meantime, the act's objective meaning will depend, from the standpoint of phenomenology, upon the frames of reference in which it is placed by an interpreter, whether he

[26] *New Science*, §§ 141, 311, 326–27, 927, 1038–39, 1044–45.
[27] Edmund Husserl, *Ideas*, §§ 51, 58.

be the agent himself or someone else.[28] If it is true that phenomenology may make no use of the notion that the wider socio-cultural context of human life and action has been instituted by providence, then this context may not be regarded as having, simply by virtue of its existence, positive value, much less as being ultimately for the best. This leaves open then the issue as to whether and in how far there is such a thing as a moral sanction for law and custom.[29]

[28] The most thorough phenomenological descriptions of this aspect of action have been developed in Alfred Shutz, *The Phenomenology of the Social World*, trans. G. Walsh and F. Lehnert (Evanston: Northwestern University Press, 1967), esp. chaps. 3 and 5. For a rough sketch of how the person's life may acquire initially the sense of being part of an historical tradition see my "Husserl's Phenomenology as an 'Historical' Science," *Social Research* 35 (1968): 256ff.

[29] The way to an affirmative resolution—though by no means unconditionally affirmative—of this issue has been indicated in Brentano, *The Origin of Our Knowledge of Right and Wrong*, pp. 4–35; see also his *Grundlegung und Aufban der Ethik*, ed. F. Mayer-Hillebrand (Bern: A. Francke, 1952), pts. 1, 2, 4, and 5 (esp. § 107).

Emanuele Riverso

VICO AND WITTGENSTEIN

The picture of Wittgenstein as a representative of logical empiricism is no longer fashionable. It has now become clear that his work contains an original mode of thought which is entirely his own and which was developed during the latter half of his life.[1] Many aspects of his later thought have been developed in the philosophies of his pupils and followers to the point that a large part of analytic philosophy in the 1940s, 1950s, and 1960s has its source in his teaching and writings. Nevertheless there are traits of Wittgenstein's thought which until recently have not received notice. These are the very traits that make his work parallel in a certain way the work of Giambattista Vico.

This essay does not intend to be an exposition of the philosophies of Vico and Wittgenstein, nor a full comparison of them. Were this to be done it would show that enormous differences exist between them. Vico and Wittgenstein are so different in the shape of their minds and so remote from each other historically, geographically, and culturally that it would be impossible to find any direct similarity between their thoughts. Nevertheless in the midst of a large field of differences some indirect but significant analogies can be found, not between their ideas and views, but between the ways they react against some significant features of their respective philosophical backgrounds. My point is that such analogies, though not great in number, are well worth consideration.

The work of Vico and that of Wittgenstein are both reactions against abstract rationalism and attempts at understanding the concreteness of life and culture. Vico reacted against mathematical rationalism supported by the followers of Descartes; Wittgenstein reacted against mathematical rationalism supported by Bertrand Russell in the Platonic stage of his philosophical development and by many students of logic in the first decades of the present century. Such reactions suggest the view that in the historical development of Western culture, useful as it may be, the flourishing of abstract thought at the same time tends to call forth a reaction in the direction of humanism and concreteness. It calls forth a

[1] E. Riverso, *Il pensiero di Ludovico Wittgenstein* (Naples: Libreria Scientifica Editrice, 1970), pp. 203–403.

need to ground abstract thought in its proper place within a humanized conception of life and the world.

Vico and Wittgenstein had different training: the one enjoyed an essentially humanistic education; the latter was trained in engineering and mathematics. But this by no means reduces the meaning of the analogy between their historical roles. The type of education that Vico enjoyed was outside the most fashionable European culture of his time, which was dominated by Cartesianism and aimed at a rigorous formulation of the concepts and methods of science rather than at a humanistic development of knowledge. Vico was educated in Naples, and Naples was not within the area of the most advanced and fashionable culture of the seventeenth century. Wittgenstein was trained in what were the most important centers of learning at the beginning of the twentieth century. Nevertheless both were self-made men in the field of philosophy, and both criticized the foremost cultural trends of their times in strictly personal ways.

Cartesianism at last won success also in Naples, where it found supporters such as Gregorio Caloprese and Tommaso Cornelio and was officially recognized under the government in Naples of the Duke of Escalona, Emanuel Pacheco (1702–1707). Although the works of Descartes found many readers in Naples at the beginning of the eighteenth century, Neapolitan Cartesianism was a way of thinking and facing general intellectual and metaphysical problems rather than a tendency towards a new method in scientific inquiry. And yet we should not be misled into thinking that the large influence that Cartesianism had in western Europe touched the scientific traits of European culture more than its ideological and emotional sides.[2]

Giambattista Vico easily realized that the role and meaning of Cartesianism in the culture of his time was not that of a purely scientific and technical procedure. Consequently he commented and criticized Cartesianism, not as a strictly technical analysis and as a procedure in the field of physics, but as a whole way of thinking and approaching the most general problems. When he argued against the refusal of what is probable (*verisimile*) and pleaded on behalf of its role in the life of mind,[3] he was suggesting a way of appraising and organizing the whole world of our knowledge. His theory of truth and probability, which opposed the Cartesian theory of truth and certainty, involves an evaluation of science, logic, mathematics, eloquence, and history which entails an assessment of what is of more or less value in life, of what is most worth caring for and looking at in the world. When he rejected the Cartesian program of accepting only what is strictly true and free from any doubt and obscurity and what is demonstrated to be such by a strictly logical or mathematical procedure, his rejection was based on an evaluation of the importance of the role of

[2] E. Riverso, *Dalla magia alla scienza* (Naples: Libreria Scientifica Editrice, 1961).
[3] *De studiorum ratione, Opere filosofiche*, III, pp. 796–99.

evidence, logic, and mathematics in human knowledge and human life generally; he was also suggesting a different appraisal of deductive and mathematical reasoning.[4]

Analogously, in the *Tractatus*, when coping with formal logic developed by Bertrand Russell, although he discusses many technical problems, Ludwig Wittgenstein aims at propounding a new way of looking at the world and a whole view of life and its values.[5] He felt that the way of looking at the world suggested and involved in Russell's formal logic was not as rigorous and consistent as it should be in order to justify the type of analysis it was intended to support. So, when Wittgenstein affirms that "the world is the totality of facts, not of things,"[6] that "feeling the world as a limited whole—it is this that is mystical,"[7] and that "even when *all possible* scientific questions have been answered, the problems of life remain completely untouched,"[8] he suggests a whole world view and a way of approaching the meaning of life. This approach was conceived as the best way to make understandable use of formal logic and to make acceptable the picture theory of language; thus it can be said that the logical technicalities—the theory of language, the mathematical operationalism, and so on—found in the *Tractatus* are strictly tied with the view that the world is the totality of facts, that the problems of life are untouched by scientific questions, and that all general and metaphysical problems should be met in the way suggested by the *Tractatus*.

Bertrand Russell, at the time Wittgenstein became acquainted with him, had himself developed an entire world view to suit his logical analysis. While such analysis was intended to express, support, and justify his metaphysical and emotional needs,[9] he still believed that "the discovery that all mathematics follows inevitably from a small collection of fundamental laws is one which immeasurably enhances the intellectual beauty of the whole; to those who have been oppressed by the fragmentary and incomplete nature of most existing chains of deduction this discovery comes with all the overwhelming force of a revelation."[10] Logic was important for having shown the perfect unity of mathematics and the way of deducing all its parts from a small collection of fundamental laws. Its study was useful to preserve the purity and strictness of reasoning,[11] to foster the austere virtues,[12] and to educate to "the refusal to regard our

[4] *Ibid.*, pp. 804–5.

[5] Riverso, *Il pensiero di Ludovico Wittgenstein*, pp. 49–82.

[6] L. Wittgenstein, *Tractatus Logico-Philosophicus*, trans. D. F. Pears and B. F. McGuinness (New York: Humanities Press, 1961), 1.1.

[7] *Ibid.*, 6.45 b.

[8] *Ibid.*, 6.52 a.

[9] Cf. E. Riverso, *Il pensiero di Bertrand Russell* (Naples: Libreria Scientifica Editrice, 1972), pp. 93–163.

[10] B. Russell, *Mysticism and Logic* (London: Allen and Unwin, 1917), p. 54.

[11] *Ibid.*, p. 53.

[12] *Ibid.*, p. 58.

own desires, tastes and interests as affording a key to the understanding of the world."[13]

When Wittgenstein in his later philosophy rejected his earlier view, in which he had attempted to assimilate Russell's logicism, it was a whole way of looking at the world and life that he rejected. He shifted the direction of his thought from the needs of scientific language to the larger needs of all the usages of language; from the quest for consistency, precision, and strictness to the quest for the understanding of the different roles of language in the cultural and historical background of its existence. In his earlier philosophy the most important function of language was that of being a representation of facts; in his later philosophy, language was seen essentially as the way men communicate with each other in the context of specific cultural conditions. It is through this change of perspective that Wittgenstein approaches a way of regarding language that Vico had suggested two hundred years before.

Of course it would be a mistake to ignore what is new in the thought of Wittgenstein, specifically in the field of semantic analysis, and of course he did not know the works of Vico nor his thought; but we cannot ignore the fact that his later philosophy and his new approach to linguistic analysis involves a new way of conceiving the nature and functions of language (although he did not develop his view systematically) that betrays the awakening of a need of concreteness and humanism felt by philosophers of other centuries. Some of the points of Wittgenstein's view are worth stressing here in comparison with some points of the philosophy of Vico, not simply to suggest surface similarities between Vico and Wittgenstein, but to contribute to discovering some deep philosophical tendencies or needs that make themselves felt in different times on changed backgrounds and in different shapes. The more remote from each other the philosophers that felt them, the more important the witness they give to such points.

The first point is the suggestion that understanding is operating. When Wittgenstein returned to Cambridge he began to try a new approach to the problem of meaning by asking the following question: What happens when I understand a sentence? In an interview with Waismann in Vienna on 21 September 1931, Wittgenstein spoke about his having been deeply concerned with the first one of such questions and strongly suggested that understanding a sentence means operating with it.[14] In a manuscript he wrote in the period from 1932 to 1934, edited by Rush Rhees under the title *Philosophische Grammatik*, this view is largely developed, though under the proviso that there is a large multiplicity of understandings.[15]

[13] *Ibid.*, p. 37.

[14] *Ludwig Wittgenstein und der Wiener Kreis*, shorthand notes recorded by F. Waismann, ed. B. F. McGuinness (Oxford: Blackwell, 1967), p. 167.

[15] L. Wittgenstein, *Philosophische Grammatik*, ed. Rush Rhees (Oxford: Blackwell, 1969), p. 11.

According to this view, to understand a word means to know how such a word is to be used,[16] and the use of a word in the language is its meaning; the function of grammar is to describe the use of words in a language.[17] A language is conceived of as a system of operations; therefore the meaning of a word and the meaning of a sentence are the roles they play in a language. Wittgenstein took up this point again in the *Blue Book*, and although he still adhered to the view that understanding is operating, he added that "the use of the word *in practice* is its meaning."[18] In his lectures he explained that "he did not mean that meaning of a word *was* a list of rules."[19]

The second point is that Wittgenstein did not continue to speak about language as something unique, the essential role of which is to represent the states of affairs existing in the world. He became conscious of the importance of the multiplicity of languages, of the plurality of uses existing in each language, and of the historical mutability of the same.[20] The analysis of language was no more conceived of as the reduction of its structures to formal logic, but as the assessment of "language games" existing in a language during a particular historical period.[21] Each language game was to be thought of as devoid of all absoluteness, and in this sense each was to be thought of as arbitrary; therefore all rules of grammar (that are the rules of language games) are arbitrary.[22] There is no possibility of giving the structures of languages a metaphysical ground; such structures can admit only of an historical and cultural ground. Only as historical facts can they be justified.

The third point is that a language, while being devoid of all metaphysical ground, is a whole world and encircles a whole culture; it involves a way of evaluating things and of coping with reality. In the *Tractatus* Wittgenstein had suggested that "the world of the happy man is a different one from that of the unhappy man"[23] and that "the limits of my language mean the limits of my world";[24] so he had implied that when ethical and aesthetical attitudes are changed, the world is also changed, but, as my world is delimited by my language, we hardly can see how the type of logical analysis suggested by the *Tractatus* could justify a multiplicity of languages, each delimiting a world. In his later philosophy Witt-

16 *Ibid.*, p. 47.

17 *Ibid.*, p. 60.

18 L. Wittgenstein, *The Blue and Brown Books* (New York: Harper, 1958), p. 69.

19 G. E. Moore, *Wittgenstein's Lectures in 1930–1933*, in his *Philosophical Papers* (New York: Macmillan, 1959), p. 258.

20 Wittgenstein, *The Blue and Brown Books*, pp. 43–44; *Philosophische Bemerkungen* (Oxford: Blackwell, 1964), pp. 52, 321; and *Philosophische Untersuchungen* (Oxford: Blackwell, 1953), p. 12.

21 *Ludwig Wittgenstein und der Wiener Kreis*, pp. 103–4.

22 Moore, *Wittgenstein's Lectures in 1930–1933*, p. 277; Wittgenstein, *Philosophische Grammatik*, pp. 29, 184, 185; and idem, *Zettel* (Oxford: Blackwell, 1967), pp. 12, 60.

23 Wittgenstein, *Tractatus logico-philosophicus*, 6.43.

24 *Ibid.*, 5.6.

genstein no longer faced such a problem because of the incorporation in his view of the multiplicity, mutability, and contingency of languages and of linguistic structures. A system of symbols is a world;[25] so a language, as a system of symbols, embraces a world, and children, when they learn to use a language, learn also to think of the world.[26] The language I learn, clasps my life[27] and gives my world structures and determinations, because a use of language is a culture;[28] "a language game does change with time,"[29] and "an entirely different game is played in different ages."[30] The arbitrariness of grammatical rules does not mean that they can be changed arbitrarily. There is a tacit agreement to this in a culture, and no single member of it can betray such an agreement, if he desires to be understood. "To obey a rule, to make a report, to give an order, to play a game of chess, are *customs* (uses, institutions)";[31] so to agree in the use of a language "is not agreement in opinions but in form of life."[32]

I want to suggest that such points of the later philosophy of Wittgenstein are comparable to some points of the philosophy of Giambattista Vico and such a comparison can be very profitable in gaining a better view of the nature of linguistic forms and their role in the life of individual minds and the development of cultures, institutions, and customs.[33]

The first point of the philosophy of Vico I want to stress here is the well-known equating of truth with that which is operational, which implies that understanding (*intelligere*, as being a perfect knowledge of something)[34] is the operation of collecting all the elements of a thing or the operation of constructing a thing. Therefore we obtain a perfect understanding of a thing only when it is we that construct it. We obtain perfect understanding and certitude in arithmetic and geometry because it is we that make its theorems, sentences, equations, and demonstrations.[35] Sciences contain less certitude, to the extent that they are less abstract, less dependent on our operations, and more merged into matter.[36]

[25] Wittgenstein, *Philosophische Bemerkungen*, p. 178.
[26] Wittgenstein, *Philosophische Grammatik*, p. 108.
[27] *Ibid.*, p. 66.
[28] Wittgenstein, *The Blue and Brown Books*, p. 134.
[29] L. Wittgenstein, *Ueber Gewissheit* (Oxford: Blackwell, 1969), p. 34.
[30] L. Wittgenstein, *Lectures and Conversations of Aesthetics, Psychology and Religious Belief* (Oxford: Blackwell, 1966), p. 8.
[31] Wittgenstein, *Philosophische Untersuchungen*, p. 81.
[32] *Ibid.*, p. 88.
[33] Obviously the views that are the most important in reference to this point are those of Ernst Cassirer, *The Philosophy of Symbolic Forms*, trans. Ralph Manheim, 3 vols. (New Haven: Yale University Press, 1953–57), vol. 1. Unfortunately I cannot enlarge the present essay to include suggestions about the way in which the ideas of Cassirer are important for understanding and employing the ideas of Wittgenstein and Vico.
[34] *De Italorum sapientia, Opere filosofiche*, I, 1, p. 63.
[35] *Ibid.*, I, 2, p. 69; *De studiorum ratione, Opere filosofiche*, IV, p. 803: "*Geometrica demonstramus quia facimus.*"
[36] *De Italorum sapientia, Opere filosofiche*, I, 2, p. 69.

Vico did not explicitly apply his operationalism to the understanding of words and sentences, like Wittgenstein, but his operationalism involves that we understand words, when we make them symbols by using them as symbols, and understand sentences, when we knowingly construct and use them, or when we construct and use them according to the structures of the language of which we are making use. Unfortunately in the *Principi di una scienza nuova* Vico did not develop further the operationalist cues he had suggested in the *De antiquissima Italorum sapientia*, but he never repudiated such views, nor do his views on the development of man and society contain anything in opposition to them.

There is considerable difference between Vico's operationalism and that of Wittgenstein. Behind Vico's views are suggestions from Hobbes and many influences of Platonism and Scholasticism. Behind Wittgenstein's views are suggestions from pragmatism, formalism, and mathematical intuitionism. Nevertheless two observations are worth making here: (1) It is probable that a reaction against the absolutism of logicism and rationalism, to be effective, should embrace operationalism in one form or another, and this means that, to disprove the abstractness of logicism and rationalism, philosophy needs to reach a new awareness of the role of human subjects in the production and the nature of the human world; and (2) it is possible to enlarge Vico's operationalism in such a way that it could embrace and improve that of Wittgenstein.

Vico's operationalism should be applied to the understanding of language and should absorb the technicalities of Wittgenstein's operationalism. As a consequence there would be a distinction between understanding a word or a sentence and understanding a thing or a state of affairs, although there is a strict correlation between them. Probably we cannot dispense with such a distinction if we are not ready to ignore what is happening in the field of psychology of intelligence, where the use of tests and measures is giving an increasing importance to the distinction between verbal and nonverbal intelligence.[37] An operational view of understanding things and facts could be properly developed with the help of Jean Piaget's theory of sensory-motor intelligence.[38] An inquiry into the correlations and mutual influences between understanding things and facts could open a new and perhaps very successful direction for inquiries into meaning and truth.

The second point in the philosophy of Vico worth mentioning here is the concept of the multiplicity and transformability of languages; their dependence on historical, cultural, and biological circumstances; and the

[37] Cf. H. J. Butcher, *Human Intelligence: Its Nature and Assessment* (London: Methuen, 1968), pp. 18, 211, 255–56, 268–69.

[38] Cf. D. Elkind and J. H. Flavell, eds., *Studies in Cognitive Development* (New York: Oxford University Press, 1969), pp. 237–55; and J. Piaget, *The Origins of Intelligence in Children* (New York: International University Press, 1952).

strict connection between uttered words, mimicry, and spontaneous gestures. This view is better understood if we realize how, in the later development of his thought (that is, in the *Principi di scienza nuova*, 1744), Vico no longer was concerned with the notion of a systematic philosophy that had been important for him when (1710) he was writing the *De antiquissima Italorum sapientia*. It would be a mistake to contend that the *Principi di scienza nuova* (1744) or the *Principi di una scienza nuova* (1725) was intended by Vico to be the outline of a new systematic philosophy any more than the *Philosophische Untersuchungen* was intended by Wittgenstein to contain a philosophical system; yet both works have a rather preemptory style, and both attempt to find something general and constant in the changing and troubling complexity of the human world.

Of course Vico's *Principi* are built according to a plan, while in the *Philosophische Untersuchungen* arguments follow each other in a less orderly way; Vico was exposing the result of his inquiry, while Wittgenstein was exhibiting his investigations in their making. Nevertheless the ideas contained in the *Principi* are far from being or pretending to be a systematic philosophy. The very principles that are formulated in the first book are in no way like the principles of a metaphysical or a logical system; they are rather the résumé of a large amount of observations and remarks in the field of history and human life. Though in the *Principi* there is a clear effort to expose the content in an orderly way, this work is very far from being the ultimate formulation of a system and should rather be viewed as the indication of a path that philosophical inquiry should follow. According to Vico, languages probably began with monosyllabic words, because of the structure of the organs by which they were first uttered and the emotional and socio-cultural circumstances of such utterances.[39] Articulated words were first formed under the influence of onomatopoeia,[40] which was determined both by natural sounds and phenomena and by emotional responses of men. But a language is not a mere set of sounds: it is composed of symbols and involves the possibility of saying something meaningful.

Wittgenstein, always concerned with the problem of meaning, took for granted the existence of an agreement among men on the usage of words and sentences, which produces meaningfulness in language. Vico was well aware of the importance of this problem, and his view of language is a very important effort to assess how it historically comes about that some particular sounds came to be used as symbols and how an agreement on such usage could occur in a people of a particular historical age. In two or three places Vico suggests that a mental language should exist, which is

[39] *Principi di scienza nuova* (1744), *Opere filosofiche*, I, sez. seconda, LX, p. 446; II, cap. 4, p. 505; cap. 5, pp. 506–7.

[40] *Ibid.*, II, cap. 4, pp. 503–5.

common to all peoples, though they have different spoken languages.[41] But it would be a mistake to think that in such places Vico was endorsing the Aristotelian view of a mental language composed of *pathémata tés psychés* or the Stoic doctrine of *leká*. We have absolutely no ground to attribute such views to Vico. In fact, he is only concerned with the finding of common features in the social and political behavior of men of different places and times.

According to Vico, a dictionary of mental terms common to all peoples should supply an explication of the substantial uniformity of their ideas concerning the most fundamental needs and utilities of men.

What we can objectively collect from his work is not the view that languages used by peoples in the various historical ages and geographical places are only expressions of one language, exempt of historical contingencies, but the view that different peoples have a common way of conceiving of the most general features of human behavior, and this uniformity could be usefully represented by a set of terms that we could suppose to be common to all peoples and that we could name "ideal language" or "mental language." In fact it would not be a true language, because a set of terms is not by itself sufficient to constitute a language.

Vico was concerned to point out that all peoples have a tendency to conceive of social life according to the same general pattern (the one illustrated by him in the *New Science*), though they give it different detailed forms. It is on the basis of such a common pattern that Vico hypothesizes the possibility of constructing a mental cross-cultural vocabulary.[42] He does not emphasize this hypothesis; rather, he is concerned to show that different forms of languages have come into existence and have been agreed upon in different times and places through a very complicated and spontaneous process in which many causes have been effective—human biological and emotional structures; natural phenomena, such as lightning, claps of thunder, and the flying of birds; and the elements and conditions of social and cultural life, such as the existence of slaves, of estates and rural properties, of money, laws, family names, marriages, and cities.

It was the compound action of such a large set of causes that was responsible for the naissance of signs which took on agreed usages. There is no metaphysical connection between a sign and the thing it refers to, but a gesture or a sound that functions as an element of a situation patterned by human behavior can become a sign of the whole situation, or of an important part of it, without separating it from the whole. In general short sounds or gestures (determined in their shape by the biological structure of men, particularly by the structure of their phonetic organs, and by their way of reacting emotionally and behavioristically to particular objects or

[41] *Ibid.*, I, sez. seconda XXII, p. 437; II, sez. seconda, cap. IV, p. 502; *Principi di una scienza nuova* (1725), *Opere filosofiche*, III, cap. XLIII, pp. 301–3.

[42] *Principi di scienza nuova* (1744), *Opere filosofiche*, I, sez. seconda, XXII, p. 438.

facts) produced by men on the occasion of certain facts were the first symbols and represented the same facts or an object existing in them.[43] In this way the first agreements of men upon the first linguistic usages were due to biological, behavioral, emotional, and natural causes and produced the simplest forms of language.[44] Obviously, against such a view it would be absurd to suggest that Vico conceived of the languages used by different peoples as the expressions of a *lógos endiáthetos,* wholly homogeneous and eternal.

According to Vico all other forms of language have developed by means of allegories, metonomies, and other poetical transformations of usages and meanings from a primary form of language, capable of referring only to material and empirical facts and itself having been produced by empirical circumstances.[45] The poetical stage was of paramount importance in the development of language because it was in this stage and by means of poetical procedures, or *tropoi,* that new linguistic usages were created and agreed upon. Such new usages generated the possibility of all sentences that do not immediately refer to material facts and things, and specifically from it were generated all abstract ways of speaking, that are essential to the development of science, philosophy, law, and other more complicated and advanced forms of culture.

The third point in the philosophy of Vico I wish to stress here is the concept that each language expresses a whole human and cultural world. I have pointed out before that Wittgenstein in his later philosophy realized this and implied or expressed such a view in several places in his manuscripts published since his death. Unfortunately he did not develop this view sufficiently for it to be exploited in a program of clarifying the problems of meaning and truth. In contrast to this, Vico assumed this view almost as a starting point of his inquiry and suggested that languages are the most serious witness of these ancient customs and ways of living followed by peoples in which the same languages originated.[46] According to Vico, each culture or each people that is the bearer of a culture is endowed with a wisdom which is embedded in the language it uses. He maintained that the wisdom embedded in a language is a philosophy and that the philosophy embedded in ancient Latin came from Pythagoreans and Etruscans.[47]

[43] *Principi di una scienza nuova* (1725), *Opere filosofiche,* III, cap. XXXVIII, pp. 294ff.

[44] *Principi di scienza nuova* (1744), *Opere filosofiche,* II, sez. seconda, cap. IV, pp. 502–6.

[45] *Principi di una scienza nuova* (1725), *Opere filosofiche,* III, cap. V, p. 260; cap. VI, p. 261; cap. XXIII, pp. 275–76; cap. XXIV, p. 276; cap. XXXVI, p. 293; cap. XXXVII, pp. 293–94; cap. XXXVIII, pp. 294–96; *Principi di scienza nuova* (1744), *Opere filosofiche,* II, sez. seconda, cap. I–VII, pp. 484–519.

[46] *Principi di scienza nuova* (1744), *Opere filosofiche,* I, sez. seconda, XVII and XVIII, p. 436.

[47] *De Italorum sapientia, Opere filosofiche,* Proemium, pp. 57–59.

Such a view is understandable as suggesting that the structures of a language are means by which the bearers of a culture are able to cope with problems of life and experience.[48] The most fundamental types of culture are three: (1) that in which human nature is subjugated by religion; (2) that in which human nature is heroic; and (3) that in which it is rational. Each type of culture is a human world specifically different from others, endowed with political structures, customs, and laws of its own and with a special form of language. In the first type there is a religious language composed mostly of gestures and cries; in the second a heroic and poetic language; and in the third a discursive language, suited to reasoning and discussing.[49]

Of course objections can be raised to this picture; nevertheless it points in a direction that complements Wittgenstein's views of language and linguistic meaning. This is a consequence of the fact that, although Vico and Wittgenstein are in fact very distant and heterogeneous philosophers, a close examination of certain points of their philosophies shows how two ways of reacting against abstract rationalism developed by two different philosophers can be seen in fact to complement each other. Modern followers of Vico could learn from Wittgenstein the use of linguistic analysis to clarify the meanings of words, phrases, and propositions more effectively than by means of Vico's etymologies. The followers of Wittgenstein could learn from Vico's work the way to expand and develop Wittgenstein's only partially developed suggestions regarding the strict connection between forms of culture and uses of language.

[48] Cf. E. Riverso, *Individuo, società e cultura* (Rome: Armando, 1971), pp. 45–91.

[49] *Principi di scienza nuova* (1744), *Opere filosofiche*, IV, sez. 5, p. 643; II, cap. IV, pp. 493–506.

Ernesto Grassi

MARXISM, HUMANISM, AND THE PROBLEM OF IMAGINATION IN VICO'S WORKS

Idealism and Marxism

THE IDEAL OF KNOWLEDGE MODELED ON MATHEMATICS AND GEOMETRY

The question of the theoretical and historical connections between Marxism, Humanism, and Vico's theory of imagination requires investigation of a vast background. The philosophical tradition of humanism stands in vivid contrast to the rationalistic school beginning with Descartes and culminating in German Idealism. It is thus understandable that since the time of Descartes the philosophical significance of humanism has been not only underestimated but virtually neglected. This general attitude has resulted in a historical tradition which has remained in force until today, namely, that of tracing the inception of modern thought to Descartes.

This gives us our first problem: What conception of philosophy and scientific thought really does begin with Descartes? Departing from the dualism of *res extensa* and *res cogitans*, philosophical and scientific thought appears possible only if it follows the mathematical and geometric ideal, for two reasons. First, if we set out from the *res extensa*, from sense perception, we attain no certainty, because no empirical phenomenon can stand up to the process of systematic scepticism, so it cannot serve as a foundation for knowledge. Second, knowledge—meaning the kind of knowledge that claims universal validity and necessity—can only depart from self-evident axioms, out of which conclusions are drawn by means of a rational process of deduction. For Descartes, such an axiom consists of his *cogito ergo sum*. The self-evidence of this principle or axiom warrants the scientific objectivity of the process to be deduced from it. The problems arising on the basis of this axiom, corresponding to the pattern set by mathematics and geometry, are solved through explanations referring back to it. A criterion thus accentuating the prevalence of truth and knowledge is bound to exclude from philosophy, and hence from scientific thought, whatever element does not have its source in truth and in logical processes.

This approach leads to a repudiation of *history*, for the latter is not in a position to contribute to knowledge or truth, since all discussions as to how events have taken place or how they are described by historians remain merely within the framework of "possibility." Nor can *philology* be attributed any philosophical significance; it can at most serve as a useful means for the understanding of ancient or foreign texts. Even then the profit expected from it is questionable, since, according to Descartes, it threatens to interfere with the authenticity of the philosophical process and to allow erroneous concepts to creep in and establish themselves. Still more dangerous is the inclusion of *art* and *poetry*, because they represent possibility rather than truth; *rhetoric*, a discipline which acquired great significance in Humanism, fares no better, because the passions impair the clarity of thought and consequently are not to be taken into account.[1] So all branches of humanism are systematically excluded from the framework of philosophy.

Kant pursues this train of thought to its logical conclusion, arriving at his *Critique*. The empirical experience emanating from the object teaches us that something has this or that quality; it does not show, however, that it cannot be otherwise. Hence empirical experience can never lead to true or strict universality, but only to hypothetical or comparative knowledge; for the universality resulting from empirical statements is merely an arbitrary exaggeration of their validity.

This accounts for Kant's critical approach. Knowledge is possible only if we succeed in discovering in ourselves a priori forms of cognition *on which* to found our understanding: these a priori forms then constitute the axioms leading to true knowledge. Reality in its various phases is *derived from the forms of human consciousness.*

Kant's own words reflect his awareness of the enormity of this conclusion, which demands that every scientific statement about reality *be derived exclusively from the a priori forms of human experience*: "However exaggerated and absurd it may sound, to say that the understanding is itself the source of the laws of nature, and so of its formal unity, such an assertion is none the less correct, and is in keeping with the object to which it refers, namely, experience."[2]

Science as an a priori structure of reality, reality as a creation of the human mind—the normal meaning of *concrete* is turned upside down. The concrete reality underlying our forms of cognition is regarded as being beyond cognizance, and nothing is concrete but the a priori forms of understanding from which reality is to be deduced. Knowledge as an a priori construction sufficient unto itself!

[1] Descartes, *Discours de la Méthode*, pt. 1, *Oeuvres*, ed. C. Adam and P. Tannery, 13 vols. (Paris, 1897–1913), vol. 10, p. 371.

[2] *Critique of Pure Reason*, trans. Norman Kemp Smith (London: Macmillan, 1933), A 127.

REALITY AS AN ACT OF CONSCIOUSNESS

It is precisely this trend of philosophizing, this method of knowledge seeking its own ends, to be derived purely from the act of consciousness as a process accomplishing itself, that is developed by Fichte. A number of statements, says Fichte, constitute a science by forming a relation with a whole and by having their roots in solid ground; hence the first essential definition of each science is its systematic form. Since philosophy claims as its function the investigation of *first causes*, it is also its task to test and to derive individual sciences. According to Fichte:

Knowledge is a building; the main purpose of this building is solidity. The foundation is solid, and as it has been laid, the purpose is already attained. But since one cannot live in a mere foundation, since it does not provide sufficient protection against the intentional attacks of the enemy or against the unintentional attacks of the weather, lateral walls are built, and over them a roof. All parts of the building fit in with the foundation and with one another, and thus the building as a whole becomes solid; but one does not build a solid building for the sake of joining it together, one joins it together to make the building solid; and it is solid if all parts of it *rest on a solid foundation.*[3]

Here also, the ideal of knowledge continues to follow the pattern of geometry and mathematics: the foundation of science is an *act* of consciousness, the original reality. How Fichte arrives at the act of self-consciousness as an original foundation we will not discuss here. We would merely recall that Fichte's aim is the apotheosis of a philosophy as a self-sufficient science deriving the whole of reality purely *from consciousness.*

Philosophy teaches us to seek everything from the I. Only through the I do order and harmony appear in the dead, formless mass. Only through man does regularity spread around him up to the limits of his observation, and as the latter is pushed forward, order and harmony are pushed forward accordingly. His reflection assigns a place to each of the infinite variety of things, so that none should displace the other; it brings unity to infinite variety. *Through it the spheres are held together . . . through it the suns run in their proper orbits.*[4]

The theory of idealistic coinage here arrives at its orgiastic culmination.

The most definite and radical example of a self-sufficient science and philosophy, with its a priori derivation from the dialectical process of consciousness and its dissolving of natural sciences, history, and art into philosophy, is represented by Hegel. How Hegel arrives at his conception of a dialectical reality is well-known: the duality of in-itself and for-us, of object and subject, to which Kant had adhered is *not primary* as far as

[3] J. G. Fichte, *Ueber den Begriff der Wissenschaftslehre* (1794), in *Sämtliche Werke*, ed. I. H. Fichte (Berlin, 1854), vol. 1, p. 42.

[4] J. G. Fichte, *Ueber die Wuerde des Menschen* (1794), in *Sämtliche Werke* (Berlin, 1854), vol. 1, p. 412.

Hegel is concerned, for it is produced by the act of thinking and therefore falls within the concept of the act of thinking. In this sense, thought carries out an "experiment": setting out from the dualism (thesis) of the in-itself and the for-us, it arrives at scepticism (antithesis), for the in-itself can, on the basis of that premise, only be arrived at *through the forms of the for-us*, and *never as it is in itself*. Thesis and antithesis are, however, by no means isolated counterpositions, for in the recognition of scepticism as a consequence of the rigid dualism presupposed, thought appears as an experimental process, that is, it becomes itself the original form of the revelation of reality (synthesis): "notion [*Begriff*] and object, 'being for another' and 'being in itself,' themselves *fall within that knowledge which we are examining*."[5] In other words, knowledge experiences itself as a process of the formation of consciousness in the dialectic form of thesis, antithesis, and synthesis.

This results in the basic thesis that *all reality is rational* and in the need to derive all reality, including history, natural sciences, and art, in its various forms of development, by an a priori dialectic process. Whatever is emotive, subjective, and perceptible must be dissolved or shown under its rational aspect.

In his *Encyclopaedia of Philosophical Sciences In Outline*, Hegel writes that philosophy is "thinking contemplation"; it substitutes "thoughts, categories, concepts, for the imagination," that is, it places the greatest value on avoiding empirical methods in order to proceed in a purely speculative manner, and it endeavors to see things dialectically in their total aspect, rather than in detail. Philosophy accordingly claims to grasp reality with the exclusive aid of logic and the dialectic of ideas.

This conception of philosophy leads to a very specific ideal of knowledge, which we can define as follows: the process of knowledge must be compelling to all, in the sense that its necessity and universal validity must make it convincing for all; it must, because of its claim to necessity and universal validity, be timeless and spaceless; it must be unemotive, because the *ratio* can only be impaired by emotions; it can have no connection with common sense or with everyday forms of speech, which are mainly obtuse forms of rational thought. Philosophy and science must become self-sufficient disciplines which, due to their autonomy, withdraw from everyday life and from the turmoil of history. The scientist, the true philosopher, must live and work *in seclusion*.

MARX'S CRITIQUE OF IDEALISM

The fundamental tenets of Idealism, as outlined above, serve as a background for understanding Marx. His critique of German Idealism was

[5] *Phenomenology of Mind*, trans. J. B. Baillie (London: Allen and Unwin, 1949), p. 141 (italics mine); cf. pp. 144–45.

already anticipated, in its essential theme, by Feuerbach. Thought, in the Idealistic sense, opposes being to itself within itself and thus assumes that it has resolved the antithesis in itself. A being of that type, however, is nothing but the object of thought, or in other words, a purely fictitious dialectic of absolute philosophy.

The function of the "new philosophy," in contrast to the idealistic tradition, is outlined by Feuerbach as follows: The "new philosophy" has as its problem of cognition, as its subject, not the I, not the absolute mind, in short, not reason *in abstracto*, but the real and entire essence of man. "The reality, the subject of reason is man alone. It is man who thinks, not the I, not reason. . . . So when the old philosophy said: only what is rational is true and real, the new philosophy says: only what is human is rational."[6]

Idealism is right in seeking the origin of ideas in man, but it is wrong in trying to derive ideas from isolated beings, from beings in themselves, from the I without a Thou supplied by the senses. According to Feuerbach, the function of science and philosophy is not to move away from sensory, that is, real things—as idealism has done—but to move towards them.

The "new philosophy" to which Feuerbach aspires is the dissolving of pure reason in the real and whole human being, in his life, in his heart, and in his blood; the new philosophy must claim to make man grounded in nature its sole and supreme object. Therefore, every philosophy ought to be a *temporal philosophy*, meaning that it ought to spring from questions arising in a concrete space and at a concrete time, for only in a space of this kind is the unity of theory and practice preserved, a unity which can never be vouchsafed by a deductive, rational philosophy following mathematical and geometrical ideals.

The affirmation of historical reality, the true achievement of a new "Humanism" having no fiercer enemy than "the speculative Idealism which replaces the real, individual human being by 'self-consciousness' or 'spirit,' " is the work of Marx. The drastic difference between Marx and Hegel consists of the fact that Hegel resolves the dualism of the in-itself and the for-us in the union of the dialectical process of the mind (whereby he has to cling to the a priori derivation of nature and of history), whereas Marx strives to reach this union in the concrete self-realization of human history. In the total process of externalization of the mind, and in the total revocation of this externalization, as described in the *Phenomenology of Mind*, Marx sees an obvious sign that all this merely centers on the "history of production" of abstract, absolute, logical, and speculative thought. The reality conceived by human history, that is, the humanization of nature through human productivity, is presented in Hegel's phenomenology merely as a product of rational mental activity:

[6] L. Feuerbach, *Philosophische Schriften* (Frankfort, 1966), p. 212.

The alienation which forms the central interest of this externalization and of its revocation, is the opposition of in-itself and for-itself, of consciousness and self-consciousness, of object and subject, that is, the opposition of abstract thought and sensory reality or real sensuousness within the thought itself. All other antitheses or antithetic movements are merely the semblance, the cover, the exoteric frame of these uniquely interesting antitheses, which provide the meaning for other profane antitheses.[7]

In his *Critique of Hegel's Philosophy of Right* (1843), Marx exemplifies his objections to Hegel by reproaching him with, among other things, the fact that in order to clarify the origin of the family, *he does not consider the true historical evolution of the family, but merely the dialectic of the idea, as though the latter in itself and by itself would act with a definitive motive*:

This fact, this actual relationship, is expressed by speculative philosophy as an appearance, as a phenomenon. These circumstances, this option, this choice of determination, this real adjustment, are the mere appearances of an adjustment which the true idea proposes to make with itself and which *goes on behind the curtain*. Reality is not expressed as itself, but as another reality. The ordinary empirical world is not ruled by its own, but by an alien mind.[8]

Marx further remarks that in his theory of law Hegel is actually interested, not in the philosophy of law, but rather in the logic that forms the philosophical element, *whereby the state merely serves to prove the logic*.[9] Hegel thus overlooks the fact that the affairs of the state and their consequences do not exist for themselves in the abstract but depend on the efficacy of special individuals, on human functions manifesting the social, impassioned, and arbitrary qualities of historically concrete man—the realm of "probabilities."

The total exclusiveness of a priori reasoning, the failure to acknowledge the independence of the historical world from the dialectic of ideas, had to lead to the phenomenon described by Marx as the "decaying process of the Hegelian system," comparable to the "putrefying process of the absolute mind."[10] Scoffing at the hermetic language of German Idealism, Marx writes: "Just as the philosophers made thought an end in itself, so they made language seek its own ends in a realm of its own. That is the secret of philosophical language, where thoughts as words have a content of their own. The problem of descending from the world of ideas into the

[7] Marx, *Ökonomisch—philosophische Manuskripte* (1884), "Kritik der hegelschen Dialektik und Philosophie überhaupt," in Karl Marx—Friedrich Engels, *Werke* [hereinafter cited as MEW], 39 vols. in 41, and a supplementary volume in two parts, separately impaginated (Berlin, 1958–68), suppl. vol., pt. 1, p. 572.

[8] Marx, *Kritik des hegelschen Staatsrechts*, (1842–44), in MEW, 1: 206.

[9] *Ibid*., p. 207.

[10] Marx-Engels, *Die deutsche Ideologie* (1845–46), in HEW, 3: 17.

world of reality turns into the problem of descending from language into life."[11]

Marx's critique of Hegel can be summarized as follows: it is not in the "flesh" of concrete history, not in the misery of the individual, that Hegel seeks philosophical history, but in the *exclusiveness of consciousness*:

> Since truth, like history, is an ethereal subject divorced from the material mass, it addresses itself not to the empirical human being, but to the 'innermost soul'; to be 'truly' experienced, it does not move the human being in his coarse flesh housed perhaps in the depths of an English cellar or on the heights of a French garret, it 'pulls' itself 'through and through' his idealistic intestines.[12]

The Humanistic, Anti-Rationalistic Tradition

THE HUMANISTIC REACTION AGAINST A PRIORI THINKING. JURISPRUDENCE AS AN ORIGINAL PHILOSOPHY.

Instead of the anonymity, the placelessness, and timelessness of a priori thought, instead of the unemotive, unrhetorical character of scientific, philosophical speculation, instead of the rejection of imagination and common sense on behalf of rationalism, the Italian humanistic tradition adopted and developed precisely the opposite viewpoints with regard to the essence of philosophy and science. It is, therefore, no wonder that rationalism and idealism brought with them a depreciation, both in the theoretical and in the historical sense, of Italian Humanism. This depreciation has led to a misunderstanding, lasting until today, of the humanistic tenets regarding the prevalence of practice, the importance of jurisprudence and rhetoric, and the philosophical impact of philology and imagination, as well as of common sense. Our interest in the forgotten, or in its essential philosophical sense, undiscovered, Italian humanistic tradition is not primarily historical, but theoretical, for we believe that particularly Vico's theory of the role of imagination, which we shall here discuss, acquires great importance in connection with Marxism.

Providing a precise analogy with Marxism's revolt against the a priori logic of German Idealism, Italian Humanism attained its own conception of philosophy through its liberating polemics against the logicism exercised towards the end of the Middle Ages in the controversy of universals. The controversy of universals, that is, of the "forms of indictment" (in Greek, *kategorein*) with which to address being in order to define it, centered around a fundamental problem. One speaks of being by defining it in

[11] Marx, *Zur Kritik der hegelschen Rechtsphilosophie, Einleitung* (1844), in *MEW*, 1: 385.

[12] Marx-Engels, *Die heilige Familie oder Kritik der kritischen Kritik* (1845), in *MEW*, 2: 83.

terms of categories such as quality, quantity, time, space, and so on. Being in its specified nature is disclosed in the framework of these universal "forms of indictment," from which the philosopher must set out to define reality. The dispute regarding universals consisted in the fact that the Realists attributed a real structure to the categories, while the Nominalists gave it a purely "logical" significance.

For the definition of philosophy, this had important consequences. The study of being as such—which was the function of metaphysics—had necessarily to begin purely from a contemplation of universals, of categories, whereby any problem of historical relevance was reduced to a subordinate importance. A decisive formulation by Johannes Scotus Erigena (810–77) shows the original abstract and a priori trend of the metaphysical philosophy of the Middle Ages. "For the rational soul can pursue knowledge *in itself*, far from the sound of the spoken word and the uttered speech."[13]

The Humanists turned precisely against this purely logical, rationalistic approach to philosophy and science. Petrarca (1304–74), C. Salutati (1331–1406), A. Politianus (1454–94), and L. Valla (1407–57), to mention only a few, turn their polemics against this a priori method. Petrarca, in his treatise, *De remediis utriusque fortunae*, writes: "I do not like that loquacious, long-winded scholastic philosophy of which they are so proud, I like true philosophy *which dwells not only in words, but in things*" ("in rebus positam non in verba.")[14]

C. Salutati, a pupil of Petrarca and first chancellor of the city of Florence, in his *De laboribus Herculis*, attacks those who are prepared to discuss everything in a purely rational way ("de cunctis disputatio et garrula discutere sunt parati") and points to the fact that their method is a purely logical one. "To the intricate cases which they turn and twist to delay their reply, many a premise is advanced, many a thesis is joined, and what is postulated follows as a final conclusion."[15] Salutati identifies these philosophers with the English logicians: ("textus Aristotelicus nec intelligunt nec legunt sed nescio quod tractatus apud 'tot divisos orbe Britannos,' quasi noster eruditioni non sufficiat situs").[16]

The campaign against an abstract, scholastic philosophy, vainly striving to define reality on the basis of a metaphysical theory of being and of the categories of being, takes place on three different planes, although they are factually interrelated. The first is the new interpretation of the essence and function of jurisprudence, done with reference to the Latin tradition

[13] J. Scotus Erigena, *De divisione Naturae* in *Patrologia Latina* (Paris, 1878), vol. 122, bk. 4, p. 869.

[14] Petrarca, *De remediis utriusque fortunae*, bk. 1, dialogue 46: "De variis titulis studiorum" in *Opera omnia*, 3 vols. (Basel, 1554), vol. 1, pp. 57–59.

[15] C. Salutati, *De laboribus Herculis*, ed. B. L. Ullman (Turici, 1951), bk. 1, chap. 1, §§ 2–4.

[16] *Ibid.*, § 2.

of Cicero and expressed in an exemplary fashion in C. Salutati's treatise *De nobilitate legum et medicinae* (1339). Here the fundamental idea is that *jus*, law, jurisprudence, as well as the appreciation of the historical situation and the state, must be derived from fundamentally human elements, not the other way round. The fundamentally human element consists in the fact that the forms of human behavior must continually be sought and defined anew and are therefore to be discovered in the historical role of man and in the elucidation of that role: it is history which differentiates the human being from the animal.

This is the realm in which questions that concern the human being impose themselves in their immediacy and urgency, without becoming isolated in the technicalities of an abstract philosophy sufficient unto itself. Jurisprudence is here shown as the only true philosophy, its object being neither nature nor abstract theories of being, that is, metaphysics, nor a science of categories, but *the concrete becoming of man.* This is the meaning of Salutati's thesis that the prevalence of jurisprudence is a result of the fact that its object is *jus. Jus*, according to Salutati, stems from *juvare*. Hence jurisprudence is a science which, through its response to the questions concerning man, is "of use" to him ("Jus igitur, quod a iuvando dicitur.")[17] If one attempts, in this manner, to avoid the theoretical discussions of philosophy and to anchor it accordingly in the concrete historicity of man, one is able to comprehend Salutati's radical thesis that the traditional seven liberal arts which, during the Middle Ages, were considered as the foundation of human culture *acquire their meaning only in and from jurisprudence.*

As an illustration of this idea, we shall mention only grammar, the first art of the trivium. A thing never exists as abstract in its meaning, but always in the framework of man's coping with things, whereby the meaning can vary radically from case to case. Correspondingly, the objectivity of language is first to be sought in man's coming to terms with things, hence in human actions. If the latter are regulated through jurisprudence, then jurisprudence acquires a dominant function. Grammar thereby manifests its historical character.

Since language has to adapt itself to facts, and since jurisprudence represents the essence of man's historical reality, lending a meaning to things, the definition of things, which grammar has made its problem, can only be sought in man's historical dealings with things and in their social arrangement. Thus jurisprudence as the theory of human actions within the community becomes the basis of grammar and philology: any purely "technical," formal, abstract grammar or philology is rejected.

[17] C. Salutati, *De nobilitate legum et medicinae*, ed. E. Garin (Florence, 1947), p. 160.

GRAMMAR AND RHETORIC AS CONCRETE PHILOSOPHY

The second phase of humanistic attempts to get away from rational, abstract philosophy is connected with the problem of words. Through his commission to translate classical texts of antiquity, Leonardo Bruni (1369–1444) became aware of the almost insuperable crisis of contemporary philosophy. Not only was there a great lack of texts of the philosophical heritage, as Bruni mentions, but the available texts were in a lamentably corrupt condition, and the translations quite inadequate.[18]

Bruni proposed to supply a philological reconstruction of ancient texts, as well as new translations. This made him discover the historical essence and transformation of the meanings of words and the fact that the naming of things can never be established on a "purely logical" basis. In *De interpretatione recta*, Bruni emphasizes the importance of the "form" of expression, of the *ornatus*, with regard to the *factual* definition of a context, though from a purely logical viewpoint the form appears to be insignificant. The pure logician, the rationalist, will consider the *ornatus* simply as an external embellishment and condemn it as part of the "irrelevant" art of the "thousand words." Bruni thinks that, in a translation, "neither the thoughts [content] should lack words, nor should the words lack charm and embellishment [form]" ("neque sensibus verba neque verbis ipsis nitor ornatusque deficiat").[19] The form (*ornatus*) of the *verba* and the *res* are inseparable, and the interpretation of the *res* is expressed in language. Thus the philosopher is, in effect, no longer the logician dealing with his theoretical problems *in abstracto*, but the "grammarian" who discloses the meaning of the *res* on the basis of the historical relevance of the word.

These ideas receive their clearest expression in the works of Agnolo Poliziano (1454–94). Poliziano establishes the thesis that philology or "grammar" ought to be, in effect, the *new form* of philosophizing. To be a *grammaticus* means to elucidate the essence of man in his development, in the process of his coming to terms with things, by means of studying the word. In his *Lamia* (the inaugural speech to his lectures about the first two Analytics of Aristotle, held in the Studio of Florence during the winter semester of 1492–93), he renounces the term "philosopher" for himself and instead claims to be a "grammarian," a representative of the "new form" of philosophy.

An insight into the function and transformation of language amounts to an insight into the historical significance of man: the philosopher as "grammarian" thus dissociates himself from the *doctores obscurae philosophiae*. Poliziano's teachings in Florence must have represented something

[18] L. Bruni, "Ad. P. P. Histrum Dialogus," in *Prosatori latini del quattrocento*, ed. E. Garin (Milan, 1952), pp. 56ff.

[19] L. Bruni, *Humanistische philosophische Schriften*, ed. H. Baron (Leipzig, 1928), p. 87.

entirely new, which explains the fact, as he himself states at the beginning of the *Lamia*, that he was repudiated by the "official" philosophers.[20]

The humanistic rejection of all a priori, "logicizing" types of philosophy also manifests itself, side by side with the renewed evaluation of jurisprudence (C. Salutati) and the identification of the new, anti-traditional philosophy with grammar (L. Bruni, A. Poliziano), on a third important plane: that of the prevalence of rhetoric.

The philosophical evaluation of rhetoric is above all carried out by Lorenzo Valla (1407–57) and Marius Nizolius (1498–1575). Owing to considerations of space, we shall restrict ourselves to Valla. He arrives at the philosophical significance of rhetoric through his radical criticism of the scholastic theory of categories. In his *Dialecticae disputationes* Valla refers to the medieval theory of categories with a clear awareness of the fact that the entire system of scholasticism was founded on it, for this tradition defines the *ens* as the supreme *genus* of all *genera*. To question the concept of *ens* would be equivalent to undermining the theory of the definitions of being (categories) related to it, as well as the entire metaphysical structure built upon them. Inevitably, the language used by this type of metaphysicians is full of "distortions and disguises" (*calumniae et involucra*).[21] Valla describes the structure of this philosophy as a maze and brands the dialecticians as *ioculatores*, as artistic players.

The only way to surmount the abstract methods of scholasticism is, according to Valla, by replacing the *ens* with the *res* and, what is more, with *concrete "res."* The first task of philosophy is, therefore, to investigate the domain in which the *res* acquires its meaning and function in relation to man. *This framework is concrete, inter-communicative language.* If philosophy is not to deal with empty concepts, it will have to adopt as the object of its investigation the significance of the *res* as a result of our daily dealings with it (*usitatissima loquendi consuetudo; vulgaris hic sermo*).[22] Concrete language always contains within itself, as an indicative expression, history and the structure of a meaningful world.

This results in the definition of rhetoric as the original domain in which language and objects appear in their concrete aspect. An orator must be capable of connecting things with man and his actions; the *copia verborum* corresponds to the *copia rerum* with which we deal. Valla formulates the contrast between abstract philosophers and rhetoricians as follows: "For how much more evident, more earnest and more magnificent is the manner in which problems are presented by orators, than the way they are analyzed by obscure, dry and anaemic dialecticians."[23] If Poliziano calls himself a "grammarian" because he is convinced that "grammar" is

[20] A. Politianus, *Lamia*, in *Opera omnia* (Basel, 1553), p. 459.
[21] L. Valla, *Dialecticae disputationes*, in *Opera omnia* (Basel, 1540), vol. 1, p. 669.
[22] *Ibid.*, p. 651.
[23] L. Valla, *De voluptate*, in *Opera omnia* (Basel, 1540), vol. 1, p. 907.

the "new" philosophy, Valla, as a philosopher, desires to be a rhetorician; for rhetoric is the queen of all things and the accomplished wisdom.[24]

Marx and Vico

MARX'S CONCEPT OF WORK AS THE ONLY CONCRETE SOURCE OF THE HUMAN WORLD

The question immediately arising from the preceding discussions is: The Humanist's emphasis on jurisprudence, on the union of *res* and *verba* (and hence on the philosophical importance of grammar as a domain of concrete philosophy), and the identification of philosophy with rhetoric—do all these tenets, which the Humanists set against the a priori philosophy of Scholasticism, actually fulfill their claim of being concrete? An objection of Marxism is here to the point. The original source of man's becoming lies in the original transformation, and thereby the humanization, of nature through work. Jurisprudence, language, and rhetoric are only concrete if they are manifestations of work, and hence manifestations of class history. Italian Humanism, therefore, despite its claim on concrete reality and its polemics against a priori methods, remains in the realm of the abstract.

The history of work is the history of the evolution of man. This thesis is introduced by Marx in the following words: "The conditions we begin with are no arbitrary conditions, no dogmas, they are real conditions which you can only abstract through the imagination. They are real individuals, with their actions and their material living conditions, those they have found as well as those produced by their own actions. These conditions are, therefore, verifiable through purely empirical methods."[25]

For the supremacy of thought in Idealism, for the prevalence of political or legal institutions in humanism, for the blind instincts and passions discussed by Machiavelli—without any consideration for the concrete economic conditions by which they are caused—Marx substitutes work, the transforming creative activity of man as the origin of society and history. "As individuals express their lives, so they are. What they are thus coincides with their productivity, both as regards *what* they produce and as regards *how* they produce."[26]

Marx's conception of work can be summarized by the following essential characteristics. First, human work is distinguished from that of animals by being the expression of a "purposeful will." This may be explained as follows: In *Das Kapital*, Marx distinguishes between human work and the animal's response to nature by describing the former as a process between

[24] L. Valla, *Elegantiarum*, in *Opera omnia* (Basel, 1540), vol. 1, p. 120.
[25] Marx-Engels, *Die deutsche Ideologie*, in *MEW*, 3: 20.
[26] *Ibid.*, p. 21.

man and nature whereby man, through his own action, freely produces, regulates, and controls a metabolism with nature. Marx literally says that this concept of work as the specific activity of man is "independent from any definite social form"[27] and, *therefore, as a theory does not represent a historical superstructure, but provides the foundation for all further economical and historical discussions.*

The animal, on the other hand—according to Marx's view—is *at one* with its vital activity: what it produces belongs directly to its physical body; that is, the forms of its basic attitude towards nature are already given and need not be sought. The animal, in this respect, is not free, for it is *in its world.* Its relation to what it produces is an *immediate* one. Therefore, says Marx, the animal has no attitude towards things; it produces under the impact of immediate physical needs, that is, under the dominion of patterns it does not design itself. Because it is not free, it lives without projecting into the future. "The animal is directly at one with its vital activity. It cannot be distinguished from it. It *is* its activity. Man makes his vital activity the object of his desire and of his consciousness. . . . His conscious activity distinguishes man directly from animal activity."[28] Thus work is conceived by Marx as a *free* process between man and nature whereby man adjusts nature through his own activity in order to appropriate the material of nature in a form that is useful to his own life.

Marx's second definition of work consists in the recognition that it represents the surmounting of immediacy through creative activity. The process of work is a transition from what does not yet exist and is only *possible* to that which becomes reality: "During the process of work, work continually changes from the shape of restlessness to the shape of being, from the shape of movement to that of object."[29] Work as a process of "metabolism" means the appropriation of nature on behalf of man. This appropriation is only possible if nature or matter undergoes a transformation leading to the surmounting of immediacy. This activity has a very definite character, one of adjustment, regulation, and control. Work as activity acquires a *formative* function with regard to nature.

A third and fourth characteristic of Marx's conception of work are its free nature and its social function. Work can only exist under the condition that man is *free.* Freedom is to be understood as a non-preconceived appropriation of nature, that is, as the faculty to transform nature into *new systems of interrelation that have not been preassigned to man.*

Work is simultaneously a *social activity.* For Marx, things have a meaning only with reference to the human being; apart from that, they are pure

[27] Marx, *Das Kapital: Kritik der politischen Ökonomie* (1867–), in MEW, 23: 196.

[28] Marx, *Ökonomisch—philosophische Manuskripte,* in MEW, suppl. vol., pt. 1, p. 516.

[29] Marx, *Das Kapital,* in MEW, 23: 196.

abstractions. Through work, man enters into relationships not only with things but also with other men. That is why Marx asserts that a humanized nature only exists for man as a social entity, as his own existence for the other and the other's existence for him.

VICO'S "THE DEED OF HERCULES"

Is it possible to find, within Italian Humanism, a theory of work as the source of history, a theory of work which simultaneously incorporates the philosophical importance of jurisprudence, philology, and rhetoric? Does the Italian humanistic conception of work bring a new contribution to the theoretical and practical complexity of questions regarding work and human historicity?

Vico, who can be said to represent the culmination of Italian Humanism, asserts—whether in opposition to the Cartesian ideal of knowledge modeled after mathematics and geometry, or against any philosophizing about nature—that *the new subject of philosophy must be history*, his reason being that history is created by man and can consequently be known by man. The sentences in which Vico outlines his plan for a "new science" are well-known:

> But in the night of thick darkness enveloping the earliest antiquity, so remote from ourselves, there shines the eternal and never failing light of a truth beyond all question: that the world of civil society has certainly been made by men, and that its principles are therefore to be found within the modifications of our own human mind.[30]

In contrast to the rationalism of Descartes and of German Idealism, Vico here attributes to history—which Descartes was not prepared to acknowledge as a philosophical science—an absolute validity and importance. History encompasses human actions which, since they can always turn out to be thus or otherwise, can never be derived a priori. That is why history is the realm of the "probable," of the *verisimile*. Actions, however, belong unconditionally to the structure of the human world, so that their realm (the realm of history) cannot simply be excluded from philosophical reflection. This type of exclusion is precisely what Vico wants to avoid in the *New Science* and is at the basis of his opposition to Descartes. The question that now arises is: What does Vico consider to be the concrete root of man's becoming? His reply points to two primal and interrelated factors: work and imagination.

Work is, to Vico, an adjustment of the direct and immediate impact of nature, an adjustment by which man steps out of nature; and here he chooses the figures of Hercules and Cadmus as symbols of it, above all Hercules. Vico symbolically places the origin of human society, or in other

[30] *New Science*, § 331.

words, of history, under *two signs of the zodiac*, which encompass the whole universe and thereby stand above all events. One is the sign of the Lion. Vico sees in Hercules, because of his extraordinary feats of work and above all because of his subduing the lion, the founder of human society. What does the lion symbolize, and what is its relation with the figure of Hercules? "The lion is here found to have been the great ancient forest of the earth, *burned down and brought under cultivation by Hercules*. . . ."[31] Hercules effects the transformations of nature, then, by subjecting it to the service of man through work.

Through the subjection of nature, and thus through the first type of work leading to the self-assertion of man, the human era is opened. That is why the Greeks counted the human era from the Olympic Games, where they celebrated the exploit of Hercules, the human deed *par excellence* of dominating the primeval forest by clearing it.[32] The development of human happenings is thus based, not on philosophy, on reflection, but on the original actions through which man built his world by adjusting nature to himself. Vico's interpretation of the ancient myth of Cadmus, in which the function of work equally plays a central role, perhaps best illustrates the concrete terms in which he conceives the origin of society to reside in work. In a fantastic, "uncritical," untheoretical manner, this myth describes the transformation of nature through the human intervention of work and, further, the origin of the first laws (agrarian laws), as well as the origin of social classes (lords and plebeians) and of sovereign power. In connection with this myth, says Vico, it is shown that the original form of human utterance was poetic and fantastic and that it is in poetic utterances that the first knowledge of man about himself is to be sought.[33] To pursue this task is to study *philosophy* as *philology*.

Vico writes:

This whole divine and heroic history of the theological poets was only too unhappily described for us in the fable of Cadmus. For first he slays the great serpent (clears the earth of the great ancient forest). Then he sows the teeth (a fine metaphor for his plowing the first fields of the world with curved pieces of hard wood, which, before the use of iron was discovered, must have served as the teeth of the first plows, and teeth they continued to be called). He throws a heavy stone (the hard earth which the clients or *famuli* wished to plow for themselves). From the furrows armed men spring forth (in the heroic contest over the first agrarian law the heroes come forth from their estates to assert their lordship of them, and unite in arms against the plebs, and they fight not among themselves but with the clients that have revolted against them; the furrows signifying the orders in which they unite and thereby give form and stability to the first cities on the basis of arms, as is all set forth above). And Cadmus is changed into a serpent (signifying the origin of the

[31] *Ibid.*, § 3, italics mine.
[32] *Ibid.*, § 733.
[33] *Ibid.*, §§ 446, 563.

authority of the aristocratic senates, for which the ancient Latins would have used the phrase *Cadmus fundus factus est,* and the Greeks said Cadmus was changed into Draco, the dragon that wrote the laws in blood. All of which is what we promised to make clear: that the fable of Cadmus contained several centuries of poetic history. . . .[34]

While the primeval forest is cleared through fire, a symbol of work, the first human center is created—the *ara,* which simultaneously becomes the first altar, for on it the human deed is celebrated. When Vico explains the symbolic drawing which serves as a frontispiece of the *New Science,* he says:

The plough rests its handle against the altar with a certain majesty, to give us to understand that ploughed lands were the first altars of the gentiles. . . . From these lands, it will be found, cities were called *arae,* altars, throughout the ancient world of the gentiles. For they must have been the first altars of the gentile nations, and the first fire lighted on them was that which served to clear the forests of trees and bring them under cultivation, and the first water was that of the perennial springs. . . .[35]

Jurisprudence, considered as the order of the human world, has its source here.

VICO ON THE FUNCTION OF IMAGINATION

In what way does Vico conceive of the second source of historical reality, that is, imagination, and in what relationship does it stand to work? The second sign of the zodiac, encompassing the whole of the universe and thus standing above all events, is the sign of the Virgin, represented by poets with a garland of ears of grain and pointing to the Golden Age ruled by imagination:

through the long course of centuries the years were counted by the grain harvests, which we find to have been the first gold of the world. This golden age of the Greeks has its Latin counterpart in the age of Saturn, who gets his name from *sati,* sown [fields]. In this age of gold, the poets assure us faithfully, the gods consorted on earth with the heroes. For we shall show later that the first men among the gentiles, simple and crude, and under the powerful spell of most vigorous imaginations encumbered with frightful superstitions, actually believed that they saw the gods on earth.[36]

The function of imagination is *threefold.* It is shown in and through imagination that the human being, unlike the animal, does not stand under the dominion of ruling patterns which give sense perceptions an unequivocal meaning. He therefore can, and does, give sensory phenomena the most varied interpretations. It is in and through imagination that he experiences his own freedom and steps out of the closed world of the

[34] *Ibid.,* § 679.
[35] *Ibid.,* §§ 15, 17.
[36] *Ibid.,* § 3.

natural forest. Thus the beginnings of human history are to be found in *poetry*, in *poetic wisdom* as the oldest form of the world order of man: "And by that trait of the human mind noticed by Tacitus whatever these men saw, imagined, or even made or did themselves they believed to be Jove; and to all of the universe that came within their scope, and to all its parts, they gave the being of animate substance. This is the civil history of the expression 'All things are full of Jove' (*Iovis omnia plena*). . . ."[37]

The second function of imagination is that of causing man to be seized by fear, by terror, in the face of things that have no direct meaning and that can be interpreted in entirely different ways. "Thus it was fear which created gods in the world; not fear awakened in men by other men, but fear awakened in men by themselves."[38] It is because of this ignorance and the fear engendered by it that he proceeds to build up an order of his own, or an adjustment of nature. "So that, as rational metaphysics teaches that man becomes all things by understanding them (*homo intelligendo fit omnia*), this imaginative metaphysics shows that man becomes all things by *not* understanding them (*homo non intelligendo fit omnia*)."[39] Imagination, based on the experience of the multiple interpretations that can be given to sensory phenomena, creates *the first analogies between these phenomena, and with them their first connections and finally definitions.* This is the first step towards an adaptation of nature, which constitutes the essence of mental activity. Vico expresses this idea in astonishingly modern terms: "when man understands he extends his mind and takes in the things, but when he does not understand he makes the things out of himself and becomes them by transforming himself into them."[40]

Since, in the beginnings of history, the understanding was not yet overrefined through the art of writing, nor spiritualized through the habit of calculating, poetic wisdom—as Vico expresses it—could, like a single stem, give rise to the development of economy, politics, logic, and ethics (all of which are poetical in nature). It is to the examination of this historical, imaginative wisdom that the "new science" is devoted, and this is what makes it a new point of departure.

The third function of imagination is that of being the *first original factor to give a meaning to work*: the intervention with nature, which, as such, is equally carried out by the animal through its work, is not limited to seeking food and preserving the species, for otherwise the human world would be no different from the world of animals. The specific human element is the experience of the "uncanniness" of nature. Even food and procreation, as primary factors in surmounting the direct impact of nature, acquire their human significance with respect to human patterns and inter-

[37] *Ibid.*, § 379.
[38] *Ibid.*, § 382.
[39] *Ibid.*, § 405.
[40] *Ibid.*

pretations, which, according to Vico's conception, *are first designed by imagination.* Here we must remember that Vico, among others, conceived ethics as an expression of the transfer of our instincts and passions, that is, of the nature in us, into a human system of relations priorly designed by our imagination and forming the roots and foundations of our ethical motivation.

Vico emphasizes the idea that linguistic images—tropes, metaphors, and other figures of speech based on a discovery of *similarities*—are not witty inventions of writers, as had been believed heretofore, but the first forms of expression through which the human world came into being. Everything invented throughout history, says Vico, came from an insight into "similarities." It was the "sight" of what men had in common that created the first forms of social and political order within nations, and with it relations among men. The original form of this "sight" was due to imagination.

All the first tropes are corollaries of this poetic logic. The most luminous and therefore the most necessary and frequent is metaphor. It is most praised when it gives sense and passion to insensate things, in accordance with the metaphysics above discussed, by which the first poets attributed to bodies the being of animate substances, with capacities measured by their own, namely sense and passion, and in this way made fables of them. . . . It is noteworthy that in all languages the greater part of the expressions relating to inanimate things are formed by metaphor from the human body and its parts. . . . Thus, head for top or beginning; the brow and shoulders of a hill; the eyes of needles and of potatoes; mouth for any opening; the lip of a cup or pitcher; the teeth of a rake, a saw, a comb; the beard of wheat; the tongue of a shoe; the gorge of a river; a neck of land; an arm of the sea . . . Heaven or the sea smiles; the wind whistles; the waves murmur . . . and our rustics speak of plants making love, vines going mad, resinous trees weeping. Innumerable other examples could be collected from all languages, all of which is a consequence of our axiom that man in his ignorance makes himself the rule of the universe, *for in the examples cited he has made of himself an entire world.*[41]

The Problem

The conclusions drawn from our preceding discussions follow. It is obvious that to mark the beginning of modern thought with Descartes is only possible if the mathematical, geometrical pattern of scientific thought is accepted as a point of departure. Should we question this pattern by pointing to the absurd consequences of an a priori conception of this type when applied to knowledge—as did Marx in the nineteenth century—we would have to raise anew the problem of the beginning of modern thought and find a new answer for it.

A second essential conclusion is the rejection of any conception of

[41] *Ibid.*, §§ 404–5, italics mine.

philosophy as a science seeking its own aims in an ivory tower of pure speculation, secluded from the concrete history of man. All the fields that were important to the Italian humanistic tradition and that were reevaluated by Vico in his *New Science*—jurisprudence, philology, rhetoric, poetry—must be reacknowledged and reinstated in their philosophical functions. It is, therefore, senseless to approach the humanistic philosophical tradition with problems of epistemology, as Cassirer unsuccessfully attempted to do. With a reassessment of the humanistic tradition, the entire Latin heritage, and above all the figure of Cicero, with his conception of jurisprudence and rhetoric, appears in a new light. "For the wisdom of the ancients was the vulgar wisdom of the lawgivers who founded the human race, *not the esoteric wisdom of great and rare philosophers*."[42]

Furthermore, the parallelism we have disclosed, between Marxist criticism of any a priori philosophy and the Humanists' rejection of speculation on the basis of an abstract theory of categories, leads from the purely historical to an essentially theoretical problem: that of the roots of man's becoming, of his historical reality: a problem that can be approached in terms of an altercation between Marxist viewpoints and the humanistic tradition culminating in Vico.

The Humanists, with their emphasis on the role of imagination, deny that the essence of man, and consequently his historical being, can be determined solely by pointing to work as an adjustment of nature, and this on the following grounds:

1. Work is the act of man's creating himself. In it and through it man develops into what he is according to his essence and species. Work is conscious activity: in it, man is no longer *im-mediate*; his attitude to himself and to the object is determined by a *mediating process*. Through work man is enabled to objectify his own essence, insofar as he engenders an objective world of his own through the forces inherent in him. In his work he is real and concrete.

2. Work is a surmounting of needs. This represents man's primary connection with the material complex of which he is a part. Need is the negation of negation, that is, affirmation as a surmounting of the first antithesis between organic and inorganic matter, the removal of a deficiency with the aim of preserving and renewing the organism.

3. Man is forced to assert himself through the negation and removal of nature as an alien force, and he does so *according to a plan* supplied by his imagination, which presupposes *his knowledge of his own essence*. Marx considers work—as the surmounting of the immediate impact of nature, as its adaptation—to be the root of history. If, however, this adaptation on behalf of man differs from that of animals because of the fact that the animal works merely for its own nourishment and the preservation of the species, and that in accordance with inborn patterns, then the question

[42] *Ibid.*, § 384, italics mine.

about the meaning of man's adjustment of nature cannot be solved simply by saying that man is a "mediating" or "adjusting" being, nor by pointing to his working activity, but only by elucidating and defining the *specific aim* of this mediation. Unless we admit the urgency of this problem, we are reduced to saying that the animal is a much higher being than man, for it also adapts nature to its ends, but without having to look for its aims and with a far greater certainty.

4. As we have seen, the essential determining factor and prerequisite for human work is freedom. That is, since nature is not transformed and adapted on the basis of preestablished patterns, the meaning of this adaptation has to be sought. The problem of the meaning of work cannot be solved by referring to work itself and remains a crucial question. The fact that the adaptation of nature cannot by itself supply the specific meaning of work can be proved by pointing out that different peoples have entirely different interpretations and evaluations of work. Imaginative cosmologies, theodicies, and magic designs determine the positive or negative judgment of work and of its execution.

5. A further essential element in defining work, apart from the element of freedom but closely connected with it, is the imagination. The transformation of nature should, of course, be realized with a view to a purpose; and the purpose, according to Marx, serves as a law to determine the ways of human activity. The purpose of work, the corresponding imagination, is *not to be derived from the concept of work itself*, for any adjustment can only be carried out with a "view" to an aim, whereas the adjustment of nature is only a *means*.

The problem regarding the meaning of work carries with it a *renewed justification of philosophy* and of its quests. For either we have to admit that human work has the same meaning as animal activity, in which case we would have to develop a theory of man as a degenerate animal—another subject for philosophizing—or we must find a meaning for human work to differentiate it from that of animals; and this, too, would be the manifestation of philosophical reflection. It would be the original function of a philosophy not conceived as a mere superstructure of a transient historical, social structure.

Any society which fails to raise and answer the question as to the meaning of man's intervention in nature, thus establishing a theory of the essence of man—a philosophical question—must degenerate into an alien form of community, despite or even through whatever social improvements it accomplishes. This alienation arises out of the fact that man ceases to concern himself with a question which is essential to him. The question regarding the nature of man was the question continually raised by the Italian Humanists in their polemics against any science seeking its own ends.

Translated by Azizeh Azodi

Donald Phillip Verene

VICO'S SCIENCE OF IMAGINATIVE UNIVERSALS AND THE PHILOSOPHY OF SYMBOLIC FORMS

Der Plan eines konstruktiven Aufbaus der Geisteswissenschaften wird in der neueren Philosophie zuerst durch Giambattista Vico scharf und bestimmt erfaßt.

Ernst Cassirer, "Die Begriffsform im mythischen Denken," *Studien der Bibliothek Warburg*, 1922

In 1884, Robert Flint, in his volume for Blackwood's Philosophical Classics for English Readers, saw the future of Vico's thought as: "The more the sciences of history, of society, and of law are cultivated, the more will his reputation grow, owing to the number of original and profound suggestions in his writings as to the subjects with which these sciences are conversant."[1] Flint's forecast, in what is still today a valuable study of Vico's thought, has not come true. Although the sciences of history, society, and law have been cultivated to a considerable extent since 1884, and Vico is not unknown to social scientists,[2] there is no evidence that the development of these fields has been based on a widespread reading of Vico. A similar state of affairs exists in regard to philosophy and philosophical theory of knowledge.

Those who have encountered the originality of Vico's ideas and the spirit of his thought firsthand frequently share Flint's impression that the true meaning of Vico's thought is about to be felt in their own time. This rather curiously looks past the fact that the course of Vico's thought has been largely a series of rescues from obscurity, whether through the interest of such figures as Michelet or Coleridge in the nineteenth century or through the philosophy of Croce or novels of Joyce in our own time.[3] It is as if the pattern of Vico's influence has illustrated something of his own principles of history, moving from course to recourse, almost slipping away, only to be revived in the thought of a new figure or figures, never

[1] *Vico* (Edinburgh and London: William Blackwood and Sons, 1884), p. 3.

[2] E.g., Marvin Harris, *The Rise of Anthropological Theory* (New York: Thomas Y. Crowell Co., 1968), pp. 19–20.

[3] The influence of Vico's thought on various thinkers is explored in many of the essays in *Giambattista Vico: An International Symposium*. For a concise account of Vico's influence arranged by country see Max Harold Fisch's Introduction to the English translation of Vico's *Autobiography*, pp. 61–107.

actually exerting a continuous influence on the general development of ideas since his time. The particular difficulties that Vico's thought has undergone are those that attend, as Isaiah Berlin has pointed out, "rich and profound but inexact and obscure thinkers, namely that their admirers read too much into them, and turn them insensibly in the direction of their own thoughts,"[4] something that Vico has suffered particularly at the hands of Michelet and Croce.

The points I wish to develop in this essay involve the view that Vico's thought has a particular significance for our age. In developing them I hope to avoid the pitfalls mentioned above, which have seemed to surround the interpretation of Vico's thought—the optimism that because Vico's thought is relevant to the present age, we are, in fact, on the edge of a new Vichian age and the transposition of Vico's ideas out of the form of his own thought. The points I wish to consider revolve around three questions: (1) In what sense can Vico's thought be understood as relevant to the conception of knowledge and life of the present age? (2) What are the central elements of Vico's theory of knowledge itself? and (3) What is the significance of Vico's theory of knowledge for contemporary theory of knowledge, in particular for the conception of knowledge as symbolic form?

More specifically, I wish to argue two points: (1) that the heart of Vico's *New Science*, epistemologically considered, lies in his conception of "imaginative universals" and (2) that the significance of this conception for contemporary epistemology lies in the fact that, through this conception, Vico's thought shows that any theory of knowledge must be grounded in a theory of myth, a viewpoint barely realized in contemporary epistemological thought. These two points state directly what is involved in the second and third of my three questions above. The first question involves the broader social setting in which these occur.

The Cartesianism of Contemporary Social Life

At the beginning of the Introduction to his English translation of Vico's Inaugural Lecture, "On the Study Methods of Our Time," Elio Gianturco writes: "We live in a Cartesian world, a world of scientific research, technology, and gadgets, which invade and condition our lives."[5]

Gianturco's remark suggests that the world of post-industrial states has at its heart a Cartesian framework, a mentality that is problem-oriented, progressive, and geometric. This is not to say that the ideas of Descartes have caused the world in which we live, nor that Descartes personally even imagined it; although his arguments are punctuated with such hypotheti-

[4] "The Philosophical Ideas of Giambattista Vico" in *Art and Ideas in Eighteenth-Century Italy* (Rome: Edizioni di Storia e Letteratura, 1960), p. 227.

[5] *On the Study Methods of Our Time* (Indianapolis, New York, Kansas City: Bobbs-Merrill Library of Liberal Arts, 1965), p. ix.

cal possibilities as machines that speak and such hypothetical doubts as whether hats and cloaks seen in the street might be concealing automata that move by springs, rather than covering men.[6] Vico saw in Descartes the opposite of his own thought. Although he minimizes the involvement of his early views with Cartesianism,[7] and although his later position is not formed as a simple opposition to it, Vico saw in Descartes' philosophy a position, and more deeply a mentality, with which his thought was fundamentally at odds.[8] What Vico experienced in his age as matters of intellectual dispute between the Cartesian position and his own have become life problems in our contemporary age.

This point can be seen if Gianturco's remark is connected with analyses of the technological character of contemporary society, such as that developed by the French thinker, Jacques Ellul.[9] The world of "scientific research, technology, and gadgets, which invade and condition our lives," on Ellul's view, functions according to a logic of its own. The world in which we live involves the transformation of all areas of human activity—productive, political, and psychological—into systems of order through technique. The logic whereby all areas of life are made part of the single phenomenon of technique is based on the ever expanding application of a single principle, which Ellul calls "efficient ordering."[10] All aspects of life are increasingly turned into procedures. Through a process of selection of the most efficient means technique becomes the medium of contemporary social life, in which all economic, political, and individual human activity is ordered into worked-out patterns and step-by-step processes, such that with every new structuring of a physical means or social relation there occurs a heightened sense of improvement and a widening sense of possibilities of application.[11] Each new technique opens up new possibilities of technical order.

On Ellul's view and that of others,[12] value experience and humanistic

[6] *Discourse*, V and *Meditations*, II.

[7] See Fisch's remarks, *Autobiography*, pp. 36–37.

[8] *Autobiography*, pp. 113 and 137–38. See also Yvon Belaval, "Vico and Anti-Cartesianism" in *Giambattista Vico: An International Symposium*, pp. 77–91.

[9] Principally in: *La Technique ou l'enjeu du siècle* (Paris: Colins, 1954); *Propagandes* (Paris: Colins, 1962); and *L'illusion politique* (Paris: Laffont, 1965).

[10] *The Technological Society*, trans. John Wilkinson (New York: Knopf, 1964), p. 110. This is a translation of Ellul's 1954 work (see n. 9); chaps. 1 and 2 comprise a general statement of Ellul's view.

[11] See Ellul's discussion of the "technical operation" and the "technical phenomenon" in *ibid.*, pp. 19–21.

[12] E.g., Herbert Marcuse states: "In the medium of technology, culture, politics, and the economy merge into an omnipresent system which swallows up or repulses all alternatives" (*One-Dimensional Man: Studies in the Ideology of Advanced Industrial Society* [Boston: Beacon Press, 1964], p. xvi). Karl Jaspers states: "In our epoch of the mass-order, of technique, of economics, when an attempt is made to render this inevitable institution absolute, there is a danger to the selfhood that the fundamental basis of the mind may be destroyed" (*Man in the Modern Age*, trans. Eden and Cedar Paul [Garden City, N.Y.: Doubleday Anchor Books, 1957, orig. pub. 1931], p. 123).

and imaginative thought have little effect in determining contemporary social order. They stand out in contemporary experience as thought forms of the past which are unconnected to and unnecessary for objective technological advance.[13] In technological life such forms of thought and experience come to serve, at most, as means for the rhetorical embellishment of its advance. Ellul's account of technological society brings into full view the single fact that is felt by intellectual thinkers and ordinary citizens alike: the centrality of technique in all affairs of modern life. What I wish to suggest is that behind this central fact stands the Cartesian model of mind. The way in which the technological ordering of human society has come about as an historical development involves all the political, economic, physical, and psychological forces that have gone into making up the modern world.[14] But if technological order is taken as it stands, it can be seen to entail a particular mentality, a conception of knowledge and truth.

No clearer or more essential account of this can be found than that way of thinking described by Descartes in the *Discourse on Method*. Here, at the beginning of modern philosophical thought, is a prescription for the step-by-step transformation of experience into a determinate series of orders. Descartes' four principal rules—(1) to begin only with what can be taken as evidently true, (2) the division of initial difficulties into parts, (3) the movement from simple to complex, and (4) the achievement of completeness by continual review and enumeration—are intended as a means for the attainment of intellectual knowledge.[15] The development of Western life since Descartes can be thought of as constituting the progressive transformation of this formula of thought into a formula for the organization of action. Although for Descartes and his age machines were largely a matter of intellectual curiosity, with the appearance of the

[13] In this regard Ellul states: "But when men found themselves going counter to the human factor, they reintroduced—and in an absurd way—all manner of moral theories related to the rights of man, the League of Nations, liberty, justice. None of that has any more importance than the ruffled sunshade of McCormick's first reaper. When these moral flourishes overly encumber technical progress, they are discarded—more or less speedily, with more or less ceremony, but with determination nonetheless" (*Technological Society*, p. 74). For a discussion of this question in terms that go somewhat beyond Ellul's view, maintaining that in technological life value experience is replaced by the revival of primitive-mythic forms of experience, see D. P. Verene's "Technology and Myth: An Hegelian View of Contemporary Culture," *Proceedings of the XVth World Congress of Philosophy*, Varna, Bulgaria, 1973. See also Ellul's comments on myth in *Propaganda*, trans. Konrad Kellen and Jean Lerner (New York: Knopf, 1965), chap. 1, esp. pp. 40–41.

[14] On Ellul's view this involves specifically the joint and unique occurrence of five factors: "They are, to summarize: (1) a very long technical maturation or incubation without decisive checks before the final flowering; (2) population growth; (3) a suitable economic milieu; 4) the almost complete plasticity of a society malleable and open to the propagation of technique; (5) a clear technical intention which combines the other factors and directs them toward the pursuit of the technical objective" (*Technological Society*, pp. 59–60).

[15] *Discourse*, II.

machine as a means of production in the 1750s the procedural ordering of experience became not simply an ideal of intellectual thought but a physical and social reality. The phenomenon of technique, first present in the machine, spread throughout modern life.

In technological life the certainty and definiteness of action, the clarity of order that is achieved in the machine, is extended to all spheres of the human world by the rational dissection of all its processes and their step-by-step reformulation as procedures.[16] In the technological universe the first condition of Descartes' fourfold conception of rules—that of beginning with what is evidently true—is always fulfilled by the definiteness of order that has been achieved by the previous application of technique, and its endpoint is always fulfilled by the need in technological life to evaluate immediately each new technique, once achieved, in terms of its possibilities for improvement and wider application within society. *In the technological world of contemporary life we experience as human agents what Descartes only conceived we could experience as seekers of intellectual truth.* The difficulty Vico saw in Descartes' conception of knowledge and truth, constructed, as it is, on the basis of mathematical and scientific thought, lies in what it excludes, the result of which is, as Vico says, to "degrade all the other studies included in divine and human erudition."[17] What is widely felt in technological life is that the process of technological ordering, particularly the techniques of individual and social order, do not generate meaning; technology never seems entirely human.

What Descartes originally excludes from knowledge in the construction of his method—the workings of the humanistic imagination—has continued to occupy its problematic position. There seems no viable place in the contemporary world for those forms of thought and feeling which have in the past in the Western tradition provided access for man to his own nature, the forms through which self-knowledge was thought possible—literature, rhetoric, the arts, history, ethics, moral discourse, dialectical and speculative thought. Hence, among intellectuals, and within universities, there is continual and wholly inconclusive talk about the relation of technology and values, the similar features of scientific and artistic creativity, and a concern to understand human development. In the society at large, there is unrelenting attention to social problems, human crises, psychological discoveries—forums are created at all levels in which these questions are discussed without end. As the life of the individ-

[16] The concept of contemporary society as technological is not the notion that technique is present as a factor in contemporary society but not in earlier forms of society. Technique, as a means of doing things, is present in all periods and forms of human society. Contemporary society is distinguished from other forms of society by the fact that it is technological in its *form*; it is in essence an "ensemble of means" (*Technological Society*, p. 19). In this connection see especially Ellul's discussion of "human techniques" (*ibid.*, chap. 5).

[17] *Autobiography*, p. 113.

ual is everywhere determined by technological advance, the freedom of the individual is at every opportunity discussed and intensely affirmed.

Traditional forms of self-knowledge occupy a place in technological life correspondent to that which they occupy in Descartes' conception of knowledge. In the *Discourse on Method* Descartes presents the reading of fables and histories in ancient literature as the study of his youth. Although they broaden and stimulate the mind, fables make one imagine events that are in reality not possible, and histories exaggerate and distort the real events they describe. Descartes, in fact, regards such forms of thought as potentially dangerous to the individual's reason; for, as he states, "those who regulate their behavior by the examples they find in books are apt to fall into the extravagances of the knights of romances, and undertake projects which it is beyond their ability to complete or hope for things beyond their destiny."[18] Such extravagances have no place in knowledge in the Cartesian conception; they also have no place in the mentality of technological life. Technique, like politics, is always the art of the possible; there is no room for men to "undertake projects which it is beyond their ability to complete or hope for things beyond their destiny."

For Descartes, "those who reason most cogently, and work over their thoughts to make them clear and intelligible, are always the most persuasive, even if they speak only a provincial dialect and have never studied rhetoric."[19] Truth has no need of eloquence or rhetoric, and all arts and activities of the mind that involve them can be replaced or superseded by a single piece of clear reasoning. For Descartes, humanistic forms of thought are to be given the respect due that which one has experienced in youth, but they are not matters for adulthood and the mature concern for knowledge. The humanities are at best ways of embellishing truths; they lack method and are thus not forms in which truth can be truly stated. Such embellishment, while it may in fact give pleasing form to truth, also contains the danger of creating a hollow center, so that when it is stripped away nothing is there. The message is clear: the humanities are one thing, truth is another, and it is eloquent in itself.[20]

[18] *Discourse on Method and Meditations*, trans. Laurence J. Lafleur (Indianapolis, New York, Kansas City: Bobbs-Merrill Library of Liberal Arts, 1960), p. 7.

[19] *Ibid*.

[20] Although Descartes excludes literary forms such as history and fable from the form of truth, he says that the *Discourse on Method* itself can be approached as a *histoire* or *fable* (see *Discourse*, I). In the "Author's Letter" to the *Principles of Philosophy* he says that his work should be read through first as a *roman*. In the same place he speaks of philosophy as a tree in which morals is a highest branch and the "last degree of wisdom," but he produces no such science. Although Descartes has views on morals, conduct, and society (in this connection see not only the *Principles*, but his letters to Princess Elizabeth, *Oeuvres de Descartes*, ed. C. Adam and P. Tannery, 13 vols. [Paris, 1897–1913], vol. 4) the relationship of knowledge to action and society remains largely that of the formulation of provisional maxims of conduct as set down in *Discourse*, III.

The failure to associate the humanities with truth that exists at the roots of the mentality which has shaped the modern age manifests itself, not as an intellectual split between the sciences and the humanities in contemporary life, but in a more generalized fragmentation between all fields of human knowledge and between the life activities of individuals and the general social order. The self-expansion of the technological process gives continual assurance of certainty and definiteness in human action, but there is no overall sense of the whole. That actuality is rational seems a fantasy; reason has no credibility as an agency to picture the human spirit as a unity. Philosophical theories of knowledge and mind are constructed which reflect this partiality; the term "epistemology" itself implies only reflection on those processes which are scientific or in some sense empirical, commonsensical, or logical. Individuals find themselves in possession of occupations and professions, but incomplete in their self-identity. Society achieves an exceptional interlocking of relationships between its economic and political functions but can create no meaningful relationship between these and natural, ethical, and aesthetic forms.

The fragmentation of intellectual and cultural experience in contemporary life creates a need for the human world to be seen as a work of reason, in the very broadest sense of this term, and to have a theory of origin. It is this kind of perspective that Vico's thought offers, and it is this kind of perspective that Vico intended his thought to offer as a counter to the Cartesianism in his own day but which in fact has had little or no effect on the development of the modern world. Crucial to this perspective is the need to understand the connections between forms of human knowledge and forms of culture and historical development. What is needed is the discovery of a way of seeing the mind as a whole that is not bought at the expense of narrowing its meaning to a single set of activities, such as science and empirical forms of thought, or to a metaphysical whole that is set off against the actual processes of human activity, such as is present in many forms of Hegelianism.[21]

[21] I have in mind here principally the Hegelianism of the late nineteenth and early twentieth centuries, in particular the absolute idealism of F. H. Bradley and Bernard Bosanquet, and that of Croce. Schelling's idealism faces similar problems of the subjugation of the particular activities of the mind to absolute mind. See Cassirer's criticisms of Schelling's theory of myth in *The Philosophy of Symbolic Forms*, trans. Ralph Manheim, 3 vols. (New Haven: Yale University Press, 1953–57), vol. 2, pp. 3–16, hereinafter cited as *PSF*. What is much needed in Vico literature is a fresh look at the relationships between Hegel's project in the *Phänomenologie des Geistes* and Vico's *New Science*. The Hegel of his "voyage of discovery" of the *Phenomenology* bears no resemblance to the Hegel that is frequently criticized and convicted without trial among contemporary non-Crocean interpreters of Vico. Much might be learned about Hegel and about Vico's thought by a direct look at the texts involved, without the assumption that what Hegel thinks is what Croce or any of the late nineteenth- and twentieth-century absolute idealists have held that Hegel thinks, and without the assumption that the principles of Hegel's philosophy are essentially to be found in his posthumously assembled *Lectures on the Philosophy of History*.

Vico's thought, which has at its heart his theory of "poetic wisdom," or mythical mentality, offers a way of understanding human knowledge that takes neither of these alternatives. It allows the human world to see itself as a unity, not by seeing itself as a unity of intellectual principles or categories, but by seeing its unity through the phenomenon of its own origin.

The Logic of Imaginative Universals

Vico's theory of "poetic wisdom," and in particular his theory of "imaginative universals" central to it, has been one of the less frequently explored themes in Vico's thought. Considerable attention has been given to Vico's view of history and his views of law and society, but less attention has been given his theory of knowledge. Vico's theory of poetic wisdom is the basis for the *New Science*.[22] The bulk of the work itself is taken up by it; his discovery of the true Homer is offered in evidence of it; and the chapters on the course and recourse of nations are developments from it.

Isaiah Berlin has discussed Vico's epistemology from the perspective of the types of knowledge which Vico distinguishes.[23] The approach I wish to take here is to consider Vico's *New Science* in its entirety from an epistemological perspective—to understand it as a kind of genetic epistemology in which forms of knowledge are seen as connected to forms of human cultural life and in which all human culture is seen as developing from an original mentality and original form of life. From this perspective Vico's theory of poetic wisdom can be seen as a primary illustration and demonstration of the correctness of his two central methodological ideas: that "Doctrines must take their beginning from that of the matters of which they treat" (§ 314) and that "philosophy undertakes to examine philology" (§ 7).[24]

Vico's theory of poetic wisdom is based on an idea generally held in the eighteenth century: that ancient primitives, contemporary savages, children, and peasants share a common form of mentality.[25] Vico associates with this mentality the "speech" of mutes and various pathological defects

[22] By the *New Science*, here and elsewhere, I mean what in the Nicolini Laterza edition of Vico's works is called the *Scienza nuova seconda*.

[23] See the Appendix to "The Philosophical Ideas of Giambattista Vico," and "A Note on Vico's Concept of Knowledge" in *Giambattista Vico: An International Symposium*, pp. 371–77. See also "The Divorce Between the Sciences and the Humanities," *Salmagundi* 27 (1974): 9–39.

[24] All citations in the text and footnotes preceded by a paragraph sign (§) are to the *New Science*.

[25] See Frank E. Manuel, *The Eighteenth Century Confronts the Gods* (Cambridge, Mass.: Harvard University Press, 1959), p. 156. In the *New Science* see §§ 206–17, 375–76, 437, 470, 498, 517, 658, 708, 841, and 1095, esp. §§ 206–17.

in normal speech; he also stresses their importance for understanding the origin and basis of language.[26] For Vico, "the first science to be learned should be mythology or the interpretation of fables" (§ 51). In this way the understanding of human mentality or human knowledge can begin where it itself begins. The means for having such a science of origins involves the combination of the propensity of philosophical thought to uncover the universal principles of order that are inherent in particulars and the power of philological thought to present the particulars of the human world in their true particularity. For Vico the science of origins, upon which all true understanding of the human world depends, requires a new method of thought, one which is at once: philosophical-philological.

Vico's theory of myth is not euhemeristic, nor does it constitute a kind of modified or neo-euhemerism, as some of his commentators have maintained.[27] Although euhemerism—that is, that myths are to be interpreted as traditional accounts of real incidents in human history—was a commonly held view in Vico's age, and although Vico frequently expresses the view that "fables were the first histories of the gentile nations" (e.g., § 51), to interpret his view of myth as euhemeristic is to overlook what Vico means by "fable." Vico defines fables as "imaginative class concepts" (§ 403). For Vico, fables are not embellishments of actual events or historical figures. There is not present epistemologically for the poetic or mythic mind: (1) an empirical or historical order of events, that is: (2) rendered into fabulous form by it. Events themselves are given form through fables.[28]

This notion of the mind's activity as giving form to perceptual experi-

[26] On mutes see §§ 225–30, 434, and 461. On the structural similarities of speech defects and first speech see §§ 453 and 462. Vico also rather unflatteringly connects poetic language with the mentality of women, see § 457. Cf. Vico's attention to speech defects with Cassirer's "Toward a Pathology of the Symbolic Consciousness," *PSF*, vol. 3, pt. 2, chap. 6, especially his concept of the importance of the theory of aphasia for knowledge of the symbolic process, speech, and representational thought.

[27] E.g., see Richard Chase, *Quest for Myth* (Baton Rouge: Louisiana State University Press, 1949), pp. 22–27; Manuel, *Eighteenth Century Confronts the Gods*, p. 160; and David Bidney, "Vico's New Science of Myth" in *Giambattista Vico: An International Symposium*, pp. 269–70 (see my criticisms of Bidney in my review of *Giambattista Vico: An International Symposium* in *Man and World* 4 [1971]: 347–50). Cf. Croce's view: "Nor does the opinion seem acceptable which attaches Vico to the Neo-Euhemeristic school. He does not indeed explicitly combat this school, and we may even grant that he presents certain superficial resemblances to it: but together with the resemblances there is the radical difference, that for Vico the stories are not alterations of actual history, but are essentially history; their supposed alteration is the actual truth as it appeared to the primitive mind" (*The Philosophy of Giambattista Vico*, trans. R. G. Collingwood [New York: Russell & Russell, 1964], p. 65).

[28] Cf. Edmund Leach, "Vico and Lévi-Strauss on the Origins of Humanity" in *Giambattista Vico: An International Symposium*, pp. 313–18. Concerning Vico's treatment of the structure of classical myths Leach states: "Logic of this kind did not reappear in myth analysis until Lévi-Strauss published 'La Geste d'Asdiwal' in 1960! . . . I am claiming that in a very tentative way Vico was already groping after this kind of analysis in 1725" (p. 315).

ence goes back as far in Vico's thought as his *De antiquissima Italorum sapientia* (1710):

Just as words are symbols of ideas, so ideas are symbols and tokens of things. Thus, just as the operation of reading consists in gathering up the elements of the alphabet which make up words, so "knowing" is the operation by which we assemble the total aggregate of the elements of an object, in order to derive from this procedure a thoroughly adequate conception of such an object. In regard to the problem of truth, we may hence conjecture that the sages of ancient Italy held truth to be identical with the act of mentally constructing truth.[29]

In the *New Science* Vico speaks of "poetic characters" (*caratteri poetici*), "imaginative genera" (*generi fantastici*), and "imaginative universals" (*universali fantastici*).[30] He uses these terms sometimes interchangeably and appears to intend them as terms that describe the same thing (e.g., §§ 34 and 209). He says the first men were poets and spoke in poetic characters. "This discovery," Vico says, "which is the master key of this Science, has cost us the persistent research of almost all our literary life . . ." (§ 34). Vico's theory of imaginative universals (imaginative genera, or poetic characters) is a theory of concept formation for poetic (or what would be today called mythic) mind. Vico contrasts imaginative universals, which are the form of thought of the first of his three ages—that of gods, that is, the age in which men thought in terms of gods—and of the second age—that of heroes—with intelligible universals or intelligible genera (*generi intelligibili*), which are characteristic of the form of thought of the third age—that of men.[31] The intelligible universal or generic concept of this third age is that of traditional Aristotelian logic.

[29] *Opere* 1: 131. Cf. Kant: "Synthesis of a manifold (be it given empirically or *a priori*) is what first gives rise to knowledge. This knowledge may, indeed, at first, be crude and confused, and therefore in need of analysis. Still the synthesis is that which gathers the elements for knowledge, and unites them to [form] a certain content" (*Critique of Pure Reason*, trans. Norman Kemp Smith [London: Macmillan, 1958], p. 111). The translation of the above passage from the *De Italorum sapientia* is from an unpublished draft of a translation by Elio Gianturco.

[30] Vico makes reference to one or more of these in §§ 34, 204–10, 403, 409, 429, 431, 460, 495–98, 808–9, 814, 832, 838, 933–35, and 1033. They are connected to particular gods or figures in §§ 74, 91, 381, 425, 508, 532, 562, 565, and 579–81. These, with perhaps a few additions, could be said to constitute the basic passages for the study of Vico's theory of imaginative universals. See also *Scienza nuova prima, Opere* 3: §§ 261–66. Cf. Vico's comments on *diversiloquia* (*Scienza nuova prima*, § 265) and *New Science*, §§ 210 and 403.

[31] The form of thought of both the age of gods and the age of heroes is the imaginative universal. The difference between the two ages in this respect is not the form of thought but the subject matter of the imaginative universals. In the first age it is gods which portray the immediately experienced forces of nature, such as Jove, or human institutions, such as Juno. In the second age it is heroes which portray various human qualities (Achilles—valiant fighting; Ulysses—cleverness). The place at which Vico makes this most clear is §§ 933–35. For intelligible universals see esp. §§ 34, 460, 499, 935, and 1040.

The generic concepts of traditional Aristotelian logic are formed by the mind's power to select from a multiplicity of particular things those features that are common to them. Objects are collected into classes in terms of their possession of some common property. The essential function of thought in this regard is that of comparing and differentiating the features of particular objects. By reflection the essential features of these objects are abstracted. As the mind rises from the perception of individual objects to the essential properties that constitute them as species and to the generic ordering of the species by omitting sensuous content from the original perceptions, so the mind can descend from genus to species to individual object by adding elements of specific content. According to this view, what is universal is that which can be conceived as a property common to the members of a given class and which can be predicated commonly of all the members of the class.

Vico's theory of imaginative universals can be conceived as a transformation of the process of concept formation present in the Aristotelian logic of genus and species. Vico regards the intelligible universal as a development from the imaginative universal. In the development of human culture the formation of human experience in terms of imaginative universals gives way to or produces the intelligible universal. For Vico, this does not simply come about by internal modifications of the imaginative universal, so that the intelligible universal is produced. This process is not accomplished simply as one of thought altering itself; instead it involves the alteration of social forms of life, specifically the movement from the age of heroes to that of men. The relationship between thought and society can be seen in Vico as one of co-determinative structures, wherein a certain type of thought is inconceivable without a certain social structure, and the reverse.[32]

If, however, the relationship between imaginative universals and intelligible universals is seen in purely logical terms, which, in fact, are the terms in which Vico frequently discusses it, the elements of the imaginative universal can be isolated. Vico's method here, like his method of constructing the *New Science* as a whole, can be conceived as one of asking the question: If we as modern thinkers form concepts in terms of intelligible genera, how are concepts formed among the first men such that our manner of concept formation can be understood as the development from this original manner of concept formation? This question can be regarded as stating the philosophical side of Vico's philosophical-philological method. The philological side is that Vico has before him his knowledge

[32] In this connection see Fisch's description of the generation of Vico's three ages, *Autobiography*, pp. 49–54. Generally speaking, I think the relationships between social conditions and forms of thought, for Vico, are more structural than causal. It is not that social conditions cause ideas, nor that thought causes certain social or political conditions; certain conditions and certain forms of thought necessarily go together and arise as co-determinative forces of history.

of the mythology of ancient Greece and Rome and the eighteenth-century insight that there is a common way of thinking that involves ancient thought, peasants, primitives, and children. What Vico wishes to see in this material is a difference in form, a difference that will reflect in logical terms the differences it more obviously has in subject matter from the writings and thought of modern men.

1. The first men, for Vico, created order in experience, not by abstracting a property held in common by a collection of particular entities, but by creating an ideal portrait. This took the basic form of the fable, a description of a particular human reality. The first men were not capable of ordering or conceiving of the perceived unities of the human world or nature through a single property abstracted from them. The first men did not encounter the world as a world of clear-cut objects and persons. They interpreted the world in divine or heroic terms.[33] They encountered it as a world of forces and emotional qualities (§§ 218–19). For Vico the poetic character or fable occupies the same central position in poetic or mythic thought that the generic concept occupies in rational or modern thought.

In the intelligible universal discreet particulars can be ordered into classes in terms of properties which can be abstracted from them and formulated in language apart from any representation of their unique properties. The intelligible universal, for Vico, is tied to the power of language to form abstract words. In the imaginative universal, language always operates metaphorically. It always preserves in its own symbolism or manner of statement something of the particulars it orders. Thus for Vico the movement from imaginative class concepts to intelligible class concepts is not simply an alteration of thought. It is accomplished through an alteration of the type of linguistic symbolism involved.[34] This idea of the connection of form of thought with form of symbolism is in itself an idea of considerable significance in contemporary semiotic science. It allows Vico to show that the first men of humanity did not think the same as modern men, but it also allows him to show that they did in fact *think*. The fact that their expressions are always poetic expressions is not the

[33] See above, n. 30.

[34] See esp. §§ 209, 225–35, 401–02, and 409. In these passages and others in his discussion of the features of poetic logic Vico expresses a view of the development of linguistic consciousness as originating in gestures and signs which have natural relations with the ideas and objects they signify and which develop through stages which stand in relation to his three ages (see, e.g., § 446). Cf. Vico's view of the origin of the linguistic function with Cassirer, "From Animal Reactions to Human Responses," *An Essay on Man* (New Haven: Yale University Press, 1944), chap. 3; and *PSF*, vol. 1, pp. 177–86; Susanne Langer, "Symbolic Transformation," *Philosophy in a New Key* (Cambridge, Mass.: Harvard University Press, 1942), chap. 2; and Ludwig von Bertalanffy, "On the Definition of the Symbol," *Psychology and the Symbol*, ed. Joseph R. Royce (New York: Random House, 1965), pp. 26–72.

result of their naiveté or inexperience with language; such poetic expressions constitute a form of thought itself that contains its own version of class logic.

The imaginative universal, the fable, or poetic character is more real than the individual, and the individual derives his reality from it. As Vico says: "poetic truth is metaphysical truth, and physical truth which is not in conformity with it should be considered false. Thence springs this important consideration in poetic theory: the true war chief, for example, is the Godfrey that Torquato Tasso imagines; and all the chiefs who do not conform throughout to Godfrey are not true chiefs of war" (§ 205). The individual is what it is because its being is the being of the type. Since the figure of the fable or poetic character is not formed by abstraction from individuals or particulars already commanding their own empirical reality, the poetic character *is* the reality, and physical reality is to shape itself in terms of it.

It is because poetic characters are themselves the conditions of reality for the poetic mind, rather than abstractions or generalizations from an empirical or physical order of individual things, that Vico can claim that the fables have: "univocal, not analogical, meanings for various particulars comprised under their poetic genera" (§ 210). For the poetic mind poetic characters are not colorful or rhetorical embellishments of genera abstracted from empirical particulars; thus the particulars are not thought of *analogically*, as being *like*, the ideal portraits of the generic individual of the fable. The individual cannot be thought of as having a reality apart from the generic character; he is what he is only through his identity with it. Thus the warrior does not conceive of his nature as apart from that of Godfrey, the true war chief. To the extent that he *is*, he and Godfrey have an identical reality. According to Vico's view, the overriding distinctive characteristic of mythic or primordial poetic thought is its power to assert *identities*, not *similarities*. The intelligible universal comes about through the development of the mind's ability to objectify experience through the discovery of similarities and differences in perceptual objects and the formulation of them in terms of common properties. The poetic mind structures experience through the formulation of immediate identities between elements.

Vico's conception of imaginative universals is not based on a nominalism in which a particular is raised to the level of a universal type and taken to stand for the nature of the class out of which it arises. Instead the reverse is true; particulars are directly conceived as universals. The primordial poetic mind can formulate relationships and make assertions that are nonsense for the modern logical mind: "we cannot at all imagine and can understand only by great toil the poetic nature of these first men" (§ 34). The poetic mind can univocally predicate a poetic genus of a collection of elements in a way that makes no sense to the mind that thinks in terms of intelligible class concepts. The way in which this univocal predication is accomplished in poetic thought involves the connection in Vico's thought between the fable and the allegory. Vico states: "Allegory is defined as *diversiloquium* insofar as by identity not of proportion but (to speak scholastically) of predictability, allegories signify the diverse species or the diverse individuals comprised under these genera. So that they must have a univocal signification connoting a quality common to all their species and individuals (as Achilles connotes an idea of valor common to all strong men, or Ulysses an idea of prudence common to all wise men)" (§ 403; cf. § 210).

For the poetic mind Ulysses is not a particular member of the class of wise men that is used to stand for the other members of the class, nor is Ulysses simply the substitution of a proper name for a class term, nor is Ulysses a kind of master type or composite individual which each member of the class of wise men could be said to be like.[35] The poetic mind can make an assertion that is nonsense for the rational mind. It can assert meaningfully for or to itself that each member of the class of wise men is literally Ulysses, not that each such individual is *a* Ulysses or is *like* Ulysses, but that each is identical with Ulysses. Each individual can be said to *be* Ulysses in the sense that Ulysses is their reality; each is to be identified as literally being Ulysses in a sense analogous to the assertion a rational mind would make in maintaining each to have the quality of being "prudent." For the mind in possession of intelligible universals and abstract words, in possession of the fundamental distinction between thing and property upon which Aristotelian class logic rests, such forms of predication by the mythic mind appear as either nonsensical thought or unnecessary literary embellishments of what are in reality common properties of a class of objects. Primitives have often been seen as naive or confused or as simply giving metaphorical accounts of ordinary empirical events, but this is not true on Vico's view.

2. A further point of Vico's theory of imaginative universals is their relationship to allegories, mythologies, and metaphors. Vico states that

[35] The imaginative universals of Ulysses or Achilles would correspond to those of the age of heroes (see above, n. 30; in *New Science* see esp. § 934). Vico's discussion of imaginative universals moves between examples of imaginative universals of gods, characteristic of his first age of humanity, and heroic figures, characteristic of his second age. He refers to imaginative universals of heroic figures when describing how imaginative universals function to form poetic classes (see §§ 205, 209, and 403). The reason for this is apparently because heroic figures are the immediate forerunners of abstract quality terms, on which the intelligible universals of the third age are based. Imaginative universals of the first age involving divine figures such as Jove, Hercules, and Juno appear to differ from heroic universals in that they represent more immediate and holistic expressions of natural forces and fundamental human institutions (e.g., marriage) than the proto-class-ordering characteristics of heroic universals. They are also expressed only quasi-linguistically, as Vico states: "the language of gods was almost entirely mute, only very slightly articulate" (§ 446; also see above, n. 32).

every metaphor is a fable in brief (§ 404), that is, when it is the result of the first men attributing their own passions to physical bodies in nature. Out of the process of these attributions, initially expressed in metaphors, arise fables. Vico does not seem to mean that metaphors as such are fables, but that the process of mind wherein metaphors arise as objectifications of nature, when carried to its furthest point, results in fable. Vico emphasizes the point that children and the first men thought in terms of imitation (§§ 215–17). The world is perceived by them as an alter ego and is given form by imitation, but putting the world into human terms that are regarded as containing the process being imitated itself, not as formulating the nature of the process in another form of symbolism. The essence of fables are poetic characters or imaginative universals. Vico says that mythologies are the allegories corresponding to the fables and that the mythologies are the "proper languages of the fables" (§ 403). The fable is a *vera narratio* (§§ 401 and 403), or true speech, the first way of forming experience.

Allegory for Vico is defined, as in the passage quoted in relation to the Ulysses example above (§ 403; see also § 210), as *diversiloquium*, or an expression "comprising in one general concept various species of men, deeds, or things" (§ 210). The allegory would appear to be the mode of speech whereby the specific is expressed in terms of the universal. Vico seems to mean that fables are the general unities between universal and particular in poetic mind and that allegories are those accounts that develop the specifics of these unities. Mythologies or allegories are the "proper languages of fables." They are the particular "stories" or accounts wherein imaginative universals are given embodiment. Mythologies and allegory seem to function in a role in poetic or mythic mind that is counterpart to the role of the hierarchy of differentiations between individuals, species, and genera that represents the overall activity of the class logic of intelligible universals. On such logic the whole of experience is formed in terms of the interlocking of genera, species, and individual through the language of subject-predicate relations. What in rational thought would be distinctions between individuals, species, and genera are collapsed through the language of mythologies into immediately apprehended wholes. The expression of imaginative universals requires, not argumentation, syllogistic inference, and definition, but the rhetorical forms and tropes of poetic logic—metaphor, metonymy, synecdoche, irony, monsters, metamorphoses, and such.

These forms which make up poetic logic (see §§ 404–11) for Vico are not simply devices for the literary embellishment of truths arrived at by logical means; they are for him features of a logic that itself precedes the logic of syllogism and rational argument. They are the means of accomplishing imaginative acts of "predication" and of conceptual interrelations.

From the fact that the forms of poetic logic are not only the forms through which the first men order experience but also the forms through which artistic or poetic expression takes place among modern men, we can conclude that imaginative universals do not disappear when men pass on to abstract modes of truth. They represent a logic of imagination itself, which for the first men is the same as thought itself but for modern man is always experienced as something in contrast to the rational forms of the concept.

3. There is a final question that should be considered at least briefly before leaving off discussion of the nature of imaginative universals. If imaginative universals provide the "master key" for Vico for a theory of mythical thought, do they also suggest a basis for philosophical thought? That the whole of the *New Science* is in some sense an imaginative universal seems evident. It is an imaginative universal, however, in a different sense than the imaginative universals of the poetic wisdom it describes. To say that the imaginative universal can be conceived as the form of philosophical thought itself is not to say that philosophy is simply the return to the thought of the first men. If the *New Science* is thought of as the formulation of imaginative universals of a meta-order, then it is possible to understand why the *New Science* seems on first encounter such a strange book. The table of contents appears more a mosaic of words than an outline of comprehensible topics. In the text itself nothing is discussed step by step; everything is woven and interwoven. The style of the text reflects Vico's methodological principle of the union of the philosophical and the philological. In understanding any form of thought Vico recreates something of the form itself, but his work is not a myth, nor is it poetry. The *New Science* represents an imaginative way of reasoning which employs both axioms and images, but in which the axioms, even in their first statement, are never divorced from content. Unlike Descartes' method, or any other mathematically modeled thought, the *New Science* does not contain abstract principles that are subsequeently applied to content.

What I wish to suggest, and I wish here only to suggest, is that Vico's *New Science* embodies in the operation of the thought it contains a version of the "philosophical universal" that is modeled neither on the intelligible universal nor on the poetic universal, but which preserves some of the characteristics of each. Both in its style of presentation and in the method of thought it advocates, the *New Science* entails a way of giving universal form to cultural content without departing from the content itself. The type of thought it involves might be called that of the "rationalized imaginative universal," in which the particular is brought together with the universal through the simultaneous employment of intellectual and imaginative means. In this sense Vico might be thought of as overcoming the Cartesian separation of reason and the humanistic imagination by generating reason within imagination.[36]

The Vichian-Cassirerian Conception of Knowledge

The conception of knowledge that is involved in Vico's theory of imaginative universals has considerable significance for contemporary theory of knowledge and the philosophical interpretation of human culture. I wish to show the nature of this claim by examining the connection between Vico's thought and Ernst Cassirer's theory of symbolic forms. Cassirer, more than any other contemporary thinker, has developed a philosophy in which types of knowledge are connected with forms of culture and in which a total account of human knowledge is based on a theory of mythical thought. Cassirer's thought, like Vico's, is not widely understood. His philosophy involves a wide number of topics—historical, linguistic, aesthetic, and scientific. I have shown elsewhere that to think of Cassirer's philosophy simply as part of Marburg Neo-Kantianism, which is its point of origin, or even to think of it only as a form of Kantianism, is mistaken.[37] What I wish to suggest here is that there is a fundamental point of contact between Vico's theory of imaginative universals and Cassirer's conception of symbolic forms which constitutes what may be called a "Vichian-Cassirerian" viewpoint for theory of knowledge and philosophy of culture. It represents an Archimedean point from which an adequate philosophical account of the questions of the origin of the human world, the unity of knowledge, and the Cartesian fragmentation of the contemporary world, discussed in the first section of this essay, can be developed.[38]

[36] Vico's production of propositions about imagination that are themselves imaginative in form can also be viewed as containing an important solution to what Plato called the "ancient quarrel between philosophy and poetry" (*Republic* X. 595a–608b). On Vico's view, philosophy can effect a relationship with poetic wisdom or myth by developing a theory of the origin of reason in the universals of poetic imagination and, through the form of thought made possible by philosophical-philological method, never separate philosophical reason from imaginative form. Vico's reformulation of this ancient quarrel can be seen as constituting the starting point for philosophy of culture as a form of philosophical thought (see D. P. Verene, ed., *Man and Culture* [New York: Dell Pub. Co., Laurel Editions, 1970], pp. 9–14 and 55–62). Vico's conception of the imaginative universal undoubtedly has considerable implications not only for a theory of philosophical propositions but also for an understanding of the logic of literary expression and aesthetic form generally.

[37] D. P. Verene, "Kant, Hegel, and Cassirer: The Origins of the Philosophy of Symbolic Forms," *Journal of the History of Ideas* 30 (1969): 33–46.

[38] My thinking on the importance of Vico for the questions of the unity of knowledge and the fragmentation of contemporary culture was first stimulated by some of the aspects of Giorgio Tagliacozzo's conception of a Vichian "tree of knowledge" in his Epilogue to *Giambattista Vico: An International Symposium*. My views on a Vichian-Cassirerian conception of theory of knowledge are a development from my initial comments on Tagliacozzo's conception in the first and fifth sections of my review of this volume (*Man and World* 4 [1971]: 342–55).

Cassirer saw Vico as the founder of the philosophy of culture and as a thinker who had a vision of the human spirit similar to his own.[39] In his study of language in the first volume of *The Philosophy of Symbolic Forms* (1923), he regards Vico as the first thinker to raise the question of a philosophy of language in terms of a general philosophy of the human spirit,[40] the approach which Cassirer saw as the distinctive mark of his own system. In the second volume of *The Philosophy of Symbolic Forms* (1925), *Mythical Thought*, he regards Vico as the first thinker to formulate a philosophy of myth and regards it as the origin point of his own theory.[41] In a later work, *The Problem of Knowledge*, he states: "Giambattista Vico may be called the real discoverer of the myth."[42]

In the *Logic of the Humanities* (1942) Cassirer makes clear the identity he sees between his general project of a philosophy of symbolic forms and Vico's science of the human world. Here he says that Vico was the first thinker to raise "with true precision" the question of the limits of the mathematical method for the philosophical understanding of historical experience; and he says that what Vico "defended with *complete decisiveness against Descartes,* was the methodological uniqueness and the distinctive value of historical knowledge."[43] In these passages Cassirer discusses Vico's conception of the *New Science* in the same terms that he conceives his own philosophy of symbolic forms. At the center of Cassirer's philosophy is the notion that each area of human culture—myth, religion, language, art, history, and science—has its own "logic," all of which are held together through the general logic of the symbolic functioning of mind, which is the one element at the basis of all human culture. Cassirer says of Vico: "Myth, language, religion, poetry—these are the objects to which human knowledge is truly commensurable. And it is

[39] Cassirer discusses Vico in his first published work, *Leibniz' System in seinen wissenschaftlichen Grundlagen* (Marburg: N. G. Elwert, 1902), pp. 447–49. His references here are to the Ferrari edition of Vico's works. It seems likely that Cassirer read Vico while a student at Marburg. Dimitry Gawronsky reports that Cassirer read classics of Italian thought with an Italian disciple of Cassirer's teacher, Hermann Cohen ("Ernst Cassirer: His Life and His Work," *The Philosophy of Ernst Cassirer* [Evanston, Ill.: Library of Living Philosophers, Inc., 1949], p. 8). Cassirer's statements about Vico in *Leibniz' System* are quite similar to the view expressed in the statement quoted as an epigraph to this essay which appeared just prior to the first volume of his *Philosophy of Symbolic Forms.*

[40] *PSF*, vol. 1, pp. 148–49.

[41] *Ibid.*, vol. 2, p. 3. A. W. Levi, *Literature, Philosophy, and the Imagination* (Bloomington: Indiana University Press, 1962), states: "But the age of Poetic Wisdom is also the age of metaphor and allegory—what Cassirer (*who owes more to Vico than he has ever explicitly acknowledged*) calls the age of mythical consciousness" (p. 222) (italics mine).

[42] Trans. William H. Woglom and Charles W. Hendel (New Haven: Yale University Press, 1950), p. 296. This is the fourth volume of Cassirer's large study, *Das Erkenntnisproblem in der Philosophie und Wissenschaft der neueren Zeit,* which was written in 1940, although its first appearance in print was in 1950 in English translation.

[43] Trans. Clarence Smith Howe (New Haven: Yale University Press, 1961), p. 52 (italics mine).

above all to these that Vico turns his gaze in constructing his 'logic.' Here for the first time logic dared to break through the circle of objective knowledge, the circle of mathematics and natural science, and dared instead to constitute itself as the logic of the humanities—as the logic of language, poetry, and history. It is with good reason that Vico's *Scienza nuova* bears its title. For it contains a truly original discovery."[44]

There are at least four basic points in which Cassirer's philosophy is similar to Vico's: (1) Both distinguish within human culture various forms of cultural experience which constitute the structures in terms of which human culture as a whole develops. In Vico these are primarily discussed as the forms of poetic wisdom—that is, poetic metaphysics, logic, morals, economics, politics, and the poetic sciences—but they are also for Vico the forms of the modern world when they are given rational rather than poetic embodiment. (2) Both have at the basis of their theories of the human world a highly original philosophical concept. For Vico it is the "imaginative universal"; for Cassirer it is the "symbolic form." (3) Both have a conception of philosophical thought that attempts to enact within their philosophies as written a union between categorical form and particular content formed. In Vico this is accomplished through his philosophical-philological method, which results in a style of presentation that is at once imaginative and rationally ordered. In Cassirer this takes the form of what at one place he calls "systematic review" (*systematischen Überblicks*),[45] in which philosophy produces an account of human knowledge and history without ending its account in a system of metaphysical categories and logical essences. (4) Both have as the basis of their accounts of human culture theories of primordial or original mentality, which Vico calls "poetic wisdom," and Cassirer calls "mythical thought." For both, theory of knowledge must presuppose theory of myth.

It is this fourth point that I wish to explore. Each of the other three points would be worth exploring, and even other points in addition to them, but it is this fourth point that goes most directly to a view absent in contemporary epistemology and at which Cassirer and Vico's thought significantly supplement each other. In contemporary theory of knowledge, human knowledge itself has come largely to be equated with that

[44] *Ibid.*, p. 54.

[45] *The Problem of Knowledge*, p. 19. Although Cassirer uses this term to characterize his method of presenting the history of "Philosophy, Science, and History since Hegel" (the subtitle of this volume), this seems a good term to apply to capture the nature of his philosophical method generally. In his philosophy of symbolic forms he is concerned to employ a method that effects the same type of union between philosophical form and content that Vico attempts through his philosophical-philological method. Cassirer regards his theory of symbolic forms as based on an attempt to escape from what he calls the "methodological dilemma" of either reducing all content of the human world of culture to a system of logical forms (which he sees as a difficulty inherent in the project of philosophical idealism itself and in particular in the philosophy of Hegel) or of simply describing the specific content of the various forms of culture resulting in a kind of pure empiricism of their actual histories (see *PSF*, vol. 1, pp. 83–84).

which occurs in commonsensical, scientific, and logical ways of thought. Philosophical theory of knowledge has been built on the Cartesian model whether it has taken language, science, or formal logic as its starting points. Epistemology has come in effect by definition to mean the analysis of theoretical and scientific thought, just as science has come to be equated with knowledge in the contemporary world generally. Theory of knowledge carried on from within this perspective faces two fundamental problems: (1) theories of knowledge are developed through reflections on linguistic, scientific, and logical data without attention to the human reality of which they are in fact a part; and (2) because theory of knowledge is thus pursued apart from a theory of the human world, it offers no account of the origin of the knowledge it investigates. Such philosophical theories of knowledge float before us unattached as timeless works of the present.

Cassirer's theory of knowledge has as its base his *Phenomenology of Knowledge* (*Erkenntnis*) of the third volume of his *Philosophy of Symbolic Forms*.[46] In it his purpose is to show how scientific or theoretical thought which is the result of the pure conceptual functioning of consciousness (*Bedeutungsfunktion*) arises from and is grounded in the representational function of consciousness (*Darstellungsfunktion*) and the expressive function of consciousness (*Ausdrucksfunktion*) that lies below it. These three functions of consciousness represent the major ways in which experience is given form in the total development of mind. They are the major relationships between subject and object that lie behind all the particular forms of human culture, and they each represent a fundamental way in which the symbol is employed to give form to experience.

Corresponding to the conceptual function of consciousness and the representational function of consciousness, on Cassirer's view, are two distinct models of concept formation. In the conceptual function the mind operates notationally: the elements of experience are apprehended serially as variables ordered by a general "law of arrangement." When the mind functions in a purely conceptual way it creates systems of order that have

[46] Cassirer regards this as a total theory of human consciousness and to be a phenomenology in the sense of Hegel's *Phänomenologie des Geistes*. As Cassirer states: "In this fundamental principle the Philosophy of Symbolic Forms agrees with Hegel's formulation, much as it must differ in both its foundations (*Begründung*) and its development (*Durchführung*). It, too, aspires to provide the individual with a ladder which will lead him from the primary configurations found in the world of the immediate consciousness to the world of pure knowledge" (*PSF*, vol. 3, p. xv). The senses in which Cassirer's phenomenology of the human spirit differs most fundamentally from Hegel's are those points at which Cassirer's thought is most close to Vico's. Cassirer regards his phenomenology as differing in its "foundations" in that it begins with a theory of mythical consciousness which is a rung lower on the ladder of consciousness than Hegel's beginning point of *sinnliche Gewissheit* and the "thing" (see *PSF*, vol. 2, pp. xv-xvi). It differs in its "development" in that it does not sublimate the specific content of the forms of the human spirit to logical form, but always presents form through its content (see *PSF*, vol. 1, pp. 83–84; vol. 2, pp. 235–37; and above, n. 42).

behind them the model of *F* (*a*, *b*, *c*, . . .), in which *F* is the principle of order that determines the arrangement of the elements (*a*, *b*, *c*, . . .).[47] It is this conceptual functioning of consciousness that makes possible mathematical forms of thought and exact natural science. In the total development of mind the conceptual function of consciousness is a development of the representational function. The representational function orders the world through thing-property relations. The model of the concept on which this function rests is the Aristotelian logic of genus and species. The representational function of consciousness is what generates the classificatory ordering of experience and levels of logical abstraction and reference to sensible particulars that occurs through language.[48]

The expressive function is the most fundamental function of consciousness, and it underlies the representational function. For Cassirer the expressive function of consciousness is what produces myth.[49] Although in the second volume of *The Philosophy of Symbolic Forms* he develops a total theory of mythical thought, in which he discusses the mythical employment of the basic categories of mind, mythic spatial, temporal, and numerical forms, and the mythic structuring of the self, he presents no general theory of the concept or model of concept formation for mythic mind.[50] It is here that Vico's thought supplies, in the form of the theory of the imaginative universal, what Cassirer's thought does not. Cassirer offers no general logic of the image or the particular synthesis between the universal and the particular that exists in the image. In the *Logic of the Humanities* Cassirer formulates a theory of concept formation for fields of humanistic knowledge, notably for history and art history.[51] But this is not grounded in terms of a logic of the imaginative act itself, the root expression of which would lie in his theory of myth.

Vico's theory of the imaginative universal provides a model of concept formation for the imaginative act itself, which is present in its purest form in myth, in the thought form of the first men, or what Vico calls poetic wisdom.[52] Thus Vico's thought adds a necessary element to Cassirer's

[47] *Substance and Function*, authorized trans. William Curtis Swabey and Marie Collins Swabey (Chicago: Open Court Pub. Co., 1923), chap. 1. The model of concept formation for what Cassirer calls in this work (orig. pub. 1910) the "functional concept" is the source in his own thought of his conception of symbolic form itself (see *PSF*, vol. 1, p. 69, and vol. 3, p. xiii; also cf. *Substance and Function*, chap. 1, and *PSF*, vol. 3, pt. 3, chap. 1).

[48] *PSF*, vol. 3, pt. 2, chaps. 1 and 2. I interpret what Cassirer calls the "generic concept" of Aristotelian logic in *Substance and Function*, chap. 1, to be the logical model for that type of thought that corresponds to the representational function of consciousness of *PSF*, vol. 3.

[49] *PSF*, vol. 3, pp. 81 and 88.

[50] D. P. Verene, "Cassirer's View of Myth and Symbol," *The Monist* 50 (1966): 554–64.

[51] "Nature-Concepts and Culture-Concepts," chap. 3.

[52] Vico's theory of the imaginative universal suggests, in addition to a model of concept formation for expressive consciousness, a logic of the mythic "archetype" as it is

first stage of consciousness, the stage of expression. Vico's age of men, or age of rational thought, which has the intelligible universal as its form, would correspond to Cassirer's second stage of consciousness, the stage of representational thought structured in terms of the generic concept. Cassirer's third stage, that of the functional concept, is beyond any form of the concept known to Vico and corresponds to the type of thinking in late modern and contemporary science and mathematics.

Cassirer's philosophy considered as a whole is a philosophy of culture in which culture is seen as a total project of the human spirit made up of the various symbolic forms such as myth, religion, language, art, history, and science. Underlying all such forms of human culture are Cassirer's three fundamental functions of consciousness, whereby the mind synthesizes the manifold of perceptual flux in ways which result in the various forms of cultural activity. The medium of all these synthetic acts of the mind is its power to symbolize, to bring the universal together with the particular through the symbol. Each symbolic form of man's cultural activity for Cassirer is a generalized form of man's self-knowledge; the symbolic forms are the human creative act carried to largest terms.[53]

Toward what does a Vichian-Cassirerian perspective ultimately point? (1) By fitting together Vico's theory of imaginative universals and Cassirer's view of the expressive function of consciousness of mythical thought, a standpoint is projected from which a logic of the imagination can be developed from within contemporary philosophical thought and from which a theory of knowledge can be developed in which all forms of knowledge can be seen as arising from the reality of the image. (2) Vico and Cassirer have philosophical temperaments of mind that are corrective of each other and which together make up an outlook not present in contemporary thought. This outlook is fundamental if theory of knowledge is to be responsive to the claims of both the imagination and the cognitive. At the points where Cassirer is the philosopher of theoretical thought,

---

employed in the work of such thinkers as C. G. Jung and C. Kerényi, *Essays on a Science of Mythology: The Myth of the Divine Child and the Mysteries of Eleusis*, trans. R. F. C. Hull (Princeton: Princeton University Press, 1969), and throughout other of Jung's works, and Mircea Eliade, *Cosmos and History: The Myth of the Eternal Return*, trans. Willard R. Trask (New York: Harper and Row, 1959), and elsewhere in his works. Although the concept of "archetype" has played an important role as an instrument in analyzing the structure of myths, and although through the work of Northrop Frye it has also been made the basis of a "science" of literary criticism, the epistemological status and the internal logical structure of the archetype remains unexplored. In relation to Northrop Frye's view see in particular the first two of his essays reprinted in his *Fables of Identity: Studies in Poetic Mythology* (New York: Harcourt, Brace, and World, 1963). It is my view that in theory of myth Vico's theory of imaginative universals suggests a view of the mythic concept that has significance, not only for Cassirer's categorical and phenomenological analysis of myth, but for the archetypal and thematic analysis of myth and also for the structural analysis of myth (see above, n. 27).

[53] *Logic of the Humanities*, chap. 5, and *An Essay on Man* (New Haven: Yale University Press, 1944), chap. 1.

Vico is the philosopher of letters and rhetoric. Where Cassirer sees thought as developing itself out of its own requirements of itself, Vico sees the connection between types of ideas and types of social organization. Both, however, understand knowledge as a concrete process that cannot be separated from its embodiment in culture or from its genesis from the origin point of the human. This perspective is not present in any of the contemporary epistemological movements such as logical analysis, linguistic philosophy, dialectical materialism, phenomenology, or pragmatism.

The total argument I have intended to present in this essay takes seriously the fact that we live in a Cartesian age—that the separation that Descartes enacted in his own thought between the reason of the intellect and the forms of the humanistic imagination has become the shape of contemporary life itself. Because of this, Vico's thought is significant, not simply for the scholarly views it contains, but because it speaks directly to the problems of the contemporary age. It holds out to us the possibility of making sense of the human world as a product of the imaginative reason. The basis for this possibility lies in Vico's theory of the imaginative universal. It provides the master key for the *New Science* and the master key for a philosophical theory of origins. When combined with Cassirer's conception of a philosophy of symbolic forms, and in particular his theory of myth, it provides the basis for a theory of knowledge that can come to grips with the fragmentation of knowledge and the separations of cultural life. It contains the possibility of philosophically giving life to the imagination, to the spiritual sense of the whole and the knowledge of origins it offers us, in the face of ongoing technological form.

Part IV VICO AND TOPICS IN HUMANISTIC AND SOCIAL SCIENTIFIC THOUGHT

Stuart Hampshire

JOYCE AND VICO: THE MIDDLE WAY

Vico's *Scienza Nuova* and *Autobiography* are related to the familiar classics of Western philosophy rather as a dream is related to the waking workaday state. They are disturbing, confusing, and they have a multiple significance. They are apt to be remembered in fragments and they mean different things to different persons: and it seems, or has seemed, that they cannot easily be put to work for any practical necessary purpose, either as guides to action in politics, or as keys to the future, or as moral exhortation, or even as advice to historians on methods of history. In this respect they are utterly unlike the works of Machiavelli, Hobbes, Locke, Condorcet, Rousseau, Hegel, Marx, Tocqueville, Durkheim. Not only are they not part of this continuous order of thought and ambition: they are opposed to it, and they would, if they could, undermine it finally. Vico's science genuinely was new, both in his theory and in his practice; and the novelty remains even now, because he has only been partially understood, and understood usually in a tame, domesticated sense, which disguises his subversive meanings.

Vico is not just one more in the line of philosophers of history and prophets of the future social sciences: rather he should be seen as the end of the line, properly read and applied. He can now be properly read, perhaps, because the famous prose theorists of history, the wide-awake thinkers and their schools, have been losing credit, and have begun to fade and to seem dull, clear daylight-error, leading us away from an inquiry that is poetical, literary, philosophical, and finally, antihistorical: an inquiry that may yield the only close knowledge of our social ways and thoughts that we can have; and that we can have particularly now, at a moment of apparent decadence, in the apparent chaos of our ways and thoughts, as cities decay and urbanity is lost, and there is a turning back toward primitive origins and toward small communities, and to the interpretation of dreams and to distrust of learning.

Prose fiction and a historical consciousness each seemed inconceivable without the other in the last hundred years, even apart from the special connections that Hegel traced and even apart from the theory of the novel as bourgeois epic. For 250 years the story of developing social forms, and the presumed patterns underlying this development, have been the proper story of humanity. Such a story can be told in prose, whether as history or as fiction: illustrations of manners and of a sentimental education in the city, or of vanishing customs in the country, and illustrations of the gradual unfolding of the great city as a modern world. Unfractured prose is the medium for representing citizens to themselves in a social and historical setting which they can recognize as their own and which they believe determines their existence and identity. Novels made self-conscious citizens of the nineteenth century even more conscious of their historical place, and of their modernity. The public, social world is the formative reality, the occasion alike of action and of feeling, and myth and poetry and every form of fiction are at once indirect comments on, and indirect reflections of, the single social reality.

Joyce turned back across 200 years to Vico, in his own *ricorso*, for a new humanism independent of social history, and independent of history of any kind: to one day in one city, and then to no clear day at all, but to nightspeech. The universal family of man is constituted by language and not by social structures. The unity of mankind is to be reconstituted, not through controlled and fact-respecting history, but through a wild, far-ranging, and imaginative philology.

The myths and puns, and metaphors and free associations, the condensations of dreamspeech and of childhood poetry and play, popular catchwords and songs, taken from many languages, are the story of mankind, except that they are not to be recaptured as story alone; they come to full consciousness as fractured prose, as a kind of pure poetry, and as an immense symbolism that combines strictly formal structures with mad, far-fetched, and also contrived, associations and coinages and metamorphoses. Fiction is rolled back to its prehistorical beginnings and prose to rituals of barbarism and to incantation, jingle, and pun. Bourgeois epic has been formalized and turned sometimes into poetry, in *Ulysses*; and in *Finnegans Wake* the dream philology, a summary of European thought in the roots of many-languaged words, has almost displaced story and wholly replaced prose. There is no public, social order.

The language is in two ways barbarously magical. First, the elaborate formal structures of *Ulysses* and *Finnegans Wake* are carried through with obsessional care, as if one careless omission, or neglected symmetry or echo, might ruin the whole, and rob it of its force and integrity, like a false step in ritual or a broken rule in children's street games. Secondly, coincidences in naming and association between names and etymological coincidences have explosive meanings that are independent of anyone's intentions. In Joyce coincidences in language are to be treated like natural portents. One stumbles across the coincidences, as in the language of oracles and in memories of dreams and in the inventions of mythology, and they carry condensed messages to be slowly, speculatively unraveled.

That words have this power is not incidental to them, and the release of this compressed power in literature is not eccentric. The deeper and shared thought, and social and family experiences, of mankind are hoarded in elaborated words and names and phrases, and literary experiment has always opened the entrance to the hoard, knowingly or unknowingly; now knowingly, because we are in the decadence that calls for renewal from the primitive sources of poetry; in the fading daylight of reason we are in need of dreamspeech and the obscure meanings of the unconscious mind, and the need to regress is a conscious one. This was Joyce's free romantic version of Vico's theory.

The confluence of Vico and Joyce, from utterly separate sources coming together, is an amazing coincidence; it is possibly a portent of our future, or of one segment of it. Joyce adopted Vico late in his own development, in the early Twenties, because Vico had said what he for his own reasons needed to hear across the 200-year chasm. It was not a case of influence, but a Joycean accident of a coinciding conclusion. Reduced to a single prose point, the common conclusion was that humanity has a unity that transcends history; it is not a false totality of diverse cultures outside biology, and humanism can be given a sense, through an imaginative philology, which is not the sense that previous humanists have given it. The unity is to be found in the universal roots of the many languages that men have imagined and invented in their poetical moments, ever since they emerged, stuttering and babbling and gesturing, from their caves, and from an inchoate state of nature, unritualized, into the first symbolisms of family relationship, and to the knowledge of fear and dependence, with transcendental imaginings to relieve the fear.

Humanists had been apt to find the unity of mankind in the exercise of sovereign reason and in the history of its supreme achievements, particularly in the philosophy of the ancient world and in Roman law. Joyce, like Vico, looked for, and played with, the universal and primitive imagery, which is overlaid by the relational structures of the famous philosophies; and his humanism put the ordinary men and women of the modern city, representing the family of mankind, in place of the heroes of the ancient world. For Vico, and for Joyce also, a representative individual preserves in microcosm through his lexicon the range of ideas which comprise the imaginative resources of the race, the spiritual capital upon which we all draw, whether in mandarin writing or in the crude patter and songs of the streets and pubs.

Joyce winds together the rough, vital language of the Dublin streets with classical and philosophical allusion into composite Joyce speech, his style from *Portrait* onward until *Finnegans Wake*. The unity of the race is to be found in the universal grammar of common imagery, buried deep in the unconscious mind, and remembered from the childhood of the individual and of mankind, and built into the archetypes of family dependence and conflict. For Joyce, even more than for Vico, the family is, alongside the use of language, the institution that constitutes a common humanity: for Vico the rituals and gestures and mute symbols that precede speech are simultaneous in the ideal order with the recognition of the family. The family is not a biological unit, but is rather the universal basis of human culture; the idea of it pervades all our perceptions of social reality. A child is born innately ready for family relationships as he is ready for speech. He enters into a third and intermediate domain, which is neither that of rational thought nor is it the state of nature studied by the natural sciences.

Joyce could be polyglot, cosmopolitan, an exile, and invent a literature that draws on many of the languages of Europe. Still the family romance, in its full complexity, is the unavoidable subject of fiction. Not only history but also nature is originally interpreted by men in terms of family relationships, and then in terms of social relationships which are derived from them. Earth Mother, God Father, the sexual symbolism of natural kinds, the ambivalences of sexuality, the metamorphoses of gods, the rivalry of brothers, the incompleteness of sons reproached by the ghost of their father, the Christ-like emigration of the son who leaves to make his way and who repudiates his fatherland and his mother for his creative mission, the wandering of the experimentalist and adventurer, ruled by curiosity, who first deserts and then returns to his home, which is the fixed center of the earth, the triangularity of sexual relations which makes jealousy an aspect of human love and which inserts the imagination into the bare couplings of nature: these are some of Joyce's themes, because they are selections from the necessary, radical themes of all European literature, which he is resuming, as Milton resumed the epic, in the form of philosophical parody. So far he and Vico are in accord.

As language constitutes the essence of man as a species, and not reason, so the family, and not the social order, is the setting that humanizes him. He is not political man at the deepest level, but family man, father, son, and brother, kinship-tied, race-respecting, inheritor of customs and rituals and songs, sometimes stranger and wanderer, the more Jewish the more representatively human, as Bloom is, always in emotion recurring in thought to the origins of his identity. But there is one divergence, or change of emphasis, which has disguised this extraordinary philosophical coincidence of view.

Joyce's early imagination was linked with erotic feeling which was to some degree autonomous and which he saw as the negation of the Manichean Catholicism of his childhood and also as part of the aestheticism of the Nineties, of the literary cultivation of the flowers of evil. The tone lingers even in *Ulysses*, though self-consciously distanced and even parodied, and it has almost disappeared in his true Viconian work, *Finnegans Wake*, which is neither specifically Christian nor pagan in a romantic sense. The original sin that comes with the thunderclap of monotheism and monogamy is no more than a humanizing sense of shame surrounding sexuality and its proper secrecies, and a humanizing fear of unknown and superhuman powers.

Such a coincidence in rejecting history for anthropology between a Neapolitan philosopher and legal theorist rejecting Descartes in the 1720s, and a Flaubertian Irishman, rejecting romantic nationalism and rivaling Dante and Milton in his literary ambitions, calls for understanding. But it also requires one to take sides for or against, to evaluate the claims made as philosophy by Vico and as fiction by Joyce.

The claims are that the story of the human race can only in part be told as a progress, as of a man growing up from childhood through maturity to old age and decay; it must also be told as an overlapping of great circles, like the circle of the seasons; so that the winter of rational argument and conceptual thought, with its bare outline of clear definitions and sparse foliage of associations, is always to be succeeded by a renewal of imagination and by untidy flowerings of poetry and linguistic invention; that mature, rational thought, whether in the individual or in the race, becomes sterile and uninteresting as soon as access to the unconscious sources of the imagination, to the sources of poetry, is lost; that the concrete thinking of childhood, with its free associations and its conflation of myth and history, its respect for the coincidences of language, for rhymes and synonymies and assonances, for primitive imagery and absurd and obscene nonsense, is always the material of literature; that language, myths, and the early literature of men are the true depositories of knowledge of human nature, because these are human creations, and men can know themselves only through their own creations, and not as observers of themselves. The claim is that the true anthropology, science of man, is therefore not an experimental science, in its methods like the physical sciences. It is rather a combination of philology and literary culture, and it is also a study of the structure of languages and of systems of myth and of the symbolic activities that complement them.

That the social orders of the past, before the ages of reason and of philosophy, are best understood through reflecting on the irrationalities and imagery preserved from childhood occurs in the thought even of the most methodical historians and most careful followers of Durkheim and Weber. But for Vico the history of nations and of races, in the great circles of their rhythmical rise and fall, is the natural history of humanity, revealing human nature, as the succession of seasons in the circling year shows the nature of speechless species. This history is the history of language; it is the recall of the unconscious, or at least of the unformulated, pictures of the social world built into the grammar and metaphors of a people's symbolic behavior; therefore the history that yields self-understanding and self-knowledge is the history of art and of literature, and particularly of the popular arts, conceived not in the linear way of social history, but as revealing the recurring archetypes of the inner world of imagination.

This is the claim, antihistorical and against prosaic knowledge and scientific method in human affairs; a defense of literature and of poetry which Shelley was to repeat; also a defense of philology, of linguistic studies generally, and of an imaginative structural anthropology. The chasm of 200 years between Vico and Joyce is the period in which historical method and the idea of social change dominated literature and popular thought; it was the period in which positivists and men of the Enlightenment, and not only they, were in accord with popular thought in seeing history as the evolution of higher forms of thought, and of a more rational social order, from lower, superstitious forms of belief and social organization; the period in which even the pessimists, such as Flaubert, thought of the modern social world as something entirely new, a unique transformation of man, whether for good or for evil.

The accompanying literary ambition was that of the realistic novel, in Lukacs's sense of realism, which shows a distinctively modern consciousness developing from an older social order and which self-consciously thought of fiction as an imaginative offshoot of social history: as in different ways Scott, Balzac, Flaubert did. The language of fiction, particularly in Flaubert's intention, gradually assumed a sophicated impersonality and objectivity which was represented as peculiarly modern, and as unattainable in other times. The story of a simple heart should be dryly told, without the induced poetry of romanticism; the power of prose, and of prose fiction, ought now to be as great as the power of poetry and of epic had been, giving back to society a noble consciousness of itself and overcoming the degeneration of the age. The nobility was to be found in subtle prose rhythms, in restraint, in literalness, in a spare beauty in describing the minutiae of the modern city and of a sentimental education, and triviality was to be redeemed by hard-won exactness on the surface.

Joyce, in accord with Vico, went beyond Flaubert into the last phase of the cycle of language, and turned back, still in the interests of a naturalism, to a portrayal of the modern city and the modern social world as an instance of the universal history of peoples and nations, at a deeper level always and everywhere the same. "Teems of times and happy returns. The seim anew. Ordovico or Viricordo." The universal, recycling family romances, and the always renewed epic of adventure and discovery, are to be presented "sub specie temporis nostri," in Joyce's words, and this calls for a combination of Defoe-like veracity in naturalistic detail with a dense, symbolic language, which condenses the myriad references to echoing themes of previous family romance and previous voyages of discovery, to primal falls and metamorphoses across literatures and mythologies of the past.

Finally, it is logical that the language of fiction should become fluid, musical, condensed, freely associating, overdetermined, dreamspeech, because dreamspeech is the furthest removed of all prose from narrative sequence, and dream happenings have the least possible temporal structure, and he who tells the story of a dream is the most unlike a historian of all storytellers. The primary processes of thought common to every man, everyman's order of imagination, are recaptured in a dreamspeech that can condense in multiple allusion: the overlapping mythologies of different cultures, the poetry of the streets and of the nursery, ancient philosophies and the adventures of world-historical heroes. Everyman's falls and fortunes, and his family's fights and returns, are, in this presentation of them, the falls and fortunes of everyman naked, unclothed in a particular historical circumstance, and in this sense natural: natural for the word-governed, mythmaking, tale-telling species that recycles its unconscious memories perpetually.

There is therefore in Joyce no intention of belittling the modern social world and the city by parody; not ancient heroes with modern little men in their place, which is the ordinary use of parody. Certainly our time, June, 1904, is a late phase in the cycle of ideal history, an age of prose and philosophy, not an early day of heroic language-making and of dark myth and poetry. Naturalists in fiction, and positivists in philosophy, in 1904, still prevailed. But it was possible to restore in a new cycle the full mythopoeic power of literature, and Ibsen had just barely begun to show the way. Everyman, complete with his family or deprived of family, is of the same stature at any time, Bloom as Ulysses, and there is no spiraling descent or ascent into the modern world for this one time only. Humanity ascends and descends only as day into night, or spring into winter, in the long cadence which allows one leading nation or leading family or leading hero to succeed another in the returning and renewing circle of spiritual seasons.

History is the nineteenth-century dream, a liberal and nationalist dream turning into nightmare, from which Joyce had awakened, confirmed in wakefulness from 1922 onward by the light from Scienza Nuova. He had slowly rejected Irish, and all, nationalism, because nationalism is a belief in a particular historical destiny and at a particular time and place: a secular derivative of a historical religion. His writing will be of and about all time. Joyce, linked to Vico, is not to be grouped with the modern writers who have seen modernity as anarchy and alienation following an Eden of pristine faith and integrity in some past age, any more than he is to be grouped with liberal humanists and Marxists who thought they were escaping from superstition and alienation.

In a famous essay, at once self-revealing and revealing of its time, T. S. Eliot wrote of *Ulysses* that the use of formal parallelisms in it is "simply a way of controlling, of ordering, of giving a shape and a significance to the immense panorama of futility and anarchy, which is contemporary history. . . . It is, I seriously believe, a step toward making the modern world possible for art." Eliot reverses the historical attitudes of liberal humanists. For him also history has a constant sense and direction, and it is temporarily downward, from the classical world and the Christian synthesis to modernity, which is disintegration. Dante is a whole writer at a center point of history and in an unfractured order. For Eliot only the self-conscious contrivances and imitations of order, obvious symbolic artifices, are now possible, because the fracture in history, modern consciousness, otherwise allows only broken speech. In orderly and aristocratic societies, in which due subordinations are recognized, the art that reflects the social order, literature, can be coherent and orderly without contrivance in its expression. Partly through F. H. Bradley these Hegelian thoughts about history and society had come to be Eliot's.

For Eliot there is an aristocracy of ages, an elite of the timely born; the new rich, the self-made in philosophy, the modern writers in serious search of a faith—Blake, Hardy, Lawrence—are censored for their hard-won beliefs, and for the earnest, vulgar, anxious display that they must make of them in their writing. For Joyce, Dante is no more a natural, rightly born, aristocrat of letters than is Giordano Bruno or Swift or Blake. In respect of historical moments, Joyce was a populist, as he was in other respects: the philosophy of cycle and renewal required him to be. All ages exhibit contingency, accidents, falls, misfortunes, conflict, and waste as part of recurring human conditions, perpetual disorder, which still has its recycling patterns and themes: and these themes from Homer and Ovid and the Old Testament wind their way in and out of Christian iconography, are reclothed and represented in Dante, and are echoed in popular songs and operettas and fairy tales, and can be found again in Irish mythology and in the sagas of the North. There never was an orderly Christian commonwealth, nor is the modern world without precedent and its alienation without a precursor. Men repeat themselves, and not least in the recurring belief that they are a generation unlike any other.

A historian, Michelet, was Vico's first effective defender, inspired by the idea of the self-creation of a people by itself through its memories of its history. History is useful in so far as it gives examples of the archetypal relationships which recur in cyclical forms from one period to another: this is the significance of the chronicles of glorious reigns, of the pageant of class war and revolution. For Joyce every true history symbolizes something in the ideal history of the human family, as does the story of Noah and his family, or the fiction of Ulysses and Nausicaa, or the story of Hamlet, Hamlet's father, and the ghost of Hamlet's father, or the tale of Humpty-Dumpty.

The institutions that historians describe have a symbolic significance in the minds of everyman, whether this symbolism is rendered explicit or not. For example, legitimacy, as from father to son, can become a grandiose legal and philosophical notion for the sake of which millions have fought and died, and they will continue to do so; its power comes, not from the arguments of philosophers, but from the deep levels of the unconscious, family-centered mind of the race. Republican brotherhood, as in ancient Rome, or among the modern and philosophical Jacobins, has equally a concrete root, which develops into an abstract, even philosophical idea, and then regresses to its primitive familiar associations. The abstract notion of emancipation, still strong in our minds and in literature, has developed from unconscious memories of slavery and from the early ceremonies and rituals which gave men freedom. The word "emancipation" condenses the history and preserves the roots of the emotional idea.

One thinks of a recent school of social anthropologists and of linguists who may be called structuralists, and particularly of Professor Lévi-Strauss. There are two closely connected features of some anthropological theories which make them seem a regression to Vico's philosophy, a recycling in which the rational empiricism of Durkheim and Radcliffe-Brown is supposed to be superseded, as Grotius's and Descartes's philosophical anthropology was to be superseded by Vico's, at least in Vico's intentions. First, some anthropologists, like Vico, find themselves interpreting the practices and institutions of a social group as parallel to a system of classifications of natural kinds, and as part of a total grammar and vocabulary which are revealed in actual family and legal relationships and in sexual conventions, and also in the forms of explanation that are given of these relationships and conventions. The way of entry into the mind of a people, and into their world as they have constituted it for themselves, is not principally through recording their behavior, neutrally described; but rather the entry is through studying the structures of their speech and of their storytelling, which will suggest the method of projection of the map of reality determining their behavior.

Such anthropologists think of the ritualized practices and institutions of a people as resembling a kind of "language," in an intelligibly extended sense of language. Therefore they find themselves coming to anthropology through a kind of philology, in the sense that understanding a phase of human development different from one's own involves entering by imagination, and by scholarship, into a different symbolic structuring of the world; and this in turn requires one to draw on some buried memory of an earlier phase of one's own experience, usually from childhood, when the structuring was still imaginative and fluid. From this Viconian standpoint, true knowledge of the past comes from an understanding of the language in which a people interpret their institutions and conduct themselves rather than from observations and description of the institutions and conduct from an external, scientific point of view, as functionalists might require. True social science therefore has more in common with literary understanding, and with a scholar's translation from one language into another, than with the methods of the physical sciences.

Secondly, there are anthropologists and others who follow Vico in being suspicious of any theory of history, or theory of human development, which makes some normative contrast between an earlier primitive and magical mentality, and the mentality of the enlightened social observer who comes after Newton and who, belonging to the modern world, has a clear, because scientific, vision of social realities. They may be merely skeptical and doubt that there is any Archimedean point from which one system of classification of human relations can be preferred to another in any absolute sense, and not relative to a particular already-formulated purpose; or they may think of the self-congratulatory culture of modern Europe and America as potentially the great destroyer of other cultures which represent equally vivid phases of development. They may therefore think of the earnest, prosaic inquirers from Europe as the destroyers of the sources of renewal for the race. Perhaps a return to a way of life which is nearer to the unconscious sources of energy is needed, and perhaps de-ritualization and faith in abstract speech and abstract argument have reached the limit of endurance; perhaps the time for recurrence is now, and perhaps the illusion of superiority has ended.

It is clear, I think, that Vico's *Scienza Nuova* offered a middle way in human knowledge; neither the study of man as the classical social scientist conceives this study nor the study of man as the historian, or the theorist of history, conceives it: a middle way also between a definition of human nature as an unchanging structure of powers and needs, and a definition of human nature as essentially always changing and as open to development without limit. Vico and Joyce were both educated to be pious Christians within the Catholic Church and both knew its philosophers. Vico was writing about the foundations of law, and looked for a middle way between the classical doctrine of natural law, everywhere the same and open to reason, and the mere relativism that made law the temporary and arbitrary will of the sovereign power: between Grotius and Hobbes. Joyce wanted a middle way between the naturalism of the best modern fiction of his time and the contrary ambitions of the Celtic revival and of poetic drama. He found a poetical naturalism, a renewal of language with a wholly modern reference in *Ulysses*.

Most of Vico's and of Joyce's readers have been educated as Christians or as Jews. Christianity is the religion that finds its theodicy in history whether one adopts the standpoint of the human race or of the individual person. From the standpoint of the race, history is to be explained by the Incarnation, and by the revelation of God's design at that time, and it moves toward a final redemption which will justify and give sense to that "immense panorama of futility and anarchy" which is otherwise inexplicable history. From the standpoint of the individual, the microcosm, his falls and recoveries are explained and justified, as he moves toward death, as being preparations for an attainable final stage of salvation, if he is a believer who accepts the history.

Judaism also places its theodicy, and consequent morality, in a historical destiny and in an anticipated prolongation of the revealed history of the Jewish people. When supernatural beliefs lost their hold upon leading political moralists and historians, they invented a humanism which still looked for explanations and justifications of contingencies, both in the race and the individual, in a development toward salvation; either they looked forward to an ideal social order or they looked back to restoring some utopian order lost in the past. For the individual, the explanation and justification of his fortunes were to be found in his historical situation and in his contribution to social improvement. This shadow of a historical theodicy is so deeply implanted in European literature that it has been almost impossible until now to be just to Vico and Joyce and to take their common thought, the middle way, seriously.

But now there are signs of a beginning, signs that there is a Joycean awakening from what he called "the nightmare of history," and a new skeptical, detached anthropology which has cut its roots to European positivism. It is skeptical and detached in that it neither finds a justification of massacres and wars and the horrors of the twentieth century in the simple-minded teleology of Marxists and of Christians and of positivists; nor is salvation to be found in an early Eden of innocence before the fall into alienation and modernity. There is no suggestion of salvation in any particular social order or political transformation or moral conversion. The story of the salvation that follows upon the fallen state, of Humpty-Dumpty put together again, is itself part of humanity's dream, and one of its perpetual myths. The fall is the beginning of a properly human culture in the age of the gods, as men emerge from the caves into monogamy and shame and ritual and into poetical speech, and as they form social orders. There is no salvation, because there is no finality. In Joyce there is only acquiescence, and harsh pleasure, in the renewing cycles of human cultures, in the rebirths of literature and of imagination, and in the return of the perpetual myths in new disguises.

In *Ulysses* and in *Finnegans Wake,* Joyce celebrates the renewals and returns and disguises in a style that takes him further from pessimism than any other modern writer. The thin complaint of modernity, the melancholy and bitterness of modern literature, persist from Tennyson and Arnold to Eliot and Lawrence and rise to a climax of self-pity in contemporary poetry and fiction. There is nothing of this in the later Joyce, for whom modernity is only one more disguise of one phase of human myth-making, an episode in the metamorphoses of the human family and of its fictions, an episode in the pageant of languages and of their renewal and of the imagination of social forms. He had found the style and form of fiction, the linguistic invention, which could be a lyrical affirmation of the continuing unity and survival of humanity through all the cycles of its ideal history.

John O'Neill

TIME'S BODY: VICO ON THE LOVE OF LANGUAGE AND INSTITUTION

Ours is an age in which everything is said clearly and concisely. What is not clear and concise only points to the need to keep up with this age. The clarity of our age is not an easy acquisition, though its style and uses are to be presumed upon among enlightened men responsible to the larger circle of those who place their faith in clarity as the fruit and sustenance of the republic of science and democracy.

Clarity in language and thought naturally allies itself with frank and open conduct. Thus we are unwilling to allow privacy to our public men; and since no one wishes to be accused of private ways, every man seeks to conduct as much of his life in public as society can conveniently cater. If obscenity and pornography are issues in our age, as indeed they are, it is only because we wish everything to be seen in the light of day, without benefit of difference, without magic, and without any appeal to poetry. Thus we are as much concerned to exhibit corruption in the body politic as we are fixed upon celebrating the conquest of body odors. For cleanliness is next to clarity.

Our age reckons upon the assumption that language is the instrument of thought and that we have nothing to find in language that we have not ourselves put into it. Thus the well-formed languages of logic and science are calculated to separate language from the history of man's speech about himself in order to make of the future a thing of rule. Language itself encourages our ambition to rule the world as a thing. For in its ordinary use language never obtrudes between us and the world, its virtue being to efface itself as the vehicle of thought and action. Thus it appears that we owe nothing to language except its proper use, which is ruled by the world's connections and not by anything our own life lends to language.[1] Clarity is therefore the only embellishment of scientific language which cultivates simplicity and precision in order to make of itself a universal prose.

The modern world holds time in its hand. We consider that we have broken with the past, and are headed towards the future launched upon

[1] Maurice Merleau-Ponty, *The Prose of the World*, ed. Claude Lefort, trans. with intro. by John O'Neill (Evanston: Northwestern University Press, 1973).

nothing but our present abilities. This is a story which is related to us by historians and social scientists in the unvarnished prose that is the emblem of our extrovert character. For we mean to make an open book of society and nature. It is essential to the success of this enterprise that we rid society and character of any universals other than those of science. Thus science is forgetful of the roots of its own practice and possibility and has no desire to be reminded of the sources of inspiration and madness which have brought history to the self-made arts of science, technology, and democracy.

It is a paradox of the age of prose that men are learning again to see and to hear, to read and to write, to talk and to listen. This is especially disturbing in a society which has made an industry of knowledge and so presumes upon its expansion that communication hardly means more than the speed with which the republic of science and commerce consumes its own self-image. For communication is the soul of extraversion; it feeds off the dead body of language and the extinction of style. Yet amidst the ruins of language and the collapse of history and character into faceless time men begin to turn over words in search of oracles, of the myths and metaphors which restore the human family and the fantastic universals of time's body.[2]

Science means to set men free from the idols of everyday language and from the mysteries of arcane speech. To achieve its purposes, scientific enlightenment must teach men to speak of history as progress and to conceive of society as the engine of character and motive. It is essential to this view that social facts are what they are only by means of clear and distinct rules of analysis and combination and are not in any way beholden to their profound interior or to their generic bonds. Thus sociological knowledge accumulates at the same time as men lose their collective memory. In this situation time's body fractures into the elements of individualism, contract, guilt, and violence. These are the material of history's progress and the daytime efforts of reason to reduce itself to an instrument without a body—a thinking calculus.

Enlightenment declares mankind to be a task of reason separated from passion and its own origins. Liberal history schedules reason in favor of the lateborn unshackled by myth, family, and the body's dreams. Liberal enlightenment rules the world by making children out of three quarters of mankind. The other quarter learns to repress its origins in order to make civilization the engine of its discontent. Thus reason's war against oracles joins in the war against the body's orifices, which are the way in and the way out of the world's round.[3]

The modern world retains its youth while all around dies young or comes to unwanted old age. Science, technology, and democracy are un-

[2] Norman O. Brown, *Closing Time* (New York: Random House, 1973).
[3] Norman O. Brown, *Love's Body* (New York: Vintage Books, 1968).

seasonable work inspired by change and progress wrought upon language, reason, and the passions in order to make a thing of mankind without any regard for the great body of human time. Thus Socrates turned from the study of science in order to live among men, to dwell upon the life that is gathered in men's language, and with a chance of wisdom to prepare for death. Socrates understood, just as Vico was to argue later, that science is a passion of youth but quite unable to make men.

And to his cost he learned that that study [Geometry] proper to minute wits is not easy for minds already made universal by metaphysics. So he gave up this study as one which chained and confined his mind, now accustomed through long study of metaphysics to move freely in the infinite of genera; and in the constant reading of orators, historians and poets his intellect took increasing delight in observing between remotest matters ties that bound them together in some common relation. It is these ties that are the beautiful ornaments of eloquence which make subtleties delightful.[4]

Science makes the world over in the name of men unconcerned with self-ignorance; it hopes to measure wisdom by what a man knows about the world outside and beyond his own life. Thus science is always defeated by death or, rather, ignores it because it presumes upon the future to accomplish its task. But Socrates understood that knowledge is redeemed only by death and community and in the gathering of men according to their own manner of speaking and living. Thus Socratic ignorance anchors upon time's body and the human family, whose conventions are the ground of man's nature. Socrates founds the tradition of vulgar metaphysics upon which Vico later builds the new science of humanity.

Kinship is the substance of this new science of man because Vico, like Socrates, understood that the good of knowledge lies in the world between men, in other words, in human institutions and not in the world outside of men, or in nature, except as science itself is a human institution. Philology is the method of the new science because language is the same thing as our humanity, the same in our childhood as in other men whose ways we learn by understanding their language. For we are just as strange to ourselves as other men in other times are to us unless we learn the history of our language. Vico's new science is therefore a science of language and kinship, a poetry of the archetypes and fantastic universals which have shaped time's body into the natural institutions of human intellect and imagination.

This was the order of human institutions: first the forts, after that the huts, then the villages, next the cities, and finally the academies. This axiom is a great principle of etymology, for this sequence of human institutions sets the pattern for the histories of words in the various native languages. Thus we observe in the Latin language that almost the whole corpus of its words had

[4] *Autobiography*, p. 123.

sylvan or rustic origins. For example, *lex*. First it must have meant a collection of acorns. Thence we believe is derived *ilex*, as it were *illex*, the oak (as certainly *aquilex* means collector of waters); for the oak produces the acorns by which the swine are drawn together. *Lex* was next a collection of vegetables, from which the latter were called *legumina*. Later on, at a time when vulgar letters had not yet been invented for writing down the laws, *lex* by a necessity of civil nature must have meant a collection of citizens, or the public parliament; so that the presence of the people was the *lex*, or "law," that solemnized the wills that were made *calatis comitiis*, in the presence of the assembled *comitia*. Finally, collecting letters, and making, as it were, a sheaf of them for each word, was called *legere*, reading.[5]

The cycle of language is the cycle of our great family history. But enlightenment seeks to dissolve the human family into a political contract grounded in fraternal guilt. In this way imagination is cut off from its universal roots. Men are forced to abandon poetry in favor of that prose which is suited to speak about what men see who no longer see into themselves. The language of imagination is therefore pushed into dreams, myths, and poetry, which store up man's common nature as a treasure to be discovered only by those who still love words, language, and song. Vico's new scientists are *philologists,* that is to say, men whose love of language loves mankind from its birth.

[The New Science] must begin where its subject matter began, as we said in the Axioms. We must therefore go back with the philologians and fetch it from the stones of Deucalion and Pyrrha, from the rocks of Amphion, from the men who sprang from the furrows of Cadmus or the hard oak of Vergil. With the philosophers we must fetch it from the frogs of Epicurus, from the cicadas of Hobbes, from the simpletons of Grotius; from the men cast into this world without care or aid of God, of whom Pufendorf speaks, as clumsy and wild as the giants called "Big Feet," who are said to be found near the Strait of Magellan; which is as much to say from the cyclopes of Homer, in whom Plato recognizes the first fathers in the state of the families.[6]

Modern man lives as unsure of birth, marriage, and death as he does of the past and the future. This is strange because modernity is essentially an historical consciousness, obsessed with the stages of its own development. But liberal individualism cannot achieve more than a guilty love of the past, for the past is beholden to its family gods, who rule the beginning and end of human life, determining its fruits and sorrows. Modern man aspires to live outside of the family; his need is to make of birth and death mere null points in order to destroy time's body. Thus modern society submits equally the womb and the grave to its cosmetic denials. The present, then, is only the dream place of beautiful losers.

Language fractures in the modern world because our speech is no longer

[5] *New Science*, §§ 239–40.
[6] *Ibid.*, § 338.

the reflection of anything that is ordered either inside or outside of us. Every historical order ultimately collapses the literary, artistic, and philosophical languages which for a time allowed an age to speak of itself and to gather its particular goods and evils. It is an axiom of Vico's new science of humanity that if history is at all saved it is saved by language. For it is in the history of our language that we recover our humanity. It is in language that we discover the gradual making of the institutions that have made us human.

But then the philologist is required against the spirit of the times to love the human family and to make a method out of remembrance and imagination. The philologist will therefore need to avoid telling mankind's story according to the pattern of progress, as though man had a future quite beyond himself or unweighted by his past. Yet to reject this story requires more strength than was needed by the early heroes, for it requires looking back into the face of the family and to our first awkward steps towards humanity. For it is easier to reject the gods than to reject man, but harder still to accept man. Such is the piety of philology.

This new science of humanity is patient with its own origins, and thus it does not speak solely through the mouths of gods and heroes. By the same token, it is not anxious about ends, and so it does not hasten man's speech with logic and science. The pillars of the poetic commonwealth are religion, marriage, and burial, which found our humanity upon what men everywhere owe to themselves and not to priests, philosophers, or scientists. For human law is nothing but the bonds men place upon themselves to clothe their nudity in the civil beauty of family, community, and speech.

Man is nothing else than the way he talks about himself. Vico's new science holds together the fractured speech of modernity because it rejoins time to its body, to its seasons and cycles of human fortune.[7] It is an axiom of the new science of humanity that science never leaves man behind; science itself is one more faith of mankind, another version of family and deliverance. This is a necessary axiom, since we should otherwise have no call to read Vico himself anymore than he had to read others before him. The call that is answered in Vico is the same call that language makes upon us today. It is the call for the renewal of the springs of language dried out in an age of precision and clarity.

But the nature of our civilized minds is so detached from the senses, even in the vulgar, by abstractions corresponding to all the abstract terms our languages

[7] Stuart Hampshire, "Joyce and Vico: The Middle Way," *The New York Review of Books* (18 October 1973). Reprinted in this volume. My own essay is merely a response to the pleasure of reading Hampshire's artful review of Norman O. Brown's *Closing Time* and my encounter with *Giambattista Vico: An International Symposium.* [*Editor's note:* that portion of Hampshire's essay which discusses Brown's work is not reprinted herein.]

abound in and so refined by the art of writing, and as it were spiritualized by the use of numbers, because even the vulgar know how to count and reckon, that it is naturally beyond our power to form the vast image of this mistress called "Sympathetic Nature." Men shape the phrase with their lips but have nothing in their minds; for what they have in mind is falsehood, which is nothing; and their imagination no longer avails to form a vast false image. It is equally beyond our power to enter into the vast imagination of those first men, whose minds were not in the least abstract, refined, or spiritualized, because they were entirely immersed in the senses, buffeted by the passions, buried in the body. That is why we said above that we can scarcely understand, still less imagine, how those first men thought who founded gentile humanity.[8]

We read Vico today because our task is to renew the names of things together with the edges of their special silence. Vico recalls that benign nominalism which brought men out of the forests into the light of language. At first men were the children of time's body; they sang out the names of things in bodily play, in pleasure, and love. They built up language through metaphor, that is, by playing upon words. And because they were not ashamed of their bodies they named things after the body and gave to nature the body's own moods and sensual speech.

The human mind is naturally inclined by the senses to see itself externally in the body, and only with great difficulty does it come to understand itself by means of reflection. This axiom gives us the universal principle of etymology in all languages: words are carried over from bodies and from the property of bodies to signify the institutions of the mind and spirit.[9]

Today we recall our ancestral condition, not because we mean to be ruled by it, but because we cannot be sure of our future without trying to hold together how man began. Vico's new science saved reason by anchoring it to time's body and its civil beauty. For reason is not the zero point of passion but rather involvement in the needs of our time acquired through a language that inhabits us and through which we in turn make our lives. The life of reason is therefore inseparable from its beginnings in poetry, myth, religion, and vulgar metaphysics. Reason is human when it is not forgetful of these origins but rather remembers them kindly for the sake of its own birth.

The most sublime labor of poetry is to give sense and passion to insensate things; and it is characteristic of children to take inanimate things in their hands and talk to them in play as if they were living persons. This philologico-philosophical axiom proves to us that in the world's childhood men were by nature sublime poets.[10]

Vico inspires us with our own language just as he renewed in himself Latin eloquence. Thus etymology is the music of Vico's new science teach-

[8] *New Science*, § 378.
[9] *Ibid.*, § 236.
[10] *Ibid.*, §§ 186–87.

ing us to hear our beginnings in the birth of language. Therefore thinking is not ahead of speaking, and speaking is not ahead of our bodies; so thinking is not ahead of time's body, which is the time our senses need to become human, to speak, and to think. In any man whose thinking listens to his speaking there is founded the soul's city, hearkening to the principles, nature, and laws of mankind. But to listen to principle and nature is to begin again, to remake sense and sensuousness, to make of time's body a renaissance of reason and its divine pleasure. This is a communal birth, and history is its only midwife, for the soul's deliverance is nowhere else than into his beautiful world.

Finally, beginning with the idea by which every slight slope was called *mundus* (whence the phrase *in mundo est, in proclivi est,* for "it is easy"; and later everything for the embellishment of a woman came to be called *mundus muliebris*), when they came to understand that the earth and the sky were spherical in form, and that from every point of the circumference there is a slope toward every other, and that the ocean bathes the land on every shore, and that the whole of things is adorned with countless varied and diverse sensible forms, the poets called this universe *mundus* as being that with which, by a beautifully sublime metaphor, nature adorns herself.[11]

Like birth itself, the human world comes about only in a given time and place marked by our weakness as much as by our strength, by pain as much as by joy, by ugliness as much as by beauty. But at no time is human nature, whether bestial or savage, heroic or divine, anything less than man's nature. This nature is not wholly passionate, for otherwise we should not have established any public grounds of truth nor any of the fixed institutions of society. Yet we ought not to attribute to men more of reason and calculation than governs the present age. For then we should make of society a preposterous contract, or else a noble lie, instead of a family which has gathered despite what it has reasoned for itself, despite its lusts and its powers.

Vico's new science is a science of reason renewed. Although it is born in the age of men, it gathers its own beginnings poetically from the temples of the sky, from which all human institutions and sciences are handed down. Vico's new science collects its own rough origins, recalling what it owes to our domestic labors in gathering acorns and animals, binding men and letters in law and parliament.

This new science of man is ultimately a life science. For he who undertakes its work must penetrate the veil of time which separates his thinking life from the brooding body, which is the place of reason and sense and their sole monument. For man is a work of his own hands and eyes, of his own lips and ears, a drama of his own passion and his own reason. Thus the eloquence of science and the civil beauty of law and religion are the true embellishment of humanity.

[11] *Ibid.*, § 725.

Robert J. Di Pietro

HUMANISM IN LINGUISTIC THEORY: A LESSON FROM VICO

In the name of linguistics devoted acolytes continue to search for a science of language. In this paper I will attempt to show how that search would be directed along meaningful paths if linguists were to gain some familiarity with Vico, a figure generally unknown to them. As the writings of various linguists will show, many developments have already occurred in their young discipline which are strongly reminiscent both of Vico's ideas and of trends to which Vico was opposed. There is a major lesson to be gained from Vico, namely, that the study of language in the twentieth century must be infused with a humanistic spirit. Hopefully an understanding of Vico's thinking about what should constitute the subject matter and the methodology of a science of man will be useful in guiding the contemporary linguist away from the present concentration on the logico-rational aspects of language and towards the emotive and communicative functions of language. Already there are signs that linguistics is moving in the direction of greater humanism, if by "humanism" we accept Vico's criterion of man's actions as a social creature, that is, as a maker of social institutions.

A brief survey of the shifts in interests and methodology in the field of linguistics over the last fifty years will serve to illustrate not only what has not changed since Vico's time but what has been lost and what is a possibility for the future. As Vico was led to formulate principles and axioms for his new science, so was Leonard Bloomfield, the so-called founder of structural linguistics, motivated to set down his "postulates for the science of language" almost half a century ago. One of Bloomfield's major concerns was to demarcate the field of language study: "Discussion of the fundamentals of our science seems to consist one half of obvious truisms, and one half of metaphysics; this is characteristic of matters which form no real part of a subject. . . ."[1]

By 1958, the major focus of interest for the linguist in the years since Bloomfield had narrowed to the so-called "central systems" of language.

[1] L. Bloomfield, "A Set of Postulates for the Science of Language," *Language* 2 (1926): 153.

Charles Hockett, a well-known structural linguist, defined these systems as (1) the grammatical system, which consists of units called "morphemes" and their arrangements, (2) the phonological system, comprising the distinctive sounds of language—the phonemes—and their patterns, and (3) the code which stands between grammar and phonology, or the morphophonemic system.[2] The semantic system which associates grammar to the extralinguistic world of meanings stood, along with phonetics, as a "peripheral subsystem."[3]

In many ways, Hockett's 1958 book, *A Course in Modern Linguistics*, marked the apex of the kind of linguistics inspired by Bloomfield. In their quest for a science of language, the Bloomfieldian linguists had decided to concentrate on the patterns of grammar and speech sounds and to pass over the semiotic functions of language. While the Bloomfieldian linguists shared with Vico the belief in the empirical observation of language phenomena, in this case, the actual utterances of people, they stood far from him in their efforts to compartmentalize language and to treat it as an autonomous system among other cultural systems devised by man.[4]

Just about the same time that Hockett published his book, Noam Chomsky's *Syntactic Structures* also appeared.[5] Modest in size, especially when compared to Hockett's highly detailed and sophisticated work, Chomsky's thin volume nonetheless engendered a new approach to language and, ultimately, a new way for the linguist to be scientific. Where the older Bloomfieldians considered carefully and separately the composition of each utterance in a language, Chomsky outlined proposals to show the interrelationship of sentences. Where care had been taken to limit the range of inquiry to corpora of sentences uttered by native subjects (and therefore attested as genuine language forms), Chomsky looked to the potential capacity of new sentence formation, which went beyond the confines of any limited corpus. As a result, the linguist found himself for the first time seriously concerned with what is grammatical and what is not grammatical in a language. The gathering of data from native speakers became less important than the invention of sentences by the linguist himself. Introspection became respectable in linguistics, much to the dismay of the Bloomfieldians.

The floodgates to mentalism in linguistics were opened wide with the appearance of Chomsky's *Cartesian Linguistics*.[6] In Descartes Chomsky had found a sympathetic forebear. Setting aside the question of whether or not Chomsky correctly interpreted Cartesian philosophy, Chomsky's particular theory, now called "transformational" or "generative lin-

[2] C. Hockett, *A Course in Modern Linguistics* (New York: Macmillan, 1958), p. 137.
[3] *Ibid.*, p. 138.
[4] *New Science*, §§ 138–40.
[5] N. Chomsky, *Syntactic Structures* (The Hague: Mouton, 1957).
[6] N. Chomsky, *Cartesian Linguistics* (New York: Harper and Row, 1966).

guistics," acquired some historical continuity.[7] Descartes' methodology was completely compatible with the speculative foundations of transformational linguistics. In an important series of lectures delivered at the University of California at Berkeley, Chomsky spoke of linguistics as a "branch of cognitive psychology" and held as unquestionable that linguistics should be a disciplinc "concerned with the study of the mind."[8] In direct antithesis to the spirit of Bloomfield's postulates, Chomsky argued against the compartmentalization of disciplines concerned with language. "It is no longer a point of honor," he wrote, "for each [discipline] to demonstrate its absolute independence of the others. . . ."[9]

Because he brought introspection to linguistics, and because he has demonstrated no particular interest in relating language to its use in society, Chomsky has taken the study of language away from its original humanistic foundations of etymology and philology, away even from the structural linguistics of Leonard Bloomfield, to what is labeled the structuralist movement in the social sciences. In so doing, however, he has also prepared the way for a Vichian influence to enter linguistics. His extremism has triggered a revolution not unlike the rebellion of Vico against the Cartesianism of the seventeenth century.[10] Many studies done recently by a group known as the sociolinguists point to the vast number of ways in which human language is intricately intertwined with human social systems. William Labov has gained prominence among the sociolinguists by cataloguing the ways in which the English language is stratified according to social levels in New York City.[11] Vico, in his concern for how language reflects the organization of society, would have been pleased with what Labov has called "linguistic variables," that is, parts of language—either grammar or pronunciation—which vary according to social class.

The attack on the formulation of grammars which are insensitive to fluctuations in the social use of language has continued to grow, and Labov has been joined by many new-found allies. Encouraged by this support, Labov has pushed his criticism of introspective linguistics even further. In a paper delivered at the Eleventh International Congress of Linguists, recently held in Bologna, Italy, he assailed the Chomskyan ideal "speaker-

[7] See H. Aarsleff, "The History of Linguistics and Professor Chomsky," *Language* 46 (1970): 570–85. Aarsleff raises serious questions about Chomsky's interpretations of Cartesian philosophy.

[8] N. Chomsky, *Language and Mind* (New York: Harcourt Brace, 1968), p. 2.

[9] *Ibid.*, p. 1.

[10] For a discussion of Vico's reaction to Cartesian mentalism see Raffaello Franchini, "Vico, Historical Methodology, and the Future of Philosophy" in *Giambattista Vico: An International Symposium*. pp. 543–52, esp. p. 549. For Chomsky's inclusion in the structuralist movement, see H. Gardner, *The Quest for Mind: Piaget, Lévi-Strauss and the Structuralist Movement* (New York: Alfred A. Knopf, 1973), pp. 240–45, esp. p. 243.

[11] W. Labov, *The Social Stratification of English in New York City* (Washington, D.C.: Center for Applied Linguistics, 1966).

hearer," who is supposedly free of involvement in social interaction: "One must look with admiration and astonishment at the boldness of linguists who have thus discarded the great body of data produced by ordinary citizens arguing, conversing, orating, corresponding, etc., proceeding with full confidence to recreate linguistics out of their own intuitions."[12] Linguistic intuitions are especially unreliable when applied to the study of how languages change over the ages. Labov continued: "We have not inherited the intuitions of the eighteenth century and it is unlikely that the twenty-first will accept ours, intermingled as they are with our theoretical persuasions." Taking the example of a vowel change in English, Labov demonstrated that its history cannot be understood without considering social class and usage: "Language is not a collection of idiosyncrasies. It is a means of communication by the use of social conventions."

With the development of sociolinguistics, we can once again appraise how much of what came before in linguistics will remain and how much of what has been added by this most recent group can be found in Vico. Clearly the most outstanding similarity is the interest by both the sociolinguists and Vico in the rapport between language and society. Vico, of course, saw the philological study of language as necessary to obtain evidence of how social institutions actually develop.[13] The sociolinguists of today make language their main concern and study the ways in which the organization of society influences the structure of grammars. Yet, Vico would have concurred with the sociolinguists in their orientation toward the observation of data from language use.

There is little accounting in sociolinguistics for the individual's idiosyncratic use of language. The linguistic behavior of classes is seen as the most regular and therefore the most significant. Vico, in a similar vein, felt that the essence of humanity lay in "the ensemble of social institutions."[14] It is unfortunate that the individual can be lost somewhere in the statistics taken on the language behavior of social classes.

As for the connections between ontogeny and thought, Vico was quite contemporary in perceiving that humans arrive at reason in maturity only after going through a stage of childhood, in which feelings and the imagination predominate.[15] Both children and primitive peoples are in a pre-rational stage. But this condition does not cut them off from perceiving truths. In Vico's interpretation, primitive societies (and children) perceive the truths of existence through their senses but do not go on to build rational concepts around their perceptions. As a result, both primi-

[12] W. Labov, "On the Use of the Present to Explain the Past," to appear in the *Proceedings of the Eleventh International Congress of Linguistics* (Bologna, 1973).

[13] *New Science*, § 138.

[14] *New Science*, Introduction, § J4.

[15] *New Science*, §§ 206, 211, 215, 218. Lev. Vygotsky, *Thought and Language* (Cambridge: M.I.T. Press, 1962) echoes Vico in arguing that speech is first learned by children for affective and social functions.

tive people and children are poetic in their use of language.[16] Advanced societies and adults, on the other hand, are philosophical in nature because they develop the intellect as a means to acquire understanding. Whatever the age of man or his culture may be, language must serve both poetic and scientific purposes.

Grammar has had such an impact on linguistics that whenever the linguist does study child language development, he concentrates on the rational, cognitive aspects of the child's expression.[17] Little, if anything, is ever done on how the child uses language to express emotion and on how new ideas grow through the use of metaphors from an imaginative base in child language.

If we think of language as being both an artifact and a tool of human expression, we can understand the far-reaching implications of Vico's ideas about language. As an artifact, language is like the other conceptual creations of man. It has a structure which can be broken down into constituent parts: nouns, verbs, phrases, clauses, sound units, idioms, and so on. There are specifiably limited ways in which these constituent parts can be put together in a given language which are subsumed under the traditional heading of syntax. When the linguist talks about the grammar of a language, he often means all of these things taken together. Chomsky has gone as far as to state that a grammar of a language is a theory of that language.[18]

At the same time, language is also a tool of man's creativity. Not only does man use language to build philosophical theories, economies, and political institutions, he also uses it to build more language. That is to say, the tool of language creation is language itself. When we talk about the creation of language through language we use the term "metaphor." In metaphor, old words and phrases are given new meanings by extending their uses to new frames of reference.

It was with great insight that Vico examined the metaphors of the *Iliad* and the *Odyssey* to discover that these two classics of Greek antiquity must have been written by different authors.[19] Although he did not articulate the tool/artifact distinction as such in language, Vico clearly understood that the way in which people *use* language depends, to a large extent, on the age of their civilization. Thus, the *Iliad* must have been written in a different age from that of the *Odyssey*.

According to Vico, human civilizations pass through a cycle of three ages. From an age of gods, in which man believes in the shaping of the world through supernatural forces, civilizations go through an age of

[16] *New Science*, § 209.

[17] See, for example, such recent studies as Carol Chomsky's *The Acquisition of Syntax in Children from 5 to 10* (Cambridge: M.I.T. Press, 1969).

[18] N. Chomsky, *Aspects of the Theory of Syntax* (Cambridge: M.I.T. Press, 1965), p. 24.

[19] *New Science*, bk. 3.

heroes, when superhuman men begin to replace the gods in shaping man's destiny. Finally, there comes the age of man himself. There are no more heroes or gods in the age of man. Man comes to see himself as he is—with his faults as well as his attributes. The understanding that the language in use in any age of man is reflective of that age led Vico to provide labels for the three types of language: sacred (or divine), symbolic, and epistolary.[20]

It is in the last of the three ages that prose style develops, with its use of metaphors which are greatly removed from their concrete references. Vico postulated that metaphors begin with body references or with human feelings and pass on to objects and occupations which are very close to mankind's physical senses. The metaphors then are extended to more abstract areas, such as science and civil institutions. Thus, one might say, in the first step of metaphorical extension from the body, "the *mouth* of the river" and "the *foot* of the mountain."[21] To illustrate the principle whereby abstract terms have basically human references as their roots, we need only consider the senses of *seminal, cultivate,* and *intercourse* in the following expressions: "a *seminal* idea," "*cultivate* one's friendship," and "engage in social *intercourse.*" Even the terminology of linguistics reflects the same kind of metaphorical extension: "generation," "nesting," "tree structure," and "sister node," to mention but a few commonly used expressions.

Wallace Chafe has recently proposed a theory which we can compare profitably with Vico's ideas about language.[22] Chafe believes that language arises from well-formed thoughts in the mind. He is therefore very much in keeping with the theory of the mind promoted by Descartes and applied to language by Chomsky. Unlike Chomsky, however, Chafe does recognize the existence of metaphors and idioms (the latter could also be termed "conventionalized metaphors"). In this respect, he approaches the views of Vico. Even more in keeping with Vico, Chafe recognizes that new meanings can sprout from old ones and lead to the formation of idioms.[23] For example, the expression "off base," taken from American baseball and having the general sense of *mistaken* or *wrong,* did not lose its original literal meaning (namely, that of "not standing on the base") but acquired an additional one. Chafe believes that the derivation of new meanings for existent expressions is by a "postsemantic process."[24] The process is post-semantic because existent expressions are assumed to have been assigned first a basic literal meaning. For Chafe, human language has evolved into

[20] *Ibid.,* § 432.

[21] *Ibid.,* §§ 237 and 240.

[22] W. Chafe, *Meaning and the Structure of Language* (Chicago: University of Chicago Press, 1970).

[23] *Ibid.,* p. 42. Compare Chafe's views with Vico's discussion of the various meanings of the Latin word *lex* in *New Science,* § 240.

[24] Chafe, *Meaning and Structure of Languages,* pp. 44–46ff.

its present form because humans became capable of conceiving many thoughts and were desirous of communicating them to other humans. A simple communicational system in which one, discrete symbol is associated with one concept or referent would not satisfy the needs of humans. Such a system would collapse under the strain of trying to keep up with the new thoughts engendered by its users. In adapting language to the needs of communication, humans tend to push their symbolizing processes further and further away from underlying semantic structures. That is why we have both literal and nonliteral meanings in language.

Unlike Vico, Chafe is not centrally interested in the ways in which new meanings for words arise. There are no cycles nor ages of man in Chafe's theory to motivate linguistic expression. What Chafe does, in essence, is to find the literal meanings of all expressions and then present the grammar of those literal meanings. Yet, even this is more than what Chomsky does. In Chomsky's standard theory (based on his 1965 book, *Aspects of the Theory of Syntax*), sentences have only literal meanings. If they have more than one literal meaning, they are termed ambiguous. The question of what is literal and what is metaphorical is not even broached. Chafe, to his definite credit, does make room in his theory for the presence of nonliteral expressions. But because idioms and metaphors do not belong in grammar, they must be explained by conversion into expressions which have literal senses and which can be subjected to grammatical systematicity.

The first major result of a Vichian attitude in linguistics would be to get rid of the notion of the well-formed ideas which are supposed to inhabit the human mind and lead to linguistic expression. In place of innate, well-formed ideas, Vico offered "imaginative class concepts"[25] which better reflect the ways in which the mind works from the outset. Vico offers the following illustration of how language shows the path from imagination and basic human feelings to reason and intellect:

Take for example the poetic phrase "the blood boils in my heart," based on a property natural, eternal, and common to all mankind. They [i.e., the peoples of the world] took the blood, the boiling, and the heart, and made of them a single word, as it were a genus, called in Greek *stomachos*, in Latin *ira*, and in Italian *collera*. . . . By means of these vulgar genera, both of words and letters, the minds of the people grew quicker and developed powers of abstraction, and the way was thus prepared for the coming of the philosophers, who formed intelligible genera.[26]

This paragraph is remarkable in many ways. More than documenting a true historical development, Vico is here reminding us of the basic metaphorical nature of even the most technical or abstract expressions. How else could the semantics of words like *anger* be discussed, if not in meta-

[25] *New Science*, § 209.
[26] *New Science*, § 460.

phorical terms? Even with recourse to sophisticated apparata to record bodily changes in instances of experiencing anger, the full meaning of the expression must include the appraisal of its psychological effects on people. Vico understood the function of language in accompanying the human mind to philosophical heights. Once these heights are reached, Vico reminds us, the mind readily ignores its dependence on the senses and its containment within the body.[27] Language remains as testimony to how the mind acquires reason.

It is not surprising that etymology would become, for Vico, a way to discover how both thoughts and institutions develop. Although his etymologies of specific words were often more imaginative than historically accurate, they do show the possible range of association of language to conceptualization and culture. For example, the derivation of *humanitas* from *humando* ("bury") enabled Vico to point out man's tendency to bury past events, then dig them up later and repeat them in cycles (*corsi* and *ricorsi* were Vico's terms). Vico's ideas about the imagination and the cycles of human history would reappear in various forms among psychologists, psychoanalysts, and historians of later times, and literary figures like James Joyce built much upon the inspiration drawn directly from Vico. An artful use of the Vichian cycle can be found in book 4 of Joyce's *Finnegans Wake*, which ends in the middle of a sentence to be completed only by returning to the first sentence of book 1.

Linguistics, unfortunately, came too late and too far away ideologically to be influenced directly by Vico. The eighteenth-century German thinker, Herder, a figure better known to linguists than Vico, shared some of Vico's ideas.[28] Both men saw language as reflecting different world views, and both recognized constant change as a vital linguistic feature. Herder, as well as Vico, believed that primitive man was poetic in nature. Yet, Herder had only indirect knowledge of Vico. Wells points out that Herder was probably acquainted with Vico's ideas through an Italian intermediary but never bothered to turn to the original writings.[29] One can only conjecture how linguistics would have developed if the nineteenth-century German philologists who were the forerunners of the linguists of this century had had some direct contact with Vico. To be sure, they would still have pursued etymological studies. However, the important link in the historicism of Vico which connects reason and logic with the imagination and the emotions was not forged in the development of linguistics. As a result, contemporary linguists have had to rediscover rationalism and the

[27] *New Science*, § 236.

[28] See, for example, H. Mueller, "On Re-reading von Humboldt," in *Report of the Seventeenth Annual Round Table on Languages and Linguistics*, ed. F. Dinneen, monograph no. 19 (Washington, D.C.: Georgetown University Press, 1966), pp. 97–107.

[29] G. Wells, "Vico and Herder" in *Giambattista Vico: An International Symposium*, pp. 93–102.

logical properties of language while rejecting all approaches which address themselves to emotional and affective expression. The keynote in contemporary linguistic methodology has been to find the elements of language which can be discretely measured. Establishing discreteness inevitably leads the linguist to be concerned primarily with language as a reflection of human cognitive powers. The result is the elaboration of grammars rather than the study of how man uses language as a tool of expression and communication.

Vico developed a philosophy of education in which the teaching of languages played a central role. As a professor on the faculty of the University of Naples, he advocated the study of foreign languages for young people. According to Vico, philosophy and logic should not be forced on young minds. He felt that the learning of languages was especially appropriate to young people because in youth the use of the imagination and the wish to associate with other people in social contacts are strong. Languages lead naturally to the play of the imagination and to interaction with others.[30] Forcing a conformity to the mathematical rigidity of logic too early in life might damage the imagination beyond repair. Vico observed that the women of his time remained more imaginative in later life than men because they were not educated so thoroughly—and therefore were spared the detrimental influence of a badly organized school curriculum!

Few took notice of Vico's educational theories, and fewer, still, of his views on language. Contemporary linguists, concerned as many of them are with the correlation of language to logic and mental concepts, have obscured the association of linguistics with language teaching. Chomsky himself, in 1966, told a large meeting of language teachers that he saw no way in which linguistics had anything to do with teaching languages.[31] The reasons for Chomsky's belief are now clear. How could linguistics have anything much to offer to the theory of language teaching if all it will do is address itself to formal grammars? The anthropologist Dell Hymes's remarks about this state of affairs have a definite Vichian flavor: "The dominant models of language in linguistics today bespeak a neutral, affectless use of language for information and report."[32]

Vico's ideas re-echo in Hymes, who goes on to state that language "must be studied in its social context, in terms of its organization to serve social ends."[33] Hymes argues in opposition to Chomsky that the study of language use is not an application of theory but is appropriate to the basic theory itself.

[30] M. Goretti, "Vico's Pedagogic Thought and that of Today" in *Giambattista Vico: An International Symposium*, pp. 553–75.

[31] N. Chomsky, "Linguistic Theory," in *Northeast Conference Reports of the Working Committees*, ed. R. Mead (Washington, D.C., 1966), pp. 43–49.

[32] D. Hymes, Introduction, *Functions of Language in the Classroom*, ed. C. Cazden, V. John, and D. Hymes (New York: Columbia University Press, 1972), p. xix.

[33] *Ibid.*, p. xviii.

It has been the purpose of this paper to direct the attention of linguists to the humanism shown by Vico in the study of man and his social institutions. Judging from what has transpired in the development of linguistics, due to its practitioners' attempts to make it a science, a touch of Vichian humanism would be very healthy at this point. Specifically, this humanism would inspire the linguist to (1) be not overly concerned with making linguistics correspond to the paradigm of a natural science, (2) realize that the detachment of a physicist or mathematician regarding the object of study is impossible for him, (3) incorporate the use of language into his theories of grammar, and (4) understand that linguistic creativity is more than grammatical, it is also metaphorical. All of these themes are discernible in Vico's writings, as I have attempted to demonstrate.

At present, the linguist likes to think of himself as a problem-solver. He judges the validity of his theories in terms of how many questions can be answered by them. A minimum criterion for new research in linguistics would be the recognition that it is language itself which the linguist uses to explain the linguistic phenomena he encounters. These phenomena are so deeply involved with the linguistic description of them that the linguist must take care to assure that they exist independently of the framework used to discuss them. An awareness of his own involvement with language is essential to the linguist, and Vico can help him find it.

Howard Gardner

VICO'S THEORIES OF KNOWLEDGE IN THE LIGHT OF CONTEMPORARY SOCIAL SCIENCE

I

That Giambattista Vico heralded a reorientation of scholarly inquiry and endorsed an alternative mode of education is clear from both the titles and the substance of his writings. While his clarion may not have been heeded immediately, the increasing recognition accorded his work testifies to its importance, at least in the view of subsequent scholars. Indeed, so rich a skein of ideas is contained in the Vichian corpus that there is an understandable tendency to marvel at the Neapolitan's prescience, to decry the void into which his works originally fell, and to dwell at sometimes excessive lengths on the links between Vico and latter-day philosophers, humanists, and social scientists. An unfortunate consequence is that the precise nature and value of Vico's contributions to scientific scholarship remain to be delineated. We are faced with a situation where Vico is universally honored as a progenitor, while the traits of his offspring are insufficiently considered.

In discussing the intellectual origins of a contemporary scientific theory, it is common to note its philosophical antecedents. Traces of Platonism, of Hegelianism, or of Humean empiricism are routinely discerned in such movements as Gestalt psychology, structuralism, or behavioristic social science. Yet, when such links are posited, the precise claims made by the earlier savants are generally not at issue; indebtedness is to a critique, a frame of reference, or a central concept. With a scholar like Vico, however, the case may be different. Vico not only claimed to discern weaknesses in contemporary scientific and pedagogical efforts; he also sought to propound the principles and the conclusions of a new branch of knowledge. Merely to discover hitherto unnoticed ties between Vico and this or that successor is to do him an injustice: should we not see where his science has gone, assess its progress, correlate more recent findings against his own claims, even reject his conclusions and principles if they are found wanting? The remainder of this essay may be regarded as the beginning of such an inquiry.

I am not concerned with the testing of specific insights or *aperçus* in

Vico's writings. Some are brilliant intuitions (for example: "When men are ignorant of the natural causes producing things, and cannot even explain them by analogy with similar things, they attribute their own nature to them");[1] others are totally unsupported and dubious at best ("The French language is abundantly endowed with words designating abstract ideas . . . this makes it impossible for the French to impart an ardently emotional tone to their ideas");[2] many contain an important scintilla of truth but must be supplemented by additions or modified by counter-examples ("The human mind is naturally impelled to take delight in uniformity";[3] "We observe children expressing nouns and particles but leaving the verbs to be understood").[4] Recent investigations in the social sciences can help sort out the more tenable from the less plausible of these assertions. What remain to be evaluated, however, are Vico's broader claims about the nature of his new science, its assumptions and principles, and its implications for pedagogy. Here we move from the realm of particular facts to the evaluation of an investigative program. In this essay I propose to examine both the substance and the approach of Vico's program, viewing each in the light of contemporary social science. Specifically, I will examine one substantive claim: Vico's assertion that there exist two fundamental ways of knowing. Then I will contrast Vico's methods and assumptions with those of the structuralist school, to which he has recently been linked by a number of commentators. In conclusion, I will take the liberty of suggesting how Vico himself might look upon the activities and theories of his intellectual successors in the social sciences. Before this critique of Vico's achievements, and his response to it, can be offered, however, I must briefly sketch the nature of Vico's program.

II

Though Vico's thought passed through discernible stages, emphases shifting with the period of writing and the audience addressed, certain central themes recur throughout his writings. Vico inveighed against the rationalist tradition, most particularly against those who came to regard the formulations of Descartes as the sole acceptable view of knowledge. Beyond mathematical laws, external to the study of natural or physical phenomena, inaccessible to deductive methods, was an enormous domain of human activity. Vico demanded investigations of human institutions, of law, custom, language, mythology, social structure, economics, politics,

1 *New Science*, § 180.

2 *On the Study Methods of Our Time*, trans. Elio Gianturco (Indianapolis, New York, Kansas City: Bobbs-Merrill, 1965), p. 39.

3 *New Science*, § 204.

4 *Ibid.*, § 453.

and other products of the activity of men and women. These areas were particularly susceptible to study because, as creations of the human mind, their principles would clearly emerge to any thoughtful individual. And yet, because of a natural tendency to turn outward, to project feelings and thoughts onto the physical world, scientists had long concentrated on the world of objects. They had unconscionably neglected the personal-social realm, which was actually much more susceptible to their understanding. Comprehension of these institutions would come about through a sensitive examination of their origins and their development; human imagination, personal experience, empathy, and searching examination of surviving texts and practices were all acceptable methods for the new science.

Applying these methods diligently, Vico concluded that human society, with its various institutions, had passed through three principal stages.[5] He was particularly intrigued by the contrast between the first phase, in which mankind was epitomized by poetic-artistic thought, and the final phase, in which civil society had evolved, and rational and mathematical-scientific thinking were highly articulated. In Vico's view the original poetic mode of thinking, in which metaphoric links between the individual and his surroundings were repeatedly realized, had given rise to two epistemological traditions: the sciences of the external world (physics, astronomy, and so on)[6] and the sciences of the human realm (morals, economics, law). As only the physical sciences had been heretofore explored, it became his mission to promulgate and outline the initial findings of a new "humanistic science."

This evolutionary course yielded deep implications for the society in which Vico lived. He deplored the increasing specialization, particularly within the sciences, the decline of poetic and artistic thought, and the neglect of those skills of rhetoric and eloquence which had flowered in classical times. Boldly he analogized the development of society with the evolution of the child. In the young child Vico found exemplified the same tendencies for discerning metaphoric links, expressing oneself poetically, relying on imaginative, mnemonic, and perceptual powers rather than on analytic, critical, and deductive skills. These youthful proclivities, critical for the full development of the child, needed gentle but persistent cultivation. Yet scholastic institutions at the start of the eighteenth century were emphasizing just those rational modes which were destined to undermine poetic thinking. Vico claimed that:

> at the very outset [children's] common sense should be strengthened so that they can grow in prudence and eloquence. Let their imagination and memory be fortified so that they may be effective in those arts in which fantasy and the mnemonic faculty are predominant. At a later stage let them learn

[5] *Ibid.*, § 31.
[6] See, for example, *New Science*, § 687.

criticism so that they can apply the fullness of their personal judgment to what they have been taught. . . . Were this done, young students, I think, would become exact in science, clever in practical matters, fluent in eloquence, imaginative in understanding poetry or painting, and strong in memorizing what they have learned in their legal studies. They would not feel the impulse to step rashly into discussions while they are still in the process of learning; nor would they, with pedestrian slavishness, refuse to accept any viewpoint unless it has been sanctioned by a teacher. In this sphere, the ancients seem to me to be superior to us.[7]

It is not possible to specify which Vichian notions were consequent upon his immersion in the lore of earlier societies, which came from a pondering of his era or reflected his own prejudices. Whatever their origins, however, Vico's conclusions were clearly propounded. A study of society reveals distinct modes of knowledge, which appear to be associated with the extent of development of the particular civilization (in the case of cultural history) or the particular individual (in the case of ontogenesis). Each of these modes of knowledge is critical, making its essential and unique contributions. Western society has increasingly emphasized the rational modes, both as an area to be studied and as a means by which to study; therefore, what is urgently needed is a reevaluation, a shift in balance, so that the poetic, intuitive, and humane aspects of society can be understood and so that these modes of knowledge can be preserved and applied where they are appropriate.

So globally phrased, Vico's claims may appear beyond evaluation. Indeed, had Vico simply pled the case of the arts, pointed up the differences between the primitive and the modern mind, or argued for a reordering of curriculum, he would merely appear as one calling for that change in emphasis which necessarily arises in the wake of any pervasive scholarly or pedagogic trend. I do not read Vico this way, however. He is claiming, as I see it, that there are fundamentally different ways of knowing and areas of knowledge, each of which must be separately examined if their complex interrelationship is to be appreciated and elucidated. It is on the basis of this claim that Vico wished to be taken seriously; and it is on this claim that subsequent scientific work may provide relevant insights.

III

Let us focus, therefore, on a claim central to Vico's argument: the necessity for fostering perceptual, rhetorical, and mnemonic skills in the young child and the desirability of postponing training in logic and deduction.[8] This program reflects Vico's belief that premature training in logical

[7] *On Study Methods*, p. 19.
[8] *Ibid.*, pp. 20ff.

scientific thinking would vitiate the child's natural proclivities toward poetic thought, thereby producing a one-sided, impoverished individual. Though there is little definitive knowledge on this issue, recent results of philosophical analysis and of empirical research in developmental psychology and in neuropsychology lend interesting support to the thrust of Vico's position; these results suggest that his strident rejection of the educational processes of his time reflected legitimate concerns.

Beginning with work on the nature of various culturally defined domains of knowledge, it has been demonstrated by a number of philosophers, and particularly by Nelson Goodman,[9] that the kinds of symbolic elements which figure in artistic products can be clearly differentiated from those involved in several of the sciences. Symbol systems employed in various art forms are characterized by the lack of clearly differentiated characters which can be unambiguously identified and which have clear one-to-one relations to the referents they denote. When confronting a painting, for example, one can make an infinite number of discriminations and classifications, many of which cut across one another; every detail and nuance contributes substantively to the work; there is no single "correct" construal of the semantic domain (the depicted elements) of the picture; it is not possible to devise a notation which captures the significant aspects of the work. This "dense" symbol system can be contrasted with an alphabetic or numerical system, in which the characters are clearly defined and segregated, no mark can belong to more than one character, and the denotations of the symbols are unambiguous and commonly agreed upon. Goodman's work demonstrates that the long-felt differences between artistic and nonartistic symbol systems can be formulated in a logically consistent manner; thus Vico's intuitive claims can now be stated in rigorous form.

While distinctions between "linguistic" (logical-scientific) and "nonlinguistic" (dense artistic) symbol systems make logical sense, it need not follow that they have psychological validity.[10] That is, it is possible that individuals might process diverse symbol systems in the same way, or bring different cognitive capacities to bear while operating upon the same symbol system. Compelling support for Goodman's position has come from a remote and rather surprising source: the study of brain function in normal and brain-damaged patients. A large number of studies now suggest that the two cerebral hemispheres, though grossly similar, mediate different psychological capacities.[11] Specifically, the left hemisphere, dominant in most individuals, seems to be especially prominent in the processing of

[9] *Languages of Art* (Indianapolis: Bobbs-Merrill, 1968).

[10] H. Gardner, V. Howard, and D. Perkins, "Symbol Systems: Philosophical, Psychological, and Educational Implications" in *Symbols and Media: The 73rd Yearbook of the National Society for the Study of Education*, ed. D. Olson (Chicago: University of Chicago Press, 1974).

[11] *Ibid.*

linguistic and language-like systems, whereas the right, or non-dominant hemisphere, seems more crucial for the processing of non-linguistic or "dense" symbolic elements. Thus an individual with injury in the left hemisphere will be unable to operate successfully with numerical and linguistic systems, while experiencing little or no difficulty in processing non-linguistic systems; indeed an aphasic can be a competent painter.[12] In striking contrast, the individual with right-hemisphere disease may succeed with linguistic, numerical, and other reasoning tasks, while exhibiting gross insensitivity to the fine details and nuances of a perceived display or of the social-emotional situation around him. It is worth noting that young children are not characterized by marked asymmetry between the two hemispheres;[13] therefore, the right hemisphere functions may be relatively more important during early childhood. As laterality develops, during the fourth through eighth years of life, linguistic functions come increasingly to the fore, perhaps at the expense of the ability to deal as centrally and successfully with dense symbol systems.

If Vico's pedagogical claims are to be critically considered, data on the development of children is most crucial. A number of studies I have conducted of children's sensitivity to dense symbol systems[14] suggest that, in the period just before adolescence, there may be a high point in the ability to discern and retain fine details of works of art; furthermore, this capacity may begin to decline at about the time of adolescence. In an effort to gain additional information on this hypothesis, I administered a large number of tasks to children of two age groups: pre-adolescents around the age of eleven and adolescents around the age of fourteen.[15] On the majority of tasks, both groups performed at an equivalent level; on a somewhat smaller number of tasks, there was improvement with age. Such improvement occurred particularly in tasks in which children were required to *operate* actively on stimulus materials, to transform them, to recode them into another symbol system or sensory modality. On the other hand, in tasks where keen memory for a stimulus, careful attention to detail, or ability to perceive many facts quickly was entailed, there was no difference among these subjects; indeed, when younger subjects were tested, little improvement was discernible from the age of seven onward. There was also a small group of tasks in which there was a decline with age. These tasks included ones in which an apparently unimportant event or element became the subject of questioning at a subsequent point, as well as others in which a compulsive attention to detail was essential. The capacities for

[12] T. Alajouanine, "Aphasia and Artistic Realization," *Brain* 71 (1948): 229–41.

[13] D. Kimura, "Functional asymmetry of the brain in dichotic listening," *Cortex* 3 (1967): 163–78.

[14] Cf. "Style Sensitivity in Children," *Human Development* 15 (1972): 325–38.

[15] "Figurative and Operative Modes of Cognition in the Arts: A Neuropsychological and Development Study," forthcoming in *Art and Cognition*, ed. D. Perkins and B. Leondar.

"incidental learning" of apparently unimportant elements[16] and for slavish attention to seemingly trivial aspects of a situation are prime candidates for processes which may decline with age. Of course, it is also widely recognized that the acquisition of entirely new skills, ranging from skiing to violin-playing to foreign language-learning, becomes progressively more difficult with age.[17] Whether cognitive, perceptual, motor, motivational, or economic factors make the most salient contribution to the increasing difficulty of these pursuits is not yet known.

When viewed in the light of other research[18] and of findings on neuroanatomical development,[19] my investigations have suggested the existence of two broad domains of tasks and skills. *Figurative* tasks, in which the ability to perceive and faithfully retain various elements is crucial, are mastered at a relatively early age by the child. These capacities seem to require intact primary and secondary cortical-sensory zones, which develop during infancy and which have a dominant role in the psychological processing by the young organism. *Operative* tasks, which include the ability to transform elements radically and to recode them in alternative sensory modalities and symbol systems, improve steadily at least through adolescence. These capacities depend upon the later-maturing "cross-modal" cortical association areas, in which inputs from different sensory modalities are combined; in these regions "amodal" aspects of spatial and temporal integration emerge. These association areas assume increasing importance in the cognitive life of the adult. While the child is impaired more severely by the destruction of primary or secondary sensory areas, which subserve figurative thought, the adult is more critically impaired when his cross-modal association areas are destroyed: he has come to depend on the logical operations which are subserved by these later maturing regions of the brain.

These considerations provide at least tentative support for Vico's claim that the young child has special proclivities in the realm of memory and perception and possesses aspects of a poetic or artistic character. In addition, they suggest that the older child is better equipped for and probably more favorably disposed toward manipulating logical and scientific symbolic materials. Vico's recommendations, therefore, are consistent with what is known about the normal course of development of the child.

However, a considerable leap is entailed in shifting from outlining normal development to implementing fundamental educational reform. Establishment of a normal developmental trajectory does not prove that

[16] H. Stevenson, *Children's Learning* (New York: Appleton-Century-Crofts, 1972).

[17] Cf. E. Lenneberg, *Biological Foundations of Language* (New York: Wiley, 1967).

[18] J. Piaget, "Piaget's Theory" in *Carmichael's Manual of Child Psychology*, ed. P. Mussen (New York: Wiley, 1970), vol. 1; see also H. Gardner, *The Arts and Human Development* (New York: Wiley, 1973), chaps. 5 and 6.

[19] A. R. Luria, *The Higher Cortical Functions in Man* (New York: Basic Books, 1966).

this trajectory is the optimal one (in other societies, different ones might be found; nature might not have evolved optimal ways). Furthermore it is as defensible on pedagogic grounds to combat dominant trends (the compensatory approach) as to reinforce them (playing to strength). Nor can it be assumed that a compensatory approach to education will undermine the natural tendencies; on the contrary, such an approach might well produce a better rounded, more versatile individual. Finally, such a legislative approach toward study methods underplays the vast individual differences among individuals. Some children are so highly figurative in their approach that they possess eidetic imagery[20] in the visual realm or equivalent facility in the auditory realm. Others are highly operative from an early age, mastering chess, mathematics, or even music at a time where other children are tone deaf, mathematically illiterate, content to parrot rhymes or learn the names of automobiles. Surely these enormous differences in early abilities reflect different hereditary proclivities and neuroanatomical organization; presumably such diverse children respond optimally to different pedagogical techniques.

Nonetheless information relevant to Vico's programs comes from two lines of research studies. First of all, some studies suggest that a concentration on operative or linguistic properties will result in a lessened sensitivity to the surface, non-linguistic properties of stimuli.[21] Second, recent findings reveal that activation of one of the cerebral hemispheres may facilitate activities mediated by that hemisphere, while impairing capacities subsumed under the opposite or rival hemisphere.[22] Surely it would be an extreme overstatement to maintain that the two approaches—figurative and operative—are irreconcilably opposed; yet information-processing limitations and the finitude of life combine to insure, in most adults, a bias toward operative, or (in fewer cases) toward figurative approaches. Exemplifying the prevalence of one-sided outcomes is the incomparable biologist Darwin, who recalled that:

> Up to the age of 30, or beyond it, poetry of many kinds such as the works of Milton, Gray, Byron, Wordsworth, Coleridge, and Shelley gave me great pleasure. . . . I have also said that formerly pictures gave me considerable, and music very great, delight. But now for many years I cannot endure to read a line of poetry. . . . I have also lost my taste for pictures and music. . . . My mind seems to have become a kind of machine for grinding general laws out of large collections of facts, but why this should have caused the atrophy of that

[20] R. N. Haber and R. B. Haber, "Eidetic Imagery: Frequency," *Perceptual and Motor Skills* 19 (1964): 131–38.

[21] Cf. L. C. Carmichael, H. P. Hogan, and A. Walter, "An Experimental Study of the Effect of Language on the Reproduction of Visually Perceived Form," *Journal of Experimental Psychology* 15 (1932): 73–86.

[22] M. Kinsbourne and J. Cook, "Generalized and Lateralized Effects of Concurrent Verbalization on a Unimanual Skill," *Quarterly Journal of Experimental Psychology* 23 (1971): 341–45.

part of the brain alone, on which the higher states depend, I cannot conceive. . . . A man with a mind more highly organized or better constituted than mine would not, I support, have thus suffered.[23]

It is worth comparing these remarks with Vico's conclusion that "By the very nature of poetry it is impossible for anyone to be at the same time a sublime poet and a sublime metaphysician, for metaphysics abstracts the mind from the senses and the poetic faculty must submerge the whole mind in the senses."[24] Yet Vico entertained the notion that the two major proclivities might yet find a common meeting-ground:

Young men should be taught the totality of science and arts, and their intellectual powers should be developed to the full . . . let their imagination and memory be fortified so that they may be effective in those arts in which fantasy and the mnemonic faculty are predominant. At a later stage let them learn criticism so that they can apply the fullness of their personal judgement to what they have been taught.[25]

IV

Vico called for the founding of a social science which devoted the same attention to human and cultural institutions as was directed by the natural scientists toward the physical world. He embraced adoption of an empathetic, intuitive manner for the study of these phenomena, with the expectation that their principal characteristics and developmental stages would thereby be revealed. His own studies suggested certain salient characteristics, and he marshaled evidence in support of his conclusions.

Nearly three centuries after the master commenced his labors, the founding of social and cultural sciences is no longer a dream. Indeed we suffer perhaps from a surfeit of social scientists—the perennial conflicts between behaviorists, psychoanalysts, structuralists, and functionalists testify to the vigor of this discipline, or at any rate to the vociferousness of its more voluble champions. Many scholars would agree with the thrust of Vico's conclusions, and a number of empirical findings and research traditions can be seen as generally consistent with his claims. And even when we examine a central Vichian tenet—the conflicting nature of scientific and humanistic ways of knowing—we find a basis for his claims.

Because of the breadth of Vico's interests, it is possible to find links between his writings and those of several contemporary social science movements. Yet, of late, it has been claimed that Vico possesses especial affinity with the structuralist movement, with the synthetic efforts of such

[23] C. Darwin, quoted in H. Read, *Education Through Art* (New York: Pantheon, 1945), p. 253.

[24] *New Science*, § 821.

[25] *On Study Methods*, p. 19.

social scientists as Jean Piaget, Noam Chomsky, and Claude Lévi-Strauss.[26] As in the case of Vico's assertions about particular phenomena, it is important to determine whether such a characterization captures merely superficial analogues or whether, in a more elemental sense, this structuralist movement has picked up and carried forward the banner raised by Vico several generations ago.

Any examination of structuralism uncovers disparate varieties, some inconsistent with one another. For example, Chomsky's epistemology entails innate ideas, while Piaget forthrightly attacks this notion. Similarly, Piaget probes the distinctive characteristics of discrete developmental levels, while Lévi-Strauss questions the existence of more "primitive" and more "developed" cognitive levels.[27] Over and above these significant divergences, however, certain broad themes characterize most contemporary structuralist writings: it is possible to assess the degree to which Vico's *oeuvre* conforms to these tenets.

Elsewhere I have described in some detail three cornerstones of structuralism: its formal, organismic, and strategic facets.[28] The *formal* portion of structuralism involves the building of logical models which isolate the basic elements in a domain of inquiry and explicate the possible transformations among them. The *organismic* aspect reflects a conviction that structures are not merely convenient fictions but rather an embodiment of the biological properties of organisms and, as such, are encountered universally. The *strategic* component alludes to the structuralist's customary mode of operation: focusing on unconscious, non-superficial aspects, emphasizing relations rather than elements per se, seeking an organized system governed by general laws.

My reading of Vico indicates that he would have little sympathy with the formal facet, which would necessitate the introduction of methods of physical science to a fundamentally alien domain.[29] Nor was Vico notably sensitive to the organismic (biological) properties of human thought, though he did share the current structuralist faith in mental configurations shared by all men. While less explicit about the methods he was employing, and unconcerned with "levels of analyses" or "relations among distinctive features," Vico did pursue the structuralist goals of a taxonomy of cultural systems and the explication of laws governing their organization.

Clearly it is overstatement to declare Vico the forefather of structuralism and, given his reservations about formal methods, he might himself have resented such an epithet. At most, Vico appears to have been a

[26] See, for example G. Steiner, "Through Seas of Thought, Alone," *The New Yorker*, 9 May 1970, pp. 154–63. Cf. also *Giambattista Vico: An International Symposium*, *passim*.

[27] H. Gardner, *The Quest for Mind: Piaget, Lévi-Strauss and the Structuralist Movement* (New York: Alfred A. Knopf, 1973).

[28] *Ibid.*, chap. 5.

[29] *On Study Methods*, pp. 23, 29, 34.

"brother under the skin" of selected contemporary structuralist thinkers, proceeding in his own way, on his own assumptions, toward the resolution of issues which were later to engage the structuralists. Vico's relation to structuralism can best be demarcated by a brief consideration of which elements he shared, and which he did not, with a few representative structuralist thinkers.

I find little in common between Vico's studies and the formal interest in the properties of syntax and phonology displayed by the linguist, Noam Chomsky. Though both share a conviction in the centrality of human language, Vico embraced an intuitive, impressionistic approach and was particularly interested in metaphor, while Chomsky has favored a systematic and formal model and has neglected, for the most part, the areas of meaning, poetry, and figurative language. Indeed Vico's nemesis, Descartes, has been designated as the spiritual forefather of Chomsky's approach to language.[30] Only in their averment of powerful commonalities among all tongues—linguistic universals, to use the current parlance—is there a significant convergence between these two thinkers.

It seems doubtful that Vico would have been comfortable with the thrust of Jean Piaget's inquiries. Like Chomsky, Piaget is bent upon producing formal models of cognitive processes; in recent years, he has spurned full, qualitative descriptions of children's behavior. Furthermore, Piaget has specifically disclaimed interest in the intuitive, imaginative, figurative ways of knowing of children[31] in order to concentrate on the very scientific-rationalist capacities from which Vico became alienated. Piaget has highlighted the difference between wisdom, the thoughtful philosophical conclusions of non-empirical scientists, and knowledge, the product of controlled investigations in the laboratory.[32] On Piaget's analysis, Vico would be engaged in *sagesse*, a form of inquiry which must inevitably be supplanted by the findings of experimental investigators.

Despite these differences, however, there are two vital threads common to the Vichian and Piagetian enterprises. The first is a steadfast conviction in the fundamental unity of all scientific inquiry, in the necessity for specifying links and arrangements among the sciences. Neither thinker was content merely to pay lip-service to this idea: both exemplified an interdisciplinary approach in their research. The other shared feature, a crucial one, is fealty to the developmental point of view. In opposition to those who forswear all qualitative differences, but also in contrast to those who feel development can process on any number of paths, both Vico and Piaget construe development as an inseparable part of existence, featuring definable stages through which organisms must pass in a specified order.

[30] N. Chomsky, *Cartesian Linguistics* (New York: Harper and Row, 1966).
[31] Gardner, *The Arts and Human Development*, Chaps. 1 and 7.
[32] J. Piaget, *Sagesse et illusion de la philosophie* (Paris: Presses Universitaires de France, 1965).

Piaget's interest has been primarily in the development of the individual, Vico's in the evolution of civilizations, but each man has been sensitive to the common features of all developmental processes, and neither has hesitated to draw analogies between individual and societal development. The common features of all men can be most compellingly discerned through adoption of a developmental perspective; this common "root metaphor" links Piaget and Vico.

We come finally to that contemporary savant with whom Vico shares the most fundamental ties. To be sure Vico would be uncomfortable with Claude Lévi-Strauss' formalism, and he might wonder at Lévi-Strauss' hesitation to invoke qualitative differences between the savage and the modern minds. Yet these differences would pale in comparison with the striking agreement on which domains of knowledge should be studied and how they can best be approached.

Products of men's minds—their laws, myths, religions, social practices—assume pivotal import in these investigators' explorations. Initially one may examine the myths of another era, or the social practices of a primitive tribe, because of their superficial bizarreness and their apparent remoteness from "civilized" society. The more one examines these practices, however, the more evident become the commonalities and even the fundamental underlying unity. The task of the scientist is to catalogue these different practices and then to show how they are related, in terms of what concepts they express, what units they employ, how they emerge in history. The parallels between these pursuits, separated by nearly three centuries, is well captured in the following quotations, the first from Vico, the second from Lévi-Strauss:

> There must be in the nature of human institutions a mental language common to all nations which uniformly grasps the substance of things feasible in human social life and expresses it with as many diverse modifications as these same things may have diverse aspects.[33]

> The ensemble of a people's customs has always its particular style; they form into systems. I am convinced that the number of these systems is not unlimited and that human societies, like individual human beings (at play, in their dreams, or in moments of delirium) never create absolutely; all they can do is to choose certain combinations from a repertory of ideas which it should be possible to reconstitute. From this one must make an inventory of all the customs which have been observed by oneself or others. . . . With all this one could eventually establish a sort of periodical chart of chemical elements analogous to that devised by Mendeleiev. In this, all customs, whether real or merely possible, would be grouped by families and all that would remain for us to do would be to recognize those which societies have, in point of fact, adopted.[34]

[33] *New Science*, § 161.
[34] C. Lévi-Strauss, *Tristes Tropiques* (New York: Atheneum, 1964), p. 160.

In addition to their attraction to the same kinds of phenomena—the details of diverse myth corpora, the burial and kinship practices of divergent societies—there is also a convergence in the methods utilized by the two men. Of necessity, in the case of Lévi-Strauss, and by choice, in the case of Vico, both men rely heavily on their own intuitive powers, on their empathy with the products of other minds, on the human capacity to discover, compare, organize, classify, and order. It must be noted that such an approach is increasingly out of favor in the social sciences. Though any thoughtful scientist naturally invokes his own hunches and examines his own responses in framing hypotheses and evaluating data, the testing of theories and hypotheses has increasingly become an interpersonal, communal affair, where results must be replicable. The Neapolitan or Parisian scholar, poring over ancient histories and ethnographies, is gradually withdrawing from the scientific chambers of the university; this pose is accepted only where absolutely necessary, for example, in the study of defunct societies; and the conclusions which can be drawn from *Verstehen* or *Einfühlung* are increasingly limited and suspect.

This review has brought out selected common features, rather than a fundamental identity, between Vico's enterprise and the efforts of contemporary structuralist thinkers. While partaking of the search for universals of Chomsky and the interdisciplinary and developmental perspectives of Piaget, Vico's disdain for formal methods and his interest in the less rationalist modes of cognition create a sizeable chasm between him and the mainstream of structuralist thought. The affinities in interest and method between Vico and Lévi-Strauss are more pervasive. Yet even here, Lévi-Strauss looks to formal methods, to agreement among observers, and to the "harder sciences" for the ultimate solutions to, or the most apt formulations of, the enigmas of the human mind.

V

Given the undeniable gap between Vico's new science and the movement which he is purported to have foreshadowed, the question arises: How would Vico survey the social sciences today? Vico envisaged a science which would focus particularly on the deep truths and which would be conducted and sustained by the profound commonalities between man as subject and man as object. Yet, as Neils Bohr once remarked, the purpose of science is to eliminate the deep truth. Looking at the majority of social scientists today, feeding punched cards into computers, testing null hypotheses, focusing on stimulus-response connections or on questionnaire responses, he might well reject the inappropriate, overly technical methods being embraced and the shallow questions being posed. He might also be dismayed by the lack of progress made in resolving the fundamental questions about human society which exercised him and by the spurning of the empathetic methods which he greatly valued. He might find many truths but little wisdom. As he became aware of the way in which data can be used and misused, in support of alternative and even conflicting theories, he might despair of providing conclusive support for his most cherished notions. He would come to see anew that "What is important?" is not a question which scientists are equipped to answer: he would realize that certain questions are inherently philosophical and that these determine how data are collected and analyzed rather than being resolved by "impartial" facts; and he would perhaps come to the reluctant conclusion that prognoses do not follow from diagnoses. Even equipped with new evidence of different ways of knowing, he would not be on much stronger ground in recommending new study methods; someone might always counter that an entirely different program of study was dictated by the data or that a meaningful test between two study programs is impossible, given the great number of variables which cannot be controlled in such a comparison.

Yet perhaps Vico would not completely despair. For if there was no proof for his claims about different ways of knowing, there is an increasingly impressive confluence of evidence from various disciplines in support of the divisions which he limned with such foresight. And, if social science has not yet found its Newton or Einstein, some medieval misconceptions about individuals and institutions have been cleared away. He might also take comfort in the fact that, even if in recent years social scientists have resisted the empathetic method, they are increasingly aware that their quantitative methods cannot provide conclusive evidence on questions of value or furnish impeccable recommendations or prognoses. Finally he might find solace in the realization that gifted social scientists of succeeding eras, in particular those of the structuralist persuasion, have continued working in those areas which his pioneering work almost single-handedly founded—the study of "simpler" societies, the developmental approach to cultural phenomena, the comparative study of economic and political systems, the examination of myths and texts—and that contemporary social scientists are coming increasingly to the conviction that there are fundamental invariants in human societies, human minds, and in the human condition.[35] Even if their resolutions and their resolve do not always coincide with that of Vico, these explorers are asking together with raised voices those questions which Vico first posed alone.

[35] Gardner, *The Quest for Mind*; see also N. Chomsky, *Language and Mind* (New York: Harcourt Brace, 1968).

George Mora

VICO, PIAGET, AND GENETIC EPISTEMOLOGY

Introduction

For two centuries Vico's prediction that his work would be either misunderstood or ignored has appeared to come true. Even those who made an attempt to grasp the meaning of his abstruse concepts could not help being influenced by their own bias, in turn, nationalistic, positivistic, and idealistic. The very disappearance of the humanistically oriented scientist, which has increasingly occurred, in connection with the overwhelming expansion and subdivision of sciences, has also hindered the comprehension of Vico's work, originally viewed in the humanistic context and now relevant to many fields of science. Thus, Vico's many facets tend to be the subject of thorough investigation by specialists in particular fields.

Yet, for all this change of perspective and fragmentation of approach, Vico's main theme, that of the progressive unfolding of reality (be this viewed in sociological or historical terms), has been universally accepted by all those interested in him. It is also true that many have accepted Vico's tenet, often stressed by him, that such an unfolding of reality through various stages can be compared to the development of the individual.

The rapid rise of psychology (including child psychology) in the past half-century should have created a situation favorable to the study of Vico in a psychological key. This did not happen, however, because most of the students of Vico, beginning with Croce, in line with their idealistic orientation, strongly objected to assigning psychology to the realm of sciences. Regardless of this epistemological issue, still controversial in the mind of some, the fact remains that many data regarding the development of the personality have been well established by modern psychology.

Under the influence of the British empirical tradition, in this country psychology has constantly aimed at achieving "hard" and "objective" data through a variety of methods (cross-sectional, experimental, and so on). In continental Europe, instead, in line with the Cartesian and Leibnizian tradition, psychology has remained affected by philosophical concepts, has relied a great deal on the personal intuition of the researcher, and has focused on the longitudinal dimension of the personality. Freud, himself, has come to represent the prototype of this kind of scientist: strongly affected by philosophical concepts *malgré lui,* he formulated a most comprehensive view of the human personality on the basis of intuitions reached from a thorough knowledge of a small number of patients.

Regardless of the criticism of Freud's methodology advanced by empirically oriented modern psychology, Freud's tenets have withstood the test of time and have become very much part of the Western culture. A similar but also dissimilar fate now appears to characterize Piaget's work, similar in the sense of methodology, inasmuch as he, like Freud, built his concepts from the thorough study of a few subjects, dissimilar in terms of the free and intellectually oriented dissemination of his notions, vis-à-vis the organizational and emotionally charged spread of psychoanalysis. Modestly initiated from the direct investigation of a few children (in contrast to Freud, who developed an entire system of child psychology from the analysis of adults), Piaget's research led him to the founding of an entire new field, that of genetic epistemology.

Vico and Piaget's Tenets

The rise of genetic epistemology leads directly back to Vico. As Piaget has put it in a succinct, comprehensive publication: "The focus of genetic epistemology is the attempt to identify the roots of the different varieties of knowledge from their most elementary forms and to follow their development through their succeeding stages up to their conceptualization in scientific terms."[1] As methodological postulates, Piaget stressed the lack of absolute beginning in the genesis of knowledge and the need for an interdisciplinary approach, by psychologists, historians of science, logicians, mathematicians, linguists, and so on, in the study of genetic epistemology.

On the surface it may appear that Vico's stance was quite alien from Piaget's: not only did he place his concepts in a humanistic, rather than scientific context, but he conceived of the human mind as an expression of God, and of human history as being led by divine providence. Yet, regardless of the humanistic (Cicero), philosophical (Plato), and theological (Christian tradition) emphasis, there is much in Vico's work which is relevant to genetic epistemology. Moreover, as with Piaget, many of Vico's themes presented in the *New Science* can be traced in other versions (that is, "genetically" speaking, in their formation and development) in preceding works, a fact often ignored by Vico's students.

Basic to Vico's philosophy is his conviction that the only approach to the study of phenomena, be those related to the individual, the nation, or

[1] J. Piaget, *L'épistémologie génétique* (Paris: Presses Universitaires de France, 1972), p. 6.

the species in its totality, is a developmental one. Indeed, in the *New Science* (1725 and 1744) he stated: "The nature of institutions is nothing but their coming into being (*nascimento*) at certain times and in certain guises" (§ 147).[2] Years before, in his *On the Most Ancient Wisdom of the Italians* (1710), he had already written: "Science consists of the knowledge of the development of things, that is of the way in which they come to be."[3]

Thus, the analogy between Vico's "humanistic" and Piaget's "scientific" study of man is certainly impressive. As H. Gardner has put it, the adoption of a developmental perspective is the common "root metaphor" linking Piaget and Vico.[4]

Vico and Piaget's Genetic Approaches to Human Psychology

CHARACTERISTICS OF THE MIND OF THE CHILD

Specifically in the field of genetic psychology, the similarities between Vico and Piaget's respective concepts are striking. In his most mature and comprehensive volume (written with B. Inhelder), *The Psychology of the Child*, Piaget has defined genetic psychology as "the study of the developmental processes that underline the mental functions investigated in general psychology (intelligence, perception, etc.). Genetic psychology tries to explain mental functions by their mode of formation: that is, by their development in the child."[5]

In this book, as in many previous publications, Piaget has described three periods between action and thought. In the first period, sensory-motor schemes develop; in the second, representations based on schemes of action internalized through semiotic relations, thought, and interpersonal connections take place; in the third, after the age of eleven or twelve, "nascent formal thought restructures the concrete operations by subordinating them to new structures";[6] that is, abstract reasoning evolves.

Now, in his famous Axiom XII of the *New Science*, Vico said: "Men at first feel without perceiving, then they perceive with a troubled and agitated spirit, finally they reflect with a clear mind" (§ 218). True, Vico based his threefold subdivision from data mainly gathered from history, be this of customs, laws, or of other institutions (as in Axioms LXV and LXVIII), rather than from experimental research. But the fact remains

[2] All citations in the text and in the footnotes preceded by a paragraph sign (§) are to the *New Science*.

[3] *De antiquissima Italorum sapientia, Opere* (Ricciardi), p. 249.

[4] See H. Gardner, "Vico's Theories of Knowledge in the Light of Contemporary Social Science" (in this volume).

[5] New York: Basic Books, 1969, p. viii.

[6] *Ibid.*, p. 152.

that, while all interested in building the foundations of the philosophy of history, Vico anticipated some basic tenets of genetic psychology.

1. *Egocentrism.* Piaget has defined as "infantile egocentrism" the stage roughly between the ages of two and eight, in which "the social exchanges characteristic of the preoperative level are precooperative, that is, at once social from the point of view of the subject and centered upon the child and his own activity from the point of view of the observer."[7] Vico expressed similar concepts in the following way: "Because of the indefinite nature of the human mind, whenever it is lost in ignorance man makes himself the measure of all things" (§§ 120, 181).

In the same volume Piaget said that for lack of consciousness of the self, "in the course of the first eighteen months . . . the child eventually comes to regard himself as an object among others in a universe that is made up of permanent objects."[8] In one of his axioms Vico said: "It is another property of the human mind that whenever men can form no idea of distant and unknown things, they judge them by what is familiar and at hand" (Axiom II, § 122).

2. *Animism.* In *The Child's Conception of the World* Piaget has convincingly demonstrated that there is a strict connection between egocentricity and animism: that is, a magic conception of reality based on the belief that all things, including inanimate ones, are endowed with the same movement, awareness, finality, and will of the animate beings. As to the concept of "animism" in children and in primitive people, Vico wrote: "It is characteristic of children to take inanimate things in their hands and talk to them in play as if they were living persons" (§ 186, as well as § 375 and § 379). "When men are ignorant of the natural causes producing things, and cannot even explain them by analogy with similar things, they attribute their own nature to them. The vulgar, for example, say that the magnet loves the iron" (§ 180), that is, "the nature of the human mind leads it to attribute its own nature to the effect" (§ 377).[9]

3. *Artificialism.* Artificialism is defined by Piaget as the belief that everything is made not only *for* man, but also *by* man.[10] In the *New Sci-*

[7] *Ibid.*, p. 118.

[8] *Ibid.*, p. 13.

[9] At times the similarities between Vico and Piaget are simply amazing. One of the answers a child gave Piaget to the question about the origin of the stars was: "People took little stones and made them into stars" (J. Piaget, *The Child's Conception of the World* [Totowa, N.J.: Littlefield, Adams & Co., 1969], p. 267). In Vico's *De constantia jurisprudentis* (1720–22), *Opere* 2: 372 one finds: "children think that stars are nails fixed in the sky . . . and that only a few yards separate the roofs of the houses from the sky." In the above-mentioned volume, Piaget stated: "For the youngest children (two to six years), the sky is situated somewhere near the height of the roofs or mountains."

[10] Thus, the idea that, for instance, the sun was not formed through a natural process, but through an act of direct intervention on the part of God, is founded (not unlike the psychoanalytic explanation) on the child's projection of the omnipotence of parents onto God. (Piaget, *The Child's Conception of the World*, p. 358.)

ence Vico said: "The nature of the human mind leads it to attribute its own nature to the effect . . . ; [the giants, that is, the early men, comparable to children] pictured the sky to themselves as a great animated body which in that aspect they called Jove, the first god" (§ 377). "And to all of the universe that came within their scope, and to all its parts, they gave the being of animate substance" (§ 379).[11]

4. *Imitation.* It is one of Piaget's tenets that the semiotic functions, that is, the relationships between verbal and other symbols and what they represent, are based on imitation, which is central to all stages of development of the child. In several of his works Vico stressed the importance of imitation for the development of the child.[12] In the *New Science* he expressed his thinking on this topic in a more general way: "Children excel in imitation: we observe that they generally amuse themselves by imitating whatever they are able to apprehend" (§ 215); "children have a powerful faculty for imitating the truth in matters within their capacity" (§ 1032).

5. *Imagination.* Disregarding the objections raised against the study of mental imagery on methodological (Würzburg school of introspection) and on critical (behavioristic school) grounds, Piaget has studied it extensively with various methods (verbal report, drawing, selection of drawings). He has found that children show first evidence of developing mental symbols, related to visual and other sensorial images rather than only to language, around the age of two. Around the age of seven or eight, which corresponds to the onset of the period of concrete operations, a major turning point occurs: mental imagery changes from static to kinetic and transformational, a change which contributes to the development of mature thinking.[13]

As early as 1699 (*First Oration*), Vico was very impressed by the power of fantasy (that is, imagination), which he defined as "the faculty of representing images of things."[14] Later on, he defined fantasy as "the faculty of unifying separate things and of correlating among themselves things proceeding from different sources."[15] In the *New Science* he said:

[11] Underlying Vico's inclination toward artificialism is the notion that "the human mind is naturally impelled to take delight in uniformity" (§ 204).

[12] Already in *De Italorum sapientia* (1710), *Opere* (Ricciardi), p. 300, Vico was impressed by the fact that "we see children doing things similar to those perceived by them, for instance 'build little houses, attach mice to a little carriage, play at odd and even, ride on top of a long stick' Horace, *Satyres*, II, 3, vv. 247–48)."

[13] J. Piaget, *Play, Dreams, and Imitation in Childhood* (New York: Norton, 1951), *passim*.

[14] As he put it: "This faculty either transforms, or connects or separates the images of things; it puts very distant things in front of the eyes, encloses things which are separated, manifests hidden things, opens a path through impervious places. It does all this with great and incredible speed! . . . It is almost impossible to explain the tremendous force, dexterity and rapidity with which the intellect compares or separates things with or from each other" (*Opere filosofiche*, p. 710).

[15] *De Italorum sapientia*, *Opere* (Ricciardi), p. 295.

"Imagination is more robust in proportion as reasoning power is weak" (§ 185). "In children memory is most vigorous, and imagination is therefore excessively vivid, for imagination is nothing but extended and compounded memory" (§ 211).[16]

THE CONSTRUCTION OF REALITY

In *The Child's Conception of the World,* Piaget has stated that "knowledge of oneself is the hardest of all knowledge,"[17] in the sense that the infant "does not distinguish his thought from that of others, not his self from the external world; in other words he is not aware of his self."[18] In the *New Science* Vico expressed the same concept in this way: "The human mind is naturally inclined by the senses to see itself externally in the body, and only with great difficulty does it come to understand itself by means of reflection" (§ 236). As an example of this, he referred to children who "looking in a mirror, try to seize their own reflection" (§ 688).

The analogies between Vico and Piaget, far from being limited to general aspects, concern specific points which have been proven by experimental investigation, in particular the development of the notions of number,[19] of sensorial functions,[20] of class,[21] and of movement.[22]

[16] Also, "Imagination, however, is nothing but the springing up again of reminiscences, and ingenuity and invention is nothing but the working over of what is remembered" (§ 699).

[17] Piaget, *The Child's Conception of the World,* p. 240.

[18] *Ibid.,* p. 152.

[19] In his studies on the development of the notion of numbers, Piaget has shown that between the ages of four and a half and five and a half children are able to count (that is, a number of bottles and an equal number of glasses) but the equality of numbers is determined solely by the equality of lengths and counting is an extraneous and irrelevant act. Only around the age of six is the child able to establish the equivalence between two sets of objects by the method of one-to-one correspondence. (J. Piaget and A. Szeminska, *The Child's Conception of Number* [New York: Norton, 1952], *passim.*) In one of his early lectures, as reported by Nicolini, Vico offered a good example of this way of reasoning, which literally anticipates Piaget's above concept: "In the early times, when a decision had to be taken concerning a matter on which opinions were divided, all the people were convoked, the facts were exposed and they were told that Smith was of this opinion, Jones of that opinion and someone else of a third opinion. Then, each of the company left his place to move either to Jones' side, or to Smith's side, or to someone else's side; finally the decision was given to the group which appeared most numerous. That happened because those primitive men were unable to say 'Jones has one hundred votes,' 'Smith fifty,' etc., in fact, it took at least two thousand years of civilization before a thing as abstract as numeration developed" (*Opere* [Ricciardi], p. 964).

[20] As part of his research on the notion of thought Piaget asked a child: "Can you give light? R. No . . . yes. How? R. With the eyes. Why? R. Because if you hadn't eyes you wouldn't see properly." Then he asked another child: "Do eyes give light or not? R. Yes, they give light. Do they give light at night? R. No. Why not? R. Because they are shut. When they are open do they give light? R. Yes. Do they give light like lamps? R. Yes, a little bit" (Piaget, *The Child's Conception of the World,* p. 40). In discussing the activities of the senses in the heroic times, Vico expressed a similar concept by stating that the ancients attributed sensorial functions to the organs of the senses.

ROLE OF LANGUAGE IN THE DEVELOPMENT OF THE CHILD

The role of language for the development of the child has become perhaps the key issue in terms of the vexing questions as to whether thought derives from language (tradition of empiricism), or language from thought (tradition of innateness of ideas). Linguists, mathematicians, logicians, psychologists, cyberneticists, structuralists, and others have often dealt with this problem in different ways.

Piaget, influenced by various philosophical and scientific trends in his youth, has continued to be concerned with this issue. Early in his experimental studies in children, he took the view that their intellectual development was strictly related to language and social factors, such as contact with parents and peers. In later years, as his orientation became more

(E. R. Dodds, *The Greeks and the Irrational* [Berkeley: University of California Press, 1951]; see also B. Snell, *The Discovery of the Mind* [Cambridge, Mass.: Harvard University Press, 1953]; B. Simon and H. Weiner, "Models of mind and mental illness in ancient Greece: I. The Homeric Model of the Mind," *Journal of the History of the Behavioral Sciences* 2 [1966]: 303–14). As for seeing, "seeing distinctly was called 'cernere oculis' (hence, perhaps, the Italian 'scenere') for the eyes are like a sieve and the pupils like two holes, and as from the sieve sticks of dust issue to touch the earth, so from the eyes, through the pupils, sticks of light issue to touch the objects which are distinctly seen" (§ 706).

[21] Piaget has experimentally proved that the child, at a concrete operational level, has a notion of class, that is, of the criteria subsumed in arranging objects in certain ways (by color, shape, and so on), particularly when concrete objects are involved. He sorts them by defining properties, understanding the relations between class and subclass, and knows some aspects of the logico-mathematical model, which he calls "grouping." However, at this stage, the child quite often shows unevenness in his response to various problems because he tends to center only on a limited amount of the information available. (J. Piaget, *The Early Growth of Logic in the Child* [New York: Harper & Row, 1964], *passim.*) This is very much in line with what Vico wrote in one of his early works: "Tell to a child, without adding anything more, to call someone, when two individuals by the same name are present. As in nature the inclination is toward the particular, the child will immediately ask: Which one of the two do you want?" (*De Italorum sapientia, Opere* [Ricciardi], p. 265).

[22] Some of Piaget's experiments have dealt with the child's ability to perceive movement by showing him a series of blocks arranged in particular situations and the various stages of a wire transformed from a semi-circle into a straight line. His conclusion is that at the pre-operational stage (age two to six or seven) the child is unable to imagine the final state accurately; moreover, he cannot give a correct rendering of the various stages of the process through which the blocks and the wire have gone. Rather, he tends to focus on one step at a time, mainly the initial and the final one, skipping the intermediate ones. (J. Piaget, *The Child's Conception of Movement and Speed* [New York: Basic Books, 1970], *passim.*) In describing the early stage of mankind which for him, as we know, parallels that of the child, Vico said: "Now, since the minds of the first men of the gentile world took things one at a time, being in this respect little better than the minds of beasts, for which each new sensation cancels the last one (which is the cause of their being unable to compare and reason discursively), therefore, their sentences must all have been formed in the singular by those who felt them" (*New Science*, § 703). Years before, in one of his lectures, he had already expressed a similar thought in a more biological fashion: "The reason why the minds of children are variable and change from moment to moment is that the fibers of their brains are mobile, so that any little thing makes an impression in their minds, which impression then is easily erased when they see another" (*Opere* [Ricciardi], p. 962).

philosophical, he de-emphasized the importance of language and of social factors and stressed action as the source of thought.[23]

As to Vico, it is certainly understandable and almost to be expected that as a professor of rhetoric (that is, the discipline dealing with the study of the elements used in literature and public speaking and with the art of oratory) for forty years, and as one rooted in the humanistic tradition, he would put a great deal of emphasis on language. In fact, toward the end of the *New Science*, with his typical incisive style, rather cryptically he stated that "speech stands as it were midway between mind and body" (§ 1045), an assertion which could lead to much discussion from more than one perspective.[24] Moreover, it is significant that for him the first type of language, in children as in primitive men, was based on body movements and actions.[25]

Traditionally, students of Vico have focused on his concept of a development from a mute to a poetic and, finally, verbal stage of language.[26] Concretely, it appears that such a threefold subdivision of language may have been emphasized by Vico in line with his almost obsessional tendency to view all expressions of reality as having gone through three stages: time (divine, heroic, human), authority (monastic, familiar, civic), government (theocratic, aristocratic, human), and so forth. In reality, his

[23] "This, in fact, is my hypothesis," he stated in a short overview of genetic epistemology, "that the roots of logical thought are not to be found in language alone, even though language coordinations are important. Rather, the roots of logic are to be found more generally in the coordination of actions, which are the basis of reflective abstraction" (J. Piaget, "Genetic Epistemology," *The Columbia Forum* 12 (1969); reprinted in R. I. Evans, *Jean Piaget: The Man and His Ideas* [New York: Dutton, 1973], p. xlvii). In fact, he has opposed the notion that logical mathematical structures are derived uniquely from linguistic form by proving that they exist before the appearance of language in the child younger than two and in deaf and dumb children and that they are independent from linguistic training.

[24] Vico's interest in language can be traced back to his *First Oration* of 1699, in which, after having hinted at the importance of word associations, he said textually: "Already at the age of two or three we memorize such an amount of ideas and words which exhaust the experience of everyday life, that a philologist interested in combining and ordering all this would have to write numerous big volumes" (*Opere filosofiche*, p. 714). Prophetically, more than two centuries had to elapse before Jean Piaget, that "philologist," would write, as in fact he did, the "big volumes."

[25] Taking as point of departure his above mentioned passage related to the inclination of the human mind to see itself externally in the body because of the difficulty in understanding itself by means of reflections (Axiom LXIII, § 236), Vico continues by saying: "This axiom gives us the universal principle of etymology in all languages; words are carried over from bodies and from the properties of bodies to signify the institutions of the mind and spirit" (§ 237). And later on: "It is noteworthy that in all languages the greater part of the expressions relating to inanimate things are formed by metaphor from the human body and its parts and from the human senses and passions" (§ 405).

[26] [The first] "was a mute language of signs and physical objects having natural relations to the ideas they wished to express (§ 32; see also § 431); [the second was a language] "spoken by means of heroic emblems, or similitudes, comparisons, images, metaphors, and natural descriptions" (§ 32; see also § 431); "[the third was] human language using words agreed upon by the people" (§ 32).

basic notion is centered on the opposition between concrete and abstract language.[27]

In line with the Aristotelian tradition, in his early treatise on education of 1709, Vico defined topics as "the middle term . . . the 'medium' . . . what the Latins call argumentum";[28] that is, topics are the commonplaces, the hypothetical or verisimilar postulates subsumed in any form of reasoning. The following year, in another writing he stated: "It is typical of children and barbarians to express themselves with universal words."[29]

Similar concepts void of their Aristotelian and philosophical flavor can be found in Piaget. In his dialogue with R. Evans, recently published, he accepted Evans's statement in regard to developmental stages:

> You are talking about universals, things that are characteristic of the cognitive structures of all human organisms, and you would probably say, in effect, that you could go to every single culture and you would find these same *universals* . . . . What you are really saying is that all societies have certain unique characteristics and all individuals in their cognitive development have universal characteristics.[30]

[27] "There is the property of the earliest peoples by which they are incapable of abstracting qualities from subjects and therefore can only designate the qualities by naming the subjects to which they belong" (§ 768). Vico called *diversiloquia* the principle by which a concrete example signifies an abstract concept, "as Achilles connotes an idea of valor common to all strong men, or Ulysses an idea of prudence common to all wise men" (§ 403, and also §§ 210 and 809), or as the expression *vera manu*, that is, "with the actual hand," means "with real force, since force is abstract and hand is concrete" (§ 1027).

[28] *On the Study Methods of Our Time*, trans. E. Gianturco (Indianapolis, New York, Kansas City: Bobbs-Merrill, 1965), p. 15.

[29] *De Italorum sapientia, Opere* (Ricciardi), p. 264. In the *New Science* he said: "The first men, the children as it were, of the human race, not being able to form intelligible class concepts of things, had a natural need to create poetic characters; that is, imaginative class concepts or universals, to which, as to certain models or ideal portraits, to reduce all the particular species which resemble them" (§ 209). Later on, in discussing the three succeeding characters, that is, forms of writing—divine (hieroglyphics), heroic, and vulgar—he mentioned that the "heroic characters . . . were also imaginative universals. . . . These imaginative universals, as the human mind later learned to abstract forms and properties from subjects, passed over into intelligible genera" (§ 934). In simple words, these topics or imaginative universals appear to be a halfway stage making possible the transition from concrete to abstract thinking. Vico refers to the "topics" or "imaginative universals" several times in his works. "Common sense arises from perception based on verisimilitude" (*On Study Methods*, p. 13); "common sense is judgment without reflection, shared by an entire class, an entire people, an entire nation, or the entire human race" (§ 142); "uniform ideas originating among people unknown to each other must have a common ground of truth" (§ 144); "the order of human ideas is to observe the similarities of things first to express oneself and later for purposes of proof. Proof, in turn, is first by example for which a single likeness suffices, and finally by induction for which more are required" (§ 424); finally, "imaginative genera, as the human mind later learned to abstract forms and properties from subjects, passed over into intelligible genera, which prepared the way for the philosophers" (§ 934).

[30] Evans, *Jean Piaget*, pp. 71–72 (italics mine).

Perhaps the most important of these "universals" is the "scheme," defined by Piaget as "what there is in common among several different and analogous actions" or as "practical, i.e., prelinguistic concepts."[31]

Typically, the new mathematics, based on general and abstract structures elicited in the child through concrete manipulations, either physical or verbal, proves beyond dispute the existence of those "imaginative class concepts or universals" through which each individual builds his own reality. For the past twenty years or so, in his numerous publications, Piaget has stressed that mental operations are not dependent on language; rather, they precede and facilitate language. Mutual operations are essentially based on the notion of structure, which, for him, "is comprised of three key ideas: the idea of wholeness, the idea of transformation, and the idea of self-regulation."[32]

In the light of all this, it was logical to expect that Piaget's concepts would be viewed from the structuralistic perspective.[33] Piaget has not been happy with the characterization of his thinking as structuralist for various reasons: the atemporal aspect of structuralism in contrast to his developmental perspective;[34] Lévi-Strauss' colorful and metaphoric way of proceeding, which is at variance with his rationalistic approach; and, finally, the preeminence attributed to language by structuralists, whether this be Jakobson or Chomsky, which is at variance with his emphasis on logic.

[31] *Ibid.*, p. 18. As theoretically, in contrast to the historical development of geometry, topology constitutes a general foundation for projective geometry and Euclidean metric geometry, Piaget concludes that "the line of development from the preoperative intuitions through the spatial operations in the child is much closer to the theoretical order than to the historical genealogy" (Piaget and Inhelder, *The Psychology of the Child*, p. 107).

[32] J. Piaget, *Structuralism* (New York: Basic Books, 1970), p. 5. In contrast to the Kantian tradition, "there are no innate structures in the human mind which simply come into being . . . all our mental structures must be constructed" (Evans, *Jean Piaget*, p. 32). Also: "Observation and experiment show as clearly as can be that logical structures *are* constructed and that it takes a good dozen years before they are fully elaborated; further, that this construction is governed by special laws. . . . There are certain given [that is, universals] from which the construction of logical structures takes off, but these 'data' are not primordial in any absolute sense" (Piaget, *Structuralism*, p. 62). In *The Psychology of the Child*, Piaget and Inhelder have stated that "a structuration is always present and stems from action or from operations" (p. 44). The subject is active even in the mechanism of perception (Piaget, *Structuralism*, p. 59). Piaget has claimed that "the major point which has been badly understood is the idea of construction" (Evans, *Jean Piaget*, p. 39).

[33] Indeed, the main theme of the recent book by H. Gardner, *The Quest for Mind: Piaget, Lévi-Strauss and the Structuralist Movement* (New York: Alfred A. Knopf, 1973), centers on the many similarities between Piaget and Lévi-Strauss—the same French intellectual tradition, methodology, theoretical derivation from Gestalt and psychoanalysis, and emphasis on equilibrium in the organism or in the culture. This justifies the assertion that they complement each other, regardless of their differences—difference in personality between the "rational" Piaget and the "intuitive" Lévi-Strauss, emphasis by Piaget on action and by Lévi-Strauss on language, a broad definition of language by Lévi-Strauss, as opposed to a strict definition by Piaget.

[34] M. Lane, ed., *Introduction to Structuralism* (New York: Basic Books, 1970), p. 17.

Nonetheless, some points of convergence between Piaget's system and structuralism are undeniable, especially in view of the antithesis between action and language. Here is where Vico comes into the picture, inasmuch as he relied both on action and language. His philosophy is essentially pragmatic, that is, a philosophy of action, but his method of acquisition of reality is mainly based on language. In fact, directly anticipating the tenets of modern epistemology, especially of the logical positivistic school, he stated: "By means of these vulgar genera, both of words and letters, the minds of the peoples grew quicker and developed powers of abstractions" (§ 460). In simple words, language is essential for abstract thinking.[35] It is no wonder then that several points of confluence between Vico and Lévi-Strauss have been brought forward.

Relevance of Vico and Piaget's Genetic Concepts for Education

Ten years ago, on the occasion of a symposium on cognitive studies and curriculum development, Piaget said:

> The principal goal of education is to create men who are capable of doing new things, not simply of repeating what other generations have done—men who are creative, inventive and discoverers. The second goal of education is to form minds which can be critical, can verify and not accept everything they are offered. The great danger today is of slogans, collective opinions, ready-made trends of thoughts. We have to be able to resist individually, to criticize, to distinguish between what is proven and what is not. So we need pupils who are active, who learn early to find out by themselves, partly by their own spontaneous activity and partly through material we set forth for them; who learn early to tell what is verifiable and what is simply the first idea to come to them.[36]

It is undeniable that from his experimental study of children Piaget has drawn conclusions which may have a far-reaching impact on education. Three main points frequently presented by him are particularly relevant for education: (1) the importance of definite stages of development; (2) the role attributed to the child's inner activity in construing his reality; (3) the recognition of an intrinsic structure of each intellectual operation as reflected in the child's action and thought.[37]

[35] This is a theme which has some connection with M. Foucault's recent book, *The Order of Things* (New York: Pantheon, 1970).

[36] R. Ripple and V. Rockcastle, eds., *Piaget Rediscovered: A Report on Cognitive Studies and Curriculum Development* (Ithaca: Cornell University, School of Education, 1964), p. 5.

[37] In regard to the first point, Piaget has emphasized the three main stages of mental growth mentioned earlier: the sensory-motor stage, the stage of concrete operations, and the stage of formal operations. As for the second point, Piaget has repeatedly emphasized the role of action in the acquisition of knowledge. Recently, in his dialogue

All this is very relevant to education on several grounds. It is true that "progressive" education carried on under various philosophies has emphasized for a long time action and spontaneity in the child, in contrast to the formality of traditional teaching. It is sufficient to mention here Dewey's definition of education as a "philosophy of experience."[38] But Piaget's main contribution lies in his emphasis on action in education based on solid experimental data rather than on a philosophical penchant. For instance, his psychogenetic method has made it possible to reach a much needed clarification of the notion of causality—so crucial for education—far from the two extremes of innateness (Kant) and empiricism (Hume).[39]

In practice, Piaget's ideas have slowly begun to influence educational practices in various ways. Of course, critics of Piaget's educational concepts have not been lacking. Some have been impressed by Piaget's "pessimism," related to the apparent rigidity and limitations of teaching children according to their developmental level, a stance opposed to the tendency of many in this country to teach a child anything at any level of development.[40] Other critics of Piaget have, of course, focused on his almost exclusive interest in cognitive processes and his unconcern for emotional factors.[41]

Turning now to Vico, his observations on child development and on education are scattered throughout his work, so that it is difficult to present them in a comprehensive way. This shortcoming is compensated,

---

with R. Evans, he said: "To me the essential aspect of thought is its operative aspect; I think that human knowledge is essentially active" (Evans, *Jean Piaget*, p. xliv). In Piaget's study of children, as Evans puts it, "One experimenter (the psychologist) arranges for the opportunities for the other experimenter (the child) to carry on his or her experiments" (*ibid.*, p. 68). Finally, in regard to structure, as Piaget and Inhelder put it, "a structuration is always present and stems from action or from operations" (*The Psychology of the Child*, p. 44).

[38] J. Dewey, *Democracy and Education* (New York: Macmillian, 1916).

[39] As Gardner put it: "One's own knowledge of states of reality comes about through transforming them; thus, the very action which constitutes thought leads ultimately to knowledge of thought. To understand a state, you must understand the transformation from which it results; to understand a structure, you must focus on its genesis and its development" (*The Quest for Mind*, p. 97).

[40] According to Kohlberg, "Basically the Piaget approach does not generate great optimism as to the possibility of preschool acceleration of cognitive development (or of compensation for its retardation) nor does it lead to a rationale in which such acceleration (or compensation) is especially critical during the preschool years" (L. Kohlberg, "Early education: a cognitive-development view," *Child Development* 39 [1968]: 1056). Yet, like others, in this same thorough study. Kohlberg has come to accept the validity of Piaget's tenets for education.

[41] In defense of Piaget, it is a fact that the main trend of ego-psychology in psychoanalysis is naturally conducive to the study of cognitive factors, a movement which may slowly lead to an integration of the psychoanalytic and the psychogenetic methods as Piaget, himself, recently indicated (J. Piaget, "Affective Unconscious and Cognitive Unconscious," in his *The Child and Reality, Problems of Genetic Psychology* [New York: Grossman, 1973], pp. 31–48).

however, by the fact that the main themes can be followed from one work to another, quite often in an increasingly refined way.[42]

Unquestionably, Vico was aware of developmental stages in human life.[43] He also believed that there was a correspondence between the development of the cultures and the increasing sophistication of the art of reasoning. As a contemporary critic put it: "Vico believes in the existence of a *psychogenetic law*, by which the individual develops through a certain series of phases, the sequential order of which is immutably fixed by nature. These stages parallel an equally immutable set of 'culture stages' which the whole of mankind has traversed in its growth from infancy to adulthood, from primitivism to civilization."[44]

In *On the Study Methods of Our Time* (1709), his only exclusively educational treatise (written to counteract the supposed dangers of Descartes' rationalistic emphasis in education), Vico's main thesis is that "since young people are to be educated in common sense, we should be careful to avoid that the growth of common sense be stifled in them by a habit of advanced speculative criticism."[45] The following year he said:

Geometry should be taught not analytically, but synthetically, so as to arrive at the demonstration by combining; which means *to create the truth instead of*

[42] His concern for education was already evident in his *First Oration* of 1699, an inspired hymn to the tremendous potentialities of the young man in his search for knowledge. It also represented the motif of his *Autobiography*, written in 1725. Indeed, this volume "will serve as a norm for anyone who, by imitating Signor Vico's generosity and his manner of laying before the public the detail of his studies, will lend a hand to the completion of this useful enterprise" (*Autobiography* p. 6). So wrote Count Gian Artico di Porcia in his "A Proposal to the Scholars of Italy," an attempt to obtain autobiographies from learned men for the edification of young students. Not only was Vico's autobiography considered excellent by Porcia, but in recent times it has been viewed by Croce as "the application of the *New Science* to the life of its author" (B. Croce, *The Philosophy of Giambattista Vico*, trans. R. G. Collingwood, [New York: Macmillan, 1913], p. 266).

[43] In his *Second Orations* of 1700 he said that "children desire perfumes, flowers, food . . . ; young men desire glory . . . ; mature men desire wealth . . . ; old men desire long life" (*Opere filosofiche*, p. 726). Later on, at the end of the *De uno principio*, he wrote: "Children choose everything arbitrarily and aim impetuously to possess what they have chosen; adolescents are dominated by a very lively imagination, while mature men judge each thing according to pure reason, and old people with a prudence full of gravity" (*De uno principio, Opere* 2: 256). Moreover, he believed that the natural course of the development of children's minds was that "they should first apprehend, then judge, and finally reason" (*Autobiography*, p. 124).

[44] E. Gianturco, Introduction, *On Study Methods*, p. xxvii. In the *New Science* (§ 499) he said that in succession, reasoning was expressed through senses (early times), moral philosophy (Aesop), dialectic (Socrates), inductive or synthetic methods (Plato), syllogism (Aristotle), and finally sorites (Zeno). Now Piaget has found that there is a correspondence between the three stages of mathematical thought throughout history and throughout the development of the child: the first period of Euclidian geometry corresponds to preoperational thought in the child; the second period of analytic geometry (seventeenth century) to concrete operational thought; the third period of sets with structures (late nineteenth century) to formal operational thought. (J. Piaget, B. Inhelder, and A. Szeminska, *The Child's Conception of Geometry* [New York: Basic Books, 1960], *passim*.)

[45] *On Study Methods*, p. 13.

finding it. To find, is work of chance, to create, of industriousness; for this reason I have asked that geometry be taught *not with the help of numbers and genders, but of forms*; so that, in learning it, the fantasy, which is the core of talent, rather than talent itself, be strengthened [italics mine].[46]

Central to Vico's thinking, as is known, is his conviction that the true (*verum*) and the made (*factum*) are convertible; that is, we can know for certain only that which we ourselves have made or created. This means that we can know with certainty only history, which is made by man, but not our own minds because the mind does not make itself. This does not mean, however, that the mind apprehends reality in a passive way.[47] At a close scrutiny, it is evident that Vico and Piaget expressed similar views in regard to children's notion of truth,[48] learning of writing,[49] and acquisition of morality.[50]

[46] *De Italorum sapientia, Opere* (Ricciardi), p. 303. Later on, in the *Autobiography*, he wrote: "If in the age of perception, which is youth, the [young men] would devote themselves to topics, the art of discovery that is the special privilege of the perceptive, they would then be furnished with matter in order later to form a sound opinion on it" (p. 124).

[47] In the *De Italorum sapientia* he said: "We are the ones who, seeing, make the color of things; tasting, the savors; listening, the sounds; touching, the heat and the cold" (*Opere* [Ricciardi], p. 292). Elsewhere, he stated that science consists of the knowledge of the genesis of things, that is, of "the way in which they come to be" and, through it, the mind "properly arranges the elements of the known thing, and, at the same time, makes the thing" (*Ibid.*, p. 249). Man "has created a world of figures and numbers which contains everything unto itself; and, by prolonging, shortening, and shaping the lines in various ways, or by adding, subtracting, and computing the numbers in various ways, is able to give life endlessly to creations" (*ibid.*, p. 253).

[48] For Vico, regardless of their developmental stage, children are always truthful: "Since the first men of the gentile world had the simplicity of children, who are truthful by nature, the first fables could not feign anything false" (§ 408). In the same paragraph he stated that "irony certainly could not have begun until the period of reflection, because it is fashioned by falsehood by dint of a reflection which wears the mask of truth." This is exactly what Piaget says: that children are always sincere in their approach to reality and that the different interpretations that they offer of reality during their development is related to their different operational levels. Naturally, irony can occur only at adolescence, at the level of formal thought, when "the subject becomes capable of reasoning correctly about propositions he does not believe, or at least not yet; that is, propositions that he considers pure hypothesis" (Piaget and Inhelder, *The Psychology of the Child*, p. 132).

[49] Vico elaborated a great deal on various characteristics of language in children, which may be relevant to psycholinguistics but not to Piaget's work proper. However, of relevance for this latter, he said that "in forming a speech, children use a certain *geometrical synthesis* [italics mine], with which they run through all the elements of language, gather those which they need and then combine them into a unity" (*Scienza nuova prima, Opere* (Mondadori) 1: 784). Writing, itself, derives from geometry (*De constantia jurisprudentis, Opere* 2: 386), a notion very much in line with Piaget's suggestion of first presenting objects to the children, then letting them manipulate and reproduce them as the best way of forming a concept of them.

[50] In regard to morality, "men were for a long period incapable of truth and of reason, which is the fount of that inner justice by which the intellect is satisfied . . . the nations were governed by a certainty of authority . . . that is a philosophy of authority, which is the fount of the *outer justice*" (§ 350; italics mine). This "outer justice" is what Piaget in his *The Moral Judgment of the Child* has called "heteron-

Vico continuously emphasized that teaching should be based on synthesis rather than on analysis. It is impossible to thoroughly know physics because we do not "make" it; on the contrary, geometrical propositions can be demonstrated because they are made by men. Consequently, it is important "to guide youngsters in mathematics not through 'species,' as they are called, but through 'forms,' that is, not through algebraic symbols but through geometrical forms."[51] This is one way to help the child "not to find the truth but to make it."[52] All this is quite close to some of the main tenets of contemporary education which have resulted from Piaget's investigations.[53]

Methodological Considerations

Piaget has employed a variety of methods in his research on children.[54] His methodology has been criticized inasmuch as it defies the application of statistical methods, while it relies on the observation and judgment of one person (particularly questionable when the researcher is the father of the subjects), and, in general, does not comply with a number of requirements accepted by many involved in research in the behavioral sciences. On the positive side, however, several points are in favor of Piaget's methodology: the advantage of longitudinal studies of a few well-known children, the high level of consistency reached by the same researcher, the generally similar results obtained by independent investigators repeating similar studies.

The criticism of Piaget's methodology, which may have accounted for

omy," that is the affective reactions and peculiarities of the morality of the child before the age of seven or eight, which is strictly dependent upon the presence of the person who gives orders and which, later on, will develop into the "autonomy" of the sense of justice. (J. Piaget, *The Moral Judgment of the Child* [New York: Harcourt, Brace & World, 1932], *passim*.)

[51] *On Study Methods*. pp. 23 and 30.

[52] *De Italorum sapientia, Opere* (Ricciardi), p. 303.

[53] For Vico education had to be based on several principles: flexibility of approach; preeminence given to language and eloquence; gradual progression in teaching from language to history, physics and metaphysics; concern for the unity of knowledge and, thus, disregard for specialization; and acceptance of emotions, and even of irrational expressions, in the child. It was his contention that education, far above learning, should aim at the moral growth of the child, so as to achieve wisdom rather than knowledge. Indeed, he, himself, considered his chair of rhetoric as a guide toward universal principles which should precede specialized teaching. (*Autobiography*, p. 199.) In this he revealed his essential humanistic background and ideals, quite apart from the scientific tradition of our time, with which Piaget is embued.

[54] He has dealt with a relatively small number of children, of which he gives no family nor developmental history. In his investigation of infant behavior he has mainly observed his own three children in their natural environment and has recorded their reactions and behavior in particular circumstances. For older children, he has applied what he called the "clinical method," consisting of eliciting verbal or non-verbal responses from children (through manipulation of objects, drawings, and so on) to questions and issues arising in the most neutral way, so as to avoid possible influence by the researcher.

the relative neglect into which his work fell for almost a decade and a half, up to the mid-nineteen-fifties, has largely subsided. After all, it is well to remember that Freud built his entire psychological system with the data subjectively obtained by the long-term study of a few cases. Both Piaget and Freud relied heavily on intuition, which is the source of creativity.

This is no different from Vico, who, endowed with an exceptional power of intuition, made use of such bold analogies and comparisons among different phenomena from the fields of history, mythology, religion, law, and science as to almost disorient today's reader.[55] The question now arises: How did Vico obtain the insight which made it possible for him to anticipate so many of the tenets of Piaget's genetic epistemology?

To be sure, Vico did not experiment with children in the way Piaget did. The fact that his pioneering psychogenetic observations are scattered throughout all his works almost as incidental remarks would indicate that he did not give too much importance to them in terms of the development of the child; rather, they represented for him additional evidence for his thesis of the philosophy of history.

He openly made reference to the methodological difficulties related to his philosophical inquiry.[56] For instance, in discussing the three words "people," "king," and "liberty," (§ 666), he took issue with the tendency of philologists to apply to early times notions related to later times. In other words, aware of the shortcomings of seeing past events in the light of the present perspective, which today is called "presentism"[57] or "inductionism,"[58] he constantly made an effort in his work to uncover the interwoven and, quite often, obscure pattern connecting all expressions of human life—language, art, polity, and religion—in the same historical period.

It is likely that, on the basis of the above, he was also aware of the

[55] He, himself, said that *ingenium* (that is, talent, genius) "is the faculty of combining separate things and of relating among themselves things from different fields" (*De Italorum sapientia, Opere* [Ricciardi], p. 295) and that "those are keen who are able to find a relationship of similarity in things very apart and different, and, disregarding incidental things, succeed in obtaining from distant points arguments appropriate to the things they deal with" (*ibid.*, p. 301).

[56] "To discover the way in which this first human thinking arose in the gentile world, we encountered exasperating difficulties which have cost us the research of a good twenty years. We had to descend from these human and refined natures of ours to those quite wild and savage natures, which we cannot at all imagine and can comprehend only with great effort" (§ 338). "It is equally beyond our power to enter into the vast imagination of those first men, whose minds were not in the least abstract, refined, or spiritualized, because they were entirely immersed in the senses, buffeted by the passions, buried in the body" (§ 378).

[57] G. W. Stocking, "On the limits of 'presentism' and 'historicism' in the historiography of the behavioral sciences," *Journal of the History of the Behavioral Sciences* 1 (1965): 211–18.

[58] J. Agassi, "Towards an Historiography of Science," *History and Theory*, Beiheft 2 (The Hague: Mouton, 1963).

methodological difficulties encountered by adults in the study of children, though he did not specifically mention them. But the point remains: How did he get the tremendous insight in regard to the psychogenetic development of the mind? The answer to this question is not easy, but at least two possibilities can be entertained.

For one thing, some scattered remarks in his works suggest that he was a very deep observer of himself.[59] The second point is that Vico lived most of his life surrounded by children.[60] Although he said very little of his direct contact with children, we can assume by inference that, being such a keen observer of all kinds of phenomena, he must have been impressed by many manifestations of the child's mind. It is also likely that he was somewhat influenced in his educational ideas by the classical (Xenophon, Plato, Aristotle, Quintilian), Christian (St. Augustin), Renaissance (Erasmus, Vives, Rabelais, Montaigne), and seventeenth-century (Fenelon) pedagogical traditions. He knew of the philosophical works of Locke, though it is unlikely that he was familiar with his book, *Some Thoughts Concerning Education*, published in 1693.

Regardless of this, Vico's approach to education was humanistic and traditional, at variance with Piaget's experimental emphasis. Thus, he may appeal even in our day for his defense of the humanistic stance, the meaning of which transcends any time and culture. But his shortcomings become noticeable when he attempts to vest his ideas with scientific data.[61]

Thus far, an effort has been made to present similarities, as well as some

[59] Typically, his insistence on the dangers of teaching logic to children too early in their development may have been related to a personal experience of similar type as reported in his *Autobiography*: "Later, having learned from his teacher that Paulus Venetus was the most acute of all the summulists, he [Vico] began also to study him, with a view to further advancement. But his mind, still too weak to stand that kind of chrisippean logic, was almost lost in it, so that to his great sorrow he had to give it up. His despair made him desert his studies (so dangerous it is to put youths to the study of sciences that are beyond their age!) and he strayed from them for a year and a half" (p. 113). A few years before, in another work, he reported that the smooth hills on which he was walking impressed him as steep mountains when he was a child (*Diritto universale*, *Opere* 2: 368).

[60] He was, himself, the sixth of eight children, of whom three died in early childhood; the seventh and the eighth were three and five years his junior. At the age of eighteen he accepted a position as tutor for the four children (then ranging from ages nine to thirteen) of the Rocca family in Vatolla and remained there for approximately nine years. Later on, after his marriage in 1699, at age thirty-one, he had plenty of opportunity to follow the development of his own children, eight in all, born between 1700 and 1720, of whom five survived beyond early childhood. At variance with his rather difficult character, he displayed a great deal of warmth toward his children. He took much responsibility for them, also in view of the intellectual limitations of his wife, and lived in close contact with them, "in the midst of the turmoil and distraction of the household" (*Autobiography*, p. 154) and "the cries of children" (*ibid.*, p. 163).

[61] For instance, in his *New Science* he wrote: "Men first became aware of weight, then of measure, and only very slowly of number" (§ 713). Now Piaget has shown experimentally that the opposite is true: the seriation of lengths is mastered at about seven years of age, that of weights at about ten. (J. Piaget and B. Inhelder, *The Child's Conception of Space* [New York: Humanities Press, 1956], *passim*.)

differences, between Vico and Piaget's concepts, mainly in relation to their psychogenetic perspectives. Also, many points of confluence in regard to the psychogenetic tenets of the child are presented in Piaget as a well construed, comprehensive theory of development of the personality, while in Vico they represent occasional and scattered remarks in support of his views on the development of humanity through various stages. Is it, then, justifiable and meaningful to attempt a comparison between Vico and Piaget, two men who lived more than two hundred years apart in situations quite different? The shortcomings of comparing two men belonging to two entirely different traditions and environments are real and should not be minimized.

First of all, the differences between them are certainly remarkable. Vico grew up and lived in the Catholic and exuberant Naples, Piaget in the Calvinist and austere French Switzerland; the one in a country affected by all kinds of upheavals, from wars to rebellions, poverty, and obscurantism, the other in a country which has become the prototype of order, affluence, and democratic institutions. Their background also could not be more different: humanistic in Vico, as proven by his admiration for eloquence and by his love for his four favorite authors (Plato, Tacitus, Grotius and Bacon), though by no means void of scientific influences, as recently shown;[62] scientific in Piaget, who came to the study of the child through zoology and biology and who, throughout all his writings, has aimed at shying away from philosophical speculations in favor of a biological orientation.

In both, the differences in personal style are most outstanding: rational, dry, and consistent in Piaget; colorful, impetuous, and uneven in Vico. This latter, who, as mentioned above, spent most of his life in close contact with adolescents, appears to have been almost affected by their *forma mentis*; Piaget, instead, never departs from the mature style of the scientist writing in an appealing French, the language of the ideas "clear and distinct."[63]

Also open to question, though worth mentioning, is the issue whether the difference in style reflects a difference in personality: even, patient, conciliatory (typically in his attitude toward the disregard and unproven criticism of his concepts by psychoanalysts) in Piaget; irritable, uneven, rather distrustful in Vico. How much of the attitude toward both of them

[62] N. Badaloni, *Introduzione a G. B. Vico* (Milan: Feltrinelli, 1961).

[63] Vico, as a matter of fact, switched from Latin to Italian early in his career to be able to better represent the immediacy of the customs, of the culture in which he lived. Whether the difference in style is also a reflection of the diffrence between these two languages may be questionable. Interestingly enough, Vico, himself, stressed the differences between French, a language which "can always condense into a small compass the essentials of things" and which is "splendidly suited for the didactic genre," and Italian, "a language which constantly evokes images" (*On Study Methods*, p. 40).

by their contemporaries was a reaction to their personalities, or vice versa, is debatable, too. One cannot gather many cues from their respective autobiographies, which, unconcerned with personal factors, essentially focus on their intellectual journey.

Of course, the main difference consists in the reaction to their work; for Piaget, enthusiasm in some psychological quarters in the twenties and thirties, followed by some degree of supercilious neglect in the forties, and, since then, by overwhelming acceptance, or at least respect and admiration for his remarkably inexhaustible creativity, up to his seventies; for Vico, puzzlement, if not opposition and, worst of all, neglect for his concepts, coupled with an inner awareness of his own greatness and contempt toward his unsophisticated contemporaries.[64]

In retrospect, it is clear that in connection with the shift of emphasis from the unconscious to ego-psychology in psychoanalysis, the *Zeitgeist* was favorable to the spread and acceptance of Piaget's ideas; on the contrary, Vico's ideas were so ahead of his time that it is no wonder that he passed unnoticed. Finally, when his greatness was recognized, as mentioned initially, his work was unilaterally viewed from the perspective of nationalism, and, more recently, of idealism by Croce and his followers. The positivistic school, which could have opened the way toward the understanding of Vico's implications for scientific thought, was of short duration in Italy in the late nineteenth century.

Yet, for all these differences, there are also many similarities between Vico and Piaget. In a way, this could be almost expected, considering that similar trends of thought may lead to similar concepts. To begin with, both remained very attached to their places of origin and of study.[65] Interestingly enough, each experienced an emotional crisis early in his life, both essentially due to the same influences.[66] It is possible that the early period

[64] Concretely, Piaget's greatness has been recognized through prestigious appointments, numerous translations of his volumes, membership in learned societies, distinguished awards, and the founding of a special institute (the International Center for Genetic Epistemology in Geneva in 1956). Vico, on the contrary, won the chair of rhetoric at the University of Naples in 1699, and, having been unanimously turned down for the chair of civil law by the faculty in 1723, maintained that small and poorly paid position for the rest of his life and had considerable difficulty in seeing his *New Science* published, let alone accepted. Though a good husband and father and a conscientious teacher, he remained virtually unknown to the intellectual elite while he was alive; in the small circle of his acquaintances he was considered brilliant, especially for his knowledge of Latin, but complex and hard to understand for his unusual ideas.

[65] Piaget, no matter how far his interests have taken him, has always gone back to his French Switzerland. Vico, as is known, never left Naples and his surroundings, which he greatly admired. Both were academicians and taught at the Universities of Geneva and Naples, respectively, for many years.

[66] Vico underwent two long periods of isolation, the first at the age of seven, for three or more years, as a result of a severe fall at home, which kept him away from school and contacts with peers (*Autobiography*, p. 111); the second, approximately at the age of eighteen, while a private tutor to the children of a noble family residing in the small town of Vatolla on the mountains south of Naples (*ibid.*, p. 119). Piaget

of isolation had a decisive influence on the emotional development of both of them. This is certainly plausible, at least on the basis of what we know today of the process of creativity. Indeed, the notion of "creative illness" has been recently introduced to signify an unusual upsurge of creative power which at times follows a physical illness or emotional disorder.[67]

Both can be considered as self-taught men. Vico, by the time he reached the age of twenty, was already called "autodidact' or "teacher of himself" because of his tendency to disregard the guidance of official teachers and to rely instead on his own inner intuition.[68] Piaget gave up the traditional way of testing children soon after his arrival at Binet's laboratory of child psychology in Paris in 1919 and embarked on his studies of genetic psychology, which eventually brought him to the creation of genetic epistemology.

What is impressive is that this tendency toward crossing and blending discipline (history, mythology, and language in Vico; biology, mathematics, and psychology in Piaget may have accounted for their unusual creativity and for the reactions of their contemporaries and, in the case of Vico, the followers of his work. The difference between them in this regard lies, of course, in the fact that Piaget developed his own cross-disciplinary interests *after* the various above-mentioned scientific fields had achieved a considerable development, Vico *before* that. Vico, himself was aware of the need for new paths in the sciences of man and wrote in 1707: "We neglect that discipline which deals with the differential features of the virtues and vices, with good and bad behavior patterns, with the typical characteristics of the various ages of man, of the two sexes, of social and economic class, race, and nation, and with the art of seemly conduct in life, the most difficult of all art."[69]

wrote in his autobiography: "Between the ages of fifteen and twenty, I experienced a series of crises due both to family conditions and to intellectual curiosity characteristic of that productive age" (J. Piaget, "Jean Piaget," in *A History of Psychology in Autobiography*, ed. E. G. Boring et al. [Worcester, Mass.: Clark University Press, 1952], vol. 4, p. 241; reprinted in: Evans, *Jean Piaget*, p. 109). Vico's famous poem "Affetti di un disperato," of 1692 (an English translation of the poem is in: H. P. Adams, *The Life and Writings of Giambattista Vico* [London: Allen & Unwin, 1935]), marked by pessimism and distrust for God, was viewed by many as the climax of a period of inner desperation and dissatisfaction with his Catholic belief (F. Nicolini, *La giovinezza di G. B. Vico* [Bari: Laterza, 1932]; A. Corsano, *Umanesimo e religione di G. B. Vico* [Bari: Laterza, 1935]; idem, *G. B. Vico* [Bari: Laterza, 1956]; A. M. Jacobelli Isoldi, *G. B. Vico: La vita e le opere* [Bologna: Cappelli, 1960]). Piaget, as he himself reports, was struck by the difficulty of reconciling a number of dogmas with biology and with the fragility of the proofs of the existence of God. Vico got over his crisis by immersing himself in the Latin and Italian classics, Piaget in the study of Bergson's "creative evolution," which offered him a much needed bridge between his passion for zoological studies (especially of mollusks), in which he had excelled since he was a teenager, and his philosophical questions.

[67] H. Ellenberger, "The concept of creative illness," *Psychoanalytic Review* 55 (1968): 442–56.

[68] *Autobiography*, p. 136.

[69] *On Study Methods*, p. 33.

Indeed, these were the disciplines of psychology and sociology, which were to develop in the nineteenth century. For Vico the problem consisted in reaching scientific—or at least, sufficiently scientific—conclusions from the study of literature, history, and language (in fact, for lack of a psychological nomenclature, he was compelled to use figures of speech to express his concepts); for Piaget the problem was that of freeing himself from the strictures of scientific knowledge accumulated in the fields of biology, mathematics, and psychology in order to be able to look at the child in a candid way and, eventually, to discover the common principles underlying these various fields. Indeed, in his dialogue with Evans, Piaget was called "a generalist in the best sense."[70]

What is clear, even at this point of preliminary inquiry, is that Vico and Piaget followed two opposite courses in their studies: from the developmental stages of humanity to the developmental stages of the child in the former; from the developmental stages of the child to the developmental stages of humanity in the latter. In Vico this course is perhaps difficult to follow, as his observations on the development of the child are scattered in the midst of his elaborate historical and mythological considerations. Furthermore, he was himself skeptical about knowing how the mind works.[71] More optimistically, Piaget, instead, has been aware of the implications of his concepts for humanity and, significantly, has written: "The fundamental hypothesis of genetic epistemology is that there is a parallelism between the progress made in the logical and rational organization of knowledge and the corresponding formative psychological processes. With that hypothesis, the most fruitful, most obvious field of study would be the reconstituting of human history—the history of human thinking in prehistoric man."[72]

The cross-disciplinary and most original aspect of Piaget's and Vico's thinking is also probably at the bottom of the difficulty in categorizing it. Piaget, himself, has complained of being misunderstood and of being wrongly considered as a neo-behaviorist, a neo-maturationist, a cyberneticist, a structuralist, or something else. His place in psychology, as one can easily find by perusing the literature, is far from being established and commonly accepted. Vico did not share Piaget's problem, as his most original contributions to psychology and even to education have remained virtually unknown until very recently.[73] Typically, Nicolini, the doyen of Vico's studies, has stated that Vico's *On the Study Methods of Our Time*

[70] Evans, *Jean Piaget*, p. 49.

[71] At variance with current scientific thinking and, in particular, with Piaget's work, he said in his Sixth Oration that logic has no history (*Opere filosofiche*, p. 778) and, later on, that as the mind does not make itself, it is unable to know how the process of knowledge occurs (*Opere* [Ricciardi], p. 254).

[72] Piaget, "Genetic Epistemology," *The Columbia Forum* 12 (1969): n.3.

[73] F. Dogana, "Il pensiero di G. B. Vico alla luce delle moderne dottrine psicologiche," *Archivio di Psicologia, Neurologia, Psichiatria e Psicoterapia* 31 (1970): 514–30.

"is the most important pedagogic essay between Locke's *Thoughts on Education* (1693) and the *Émile* (1762) of Rousseau."[74] Yet Vico's name has hardly been mentioned in histories of education, even in the Italian literature.[75]

Vico and Genetic Epistemology on the Zeitgeist *of the Eighteenth Century*

Thus far, a comparison of Vico and Piaget has brought forward, perhaps unexpectedly, many similarities. The history of science cannot be presented, however, from the perspective of the "great men," that is, as a disconnected succession of fortuitous anticipators of contemporary concepts, on the basis of an assumed dichotomy between "true" and "false" forerunners.[76]

In the history of science, it has been said, advances occur, rather than purely accidentally, according to a "continuity theory," that is, as a continuous refinement of notions transmitted more or less unconsciously (or preconsciously) from one generation to another and at times embodied in the work of a particular man. In *The Structure of Scientific Revolutions,* Kuhn has submitted that scientific principles are meaningful and understandable in the context of a paradigm, that is, a disciplinary world view which is culturally transmitted and sustained by a set of social institutions. Scientific revolutions occur when the introduction of new notions provokes a crisis which necessitates the creation of a new paradigm.[77]

The situation is complicated for the behavioral sciences, and in particular for psychology, as they are still at a "pre-paradigmatic" level,[78] for two reasons: first, because of the universality of their postulates, essentially the same, at least from the Greeks on; and, second, because of the uncertainties regarding the body-mind issue, uncertainties which reflect the difficulty of defining their focus, their methodology, their boundaries, and their reciprocal relations. This state of things is even more complicated in the

[74] F. Nicolini, *Vico e Rousseau* in *Atti dell'Accademia Pontaniana* 1 (1947–48 (new series); reprinted in *Vico e Rousseau* (Naples: Giannini, 1949).

[75] For a recent and thorough presentation of Vico's educational thought: R. Fornaca, *Il pensiero educativo di Giambattista Vico* (Turin: Giappichelli, 1957).

[76] As Boring put it years ago, "it may be true that it is the 'great' man who perceives significance, but it is also true that the significance shows the problem to the 'great' man. This is why great discoveries do not occur until times are ready for them or, when they occur too early, are not great. In other words, the state of the times works both before and after discovery" (E. Boring, "The problem of originality in science," *American Journal of Psychology* 39 [1927]: 70–90; reprinted in E. Boring, *History, Psychology, and Science: Selected Papers* [New York: Wiley, 1963].

[77] T. Kuhn, *The Structure of Scientific Revolutions,* 2d ed (Chicago: University of Chicago Press, 1970).

[78] R. Watson, "Psychology: a prescriptive science," *American Psychologist* 22 (1967): 435–43.

case of genetic epistemology because of its interdisciplinary aspect, halfway between science and philosophy.

The point is that, at present, there is no history of genetic epistemology. As in the case of Freud, Piaget's discoveries appear to have no antecedents. The analogy with Freud may be relevant here on more than one count. Freud, too, tried to remain a scientist; yet, as he advanced in age, he turned more and more into a philosopher. Also, in the case of Freud, his discoveries were seen as priorities void of antecedents; only later their antecedents were traced back, mainly from the fields of philosophy and religion.

Both Freud and Piaget were so involved with their clinical and genetic discoveries, respectively, that they were not able to devote time to the history of their concepts. It is likely that even Piaget's antecedents will be discovered in the field of philosophy, and particularly of logic, which, until recently, was not subjected to scientific investigation.[79] The search for Piaget's antecedents is just beginning.

As shown above, Vico anticipated both the philosophical and experimental tenets of Piaget's system. True, he reported his findings in a scattered, unpretentious way, merely as additional support to his theory of three stages of development of mankind. Yet, in spite of their incidental character, there is some sort of unifying trend which connects them. Thus, it is likely that no matter how many other Piagetian concepts may have been anticipated by others, Vico's importance as predecessor of Piaget may remain unique.

Assuming that this is the case, some important questions emerge, over and above a comparison of their tenets and of their personalities: Are their similarities an expression of a common *Zeitgeist*? Is their interdisciplinary approach an expression of a common orientation and, perhaps, need of their contemporary society?

The answers to these questions lie in the future. Even so, it is possible to venture some conjectures regarding their similarities. One obvious point is that both have come to represent an attempt to bridge the gap between sciences and humanities. Could it then be that their systems respond to a need to bridge such a gap, common in the early eighteenth century as in

[79] In a brief historical review on child animism, W. Dennis, a psychologist, has pointed out that predecessors of Piaget include Hume (1757), D. Tiedemann (1787), Maine de Biran (1803), and, later on, Comte, E. B. Taylor, W. Preyer, S. Hall, J. Sully, and others. Vico, however, not mentioned in this review, preceded all these authors. (W. Dennis, "Historical notes on child animism," *Psychological Review* 45 [1938]: 257–66.)
A feeble attempt has just been made of comparing Piaget's "image mentale" and "intelligence" with St. Thomas Aquinas' "imaginatio" and "intellectus;" a comparison also of relevance to Vico in the light of his assent to the Catholic philosophy, though, undoubtedly, more in the direction of the Platonic than of the Aristotelian tradition. Such a comparison, however, presents many limitations, as it refers to the philosophical rather than to the experimental aspects of Piaget's work (K. Bürgi, *Imaginatio und Intellectus bei Thomas Aquinas und Jean Piaget* [Zurich: Juris, 1972]).

our time? One main common aspect seems to stand out. Then, in the early eighteenth century, in attempting to define the tenets of the philosophy of history, Vico was in reality anticipating the main themes of the Enlightenment of the succeeding decades. As a matter of fact, his system has a more palatable and scientific appeal, at least today, than the vagueness of English deism or French ideology. In retrospect, Vico's system appears to fit in much better with the practical (that is, the social and especially economic) aspect of the Italian Enlightenment, which, as pointed out by recent historiography, is at variance with the more speculative character of French, British, and German Enlightenment.[80] Vico's work signifies a strong emphasis on considering man as the most proper study for man, relying almost exclusively on a humanistic background. Such a humanistic background will be later disposed of by the quickly rising sciences of man in the latter eighteenth and nineteenth centuries. But this new scientific orientation will also mean the loss of that ample breadth of perspective which is intrinsic to the humanities.

Today, a century and a half after all sorts of scientific approaches based on the most varied methodology have been attempted for the study of man and society, a feeling of dissatisfaction is becoming increasingly manifest in many quarters. Obviously, this is related to the feeling of alienation for the loss of the humanistic background and of the widening gap between the "two cultures" (that is, the humanistic and scientific), as brought forward by many, notably C. P. Snow.[81] The answers to this unfortunate polarization have been many, ranging from Marxism to a variety of neo-Humanisms. As mentioned above, Piaget's work is hard to categorize; moreover, he has constantly made an effort to dissociate himself from philosophical movements and to present his work in strictly scientific terms. Yet, for all this effort, his work, ranging from purely psychological to philosophical and moral issues, represents in many ways a concrete attempt to overcome the strictures of the above polarization. Thus, the analogy between Vico and Piaget may have deeper roots than may appear on the surface.

These broad common aspects between Vico and Piaget, though appealing, may give the impression of being too speculative for many. Perhaps a comparison between the two from the perspective of child psychology may be more relevant and convincing. Child psychology is a relatively new field which emerged from the confluence of several trends from the second half of the nineteenth century on.[82] Prior to them, in the eighteenth cen-

[80] S. Moravia, "An outline of the Italian enlightenment," *Comparative Literature Studies* 4 (1969): 380–409.

[81] C. P. Snow, *The Two Cultures and the Scientific Revolution* (London: Cambridge University Press, 1959).

[82] Considered especially important are Wilhelm Preyer's account of his son's mental development during the first four years, Charles Darwin's diary of his infant son, Francis Galton's psychometric experiments, Stanley Hall's content of the children's mind, up

tury, the few direct reports on children that appeared were anecdotal rather than scientific.[83]

Even the various authors who followed the early pioneers in child psychology were interested primarily in the developmental process and in the developmental stages of the child, probably under the influence of the Darwinian theory of evolution and of educational concepts. The importance of these studies cannot certainly be minimized, especially in relation to clinical and educational matters. They have not been concerned, however, with the epistemological aspects, that is, the general laws of the development of the child's mind, indeed, the area in which Vico stands out as a unique precursor of Piaget.

In order to assess such a singular role of him, it is necessary to place his notions about childhood in a much broader context than the rather limited one of child psychology. Namely, it is important to attempt to recapture the position in which Vico held childhood against the background of his time, that is, from the perspective of the concept of childhood throughout history, a challenging and interdisciplinary field of contemporary historiography.

Traditionally, it has been maintained that 1762, the year of the publication of *Émile* by J. J. Rousseau, represented a milestone in the concept of childhood. As George Boas recently put it, "Rousseau seems to have initiated the idea that childhood is something different from manhood and—but this not necessarily follows—it has its rights and privileges. The chief of these was the right to be itself;" and somewhere else, "the child is neither a beast nor a man: he is a child."[84] Thus, Rousseau has been considered as the greatest revolutionist in the field of education. Less emphasis has been put on his psychological concepts, although it has been suggested that he anticipated modern notions of developmental stages and even some psychological laws.[85]

Again, turning from the history of great men to the history of ideas, Rousseau's apparent discovery was in reality the crystalization of a long process whose roots can be traced back to as early as the sixteenth century. Then, in the Renaissance, a number of pedagogical treatises, as well as expressions of the figurative arts, had focused on the importance of the family as a natural background for childhood. Later on, the movement of

---

to Alfred Binet's tests of intellectual development (W. Dennis, "Historical beginnings of child psychology," *Psychological Bulletin* 46 [1949]: 224–35; idem, *Historical Readings in Developmental Psychology* [New York: Appleton-Century, 1972]; J. Anderson, "Child development: An historical perspective," *Child Development* 27 [1956]: 181–96).

[83] W. Dennis, "A bibliography of baby biographies," *Child Development* 7 (1936): 71–73.

[84] G. Boas, *The Cult of Childhood* (London: The Warburg Institute of the University of London, 1966), p. 31.

[85] E. Claparède, "J. J. Rousseau et la conception functionelle de l'enfance," *Revue de Métaphysique et de Morale* 20 (1912): 391–416.

the Reformation, by linking the idea of childhood to that of original sin, contributed to maintaining the view of the child as undifferentiated from the adult. True, as brilliantly shown by Ariès, the process of de-differentiation of childhood from adulthood became manifested in the seventeenth century, especially in the upper class, mainly as a result of the new educational system introduced by Jesuits and others on the wave of the Counter-Reformation.[86] But, essentially, the notion of the child as an adult in miniature persisted until the late eighteenth century.

It is from this perspective that Vico's anticipatory role of genetic epistemology acquires depth, that is, as a precursor of the idea of the individuality of childhood. His theme of the analogy between the mind of the child and that of the primitive, which will be put in biological terms by Haeckel at the end of the nineteenth century,[87] in reality anticipates some important trends which have surfaced only recently.

For one thing, as George Poulet put it: "The great discovery of the 18th century is the phenomenon of memory"; and, elsewhere: "The secular thought of the 18th century conceives and tries to realize a *philosophical duration* which would be the continual renewal of thought, sentient in its origin and continuously sentient by regaining touch with its origin and the past."[88] This memory can be followed along two dimensions: the individual and the social. From the individual perspective, memory led to nostalgia—indeed a pervasive theme of the eighteenth century.[89] Kant stated in his *Anthropology* (1798) that what a person wishes to recover from is not so much the actual *place* where he passed his childhood but his youth itself.[90] Likewise, in a more poetic vein Schiller said that "children *are* what we *were*."[91] From the social perspective, memory led to the nostalgia for the forgotten world of the primitive ("the noble savage") of antiquity and especially of the Middle Ages, which was to become in later decades the common theme underlying the revival of the study of archaeology (J. Winkelmann), language (J. Herder), mythology and sagas (the Grimm brothers)—trends forerunning cultural and political nationalism in various ways.

Moreover, the eighteenth century also signifies the beginning of the interest in autobiography, obviously related to memory and to nostalgia. Rousseau (*Confessions*), Wordsworth (*Prelude*), and Goethe (*Poetry and Truth*), it has been said, "are the first to see themselves as a complex process of 'becoming' in which the past always resounds in the present"; and

[86] P. Ariès, *Centuries of Childhood* (New York: Vintage, 1965), *passim*.

[87] As is known, the German zoologist and philosopher E. Haeckel in 1872 formulated the "biogenetic law:" that ontogenesis is a brief and rapid recapitulation of phylogenesis.

[88] G. Poulet, *Studies in Human Time* (Baltimore: Johns Hopkins Press, 1956), pp. 23–24.

[89] J. Starobinski, "The idea of nostalgia," *Diogenes* 54 (1966): 81–103.

[90] I. Kant, *Anthropologie* (Königsberg: Nicolovius, 1798), *passim*.

[91] Quoted from Boas, *The Cult of Childhood*, p. 73.

"their importance lies not just in the discovery of the child world but in the recognition . . . of the great complexity of the human psyche, and this is ultimately related with the discovery of the relationship between self and circumstances."[92] For the rise of autobiography, G. Gusdorf wrote, "it is necessary for mankind to have overcome, through a cultural revolution, the mythical picture of traditional wisdom to enter the dangerous realm of history."[93]

Finally, the role of adolescence as distinct from childhood and adulthood, though an eternal (M. Debesse)[94] and universal (N. Kiell)[95] experience, was discovered in the late eighteenth century. As recently brought forward, the earliest awareness of the so-called *Flegejahre* ("awkward years," an expression introduced in the German literature around 1770) reached its peak in the early nineteenth century, when Jean Paul Richter, one of the greatest representatives of German romanticism, published his four-volume fiction by the homonymous title.[96]

Now, Vico anticipated these same themes of memory (through his novel revival of the past), of autobiography (through an account of his intellectual journey), and of adolescence (through the impetuous style of life reflected in his writings). The important point here is that these three themes are closely related to a new emphasis on childhood, an emphasis which, indirectly, may throw some light on his interest in identifying the psychogenetic laws of the individual and of society.

Again, the question can be raised: Is there a relationship betweeen Vico and Piaget's *Zeitgeist* in the light of these various themes? A more than casual relationship may be found between Vico's image of man and modern man's new awareness of the ambivalence of his motives and feelings and of the unconscious depth of his personality, in line with the inclination to see the future in the light of the past, at variance with the harmonious and unbroken unity of the classical image of man.[97]

This point also brings forward P. Rieff's opposition of "kairotic time," the crucial, cyclic, past-oriented time exemplified by the collective memory of society for ancestral events, and "chronological time," the unilateral

[92] R. Pascal, *Design and Truth in Autobiography* (Cambridge, Mass.: Harvard University Press, 1960), chaps. 3 and 4.

[93] G. Gusdorf, "Conditions et limites de l'autobiographie" in *Formen der Selbstdarstellung: Analekten zu einer Geschichte des literarischen Selbstportrait, Festgebe für Fritz Neubert*, ed. G. Reichenkron and E. Hasse (Berlin: Duncker & Humblot, 1956), p. 107.

[94] M. Debesse, *La crise d'originalité juvénile*, 3d ed. (Paris: Presses Universitaires de France, 1948).

[95] N. Kiell, *The Universal Experience of Adolescence* (New York: International Universities Press, 1964).

[96] H. Muchow, "Die Flegejahre als Zivilisationphänomen. Eine Theorie der Vorpubertät," *Studium Generale* 5 (1952): 280–86; and H. Muchow, *Flegejahre. Beiträge zur Psychologie und Pädagogik*, 2d ed (Ravensburg: Maier, 1953).

[97] A. Chorus, "The image of man in the older biography," *Journal of the History of the Behavioral Sciences* 2 (1966): 225–32.

future-oriented model of radical religious and secular thought.[98] In other words, is there a common *Zeitgeist* underlying the relationship between Piaget's present emphasis on developmental cycles and Vico's main concern with course and recourse, to which the psychogenetic laws bring additional support and evidence?

Finally, Vico and Piaget's concepts have relevance to the archetypal image of the child as the "child god," the *puer aeternus*, a theme common to many religions and cultures. On the one side, as the sociologist Durkheim wrote, the child is "*un petit traditionaliste*,"[99] a statement echoed by that of Ariès that "children form the most conservative of human societies."[100] Increasingly, some have embraced the notion that since the eighteenth century, childhood has essentially signified a repository of ancestral mores and cultural patterns. On the other side, "childhood sees big," the French philosopher Alain at one time said, "because of the growth which it is in itself." Indeed, the child god, Eros, was the oldest of the Greek deities because from him all proceeds. Thus, the child, representing the potential future, continuously breaks the existential barrier of human existence toward endless new horizons.

From this perspective, Piaget and Vico could not be further apart: the first always rational and scientifically convincing, the latter often emotional and perplexing. The forceful and restless style with which Vico has presented his bold concepts has been, in fact, viewed as an anticipation of an expression of existentialistic pathos.[101]

Yet, to conclude, both Vico and Piaget, by following opposite courses, arrived at conclusions which, independent from their different contexts and *Zeitgeist*, present striking similarities. Both intuitive, both solitary giants of knowledge, they focused their entire work on the "poetic," that is, according to the Greek etymology, "creative" characteristic of the human mind. By construing his reality in the act of knowledge "the child is a philosopher," Piaget has repeatedly said.[102] This appears to echo Vico's statement in his *First Oration* of 1699: "Each of you, during childhood, is a great philosopher."[103] True, in Vico the emotional momentum prevails, in Piaget the rational. But the difference in style should not overshadow the fundamental similarity of content, as "the poet teaches by delighting what the philosopher teaches austerely."[104]

[98] P. Rieff, "The meaning of history and religion in Freud's thought," *The Journal of Religion* 2 (1951): 114–31; reprinted in *Psychoanalysis and History*, ed. B. Mazlich (Englewood Cliffs: Prentice-Hall, 1963), pp. 23–44.

[99] E. Durkheim, "Enfance," in *Dictionaire Pédagogique*.

[100] Ariès, p. 68.

[101] E. Paci, *Ingens Sylva* (Milan: Mondadori, 1949).

[102] J. Piaget, "Children's Philosophies" in *A Handbook of Child Psychology*, ed. C. Murchinson (Worcester, Mass.: Clark University Press, 1931), p. 377.

[103] *Opere filosofiche*, p. 714.

[104] *On Study Methods*, p. 43.

Part V VICO AND PRAXIS

Pietro Piovani

APOLITICALITY AND POLITICALITY IN VICO

1. The problem of the political classification of a philosopher, even one of the classical, completely scholastic type, is a problem to which our age is particularly sensitive. In this curiosity about politics, prevalent in our time to the point of obsession and indentured by its very nature to the most awkward anachronisms, there is an inquisitorial aspect. Not for nothing did Nietzsche accuse "modern philosophizing" of always having a "political and policelike coloration." There is no doubt that the attempt to arrive at the precise political classification of a thinker is all the more vain, the more complex his thought. If a thinker is truly a genius and his thought is complex, it will be impossible to confine him within any specific category that might characterize him by criteria different from those used by the philosopher himself in his thought, and also in the *nuances* of a variegated discourse which the historian ought to seek to understand and develop in its full richness. Besides, the classics of philosophical thought resist the repeated attempts to place them within given ideological positions by providing involuntary theoretical support to different or even contradictory interpretations. One need only think of the contrasting *readings* of the political intentions behind the thought of, say, Socrates and Plato. Or one should recall the irony—truly dominated by a subtle, involuntary cunning—of Hegel's *political* destiny, this apologist of the Prussian state who became, especially among his interpreters of the second half of the nineteenth century, the precursor and essential dialectical ally of Marx's criticism of the modern state and almost the theoretician (more or less unconsciously) of the proletarian revolution. For a more striking example, closer to our own unquiet times, one might think of the fruits born in the twentieth century of the seeds sown by Heidegger, seeds which took root in lands that were both distant and adverse to the political feelings of the German thinker.

In any case, it would be wrong to reduce to a crude, myopic politicism the curiosity directed at discerning the political implications contained in the speculation of a philosopher. There is no need to stress how narrowly vulgar is the critical attitude of the person who might limit himself to asking, What is the position—latent or manifest—of a philosopher, regardless of whether he lived three decades or three centuries ago, with respect to the current political cause that I favor? The *politicization* of a philosopher is not achieved by means of such naive exegeses, which fundamentally are not worth anyone's time. More correct is the hermeneutic attitude which seeks to understand the political reasoning that might be expressed or implied in a philosophical system and that might serve as a valuable guide to the *ideology* of an epoch and of a social condition, intellectually evaluated. The sociology of knowledge, influenced by ideas in part Hegelian and in part Marxian and brought to fruition in the teachings of Karl Mannheim, taught intellectuals to see in philosophies the symbols of a situation, the forms placed over a deeper ideology born of structures in evolution—an epochal condition condensed in the representativity of a single system of thought. It is in this sense that most critics working in Italy after World War II have most often interpreted Vico.

2. The interest in the political representativeness of Vico led many critics to revise the drastic opinion of Benedetto Croce, who wrote in 1909:

> He was really an apolitical man. . . . There was nothing in him of the combative spirit of an apostle, propagandist, agitator, or rebel, which characterized many of the philosophers of the Renaissance: especially Bruno and that Campanella whom Vico (although, and perhaps because, he was a Neapolitan) never mentions. To be sure, his age and his country were neither the time nor the place for rebellions, revolutions, and those ardent conflicts that give rise to great actions and political passions. And yet, political parties (French and Austrian) did exist there; one could discern a certain desire for national independence; and men appeared who dedicated their work and lives to these ends, and were persecuted and went into exile. Moreover, during that time occurred the high point of the battle between church and state, and between Naples and Rome, with Pietro Giannone, about whom, as of all that activity, Vico remained silent and apparently ignorant.[1]

Thus formulated, the thesis of Vico's non-politicality has been often repeated, with diverse tones and emphases; and almost all the reiterations of Croce's thesis are turned to the attention and revision of its drastic nature, even while confirming the general judgment.

The neatness of this view, expressed so openly, in assuming its own hermeneutical responsibilities without taking refuge in prudential half-measures, has become an object of criticism. And since to criticize is easy, while to analyze calmly is difficult, the successive polemics directed against the thesis have ignored certain fundamental truths. In the first place, we should note the partial revisions of this thesis made both by Croce himself and then, later, in certain formulations of Nicolini. In the second place, we should mention the biographical and psychological acuity of the pages written about Vico by Croce in 1909 ("Intorno alla vita e al carattere di G. B. Vico"), in which certain elusive features of Vico's nature are firmly

[1] B. Croce, *La filosofia di Giambattista Vico*, 4th ed. (Bari, 1947), pp. 288–89.

grasped—pages destined to be re-examined rather than forgotten by the minute investigations undertaken in succeeding decades. In the third place, it is necessary above all to note that many revisions of Croce's original judgment came from men and groups near to Croce, with investigations directly or indirectly stimulated, promoted, or encouraged by him, especially in the more liberal years of the first decade of the twentieth century. The examples are numerous, and it is sufficient to record only a few.

In 1914 Laterza Press published in one volume a collection of essays by Raffaele Cotugno, with an introductory dedication to Croce, in which Vico's involvement in the problems of his own century is set forth with learning and spirit.[2] In the same period, *La critica* published some of Giovanni Gentile's essays, later reprinted in 1915 in the first edition of his *Studi vichiani*, in which reappears Bertrando Spaventa's old argument regarding the isolation of Vico. Gentile's essays contain other points, however, which lead to new historical and scholarly explorations of Vico's youth and early life and the culture of pre-Vichian Naples. These same topics are covered by such talented scholars as Fausto Nicolini and Nino Cortese who, in respective works entitled *La giovinezza di Giambattista Vico (1668 1700)* and *Franceso D'Andrea e la rinascenza filosofica in Napoli nella seconda metà del Seicento*, initiated investigations of Vico, not only *against* the background of the political and ethical life of his time, but *within* that time, and as a participant in its movements. To be sure, once Croce's great work on Vichian themes had ended and the time for a comprehensive defense of his achieved critical system had come, Nicolini himself often preferred to view Vico as removed from his times and as the ideal contemporary and interlocutor of that Romantic philosophical tradition which culminates in Hegel.[3] But this is not to deny that Nicolini was certainly among those who sought to correct the representation, now conventional, of Vico as a *solitario*,[4] thus apolitically inaccessible to the surrounding ideas of this time.

To show the distance between the theses offered by Croce in 1909 and the investigations undertaken immediately thereafter by members of the Neo-Idealist school, we need only recall the first chapter, "Vico and Giannone," in Guido De Ruggiero's *Il pensiero politico meridionale nei secoli XVIII e XIX*, written in 1921 but, as the preliminary acknowledgment indicates, ripened in the atmosphere of the *Società Napoletana di Storia Patria*, of which, in those years, the *magna pars* was Croce. Subsequently, Vico's well-known youthful religious doubts (doubts that were more or less limited) were sufficient to modify the image of Vico which had appeared in previous decades. Such doubts, in late-seventeenth-century

[2] *La sorte di Giovan Battista Vico e le polemiche scientifiche e letterarie dalla fine del XVII alla metà del XVIII secolo* (Bari, 1914).

[3] See, for example, F. Nicolini, Introduction to Vico, *Opere* (Ricciardi), p. x.

[4] F. Nicolini, *La giovinezza di Giambattista Vico*, 2d ed. (Bari, 1932), p. 8.

Naples, were inevitably connected with—in fact implied—hidden political sympathies taken in a broad sense. And the first to discuss these religious doubts in a full and adequate manner were Antonio Corsano and Fausto Nicolini, in well-known books published by the Biblioteca di Cultura Moderna.[5]

3. It is undeniable, therefore, that in the cultural circle strongly influenced by Croceanism the progressively broadened investigations (already begun towards the end of the first half of the twentieth century) led to the placing of Vico in his times, in his society, in the midst of the men and the problems of his city. This tendency often attenuated the argument which, by insisting on the anti-Enlightenment attitude of Vico and on his isolation from the surrounding "Cartesian" and "Illuminist" culture, transferred Vico in an ideal sense into the Romantic nineteenth century. Thus, in contrast with the progress in research, there was a brisk return to the thesis of Vico's *apoliticality*,[6] undertaken by polemical thinkers especially interested either in refuting the non-documentable hypothesis of Vico's hidden political predilections for the *Gallispani* against the Austrians or in opposing a rich but forced thesis ascribing Vico to the European Enlightenment, or at least to certain aspects of it.

In this chaos of arguments, polemically stimulating but calculated to inflate artificially the contradictions, the actual condition of scientific research became greatly altered. One such alteration was a change in viewpoint often exhibited by the very scholars who had contributed essential results to the attainment of a wider knowledge of Vico. In view of these schematized oppositions, the intervention of historians of Neapolitan culture and society in the seventeenth and eighteenth centuries, while opening new perspectives and clearing rough ground, contributed to the rigidification of the schematization which opposes the idealistic image of an "apolitical" Vico, unrelated to his time, to a "post-realistic" Vico, relatively aware of the political situation of his time.

Many sophisticated historians—often experts in multinational historiographical experiences—turned their attention to the Naples of the seventeenth and eighteenth centuries and dissolved those theses created on the basis of such criticizable formulas as "pre-Vichianism" and "post-Vichianism." These historians rightly reject an examination which, by overevaluating the philosopher in Vico, claims to re-endow him with a "corporeal" reality composed of economic, social, and political phenomena,

[5] A. Corsano, *Umanesimo e religione di G. B. Vico* (Bari, 1935); idem, *Il pensiero religioso italiano dall' umanesimo al giurisdizionalismo* (Bari, 1937); and F. Nicolini, *La religiosità di G. Vico* (Bari, 1949).

[6] F. Nicolini, "Fu il Vico uomo di partito? Ancora dell' apoliticità del Vico; Sempre sull'apoliticità di Vico" in *Atti della Accademia Pontaniana*, new series, 5 (1952–55): 289–317, 402–6; idem, *Il Croce minore* (Milan and Naples, 1963), pp. 80–93. Cf. P. Piovani, "Per gli studi vichiani" in *Studi in onore di Antonio Corsano* (Bari, 1970), pp. 613–15.

which it is absurd to evaluate with principal reference to the task of a philosophy. Still, it is legitimate to suspect that the years of Naples "before Vico" and "during Vico's time" would have been studied with less frequency, breadth, and intensity if the great emblematic figure of Vico had not been authoritatively etched on that city's horizon. Thus many investigations of political history, even those distant from the history of philosophy, have managed to bring themselves closer to Vico, so as to consider him at least from a specific perspective, one able to support a thesis and conducive to understanding, if not engaging, him in some way. In sum, to have inspired historical investigations, often of the first order, rich in their diversity and variety,[7] is one posthumous merit that we can attribute in part to Vico.

As we have noted, it was a datum well established by research that Vico was not insensitive to the ferments and the heresies (even literary) circulating in Neapolitan culture. This theme is specified, especially under the influence of studies investigating the exact composition of the philosophical and scientific culture of Naples prior to and contemporary with Vico,[8] by a methodology progressively turned, by means of the whole philosophical history of Italy, to an intimate understanding of those connections deepened in the actual circulation of ideas.[9]

In the new spirit of research, the intellectual unrest of Naples in the last decades of the eighteenth century is seen as proof of a true and proper cultural "libertinism,"[10] to be set in relation to social phenomena now observed with a new critical acumen. Thus Vico is located in the fullness of a moment of transformation in the ordering of the social classes of his city, a reality which could not be ignored, however it might be assessed:

In Naples, during the second half of the seventeenth century, men of the civil class (*ceto civile*) were slowly taking the place of the established nobility (*nobili di sedile*) in the management of public affairs and in the direction of administrative institutions. Certain members of the *ceto civile* were opposed to

[7] For detailed references to the contributions of these authors (Raffaele Ajello, Nicola Badaloni, Sergio Bertelli, Vittor Ivo Comparato, Biagio de Giovanni, Romeo de Maio, Giuseppe Galasso, Giuseppe Giarrizzo, Lino Marini, Salvo Mastellone, Amedeo Quondam, Michele Rak, Giuseppe Ricuperati, Silvio Suppa, Franco Venturi, Brunello Vigezzi, Pasquale Villani, Lucio Villari, Rosario Villari, Paola Zambelli) see the bibliographical notes in vols. 5–7 of *Storia di Napoli* (Naples, 1970–72).

[8] See B. De Giovanni, *Filosofia e diritto in Francesco D'Andrea—Contributo alla storia del del previchismo* (Milan, 1958); N. Badaloni, *Introduzione a G. B. Vico* (Milan, 1961); and G. Fassò, *Vico e Grozio* (Naples, 1971). For the orientations of the various critical traditions, see Paolo Rossi, Lineamenti di storia della critica vichiana, in vol. 2 of "*I classici italiani nella storia della critica*," ed. W. Binni (Florence, 1961).

[9] The most creative influence on this methodological orientation has been exercised by the magisterial work by E. Garin, *Storia della filosofia italiana* (Turin, 1966), the first edition of which was issued in 1947.

[10] See S. Mastellone, *Pensiero politico e vita culturale a Napoli nella seconda metà del Seicento* (Florence, 1965), p. 85; and idem, *Francesco D'Andrea politico e giurista (1648–1698)—L'ascesa del ceto civile* (Florence, 1969), p. 168.

the social dominance of the feudal aristocracy and, with the consent of the Spanish government, condemned their abuses, invoking the ancient legislative tradition and reaffirming the rights of the state.[11]

If the historian is concerned to establish useful chronological limits of the phenomenon, perhaps even distinguishing different times, distinct periods, and separate events, the reader of Vico is quite likely to reach, so to speak, *ultra petita et visa.* It is not enough for him to see Vico as more or less tied to this web of moral and political forces. Going directly to the heart of the matter, he is forced to present Vico as the philosopher of the new, rising classes or, conversely, as the thinker ready to place himself at the service of the adversaries of these new classes. We should remember that practitioners of the most rigorous historical research do not abandon themselves easily to such speculation. For all of them, however, Vico enters into this predominantly historical-political play of interpretations.

The most explicit proponent of the "substantial *politicality* of Vichian thought," in declared contrast with Croce's and Nicolini's defense of the "apoliticality" of Vico, is Giuseppe Giarrizzo. His work is based on an independent and subtle rereading of Vico's corpus "from the first poetic compositions to the *New Science* of 1744," but with specific attention to Vico's known consonances with rethinkings of classical suggestions transfigured by modern European authors (and especially Bacon).[12] Giarrizzo, while maintaining that many consequences have to be derived from the Vichian judgment "on the formation and civil function of the *literati*"[13] and while never losing sight of "the social profile of Vico's conception" of *dominium*,[14] refuses to consider Vico only in terms of the rise of the *ceto civile*. But his reservations are intended to expand, rather than to limit, the problem. Giarrizzo believes that one ought not "limit oneself to defining Vico's position as anti-baronial [especially] from the point of view of the *ceto intellettuale* (the intellectual class)"[15] because he thinks that by now it is necessary to expose "the political basis of all of his thought."[16] This political basis, he maintains, can be grasped in its entirety if placed in relation, not only with the transformations and the specific claims of the dominant class of citizens in Naples, but, even more, with the entire "southern agrarian world which Vico indicates that he understood in all of its conflict and drama."[17] Such discussions, however, do not concern only the city or the Kingdom of Naples: they touch upon problems that

[11] *Ibid.*, p. 12.

[12] See G. Giarrizzo, "La politica di Vico," in *Quaderni contemporanei*, dedicated to G. B. Vico and published by the Istituto Universitario di Salerno (Salerno, 1968), no. 2.

[13] *Ibid.*, p. 80.

[14] *Ibid.*, p. 117.

[15] *Ibid.*, p. 74.

[16] *Ibid.*, p. 83.

[17] *Ibid.*, p. 128.

belong to the formation of the modern state and of capitalistic and pre-capitalistic social structures—"these are features which place Vico in the center of a European debate."[18] In this respect, Giarrizzo approaches the position of Badaloni, especially in the belief that, in the *Orations* and the *Coniuratio*, one can discern a Vico who, setting out to evaluate "social problems by means of a rational analysis . . . recognizes the healthy forces . . . in the working classes, in the middle classes, in the lower nobility, and finally in those who, whatever might be their social origin, constituted the *ordo*, that is to say, those groups, intellectual and noble, which possessed political power during the last period of Spanish domination."[19] It is not surprising, therefore, that similar considerations permit the rejection of the thesis of Vico's apoliticality and the acceptance of the "preeminence" in him "of political feeling . . . the dominance not of his historical imagination, but of his political passion, the only force able to endow with critical and argumentative solidity his boldest conjectures."[20]

4. The "political" interpretations of Vico, when conducted with appropriate tact and exegetical prudence, when they are based on a constant and detailed reference to the texts, when they do not rest upon argumentation so subtle as to become tiresomely carping, have a certain persuasiveness and suggestibility. Even when they do not succeed in canceling perplexities, they ought not to go unnoticed. They present, to be sure, numerous risks, some of which are especially dangerous for the understanding of Vico's philosophy. First of all, the search for the political implications of Vico's discourse can rapidly become a tiresome *maniera*, whose vices can only become exaggerated in the awkward hands of epigones. Next, the recognition of a basic political attitude in Vico can give way to an exaltation of Vichian political doctrines, which often have original applications but which, in and of themselves, are either modest or are valuable primarily for the transformations—genial or not—of other people's political doctrines, and thus ought to be considered more as effects than as causes. Reduced to pure political thought, Vico's ideas not only lose much—their best part—but are of modest stature when compared with the political theories of many of his philosophical contemporaries in Europe. These theoreticians had quite a different sensibility regarding the problematics of the formation of the modern state, due to their direct experience of it in those practical laboratories of political science which were the great national states of Europe of the seventeenth and eighteenth centuries. In our view, however, it is doubtful that Vico ever possessed anything more than a random, crude, and occasional suspicion of the true problems of the formation of the modern state. Certainly, he never had any clear understanding of them.

[18] *Ibid.*, p. 129.
[19] *Ibid.*, p. 71; Badaloni, *Introduzione a G. B. Vico*, pp. 311–12.
[20] Giarrizzo, "La politica di Vico," pp. 99, 113.

The "political" key, if used with a delicate touch, can be one of the keys to the reading of Vico's difficult thought. But one ought not exclude the use of other keys, which can also be used to open that armored strongbox. When a historian of culture looks at Vico as a witness, to be used for the understanding of both the "ideal" and "material" forces operating in a political situation, he will penetrate Vico's thought with a thoroughness equal to the complexity of the task. But such a reading runs a more insidious risk when used by predominantly "literary" and "philosophical" interpreters who pose as experts on political-historical situations. In such cases, the political interpretation only produces bad literature and exiguous philosophy. Anyone who knows philosophy finds in the *New Science* a hundred motifs for independent meditation and personal confrontation and thus has no need to use a mode of reading which repeats past forms and models. Those who have been aware of this truth are, naturally, those historians who have sought to interrogate Vico as their witness independently.

The risks involved in the political interpretations of Vico, particularly the great risk of a vulgarization of this type of reading, ought not to obscure the nucleus of rich truth contained in these interpretations. As suggested by the critical works indicated above, in pointing to this nucleus of truth, we do not wish to refer to a theme so often stressed, from Carlo Pisacane to Benedetto Croce: that of the higher politicality of the apolitical and impolitical Vico, one who was distracted from immediate problems because his attention was turned to general political and metapolitical ideas. It would be difficult for anyone, in fact, to maintain that the *New Science*, a "history of human ideas," is not in certain respects a history of political ideas: in the civil orders human ideas are realized by their historization.[21] On the other hand, however, the aversion of Vico, the "political philosopher," for "monastic and solitary philosophers"[22] is among the well-known presuppositions of his "civil philosophy." But the critical approach which we have indicated does not stop with this recognition: it wants to grasp the politicality of Vico in an even more immediate connection, to isolate those forms of sensibility which would link Vico to the political-ethical struggles of his time, by means of direct or indirect statements present in his thought. Now, this proposed reading, no matter how much confusion it causes and how many risks it runs, certainly has one merit, which is its credibility: it shows us a Vico anything but unaware of the political-social innovations of his century. Thus, the proposal for a political reading of the more rhetorical and traditional works of Vico strikes a new blow at the image of a totally anti-Cartesian Vico, the anachronistic follower of a revived Plato, promoter of a restored pure metaphysics then transformed into an arbitrary philosophy of history—in sum, a blow against

[21] See especially, *New Science*, §§ 348–50.
[22] *Ibid.*, § 130; and The Autobiography, *Opere*, p. 11.

the image of Vico as the anti-Enlightenment philosopher and enemy of modern European philosophy. Such an image of Vico was agreeable to Catholic traditionalism as well as to the programmatic anti-traditionalism of the hostile interpreters of a "new science" which refuses to be merely a philosophy of the natural sciences. However, the investigation of Vico in the context of his own history indicates how one can securely maintain that the Vichian "philosophy of *auctoritas* . . . is not at all a philosophy of *traditio*."[23] In evaluating this perspective, one might doubt whether "all of Vico's intentions" were turned to "creating a modern, socially conditioned intellectual figure,"[24] but one can understand how the appeal to this implicit *sociality* and *politicality* of Vico's discourse reveals a side of Vico that it would be wrong to ignore.

To summarize, one could discuss at great length the ideological "conditioning" of Vichian philosophy, either in terms of criteria of general methodology or with specific reference to the author. And we are not inclined to view Neapolitan philosophy simply as the forerunner of an ideology or of a political conception. But one cannot ignore the fact that in the history of Vico's critical fortune, we find recurrent sympathies for a Vico responsive to the problem of the subterranean development of social forces within the context of an articulated vision of society, endowed with its own dialectic and its own dynamism. Whether we like it or not, such constant and repeated critical sympathies are not an invention of the current "political-social" interpretations of Vico; they are facts which should be remembered and which serve to confirm Vico's authorization of such readings.

There is no doubt that Vico—like all great philosophers—has been, according to the different assessments of his interpreters, an involuntary standardbearer of many ideals. And there is no doubt that, to push "Vichianism" to its inevitable ideological and philosophical conclusions,[25] one must study him in each of several situations: a requirement that is obligatory for every historical characterization. Whatever is omnivalent and omnicomprehensive must dissolve, finally, into generality. As an inspirer of F. Mario Pagano, one of the most noble and knowledgeable victims of the Bourbon terror of 1799, Vico was borrowed as the tutelary spirit of the *cultura meridionale*, the extreme effort made by the Bourbons to establish a dialogue with Italian intellectuals at the VII Congresso degli Scienziati of 1845, three years before the definitive break between the Neapolitan crown and the Italian nationalists.

As often happens, Vico has been used repeatedly as pretext and symbol of ideological causes and programs which bear little relationship to him.

[23] N. Badaloni, "La cultura" in *Storia d'Italia: Dal primo Settecento all'Unità* (Turin, 1973), vol. 3, p. 770.

[24] *Ibid.*, p. 772.

[25] G. Oldrini, "La questione del vichismo meridionale," in *Ricerche sulla cultura dell'Italia moderna*, ed. P. Zambelli (Bari, 1973), pp. 199–213.

And yet, it is significant that he enjoys such favor among readers sensitized to the dynamics of political ideas and interests seen in their intrinsic sociality, potential or realized. If the Vichian "philosophy of man" assumes in Genovesi tints which will by themselves color his numerous followers, these colorations favor the confrontation between Vico and the *Ideologi*,[26] which, after Romagnosi, assumes the tone of a new and lasting synthesis in Cattaneo and Ferrari, respectively.[27] On the other side, it is the exhortation to the verifying comprehension of the fact, to create an aversion to the *chimerical*, to the abstractly ideal, that suggests to Cuoco's Vichian spirit words similar to those already uttered with clear methodological purpose by F. M. Pagano: "Science which does not correspond to the fact is for Vico chimerical: in his philosophy the true is that which exists. In order, therefore, to create a science of man that is not chimerical, one must start from the facts."[28] The manifest Vichian exhortation to seek the facts and to comprehend their ethical-social historical realization prevents to the heirs of Scholasticism an adherence which might go beyond generic praise. But it does not prevent the formation in southern Italian political thought of an independent "Vichian Right," which might well be studied with profit.[29] After Cuoco, the majority of nineteenth-century Italian liberals never denied to Vico the authoritative prestige granted by Cousin's eclecticism, with which, it should not be forgotten, the historiography of the French Restoration was concerned. This historiography was exceedingly sensitive to the development of the internal structures of civil society, in view not only of the difficulties of the post-Revolutionary state, but also in view of the needs not fulfilled by the history of the state and by the citizens' demand for guarantees.[30] This generated different dissatisfactions, which, because they drew attention to social, structural, and

[26] On the nature of these encounters see especially the reflections and documentations offered in chaps. 3 and 4 of part 5 of Garin's *Storia della filosofia italiana*; and F. Tessitore, "Tra vichismo e ideologia," in vol. 9 of the *Storia di Napoli* (Naples, 1972). As P. Casini notes in chaps. 4 and 7 of his *Introduzione all'Illuminismo* (Bari, 1973), it is difficult to distinguish, in certain aspects of Italian culture of the eighteenth century, between defenders and enemies of the Enlighteners and their relative successive repercussions on the influence of the *Ideologi*.

[27] While it is necessary to await the outcome of critical studies concerned with Cattaneo and his relations with Vico, which might take up once more the path marked out by Alessandro Levi, we can be grateful still for the studies on Ferrari and Vico provided by C. D'Amato, "Le basi ideologiche della filosofia della storia di Giuseppe Ferrari," in *Ricerche sulla cultura dell'Italia moderna*, pp. 237ff., and "La formazione di Giuseppe Ferrari e la cultura italiana della prima metà dell' '800," in *Studi Storici* (1971), pp. 701ff., thanks to which we are finally liberated from old, tenacious and repeated preconceptions, such as those of S. Onufrio, "G. B. Vico e il liberalismo moderato," in *Rassegna di politica e di storia* (1968), p. 163.

[28] V. Cuoco, *Scritti vari*, ed. N. Cortese and F. Nicolini (Bari, 1924), pt. 1, p. 318.

[29] On this topic, see F. Tessitore, *Aspetti del pensiero neoguelfo napoletano dopo il Sessanta* (Naples, 1962).

[30] On aspects of such a political-historical sensibility in Restoration France, see the relevant chapters, "La germinazione delle idee" and "La genesi della concezione classistica" of A. Omodeo, *La cultura francese nell'età della Restaurazione* (Milan, 1946).

infrastructural developments, created strange theoretical consonances between revolution and conservation, between post-Enlightenment reformers and Romantic revisionists, and then between the leftist and rightist Hegelians. Within this framework, one can understand the interest in Vico shown by thinkers such as Marx and, later, Antonio Labriola, an interest which permits one to say, with only slight distortion, that certain Vichian methods and ideas represent "the first effective attempt at a dialectical understanding of social-historical reality."[31] And a critical tradition has arisen which is based on this possible interpretation and in great part confirms it.

5. Actually, whatever consequences have to be drawn from it, there is a social vision of history standing at the heart of Vico's philosophy of history and constituting one of the criteria which modify and control its universalist aspirations. By virtue of this implicit vision, Vico has no need to raise the problem (raised for the first time by Voltaire) of a broadened historical conception which would not be merely a narrative of the virtues and vices of kings, courts, governors, and chancellories, that is, of only rulers, but which might take serious account of other creative forces, less exalted but nonetheless effective. Although he was apparently less modern in his methodological concerns, inclined to write apologetic biography, susceptible to the most reverent obsequiousness, and alien to any tendency to criticize power, Vico did possess a dramatic view of history. Because of this view, Vico was inclined indeed to justify power, but he wished first of all to explain it by investigations that were not pure logical exercises but historical conjectures and—true or presumed—documentations. For Vico, it is not a question of widening one's scope to include other powers in their novelty and range; it is a question of seeing by which actions authority had gained its claim to be authoritative. Thus, in this rigid philosophy of authority, the "authoritarian" can even be confirmed, but only if subjected to a radical examination which exposes its modes, motives, and modifications, showing openly how and when it might be *stopped*, and might succeed in achieving its own stability. This Vichian penetration of *natures* up to their *nascimenti* (births) is a subtle rationalization of them. This excavation to the roots already implies a radicalization of the themes examined, within an analysis so pitiless as to render nude the most hidden anatomical secrets of institutions. The rational comprehension of the sacredness of the sacred, even when it ends in confirmed and renewed respect, is already in itself a desacralization. The clarification of the motives behind the formation and consolidation of a myth is an implicit philosophy of myth, which is already a demythification. A history which claims to explain historical forces by following them in the discovered totality of their evolution is a history which submits those forces to a tendentiously analytical dismantling. Such a history, whether or not one program-

[31] N. Badaloni, Introduction, to Vico, *Opere filosofiche*, p. liv.

matically desires it, seeks to understand their assets, movements, balances, and imbalances and thus inevitably intuits their immanent dialectical nature.

Writing after, and against, the Revolution, De Maistre enunciated the whole of his reactionary philosophy when, with disquieting insight, he warned that "one must hide the origins of power." Writing before the Revolution and far away from it, Vico goes beyond any specific criticism of power by proposing a history totally dedicated to unveiling the origins of the powers and even theorizing the universal reasons for this unveiling. His true "rationalism" lies precisely in this anticipation of the criticism of historical reasoning, which does not discuss the political forms as they ought to be, but shows them as they are, thus revealing them in the admonitory truth of their greatness and wretchedness, and thereby participating in the great eighteenth-century inquiry into the virtue and decadence of nations and their regimes.

The "philological" interest in the genesis of things pays homage to their greatness, yet progressively strips them of their superficial glitter. In the childhood of mankind, glimpsed at its beginnings, there is nothing which does not become diminished in some way. The genetic way of knowing is a critical process. For Vico, the birth of cities is a dramatic, and not an irenic, event; it originates from the force able to blunt violence, from a demand which opposes another demand and bridles it with the fantasy that necessity suggests. Thus society cannot have originated in a peaceful social contract. The principles of European political thought are not ignored but are rather absorbed and revived in the light of a dawnlike vision of civilization, more weighty and more tragic. Vico's vision is not a political doctrine in the narrow sense, because it is much more than simple political theorization:

> Grotius's simpletons and Pufendorf's abandoned men had recourse to the altars of the strong to save themselves from Hobbes's violent men, even as beasts driven by intense cold will sometimes seek salvation in inhabited places. Thereupon the strong, with a fierceness born of their union in the society of families, slew the violent who had violated their lands, and took under their protection the miserable creatures who had fled from them.[32]

The history of man, born of such ferocity, continues as a permanent testimony to miseries to be overcome, needs to be satisfied, abuses to be opposed, and arrogance to be dissolved. In this history, every institution is in its origin a remedy for an evil, refuge from a peril, or salvation from an impending danger. Even the times in which intellects, academies, kingdoms, and wealth flourish are only more or less durable points of arrival in a process dominated by harsh necessities: their glorious tranquility stands, more or less vigilant, above an abyss of sharp precipices. Little is

[32] *New Science*, §§ 553.

needed to cause their fall into the renewing epochs of the dark age, a stimulus and destiny from which no human culture is immune.

Because of this constant and inexhaustible mobility, the history which would be truly conscious of its own understanding must trace the forces that control the various unstable balances into the corporeality in which they are formed and delineated. In the alternations between dominating and being dominated, the events of history, in order to be understood, must be observed in the fiber of their social fabric. The sociality found in Vico's history is a polemical one. In this sense, and only in this sense, can it be seen as class warfare. But it can be seen in this way only from within a movement of institutions which are born, consolidated, elaborated, weakened, and fall apart. Individuals, in any case, are objectified in the institutions in which their subjectivity is expressed. The Vichian moment of the "objective spirit" (if we may call it such) is only institutional. Religions, languages, dominions, laws, and arts are objectified in their historical reality insofar as they become institutionalized, and they must be sought and evaluated in this, their concrete self-realization. This is their actual socialization, which takes account of the differences of property, classes, and of *status* so as to be able to grasp such a fleeting, mobile institutionality.

Social objectification is, for Vico, proper to wills which, so to speak, coagulate and become stratified in institutions. He is drawn to the *social* by the effort to grasp the ways in which these institutions were formed. To grasp such a movement, one must perceive in the *structured* as it appears that which is *under* the structure. But this interest was suggested to him by his fundamentally moral concern never to lose sight of the ethical value of the activity of those men who laboriously construct their painful and noble history. And this concern is, in its essence, a defense of "industry" and a condemnation of "laziness." Yet this concern does not degenerate into a generic moralism but is fashioned into a new historical method, thanks to the limitation of the juridical forms which this scholar of juridical civilizations points out. Vico was more aware than most thinkers of the profundity of meaning implied in every legal *fictio*, and he pays homage to the deep historicity contained in the wisdom of artifices. And yet in explaining the rationality of the artifice, he seeks to understand from what needs it might have arisen, what interests it might have expressed, and what conflicts it might have hidden. The Roman legal experience, fundamental to Vico's philosophy and to his entire conception of history,[33] furnished him with rich materials for meditating on problems which he saw revived and repeated in the structures of the Middle Ages, in the post-feudal and anti-feudal transformations in process during the modern age, which had become progressively more visible and more "exemplary" in their new proclaimed dynamism. It is the same juridical

[33] See S. Mazzarino, *Vico, l'annalistica e il diritto* (Naples, 1971).

sense of the *institution* and its complex significance which furnishes Vico with social interests translatable into specifically political intentions, either latent or explicit. This juridicity is the premise of all *politicality* and *sociality* in Vico and is an aspect which should never be lost sight of. Thus, at the moment of the foundation of the human sciences, law enriches Vichian philosophy with a curiosity which will be suggested to other eighteenth-century philosophers by other experiences, such as, for example, political economy. In these cases, the "political" issue should be comprehended more as a result than as a cause, and therefore its evidence is presented in chiaroscuro: a chiaroscuro that would be changed by an interpreter who might wish to show it in full light. To understand this "political" issue as it is, one must accept it and study it as it presents itself.

Translated by Margaret Brose

Angela Maria Jacobelli

THE ROLE OF THE INTELLECTUAL IN GIAMBATTISTA VICO

The philosophical tradition which begins with Greek thought attributes to the sage, that is to say, the most representative intellectual, a fundamental role, inasmuch as it assigns to him the task of discovering first principles and providing for human beings and the world a firm foundation. The contemplative nature that seems to be proper to the mental operation necessary for the discovery of first principles or metaphysics constitutes the main target of a critical tradition which accuses metaphysics of deriving its essential principles from an abstract reality constitutionally extraneous to the concreteness of real life. Actually, it is easy to meet this accusation of abstractness, as many contemporary critics have done, by recalling not only that research is motivated by vital interests of safety and organization but that primary truths are lived as normative principles.

Undoubtedly, the grafting of a religious dimension onto the theoretical enterprise accentuated that redemptive impulse which orients existence toward the supernatural or transcendent. The normative implication deduced from this reference to divine transcendence assumed that ascetic character which derived from the radical dualism between the natural and the supernatural characteristic of a religious perspective. In this case too, however, it should be stressed that it was precisely the action of the intellectual which redefined the redemptive impulse in less radical ways, by a revindication of human reality even in its earthly aspect. Scholasticism tried, in fact, to elaborate revealed truths by theoretical means, to constitute theology as a science. The impossibility of successfully completing this task favored the development of a type of theory especially concerned with the systematic investigation of nature.

From this division there arose two different types of theorizing and therefore two types of intellectuality: one based on the conviction that the proper object of theory is the supernatural world, since from it alone can one derive those universally valid and immutable principles necessary for a properly lived life; the other dedicated to showing that theorizing is authentic only when it avoids transcendental abstractions and concentrates on the natural world. Intellectuals thus became divided into two groups, the speculative and the scientific, both fighting to defend contradictory principles; and this division persists even today.

Contemporary society, however, has a characteristic uniquely its own. It is, in fact, always more deeply involved in a process of increasing realization of the problems that the role of the intellectual involves. From all sides we hear warnings of the dangers implicit in the process of reflection characteristic of theorizing, a process which seems to place a barrier between the natural world and the possibility of acting within and transforming that world.

The most striking example of this type of warning is inspired by Marx's criticism of bourgeois thought and gave rise to the different positions taken by revolutionary movements with respect to elites. Leftwing intellectuals have tended towards a corrosive self-criticism, which often results in a loss of faith and a renunciation of their own specific commitment, in their efforts to transform that commitment into rigorously scientific and technical forms or, seen in its best light, in the frantic search for a living space in which their existence might be justified. On the other hand, even Western Neo-capitalism, supported and comforted by the sensational developments of a scientific technology, looks with diffidence at those "eggheads" who might represent sources of grave danger for the established powers.

In the modern world, an absurd situation is therefore developing, in which the suspicion of intellectuals, on the one side, feeds their proud isolation and thus reinforces their abstractness and, on the other side, forces them to prostitute themselves to the powers that be, in exchange for their acceptance by the established society. The abundant literature on the problem of the role of the intellectual is testimony to the profound discomfort of the intelligentsia when confronted with this dramatic alternative: suicide or prostitution.

In the various attempts to find a way out of this dilemma, there seems to be a common element, even among the diverse opinions which might appear at times to be radical, that is to say, the desire to demonstrate that the type of reflection proper to the role of the intellectual is not extraneous to the dynamics of life and to concrete reality but is in fact its very base. The recognition of the role of reflection in the constitution of society and history is affirmed, ever more self-consciously, as the only remedy by which to bring civil life out of that condition of suffocation which bodes ill for society. Only the development of an adequate awareness of the true role of theorization can effectively prevent the manipulation of culture for ends that are extraneous to it, can reactivate that self-reflection and posing of problems capable of renewing within the socio-historical reality of man that utopian impulse, that ideal capacity for projection and that imaginative extrapolation, which negate what has already been achieved in the interest of a revolutionary notion of "what ought to be." Theorization should be able to refute every extrinsic mediation with praxis, recognizing its own inherent constitutive practical powers, which only its own degeneration can destroy. Phenomenology and Existentialism, the sociology of knowledge, philosophical anthropology and the "Frankfurt School," revisions of neo-positivism, neo-empiricism, linguistic analysis, pragmatism, the evolution of Marxism, and the reassessment of neo-idealism all attest to the need for a reconfirmation of the positive role of the intellectual by means of a new definition of the true and practical dimensions of intellectual consciousness.

In the context of this need to overcome the crisis of intellectuality, it might be interesting to reconsider the terms in which the problem of the intellectual is discussed in Vico's philosophy. Beyond his historical misfortune and the abstruseness of his style and even his thought, which is characteristic of the seventeenth century, Vico still offers some suggestions for understanding the practical dimension inherent in all theorizing. The first instance that comes to mind concerns the remarks made by Vico in his *Pratica della Scienza nuova.* These remarks may be confusing, however, in that the role of philosophers seems to be only to "recall the peoples to their *acme* or perfect state,"[1] insofar as they have come to know this through the contemplation of the cycle of nations and thus are able to give good orders, laws, and examples. The references to the dualism of body and soul and to the necessity that the body should serve and the mind command give to the *Pratica* the aspect of a traditional form of Platonism. In reality these notes, left at the stage of a sketch, can be adequately understood only if they are placed within the total meaning of Vico's thought, which can be condensed into two basic points: his criticism of the culture of his own age and the elaboration of a "new science" in opposition to that culture.

Already in the first *Oration* (1699), Vico observed that the tendency to promote the concreteness of experimental science against the abstractness of theology and moral philosophy could lead to the aridity of mathematics and intellectualism. To ward off this danger Vico defends self-knowledge, that reflection upon one's self which, although combining many different influences, from Platonic-Augustinian to Cartesian ones, opens the way to a new meaning of rationality. In the *Orations*, Vico above all points to the social dimension of a wisdom elaborated through a stressing of the injunction "Know thyself." And even if the associative force of this reflection concerns only the *societas litteraria* (*Third Oration*), and even if it is defined as a concern for the common good and the utility of the nation (*Fourth Oration*), there still arises from it an essential connection between *rerum divinarum cognitio, humanarum prudentia,* and *veritas et dignitas orationis* (*Fifth Oration*), which will constitute the object of his famous oration *De nostri temporis studiorum ratione.*

[1] "Pratica della Scienza nuova," *Opere* (Ricciardi), p. 875. See also "Practic of the New Science," trans. Thomas G. Bergin and Max H. Fisch, § 1405 (in this volume).

In this more extensive discussion Vico delineates the crisis of a knowledge concentrated on an eminently contemplative rationality, the crisis of the *isolated philosopher*. The necessary involvement of the sage in the *societas litteraria*, and of this literary society in the *societas civilis*, becomes an ever more pressing concern for Vico and leads him to a re-examination of both common sense and the concept of verisimilitude. Although at this point the problem remains vague for Vico, he seeks to defend acceptance of a notion of knowledge as wisdom equally different from a servile cleverness and a doctrinaire abstractness, a prudential wisdom which rejects the dogmatic adherence to "truth" in favor of the flexibility of the verisimilar.

The fundamental step in determining the nature of this wisdom is taken in the *De antiquissima Italorum sapientia*. The mediating presuppositions of the traditional theory of knowledge lead to scepticism, since a finite reason can never know a reality which is the creation of an infinite divine mind. The only escape from this scepticism seemed to be that offered by the Cartesian doctrine of innateness; but Vico denies this doctrine and maintains that the principle of *verum et factum convertuntur*, on which the denial of finite reason is based, can in fact be interpreted in a positive sense.

Being finite, the human mind cannot create the world of nature and thus cannot truly know it; but since this mind is in fact a divine creation, it has its own inherent excellence (*bontà*), by virtue of which its aspiration to truth cannot be totally groundless. If this aspiration were groundless, the human mind would contain an intrinsic contradiction, which would compromise its excellence. Consequently, human intelligence must have in itself some capacity for true knowledge and thus, according to the principle of *verum et factum*, for creating something. Thus the excellence of the human mind assumes for Vico the meaning of a participation, even though limited, of the creative activity of the divine mind in the human mind, by assimilating to it an experimental mode of operation, as against the doctrine of innate ideas. In the *De antiquissima Italorum sapientia*, the creativity of the human mind is limited to the realms of mathematics and, more marginally, language. But Vico's long study of the problems of law suggested to him a new field of human creativity on which to found a "new science."

In the *Diritto universale* Vico's reflection on the nature of positive law suggests the problem of the transition from animal to civil life. Vico singles out a fundamental difference between the animal and the savage: the former lives an instinctively balanced existence, while the latter remains prey to conflicts among his various instinctive drives which might lead him to self-destruction. If he does not destroy himself, it is because there is also present in the savage a balancing force, which Vico conceives as *vis rationis*. Vico is not concerned with the possibility that this *virtus* might be considered, as it is in the Biblical notion of original sin, as a degraded form of the *ratio integra* which God gave to the first men. He uses this point only to establish that it introduces an avenue to the supernatural into the experience of natural facts. This avenue endows the natural experiences of men with an emotional weight by which events, especially exceptional ones, become endowed with fantastic and mythical meaning. The elaboration of myths constitutes those mythical hypostases on the basis of which man is able to exercise a control, an *auctoritas*, over his passions. This elaboration of myths has its own truth, although quite different from any logically determined one, which produces a *honestas naturalis* that informs man's search for well-being, as the result of a modesty which constitutes, as *conscientia prave facti*, the vital nucleus of morality.

If the *vis rationis* is inherent in human sensibility and gives rise to the *auctoritas monastica*, it also determines the transition to *auctoritas familiaris* and *auctoritas oeconomica*, that is to say, civil life. Inasmuch as *vis rationis* provides a point of common reference to the supernatural (however fantastic), it promotes a convergence among individuals, a cohesion which first emerges as an apportioning of things useful but is then developed into the notion of *iustitia*. The constitution of civil society as apportioning implies as well the attainment of a basis for communication between men. If in a hypothetical Edenic state men may have been able to communicate with one another because of their common involvement in the divine, in a condition of savagery this could occur only because human sensibility maintains in them, due to its emotional and fantastic nature, a creative power, a capacity for *poiesis* which, while creating myths to explain the supernatural, expresses them by means of the creation of language. The *poiesis* peculiar to human sensibility is therefore the basis of communication and apportioning, which are the constitutive elements of the civil life.

The most striking motif in Vico's theory is his reduction of reason from *res cogitans* to *virtus*, that is to say, to *vis rationis*, as a way of highlighting reason's dynamic function in terms of a human existence, which therefore reveals itself in a historical, evolutionary development. The peculiar nature of this development consists precisely in the process of becoming aware of the processes which render it possible. Initially, the *vis rationis* acts as an instinctive force which, moving from within pure sensibility, constitutes a *conscientia*, that is to say, a knowing of things in terms of one another (*conscientia est cum alio noscere*).[2] *Conscientia* makes us aware of something but remains unaware of itself, except in a purely mythic form. In the development of civil life and its progressive articulation, the power of myth is dissolved, and man explicates with growing clarity and understanding the operations of consciousness. In this process of growing self-awareness, the *vis rationis*, the implicit basis of civil life, becomes its own ideal reference, to which life must always adjust. It is within terms of this

[2] *Diritto universale, Opere* 2: 73.

vital circularity that the principle of *verum et factum convertuntur* assumes its positive valence.

In the *Diritto universale* the regulative function, which is realized by means of the growing awareness of the nature of human poeticity, reaches maturity in the concept of *constantia iurisprudentis*. The jurisconsult actively intervenes in the development of law itself, determining the direction of its evolution in his efforts to conserve *constantia*, the stability of law, while recongizing the necessity of understanding the variety of life's continually changing forms. The jurisconsult represents a true synthesis of *truth* and *certitude*, an adjustment to the facts which, by apprehending the ideal force, the truth, which constitutes them, seeks to orient them in terms of that truth. In this sense, the jurisconsult appears as the expression of that acuity in which *sapientia* assumes a healing function, that is, inserts itself into civil life as a fashioning agent.

As long as the discourse remains on the level of law, its implicit problems remain partly hidden. But the examination of positive law and of its connection with civil life leads directly to *history*, and here the problems appear in all their gravity. On the level of history, one perceives, in fact, a division between the mythical poetizing which makes history possible, in the sense of what might be called the *res gestae*, and the reflection which produces the *historia rerum gestarum*. Out of this division arises the doubt that reflection might exhaust the poetic capacity; for even if reflection on history might result in a true wisdom (*sapienza vera*), it is doubtful whether this wisdom could be easily converted into the knowledge of new facts. Since "the world of gentile nations has certainly been made by men,"[3] on the basis of the principle of *verum et factum convertuntur* we are permitted to believe that we can truly know that world; but we must also believe that from that knowledge new facts can and indeed must arise. Hence Vico's speculative effort was directed to determining the possibility of a "new science," that is, a *sapienza riflessa*, in which the creativity of the human mind would not be dissolved and which would thus confirm the reciprocal conversion of *verum* and *factum*.

In order to clarify the significance of a "new science" one must first rise above the sterile opposition between philosophy and philology, of which even Vico seems to remain a victim when, in *Axiom* X, he writes:

> Philosophy contemplates reason, whence comes knowledge of the true; philology observes that of which human choice is author, whence comes consciousness of the certain. . . . This same axiom shows how the philosophers failed by half in not giving certainty to their reasonings by appeal to the authority of the philologians, and likewise how the latter failed by half in not taking care to give to their authority the sanction of truth by appeal to the reasoning of the philosophers.[4]

[3] *Scienza nuova prima*, *Opere* 3: 29.

[4] *New Science*, §§ 138, 140. All citations in the text preceded by a paragraph sign (§) are to the *New Science*.

Here it appears to be more a matter of the complementarity of two disciplines than of an actual resolution of their opposition. In reality, Vico's position, although beginning with this traditional dualism, introduces a dynamic tension between its terms which transforms its meaning.

It cannot be denied that the *New Science* contains a manifest ambiguity. The relating of the *true* to the *certain* is presented as a "new critical art" by which "we consider at what determinate times and on what particular occasions of human necessity or utility felt by the first men of the gentile world, they . . . imagined first such and such gods and then such and such others" (§ 7). This formulation of the "new critical art" might seem to anticipate the kind of research which today is known as the sociology of knowledge or cultural anthropology. But Vico wished to distinguish this "new critical art" from the traditional science of philology, because he felt that, although it is necessary to relate truth to "determine times and particular occasions," it would be then a grave deficiency if inquiry became mired down in the "deplorable obscurity of causes and almost infinite variety of effects." But, when he seeks to explain how one might avoid this danger, Vico affirms that in order to reduce philology to "the form of a science" it is necessary to discover "in it the design of an ideal eternal history traversed in time by the histories of all nations . . ." (§ 7).

The concept of "an ideal eternal history" is undoubtedly the source of serious ambiguities of Vico's thought, since the term "ideal" does not always succeed in maintaining a correct balance between "history" and "eternal"—and the latter seems to prevail over the former. In fact, the principle of *corsi* and *ricorsi*, the formally changeless recurrence of certain historical structures, appears to suggest the presumption by Vico that the triadic schema which he elaborated (the three ages, divine, heroic, and human) might have an absolute value, possess eternal validity, and thus ought to be considered as an immutable criterion of historical becoming.

The "new critical art" which had to find in the "philosophy of authority" the ideal complement of "certainty" would be in this way reabsorbed into the systematic consistency of a "philosophy of history." This systematic reversal may seem to be confirmed by the connection which links the "philosophy of authority" with the "metaphysics of the world of nations" and this latter with a "reasoned civil theology." Actually, however, the opposite is the case. The particular character which a metaphysics assumes, inasmuch as it leads to a "reasoned civil theology," in fact constitutes, paradoxically, a check on the absolute claims of the metaphysics. Any investigation of the historical and social structuration of the human world, in concluding with a reference to a divine world, reveals the limitations of human consciousness or knowledge and thus brings into question the claims to absolute validity of its notions. If man can truly know the certainty of civil life only insofar as he is able to make explicit the connection between human consciousness and God, he must then admit that he does not have the ability to understand the infinite essence of the divine. By means of reflection on the world of nations, Vico can explicate the fundamental role that the idea of God plays in the development of civil life. The presence of this idea, even in its primordial, emotional and fantastic form, in a consciousness still dominated by sensation established indisputably for Vico the ontological connection between the human mind and the divine mind and thus the existence of the latter. But the echo of the basic patristic argument, which descends through a set of successive elaborations to Descartes, has in Vico such an accentuation of the transcendence of the divine that it practically renders his discussion of it devoid of content. The discussion, still present in the *Diritto universale*, concerning the divine *aseitas* and its articulation in *posse, posse, velle infinitum* as the basis of the human *suitas*,[5] disappears in the *New Science*, where every kind of revelation is absorbed into the "reasoned civil theology." What remains valid for Vico is the idea that if the human mind is turned towards God, that means that God is turned towards men, that He has given His own eternal infinity to our temporal finitude by informing and preforming us: man understands God only as providence.

In whatever guise, then, the infinite may have descended into these finite things, we would not be able to understand even if God were to explain it to us, it belonging to the truth peculiar to the divine mind, in which knowing and making are the same act. The human mind, by contrast, is limited and formed, which is why it is able to conceive of formless and boundless things but cannot understand them.[6]

The inexhaustable nature of the divine to the human mind thus appears as an insurmountable obstacle to the human attempt to grasp the essence of the eternal and to derive from it the immutable norm of the temporal. But, despite the indissoluble ontological connection which seems to exist between the human and the divine mind, this limitation undermines the possibility of applying the principle of *verum et factum convertuntur* to history. Men, in fact, ought to be able to know history truly, inasmuch as they are themselves the makers of the civil world. But if the idea of God, which constitutes the prime motive of human mental processes, suggests a participatory relation between man and God, then human responsibility for the making of history is placed in doubt. In fact, Vico says, human will is the *Fabro* (artificer) of history but obeys the "divine architect," that is to say, providence.[7] Human will is an instrument which divine providence uses for the realization of its plans.

It is from these notions that is born that ambiguous Vichian theory of the "heterogenesis of ends," that is, the imbalance between the particular ends that men propose for themselves and that universal end which pro-

[5] *Diritto universale, Opere* 2: 43.
[6] *De Italorum sapientia, Opere* (Ricciardi), p. 277.
[7] *Scienza nuova prima, Opere* 3: 39.

vides the cohesive force of history and which is the result only of providence. Consequently, men cannot truly know history, since they make it only as instruments.

In reality, if many of Vico's assertions express the need to ground ontologically the creativity of human consciousness in divine creativity, this ground is ultimately reduced to two very restricted functions. On the one side, providence preforms human nature so as to render it capable of those processes of consciousness which, by producing common sense, make possible intersubjective communication. On the other side, it prevents, by virtue of its eternal changelessness, the historical degeneration of humanity from ending in total destruction and guarantees to it the possibility of renewal.

Beyond these functions, which might be considered objective, there remains only the capacity of human consciousness to elaborate, even if in fantastic and emotional forms, that idea of God, that is to say, that opening to the idea of infinite transcendence, which is the matrix of any further operations of human consciousness and of the intersubjective range that these operations have. It is the force and authenticity of this idea of infinite transcendence which guarantee, according to Vico, the poetic capacity (*poiesis*) of human consciousness; and it is by the weakening of this capacity that historical degeneration is determined. The forms which permit the transition from poetic-mythic consciousness, that is, *sapienza poetica*, to civilized consciousness, that is, *sapienza riflessa*, constitute, according to Vico, the prime cause of the crisis which was taking shape in the society of his time, precisely because in those forms the idea of God was becoming weakened.

The vital core of Vico's work, which extends far beyond the many observations he makes regarding his unquestioning acceptance of his Catholic faith and his obsequious respect for the established authorities, consists in the conviction that, besides that drastic remedy for the crisis preordained by providence by means of the fall into barbarism and a successive return to *sapienza poetica*, there is within the *sapienza riflessa* the capacity to oppose the fall into degeneration and to recover, on the plane of a fully developed reason, the creative power.

The possibilities of this recovery become clarified by degrees. In a first stage, in revision of his previous judgments on civil poetry, Vico accepts the possibility that the ideas formulated by philosophy, metaphysics, and theology in civil times might have been felt, as possibly happened in Dante and Petrarch, with such a deep emotional fervor that it was possible to effect their translation into poetic forms. In this way the *sapienza riflessa* would have become transformed into mythic consciousness, thereby recovering its creative force. All this notwithstanding, it could be said that this reconsideration of the value of civil poetry still reflects that basic dualism which seemed to oppose "perceiving with a troubled and agitated spirit" to "reflecting with a clear mind" (§ 218). The effective resolution of the dualism which Vico had attempted by his criticism of the Cartesian *res cogitans* and the alternative of the *vis rationis* leads to the development of the very concept of *sapienza riflessa* into the concept of *sapienza eroica.*

The strength of primitive poetic minds resulted precisely from the synthesis of *mens* and *animus*, of reason and passion. These minds functioned within this synthesis, or better yet, were themselves unities which preceded the division between reason and passion, unities in which universality, emerging as poetic form, revealed its creative power. In civil times, which are human and no longer divine or heroic, one passes from a spontaneous orientation towards the universality of the supernatural and from an emotional self-disciplining of the senses and passions to a process of self-awareness in which the assumption of responsibility is based precisely upon the juxtaposition of feeling and intellect, of particular and universal. In this form, however, there is realized a very limited condition, one wanting in self-consciousness, which might be the cause of a fatal degeneration of the human processes.

Not even the capacity to reendow universal abstractions with creative force by means of their translation into poetic forms is sufficient to meet this danger. What Vico aims at is the realization of a wisdom that might succeed in developing the processes of reflection so as to produce a self-reflection by which one might grasp the indissoluble unity of consciousness beyond its various manifestations. This wisdom makes explicit the "almost divine strength of human minds"—their creative capacity to imbue themselves with both science and virtue.[8] This *sapienza eroica* is called "healing" because it provides the only effective "therapy" for humanity in its decadent phase. Insofar as it is a "healing wisdom," it must know how to move ceaselessly from concrete facts to the ideas from which these facts have sprung, rescuing them from what we would call today an exclusively positivistic description, in order to grasp their significative value; and it must know how to return from these ideas to the facts considered as the actualization of the poeticizing force proper to that ideality. Only thus can the *being* of men, their factual determination, cease to be experienced as a weight which immobilizes and become involved instead in the "ought" kept open and vital by the tension of ideas.

It is true that for Vico this ideal tension is characterized by its grounding in the idea of God. But it is also true that, since this idea is unable in principle to eventuate in a true knowledge of God, but halts at the idea of a providence, which is by itself a problem, it assumes only the function of justifying and intensifying the tension between the infinite and the finite, the universal and the particular. The awareness of this complex articulation and functioning of ideality, which sees in man that entity in which "to be" is "to aspire" (*essere è un dover essere*) constitutes the

[8] "Della mente eroica," *Opere* (Ricciardi), p. 914.

culmination of *sapienza riflessa* which, by means of self-reflection, authentically realizes the synthesis of philology and philosophy, of facts and ideas.

In the last chapter of the *New Science*, after having described the development of the concept of "heroism" in various manifestations of the social life, Vico observes:

> These commonwealths gave birth to philosophy. By their very form they inspired it to form the hero, and for that purpose to interest itself in truth. All this was ordained by providence to the end that, since virtuous actions were no longer prompted by religious sentiments as formerly, philosophy should make the virtues understood in their idea. . . . And from the philosophies providence permitted eloquence to arise and . . . become impassioned for justice, and from these ideas of virtue to inflame the peoples to command good laws (§ 1101).

Even though Vico, living in a monarchy, sought to exhalt the monarchical form of government, there is no doubt that his ideal was identifiable with the republican ideal and the corresponding form of heroism of a philosophy which might produce an eloquence capable of inspiring that ideal power from which good laws come.

Reflecting on Vico's position, one might conclude that it was not by chance that Herbert Marcuse called that type of theorizing intended to unleash the ethical-utopian dimension of society a "new science." In reality, in spite of the obvious differences between Vico and the social and cultural concepts of the "critical theory" of the Frankfurt School and particularly of Jürgen Habermas, the latter's aim of recovering "the practical dimension of reason and the ethical dimension of theorizing" can be seen as a commentary on that "heroic philosophy" which is the most authentic expression of the "praxis" of the *New Science*. The *Pratica* is not simply a corollary of Vico's great work but is inherent in the very process of self-reflection which informs it. If we have sometimes used expressions with overtones of existentialism, phenomenology, or specifically Marcuse and Habermas' "critical theory," it was exactly in order to stress the possibiilty of seeing in Vico's thought motifs and suggestions much more vital than a superficial reading might permit.*

* Another figure of the Frankfurt School, in fact its director during its most creative years, Max Horkheimer, had a definite interest in Vico's conception of history. His work, *Die Anfänge der bürgerlichen Geschichtsphilosophie* (*The Origins of the Bourgeois Philosophy of History*) published in Stuttgart in 1930, which served as part of his credentials for assuming the directorship of the Institut für Sozialforschung in that same year, had as part of its concern a discussion of Vico's views as well as those of Machiavelli, Hobbes and others. Martin Jay reports in *The Dialectical Imagination: A History of the Frankfurt School and the Institute of Social Research 1923–1950* (Boston and Toronto: Little, Brown and Co., 1973) that "in fact, Vico was one of Horkheimer's early intellectual heroes" (p. 49). Horkheimer admired Vico's attack on Cartesian thought and Vico's principle that man being himself the maker of history can understand history in a more fundamental sense than he can understand nature. Jay sums up Horkheimer's relationship to Vico as: "Vico's attack on Cartesian meta-

Poetry, literature, eloquence, and philosophy are the specific domains of the Vichian intellectual, to whom is entrusted the principal responsibility of avoiding the drastic remedy which providence provides for the degeneration of peoples, that is, the fall back into the "*barbarie del senso.*" Standing between the "*barbarie della riflessione*" and the "*barbarie del senso*" is the capacity of the intellectual to develop an awareness of his own *heroism*, of the *poiesis* proper to reason, by liberating it from the deformations which weaken it and thus making possible the creation of the civil, socio-historical world. That Vico did not determine the political forms which the renewal of *heroic philosophy* would take testifies above all to the fact that this renewal might be linked to the forms which civil life in fact assumes. Moreover, Vico's undeniably Platonic treatment of heroic philosophy, in the framework we have indicated, may be taken as a warning against giving the intellectual tasks not proper to his calling. The notion that the intellectual should bear witness to the concreteness of his theorizing by involving himself directly in politics is an example of the deformation of the role of the intellectual caused by his sense of guilt for having allowed theorizing to become an incentive to social degeneration. The intellectual is not aware that in this self-laceration he denies his most authentic role and subjugates himself to the established political power.

The intellectual has a role which is bound to influence politics, but his own political action consists in the commitment to develop a "heroic" rather than a "barbaric" reflection in men, one that would favor men's natural tendency *ad communicandum*, and to construct a civil life on the basis of this communication. This, in Habermas' terms, is the reconfirmation or recovery of that "intersubjective, communicative action" which permits an authentic development of social life. If the intellectual must use self-criticism as a defense against the dangers of a degenerative involution of culture, he must also be aware that the particular nature of his role does not require his participation in a concrete process which would always remain extrinsic to him and which would end by making him their instru-

---

physics and the growing idolatry of mathematics set him apart from his contemporaries. So too did his insight that man could know history better than the natural world because man was history's maker. Vico had also transcended the limitations of the Enlightenment interpretation of the origins of myths, which he saw less as priestly tricks than as the projection of human needs onto nature. In so arguing, Vico had anticipated the later Marxist view of ideology. Thus, despite his cyclical theory of the rise and fall of civilizations, which was similar to Machiavelli's, he was unique in seeing that human activity was the key to understanding historical development. Vico had understood that *praxis* and the domination of nature were not the same. Although he separated man and nature, he did so in a way that avoided placing one above the other. By insisting on the subjectivity of man, he preserved the potentiality of the subjectivity of nature. In his subsequent writings [after *The Origins of the Bourgeois Philosophy of History* of 1930] Horkheimer spent little time with Vico, but the critique of the Enlightenment made by the Italian theorist was one he continued to share" (pp. 257–58). [*Editors' note.*]

ment. He must be able to recognize the concrete *poiesis* which is proper to him and, by means of self reflection, work to affirm and defend it. This, is the intellectual's specific task, a task which Vico held to be essential for the realization of a sound social order, inasmuch as its validity rests on an ideal tension of knowledge, continually reconfirmed and reborn in the awareness of that creativity which can only be born from that tension.

Translated by Margaret Brose

Max H. Fisch

VICO'S *PRATICA**

So that the art and practic part of life
Must be the mistress to this theoric.

Henry V

Even before the second edition of his *New Science* appeared in 1730, Vico began revisions looking toward a third. In the summer of 1731 he drafted an entirely new concluding chapter to follow that of the second edition. He devoted this new final chapter to what he called the *pratica* of the new science. But when the third edition appeared in 1744, it ended as the second had, with "On an Eternal Natural Commonwealth." It is probable that the omission was not an oversight of the last months or weeks of Vico's life, but resulted from a decision taken as early as 1731, and for good reasons.

Nicolini, the leading editor of Vico in the present century, nevertheless included the *Pratica* in all four of his editions of the *New Science*. Partly because he made it so readily accessible, and partly because of the rise of such movements as Marxism, fascism, pragmatism, instrumentalism, operationalism, and praxiology, it has come to be referred to with some frequency.[1] The editors of the present volume therefore asked Bergin and me to contribute an English translation of the *Pratica*. And I offer here a few reflections concerning it, as a supplement to my previous essay on "Vico and Pragmatism."[2]

The most obvious questions concerning the *Pratica* are: (1) Why did Vico write it? (2) Why was it to serve as the concluding chapter? (3) Why did he withhold it from publication? (4) What is the meaning of *pratica* here, and how should it be rendered in English?

Vico nowhere answers any of these questions. Concerning the first three, and above all concerning the third, we are reduced to conjecture. But the *Pratica* itself supplies a clue which will lead us to a confident answer to

* See below in this volume the translation of the *Pratica*, "Practic of the New Science."

[1] There is at least one previous translation, by Carlo Sganzini, under the title "Ueber politische Erziehung (Praxis der Neuen Wissenschaft)," appended to his essay, "Das politische Denken Giambattista Vicos und die Gegenwart," *Philosophia* 3 (1938): 359–72. Sganzini rightly rejects the fascist interpretation of Vico by Walther Witzenmann, which made Sorel the father of fascism and Vico its grandfather.

[2] In *Giambattista Vico: An International Symposium*, pp. 401–24. For some notes on this essay see Appendix below.

the fourth, and that answer will afford a basis for conjectures concerning the first three. The clue is in the opening sentences:

This entire work has so far been treated as a purely contemplative science. . . . It consequently seems to be lacking in the *pratica* that all those sciences should have which are called "active," as dealing with matters that depend on human choice. That *pratica* can easily be derived from contemplation of the course the nations run. . . .

Pratica, like *contemplativa* and *attive,* is a technical term in what we now call the philosophy of science. The philosophy of science proceeds on the assumption that there is a plurality of sciences; that science is either what they have in common or an ideal to which they approximate in varying degrees; that there are nevertheless divers kinds of sciences; and that the philosophy of science must not only determine what science is but distinguish the kinds. These particular technical terms belong to a vocabulary for distinguishing the kinds that goes back to Plato and Aristotle.

Aristotle distinguishes three kinds of science, which he calls *theôrêtikê, praktikê,* and *poiêtikê*—theoretical, practical, and "poetical," that is, creative or productive. They are distinguished in the first place by their aims—knowing, doing, making—according as the knowing they aim at is knowing for the sake of knowing on the one hand or knowing for the sake of doing or making on the other. But they are distinguished in the second place by the objects they study. The objects of theoretical science are none of our doing or making; they cannot be otherwise than as they are; our knowing or not knowing them makes no difference to them; the only difference it makes is to us. The objects of practical and productive science, on the other hand, are precisely our own doings and makings, the things we have done or made or intend doing or making. And since our doings and makings depend on our knowledge, so also do the objects of practical and productive science.

The theoretical sciences recognized by Aristotle are theology or first philosophy (later called metaphysics), physics, and mathematics. The only autonomous practical science he recognizes is *politikê*—not politics in our sense but the poliscraft.[3] (*Oikonomikê,* household management, is included in the poliscraft; but *êthikê,* ethics, is nowhere mentioned.) Productive science embraces all the other arts and crafts, including medicine, the one most frequently brought into analogy with the poliscraft.

In Latin and in modern languages derived from Latin, Aristotle's Greek terms were sometimes translated, sometimes domesticated. Latin writers who sought to adhere as closely as possible to Aristotle's classification, and yet to translate, came out with:

[3] Max H. Fisch, "The Poliscraft" in *Philosophy and the Civilizing Arts: Essays Presented to Herbert W. Schneider on his Eightieth Birthday,* ed. Craig Walton and John P. Anton (Athens, Ohio: Ohio University Press, 1975), pp. 24–48.

scientia	*speculativa* or *contemplativa* *activa* *factiva*	=	*epistêmê*	*theôrêtikê* *praktikê* *poiêtikê*

But Latin writers less concerned with translation freely modified his scheme on the one hand and domesticated some of his terms on the other.

Since the autonomous *polis* no longer existed, Aristotle's identification of practical science with *politikê* was uncomprehended, and it was easy to insert ethics and economics before politics and at the same time to give politics a more general meaning. By a grotesque misinterpretation that still prevails, all this was read into Aristotle himself.[4]

Such writers rightly sensed, however, that the theoretical/practical distinction was much more important for Aristotle than either the practical/productive or the theoretical/productive distinction, and they tended either to omit productive science altogether or to make it a species of practical science or even in some respects of the theoretical science of physics. They could not quite make factive science a species of active, so they domesticated Aristotle's *praktikê* as *practica*, and made *activa* and *factiva* two species of *practica*. Having thus domesticated *praktikê*, they went on to domesticate *theôrêtikê* also, or rather the short form *theôrikê*, as *theorica*. The resulting Latin variation on Aristotle's classification thus became:

scientia	*theorica* (*metaphysica, physica, mathematica*)	
	practica	*activa* (*ethica, economica, politica*)
		factiva (e.g., *medica*)

At the same time there were numerous other variations on the theoretical/practical distinction, having little in common but the names, which had lost their Aristotelian precision. It was frequently observed, for example, that within any one science, whether theoretical or practical, and, if the latter, whether active or factive, there might be *relatively* theoretical and *relatively* practical *parts*. The theoretical science of geometry, for example, had a practical part in which it was brought to bear on the art of surveying; and the practical (and more specifically factive) science of medicine had a theoretical part, much of it borrowed from physics (as including chemistry, biology, and psychology). (Among the more practical parts of medicine, of course, were diagnostics and therapeutics.)

It was in this way that Italian *pratica*, like Latin *practica*, had come to have two technical meanings in Vico's time: (1) as the name for a *kind* of science to be distinguished always from theoretical science on the one hand, and sometimes also from productive science on the other, but more

[4] *Ibid.*

commonly including the latter as a species; and (2) as the name for a *part* of a science, as distinguished always from a more theoretical part of the same science, whether that science as a whole, by Aristotle's two criteria, be theoretical or practical. In both these technical senses, the commonest opposite of *pratica* was *teorica*. Their English equivalents, now obsolete, were *practic* and *theoric*. In both senses, *teorica* and *pratica* are feminine singular adjectives used as nouns. In sense 1 the noun understood is *scienza*; in sense 2, *parte*. Thus, in the case of medicine:

$$(\textit{scienza})\ \textit{medica}\left\{\begin{array}{l}(\textit{parte})\ \textit{teorica}\\ (\textit{parte})\ \textit{pratica}\end{array}\right.$$

It is true that *pratica* had also acquired a non-technical sense for which English *practice* may serve; and even within the *Pratica* Vico once inadvertently uses *le pratiche* in that non-technical sense, "the practices."[5] But for the technical senses modern English has no equivalent; only the obsolete *practic* will do.[6]

We are now ready to answer question 4: What is the meaning of *pratica* in Vico's *Pratica*, and how should it be rendered in English? Our answer is: Except for that one lapse into non-technicality, *pratica* is used in the second of its two technical senses and means the (or a) more practical part of the new science of humanity; and the only possible English rendering is *practic*. (*Practic*, I have granted, is obsolete; but so is the *Pratica*.)

If the reader is still in doubt, a glance at the first edition of the *New Science* may help. Vico there says that it has two practics:

> One of these is that of a new critical art to serve as torch for distinguishing the true in obscure and fabulous history. Beyond this, the other practic is a sort of diagnostic art which, guided by the wisdom of mankind, from the order itself of the institutions of humanity determines the degrees of their necessity or utility and, as its last consequence, determines the chief end of this science, that of discerning the indubitable signs of the state of the nations.[7]

The two practics are clearly the two arts, one critical the other diagnostic, each a part of the new science itself. And the new science, like medicine, not only *has* at least two practics but *is* a science of the practical *kind*, though of the active rather than the factive species of that kind.

[5] *Scienza nuova*, *Opere* 4: § 1410. In Greek, this non-technical sense was unambiguously expressed by the noun *praxis*. Neither Latin nor Italian had an unambiguous equivalent. In the end they domesticated *praxis* (Italian, *prassi*); but it had little currency until Duns Scotus defined and used it in arguing that theology is a practical science (*Opus Oxoniense*, Prologus, Pars V). Vico had a Scotist teacher but did not follow suit, though this may have been one of the sources of his *verum-factum* principle.

[6] In the preceding ten paragraphs I have given the barest possible sketch of a long and complicated story, to which the best introduction, though itself only a sketch, is part 1 of Nicholas Lobkowicz's *Theory and Practice* (Notre Dame: University of Notre Dame Press, 1967). A much more detailed study is greatly needed.

[7] *Scienza nuova prima*, *Opere* 3: § 391.

I return now to my first three questions, to which only conjectural answers are possible. (1) Why did Vico write the *Pratica*? In the first place, I conjecture, because he was accustomed to think in terms of Aristotle's classification of the sciences and of later variations on it. His *Ancient Wisdom of the Italians* was to consist of three books: metaphysics, physics, and ethics—two of Aristotle's theoretical sciences and (according to the misinterpretation mentioned above) the first of his practical sciences. When in his *Universal Law* Vico went on to deal with jurispudence, he of course understood that he was dealing with that part of Aristotle's third practical science, politics, which had a place in the faculties of the universities of Vico's time. And in the *New Science* itself, as a glance at the table of contents of book 2 will show, he divides "Poetic Wisdom" into metaphysics, logic (including semiotic, grammar, and rhetoric), morals, economy, politics (the three practical sciences), and physics (including cosmography, astronomy, chronology, and geography)—all poetic, that is, the wisdom of the makers of humanity.

In the second place, because he therefore anticipated the question, "Is your new science of humanity contemplative, practical, or productive?"

And, in the third place, because it came over him, when the second edition was already in print, that he had given no such clear indication in it as he had in the first that, by Aristotle's two criteria, the new science of humanity was a practical, not a theoretical, science. In the first edition he had said that the second practic, the diagnostic art, "determines the chief end of this science, that of discerning the indubitable signs of the state of the nations," that is, of the stage that a given nation has reached in "the ideal eternal history," in "the course the nations run"—so that its statesmen may be guided accordingly. The new science of humanity was to take the place of that "philosophy concerning things human" (*hê peri ta anthrôpina philosophia*)[8] which Aristotle's *Politics* was meant to complete; but perhaps few readers of Vico's second edition would have guessed it.

(2) But why did Vico write the *Pratica* to serve as the concluding chapter in the third edition? In the first place, I conjecture, because that was the remedy that called for the least rewriting, the least disruption of the general plan of the second edition.

In the second place, because, in any science that had both a theoric and a practic, the natural, the accepted, the expected order was first the theoric and then the practic.

So Vico imagines a reader coming up to the end of the second edition and asking, like a medical student impatient to get to diagnostics and therapeutics, "But is your new science of humanity a purely contemplative one?" And the answer he starts to give in the third edition is, "Up to this point it may have seemed so, but I turn now from theoric to practics." One of these practics he says "can easily be derived from contemplation

[8] *Nicomachean Ethics,* 1181^b15.

of the course the nations run"; but he leaves the derivation to "the wise men and princes of the commonwealths." This is the diagnostic art which was the second practic named in the first edition. It corresponds to Aristotle's *Politics*, reconstructed in the light of the new science and brought within its scope. (The reconstruction had begun in Vico's *Universal Law*, in which the new science itself had first been broached, in a chapter entitled "Nova Scientia Tentatur.")

"The practic that we as philosophers can supply," he goes on, "is one that need not take us outside our academies." This, it turns out, corresponds to the other two practical sciences of the Aristotelian tradition—ethics and economics. As Vico says toward the end, "By these principles of metaphysics brought down into physics and thence through morality carried into household management (*iconomica*) and thus into their own education, let the young be guided into good politics, and with their minds so disposed let them finally move on into jurisprudence."[9] They will then be prepared to become "the wise men and princes of the commonwealths" and derive the practic first mentioned, the diagnostic art, "from contemplation of the course the nations run."

I come, finally, to the most difficult question of all: (4) Why did Vico nevertheless withhold the *Pratica* from publication? In the first place, I conjecture, because he quickly came to see its utter insufficiency. It was a pathetic dodge to dismiss the diagnostic art in a single sentence (which has become two in our translation), by leaving its derivation to "the wise men and princes of the commonwealths." And as a replacement for the *Nicomachean Ethics* and the *Economics* of the Aristotelian corpus, the hasty, sketchy, and preachy remainder of the *Pratica* was a miserable failure. If he could not do vastly better than that, it were better to omit the *Pratica* altogether.

In the second place, and much more importantly, Vico must have concluded on reflection that the *Pratica* conceded too much to the Aristotelian trichotomy and hierarchy of the sciences. The new science of humanity is not just one more science, waiting to be assigned to one of the three kinds. It will not leave the hierarchy standing, with all previously assigned sciences remaining safe in their slots. It is a practical science, in the sense of bringing replacements for the three practical sciences of the Aristotelian tradition. But it is no more practical than contemplative or productive. It is contemplative, but it contemplates a world we ourselves have made, the world of nations; and that world has not been finished and fixed for our contemplation. It is still in the making—*our* making—and it can be made better. So the new science is productive, and doubly so.

The superiority that the tradition ascribes to contemplative knowledge over practical, and to practical over productive, is illusory. The reason we

[9] *Scienza nuova, Opere* 4: § 1411. See below in this volume the translation, "Practic of the New Science."

can know the human world, the world of nations, is not the eternity of its ideal eternal history, but the fact that we have made it. Only one of Aristotle's three theoretical sciences, namely mathematics, shares that prerogative, but in an inferior, not a superior, degree. We have scientific knowledge in mathematics, not because mathematical objects are eternal objects awaiting our contemplation, but because they are objects of our own creation. And it is not the case that mathematics is cognitively superior to the new science because it is contemplative and the new science productive. On the contrary, both are productive, but, of the two, mathematics is cognitively inferior because what we create in mathematics are fictions, and what we create in the world of nations are realities.

And as for physics, another of Aristotle's theoretical sciences, such knowledge as we can have of the human world, because we have made it, we cannot have of the physical or natural world because it is not we but God who has made that. A quasi-knowledge of some parts of the natural world, to be sure, is open to us; but it can extend only as far as experiments of our own making will carry us, that is, only so far as physics becomes a productive science.

It is fair to add that Aristotle himself is of two minds about physics. In the *Metaphysics* he makes it theoretical, but in the *Parts of Animals*, thinking of nature as craftsman, he makes it productive.[10]

Logic has always been a problem in the Aristotelian tradition. Neither its theoretical, its practical, nor its productive aspects have seemed to justify assigning it to any one of the three kinds. Calling it an organon was a way, not of deciding for the third, but of avoiding a decision. The new science makes it all three, but in the first place productive, as studying signs of our own making and relations among them.

In sum, the trichotomy of knowing, doing, and making is untenable. What is none of our doing or making is none of our knowing either. And not only are doing and making prerequisite to further knowing, but knowing cannot later detach itself from them or be made to precede them. No point is reached at which theoric can be got out of the way before practic and poetic or technic begin.

If Vico had such thoughts as I conjecture, he may then have proceeded to these: "Clearly the *Pratica* must be suppressed. And, as for these other thoughts, I cannot now express them better than I already have, in the *Ancient Wisdom*, the *Universal Law*, and the first and second *New Science*. It will not avail to lift them out of context and resay them here. The new critical art, for example, belongs where I now place it, among the principal aspects of the new science.[11] The diagnostic and therapeutic practices are so far only projects; even the theoric, though newly created,

[10] Fisch, "Vico and Pragmatism" in *Giambattista Vico: An International Symposium*, p. 404.
[11] *New Science*, § 392.

is not finished but will develop in ways I cannot foresee. The new science of humanity cannot be pressed between the covers of a book. The end of the book is not the end of the science. If the science is to live and flourish, and if my book is to be a means of its doing so, I must trust all to my discerning readers, and to their students—and mine."

APPENDIX

Some Notes Concerning My Essay, "Vico and Pragmatism," in Giambattista Vico: *An International Symposium* (1969)

1. Though "Peirce nowhere mentions Vico" (p. 401), he does mention Flint's *Vico* as though he were acquainted with it, in reviewing another work by Flint in *Nation* 80 (1905): 360.

2. The Ph.D theses referred to in notes 11 and 18 have since been completed, both at the University of Illinois at Urbana-Champaign in 1969: Donald R. Koehn, *Peirce's Explanation of the Validity of Synthetic Inference in the "Illustrations of the Logic of Science"*; Willard M. Miller, *C. S. Peirce on the Philosophy of History.*

3. In the important quotation from *Collected Papers* 5.311 on pp. 416f., an error can now be corrected from an errata list of which the editors were unaware. Peirce there corrects "capable of a definite increase of knowledge" to read "capable of an indefinite increase of knowledge."

4. To footnote 19 add: Robert G. Meyers, "Peirce on Cartesian Doubt," *Transactions of the Charles S. Peirce Society* 3 (1967): 13–23.

Alain Pons

PRUDENCE AND PROVIDENCE: THE *PRATICA DELLA SCIENZA NUOVA* AND THE PROBLEM OF THEORY AND PRACTICE IN VICO

For Vico, as later for Hegel, the importance of the concept of history was primarily theoretical. It never occurred to either of them to apply this concept directly by using it as a principle of action. Truth they conceived of as being revealed to the contemplative, backward-oriented glance of the historian, who, by being able to see the process as a whole, is in a position to overlook the narrow aims of acting men, concentrating instead on the higher aims that realize themselves behind their backs (Vico).

Let us compare these lines of Hannah Arendt, from her "The Concept of History,"[1] with a text of Vico himself:

This entire work has so far been treated as a purely contemplative science concerning the common nature of nations. It seems for this reason to promise no help to human prudence toward delaying if not preventing the ruin of nations in decay. It consequently seems to be lacking in the practic that all those sciences should have which are called "active," as dealing with matters that depend on human choice.

That practic can easily be derived from the contemplation of the course the nations run. Instructed by such contemplation, the wise men and princes of the commonwealths will be able, through good institutions, laws, and examples, to recall the peoples to their *acme* or perfect state. The practic of the science that we as philosophers can offer is such as can be completed within the academies.[2]

These are the first two paragraphs of a chapter which appears in the *Correzioni, miglioramenti e aggiunte*, written by Vico in 1731 as an addition to the 1730 edition of the *New Science*. This chapter, entitled *Pratica della Scienza nuova*, was to be included in the *Conclusione dell'opera*, but it was not retained in the definitive edition of 1744, which, as is well known, was prepared by Vico himself.[3]

[1] *Between Past and Future: Six Exercises in Political Thought* (Cleveland and New York, 1963), p. 77.

[2] See below in this volume, "Practic of the New Science," trans. Thomas G. Bergin and Max H. Fisch, §§ 1405–6.

[3] The *Pratica della Scienza nuova* was first published by Del Giudice in *Scritti inediti di Giambattista Vico tratti da un autografo dell'autore* (Naples, 1862). It is republished in vol. 2 of the *Opere*, ed. Fausto Nicolini (Bari, 1928), following the text of the 1744 edition of the *Scienza nuova*.

The comparison of these two texts is not lacking in irony, for Vico seems to contradict in advance the author of *The Human Condition* and to foresee and to contest almost point for point the interpretation which makes of him a pure *theoretician* of history. This interpretation is not, however, new; one finds it among both those who see in Vico's work "philosophy of history" in the Romantic sense of the term and those who would modernize the epistemological structure of the Vichian "new science" and define its object and its method in terms of our modern "human" or "social" sciences. But if we have retained the formulation of Hannah Arendt, it is because it has the merit of a perfect clarity, especially in the light of another of her remarks in which, while opposing the Vico of the *De nostri temporis studiorum ratione* to the Vico of the *Scienza nuova,* she speaks of "this biographical development" which, "though quite extraordinary in the early eighteenth century, became the rule approximately one hundred years later: each time the modern age had reason to hope for a new political philosophy, it received a philosophy of history instead."[4]

If one follows Hannah Arendt, it is necessary then to admit that Vico only discovered the modern concept of history by breaking completely with the tradition of classical political philosophy, which refused to dissociate theory and practice, the analysis of political society, of its bases and end, and the search for principles of action applicable to contemporary situations. According to Arendt, the view which Vico brings to bear on the new world of history which reveals itself to him is purely retrospective, therefore contemplative—"theoretical" in the etymological sense of the word, in the way that the Greek natural philosophers' view of nature would be theoretical. To understand all is not only to accept all: it is also to justify all and to sanctify it. Thought and reality are reconciled, as they are with Hegel; but what then of *praxis,* that is to say, free and creative human action? What could be the relationship of *praxis* to a theory which is a theory only in virtue of its exclusion from history of the arbitrary, whether it be that of human wills or of the divine will?

The "new science" of Galileo allowed Descartes to affirm that man is now able to make himself "master and owner of nature"; but Vico, according to Hannah Arendt, would not have dared to conceive of so typically modern, or Promethean, an idea, according to which his "new science" could be put to the service of action and could serve to give direction to political practice by illuminating its means and ends. One had to wait for Marx to draw the full implication of the Vichian principle which affirms that history is "made" by men: these implications are not only epistemological but also practical. The science of history will serve then to control history, no longer to subjugate it but truly to "make" it, to the point where theory and practice are no longer separated, but united

[4] *The Human Condition* (New York, 1959), p. 373, n. 62.

and even identified. Thus it is that Hannah Arendt could oppose to Vico and Hegel in the same text the figure of Marx who "combined this notion of history with the teleological political philosophies of the earlier stages of the modern age, so that in his thought the 'higher aims'—which according to the philosophers of history revealed themselves only to the backward glance of the historian and philosopher—could become intended aims of political action."

This picture, at least in the case of Vico, needs to be refined. A text such as the *Pratica della Scienza nuova* suffices by itself alone to show that in the path which led from the *Orazioni inaugurali*, and especially from the *De nostri temporis studiorum ratione*, to the *Scienza nuova*, Vico never forgot his interest in combining philosophical theory with practice considered as the introduction of wisdom into civil life. But why, instead of developing this theme, did he choose to exclude the *Pratica* from the 1744 edition? Here commentary becomes risky in looking for an explanation of this exclusion and of this void in the general economy of Vico's work. The terms in which the question might be posed are clear. Vico perceives the fundamentally theoretical nature of his *Scienza nuova*. He undertakes therefore to show, in the *Pratica*, that his theory is susceptible to a practice, that is to say, to applications, whether on the level of direct political action or on that of cultural action considered in its relations with the sphere of public life. Then, however, he neglects to publish these pages, thereby exposing himself to the reproach, formulated by himself, of having set forth only a *scienza contemplativa*, one lacking in practical applicability. Purely psychological or historical explanations, which pretend to perceive Vico slipping from a *political* into an *apolitical attitude*, are bound to be inadequate.[5] A question which brings under consideration the internal meaning and coherence of a philosophical work can be answered only on the philosophical plane. I shall attempt to show here, therefore, that what Hannah Arendt calls a "biographical development," which portrays Vico as passing from the announcement of a new political philosophy in the *De nostri temporis studiorum ratione* to the realization of a philosophy of history in the *Scienza nuova*, presupposes what has come to be called an "epistemological break" (*coupure epistemologique*) such that, at one stroke, the relations between theory and practice become totally

[5] It is not, to be sure, a question of denying the considerable interest of those researches which, over the past years especially, try to make better known the cultural and political environment of Vico's thought. A deeper study of the problem of practice in Vico would necessarily have to refer to these works, and especially to the following among them: Biagio de Giovanni, *Filosofia e diritto in Francesco d'Andrea—Contributo alla storia del previchismo* (Milan, 1958); idem, "Il *De nostri temporis studiorum ratione* nella cultura napoletana del primo Settecento," in *Omaggio a Vico* (Milan, 1961); Nicola Badaloni, *Introduzione a G. B. Vico* (Milan, 1961); Salvo Mastellone, *Pensiero politico e vita culturale a Napoli nella seconda metà del Seicento* (Messina and Florence, 1965); Giuseppe Giarrizzo, "La politica di Vico," in *Quaderni Contemporanei*, no. 2, *Giambattista Vico nel terzo centenario della nascita* (Salerno, 1968).

transformed. Would not, then, the answer to the question which interests us reside in the contradiction, more or less consciously apprehended by Vico, between his fidelity to the classical ideal of political action and his desire to found a genuine science of history and society, a desire which supposes the abandonment of the theoretical presuppositions of this ideal?

The importance which Vico grants to practice, considered in the most classic sense of the term as the activity of the citizen in the city, and the manner in which he conceives the strict connection which has to be established between practice thus understood and theoretical knowledge, appeared clearly in the *Orazioni inaugurali* (which, let us not forget, are discourses delivered by a professor of rhetoric addressing himself, before civil and religious authorities, to young men destined to form the cadres of the Neapolitan state). But it is in the *De nostri temporis studiorum ratione* that this connection is affirmed with the greatest force and analyzed most profoundly.[6]

In chapter 7 of the *De nostri temporis studiorum ratione* Vico in effect condemns the modern *ratio studiorum*, dominated by Cartesianism, for its interest in the natural sciences to the detriment of the *moralis doctrina* and "especially that part which, in relation to the civil life and eloquence, is concerned with human character, with its dispositions and its passions, with the properties of the virtues and the vices, of good and evil principles of action, with the characteristics of the customs according to age, sex, condition, fortune, race, nationality, and with that art of *decorum* which is the most difficult of all." And he adds that, for this reason, "the *de republica doctrina*, so important and so noble, is among us almost completely allowed to lie fallow."[7] It should be noted that, in the enumeration of the tasks which Vico assigns to the *moralis doctrina*—which seems to cover, in great part, the field investigated today by our "human sciences"—the study of men, their nature, and their condition is considered only "in relation to the civil life and eloquence." It would thus be an error to think that this text prefigures the opposition which has become familiar to us between the "sciences of nature" and the "sciences of the spirit" or the "human sciences" (which is why, in our citation of Vico above, we did not translate the Latin word *doctrina* by the word *science*). In fact, this opposition is entirely modern, supposing a common ground which is that of a certain "scientific" ideal of a rigorous and distinterested knowledge, neutral with respect to moral values and the practical ends of man, a knowledge which is, in a word, completely "theoretical." Now, the ideal which Vico defends here is not that of a disinterested scientific research applied to the study of man, but rather that of *prudentia*, which he distinguishes radically from *scientia*.[8] The list which he establishes of the

[6] *Opere* 1: 69ff.
[7] *Ibid.*, pp. 90–91.
[8] *Ibid.*, p. 91.

principal objects of study of moral doctrine applied to the civil life only recapitulates, almost word for word, a passage of the *De dignitate et augmentis scientiarum,* in which Bacon, that "universal man in theory and practice," that "rare philosopher and great minister of state" (according to the *Autobiography*), develops a remark of Aristotle, who, in the *Rhetoric*, announces that he is going to "treat human nature in terms of passions, habits, ages, and conditions of fortune."[9] The knowledge of men permits them to influence these things, especially by means of the art of rhetoric, which is one of the essential instruments of political action.

At the very moment in which the humanistic-rhetorical tradition is progressively losing its prestige, Vico thus celebrates with an almost pathetic fervor the ideal, at once theoretical and practical, represented by the notion of prudence. It is not necessary here to recall the significance and importance of the Aristotelian notion of *phrónesis*, which, under the name of *prudentia*, had been transmitted to the Christian West by the Romans. It is only necessary to stress one essential point. The modern attitude toward action consists in the desire to base action on a science of society and its laws, in order to make of practice the "practice of a theory" or the "application of a scientific theory." For Aristotle, by contrast, there could be no science of human things, which are contingent, governed by chance, time, and circumstances, since the *epistéme* applies only to things necessary and immutable. There is no possibility therefore of *praxis* being based on "scientific" knowledge: *praxis*, on the contrary, is only possible because of what Aristotle calls "gaps in nature." The sublunar world is subject to a contingency which is not a function of the imperfection of human intelligence but which is objective or ontological. *Phrónesis* cannot be a science, since "of chance there can be no science." It does not have the status of "theoretical" knowledge, since its object is human *praxis*, and its norm is human well-being. "It is absurd to think," Aristotle says, "that prudence could be the highest form of knowledge, if it is true that man is not the highest being in the universe."[10] But prudence is not simply instinctive flair, empiricism without principle. In characterizing it as "dianoetic virtue of the calculative or operative part of the soul which knows contingent things," Aristotle makes of it an intellectual virtue presupposing a certain expedient and effective knowledge of action. Prudence consists of discerning what is useful and desirable for man and in finding the best means of attaining it. But this knowledge is not infallible; human action unfolds in time and is thus only effective when it is undertaken at the right moment (*kairós*). Now, no science or art can distinguish the *kairós* without risk of error, and the possibility of defeat is inherent in any action, however prudent it might be.[11]

[9] Cf. Bacon, *De dignitate et augmentis scientiarum,* bk. 7, chap. 3; Aristotle, *Rhetoric* II. 12. 1388b.

[10] Aristotle, *Nichomachean Ethics* VI. 7. 1141ff.

[11] See especially Pierre Aubenque, *La prudence chez Aristote* (Paris, 1963).

In giving preeminence to the contemplative virtues, the Middle Ages had relegated prudence to a subordinate position. The Renaissance, by contrast, followed Cicero and, as a result, Aristotle (not the metaphysical and logical Aristotle of the Scholastics, but the author of the *Ethics* and the *Rhetoric*) and made prudence the supreme virtue, placing it at the center of every ethical and political discussion.[12] It is to such discussions, which agitated the thought of the Renaissance and the baroque age and which bore upon the relations between wisdom, prudence, and cunning, that Vico constantly refers in the *De nostri temporis studiorum ratione* (hence his opposition of a "false" reason of state to "that which the Italians call *giusta ragione di Stato* and which is known only by prudent men").[13] This interest in the problematics of prudence and the ideal of action during the sixteenth and seventeenth centuries takes on an anachronistic quality at the dawn of the Enlightenment. That Vico was conscious of it seems to be shown by the provocative praise which he gives to the by now discredited figure of the courtier: "It may be that wise men will object to what I have said about civil prudence, that I want to make courtiers and not philosophers, to teach them to neglect virtue and to cultivate the appearance of it, to trample on virtue while putting on a deceitful front. I have no intention of it; instead, I would like to have them act like philosophers at court."[14]

The opposition which Vico sets up, between "baroque" prudence and the "modern" spirit that inspires the mechanists, Cartesians, and Jansenists, can be likened to the famous distinction made by Pascal between the *esprit de finesse* and the *esprit de geometrie*. On the one side, there is the "flexible" nature of the rules of prudence which embrace the sinuosities of circumstances (*anfractuosa vitae*), take account of the mobility and mutability of the things of life, and follow "oblique" ways in order to avoid obstacles. On the other side, there is the "rectilinear" and "rigid" aspect of the criteria of truth utilized by the moderns.[15] One would be tempted to find there an almost aesthetic opposition of two styles, Neapolitan baroque and French classicism; but, more deeply, it is two worlds which oppose each other, the living, colored, and varied world of men and the cold and abstract world of mathematics, logic, and mechanics.[16]

[12] See in particular Rodolfo de Mattei, "Sapienza e Prudenza nel pensiero politico italiano dall'umanesimo al secolo XVII," in *Umanesimo e scienza politica* (Milan, 1951); and Mario Santoro, *Fortuna, ragione e prudenza nella civiltà letteraria del Cinquecento* (Naples, 1966).

[13] *Opere* 1: 111.

[14] *Ibid.*, p. 93.

[15] *Ibid.*, pp. 91–92.

[16] In his letter to F. S. Estevan of 12 January 1729, Vico takes up again the same themes of the *De nostri temporis studiorum ratione* in order to denounce the education which prepares youth to enter the world of men "as if this world were composed of lines, numbers, and algebraic signs" (*Opere* 5: 201). This letter should be quoted in its entirety, since it demonstrates to what extent, twenty years later, Vico remains faithful to the inspiration of the *De nostri temporis studiorum ratione*.

The world of men is the world of time, of change, of appearance, of circumstance, and of contingency. To take account of a single human phenomenon is an endless task, because its causes are innumerable and extended throughout time (*in temporis longitudinem*).[17] And yet, as long as men have existed, they have learned to act both well and badly in this their world; and this instinctive practical knowledge, which is innate in the species, is called "common sense." Prudence, possessed by everyone, rests on common sense, to which it gives the benefit of surety. The world of mathematics, logic, and mechanics ignores these approximations, these oscillations, this art of the *Je ne sais quoi* dear to Balthasar Gracian, the Spanish Jesuit who wrote the *Oraculo Manual y Arte de Prudencia*. It recognizes only one value, truth, and its opposite, error. Scientific propositions have a universal and necessary character; they are apodictically certain, and they permit the explanation of a multiplicity of natural phenomena by means of a single unique cause. It is impossible, according to Vico, to reconcile these two worlds. Scientific reason is formed, in effect, *against* common sense. This is what allowed scientific reason to triumph in the domain of the knowledge of nature but at the same time precludes knowledge of social and political man. Vico does not deny the possibility of arriving at the truth by means of the study of human things, but this truth, according to him, has nothing to do with logical-mathematical truth. "Prudence," he writes, "seeks out in human actions the truth as it is, even when it proceeds from imprudence, ignorance, desire, necessity, or chance."[18] As we shall see, Vico will take a decisive step when he conceives the possibility of laying the foundations of an authentic *science*, permitting the discovery in human actions of "the truth as it is."

The possible positions one can occupy vis-à-vis that ideal unity of theory and practice represented by the notion of prudence are incarnated, in the *De nostri temporis studiorum ratione*, by "figures" offered in the manner of Aristotle when he paints the figure of the *phrónimos*. Between the *tabula rasa*, which is the *stultus* (a familiar figure since the second *Orazione inaugurale*) and the perfect union of thought and action in the *vir sapiens*, there are the two dialectically opposed moments. There is the *illiteratus astutus*, whose ability is manifested only on the level of detail and who is unable to conceive general principles, and the *doctus imprudens*, who reminds us of such traditional sages as Anaxagoras or Thales, whose knowledge, according to Aristotle, is "admirable, difficult, and divine" but "lacking in utility"—unlike the knowledge of the *phrónimos*. But in the eyes of Vico, the *doctus imprudens* represents above all the man who has the courage to create modern culture; he desires, in effect, to pass directly from eternal to particular truths, without taking account of necessary delays and detours. As for the *vir sapiens*, he always looks to eternal truth

[17] *Opere* 1: 92.
[18] *Ibid.*, p. 97.

without ignoring for all that the difficulties of action or losing himself in them. His task, as the sixth *Orazione inaugurale* indicates, is "to join the study of wisdom to that of eloquence," so as to "be worthy of human society and to serve the greatest number."[19]

Nothing shows better the extent to which Vico, in his first works, remains attached to the classical problematics of action than his attitude towards history. In the *De nostri temporis studiorum ratione*, history is never treated as an autonomous discipline, having a theoretical interest in itself. History is classified among the "aids," "the arts which are related to prudence," on a par with the art of oratory and that of poetry.[20] Prudence, as Aristotle had already shown, is the art of seizing the occasion and cannot, therefore, properly speaking, be "taught." It is impossible to fix its rules in a list of precepts, in a general and abstract code, since all situations are different. The role of history is thus to "show" rather than to "demonstrate." Each person must derive from the examples supplied by history the lessons to be followed or not to be followed. Already, in the fifth *Orazione*, Vico had stressed the importance of examples in learning the art of war, in which it is crucial to recognize "the moment when one must fight." In this field, "as in everything that depends on prudence, nothing can be fixed," and one must have recourse to examples and models, both literary and historical: Achilles served as a model to Alexander, who, in turn, served as a model to Caesar.[21] The sixth *Orazione* analyzes in even greater depth the practical role assigned to history and its subordinate status in comparison with "civil and moral doctrine":

Commentaries, annals, lives of famous men, all that remains to states and perpetuates their memory, belong then to the moral and civil doctrines which are commonly called "histories." There are also histories of jurisprudence, which include the laws published by the state at various moments, the interpretations which the jurisconsults have given to them, and examples of judgments handed down. Mathematics, by contrast, does not have histories,

[19] *Ibid.*, pp. 66–67. In much the same way, in the *De rebus gestis Antoni Caraphaei* (1716), Vico speaks of the "politicians" who "observe more attentively than other men the customs of nations, explore more profoundly the taste of courts, scrutinize more ably the secrets of governments [because they] are interested in knowing the greatest possible number of individual details which permits them to understand in what way and to what extent each part fits into the whole, since those who cultivate the most severe disciplines, keeping their gaze turned upon the highest classes of things, neglect the details, on the attentive observation of which completely depends the utility of things" (*Opere*, 6: 19).

[20] *Opere* 1: 99.

[21] *Ibid.*, p. 54. The same idea is expressed with even greater clarity in the *De rebus gestis Antoni Caraphaei*: "Those who offer an example of kings or free peoples produce a richer civil doctrine than those who speak of it in precepts. For the useful and the worthy, the two ends which politicians seek above all to realize, are perceived in the same act by which these things are produced; and as they cannot bear being closed, as if behind bars, in the precise definitions of science, they are left to the will of prudence" (*Opere* 6: 19).

because it does not use examples; nor does logic because it utilizes examples taken from other realms, and when it has no examples, invents them; and metaphysics even less, since it only contemplates the human spirit and God in their perfectly pure and simple natures.[22]

Nothing is more characteristic of the rhetorical-humanist tradition than this manner of conceiving history as a depository of examples. This is found in Cicero and even more among those to whom we commonly attribute a modern and scientific historical consciousness, as for example Bodin and Bacon.[23] For all these authors, "the principal and proper work of history (is) to instruct and enable men, through the knowledge of past actions, to comport themselves prudently in the present and providently toward the future," as Hobbes writes in the introduction to his translation of Thucydides.[24] But if Vico, in the *De nostri temporis studiorum ratione*, remains faithful to this tradition and makes history the handmaiden to prudence, one must insist on the unique importance of chapter 11 of this same work, which deals with the "prudence of law," that is, of jurisprudence. In these pages, in fact, we see that the classical problem of the relation of knowledge and action is transcended by the formulation of the notion of history, considered no longer as a collection of examples but as a temporal dimension.

Already, in the sixth *Orazione*, Vico had stressed that jurisprudence, which "combines and fuses moral doctrine, civil doctrine, and moral theology," is "neither science nor art, but prudence."[25] This definition reveals the indissociably theoretico-practical aspect of law. Now, the *De nostri temporis studiorum ratione* insists that this union was achieved only in Rome. In Athens the elements of prudence were separated: "The philosophers displayed the relationship of the philosophy or doctrine of right to the state, justice, and the laws," while the practitioners collected laws in order to permit the orators to practice their eloquence. In Rome, by contrast, "the philosophers were themselves jurisconsults, in the sense that they turned all their wisdom to the practice of law. That which, in Greece, was taught by the philosophers, in Rome was learned by political practice itself (*ipso usu reipublicae*)."[26]

[22] *Opere* 1: 63.

[23] On this problem, see in particular Leo Strauss, *The Political Philosophy of Hobbes* (Chicago, 1963), chap. 7; and Max H. Fisch's Introduction to the English translation of Vico's *Autobiography*.

[24] Hobbes, *English Works*, vols. 7 and 8. To be sure, here we are dealing with Hobbes in his humanist period, still under the influence of Aristotle. As soon as he decides to apply the method of Galileo to social philosophy, that is to say, to open to a science which he wishes to be as certain as geometry the field hitherto reserved for prudence, Hobbes insists on the purely conjectural character of what he defines as "a presumption of the future, contracted from the experience of time past" (*Leviathan*, chap. 3). For him, from now on, "Prudence is no part of philosophy" (*ibid.*, chap. 46).

[25] *Opere* 1:62.

[26] *Ibid.*, p. 101.

In Roman law, theory is therefore inscribed in the practice; this permits Vico to sketch in the *De nostri temporis studiorum ratione* a historical interpretation that will be fleshed out in the *Diritto universale* and the *Scienza nuova.* History is no longer used, then, to furnish examples and specific references to prudent acts; rather it constitutes the temporal element, in which juridical institutions are born, develop, and expand and in which oppositions that seem insurmountable are dialectically resolved. The opposition, in the case of Roman law, is between *justum* and *aequum.* The "heroic age" was characterized by the rigorous observance of the letter of the laws, which established in a strict manner the limits separating the just from the unjust, the permitted from the prohibited. In order to evoke this wisdom of the "heroic age," Vico cites four verses of Horace which seem to prefigure the chapters of the *New Science* devoted to the origins of humanity and to "divine" and "heroic" times:

> haec fuit sapientia quondam,
> publica privatis secernere, sacra profanis,
> concubitu prohibere vago, dare jura maritis,
> oppida moliri, et leges incidere ligno.[27]

Under the Roman Empire, and during the epoch corresponding to it in the history of Western civilization, which is to say, according to Vico, his own era, jurisprudence was concerned primarily with *aequum,* or equity, with the spirit of the law, and was therefore "particular and flexible" inasmuch as it was an *ars aequi.* While ancient jurisprudence was almost entirely constituted by public law and subordinated to the interest of the state, imperial jurisprudence (like modern European jurisprudence) increasingly stressed private law, which resulted in the progressive humanization of the law. But Vico sees the danger of such an evolution: Do not imperial and modern law, in becoming identified more and more with private law, run the risk of ignoring their origins and losing sight of their primary function, which is to assure "the higher interest of the state"? In this regard, Roman history already assumes for Vico the paradigmatic role that it will play in the *New Science.* It is necessary, he writes, to study "the origins, the consolidation, the form, the increase, the period of stabilization, the dissolution of the Roman principate, and to compare all that with reigns in our era." One will then perceive that "weak jurisprudence was the main cause of the corruption of eloquence and of Roman political power."[28] History, here, does more than furnish an example; it permits the understanding of the general process. History shows that the ties which bind theory and practice are not analyzable in terms of pure logic, but only reveal themselves in and through history. But it was only in the writing of the *Diritto universale* and above all the *New Science* that the full implications of this principle were developed.

[27] *Ep. ad Pis.* 396–99.
[28] *Ibid.,* pp. 111, 113.

Thus, for the Vico of the *De nostri temporis studiorum ratione*, we would maintain, there can be no science of action, in the strict sense of the word *science*, nor, consequently, a science of society; and practice continues to be presented as a kind of Aristotelian prudence. It can be seen that behind the critique of modern education, which gives a privileged place to the mathematical and physical sciences to the detriment of "political and moral doctrine," there is a more fundamental critique of any attempt to construct a science of human things and, consequently, of any effort to reduce practice to the simple application of laws enunciated by a science of society. The Vichian "philosopher of the court" stands opposed to the Cartesian sage, "spectator of, rather than actor in, all of the dramas played in the world,"[29] who withdraws from action not to contemplate eternal truths, but to develop a science of nature capable of technical application; he also stands opposed to the Hobbesian "social engineer," capable of dismantling the machinery of the body politic. To be sure, in 1708 Vico ignored the work of Hobbes, but Jürgen Habermas is right to make of the author of the *De cive* the "ideal" target of the attacks mounted by Vico in the *De nostri temporis studiorum ratione*, in the name of the classical tradition, against those who wished to construct a hypothetico-deductive science of society.[30]

We can now perceive more clearly the path traveled from the *De nostri temporis studiorum ratione* to the *Scienza nuova*, can better comprehend how Vico both broke with the classical tradition and remained faithful to it. The break is marked in the epistemological presuppositions, in the claim to found a "new science of the world of nations" which, on the Galilean model, elaborates universal and necessary propositions about phenomena which, in their Aristotelian conception, would not sustain a true *epistéme*. Considered in this light, Vico is boldly modern, in the same way as Descartes and Hobbes. But he differs from them and displays his loyalty to humanistic rhetoric by refusing to assimilate the knowledge of the human world to the knowledge of mathematical ideals or physical realities. Such an assimilation presupposes, in fact, a coherence and permanence in human affairs that they do not possess, since they are bound, as we have seen, "to imprudence, ignorance, desire, necessity, and fortune," that is to say, to all that which eludes a deductive type of logic. Vico's brilliant stroke was to reverse the postulate on which modern rationalism rests, by asserting that the only true science that could be created had to be of the human world, in so far as this world is "made" by man, while the natural world, the work of God, is known only by God. By the same stroke Vico transcended and perfected the classical doctrine of prudence, which was content to teach men to act in the best possible way in a world

29 Descartes, *Discours de la méthode*, pt. 3.

30 See Jürgen Habermas, "Die klassische Lehre von der Politik in ihrem Verhältnis zur Sozialphilosophie," in *Theorie und Praxis* (Frankfurt, 1972), pp. 48ff.

governed by contingency and irrationality. Vico's science was not constructed *in spite* of contingency and irrationality; it seeks to dispell these latter, by showing the necessity and rationality of human phenomena, which assume significance and value once they are located in the general historical process in which they appear and develop.

I shall not try to show here how Vico attempted to implement his program. The point to be stressed is that the "philosophy of humanity" of Vico leads to a theory of human nature and that this theory is only possible because human nature reveals itself in the *practice* constituted by "the universal history of nations." Knowledge and action, theory and practice, coincide; they do not have separate histories. The fundamental principle according to which men might arrive at a science of the world of nations or the civil world, because they have made it (§ 331),[31] assumes that the activities of knowledge and those activities properly called practical develop at the same time and according to the same rhythm. The whole of humanity is manifested in each moment in history, in a manner that is indissolubly theoretical and practical at one and the same time.

The notion of wisdom (*sapienza*), as it is defined in book 2 of the *New Science* (§§ 364ff.), illustrates this integral union of knowledge and action. Wisdom is "the faculty which commands all the disciplines by which we acquire all the sciences and arts that make up humanity" (§ 364). Wisdom "perfects man," that being who is at one and the same time "mind and spirit," intellect and will. "Poetic wisdom," for example, which characterizes men still dominated by sensation and imagination, is a "crude metaphysics" in which one can distinguish an ethics, an economics (that is to say, a doctrine of the government of the family), and a politics, as well as a physics, a cosmography, and an astronomy (§ 367).

The use of the term "wisdom" in relation to ethics, economics, and politics, traditionally governed by the more modest notion of "prudence," is revealing. This lexical difference signals well the great difference between the *New Science* and the *De nostri temporis studiorum ratione*. If Vico can speak of the "wisdom" of men, it is because he perceives, behind their actions, a directing power which infallibly guides them—providence. Here it is well to recall that *providentia* and *prudentia* are the same word. Vico uses the notion of prudence to give himself a wider scope: prudence is no longer the heritage of a few privileged people; it belongs to all of humanity. Human designs are transcended by those of providence, which makes use of men, such as they are, with their passions and their intelligence, which develops only gradually; providence makes them realize, at the appropriate moment (the Greek *kairós*), what they must realize in order to "conserve human society" and to "practice justice as a member of the society of the family, of the city, and finally, of mankind" (§ 341).

The order of appearance and succession of human phenomena, the

[31] All citations in the text preceded by a paragraph sign (§) are to the *New Science*.

manner in which they are produced, and the times and places of their manifestation are all fixed by providence, which does not act arbitrarily, but develops over time the "nature of nations."[32] The *De nostri temporis studiorum ratione* deplored the fact that moral and civil doctrines had been weakened because their object, human nature, is "uncertain about the existence of free will." Now that this uncertainty has been dissolved, the "nature" of men is revealed in the "certainty" of the "birth" of human things in determined times and places, according to determined modes. History is no longer a collection of examples and models for prudent action; it is exemplary in itself. History no longer gives counsels of prudence; it is prudence realized, since it is divine providence which is its principle. On the plane of universal history, providence acts as a *phrónimos* or a *prudens* would, or like an orator possessed of a perfect rhetorical art, who understands human nature completely, with all its strengths and weaknesses, its virtues and vices, and who uses these to lead men toward the best possible common life, guiding them by the hand, step by step, without letting them skip levels, without imposing upon them any abstract ideal, but leading them through the necessary detours, like a good politician of the baroque age.

It can be seen that Vico relies on some religious and almost mystical accents in order to promise that "the reader will experience in his mortal body a divine pleasure" (§ 345). Pythagoras spoke of the *θεωρία τῶν καλλίστων*, the contemplation of the perfect order which governs celestial bodies. In the same way, the *New Science* is "theory," contemplation of the perfect order which governs the course of the history of nations, or the human world. The pleasure which it gives us is infinitely superior to that of Greek *theoria*, which remains passive. Since "the world of nations was certainly made by men," the "new science" procures for men the "truly divine" pleasure of simultaneous knowing and doing, the conjuncture of the theoretical and the practical (§ 349). Here we reach the extreme point of modern *hubris*, humanism pushed to its final limits. And it is well that later Michelet and Marx would understand it thus and make of the Vichian formula, according to which it was men who made the world of nations, the Promethean motto *par excellence.*

But is this formula not ambiguous? What does the verb *to make* signify? *To make* in Greek is *poīeīn*, "to fabricate" or "to construct" according to a model or plan. Now, men are incapable of making their history in this sense, and it is divine providence which must work for them. Their "making" is thus reduced to an activity that one might call passive, since it does not find in itself its origin or end. Action as *praxis*, as free political activity, oriented towards the "total well-being," open to success as well as to failure, is indeed forgotten.

That Vico had perceived the risk is shown by the first paragraph of the

[32] *Scienza nuova prima, Opere* 3: 223; *New Science,* § 346.

Pratica della Scienza nuova, quoted at the beginning of this essay. This text insists on the fact that the *New Science* is a part of the sciences "which relate to matters depending upon human free will and which are all called 'active.'" Now, what "practical" consequences could be drawn from a theory which consists in showing the comprehensible necessity for all that was, is, and will be in the history of the nations? Does not the wonder thus obtained end, if not in fatalism, then at least in a kind of quietism? Does not exchanging the role of the "philospher of the court" for that of the more grandiose "confidant of providence" suggest a "lack of practice"?

The *New Science* of 1725 already poses the problem, but in different terms, in its short book 4 (it should be noted that in this first version only three pages are devoted to the "praxis" of the *New Science* and that in the last edition, that of 1744, all reference to this question has disappeared). "Of this science, thus outlined and with such kinds of proofs, there are two practices," Vico writes.[33] The first consists of a *critical* art, which permits us to "distinguish the true in obscure and fabulous history," and the other of a *diagnostic* art, which permits us "to know the indubitable signs of the state of the nations." But these two practices remain theoretical; they are only specifications of the fundamental science carried to such a point that the "critical" developments come to occupy the dominant place in the work. It remains to see what "practical" consequences, concerning human or political action, might be derived from this critical art and especially from the diagnostic art which Vico says constitutes "the principal aim of this science."[34] In other words, it remains to be seen what role the philosophers, armed with the new science which Vico gives them, might play in the city.

One answer, or a hint of an answer, to this question is found in the *Pratica della Scienza nuova*. In this text, Vico, without explicitly referring to the diagnostic art of which he spoke in 1725, specifies the use that might be made of an art which gives us knowledge of the stage of develop-

[33] *Scienza nuova prima, Opere* 3: 224. We should note that the term "pratica" is not used here in the sense of the Greek word *praxis*, but in the sense of *practica theoriae*, that is to say, the application of a science, therefore of an art, of technique which rests upon theoretical knowledge. It seems to have been Hugh of Saint Victor who, in the twelfth century, first used the nominalized adjective *practica* to mean "concrete application," thereby distinguishing within a fundamentally theoretical science, one part that was specifically "theoretical" and another part "practical." See Nicholas Lobkowicz, *Theory and Practice* (Notre Dame and London, 1967), pp. 82ff. As thus conceived, practice no longer has anything to do with Greek *praxis*, which designated a kind of life consecrated to political action. When Vico speaks of the *Pratica della Scienza nuova*, he uses the word *pratica* in the modern sense of "the application of a science," but he limits this application to political action, to the question of a good and just common life. This shows that Vico was well aware of the meaning of the ancient notion of *praxis* or *vita activa*. See Arendt, *The Human Condition*, on the notion of *vita activa*.

[34] *Opere*, III, p. 224.

ment of nations as well as of their state of health. The word *diagnostic* is borrowed, characteristically, from the vocabulary of medicine, which suggests that the philosopher's task is to read and interpret symptoms (it is difficult here not to think of Spengler). But will he be content to examine and analyze or will he also try to treat and to cure? Vico chooses the latter. The "practice" of the *New Science* will consist of halting nations on the point of perishing from falling into complete ruination, of retarding their march toward destruction, or better yet, leading peoples to their *acme*. This practice will be either directly political (the work of governments enlightened by the reading of the *New Science*) or cultural (the work of philosophers in the academies).

In order to understand the importance of these assertions, it is necessary to remember that Vico places the *acme* of the life of nations in the "human" and "free" governments which correspond to the stage of "completely developed" reason (§ 1097). This state of balance is not definitive, since the law of life governs social organisms as it does all living things. Popular liberty runs the risk of degenerating into anarchy or a lawless freedom. But providence brings to this disaster of cities three possible remedies (§ 1103). These are: an internal remedy, the establishment of a monarchy, which stabilizes the liberty of a nation and assures its conquests; an external remedy, in which a corrupted people becomes the subject of better nations, by virtue of that great law of natural right, which desires that "those governing the world are always by nature the best"; and, finally, the extreme remedy, when the sickness itself has become extreme and the "barbarism of civilization" has replaced true civilization or "humanity," the return to the original point, to that "primitive simplicity of the original world," which will give birth to a new *corso*, to a *ricorso*. This last solution is that which, because of its spectacular nature, was most striking to readers. But one must not forget the first, even if it is less radical. It is there, in fact, that the "practice" of the *New Science* can intervene and "help human prudence," which, scientifically enlightened, plays in some way the role of divine providence, trying to dominate the course of events, to bend, slow it down, indeed even turn it backwards on its course. And it is only in the case of a failure of human prudence that divine providence will be forced to take things in hand and employ extreme measures.

The specifically political implications of this recourse to monarchy as remedy, its significance for the Neapolitan and European context of the epoch, have been much studied, especially in recent Italian criticism; and therefore we will not linger on them here.[35] What should be stressed is the use Vico makes of history in his search for a remedy. The strictly conservative and even reactionary end of knowing how to forestall the *ricorso* by halting decadence, by retarding it, or by reversing its course

[35] See above, n. 5.

towards the *acme*, is not at all original. This was a commonplace of political thought since antiquity. The novelty resides in the fact that the measures recommended have to be taken in virtue of a historical diagnosis which provides knowledge of the "state" of nations, which is to say, the stage of their evolution in relation to a well-defined *acme*. The intervention, therefore, is only possible on the basis of a historical analysis of a situation. Here one can see easily the difference between Vico and an author like Hobbes, who also assigns to his civil philosophy the task of forestalling the corruption of the state and of remedying it, but who works in the totally atemporal and ahistoric perspective of a pure political logic.

Even more, with Vico we meet for the first time a theory which seeks to be scientific and locates itself historically by analyzing the possible conditions of its appearance, of its validity, and of its practical efficacity. Philosophy, for Vico, only appears at a certain moment in the development of reason, that is to say, in the history of the nations. This moment marks the summit, the full development of humanity, but it brings with it also a grave and inevitable danger, that of the dissociation of thought and action, of theory and practice. This dissociation did not exist in the "divine" and "heroic" ages, for in those times wisdom was indissolubly theoretical and practical, and the degree of religious, moral, and intellectual development of humanity was immediately linked to the customs, institutions, and laws, so that there was no distance between the real and the ideal. But "fully developed" reason is characterized by reflection, that is to say, by the possibility of a schism between real and ideal, practice and theory, will and intelligence, common sense and *sapienza riposta*. Philosophy necessarily presupposes such a schism; this is its *raison d'être*. Vico tries to give to philosophy the function of combating, by its own means, the evil which it risks giving birth to, and of opposing the schism by developing itself and forestalling what he calls the "barbarism of reflection" which is manifested in the total divorce of the spirit from the letter of institutions.[36] The violent criticism which he makes of the culture of his times can have no other meaning. By concentrating their theoretical efforts on a science of nature, modern philosophers abandon the world of practice to the unenlightened initiative of the rulers. The task of the "science of the world of nations" is to reestablish the link between reason and action and to rediscover that "beautiful wholeness," to speak in Hegelian terms, which the men of "divine" and "heroic" ages realized spontaneously with their wisdom.

Thus we see appearing in Vico the idea which later, with Hegel and Saint-Simon, comes to dominate Western thought: namely, that philosophy and the human sciences appear at moments of crisis, that they are

[36] *Pratica, Opere* 4: § 1406, gives the example of Messalina and Nero, who sought to give to the worst debaucheries the sanction of solemn ceremonies.

at once consequences, symptoms, and also means for overcoming the crises of which they are the issue. But what is lacking in Vico is precisely the modern idea of "crisis," which would have permitted him to recognize the fecundity of those events in which he sees only the signs of sickness and decadence. No one more than he, however, understood the agonistic nature of history which progresses only by means of battles and internal tensions (his familiarity with Roman history was, in this respect, determining). But he remained a prisoner of traditional political thought and of his own cyclical schema, so that, for him, once the *acme* was reached, crisis could only have negative and destructive results. The limitations of his historical experience prevented him from understanding, as Hegel and Saint-Simon were able to do in the wake of the French Revolution, that the dissolution of an apparently stable state of things could signify that a new order was in process of being born—an idea which permitted Marx to transform the notion of "crisis" into the more catastrophic but at the same time more optimistic notion of "revolution."

The social basis on which Vico builds the theory which he calls "practice" is narrower than that of Marx, who justifies and guarantees his identification of theory and practice by the revolutionary action of the proletariat considered as a universal class. The Vichian practice is reduced to an attempt to affect the governing class (his is the classic role of the counselor of a prince) and to a specifically cultural action within the academy to which, let us remember, the *New Science* of 1725 is dedicated, and which will be, Vico hopes, the ideal vehicle for the diffusion of his ideas in Europe. At the end of the *Pratica* (§ 1411), Vico adds to the academies, the universities in which is effected the fusion of theoretical research and political practice, for the formation of future rulers and members of the cultivated class, on which the institutions of modern Europe depend.

The practice of the new science is thus limited to a small number. There is nothing surprising in this, if we recall that the Vichian conception of providence, considered as historical prudence, possesses, as does the Aristotelian concept of prudence, an expressly "aristocratic" character, in the etymological sense of the word. In the *Conchiusione dell'opera*, he returns several times to what he calls the "true natural aristocracy" (§ 1097) and affirms that "it is always those who are by nature the best who govern the world" (§ 1105). But it is in the *Pratica* above all that he insists on this aristocratic vision of history and develops, as Fausto Nicolini has noted, some "stupefying philosophical notions of the role played in states by the 'few' or, as one would say today, the ruling classes."[37] The opposition which existed, in the *De nostri temporis studiorum ratione*, between the *stultus* and the *vir sapiens* becomes here an opposition be-

[37] Fausto Nicolini, *Commento storico alla seconda Scienza nuova* (Rome, 1949), vol. 2, p. 201.

tween the "vulgar" and the "wise" or the "strong"; and this opposition is developed across the whole line of history. The "vulgar" is the "material," the "body of the world of nations," while "the men who can counsel and defend others" are the "form" and "spirit" of it (§ 1407). We noted earlier that the Vichian theory of providence gave to the whole of humanity the task of working for the common good and of realizing providential designs. This affirmation does not contradict the elitist spirit of Vico's statements about the role of the "wise" and "strong," that is to say, the "prudent." The wisdom of the strong is rooted, in fact, in the common sense of the people and expresses their deep needs. Providence works to realize in history the city of which Plato dreamed, and the privileged individuals of which providence makes use are necessarily the best. The historical sociology of Vico, which emphasizes the role of active minorities and self-conscious avant-gardes, is only a translation of an optimism that is fundamentally metaphysical. And if we must at any cost look for "progressivist" guarantees, are we not close, if not to Marx, then at least to Lenin and Gramsci?

The *Pratica* dates from 1731. In 1732, Vico delivered his discourse *De mente heroica*, which is a hymn to the glory of the heroic virtues of the human spirit and an act of faith in the immense possibilities of the educational practice in the universities and academies. In 1744, he chose not to integrate the *Pratica* into the definitive edition of the *New Science*, at the risk of being accused of "failing to come to the aid of human prudence" or of "wanting in practice." Was he discouraged by failure? Was it impossible for him to transcend a narrow class viewpoint? All these answers are possible, but, in any case, everything occurred as if Vico completely and definitively entrusted to providence, that is to say, to the movement of history, the responsibility of human practice. The circle is complete. The modern age did not get a new political philosophy, but a philosophy of history.

Translated by Margaret Brose

PRACTIC OF THE NEW SCIENCE

Giambattista Vico

PRACTIC OF THE NEW SCIENCE

Translated by Thomas G. Bergin and Max H. Fisch

Preliminary Note

The pages here translated form part of the *Correzioni, miglioramenti ed aggiunte terze,* the third of the four sets of corrections, revisions, and additions to the second edition of the *New Science* that were drafted by Vico for incorporation in his third edition. This set was composed in the summer of 1731. The manuscript is preserved in the *Biblioteca nazionale* at Naples, as no. XIII, D.80. The *Pratica* was intended to be added to the Conclusion as a second chapter, following directly upon paragraph 1112, but Vico soon (and wisely) gave up that plan. The text of the *Pratica* is included, however, in all four of Fausto Nicolini's editions of the *Scienza nuova* of 1744: that of 1911–16 in the *Classici della filosofia moderna,* on pp. 1052–58 of volume 3; those of 1928 and 1942 in the *Scrittori d'Italia,* on pp. 268–71 and 274–77, respectively, of volume 2; and that of 1953 in the Vico volume in *La letteratura italiana,* on pp. 875–77. For commentary see the first of these, and also Nicolini's *Commento storico alla seconda Scienza nuova* (1950), volume 2, pp. 201–3. As in our translation of the *New Science* (Cornell University Press, 1948; revised edition, 1968), we here follow Nicolini's edition of 1928, with one exception, which is indicated in note 7 below. For abbreviations and references and for the policies of our translation, see pp. v–viii and xvii–xviii of our 1968 edition. For the obsolete *practic* as our rendering of *pratica,* see above, "Vico's *Pratica.*"

1405 This entire work has so far been treated as a purely contemplative science concerning the common nature of nations. It seems for this reason to promise no help to human prudence toward delaying if not preventing the ruin of nations in decay. It consequently seems to be lacking in the practic that all those sciences should have which are called "active," as dealing with matters that depend on human choice.

1406 That practic can easily be derived from the contemplation of the course the nations run. Instructed by such contemplation, the wise men and princes of the commonwealths will be able, through good institutions, laws, and examples, to recall the peoples to their *acme* or perfect state. The practic of the science that we as philosophers can offer is such as can be completed within the academies. What it requires of us is that, from these human times of acute and intelligent minds in which we are born, we should here at the end look back to the picture that was placed at the beginning.[1] And it requires that the academies, with their sects of philosophers, should support not the corruption of the sect of these times [viii, 978f.] but the three principles upon which this Science has been founded. These are: that there is divine providence; that human passions must be moderated since they can be; and that our souls are immortal [333, 337, 340, 342, 504]. And [they must uphold] this criterion of truth: that we must respect the common judgment of men—the common sense of mankind [142, 145]—which God, who does not allow himself to be forgotten even in the most abandoned nations, never rouses to more vigorous reflection than when they are most corrupt. The reason for this is that so long as the peoples keep to good customs, they do decent and just things rather than talk about them, because they do them instinctively, not from reflection. But when they are corrupted and ruined, then, because within themselves they ill endure their sense of lacking such things, they speak of nothing but decency and justice, just as it comes naturally for a man to talk of nothing but what he affects to be and is not. And because they feel themselves resisted by their religion (which naturally they cannot disavow or repudiate), in order to console their errant consciences they use that same religion with impious piety to consecrate their wicked and nefarious actions. Hence those two dreadful human phenomena of which we read in the history of decadent Rome. The first is that of Messalina, who, living with the dull and foolish Claudius, enjoyed full ease, license, and liberty to spend whole nights venting her insatiable lust in the brothel, and yet, though all the while married to the emperor, wants to enjoy Gaius Silius with all nuptial sanctity and propriety.[2] The second is that of Domitius Nero, who, having disgraced the majesty of the Roman empire by performing as a musician in the public theaters, wanted to be nefariously married to [his freedman] Pythagoras with the sacrifices and auguries and all the other divine ceremonies.[3]

1407 Considering all this, let the masters of wisdom teach the young how to descend from the world of God and of minds into the world of nature, in order to live a decent and just humanity in the world of nations [2, 331]. Which is to say that the academies, holding such principles and such a criterion of truth [1406], should teach the young that it is the nature of the civil world, which is the world that has been made by men [331], to

[1] It may be that *guardare a rovescio* here means not "to look backwards at" but "to look at in reverse"; that is, contrariwise, as if everything in it were replaced by its opposite, as often seemed to Vico to be the case in the philosophic "sects" of his day.

[2] Tacitus A.11.26ff.

[3] Tacitus A.15.37; Suetonius, *Nero* 29.

have just such matter and form as men themselves have. And, accordingly, that of the two principles that compose the civil world, the one is of the same nature and has the same properties as our body, the other as our rational soul has—of which two parts the first is the matter and the second the form of man.

1408 The properties of matter are to be formless, defective, dark, sluggish, divisible, mobile. It is, as Plato calls it,[4] "other"; that is, always diverse from itself. By reason of all these properties matter has the nature of being disorder, confusion, and chaos, greedy to destroy all forms [688]. The properties of form are to be perfection, luminous, active, indivisible, constant. That is, it strives to remain as far as it can in the state in which it is. This is why Plato is wont to call it "itself."[5] By reason of all these properties the nature of the form of man is to be order, light, life, harmony, and beauty.

1409 Hence the men who have neither counsel nor virtue of their own are the matter which is the body of the world of nations, in respect of matter's property of being formless. In respect of its property of being defective, the matter is vicious men, for all vices are nothing but defects. In respect of the property of darkness, it is the men who are indifferent not only to glory, which is a great and dazzling light, but even to praise, which is a faint and small light. In respect of the property of being sluggish and lazy, it is all the delicate soft and dissolute idlers. In respect of divisibility, it is the men who pursue nothing but their own private interests, which divide men; or bodily pleasures or preferences of taste, which are as many as there are men. In respect of mobility, it is all the doltish men who are always changing their minds, who never remain content with the same thing, who always love and affect new things; who in a word are called the *vulgus*, whose fixed epithet is *mobile*.[6] In respect of disorder and confusion, it is the men who, by reason of all these properties of matter, would, as far as in them lies, reduce the world of nations to the chaos of the theological poets, which we have found to signify the confusion of human seed [688]; and consequently to the nefarious bestial life when this earth was an infamous jungle of beasts.

1410 On the other hand, those who are the form and mind of this world of nations, in respect of form's property of being perfection, are the men who can counsel and defend themselves and others, and these are the wise and the strong. In respect of activity, the industrious and diligent men. In respect of being luminous, the men adorned with praise in private life and with glory in public. In respect of indivisibility, the men who in

[4] *Sophist* 258d–259b.

[5] As in such phrases as "justice itself" (*Republic* 363a), "virtue itself" (*Protagoras* 360e), "likeness itself" (*Parmenides* 130b), "man himself" (Aristotle, *Nicomachean Ethics* 1096^a35, *Metaphysics* 991^a29).

[6] *Mobile vulgus* is equivalent to "the fickle vulgar," "the lawless rabble, "or, for short, "the mob" (since English *mob* is short for Latin *mobile*).

every pursuit or profession are engaged with all their powers and with all propriety: the knight in knightly arts, the scholar in studies of the sciences, the statesman in the practices of the court, and every artisan in his own craft. In respect of constancy, the serious and grave men. In respect of the property of being "itself" [1408], the men of integrity, circumspect, proper and decorous. And finally in respect of being order, beauty, and harmony, the men who, each one fulfilling the duties of his own order, cooperate toward the harmony and beauty of the commonwealths, and, by means of all these civic virtues, exert themselves to preserve their states. And since from their weak and corrupt nature they cannot bring forth this exertion, providence has set up such orders for human institutions that religions and laws, assisted by the force of arms, may move them to it. This force began among the gentiles with the force of Jove through religions, which force instigated the exertion of the few more robust giants to found humanity [377]. To this force the few strong are drawn by nature and consequently with pleasure, for it moves them to exertion, which is connatural with the strong; and the many weak are bound therein despite themselves, to the end that they may not dissolve human society. And this is the spirit of this entire work.

1411 By these principles of metaphysics [1406] brought down into physics and thence through morality carried into family government and thus into their own education [1407–1409], let the young be guided into good politics, and with their minds so disposed let them finally move on into jurisprudence. Wherefore in [the dedication of] the first [edition of the] *New Science* [in 1725] we proposed to the universities of Europe that jurisprudence should be treated in the whole context of human and divine erudition, and on that account we put it above all the other sciences. It is by being prepared in this way that the youths to be taught will learn the practic of this Science founded on the eternal law that providence has established for the world of nations. This is that nations are secure and flourish in felicity so long as the body in them serves and the mind commands. And the youths will thus be brought to the true crossroads of Hercules, who founded all the gentiles [514]. Namely, whether they[7] will take the road of pleasure, with baseness, scorn, and slavery for them and for their nations, or the road of virtue, with honor, glory, and happiness.

[7] Nicolini's edition of 1911–16 reads *vogliano*. His three later editions all read *vogliamo*. At this one point we follow his first reading.

CRITICAL WRITINGS ON VICO IN ENGLISH

Molly Black Verene

CRITICAL WRITINGS ON VICO IN ENGLISH

This bibliography is in three parts. Part I lists books and articles devoted in whole or specific part to the thought of Vico; Part II lists various works which, although not primarily concerned with Vico, make some reference to his thought or very briefly discuss it; and Part III lists reviews of works on Vico.

The aim of this bibliography is to provide a comprehensive list of works on Vico which have been published in English or in English translation from the nineteenth century to the present. It does not claim to be wholly without omission, but completeness has been the ideal which has guided its preparation. Part II is an exception to this. It is not feasible to be exhaustive, or even nearly so, of works that under various titles and in the course of pursuing other topics cite or briefly discuss Vico. Undoubtedly any student of Vico will be aware of additions that might be made to this list. Part II does not represent a systematic search but simply lists references to Vico that have been discovered by the editors. It owes much to mentions of Vico that Dr. Tagliacozzo has gathered over a period of years while pursuing topics of a Vichian nature. In general, titles have been included in this second part for one of two reasons: in some cases, it is thought to be of interest in itself that a given author cites Vico, while in others, what is said, although brief, is of interest as such and in fact is often of as much interest as what is said in works specifically directed to the examination of Vico's thought.

A much larger number of works on Vico exist in Italian than in English; the number in other European languages is also fairly large. Most of these can be found through the three bibliographies listed below. In restricting the scope of this bibliography to works existing in English on Vico the aim has been twofold: (1) to establish with some exactitude what has in fact been done in English on Vico; and (2) to aid one of the overall goals of the volume, that of promoting further thought on Vico among English-speaking scholars.

This bibliography incorporates the one contained in *Giambattista Vico: An International Symposium* (pp. 615–19), which listed many works published in English during the last fifty years. There has been an attempt in preparing this bibliography to verify directly the information given in the entries with the works themselves, but available facilities have not made this possible in all cases. Thus some entries reflect information obtained only through other general bibliographical sources, but such titles are included because there is no apparent reason to doubt their accuracy, and on the view that it is preferable that they appear here known than remain elsewhere perhaps unknown to a given researcher. For a general account of the entry of Vico's thought into English letters and scholarly thought see Max Harold Fisch's Introduction to *The Autobiography of Giambattista Vico* (pp. 80–103).

The following bibliographies have been of assistance in preparing this bibliography:

Croce, Benedetto. *Bibliografia vichiana.* Revised and enlarged by Fausto Nicolini. 2 vols. Naples: Riccardo Ricciardi Editore, 1947–48.

Gianturco, Elio. *A Selective Bibliography of Vico Scholarship* (1948–1968). *Forum Italicum,* Supplement. Florence: Grafica Toscana, 1968.

Donzelli, Maria. *Contributo alla bibliografia vichiana* (1948–1970). Naples: Guida Editori, 1973.

I. Works on Vico

Adams, Henry Packwood. "Giambattista Vico." *Contemporary Review* 148 (1935): 79–85.

———. *The Life and Writings of Giambattista Vico.* London: Allen & Unwin, 1935. Reprinted, New York: Russell & Russell, 1970.

Auerbach, Erich. "Vico and Aesthetic Historism." *Journal of Aesthetics and Art Criticism* 8 (1949): 110–18. Reprinted in *Scenes from the Drama of European Literature.* New York: Meridian, 1959, pp. 183–200.

———. "Vico's Contribution to Literary Criticism." In *Studia philologica et litteraria in honorem L. Spitzer.* Bern: Franke, 1958, pp. 31–37.

Badaloni, Nicola. "Ideality and Factuality in Vico's Thought." In *Giambattista Vico: An International Symposium,* pp. 391–400.

Bank, Bruce H. "Where Terms Begin: Giambattista Vico and the Natural Law." Ph.D. dissertation, Harvard University, 1966.

Beckett, Samuel. "Dante . . . Bruno . . . Vico . . . Joyce." In *Our Exagmination Round His Factification for Incamination of Work in Progress,* edited by Samuel Beckett et al. Paris: Shakespeare & Co.; Norfolk, Conn.: New Directions, 1929, pp. 1–22.

Belaval, Yvon. "Vico and Anti-Cartesianism." In *Giambattista Vico: An International Symposium,* pp. 77–91.

Bergel, Lienhart. "Vico and the Germany of Goethe." *Forum Italicum* 2 (1968): 566–88.

Bergin, Thomas Goddard. "Giambattista Vico." In *Collier's Encyclopedia.* 1974.

Berlin, Isaiah. "The Philosophical Ideas of Giambattista Vico." In *Art and Ideas in Eighteenth-Century Italy*. Rome: Edizioni di Storia e Letteratura, 1960, pp. 156–233.

———. "A Note on Vico's Concept of Knowledge." In *Giambattista Vico: An International Symposium*, pp. 371–77. Also published in *The New York Review of Books*, 24 April 1969, pp. 23–26.

———. "One of the Boldest Innovators in the History of Human Thought." *The New York Times Magazine*, 23 November 1969, pp. 76, 77, 79, 80, 82, 84, 86, 89, 92, 97, 99–100. Reprinted in *Molders of Modern Thought*. Edited by Ben B. Seligman. Chicago: Quadrangle Books, 1970, pp. 41–56.

———. "Giambattista Vico." *The Listener* 88 (1972): 391–92, 394–98.

———. "The Divorce Between the Sciences and the Humanities." *Salmagundi* 27 (1974): 9–39. Also published in booklet form as *The Divorce Between the Sciences and the Humanities* (The Second Tykociner Memorial Lecture), Champaign: University of Illinois, 1974.

Berry, Thomas M. *The Historical Theory of Giambattista Vico*. Washington, D.C.: Catholic University of America Press, 1949.

Bevilacqua, Vincent M. "Vico, 'Process,' and the Nature of Rhetorical Investigation: An Epistemological Perspective." *Philosophy and Rhetoric* 7 (1974): 166–74.

Bidney, David. "Vico's New Science of Myth." In *Giambattista Vico: An International Symposium*, pp. 259–77.

Brown, Norman O. *Closing Time*. New York: Random House, 1973.

Cairns, Grace E. "Giambattista Vico: The 'Science' of the Culture Cycle." In *Philosophies of History*. London: Peter Owen, 1963, pp. 337–52.

Cambon, Glauco. "Vico as Poet." *Forum Italicum* 2 (1968): 326–31.

———. "Vico and Dante." In *Giambattista Vico: An International Symposium*, pp. 15–28.

Caponigri, A. Robert. "Giam Battista Vico." In *A History of Western Civilization*. 5 vols., edited by A. Robert Caponigri and Ralph M. McInerny. Notre Dame: University of Notre Dame Press, 1963–71. Vol. 3, *Philosophy from the Renaissance to the Romantic Age*, pp. 481–95.

———. *Time and Idea: the Theory of History in Giambattista Vico*. London: Routledge and Kegan Paul, 1953. Reprinted: Notre Dame: University of Notre Dame Press, 1968.

———. "Vico and the Theory of History." *Giornale di metafisica* 9 (1954): 183–97.

———. "Vico." In *The New Catholic Encyclopedia*. 1967.

———. "Umanità and civiltà: Civil Education in Vico." *The Review of Politics* 31 (1969): 477–94.

Caramella, Santino. "Vico, Tacitus, and Reason of State." In *Giambattista Vico: An International Symposium*, pp. 29–37.

Ceñal, Ramón. "Vico and Nineteenth Century Spanish Thought." In *Giambattista Vico: An International Symposium*, pp. 187–201.

Chaix-Ruy, Jules. "Giambattista Vico." In *Encyclopaedia Britannica, Macropaedia*. 1974.

Chambliss, Joseph James. "Vico: Poetic and Rational Metaphysics." In *Imagination and Reason in Plato, Aristotle, Vico, Rousseau and Keats: an Essay on the Philosophy of Experience.* The Hague: Martinus Nijhoff, 1974, pp. 29–43.

Child, Arthur. *Making and Knowing in Hobbes, Vico, and Dewey.* Berkeley: University of California Press, 1953.

Church, Margaret. "Dubliners and Vico." *James Joyce Quarterly* 5 (1968): 150–56.

———. Vico and 'Ulysses.'" *Proceedings of the Third International James Joyce Symposium, 14–18 June, 1971.* Edited by the Facoltà di Magistero, University of Trieste. Trieste: La Editoriale Libreria, 1974, pp. 343–47.

Clark, M. A. "Rimbaud—Michelet—Vico." *Modern Language Review* 37 (1942): 50–55.

Clark, Robert T., Jr. "Herder, Cesarotti and Vico." *Studies in Philology* 44 (1947): 645–71.

Collingwood, Robin G. "Anti-Cartesianism: Vico." In *The Idea of History.* Oxford: Clarendon Press, 1946, pp. 63–71.

Copleston, Frederick. "Bossuet and Vico." In *A History of Philosophy,* 8 vols., 1948–66. London: Burns & Oates, 1964, vol. 6, *Wolff to Kant,* pp. 150–63.

Corsano, Antonio. "Vico and Mathematics." In *Giambattista Vico: An International Symposium,* pp. 425–37.

Cotroneo, Girolamo. "A Renaissance Source of the *Scienza nuova:* Jean Bodin's *Methodus.*" In *Giambattista Vico: An International Symposium,* pp. 51–59.

Cousin, Victor. "Historians of Humanity." In *Course of the History of Modern Philosophy.* Translated by O. W. Wright. New York: Appleton, 1872, pp. 211–27.

Croce, Benedetto. "Giambattista Vico." In *Aesthetic, As Science of Expression and General Linguistic.* Translated by Douglas Ainslie. New York: Macmillan, 1909, pt. 2, chap. 5. Rev. ed. 1922. Reprinted: New York: Noonday, 1956.

———. *The Philosophy of Giambattista Vico.* Translated by Robin G. Collingwood. London: Howard Latimer, 1913. Reprinted: New York: Russell & Russell, 1964.

———. "Vico." In *Encyclopedia of the Social Sciences.* 1935, 1962.

———. "Vico and the Subsequent Development of Philosophic and Historic Thought" and "Machiavelli and Vico." In *Philosophy, Poetry, History: an Anthology of Essays.* Translated with an introduction by Cecil Sprigge. London: Oxford University Press, 1966, pp. 138–44 and 655–70.

Daffina, Paolo. "China in Giambattista Vico's Judgment." *Philosophy East and West* 9 (1958): 65–73.

D'Arcy, Martin C. "The New Science of Vico." In *The Meaning and Matter of History. A Christian View.* New York: Farrar, Straus, and Cudahy, 1959, pp. 122–32. Published in Great Britain as: *The Sense of History, Secular and Sacred.* London: Faber & Faber, 1959, pp. 122–32.

Day, Paul W. *Matthew Arnold and the Philosophy of Vico.* University of Auckland, bulletin 70 (English ser. 12), Auckland, New Zealand, 1964.

DeGennaro, Angelo. "Croce and Vico." *Journal of Aesthetics and Art Criticism* 22 (1963): 43–46.

———. "The Lasting Influence of Vico: On the Tercentenary of His Birth." *Italica* 35 (1968): 403–9.

———. "The Relevance of Vico's Thought in the Tercentenary of his Birth." *Forum Italicum* 2 (1968): 299–304.
———. "The Vico Tricentenary 1668–1744." *Personalist* 49 (1968): 153–58.
———. "Vico and Croce: The Genesis of Croce's Aesthetics." *Personalist* 50 (1969): 508–25.
De Mas, Enrico. "Vico and Italian Thought." In *Giambattista Vico: An International Symposium*, pp. 147–64.
———. "On the New Method of a New Science—A Study of Giambattista Vico." *Journal of the History of Ideas* 32 (1971): 85–94.
———. "Vico's Four Authors." In *Giambattista Vico: An International Symposium*, pp. 3–14.
de Mauro, Tullio. "Giambattista Vico: From Rhetoric to Linguistic Historicism." In *Giambattista Vico: An International Symposium*, pp. 279–95.
DeSantillana, Giorgio. "Vico and Descartes." *Osiris* 21 (1950): 565–80. Reprinted in *Reflections on Men and Ideas*. Cambridge: Massachusetts Institute of Technology Press, 1968, pp. 206–18.
Dieckmann, Liselotte. "Giambattista Vico's Use of 'Renaissance Hieroglyphics.'" *Forum Italicum* 2 (1968): 382–85.
Dismukes, W. P. "Michelet and Vico: A Study of Michelet's Use of Vichian Principles." Ph.D. dissertation, University of Illinois, 1936.
Donagan, Alan, and Donagan, Barbara. "Giambattista Vico: A New Conception of Historiography." In *Philosophy of History*. New York: Macmillan, 1965, pp. 44–52.
Dorfles, Gillo. "Myth and Metaphor in Vico and in Contemporary Aesthetics." In *Giambattista Vico: An International Symposium*, pp. 577–90.
Downs, Robert B. "Vico." In *Molders of the Modern Mind: 111 Books That Shaped Western Civilization*. New York: Barnes & Noble, 1961, pp. 112–14.
Eberhard, John P. "A New Science Needed for Man." *Transactions of the New York Academy of Science* 32 (1970): 806.
Edie, James M. "Vico and Existential Philosophy." In *Giambattista Vico: An International Symposium*, pp. 483–95.
Fáj, Attila. "Some Important, Hitherto Unnoticed, Sources of Finnegans Wake." *Proceedings of the Third International James Joyce Symposium, 14–18 June, 1971*. Edited by the Facoltà di Magistero, University of Trieste. Trieste: La Editoriale Libreria, 1974, pp. 358–74. Reprinted in *A Wake Newsletter* 10 (1973): 3–12, and in *Neuphilologische Mitteilungen* 76 (1974): 650–62.
Falzon, Paul L. "Some Additions to Croce's Bibliography of Vico." *Melita Theologica* 1 (1921): 488–95, 526–33.
Faucci, Dario. "Vico and Grotius: Jurisconsults of Mankind." In *Giambattista Vico: An International Symposium*, pp. 61–76.
Feder, Lillian. "The Cyclic View: Giambattista Vico and Oswald Spengler." In *Ancient Myth in Modern Poetry*. Princeton: Princeton University Press, 1972, pp. 270–76.
Feibleman, James. "Toward the Recovery of Giambattista Vico." *Social Science* 14 (1939): 31–40.
Feldman, Burton, and Richardson, Robert D. "Giambattista Vico (1668–

1744)." In *The Rise of Modern Mythology 1680–1860*. Bloomington: Indiana University Press, 1972, pp. 50–61.
Fisch, Max Harold. "The Coleridges, Dr. Prati and Vico." *Modern Philology* 41 (1943): 111–22.
———. Introduction to *The Autobiography of Giambattista Vico*, translated by Max H. Fisch and Thomas G. Bergin. 1944, pp. 1–107. Reprinted: Ithaca: Cornell University Press, Great Seal Books, 1963.
———. "Vico on Roman Law." *Essays in Political Theory Presented to George H. Sabine*, edited by Milton R. Konvitz and Arthur E. Murphy. Ithaca: Cornell University Press, 1948, pp. 62–88.
———. Introduction to *The New Science of Giambattista Vico*, translated by Max H. Fisch and Thomas G. Bergin. 1951 (abridged translation). Reprinted: Ithaca: Cornell University Press, 1968 (complete translation); 1970 (reissue of 1951 edition).
———. "Giambattista Vico." In *Encyclopaedia Britannica*. 1959, 1973.
———. "Vico and Pragmatism." In *Giambattista Vico: An International Symposium*, pp. 401–24.
Fitzmorris, T. J. "Vico Adamant and Some Pillars of Salt; Neapolitan Philosopher of the Eighteenth Century." *Catholic World* 156 (1943): 568–77.
Flint, Robert. *Vico*. Edinburgh: Blackwood, 1884.
Fox, June, "Giambattista Vico's Theory of Pedagogy." *British Journal of Educational Studies* 20 (1972): 27–37.
Franchini, Raffaello. "Vico, Historical Methodology, and the Future of Philosophy." In *Giambattista Vico: An International Symposium*, pp. 543–52.
Gadol, Eugene T. "The Idealistic Foundations of Cultural Anthropology: Vico, Kant and Cassirer." *Journal of the History of Philosophy* 12 (1974), 207–25.
Gardiner, Patrick, "Vico." In *Theories of History*. Glencoe, Ill.: The Free Press, 1959, pp. 9–21.
———. "Vico." In *The Encyclopedia of Philosophy*. 1967.
"Giambattista Vico." In *Encyclopaedia Britannica*. 1911.
Gianturco, Elio. "Suarez and Vico: A Note on the Origin of the Vichian Formula." *Harvard Theological Review* 27 (1934): 207–10.
———. "Character, Essence, Origin and Content of the Jus Gentium According to Vico and Suarez." *Revue de littérature comparée* 10 (1936): 167–72.
———. "On Suarez and Vico." Abstract. *Italica* 13 (1936): 116.
———. *Joseph de Maistre and Giambattista Vico: Italian Roots of de Maistre's Political Culture*. Washington, D.C.: Murray & Heister, 1937.
———. "Bodin and Vico." *Revue de littérature comparée* 22 (1948): 272–90.
———. Introduction to Giambattista Vico's *On the Study Methods of Our Time*, translated by Elio Gianturco. Indianapolis, New York, Kansas City: Bobbs-Merrill Library of Liberal Arts, 1965, pp. ix–xxxiii.
———. Translation of "Letter of Giovanni Antonio Chiajese to Nicola Geremia (August 13, 1721)." *Forum Italicum* 2 (1968): 315–25.
———. Translation of "G. A. Chiajese's letter on the *De Uno*." *Forum Italicum* 2 (1968): 370–81.
———. *A Selective Bibliography of Vico Scholarship (1948–1968)*. *Forum Italicum*, Supplement. Florence: Grafica Toscana, 1968.

———. "Vico's Significance in the History of Legal Thought." In *Giambattista Vico: An International Symposium*, pp. 327–47.

Gilson, Étienne, and Langan, Thomas. "Vico and the New Science." In *Modern Philosophy: Descartes to Kant*. New York: Random House, 1963, pp. 341–49.

Goretti, Maria. "Vico's Pedagogic Thought and That of Today." In *Giambattista Vico: An International Symposium*, pp. 553–75.

Grassi, Ernesto. "Critical Philosophy or Topical Philosophy? Meditations on the *De nostri temporis studiorum ratione*." In *Giambattista Vico: An International Symposium*, pp. 39–50.

Grimaldi, Alfonsina Albini. *The Universal Humanity of Giambattista Vico*. New York: Vanni, 1958.

Haac, O. A. "Vico and Michelet." *Forum Italicum* 2 (1968): 483–93.

Hall, Robert Anderson, Jr. "G. B. Vico and Linguistic Theory." *Italica* 18 (1941): 145–54.

———. "Benedetto Croce and the Influence of G. B. Vico." In *Idealism in Romance Linguistics*. Ithaca: Cornell University Press, 1963, pp. 21–36.

Hampshire, Stuart. "Vico and His 'New Science.'" *The Listener* 44 (1949): 569–71.

———. "Vico and Language." *The New York Review of Books*, 23 February 1969, pp. 19–22.

———. "Vico and the Contemporary Philosophy of Language." In *Giambattista Vico: An International Symposium*, pp. 475–81.

———. "Joyce and Vico: The Middle Way." *The New York Review of Books*, 18 October 1973, pp. 8, 9, 12, 14, 16, 21.

Harris, Henry S. "Vico." In *Encyclopedia Americana*. 1974.

Henseler, Donna Leah. "Vico's Doctrine of Ricorso in James Joyce's Finnegan's Wake." Ph.D. dissertation, Michigan State University, 1970.

Hodgart, Matthew. "A Viconian Sentence in Ulysses." *Orbis Litterarum* 19 (1964): 201–4.

Hodges, Herbert Arthur. "Vico and Dilthey." In *Giambattista Vico: An International Symposium*, pp. 439–45.

Hughes, H. Stuart. "Vico and Contemporary Social Theory and Social History." In *Giambattista Vico: An International Symposium*, pp. 319–26.

Hutton, Patrick H. "The New Science of Giambattista Vico: "Historicism in Its Relation to Poetics." *Journal of Aesthetics and Art Criticism* 31 (1972): 359–67.

Johnston, William M. "The Influence of Croce, Gentile and Vico on Collingwood during the Early 20's." In *The Formative Years of R. G. Collingwood*. The Hague: Martinus Nijhoff, 1967, pp. 81–90.

"Joyce and Vico." *Proceedings of the Third International James Joyce Symposium, 14–18 June, 1971*. Edited by the Facoltà di Magistero, University of Trieste. Trieste: La Editoriale Libreria, 1974, pp. 342–78. [Papers on Vico in this volume are listed separately in this bibliography.]

Kamenka, Eugene. "Vico and Marxism." In *Giambattista Vico: An International Symposium*, pp. 137–43.

Kenrick, John. "Vico." *Philological Museum* 2 (1833): 626–44.

Klein, A. M. "A Shout in the Street." *New Directions in Prose and Poetry* 13 (1951): 327–45.

Kline, George L. "Vico in Pre-Revolutionary Russia." In *Giambattista Vico: An International Symposium*, pp. 203–13.

Knox, Thomas Malcolm. "Vico." In *Chamber's Encyclopaedia*. 1966.

Leach, Edmund. "Vico and Lévi-Strauss on the Origins of Humanity." In *Giambattista Vico: An International Symposium*, pp. 309–18.

Lifshitz, Michele A. "Giambattista Vico (1668–1744)." Translated by Henry F. Mins, Jr. *Philosophy and Phenomenological Research* 8 (1948): 391–414.

Lion, Aline. "Giambattista Vico." In *The Pedigree of Fascism: a Popular Essay on the Western Philosophy of Politics*. London: Sheed & Ward, 1927, pp. 125–36.

———. *The Idealistic Conception of Religion: Vico, Hegel, Gentile*. Oxford: Clarendon Press, 1932.

Litz, A. Walton. "Vico and Joyce." In *Giambattista Vico: An International Symposium*, pp. 245–55.

Löwith, Karl. "Vico." In *Meaning in History: The Theological Implications of the Philosophy of History*. Chicago: University of Chicago Press, Phoenix Books, 1949, pp. 115–36.

Manson, Richard. *The Theory of Knowledge of Giambattista Vico: On the Method of the New Science Concerning the Common Nature of the Nations*. Hamden, Conn.: Archon Books, 1969.

Manuel, Frank. "Vico: The 'Giganti' and their Joves." In *The Eighteenth Century Confronts the Gods*. Cambridge, Mass.: Harvard University Press, 1959, pp. 149–67.

Mason, Ellsworth G. "James Joyce's 'Ulysses' and Vico's Cycle." Ph.D. dissertation, Yale University, 1948.

———. "Joyce and Vico—Gemelli." *Proceedings of the Third International James Joyce Symposium, 14–18 June, 1971*. Edited by the Facoltà di Magistero, University of Trieste. Trieste: La Editoriale Libreria, 1974, pp. 353–57.

Maurice, Frederick Denison. "Vico." In *Modern Philosophy; or, A Treatise of Moral and Metaphysical Philosophy from the Fourteenth Century to the French Revolution, with a Glimpse into the Nineteenth Century*. London: Griffin, Bohn, & Co., 1862, pp. 500–504.

Mazlish, Bruce. "Vico." In *The Riddle of History. The Great Speculators from Vico to Freud*. New York: Harper & Row, 1966, pp. 11–58.

McReynolds, J. W. "Giambattista Vico on Education." *School and Society* 71 (1950): 149–51.

Meinecke, Friedrich. "Vico/Lafitau." In *Historism: the Rise of a New Historical Outlook*. Translated by J. E. Anderson. New York: Herder and Herder, 1972, pp. 37–53.

Metastasio, Arthur Paul. "Vico and French Romanticism." Ph.D. dissertation, Boston University, 1963.

Momigliano, Arnaldo. "Vico's *Scienza Nuova:* Roman 'Bestioni' and Roman 'Eroi.'" *History and Theory* 5 (1966): 3–23.

Montano, Rocco. "Vico's Opposition to Enlightenment." *Italian Quarterly* 17 (1974): 3–34.

Nash, Ronald H. "Giambattista Vico (1668–1744)." In *Ideas of History*. Edited by Ronald H. Nash. New York: Dutton, 1969, vol. 1, *Speculative Approaches to History*, pp. 25–47.

Noether, Emiliana P. "Giambattista Vico." In *Seeds of Italian Nationalism, 1700–1815*. New York: Columbia University Press, 1951, pp. 48–62.

———. "Giambattista Vico and the Risorgimento." *Harvard Library Bulletin* 17 (1969): 309–19.

Paci, Enzo. "Vico and Cassirer." In *Giambattista Vico: An International Symposium*, pp. 457–73.

———. "Vico, Structuralism, and the Phenomenological Encyclopedia of the Sciences." In *Giambattista Vico: An International Symposium*, pp. 497–515.

Palmieri, Mario. "Two Forerunners of Fascism." In *The Philosophy of Fascism*. Chicago: The Dante Alighieri Society, 1936, pp. 191–200.

Pasotti, Robert Neil. "Giambattista Vico and the Psychology of History." Ph.D. dissertation, Columbia University, 1963.

Perkinson, Henry J. "Giambattista Vico: Philosopher of Education." Ph.D. dissertation, Harvard University, 1959.

Perotta, P. C. "Giambattista Vico, Philosophic Historian." *Catholic Historical Review* 20 (1935): 384–410.

Piovani, Pietro. *Giambattista Vico—Our Perennial Standard*. New York: Istituto Italiano di Cultura, 1969.

———. "Vico Without Hegel." In *Giambattista Vico: An International Symposium*, pp. 103–23.

Pompa, Leon. "Vico's Science." *History and Theory* 10 (1971): 49–83.

———. *Vico: A Study of the "New Science."* Cambridge: The University Press, 1975.

Pons, Alain. "Vico and French Thought." In *Giambattista Vico: An International Symposium*, pp. 165–85.

Prezzolini, Giuseppe. "Vico: the Discovery of Poetry." In *The Legacy of Italy*. New York: Vanni, 1948, pp. 169–76.

Randall, John Herman, Jr. "The Science of Society: Montesquieu, Vico, the Physiocrats, and Rousseau." In *The Career of Philosophy*. 2 vols. New York: Columbia University Press, 1962–65. Vol. 1, *From the Middle Ages to the Enlightenment*, pp. 940–83.

Read, Herbert. "Vico and the Rise of the Genetic Concept of Art." In *Art Now: An Introduction to the Theory of Modern Painting and Sculpture*. London: Harcourt, Brace & Co., 1933, pp. 32–34. Rev. ed. London: Pitman, 1948, pp. 35–37. Rev. ed. London: Faber & Faber, 1960, pp. 24–26.

———. "Vico and the Genetic Theory of Poetry." In *Giambattista Vico: An International Symposium*, pp. 591–97.

Ricciardelli, M., ed. *A Homage to G. B. Vico in the Tercentenary of His Birth. Forum Italicum* 2, no. 4 (1968). [Special issue. Articles in English are listed separately in this bibliography.]

Rickman, H. P. "Vico and Dilthey's Methodology of the Human Studies." In *Giambattista Vico: An International Symposium*, pp. 447–56.

Robertson, J. G. "Giambattista Vico." In *Studies in the Genesis of Romantic Theory in the Eighteenth Century*. Cambridge: The University Press, 1923, pp. 179–94.

Rockey, Palmer. "The Moral Philosophy of Giambattista Vico." Ph.D. dissertation, St. Louis University, 1955.

Said, Edward W. "Vico: Autodidact and Humanist." *Centennial Review* 11 (1967): 336–52.

Salomone, William. "Pluralism and Universality in Vico's *Scienza nuova*." In *Giambattista Vico: An International Symposium*, pp. 517–41.

Saunders, J. J. "Giambattista Vico, 1744–1944." *Dublin Review* 214 (1944): 137–44.

Sewell, Elizabeth. "Bacon, Vico, Coleridge, and the Poetic Method." In *Giambattista Vico: An International Symposium*, pp. 125–36.

Slomich, Sidney J. "Studies in Eschatological Politics: Reason, Fact, Value, and Law in the Historical Political Theories of Vico, Marx, Hegel, Mazzini, and Kant." Ph.D. dissertation, Harvard University, 1951.

Stadelmann, R. "Giam Battista Vico's Philosophy of History, *Scienza nuova*." *Tübingen University Lecture Series*, nos. 3–4 [n.d.], pp. 72–75.

Stark, Werner. "Giambattista Vico's Sociology of Knowledge." In *Giambattista Vico: An International Symposium*, pp. 297–307.

Stevenson, W. Taylor. "Giambattista Vico and the Modern Historical Consciousness." In *History as Myth: The Import for Contemporary Theology*. New York: Seabury Press, 1969, pp. 33–57.

Swinny, S. H. "Giambattista Vico." *Sociological Review* 7 (1914): 50–57.

Tagliacozzo, Giorgio. "Economic Vichianism: Vico, Galiani, Croce—Economics, Economic Liberalism." *Quarterly Review of the Banca Nazionale del Lavoro*, no. 85 (1968): 95–119. Reprinted in *Giambattista Vico: An International Symposium*, pp. 215–23.

———. "Epilogue" ["Unity of Knowledge" and "General Education"]. In *Giambattista Vico: An International Symposium*, pp. 599–613.

———, and White, Hayden V., eds. *Giambattista Vico: An International Symposium*. Baltimore: Johns Hopkins Press, 1969. [Essays in this volume are listed separately in this bibliography.]

———. "Vico and Joyce." *Proceedings of the Third International James Joyce Symposium, 14–18 June, 1971*. Edited by the Facoltà di Magistero, University of Trieste. Trieste: La Editoriale Libreria, 1974, pp. 374–78.

Toulmin, Stephen, and Goodfield, June. "Vico: The Mendel of History." In *The Discovery of Time*. New York: Harper & Row, 1965, pp. 125–29.

Vaughan, Charles E. "Giambattista Vico, An Eighteenth-Century Pioneer." Deansgate, Manchester, *John Rylands Library Bulletin* 6, no. 3, 1921.

———. "The Eclipse of Contract: Vico, Montesquieu." In C. E. Vaughan, *Studies in the History of Political Philosophy Before and After Rousseau*. 2 vols., edited by A. G. Little. Manchester: The University Press, 1925. Vol. 1, pp. 204–302.

Vaughan, Frederick, "La 'Scienza nuova': Orthodoxy and the Art of Writing." *Forum Italicum* 2 (1968): 332–58.

———. *The Political Philosophy of Giambattista Vico: an Introduction to La Scienza nuova*. The Hague: Martinus Nijhoff, 1972.

"Vico—*New Science*, and *Ancient Wisdom of the Italians*." *Foreign Review and Continental Miscellany* 5 (1830): 380–91.

Vittorini, D. "Giambattista Vico and Reality: an Evaluation of the 'De nostri temporis studiorum ratione' (1708)." *Modern Language Quarterly* 13 (1952): 90–98.

Wellek, René. "The Supposed Influence of Vico on England and Scotland in the Eighteenth Century." In *Giambattista Vico: An International Symposium*, pp. 215–23.

Wells, George A. "Vico and Herder." In *Giambattista Vico: An International Symposium*, pp. 93–102.

Whalley, George. "Coleridge and Vico." In *Giambattista Vico: An International Symposium*, pp. 225–44.

White, Hayden V. "Giovanni Battista Vico." In *International Encyclopedia of the Social Sciences*. 1968.

———. "What is Living and What is Dead in Croce's Criticism of Vico." In *Giambattista Vico: An International Symposium*, pp. 379–89.

———. "Croce contra Vico." In *Metahistory: the Historical Imagination in Nineteenth-Century Europe*. Baltimore: Johns Hopkins Press, 1973, pp. 415–22.

White, Patrick T. "James Joyce's 'Ulysses' and Vico's 'Principles of Humanity.'" Ph.D. dissertation, University of Michigan, 1963.

———. "Ulysses and Vico's 'Principles of Humanity.'" *Proceedings of the Third International James Joyce Symposium, 14–18 June, 1971*. Edited by the Facoltà di Magistero, University of Trieste. Trieste: La Editoriale Libreria, 1974, pp. 348–53.

Whittaker, Thomas. "Vico's New Science of Humanity." *Mind* 35 (1926): 59–71, 204–21, 319–36. Reprinted in *Reason: a Philosophical Essay, with Historical Illustrations—Comte, Mill, Schopenhauer, Vico, Spinoza*. Cambridge: The University Press, 1934.

II. Some Works Which Cite Vico

Arendt, Hannah. "History and Immortality." *Partisan Review* 24 (1957): 23–24.

———. *Between Past and Future*. New York: Viking Press, 1961, pp. 50, 57–58, 77, 82, 84.

Arieti, Silvano. *Interpretation of Schizophrenia*. New York: Brunner, 1955, pp. 6, 206–7, 221, 280, 312. Rev. ed. New York: Basic Books, 1974, pp. 7, 238, 243, 293, 366, 377n., 546, 735.

———. *The Intrapsychic Self*. New York: Basic Books, 1967, pp. 122, 125n., 148, 400, 408.

Atherton, James S. *The Books at the Wake: a Study of Literary Allusions in James Joyce's Finnegans Wake*. New York: Viking Press, 1960, pp. 18, 19, 22, 28, 29–34, 52, 53, 54, 111, 126, 136, 149, 150, 260, 267, 268, 287.

Avineri, Shlomo. *The Social and Political Thought of Karl Marx*. Cambridge: The University Press, 1968, p. 77.

Auerbach, Erich. *Mimesis: the Representation of Reality in Western Literature*. Translated by Willard R. Trask. Princeton: Princeton University Press, 1953, pp. 34, 381n.

———. *Literary Language and Its Public in Late Latin Antiquity and in the Middle Ages*. Translated by Ralph Manheim. New York: Pantheon Books, 1965, pp. 7–24, 122.

Becker, Ernest. *Beyond Alienation: a Philosophy of Education for the Crisis of Democracy*. New York: Braziller, 1967, pp. 5, 15, 24, 27, 102, 117, 168, 232, 252.

———. *The Structure of Evil: an Essay on the Unification of the Science of Man*. New York: Braziller, 1968, pp. 27–28, 31, 219, 227, 329, 340, 341, 398n.

Berlin, Isaiah, ed. *The Age of Enlightenment*. New York: New American Library of World Literature, Mentor Books, 1956, pp. 273–75.

———. "History and Theory: the Concept of Scientific History." *History and Theory* 1 (1960): 6, 24, 26, 28, 30.

———. "Herder and the Enlightenment." In *Aspects of the Eighteenth Century*, edited by Earl R. Wasserman. Baltimore: Johns Hopkins Press, 1965, pp. 49, 50, 51, 52, 67, 69, 71, 80, 84.

———. "Georges Sorel." *The London Times Literary Supplement*, 31 December 1971, pp. 1617–22.

Bloom, Harold. *The Anxiety of Influence. A Theory of Poetry*. New York: Oxford University Press, 1973, pp. 59–62.

———. *The Ringers in the Tower. Studies in Romantic Tradition*. Chicago: Chicago University Press, 1975, pp. 4, 6.

Boas, George. "In Search of the Age of Reason," In *Aspects of the Eighteenth Century*, edited by Earl R. Wasserman. Baltimore: Johns Hopkins Press, 1965, pp. 13, 14, 15, 18.

Bridenthal, Renate. "Was There a Roman Homer? Niebuhr's Thesis and its Critics." *History and Theory* 11 (1972): 193–213.

Brown, Norman O. "Rieff's 'Fellow Teachers.' " *Salmagundi* 24 (1973): 34–45.

Brown, Roger L. *Wilhelm von Humboldt's Conception of Linguistic Relativity*. The Hague: Mouton, 1967, pp. 30, 31, 32, 34.

Brownson, Orestes A. "The Philosophy of History." In *The Works of Orestes A. Brownson*. 20 vols, edited by Henry F. Brownson. New York: AMS Press, 1966, vol. 4, pp. 392–401.

Buckle, H. T. *Introduction to the History of Civilisation in England*. Edited by J. M. Robinson. London, 1904, pp. 91 n.8, 466 n.131, 500.

Bultmann, Rudolph. *The Presence of Eternity*. Harper & Row: New York, 1957, pp. 64, 65, 69, 79, 80, 81, 85, 86.

Bury, John Bagnell. *The Idea of Progress: an Inquiry into Its Origin and Growth*. New York: Macmillan, 1932, pp. 267–71, 277, 308.

Cahnman, Werner J. and Boskoff, Alvin, eds., *Sociology and History: Theory and Research*. New York: The Free Press of Glencoe, 1964, pp. 46–48, 51, 138n.

Cammet, John M. *Antonio Gramsci and the Origins of Italian Communism*. Stanford: Stanford University Press, 1967, pp. 42, 60, 203.

Caponigri, A. Robert. *History and Liberty: the Historical Writings of Bene-*

detto Croce. London: Routledge & Kegan Paul, 1955, pp. 3, 14, 117, 122, 163, 180, 182, 231.
———. "The Nature of History." *Giornale di metafisica* 17 (1962): 338, 339, 363, 376.
Casserly, Julian Victor Langmead. *The Christian in Philosophy*. New York: Scribner, 1961, pp. 46, 66, 67, 118–21, 123, 207, 208, 237, 238.
Cassirer, Ernst. *An Essay on Man*. New Haven: Yale University Press, 1944, pp. 114, 153, 172.
———. *The Problem of Knowledge*. Translated by William H. Woglom and Charles W. Hendel. New Haven: Yale University Press, 1950, pp. 217, 296.
———. *The Philosophy of the Enlightenment*. Translated by Fritz C. A. Koelln and James P. Pettegrove. Princeton: Princeton University Press, 1951, p. 209.
———. *The Philosophy of Symbolic Forms*. 3 vols., translated by Ralph Manheim. New Haven: Yale University Press, 1953–57. Vol. 1, *Language*, pp. 147–55, vol. 2, *Mythical Thought*, p. 3.
———. *The Logic of the Humanities*. Translated by Clarence Smith Howe. New Haven: Yale University Press, 1961, pp. 52–55.
Chambliss, Rollin. *Social Thought*. New York: Dryden Press, 1954, pp. 366–91.
Clark, Robert T., Jr. *Herder—His Life and Thought*. Berkeley: University of California Press, 1955, pp. 24, 31, 179–80, 188, 191, 314, 381.
Cochrane, Eric. *Florence in the Forgotten Centuries, 1527–1800*. Chicago: University of Chicago Press, 1973, pp. 326, 334, 388, 552.
Collingwood, Robin G. *Speculum Mentis or The Map of Knowledge*. Oxford: Clarendon Press, 1924, pp. 53, 74, 216.
———. *Principles of Art*. Oxford: Clarendon Press, 1938, pp. 80, 138.
Croce, Benedetto. *History, its Theory and Practice*. Translated by Douglas Ainslie. New York: Harcourt, Brace, & Co., 1923. Reprint ed. New York: Russell & Russell, 1960, pp. 31, 79, 96, 102–3, 105, 124, 164, 171, 191, 229, 269–70, 275, 277–78, 285–86, 304.
———. *European Literature in the Nineteenth Century*. Translated by Douglas Ainslie. New York: Knopf, 1924, pp. 83, 85, 155, 268.
———. *History as the Story of Liberty*. Translated by Sylvia Sprigge. New York: Norton, 1941, pp. 17, 35, 40, 60, 71, 72, 73, 73n, 74, 78, 79, 82, 113, 118, 142, 143, 211, 231, 247, 269, 270, 293, 299, 300.
———. *My Philosophy: Essays on the Moral and Political Problems of Our Time*. New York: Collier Books, 1962, pp. 13, 91, 205.
———. "An Unknown Page from the Last Months of Hegel's Life." Translated by James W. Hillesheim and Ernesto Caserta. *The Personalist* 45 (1964): 344–45, 351.
———. *Guide to Aesthetics*. Translated by Patrick Romanell. Indianapolis, New York, Kansas City: Bobbs-Merrill, 1965, pp. ix, xiii–xviii, 19, 56, 84.
———. *History of the Kingdom of Naples*. Translated by Frances Frenaye. Edited by H. Stuart Hughes. Chicago: University of Chicago Press, 1970, pp. 9, 10, 39, 40, 83, 150, 157, 158, 159, 197, 198, 220, 236, 248.
Dallmayr, Fred. "Political Science and the 'Two Cultures.'" *Journal of General Education* 19 (1968): 274.
D'Entrèves, Alessandro Passerin. *Natural Law: an Introduction to Legal Phi-*

losophy. London: Hutchinson's University Library, 1951. Reprint ed., *Natural Law: a Historical Survey*. New York: Harper & Row, Harper Torchbooks, 1965, pp. 28, 54, 118.

De Sanctis, Francesco. *History of Italian Literature*. 2 vols., translated by Joan Redfern. New York: Harcourt, Brace and Co., 1931, Vol. 2, pp. 782, 789, 792–812, 813, 818, 820, 823, 827, 844, 891, 906, 907, 909, 916, 918, 923, 926, 927, 944.

deVries, Jan. *The Study of Religion: a Historical Approach*. Translated with an introduction by Kees W. Boole. New York: Harcourt, Brace, & World, 1967, pp. 34–35.

DiPietro, Robert. "The Discovery of Universals in Multilinguism." In the *21st Annual Roundtable*, edited by James E. Alatis. Washington: Georgetown University, School of Languages and Linguistics, *Monograph Series on Languages and Linguistics* 23 (1970): 20.

Dyson-Hudson, Neville. "Structure and Infrastructure in Primitive Society: Lévi-Strauss and Radcliffe-Brown." In *The Structuralist Controversy: the Languages of Criticism and the Sciences of Man*, edited by Richard Macksey and Eugenio Donato. Baltimore: Johns Hopkins Press, 1970, p. 222.

Edie, James M. "Expression and Metaphor." *Philosophy and Phenomenological Research* 23 (1963): 548.

Ellmann, Richard. *Ulysses on the Liffey*. New York: Oxford University Press, 1972, pp. 52–53, 58–59, 84, 118–23, 136, 141–42, 178–83, 190, 192.

Everett, Alexander Hill. "Progress and Limits of Social Improvement." *North American Review* 38 (1834): 513.

Farrar, C. C. S. "The Science of History." *De Bow's Review* 5 (1848): 58, 133, 211–14.

Fisch, Max H. "The Academy of the Investigators." *Science, Medicine, and History: Essays in Honour of Charles Singer*. 2 vols., edited by E. A. Underwood. London and Toronto: Oxford University Press, 1953, Vol. I, pp. 521–63.

———. "The Critic of Institutions." *Proceedings and Addresses of the American Philosophical Association* 29 (1956): 42–56. Reprinted in *Studies in Philosophy and in the History of Science: Essays in Honor of Max Fisch*, edited by Richard Tursman. Lawrence, Kans.: Coronado Press, 1970, pp. 182–92.

———. "The Philosophy of History: A Dialogue." *Philosophy (Tetsugaku)* 36 (1959): 149–70, published by the Mita Philosophy Society, Keio University, Tokyo. Reprinted in *Studies in Philosophy and in the History of Science: Essays in Honor of Max Fisch*, edited by Richard Tursman. Lawrence, Kans.: Coronado Press, 1970, pp. 193–206.

Fisch, William B. "Max Harold Fisch. A Bio-Biographical Sketch." In *Studies in Philosophy and in the History of Science: Essays in Honor of Max Fisch*, edited by Richard Tursman. Lawrence, Kans.: Coronado Press, 1970, pp. 207–10.

Flint, Robert. *The Philosophy of History in Europe*. Edinburgh: Blackwood, 1874. Vol. 1, *The Philosophy of History in France and Germany*, pp. 26, 77, 96 n. 1, 206, 286–87, 289, 290, 320–21, 324, 351 n. 1.

———. *Historical Philosophy in France and French Belgium and Switzerland*.

London: Blackwood, 1893, pp. 77, 124, 126, 158, 211, 227, 255–56, 264, 265–66, 321, 352, 382, 383, 389–90, 480, 526, 530–32, 536, 568, 677, 684.

———. *Philosophy as Scientia Scientiarum and A History of Classifications of the Sciences*. Edinburgh and London: Blackwood, 1904, pp. 127–29.

Forbes, Duncan. *The Liberal Anglican Idea of History*. Cambridge: The University Press, 1952, p. 17, 156.

———. " 'Scientific' Whiggism: Adam Smith and John Millar." *The Cambridge Journal* 8 (1954): 658.

France, Peter. *Rhetoric and Truth in France*. Oxford: Clarendon Press, 1972, pp. 3–33, 69–111.

Fromm, Eric. *Marx's Concept of Man*. New York: Ungar, 1961, p. 15.

Frye, Northrop. *The Critical Path*. Bloomington: Indiana University Press, 1971, pp. 34, 38.

Fugate, Joseph K. *The Psychological Basis of Herder's Aesthetics*. The Hague: Mouton, 1966, pp. 113, 115.

Gallie, W. B. *Philosophy and the Historical Understanding*. New York: Schocken Books, 1964, pp. 11, 55, 127, 174.

Gardner, Howard. *The Quest for Mind*. New York: Knopf, 1962, p. 238.

Gilbert Katherine Everett. "Cassirer's Placement of Art." In *The Philosophy of Ernst Cassirer*, edited by Paul Arthur Schilpp. New York: Tudor, 1958, p. 616.

———, and Kuhn, Helmuth. *A History of Esthetics*. New York: Macmillan, 1939, pp. 268–74.

Gilbert, Stuart. "Prolegomena to *Work In Progress*." In *Our Exagmination round His Factification for Incamination of Work in Progress*, edited by Samuel Beckett et al. Paris: Shakespeare & Co., Norfolk, Conn.: New Directions, 1929, pp. 51–56.

Giles, Henry. "The Leading Theories on the Philosophy of History." *North American Review* 95 (1862): 167–70.

Gorman, Herbert. *James Joyce*. New York and Toronto: Farrar & Rinehart, 1939, pp. 332–35.

Gross, John. *James Joyce*. New York: Viking Press, 1970, pp. 25, 79.

Grote, George. *A History of Greece*, 12 vols. 2d ed., London: John Murray, 1869–70. Vol. 1, ch. 16, pp. 341–43, n.

Gutmann, James. "Cassirer's Humanism." In *The Philosophy of Ernst Cassirer*, edited by Paul Arthur Schilpp. New York: Tudor, 1958, p. 448.

Hamilton, Peter. *Knowledge and Social Structure: an Introduction to the Classical Argument in the Sociology of Knowledge*. London: Routledge & Kegan Paul, 1974, pp. 1–14.

Harris, Marvin. *The Rise of Anthropological Theory: a History of Theories of Culture*. New York: Crowell Press, 1968, pp. 19–20, 27–28, 65, 269, 759.

Hazard, Paul. *European Thought in the Eighteenth Century*. Translated by J. Lewis May. New Haven: Yale University Press, 1954, pp. 33, 35, 36, 37, 152, 246, 406.

———. *The European Mind, 1680–1715*. Translated by J. Lewis May. New York: World Publishing Co., Meridian Books, 1963, pp. 76, 130, 311, 412–14.

Hodgen, Margaret Trabue. *Early Anthropology in the Sixteenth and Seven-*

teenth Centuries. Philadelphia: University of Pennsylvania Press, 1964, pp. 492–97, 513.

Hodges, Herbert Arthur. *The Philosophy of Wilheim Dilthey*. London: Routledge & Kegan Paul, 1952, pp. xiii, xvi, 186, 190, 236.

Holmes, George F. "Schlegel's Philosophy of History," *Southern Quarterly Review* 3 (1843): 274–79.

Hughes, H. Stuart. *Oswald Spengler, a Critical Estimate*. New York: Scribner, 1952, pp. 38–40, 53, 81, 94, 141.

———. *Consciousness and Society: the Reorientation of European Social Thought, 1890–1930*. New York: Random House, 1958, pp. 171–72, 198, 202, 205–6, 208–9, 212, 270, 428.

———. *History as Art and as Science*. New York: Harper & Row, 1964, pp. 26–30, 36.

Hughes, Peter. *Spots of Time*. Toronto: CBC Publications, 1969, pp. 23–36.

———. "Language, History and Vision: an Approach to Eighteenth-Century Literature." In *The Varied Pattern: Studies in the Eighteenth Century*, edited by Peter Hughes and David Williams. Toronto: A. M. Hakkert, 1971, pp. 83, 88, 90, 92.

Huppert, George. *The Idea of Perfect History*. Urbana: University of Illinois Press, 1970, pp. 166–67.

Jay, Martin. *The Dialectical Imagination: a History of the Frankfurt School and the Institute of Social Research, 1923–50*. Boston: Little, Brown, 1973, pp. 25, 49, 81, 257, 258, 269.

Kaempffert, W. "Story of a Materialist." *Saturday Review of Literature*, 17 June 1944, p. 40.

Kaufman, Edgar J., Jr. "Memmo's Lodoli." *Art Bulletin* 46 (1964): 167–68, 170, 172.

Kelley, Donald R. *Foundations of Modern Historical Scholarship*. New York: Columbia University Press, 1970, pp. 1, 6, 7, 44, 301, 303–5.

———. "History as a Calling: The Case of La Popelinière." In *Renaissance Studies in Honor of Hans Baron*, edited by Anthony Molho and John A. Tedeschi. DeKalb: Northern Illinois University Press, 1971, p. 773.

Kristeller, Paul Oskar. *Renaissance Thought: the Classic, Scholastic, and Humanist Strains*. New York: Harper & Row, Harper Torchbooks, 1961, p. 18.

———. *Renaissance Thought II: Papers on Humanism and the Arts*. New York: Harper & Row, Harper Torchbooks, 1965, p. 188.

Labriola, Antonio. *Essays on the Materialistic Conception of History*. Translated by C. H. Kerr. New York and London: *Monthly Review Press*, 1966, p. 76.

Lafargue, Paul. "Reminiscences of Marx." *Reminiscences of Marx and Engels*. Moscow: Foreign Languages Publishing House [n.d.], p. 78.

Land, Stephen K. "Universalism and Relativism: a Philosophical Problem of Translation in the Eighteenth Century." *Journal of the History of Ideas* 35 (1974): 606–8.

———. *From Signs to Propositions: the Concept of Form in Eighteenth-Century Semantic Theory*. New York: Longman, 1974, pp. 50–74.

Leach, Edmund. *Claude Lévi-Strauss*. New York: Viking Press, 1970, pp. 35, 129n.

Levi, Albert William. *Philosophy and the Modern World*. Bloomington: Indiana University Press, 1959, pp. 108, 520.
———. *Literature, Philosophy, and the Imagination*. Bloomington, Indiana University Press, 1962, pp. 60, 221–25.
Levin, Harry. *James Joyce: a Critical Introduction*. Norfolk, Conn.: New Directions, 1941, pp. 133, 142–48, 156, 157, 166, 168, 172, 181, 182, 183, 190, 199.
Lichtheim, George. *George Lukacs*. New York: Viking Press, 1970, pp. 16, 21, 22, 33, 121, 132.
———. *Europe in the Twentieth Century*. London: Weidenfeld and Nicolson, 1972, pp. 221, 357, 358–61, 362, 371.
Malefijt, Annemarie de Waal. *Religion and Culture*. New York: Macmillan, 1960, pp. 29–32, 34.
Mandelbaum, Maurice. *History, Man and Reason: a Study of Nineteenth-Century Thought*. Baltimore: Johns Hopkins Press, 1971, pp. 182, 481n.
Manuel, Frank E. "In Defense of Philosophical History." *Antioch Review* 20 (1960): 331–43.
———. *Isaac Newton Historian*. Cambridge: Harvard University Press, 1963, p. 43.
———. *The Prophets of Paris*. Reprinted: New York: Harper Torchbooks, 1965, pp. 14, 23, 31, 35, 48, 63, 64, 165, 169, 277, 281, 300.
———. *Shapes of Philosophical History*. Stanford: Stanford University Press, 1965, pp. 40, 47, 49, 55, 58, 93, 139, 158.
———. "The Use and Abuse of Psychology in History." *Daedalus* 100 (1971): 188–90.
———. *Freedom From History and Other Untimely Essays*. New York: New York University Press, 1971, pp. 7, 18, 19, 25–26, 27, 54, 55, 56, 58, 61, 62, 63, 64, 244.
Marx, Karl. *Capital*. Edited by Friedrich Engels. Translated by Samuel Moore and Edward Aveling. Moscow: Progress Publishers, 1965, p. 372 n.3. New York: International Publishers, 1967, p. 367 n.1.
Mazzeo, Joseph A. "Some Interpretations of the History of Ideas." *Journal of the History of Ideas* 33 (1972): 381.
Meisel, James H. *The Myth of the Ruling Class: Gaetano Mosca and the 'Elite.'* Reprinted: Ann Arbor: Ann Arbor Paperback, 1962, pp. 30, 39, 139, 200, 242, 258, 267.
Melko, Matthew. *The Nature of Civilizations*. Boston: Porter-Sargent Books, 1969, pp. 5, 189, 194, 197.
Miller, Willard M. "A Bibliography of the Writings of Max Harold Fisch." In *Studies in Philosophy and in the History of Science: Essays in Honor of Max Fisch*, edited by Richard Tursman. Lawrence, Kans.: Coronado Press, 1970, pp. 211–19.
Mohan, Robert Paul. *Philosophy of History*. New York: Bruce, 1970, pp. 51–65.
Montagu, M. F. Ashley. "Cassirer on Mythological Thinking." In *The Philosophy of Ernst Cassirer*, edited by Paul Arthur Schilpp. New York: Tudor, 1958, p. 368.
Munz, Peter. *When the Golden Bough Breaks: Structuralism or Typology?* London: Routledge & Kegan Paul, 1973, pp. 107, 120.

Neff, Emery. *The Poetry of History*. New York: Columbia University Press, 1947, pp. 83–87, 88, 96, 98, 131, 132, 133, 136, 137, 140, 157.
Ollman, Bertell. *Alienation: Marx's Concept of Man in Capitalist Society*. Cambridge: The University Press, 1971, p. 259 n.24.
Pachter, Henry. "Defining an Event: Prolegomenon to any Philosophy of History." *Social Research* 41 (1974): 439.
Peirce, Charles Sanders. Unsigned review of Robert Flint's *Philosophy as Scientia Scientiarum and A History of Classifications of the Sciences*. *Nation* 80 (1905): 360.
Perelman, Ch. and Olbrechts-Tyteca, Lucie. *The New Rhetoric: a Treatise on Argumentation*. Translated by John Wilkinson and Purcell Weaver. Notre Dame: University of Notre Dame Press, 1969, pp. 23, 84, 144, 175, 176, 178, 217, 218, 236, 392, 393, 408, 429, 444, 448, 488.
Price, Martin. *Swift's Rhetorical Art*. New Haven: Yale University Press, 1953, pp. 1–35.
Psathas, George, ed. *Phenomenological Sociology: Issues and Applications*. New York: John Wiley, 1973, pp. 113, 124n., 344, 345, 346n.
Rand, Calvin. "Two Meanings of Historicism in the Writings of Dilthey, Troeltsch and Meinecke." *Journal of the History of Ideas* 25 (1964): 503–18.
Read, Herbert. *Form in Modern Poetry*. London: Sheed & Ward, 1932, pp. 36–38.
———. *The Forms of Things Unknown: Essays Towards An Aesthetic Philosophy*. New York: Horizon Press, 1960, pp. 109–11, 115–16, 118, 119.
———. *In Defence of Shelley and Other Essays*. Freeport, N.Y.: Books for Libraries Press, 1968, pp. 151–56.
Russell, Bertrand. *Wisdom of the West*. Edited by Paul Foulkes. New York: Doubleday, 1959, pp. 206–9, 216, 217, 271, 274, 275, 277, 290.
Said, Edward W. "Labyrinth of Incarnations: the Essays of Maurice Merleau-Ponty." *Kenyon Review* 29 (1967): 67.
———. "The Text as Practice and as Idea." *Modern Language Notes* 88 (1973): 1073, 1078, 1080, 1090, 1100.
Saintsbury, George A. *History of Criticism and Literary Taste in Europe From the Earliest Texts to the Present Day*. 3 vols. 2d. ed. New York: Dodd, Mead, 1902–05, vol. 3, pp. 152–57.
Schumpeter, Joseph A. *History of Economic Analysis*. New York: Oxford University Press, 1954, pp. 28, 135, 136, 137, 300, 791–92.
Sewell, Elizabeth. *The Orphic Voice: Poetry and Natural History*. Reprinted: New York: Harper & Row, Harper Torchbooks, 1971, pp. 181–84.
Shibles, Warren A. *Metaphor: an Annotated Bibliography and History*. Whitewater, Wis.: Language Press, 1971, pp. 88, 92, 207, 366, 383, 402.
Sorokin, Pitirim A. *Society, Culture and Personality: a System of General Sociology*. New York: Cooper Square, 1962, pp. 15, 20, 21, 31, 110, 538, 588, 686, 687.
———. *Sociocultural Causality, Space, Time*. New York: Russell & Russell, 1964, pp. 34, 234.
Stapleton, Laurence. *Justice and World Society*. Chapel Hill: University of North Carolina Press, 1944, pp. 34–35, 37–48.

Stark, Werner. *The Sociology of Knowledge*. London: Routledge and Kegan Paul, 1958. Reprinted, 1960, pp. x, 115, 160, 165, 328.

———. *Montesquieu: Pioneer of the Sociology of Knowledge*. London: Routledge and Kegan Paul, 1960, pp. ix, x, 52.

———. *The Fundamental Forms of Social Thought*. Reprinted: New York: Fordham University Press, 1964, pp. 8, 11, 12, 219–22.

Steiner, George. "Orpheus with his Myths: Claude Lévi-Strauss." *Psychiatry and Social Science Review*, 15 August 1970, pp. 15–20; 15 September 1970, pp. 13–15.

———. "Whorf, Chomsky, and the Student of Literature." *New Literary History* 4 (1972): 15–34.

Stromberg, Roland N. *An Intellectual History of Modern Europe*. New York: Appleton-Century-Crofts, 1966, pp. 163–64, 65, 69, 267.

Struever, Nancy. *The Language of History in the Renaissance*. Princeton: Princeton University Press, 1970, pp. 57n, 65, 71, 95, 132.

———. "Rhetoric and Philosophy in Renaissance Humanism." *Journal of Interdisciplinary History* 2 (1972): 64–72.

———. "The Study of Language and the Study of History." *Journal of Interdisciplinary History* 4 (1974): 401–13.

Sumner, Charles. "The Law of Human Progress." In *The Works of Charles Sumner*, Boston: Lee and Shepard, 1849, pp. 14–15.

Teggart, Frederick J. *Theory and Processes of History*. Berkeley and Los Angeles: University of California Press, 1960, p. 1.

Thompson, James Westfall, and Holm, Bernard J. *A History of Historical Writing*. 2 vols. New York: Macmillan, 1942, vol. 2, pp. 92–94.

Thompson, John Hinsdale. "Finnegans Wake." In *Modern Poetry: American and British*, edited by Kimon Friar and Malcolm J. Brinnin. New York: Appleton-Century-Crofts, 1951, pp. 88–97.

Tindall, William York. *James Joyce, His Way of Interpreting the Modern World*. New York: Charles Scribner's Sons, 1950, pp. 64, 70–77, 79, 83, 85, 86, 97, 99–100, 104, 112, 115.

———. *A Reader's Guide to Finnegans Wake*. New York: Farrar, Straus, and Giroux, 1969, pp. 8–10, 30, 35, 44, 79, 80, 81, 84, 85, 95, 96, 103, 104, 106, 109–10, 112–13, 127, 137, 138, 139, 154, 158, 164, 165, 176, 178, 182, 187, 193, 201, 204, 206, 210, 216, 217, 223, 225, 231, 242, 247, 255–56, 267, 283, 294, 297, 305, 309, 310, 318, 321, 322.

Toynbee, Arnold J. *A Study of History*. 12 vols. Oxford: The University Press, 1961, vol. 12, pp. 40n., 131n., 161n., 252, 584, 585, 586–87, 607, 653n.

Trotsky, Leon D. *The History of the Russian Revolution*. 3 vols., translated by Max Eastman. Ann Arbor: University of Michigan Press, 1932, vol. 1, p. 3.

Ullmann, Stephen. "Semantic Universals." In *Universals of Language*, edited by J. H. Greenberg. 2d ed., Cambridge: Massachusetts Institute of Technology Press, 1963, p. 241.

Venturi, Lionello. *History of Art Criticism*. New York: Dutton, 1964, pp. 137, 161–62, 330.

Verene, Donald Phillip. "The Philosophy of Culture and the Problem of Human Existence." In *Akten des XIV. Internationalen Kongresses für Philosophie*. Vienna: Herder, 1968, p. 497.

———, ed. *Man and Culture: a Philosophical Anthology*. New York: Dell Laurel, 1970, pp. 56–58, 63–75.

Walsh, William H. *An Introduction to Philosophy of History*. London, New York: Hutchinson's University Library, 1964, pp. 11, 121, 165, 166.

Wellek, René. *The Rise of English Literary History*. New York: McGraw-Hill, 1966, pp. 74, 86.

———, and Warren, Austin. *Theory of Literature*. New York: Harcourt, Brace and World, 1956, pp. 113, 191.

White, Hayden V. "Foucault Decoded: Notes from Underground." *History and Theory* 12 (1973): 48.

Whyte, Lancelot Law. *Essay on Atomism: From Democritus to 1960*. Middletown, Conn.: Wesleyan University Press, 1961, p. 53.

———, ed. *Roger Joseph Boscovich: Studies of his Life and Work on the 250th Anniversary of his Birth*. London: Allen & Unwin, 1961, pp. 118–19, 125.

———. *The Unconscious Before Freud*. Garden City, N.Y.: Doubleday, 1962, pp. 45, 93–97, 186, 188.

Wilson, Edmund. *To the Finland Station*. Reprinted: New York: Farrar, Straus & Giroux, 1972, pp. 1–7, 62, 141, 193, 467.

Winch, Peter. "Understanding a Primitive Society." *American Philosophical Quarterly* 1 (1964): 324.

Wright, O. W. "Primary Law of Political Development in Civil History." *North American Review* 88 (1859): 387–88.

III. Reviews

Listed alphabetically by author of work reviewed

Adams, H. P. *The Life and Writings of Giambattista Vico*. London: Allen & Unwin, 1935.

REVIEWS:

Gianturco, Elio. *Italica* 13 (1936): 132.

Jessop, T. E. *Philosophy* 11 (1936): 216–18.

Atti del convegno internazionale sul tema: Campanella e Vico. N. 126 of the *Problemi attuali di scienza e cultura*. Rome: Accademia Nazionale dei Lincei, 1969.

REVIEW:

Gianturco, Elio. "Vico's Commemoration at the Accademia dei Lincei." *Forum Italicum* 4 (1970): 421–34.

Brown, Norman O. *Closing Time*. New York: Random House, 1973.

REVIEWS:

Goldfein, Alan. "The End?" *Commentary* 57 (1974): 84–85.

Hampshire, Stuart. "Joyce and Vico: The Middle Way." *The New York Review of Books*, 18 October 1973, pp. 8, 9, 12, 14, 16, 21.

Said, Edward. *The New York Times Book Review*, 9 September 1973, pp. 31, 32, 34.

Schwartz, Albert. "In the Waiting Room." *The New Republic*, 22 September 1973, pp. 23–25.

Caponigri, A Robert. *Time and Idea: the Theory of History in Giambattista Vico*. Chicago: Regnery, 1953.
REVIEWS:
Fisch, Max H. *Journal of Philosophy* 54 (1957): 648–52.
Shanahan, W. O. *Review of Politics* 17 (1955): 136–42.

Croce, Benedetto. *The Philosophy of Giambattista Vico*. Translated by Robin G. Collingwood. New York: Macmillan, 1913.
REVIEWS:
"Beginnings of Sociology." *Nation* 99 (1914): 46–47.
Cohen, Morris R. *Philosophical Review* 23 (1914): 677–82.

Daus, H. J. *Selbstverständnis und Menschenbild in den Selbstdarstellungen Giambattista Vicos und Pietro Giannones: Ein Beitrag zur Geschichte der italienischen Autobiographie*. Geneva: Librairie E. Droz; Paris: L. Minard, Kölner Romanistische Arbeiten, Neue Folge, 1962.
REVIEW:
Scott, J. A. *Modern Language Quarterly* 25 (1964): 365–67.

Donati, Benvenuto. *Nuovi studi sulla filosofia civile di G. B. Vico*. Florence: Le Monnier, 1937.
REVIEW:
Gianturco, Elio. *Journal of Modern History* 9 (1937): 514–16.

Flint, Robert. *Vico*. Edinburgh: Blackwood, 1884.
REVIEW:
"Flint's Vico." *Saturday Review* (London) 58 (29 November 1884): 699–700.

Gianturco, Elio. "Suarez and Vico. A Note on the Origin of the Vichian Formula." *Harvard Theological Review* 27 (1934): 207–10.
REVIEW:
Italica 13 (1936): 132.

———. *A Selective Bibliography of Vico Scholarship* (1948–1968). *Forum Italicum*, Supplement. Florence: Grafica Toscana, 1968.
REVIEW:
Palmer, Lucia M. *Journal of the History of Philosophy* 8 (1970): 220–22.

Grimaldi, Alfonsina Albini. *The Universal Humanity of Giambattista Vico*. New York: Vanni, 1958.
REVIEW:
Berry, Thomas M. *Thought* 34 (1959): 456.

Manson, Richard. *The Theory of Knowledge of Giambattista Vico*. Hamden, Conn.: Archon Books, 1969.
REVIEWS:
Beitscher, Henry. *Review of Metaphysics* 23 (1970): 342.
Caponigri, A. Robert. *Journal of the History of Philosophy* 9 (1971): 98–101.
Wolff, Kurt H. *Annals of the American Academy of Political and Social Science* 391 (1970): 239–40.

Nicolini, Fausto. *Bibliografia vichiana*, by Benedetto Croce, revised and enlarged by Fausto Nicolini. 2 vols. Naples: Ricciardi, 1947–48; *Autobiografia di Giambattista Vico (1725–28)*, edited by Fausto Nicolini. Milan: Bom-

piani, 1947; and *Uomini di spada, di chiesa, di toga, di studio ai tempi di Giambattista Vico*, by Fausto Nicolini. Milan: Hoepli, 1942.
REVIEW:
Fisch, Max H. *Philosophical Review* 58 (1949): 528–29.

———. *La religiosità di Giambattista Vico: quattro saggi*. Bari: Laterza, 1949.
REVIEW:
Gianturco, Elio. *Journal of Philosophy* 48 (1951): 153–57.

Per il secondo Centenario della "Scienza Nuova" di G. B. Vico (1725–1925). Rome: Edizioni di *Rivista internazionale di filosofia del diritto*, 1925.
REVIEW:
Whittaker, T. *Mind* 35 (1926): 519–20.

Pompa, Leon. *Vico: A Study of the "New Science."* Cambridge: The University Press, 1975.
REVIEW:
Abel, Betty. "The Proper Study of Mankind." *Contemporary Review* 226 (1975): 221.

Tagliacozzo, Giorgio, and White, Hayden V., editors. *Giambattista Vico: An International Symposium*. Baltimore: Johns Hopkins Press, 1969.
REVIEWS:
Beitscher, H. *Review of Metaphysics* 24 (1971): 762.
Bergel, Lienhart. "Vico For Our Time." *Forum Italicum* 6 (1972): 575–83; also published in *Rivista di studi Crociani* 9 (1972): 135–42.
Bevilacqua, Vincent M. *Quarterly Journal of Speech* 57 (1971): 124–25.
Bobick, M. T. *American Sociological Review* 35 (1970): 926–27.
Brunius, Teddy. *Journal of Aesthetics and Art Criticism* 30 (1971): 129–31.
Caponigri, A. Robert. *Philosophy and Rhetoric* 4 (1971): 135–36.
Casagrande, Joseph B. *American Anthropologist* 74 (1972): 11–12.
Choice 7 (1970): 240.
Collins, James. *The Modern Schoolman* 48 (1970): 64–65.
Costa, Gustavo. *Journal of the History of the Behavioral Sciences* 8 (1972): 441–43.
DiPietro, Robert J. *Foundations of Language* 9 (1973): 410–21.
Dye, James Wayne. *Bibliographie de la Philosophie—Bibliography of Philosophy* 19 (1972): 76.
Fox, June. "The Pedagogical Theory of Giambattista Vico: In Appreciation of an International Symposium." *Educational Theory* 20 (1970): 292–303.
Gardiner, Patrick. "Sleeper Awake." *The New York Review of Books*, 20 May 1971, pp. 35–40.
Gianturco, Elio. *Italian Quarterly* 9 (1970): 108–11.
———. *Renaissance Quarterly* 24 (1971): 419–22.
Giorgi, Amedeo P. *Journal of Phenomenological Psychology* 1 (1971): 263–64.
Goudge, Thomas A. *Philosophy of the Social Sciences* 1 (1971): 350–52.
Grande, Frank. "Review Article: Vico Without Hegel." *Review of National Literatures* 1 (1970): 293–99.

Gutmann, James. *Saturday Review*, 18 April 1970, p. 41.
Harris, Henry S. *Dialogue* 9 (1970): 410–14.
Henderson, James L. *British Journal of Educational Studies* 18 (1970): 224–25.
Hershbell, Jackson P. *The Library Journal* 95 (1970): 2485.
Kelley, Donald. *Journal of Interdisciplinary History* 3 (1973): 772–75.
Littleford, Michael S. "Vico's Legacy to Contemporary Education." *Educational Forum* 36 (1972): 393–401.
Malefijt, Annemarie de Waal. *Critical Anthropology* 2 (1971): 82–84.
———. *Man* 6 (1971): 501–2.
McClintock, Robert. *Comparative Education Review* 16 (1972): 376–78.
Mohan, Robert P. *Catholic Historical Review* 59 (1973): 452.
Mora, George. *Psychoanalytic Quarterly* 41 (1972): 119–22.
Musto, David F. *American Journal of Psychiatry* 127 (1971): 1710–11.
Nisbet, Robert. "Vico: The Anti-Descartes." *The American Scholar* 39 (1970): 714, 716–18.
Noether, Emiliana P. *American Historical Review* 76 (1971): 476–79.
Orsini, G. N. G. *Comparative Literature* 23 (1971): 365.
Palmer, Lucia. *Studi Internazionali di Filosofia* 3 (1971): 231–33.
Pasotti, Robert. *Journal of Value Inquiry* 6 (1972): 77–80.
Perkinson, Henry J. *Main Currents of Modern Thought* 27 (1971): 167–68.
Pompa, Leon. *Philosophy* 47 (1972): 162–69.
———. "Vico In Review." *Studi Internazionali di Filosofia* 5 (1973): 215–19.
Robinson, Daniel S. *The Journal of Philosophy and Phenomenological Research* 31 (1970): 133.
Schneider, Herbert W. *The Journal of the History of Philosophy* 8 (1970): 467.
School and Society 97 (1969): 514.
Shiner, L. E. *Journal of the American Academy of Religion* 39 (1971): 535, 538.
Steiner, G. "Through Seas of Thought, Alone," *The New Yorker*, 9 May 1970, pp. 154–56.
Stromberg, Roland N. *Comparative Literature Studies* 8 (1971): 79–80.
Struever, Nancy S. *The Journal of Philosophy* 70 (1973): 801–4.
Verene, Donald Phillip. *International Philosophical Quarterly* 11 (1971): 260–62.
———. *Man and World* 4 (1971): 342–54.
"Vico in Our Time." *The London Times Literary Supplement*, 1 October 1970, pp. 1161–63.
Virginia Quarterly Review 46 (1970): lxxvi.

Vico, Giambattista. *The Autobiography of Giambattista Vico*. Translated by Max H. Fisch and Thomas G. Bergin. Ithaca: Cornell University Press, 1944.
REVIEW:
Wellek, René. *Philological Quarterly* 24 (1945): 166–68.

———. *La Scienza nuova*. Translated into French by Princess Cristina Belgiojoso. Paris, 1844.

REVIEW:
"*The New Science*: by Vico. Translated by the Author of the Essay on the Formation of Catholic Doctrine. With an Introduction on Vico and his Works." *Foreign Quarterly Review* 34 (1845): 289–303.
———. *The New Science of Giambattista Vico*. Translated by Thomas G. Bergin and Max H. Fisch. Ithaca: Cornell University Press, 1948.
REVIEWS:
Edie, James M. "Giambattista Vico: The New Science." *Italica* 39 (1962): 147–49.
Gianturco, Elio. *Ethics* 60 (1950): 140–41. Response: Arthur Child, "Vico in Translation." *Ethics* 60 (1950): 292–93. Reply: Elio Gianturco, "Words and Meaning in Vico." *Ethics* 61 (1951): 151–53.
———. *Oeuvres choisies de Vico, contenant ses memoires, écrits par lui-même, La Science Nouvelle, &c. Précédées d'une introduction sur sa vie et ses ouvrages*. Translated by Jules Michelet. Paris: Hachette, 1835.
REVIEW:
Walker, James M. *Southern Quarterly Review* 1 (1842): 404–16.
———. *On the Study Methods of Our Time*. Translated with an introduction and notes by Elio Gianturco. Indianapolis, New York, Kansas City: Bobbs-Merrill Library of Liberal Arts, 1965.
REVIEW:
Bergin, Thomas G. *Journal of Modern History* 30 (1968): 691–92.

Index

Library of Congress Cataloging in Publication Data
Main entry under title:

Giambattista Vico's science of humanity.

"Vico's writings": p. xiii
"Critical writings on Vico in English, [by] Molly Black Verene": p. 457
Includes bibliographical references and index.
1. Vico, Giovanni Battista, 1668–1774—Addresses, essays, lectures. I. Tagliacozzo, Giorgio.
II. Verene, Donald Phillip, 1937–
B3583.G48 195 75–26753
ISBN 0–8018–1720–X

THE JOHNS HOPKINS UNIVERSITY PRESS

This book was composed in Electra text and display type by the Maryland Linotype Composition Company. It was printed on Warren's 50-lb. Publishers Eggshell Wove paper and bound in Columbia Fictionette cloth by Universal Lithographers, Inc.

Da